ASHIS NANDY

RETURN FROM EXILE

Alternative Sc
Illegitimacy of Nationalism
The Savage Freud

OXFORD
UNIVERSITY PRESS

OXFORD
UNIVERSITY PRESS

YMCA Library Building, Jai Singh Road, New Delhi 110 001

Oxford University Press is a department of the University of Oxford. It furthers the University's objective of excellence in research, scholarship, and education by publishing worldwide in

Oxford New York

Athens Auckland Bangkok Bogota Buenos Aires Cape Town Chennai Dar es Salaam Delhi Florence Hong Kong Istanbul Karachi Kolkata Kuala Lumpur Madrid Melbourne Mexico City Mumbai Nairobi Paris São Paulo Shanghai Singapore Taipei Tokyo Toronto Warsaw

with associated companies in Berlin Ibadan

Published in India
By Oxford University Press, New Delhi

First published 1998
Second impression 2001

ISBN 019 564178 7

Printed by Sai Printo Pack Pvt. Ltd., New Delhi 110 020
Published by Manzar Khan, Oxford University Press
YMCA Library Building, Jai Singh Road, New Delhi 110 001

To the memory of three friends who recently called it quits:

Bashiruddin Ahmed, a scholar whose romance with
Indian democracy, yoghurt and hypochondria never ended;
Surapriya Mookerjee, half-hearted doctor,
gifted raconteur, grand eccentric;
and Bulu Bannerji, compulsive gambler
and occasional card-sharper,
who dreamt all his life of quick money and yet
treated poverty and wealth with equal disdain.

INTRODUCTION:
The A, B, C, D (and E) of Ashis Nandy

ZIAUDDIN SARDAR

Ashis Nandy's *The Savage Freud* is dedicated to 'three Indians who symbolize the hundred-and-fifty-year-old attempt to re-engineer the Indian':

> Vinayak Damodar Savarkar (1880-1965), unflinching warrior for Hindu nationalism, who spent his life trying to make the Hindu more martial, masculine, cohesive and organized;
>
> Damodar Dharmanand Kosambi (1907-1960), indefatigable rationalist and progressive thinker, who never gave up his efforts to make Indians more scientific, objective and historically minded;
>
> and Nirad C. Chaudhuri (1897-) the last of the great Edwardian modernists of India, who has always thoughtfully shared the white man's burden, especially Europe's educational responsibilities in South Asia.[1]

It would be safe to assume that Nandy himself is not in favour of re-engineering the old-fashioned, traditional, but somewhat world-wary *hindustani*. After all, the less than 'masculine' and 'scientific' Indian has survived centuries of colonization and decades of modernity and instrumental development—and survived with his sanity and identity more or less intact. Even now, in the closing years of the western millennium, the *hindustani* seems to demonstrate a stubborn resilience in the face of the all-embracing embrace of post-modernism and 'globalization', and appears ever ready to preserve his or her Selfhood from whatever else the twenty-first century may

[1] Ashis Nandy, *The Savage Freud, and Other Essays on Possible and Retrievable Selves.* (Delhi: Oxford University Press, 1985). See the dedication.

throw at him or her. If Nandy stands *for* anything, it is the traditional *hindustani* ; that is, some one who is much more than a mere 'Indian', a citizen of a nation-state called 'India'; someone whose Self incorporates a civilization with its own tradition, history (however defined), life-styles and modes of knowing, being and doing.

Counterpoising the author of *The Intimate Enemy* with others amounts to comparing his thesis (tradition, civilization, the total Self) with their anti-thesis (nationalism, rationalism, secularism, etc.). Nandy is not amenable to this kind of dualistic logic. There are three prerequisites for understanding Ashis Nandy and his thought. First, it is important to appreciate that he operates on a non-dualistic, four-fold logic where relationships of similarity and convergence are more important than cold, instrumental rationality, and the universe has more options than simply either/or duality. Second, he functions beyond (rather than outside) the established conventions of western thought. His ideas span a universe that includes 'the West' but only as one civilization in a multicivilizational world and then largely—and this may come as a surprise to many—as a victim. Nandy categorically locates himself with the victims of history and the casualties of an array of grand western ideas such as Science, Rationality, Development, Nation-State; but the victims of *zulm* or tyranny in history, and conceptual and ideational oppression in our time, are located as much in a geographical, civilizational, intellectual and conceptual space called 'the West' as in the non-West. Nandy seeks both to unite the victims and to increase the awareness of their victimhood. Third, Nandy has no respect for disciplinary boundaries. Indeed, to accept the disciplinary structure of modern knowledge is to accept the worldview of the West. But his scholarship is not interdisciplinary or transdisciplinary in the conventional sense; he is no 'Renaissance Man'. He is a polymath in the traditional sense, operating beyond the disciplinary structure of knowledge, *and* regarding all sources of knowledge—revelational as well as non-revelational, traditional as well as modern, tacit as well as objective—as equally valid *and* all methods and modes of inquiry as equally useful.

Alternatives, Androgynous

Nandy's first book, *Alternative Sciences: Creativity and Authenticity in Two Indian Scientists,* is dedicated to 'the Ramanujans who walk the dusty roads of India undiscovered and the Boses who almost make it but never do'.[2] The book analyses the life and work of Jagadis Chandra Bose, the Indian physicist and botanist, and Srinivasa Ramanujan, the brilliant mathematician. Bose tried to give a special Indian perspective to world science. He was one of the earliest modern scientists to do interdisciplinary research and mapped out a philosophy of science which anticipated a number of major present-day themes in it. In the West, he was considered a genius and a missionary-scientist; in India, he was a national hero. Unlike Bose, Ramanujan was totally a product of traditional India. Despite the fact that he failed most of his academic examinations, Ramanujan emerged a world-class mathematician, using as his base a neat, non-dualistic science that has been the forte of Indian thought since the eighth century. Through an analysis of their lives, Nandy explores how modern and traditional India tried to cope with the culture of modern science, and how their personal search for meaning personified India's search for a new self-definition.

While Bose had a total belief in science, he was concerned with the parochialism of western science and the hostility of western scientists towards India and all things Indian. He suffered, Nandy alleges, from a double bind: on the one hand, the perceived hostility of the West led to a growing hostility towards the West; and, on the other, he felt a sense of inferiority in relation to the West. He loved to have his wife and assistants sing western scientists' eulogies of his work to his visitors. Ramanujan's science relied as much on mysticism, metaphysics and astrology as it did on the abstract ideas of mathematics. He developed his own philosophy of life and his mathematics formed an integrated whole with his metaphysics and astrology. Nandy is sympathetic to both scientists—indeed, to their predicament, too—but he finds both their lives as well as their perceived alternatives wanting.

What exactly is Nandy rejecting in *Alternative Sciences*? He clearly

[2] Ashis Nandy, *Alternative Sciences: Creativity and Authenticity in Two Indian Scientists,* (Delhi: Oxford University Press, 1995). See the dedication.

rejects the dominant mode of western science. But he also rejects Bose's attempts to seek an alternative within western science—an Indian science that is actually an appendage to the 'universal model' of western science. And to a lesser extent, he rejects Ramanujan's version of traditional Indian science too, even though it is rooted in folk history. Both use a strategy that uses the West as a yardstick and consider their Indianness as a negative identification. And, as such, both alternatives are derived from the western notion of what is science, striving 'to be the exact reverse of what a hypothetical model of western analysis is'.[3] For Nandy, an alternative that is genuinely an alternative cannot take the West as its reference point.

So what is Nandy's alternative, alternative to? To begin with, it is an alternative to a worldview that 'believes in the absolute superiority of the human over the non-human and the sub-human, the masculine over the feminine, the adult over the child, the historical over the ahistorical, and the modern or progressive over the traditional or the savage'; it is an alternative to a view that has its roots in 'anthropocentric doctrines of secular salvation, in the ideologies of progress, normality and hyper-masculinity, and in theories of cumulative growth of science and technology'.[4] It is also an alternative to 'a fully homogenized, technologically controlled, absolutely hierarchized world' based on a dualistic logic of 'the modern and the primitive, the secular and the non-secular, the scientific and the unscientific, the expert and the layman, the normal and the abnormal, the developed and the underdeveloped, the vanguard and the led, the liberated and the savable'.[5]

But this alternative is not, and cannot be, an alternative to the West per se. For Nandy, the West is more than a geographical and temporal entity; it is psychological category. Now the West is everywhere: within and without the West, in thought processes and liberative actions, in colonial and neo-colonial structures and in the minds of oppressors and the oppressed—the West is part of the oppressive structure; it is also in league with the victims. Thus, to be anti-West is itself tantamount to being pro-West; in Nandy's

[3] Ibid., p. 15.

[4] Ashis Nandy, *The Intimate Enemy: Loss and Recovery of Self Under Colonialism*, (Delhi: Oxford University Press, 1983), p. x.

[5] Ibid., p. x.

words, 'anti-colonialism, too, could be an apologia for the colonization of minds'.[6]

Nandy's alternative then is located beyond the West/anti-West dichotomy, even beyond the indigenous constructions of modern and traditional options, in a different space. It lies in a new construction: a 'victims' construction of the West, a West which would make sense to the non-West in terms of the non-West's experience of suffering'.[7] This construction, both of a 'victims alternative' as well as of an alternative West, turns out to be a strategy for survival. Modern oppression, Nandy asserts, is unique in many respects. Unlike traditional oppression—which is an encounter between the self and the enemy, the rulers and the ruled, the believers and the infidels—modern oppression is 'a battle between dehumanized self and the objectified enemy, the technologized bureaucrat and his reified victim, pseudo-rulers and their fearsome other selves projected on to their "subjects"'.[8] This is the difference between the Crusades and Auschwitz, between Hindu-Muslim riots in India and the Gulf War. And this is why Nandy's alternative is the alternative of the victims; and whenever the oppressors make an appearance in this alternative, they are revealed to be *disguised victims* 'at an advanced stage of psychosocial decay'.[9] The construction of their own West allows the victims to live with the alternative West 'while resisting the loving embrace of the West's dominant self'.[10]

India, then, is not the non-West. It is India and it cannot be defined in relation to the West. The ordinary Indian has no reason to seek his/her self-definition in relation to the West or to see himself/herself as a counter-player or an anti-thesis of the western man or woman. The strain to be the opposite of the West distorts the priorities of the traditional worldview of India, dissolves the holistic nature of the Indian view of humanity and its place in the universe, and destroys Indian culture's unique *gestalt*. The search for alternatives is not a choice between East and the West or between the North and the South: 'it is a choice—and a battle—between the Apollonian and the Dionysian *within* India and *within* the

6 Ibid., p. xi.
7 Ibid., p. xiii.
8 Ibid., p. xvi.
9 Ibid., p. xvi.
10 Ibid., p. xiv.

West'.[11] Even if such a distinction does not exist in an oppressive culture, Nandy asserts, 'it has to be presumed to exist by its victims for maintaining their own sanity and humanness'.[12] There is thus no need to look elsewhere for an alternative social knowledge that is ethically sensitive and culturally rooted for it is already partly available outside the framework of modern science and social sciences —'in those who have been the "subjects", consumers or experimentees of these sciences'.[13]

Nandy's search for alternatives beyond the dichotomy of Hegelian thesis and anti-thesis has an interesting gender dimension. Colonial India, taking the cue from the colonizers, went through a radical shift in its gender consciousness. Traditionally, Indian thought has given greater preference to ***naritva*** (the essence of femininity) and *Klibatva* (the essence of androgyny or hermaphroditism) in comparison to ***purusatva*** (the essence of masculinity). Colonial India came to perceive the notion of *naritva* and *Klibatva* as pathologies that could only lead India to a negation of masculine identity. All forms of androgyny were lumped together as a dangerous anti-thesis of beneficial, undifferentiated masculinity. Nandy leans towards the traditional by carefully choosing the subjects of his inquiry. Thus Ramanujan is deliberately counterpoised against Bose because of the extent to which he can accept elements of feminity in him —his resemblance to his mother and grandmother in looks, his 'delicate and conspicuously feminine build and appearance', his 'velvety soft palms and long tapering fingers'.[14] The British mathematician George Hardy, who gave Ramanujan the one break his genius deserved, also turns out to be a 'queer'. Most of the characters in *The Intimate Enemy*, perhaps Nandy's most influential book, have ambiguous sexualities which are deliberately played upon: Gandhi, Oscar Wilde, Kipling, C.F. Andrews (the English priest described by Gandhi as Indian at heart and a true Englishman), Aurobindo. However, this should not be read as an uncritical endorsement of the feminine principle. Under specific conditions, Nandy argues (thinking perhaps of Indira Gandhi and Margaret

[11] Ibid., p. 74.

[12] Ibid., pp. 74–5.

[13] Ibid., p. xvii.

[14] *Alternative Sciences*, p. 100.

Thatcher) femininity can carry intimations of certain forms of masculinity.

The point here is that traditional Indian society, despite its patriarchal dimensions, does not allow gender, age and other biological differences to be easily transformed into principles of social stratification. On the contrary, it sees the masculine and the feminine, the infant, adult and the aged as a continuum. The differences are acknowledged, but the boundaries are open and diffused.

Boundaries, biographies

The dedication in *Science, Hegemony and Violence*, an anthology of essays edited by Ashis Nandy that deconstruct modern science with devastating power, reads: For A.K. Saran, Dharampal and Mohamad Idris 'who have tried to keep the future open for our generation of South Asians'.[15] Perhaps it is not widely know that Nandy is a futurist—but a futurist of a particular type. As opposed to the likes of Daniel Bell and Herman Kahn who would turn future studies into a closed discipline with its own priesthood, sacred texts and formal content, Nandy's concern is to keep the boundaries of future studies, and the future, completely open. In their own way, the three to whom the book is dedicated have tried to do the same: Saran has spent all his intellectual energies demolishing the positivist boundaries of Indian social science disciplines;[16] Dharampal tried to rescue the history of Indian science and education from the clutches of western and westernized historians and open it up to new interpretative possibilities;[17] and Mohamad Idris has devoted his life to saving the environment and cultural ecology of South East and South Asia.[18] Nandy stands for a plural future. Much of

[15] Ashis Nandy, *Science, Hegemony and Violence: A Requiem for Modernity*, (Delhi: Oxford University Press, 1990; Tokyo: The United Nations University, 1988). See the dedication.

[16] A.K. Saran is a thoroughgoing anti-positivist who is totally disdainful of all social science discourse. He is heavily influenced by Coomaraswamy as well as by marginalized western traditions, represented by such people as Marco Pollis, Simone Weil, Wittgentstein, and others. He writes in a peculiar style in which footnotes often tend to be longer than the text itself.

[17] See Dharampal's classic studies *Indian Science and Technology in the 18th Century* (Delhi: Impex, 1971) and *The Beautiful Tree* (Delhi: Impex, 1983).

[18] Mohamad Idris founded and led the Consumer Association of Penang (CAP) which

his thought is concerned with the survival of cultures incompatible with western notions of modernity, science, progress, and rationality. The survival, and hence the future, of non-western cultures, he has maintained, depends on pluralizing human destiny; and future studies, in its current incoherent form, offers escape routes that history, in its current institutionalized, disciplinary form, does not.

Nandy's concern for ensuring that boundaries—of disciplines, cultures, genders, futures, alternatives—remain open and diffused, combined with his aggressive stance against western grand narratives —Science, Reason, Progress, Nationalism—appear to locate him within the domain of postmodernism as does his deliberate attempt to dissolve the difference between high and low art and culture. But this location is more apparent than real. Nandy has some subtle and some serious differences with many of the postmodern persuasion. Postmodernism celebrates difference but blurs the boundaries that maintain difference. Nandy celebrates difference but not for its own sake: he wants different cultures to survive, indeed thrive, and remain different with their distinctive traits intact. In his thought, boundaries are needed, so that difference can retain its difference; but one must have an open attitude to boundaries to avoid falling in the trap of 'fundamentalism', 'puritanism' and 'nationalism'. Unlike many postmodern writers, Nandy does not recognize a category called 'ethnicity' which sharply demarcates between 'true insiders' and the constructed Other, the outsider. All those people who are described as ethnic, whether in the United States—where, apart from the white Anglo-Saxons, all other communities, from the Jews to Greeks, Irish, Hispanics and Asians, are termed ethnic, thus confirming their status as outsiders—or in India, are primordially deemed to be Others. His basic elements of analysis are culture and civilization (which assumes grand narrative proportion in Nandy's writings); he wants to retain both categories as analytical tools as well as distinctive and different entities. The cultural subjects of difference, the non-western cultures and civilizations, Nandy has argued forcefully, must be accorded the right and the space to

---

is perhaps one of the most influential environmental pressure groups in the Third World. He also established the Third World Network, an information and media service on Third World issues based in Penang; and the Kuala Lumpur based Just World Trust which campaigns for social justice and champions the cause of the marginalized and the oppressed.

negotiate their own conditions of discursive control and to practise their difference as a rebellion against the hegemonic tendencies of both modernity and postmodernism. The differences and diversities in Indian culture, he writes, are often sought in

> the uniqueness of certain cultural themes or in their configuration. This is not a false trail, but it does lead to some half-truths. One of them is the clear line drawn on behalf of the Indian, between the past and the present, the native and the exogenous, and the Hindu and the non-Hindu. But ... the West that is aggressive is sometimes inside; the earnest, self-declared native, too, is often an exogenous category, and the Hindu who announces himself so, is not that Hindu after all. Probably the uniqueness of Indian culture lies not so much in a unique ideology as in the society's traditional ability to live with cultural ambiguities and to use them to build psychological and even metaphysical defences against cultural invasions. Probably, the culture itself demands that a certain permeability of boundaries be maintained in one's self-image and that the self be not defined too tightly or separated mechanically from the not-self. This is the other side of the strategy of survival—the clue to India's post-colonial worldview.[19]

For non-western cultures and civilizations, as well as for Nandy, relativism cannot be absolute: it must be conditional, critical and concise, postmodernism notwithstanding.

In postmodern thought and practice, past and future implode into the present. Thus both history and (western) utopias/dystopias become instruments of dominance and techniques of rewriting the life plan of the lesser mortals of the world. For Nandy, all politics of the past, as well as those of the future, are attempts to shape the present. And the search for a non-oppressive present or a just and sustainable future often ends with new modes and techniques of oppression. The past is often used to keep non-western cultures and civilizations in a vice-like grip: and it comes in useful for imposing limits on visions of the future. The present of the non-West is often projected as the past of the West; and the future of non-West, in such a straitjacket, can only be the present of the West. This linear, progressive and cumulative notion of history, a product of liberal, humanistic ideologies, is used to curb the emergence of genuine alternative worldviews, alternative visions of the future and

[19] *The Intimate Enemy*, p. 107.

even alternative self-definitions and self-concepts. This is why, Nandy contends, 'the peripheries of the world often feel that they are victimized not merely by partial, biased or ethnocentric history, but by the idea of history itself'.[20]

How can we ensure that alternative visions of the future do not simply become steps towards new forms of oppression? Future utopias and visions, Nandy contends, must have an in-built ability to account for their legitimate and illegitimate offsprings. The oppressive actions of zealous visionaries in the name of their visions cannot be explained away as simply the actions of misguided adherents or products of misuse or deviations and false interpretations. A vision must take the responsibility of what is undertaken in its name. What this actually means is that the vision itself must have some capacity to liberate the visionaries from its own straitjacket. It cannot claim 'a monopoly on compassion and social realism, or presume itself to be holding the final key to social ethics and experience. Such a mission not merely devalues all heretics and outsiders as morally and cognitively inferior, it defines them as throwbacks to an earlier stage of culture and history, fit to be judged exclusively by the norms of the vision'.[21]

When Nandy uses biography and narratives as tools of cultural analysis, he deconstructs them using these criteria. In postmodernism, the narrative—particularly fiction—has itself become a theory of salvation. For example, Richard Rorty argues that philosophy and theory can no longer function to ground politics and social criticism; only fiction (he is particularly partial towards Nabokhov and Orwell) can give us insight into the sorts of cruelty we are capable of, and awaken us to the humiliation inflicted by particular social practices.[22] In British cultural studies, biography has acquired a similar role. Our salvation lies in art, argues Fred Inglis, and 'the art-form for each of our ordinary lives is, of course, biography'.[23] Thus, biography makes sense of our experiences and gives meaning to our individual

[20] Ashis Nandy, *Traditions, Tyranny, and Utopias: Essays in the Politics of Awareness* (Delhi: Oxford University Press, 1987), p. 46.

[21] Ibid., p. 11.

[22] Richard Rorty, *Philosophy, the Mirror of Nature* (Princeton: NJ, Princeton University Press, 1979).

[23] Fred Inglis, *Cultural Studies* (Cambridge: Massachusetts: Blackwell Publishers, 1993), p. 204.

lives: it teaches us how to live and how not to live. And cultural studies, particularly in its British form, is going to be the new theology that will teach the young how to think, what to feel, how to live, and what it is to be good. The assertions, writes Inglis,

> arise distinctly from the structure of feeling and frame of thought which, in small corners of non-elite academies, have formed Cultural Studies. And elite or not, there is no doubt in my mind that the strong tide of interest running through a generation in the style and preoccupations of Cultural Studies however named is evidence of the subject's larger timeliness. I will risk declaring that *this is the way the best and brightest of present-day students in the human sciences want to learn to think and feel.* And having learned to think and feel thus, this is how they want to act and live... There is, as always, a story hidden in these assertions. It is the story of how Cultural Studies will make you good. (Italics in the original.)[24]

It is beyond Nandy's intellectual constitution to be so coarse. For him, biography is a ground for mining psychological insights, for understanding how the Indian Self survived, or failed to survive, the onslaught of colonialism, for constructing a politics of awareness—not a new theology of deliverance.

But deliverance is what western thought is all about, Nandy would argue. In modernity, of course, the grand narratives are essentially vehicles of salvation. Having swept all grand narratives aside, postmodern thought generates the illusion that there is nothing for us to do than to live with the horror of meaninglessness. Both modernity and postmodern thought, however, fall back on a single theory of salvation: the secular imagination. It is not by accident that Rorty suggests that the real goal of postmodernist thought is to de-divinize the world, to expunge all traces of religious thought;[25] and Inglis suggests 'that the study of culture, as of nature, teaches atheism'[26]—this is not a conclusion of philosophical or cultural inquiry but a deep seated assumption that is an essential component of dominant western consciousness. This insistent falling back on secularism—disguised as 'liberal humanism' or 'biography' or 'cul-

[24] Ibid., p. 229.

[25] Richard Rorty, *Contingency, Irony and Solidarity* (Cambridge: Cambridge University Press, 1989).

[26] *Cultural Studies,* p. 231.

tural studies'—has led Nandy to argue that the West and its relationship with the non-West have become deeply intertwined with the problem of evil in our time. The West can now appreciate only the secularized aspects of the non-West. Thus, Inglis cannot see any good in Islam and is happy to dismiss it as 'angry and vengeful'.[27] He lionizes neo-orientalists like V.S. Naipaul (described by Nandy as 'ethnocidal') who portray the non-secularist people as puritanic savages. Inglis represents the westernized Jawaharlal Nehru as 'India' and sees in his biography the vision of what India should be because 'Nehru took the narratives embodied in the biographies of J.S. Mill and William Morris, and turned them to Indian account.'[28] The India imagined by Nehru, Inglis asserts, 'would be peaceable, independent, industrialized, united, social-democratic. It would not be Gandhi's peasant homeland with a loom in every cottage and his creaking, cranky ideas about sex, the deity, asceticism and whatnot.'[29] Inglis is not inclined to ask questions such as whether, without Gandhi, there would have been an independent India; and whether it is a part of Nehru's legacy that we have an aggressive, warring nation state in India nursing Hindu nationalism and disunited communities perpetually fighting for 'autonomy' or 'independence'! Grand narratives may damage your health, as Inglis suggests, but, Nandy would insist, the western secular imagination itself has become, in the context of the non-West, pathological and intrinsically, if unconsciously, part of the landscape of evil.

Inglis' perception of Gandhi echoes George Lukacs' criticism of Rabindranath Tagore. Reviewing Tagore's *The Home and the World*, Lukacs makes some bold claims:

> Tagore himself is—as imaginative writer and as thinker—a wholly insignificant figure. His creative powers are non-existent; his characters pale stereotypes; his stories thread-bare and uninteresting; and his sensibility is meagre, insubstantial ...
>
> The intellectual conflict in the novel is concerned with the use of violence ... The hypothesis is that India is an oppressed, enslaved country, yet Mr Tagore shows no interest in this question ....

[27] Ibid., p. 215. On neo-orientalism in general, and Naipaul in particular, see Ziauddin Sardar and Merryl Wyn Davies, *Distorted Imagination: Lessons from the Rushdie Affair* (London: Grey Seal, 1989).

[28] Ibid., p. 218.

[29] Ibid., p. 220.

> ... A pamphlet—and one resorting to the lowest tools of libel—is what Tagore's novel is, in spite of its tediousness and want of spirit.
>
> This stance represents nothing less than the *ideology of the eternal subjection of India* ...
>
> This propagandistic, demagogically one-sided stance renders the novel completely worthless from the artistic angle ...
>
> But Tagore's creative powers do not stretch to a decent pamphlet ... The 'spiritual' aspects of his story, separated from the nuggets of Indian wisdom into which it is tricked out, is a petty bourgeois yarn of the shoddiest kind ... (his) 'wisdom' was put at the intellectual service of the British police.[30]

Lukacs was writing in 1922. Inglis is writing in 1992. Seventy years on, the critical apparatus of western scholarship still sustains a hegemonic cultural discourse. What is it about Tagore and Gandhi that so frightens western intellectuals in general, and cultural critics in particular? Both saw themselves as members of a civilization that, in the words of Nandy, 'refuses to view politics only as a secularised arena of human initiative. While associating the country with maternity and sacredness, they insisted that the association imposed a responsibility on the individual to maintain that sacredness.'[31] The position taken by both had an intrinsic, in-built critique of nationalism and the idea of the 'nation state'.

In *The Illegitimacy of Nationalism*, Nandy explores the biography of Tagore to reveal how the Bengali poet developed his anti-nationalist views. It is an excellent example both of concise, pithy writing and the use of biography in cultural analysis. Unlike western art criticism, where an artist's work is often seen to be independent of his life, Nandy insists on looking at Tagore's biography through a pluralist framework. Tagore's worldview is unfolded through ideological and mythical constructions as well as through the examination of his novels and his life. Thus Tagore's divided selves—his modernist upbringing and appreciation of British culture, his innate traditionalism and consequent distaste for British culture—are brought together both through confrontation and synthesis. Tagore was, indeed is, one of the founding fathers of the modern consciousness in India. So it is somewhat of a paradox that he ended

30 Quoted by Nandy, *The Illegitimacy of Nationalism* (Delhi, OUP, 1994), p. 16.

31 Ibid., p. 85.

up, against his own instincts and upbringing, as an ardent critic of modernity. Nandy explains the paradox by using a technique that is almost a hallmark of his scholarship. Just as he counterbalances, in *Alternative Sciences*, the life of Bose with Ramanujan, in *The Illegitimacy of Nationalism*, he juxtaposes Tagore with what he calls his 'political double': the writer and activist Brahmabandhab Upadhyay. Both Tagore and Upadhyay were patriots who had great respect for each other. But while Upadhyay used nationalism, both in his life and his writing, to fight imperialism, Tagore was concerned about the hidden costs of nationalism. He came to see it as a dualistic counter-ideology of imperialism, both having moorings in a single worldview. Thus the author of the national anthem of India, who has influenced Indian nationalism through his poetry, songs and participation in the struggle against the Raj, could speak of nationalism as 'a *bhougalik apadevata*, a geographical demon, and Shantiniketan, his alternative university, as a temple dedicated to exorcise this demon'.[32]

Tagore's analysis of his own culture and its power to resist physical, mental and spiritual colonization, leads him to a conclusion often diametrically opposed to that of his contemporaries. Nandy shows that cultural analysis itself can be a tool of dissent and resistance. Cultural studies need not desacralize, as Inglis contends; it can lead to sacralization, and towards strategies for surviving—in the case of the non-West—and curing—in the case of the West—the pathologies of the dominant, still inherently colonial, modes of thought. Nandy uses psychological biography to exorcise the demons within the modern nation state of India and heal its split, disintegrating selves. He shows how cultural studies can be, and must be, about liberating western and non-western civilizations from the suffocating embrace of both old and new versions of colonialism.

Colonialism, civilizations

The dedication in *The Tao of Cricket* could not be simpler: 'To Uma'.[33] In the preface to *The Intimate Enemy*, Nandy confesses

[32] Ibid., p. 7.

[33] Ashis Nandy, *The Tao of Cricket: On Games of Destiny and the Destiny of Games* (Delhi: Penguin Books, 1989). See the dedication.

that 'without my wife Uma and my daughter Aditi I would have finished the work earlier but it would not have been the same'.[34] Wives and children, as any Sufi manual of a good life will confirm, have a great deal to teach husbands and parents. Traditional societies do not assign different categories of thought to different sexes or to different stages of human biological growth. Men are capable of feminine thoughts, just as children can have 'adult' ideas. But in the ideology of colonialism, thought and education flowed only one way: the aggressive, masculine colonizer taught the cowardly, feminine colonized subject. The subjugated non-West, with its primitive and child-like cultures, had nothing to teach the imperial West. The adult, male and virile western civilization had a responsibility to husband the weak, docile, passive cultures of the Orient.

This self-image of the colonial powers produced a counter-image in its dissenters. The conventional view holds that the only victims of colonialism were the subject cultures and societies. So colonialism is seen essentially as a political economy designed to ensure one-way flow of goods and benefits with the non-western communities as passive and perpetual losers: 'behind all the rhetoric of the European intelligentsia on the evils of colonialism lay their unstated faith that the gains from colonialism to Europe, to the extent that they primarily involved material products, were real, and the losses, to the extent they involved social relations and psychological state, false'.[35] But this is a vested view of colonialism propagated by colonialism itself. It suppresses the fact that the colonizers too were devoured by the ideology of colonialism.

Colonialism dehumanized the colonizers as much as it brutalized the colonized. The relationship it produced between the rulers and the ruled was akin to that in a family headed by a tyrannical husband and father who maintains his authority by sheer terror. But the more he abuses the family the more he loses his own humanity and the more the family disintegrates into a group of victims. What the European imperial powers did in the colonies bounced back to the fatherland as a new political and public culture. Colonialism transformed Britain culturally by declaring tenderness, speculation and introspection as feminine and therefore unworthy of public

[34] *The Intimate Enemy*, p. xx.

[35] Ibid., p. 30.

culture and by bringing to the fore the most brutish, masculine elements of British colonial life. It justified a restricted cultural role for women and promoted an instrumental notion of lower classes; both now became slightly modified versions of the colonial concept of hierarchy. Thus the calamity of colonialism for Britain was the tragedy of the women, the children, the working classes and others placed at the bottom of the heap by a set of oppressive masculine virtues. The models of punishment, discipline, productivity and subjugation, that were used in the colonies to whip the subjects into shape, were used in the fatherland to encourage new forms of institutionalized violence and ruthless social Darwinism.

In George Orwell's classic essay, 'Shooting an Elephant', Nandy finds the most profound description of the trepidation and terror induced by colonialism in the colonizers: 'the reification of social bonds through formal, stereotyped, part-object relationships; an instrumental view of nature; created loneliness of the colonizers in the colony through a theory of cultural stratification and exclusivism: an unending search for masculinity and status before the colonized'.[36] The perception of the subject people as simple children who had to be impressed with 'conspicuous machismo' forced the colonizers into perpetual suppression of their own self for the sake of an imposed imperial identity. Over a period of time, this inauthentic, murderous identity would be internalized. It is hardly surprising then that all the themes that can be identified with the present cultural crisis of the West are present in Orwell's essay.

The imperial powers also created a self-image for those who were being husbanded by colonialism. In as much as this self-image is a dualistic opposite, it is and remains in essence a western construction. Colonialism replaced the Eurocentric convention of portraying the Other as an incomprehensible barbarian with the pathological stereotype of the strange but predictable Oriental. He was now religious but superstitious, clever but devious, chaotically violent but effeminately cowardly. At the same time, a new discourse was developed where the basic mode of breaking out of these stereotypes was to reverse them: superstitious but spiritual, uneducated but wise, womanly but pacific. 'No colonialism could be complete', writes Nandy, 'unless it "universalized" and enriched its ethnic stereo-

[36] Ibid., p. 40.

types by appropriating the language of defiance of its victims. That was why the cry of the victims of colonialism was ultimately the cry to be heard in another language—unknown to the colonizer and the anti-colonial movements that he had bred and then domesticated'.[37]

The victim's language of defiance may be totally different, but the agony caused by centuries of colonialism and the experience of authoritarian imperial rule equally distorted the minds and cultures of both, the imperialists and their prey. Moreover, after a while, the distortion did not look like a distortion. The mutual bondage in anguish generated strong justifications for this suffering on both sides of the colonial divide. The forces that unleashed and sustained the agony shape almost every aspect of our history, our contemporary lives and our imagined futures. Indeed, the institutionalized suffering flowing out of the system has acquired its own momentum and has become self-perpetuating.

Nandy's perspective on dealing with institutionalized suffering is based on three assumptions. First, he asserts, no civilization has a monopoly on goodness and humane values. All civilizations share certain basic values and cultural traits that derive from our biological self and social experience. What is unique about a given civilization is not its values but the framework within which these values are actualized and the emphasis and priorities it assigns to these values. Thus certain values, or traditions based on these values, may, at a given point, recede or acquire dominance in a civilization but they are never solely absent or exclusively present: 'what looks like a human potentiality which ought to be actualized in some distant future, is often only a cornered cultural strain waiting to be renewed or rediscovered'.[38] Second,

> human civilization is constantly trying to alter or expand its awareness of exploitation and oppression. Oppressions which were once outside the span of awareness are no longer so, and it is quite likely that the present awareness of suffering, too, will be found wanting and might change in the future. Who, before the socialists, had thought of class as a unit of repression? How many, before Freud, had sensed

[37] Ibid., p. 73. For a more detailed discussion of the relationship between the colonizer and the colonized see Ziauddin Sardar, Ashis Nandy and Merryl Wyn Davies, *Barbaric Others: A Manifesto on Western Racism* (London: Pluto Press, 1993).

[38] *Traditions, Tyranny and Utopias*, p. 22.

> that children needed to be protected against their own parents? How many believed, before Gandhi's rebirth after the environmental crisis in the West, that modern technology, the supposed liberator of man, had become his most powerful oppressor? Our limited ethical sensitivity is not a proof of human hypocrisy; it is mostly a product of our limited cognition of the human situation. Oppression is ultimately a matter of definition, and its perception is the product of a worldview. Change the worldview, and what once seemed natural and legitimate becomes an instance of cruelty and sadism.[39]

Third, all civilizations, in as far as they are human, are imperfect; and imperfect civilizations can only produce imperfect solutions for their cultural and social imperfections. Solutions, after all, emerge from exactly the same cultural and social experience as the problem and, as such, the same thought or consciousness as well as the same unthought, or unconsciousness, informs them.

What, then, are the possible boundaries of a solution? Our release from institutionalized suffering, Nandy argues, must involve both the non-West and the West. But this is not an invitation for the masculine, oppressive West to transform itself: it is the recognition that the oppressed and marginalized selves in the West need help and that they can be recognized and used as civilization allies in the battle against institutionalized suffering. It is non-western civilizations that must give collective representation to all institutionalized suffering everywhere—the suffering of the pasts as well as the present. And, as such, non-western civilizations have to be aware of both: the outside forces of cruelty and grief as well as the 'inner vectors' that have dislodged their true Selves. Non-western cultures have to do much more than simply resist the West: they have to transform their cultures into cultures of resistance. They have to rediscover their traditions of reinterpreting traditions to create new traditions—including new traditions of dissent.

Dissent, definitions

'For those who dare to defy the given models of defiance' reads the dedication in *Traditions, Tyranny and Utopias,* which is subtitled:

[39] Ibid., p. 22.

'Essays in the Politics of Awareness'.[40] Dissent, in Nandy's thought, is about awareness and it must begin with two realizations. First, 'yesterday's dissent is often today's establishment and, unless resisted, becomes tomorrow's terror'.[41] Second, dissent itself has been colonized. The dissenters, the counterplayers to the game of western imperialism and domination, work *within* the dominant model of universalism and *with* the dominant consciousness. Western categories and system of knowledge, argues Nandy, have been much more successful in ensuring dominance than naked political and economic power. The true power of the West lies not in its political and technological might, but in its power to define. The West defines freedom, history, human rights, dissent; the non-West accepts these definitions. This unquestioned, often unrecognized power of the West to define, and the game of categories the West plays with the non-West, ensures that dissent not only remains docile and confinable but serves as an illustration of the West's democratic spirit. Witness how easily the dominant academic culture took over 'disciplines' that began as attempts to break out of the straitjacket of conventional knowledge systems. Ecology, feminism and cultural studies have been successfully domesticated and professionalized as new specializations in the knowledge industry. Thus, by subtle but well organized means, the dominant knowledge industry ensures that the capitals of dissent, along with the capitals of global political economy, are located in the stylish universities, think tanks and other intellectual centres of the First World. Domination is only complete when dissent can be foreseen and managed; and this cannot be done unless definitional criteria has been established to determine what is genuine, sober dissent and these criteria have been systematically institutionalized through the university system. This is what fashionable academic and intellectual trends, such as post-modernism, post-colonialism and post-structuralism, are designed to do. Appreciating how dissent is predicted and controlled, Nandy confesses,

> explained to me some of my earlier disappointments with western dissenters, particularly from the left. Many of them are not only eminent scholars in their own right but have brought up, with paternal concern,

40 Ibid. The dedication.

41 Ibid., p. 13.

> at least three generations of non-western dissenting scholars, teaching them with loving care the meaning of 'true' dissent and the technology of 'authentic' radicalism. But copious tears shed for the Third World and its exploited masses, I was gradually to find out, rarely went with any respect for the Third World's own understanding of its own plight (as if that understanding had to be hidden like a family scandal from the outside world).[42]

But it is not just that the West domesticates dissent; official India too has its versions of managed dissent. The Indian public life gives voice to all types of nonconformity; indeed there is a culture of in-house dissent that is part of the Indian political scene. The radical Marxist movement, the thundering editorials of the nation's newspapers and magazines, the popular new video newsmagazines —these are all examples of dissent that Indian state has nurtured and can comfortably contain. However, there is one thing that domesticated dissent can never do, or is never allowed to do: to challenge, compromise or remove the 'core components', the founding pillars of 'India'. Amongst these, writes Nandy,

> are the state (by which is meant the nation-state); nationalism (defined as allegiance to a steam-rolling monocultural concept of India, composed out of the nineteenth-century European concept of nationality); secularism (used not as one possible way of containing religious strife but as a synonym for the promotion of supra-religious allegiances to the now-dominant idea of the Indian state); development (which has now fully colonised the idea of social change); history (paradoxically seen as an ahistorical, linear, scientific enterprise); rationality (as an allegedly non-partisan, contemporary embodiment of the post-Enlightenment theories of progress) and a totally romanticized concept of *realpolitik* that is neither realistic nor truly political in its content.[43]

The ideal western, and hence 'universal' notion of cultural dissent is well captured by the story of fifteenth-century Aztec priests who were rounded up by their Spanish conquerors and given two choices: to convert or to die. The priests responded that if their gods were dead, as alleged by the Jesuit priests, then they too would rather die. The Spanish took no time to unleash their war dogs on the

[42] Ashis Nandy, 'Bearing Witness to the Future,' *Futures* 28 (6/7) Aug/Sept 1996, p. 638.
[43] *The Savage Freud*, p. ix.

Aztec priests. What would, Nandy asks, be the response of Brahman priests if they were given the same choice? They would readily convert to Christianity; some of them would even write treatises praising the colonizers and their gods. However, their Christianity would soon reveal itself to be a minor variation of Hinduism. Why does the dominant culture regard the Aztec priests as models of courage and the Brahman priests as hypocritical cowards? On one level, the answer is simple. After their last defiant act, the Aztec priests die, leaving their killers free to continue with their rampage and to sing praises of the courage of their dead enemies. The Aztec priests also set a good example, from the perspective of the dominant culture, for all dissenters to follow: die in glorified dissent. The Brahmanic response ensures that 'unheroic cowards' are always there, ready to make their presence felt when opportunities arise.

There is also another answer:

> the average Indian has always lived with the awareness and possibility of long-term suffering, always seen himself and protecting his deepest faith with the passive, 'feminine' cunning of the weak and the victimized, and surviving outer pressures by refusing to overplay his sense of autonomy and self-respect. At his heroic best, he is a *satyagrahi*, one who forges a partly-coercive weapon called *satyagraha* out of ... 'perfect weakness'. In his non-heroic ordinariness, he is the archetypal survivor. Seemingly he makes all-round compromises, but he refuses to be psychologically swamped, co-opted or penetrated. Defeat, his response seems to say, is a disaster and so are the imposed ways of the victor. But worse is the loss of one's 'soul' and the internalization of one's victor, because it forces one to fight the victor according to the victor's values, within his model of dissent. Better to be a comical dissenter than to be a powerful, serious but acceptable opponent. Better to be a hated enemy, declared unworthy of any respect whatsoever, than to be a proper opponent, constantly making 'primary adjustments' to the system.[44]

By accepting a violent end to their dissent, the Aztec priests, Nandy seems to be saying, unwittingly collude with the worldview of their oppressors. In some celebrated non-western dissenters, this collusion is more open and conscious. For example, violence has a central, cleansing role in Frantz Fanon's vision of a post-colonial society.

[44] *The Intimate Enemy*, p. 111.

This is why his vision, which is so alien to many Africans and Asians, has been so readily accepted in the West. Fanon argued that the oppressor is often internalized by the oppressed. So it becomes necessary for the oppressor to be confronted in violence not just to liberate oneself from his oppression but also to mark an agonizing break with a part of one's own self.[45] Nandy argues that if Fanon had more confidence in his culture (this is a problematic assertion as Fanon had no notion of what *his* culture was) he would have realized that his vision tied the victims more deeply to the culture of oppression than straightforward collaboration. By accepting the oppressors' principle of violence, the victims further internalize the basic values of the oppressors. And once violence is given cultural legitimacy, it transforms the battle between two visions and worldviews into a struggle for power and resources between two groups with identical values.

This stance against violence and militarism, however, should not be confused with pacifism. Pacifism, like environmental consumerism, is often a luxury and can be a symbol of status. The rich and well-connected dodge the contaminated world of military violence more easily and skillfully; those sent to fight distant wars to protect 'national interests', are often the under-privileged and the marginalized. During the Vietnam war, for example, 'conscientious objectors' and draft dodgers were mostly well-to-do whites. Those shipped to fight in Vietnam were predominantly blacks and poor whites who 'neither had any respite from the system nor from their progressive, privileged fellow citizens protesting the war and feeling self-righteous'.[46] They were men who had experienced direct and institutionalized violence at home in the form of overt and latent racism, oppressive labour regulations and other discriminatory practices. The stereotyping of the 'commie' Vietcong and the genocidal behaviour of many of these soldiers is not surprising: 'the Vietnam war on this plane was a story of one set of victims setting upon another, on behalf of a reified, impersonal system of violence'.[47]

Beyond violence and pacifism, there is a third option: the dissenter as a non-player. Here the oppressed, refusing to be a first-class

[45] *Traditions, Tyranny, and Utopias*, p. 34.

[46] Ibid., p. 30.

[47] Ibid., p. 31.

citizen in the world of oppression, is neither a player nor a counter-player: he or she plays another game altogether, a game of building an alternative world where there is some hope of winning back his or her humanity. This is a game that someone like Radhabinod Pal played. Pal was a member of the International Military Tribunal for the Far East that conducted the Tokyo war crimes trial from 1946 to 1948. He found the Japanese accused of war crimes to be not guilty—the only one of the judges to do so. Not that Pal was unaware of Japanese atrocities—he was simply playing a game that involved going beyond the dualistic logic of the accused and the accusers. He was, as Nandy so elegantly shows, acknowledging the symbiosis of adversaries, a game Nandy himself plays rather well. In Pal's dissenting judgement there was a silent summons not merely for the accused to reflect on their guilt but to the plaintiffs and the judges, 'to discover the accused in them'.[48]

Hope as a Weapon

In the final analysis, it is a game of dissenting visions and futures. The future itself is a state of awareness. And the main aim of the game is to transform the future by changing human awareness of the future. By defining what is 'immutable' and 'universal', the West silences the visions of Other peoples and cultures to ensure the continuity of its own linear projections of the past and the present on to the future. By avoiding thinking about the future, Other cultures and societies become prisoners of the past, present and future of the western civilization. As Thomas Szasz had declared, 'in the animal kingdom, the rule is, eat or be eaten; in the human kingdom, define or be defined'.[49] Hence the need for non-western cultures to define their own future in terms of their own categories and concepts and to articulate their visions in a language that is true to their own Self, even if not comprehensible 'on the other side of the global fence of academic respectability'.[50] The plurality of dissent can only be ensured if human choices are expanded by 'reconceptualizing political, social and cultural ends; by identifying

[48] *The Savage Freud*, p. 59.

[49] Thomas Szasz, *The Second Sin* (London: Routledge and Kegan Paul, 1974), p. 20.

[50] *Futures*, p. 638.

emerging or previously ignored social pathologies that have to be understood, contained or transcended; by linking up the fates of different polities and societies through envisioning their common fears and hopes'.[51]

Hope is perhaps the last weapon in the armoury of those who reside outside the 'civilized' world. But hope alone is not enough: 'the meek inherit the earth not by meekness alone'.[52] Nandy seeks to furnish the victims with a host of other tools that have always been there, but have been buried under the mental constructions of internalized colonialism and modernity.

This gives Nandy's thought its hallmark of consistency. Not that he was not modified his ideas, refined and sharpened them, or that he is unaware of his own failures. For example, the preface to the second edition of *Alternative Sciences* provides a critique of the book pointing out where it has failed, where he has refined his ideas, and where it could be improved if he were to rewrite it. The consistency comes from two sources. Firstly, he is always true to his own roots. His ideas are a distillation of the plurality of India; they emerge from examinations of things Indian, and tend to rely almost exclusively on Indian myths and categories for analysis and on Indian examples for explanation. Anyone who has seen Nandy in action at a seminar or a conference knows that he is totally open to ideas, whatever their source, and is scintillated by the power of ideas to move people and societies. In particular, and in line with his own position, he relishes the ideas that seek to sabotage his position. He is ever ready to grant that his ideas may be rendered irrelevant by new readings of traditional visions or by new visions with changed perceptions of evil. But he measures the quality of ideas by their non-dualistic content and the import they may have on the victims of manufactured oppression. In this respect, he is a true friend of all victims—everywhere.

Secondly, Nandy is consistent in his critique and equally harsh on the West and the non-West. The colonial attitudes to Indian culture split the Indians into the this-worldly (exceedingly shrewd, greedy, self-centred, money-minded) and the overtly other-wordly (too concerned with spirituality, mysticism and transcendence, not

[51] Ibid., p. 637.

[52] *The Intimate Enemy*, p. xiii.

fit for the world of modern science and technology, statecraft and productive work). Nandy, on the other hand, sees India as a consistent whole. He is not concerned with romanticizing Indian tradition. He is always eager to expose the folly of fossilized, suffocating tradition ('the blood-stained, oppressive heritage of a number of oriental religious ideologies') as well as tradition constructed under the impulse of modernity (so 'immaculate in the hands of their contemporary interpreters'). It is this consistency that makes Nandy truer to his own self.

The qualities of Ashis Nandy's mind are in full evidence in the three books brought together in this omnibus edition: *Alternative Sciences, The Illegitimacy of Nationalism* and *The Savage Freud.* One could see them as three different and distinct books; but they could easily be read as a unified collection of essays. As a writer, Nandy is, above all, an essayist. And, in their own different ways, all of these essays explore, expand, interrogate, a single theme—a theme that could be described as the dominant ambition of the civilization that is India: 'to be the cultural epitome of the world and to redefine or convert all passionate self-other debates into self-self debates'.[53]

[53] *The Illegitimacy of Nationalism,* p. 82.

ALTERNATIVE SCIENCES

Creativity and Authenticity in Two Indian Scientists

Contents

Preface to the Second Edition

Twelve years is a long time in a person's life; it is an even longer time in the life of a book; and nothing can be as startlingly educative as reading one's own work after such a gap. The earlier introduction to *Alternative Sciences* reflects that discovery. It was written, as I make clear in it, some years after the work on the book was completed and gave me a chance to have a second, more dispassionate look at the whole endeavour. It was in fact an author's attempt to mark out a possible baseline for criticism of his own book. I propose to use this preface to strengthen that process.

I am still fond of *Alternative Sciences*, and I still wistfully remember the leisurely pace at which I worked on the two life histories included in the book. It was after all my first independent work of scholarship. However, when I wrote the book, my primary emphasis was on the social psychology of creativity. So I accepted, even if grudgingly, the standard two-fold division of science into its text and context. Over the years I have given up this two-fold division, and come to believe that there is no Orwellian thought-police guarding the borders between the contents and contexts of modern science. The main function of the dichotomy has been to deflect all criticism of science away from the scientist, towards the forces that control the externalities of modern science—some well-known candidates being the military–industrial complex, American hegemony, Stalinism, Oriental despotism, and religious bigotry. This is what I have elsewhere called the principle of split legitimation, influenced partly by the work of my friend J. P. S. Uberoi. According to this principle, only the good that science does need be owned up by scientists, never the evil. The politically powerful play up to the split, for it allows them to bypass the scientists' moral selves while appropriating their professional skills. Few claim that the Weimar Republic played any role in the creation of quantum mechanics or the theory of relativity. Almost everybody believes they were the discoveries of gifted scientists; it was nuclear weaponry that was the doing of necrophylic establishments.

In that sense I now find *Alternative Sciences* not adequately critical. The two scientists I have constructed in its pages are ambivalent towards modern science. They do use traditional cognitive orders as a baseline for social criticisms of modern science, but they both feel uncomfortable with the idea of the plurality of science and the proposition that there can be politics or culture in the content of science. Like the author when he wrote the book, they want to give modern science a richer, more plural context and to bring that context to bear upon the creative process in science.

In other words, I blame myself for not pursuing systematically the alternative frames of knowledge that the two scientists used and leaned against. For instance, in the section on Srinivas Ramanujan, there is no discussion of the indigenous schools of mathematics which had survived in vestigial form in South India, specially in Kerala, and which shaped his mathematical worldview. Even in the case of Jagadis Chandra Bose, there is insufficient effort to set Bose's vitalistic biophysics within the tradition of Indian science. To those who know my subsequent work, I must issue the warning that this is not a book on knowledge systems; it is a book on the personal contexts of scientific creativity outside the normal habitat of modern science. This has given a touch of incompleteness to the two life stories, especially to my profiles of the two scientists as functioning, creative individuals. Fortunately other scholars have in the meanwhile worked on this part of Ramanujan's heritage and what I left undone in his case has not remained an area of darkness any more.

If I were to write this book today, I should define my responsibility slightly differently. Taking a position with the victims of modern science outside the perimeters of the 'civilized' world, I shall offset myth against science and history. These victims, for good or for ill, tend to speak the language of myths; their rulers and their self-declared emancipators both speak the language of science and of history. My inability to build that into the very framework of my analysis would be a more serious criticism of this book than that new philosophical insights have led to a revaluation of Bose's plant physiology, or that new data have been amassed on Ramanujan's life and work.

Some other opportunities which I did not exploit sufficiently are probably now, sadly enough, no longer open to exploration. I did not fully know what to make of the rich experience of interviewing

Janaki, Ramanujan's greatly-suffering wife. I could sense her powerful presence, her meaningful though sad life after her husband's death, and her instinct for survival. She was an interesting person in herself, not merely as her husband's shadow or her mother-in-law's other. Similarly with John Littlewood and C. P. Snow. My framework did not have much space for their captivating personalities which told me so much about the pre-war culture of science. Even though I sensed that these men bridged, through their self-definitions, different eras and traditions of science, I did not know how to integrate these experiences into my narrative. I had spent hours with all three of them and my encounter with Janaki was particularly moving; but I stuck to the personality of Ramanujan and the environment that shaped it, and did not digress into the trajectories of others who had played a role in his life. Similarly, towards the end of my work on the book, I came to know that Mrs Boshi Sen—her husband was at one time one of Bose's intimates who parted company with his hero as a disappointed and slightly bitter apostate—lived at Almora at the foot of the Himalaya. Reportedly she was a storehouse of information on the later Bose, his style of research, his organizational and interpersonal skills. Alas, I felt I knew that part of the story rather well and did not need to reopen the case I had already studied.

Probably, *Alternative Sciences* would have been a more acceptable book for me today if I had consciously allowed it to be something more than a book on the cultural psychology of scientific creativity.

Yet, despite being unavailable for over five years, this book has continued to enjoy a certain patronage from critics and students of the sociology and culture of science. Some readers have generously continued to look at it as a step towards the identification of a more humane, culturally rooted system of science. Even if this is not so, the book remains to this day one of the few available on the cultural context of individual creativity in science in the non-western world. It is with that awareness that this paperback edition is being issued. I hope it still manages to convey to the reader, however imperfectly, something of the anguish of being a dissenting scientist in this part of the world, with the defence of cultural and intellectual values from the point of view of defeated systems of knowledge, and with the psychological costs of confronting an imperial system of knowledge outside the western world.

I am grateful to my editor at the Oxford University Press who took the initiative of republishing the book and also helped me get rid of the touch of pomposity that often informs an author's first work, to Punam Zutshi who provided editorial help and words of wisdom, and to Bhuwan Chandra for his secretarial services.

Finally, two warnings to the reader that I should have given when the book was first published. Many technical terms used in the following pages do not appear to be so. I have in mind especially clinical terms borrowed from psychoanalytic psychology such as projective system (*à la* Abraham Kardiner) and projection, identification, reality-testing, rationalization, ritual and ritualization, orality, compensation, reparation, reality-testing, regression, cathexis and concretism. Even apparently everyday words such as need and nurture (both used in Henry Murray's sense), self, denial, identity, development (in the sense of personality development), motive and defence have technical meanings. I hope that the sense in which I have used them is clear from the context; nevertheless, the qualification should be borne in mind.

Second, I have not come across any important new work on Bose during the last two decades. The brief chapter on him in Peter Tomkins and Christopher Bird's *The Secret Life of Plants* is primarily a response to the changing attitude to science in the early 1970s. In the case of Ramanujan, however, there is now a charming new biography, Robert Kanigel's *The Man Who Knew Infinity*. There have also been new developments in the study of his work, thanks to the rediscovery of some of his notes.

Delhi, 1993

A. N.

Preface to the First Edition

Psychologists analysing biographical data are twice privileged. They may write bad life histories because they are psychologists and they may produce bad psychology because they are dealing with history. I have brazenly exploited both the privileges in this book. The only mitigating circumstance I can claim is that somebody had to raise the issues raised here. This is one book which was in search of an author. That it found one in me is an irritant which the reader will, regrettably, have to endure.

I have another confession to make. The science of science is today a specialized discipline. It was less so when I started this work some years back. So the reader may find in the following pages a certain naïveté, theoretical as well as methodological. Unfortunately, without rewriting the entire book it was impossible to utilize fully the new developments which have since taken place in social studies of sciences and to remove this naïveté. I am ashamed to say that I have shirked that responsibility. While that makes this book technically a less competent enterprise, I hope it still communicates some flavour of the inner world of two Indian scientists.

To make the task of my reviewers easy, let me briefly state at this point what this book is about. In the following pages I have analysed the life histories of two scientists who at one time seemed to promise new paradigms of science as well as new models of scientific creativity.

The first essay is on Jagadis Chandra Bose (1858–1937) who started his career as a brilliant physicist, changed his discipline to become an even more influential plant physiologist, and died a lapsed scientist and half-forgotten mystic. In his heyday, his admirers such as Albert Einstein, Bernard Shaw, Henri Bergson, Aldous Huxley, and Romain Rolland found in him the personification of a historical civilization which had a more humane concept of science and a more integrated view of the organic and inorganic worlds than the West would offer. Even when he had fallen from grace in the world of science, his compatriots continued to see in him a symbol of Indian science and a pioneer who had Indianized modern science to make it compatible with the culture of an ancient society. The essay traces Bose's science to his early socialization, the distinctive concept of science in his society, and the needs of modern science at his time. It also shows how his professional degeneration reflected the interactive demands of his subject society, his personality, and the apparently universal culture of world science dominated by societies which in the context of India aroused deep feelings of personal inadequacy and a painful search for parity.

The second essay is on Srinivasa Ramanujan (1887–1920), one of the greatest untrained mathematical geniuses ever known. When this was accidentally discovered at the age of twenty-five, he was working as a clerk in Madras on a salary of twenty-five rupees a month. But on his own, helped by a hopelessly out-of-date, second-rate textbook for undergraduates, he had re-made some of the major mathematical discoveries of the previous hundred years and was in many fields far ahead of his contemporaries. The essay analyses the sources of Ramanujan's mathematical thinking, the association between it and his magical–ritualistic concepts of numbers and manipulation of numbers, his uncontaminated orthodoxy and pride in it, and the psychosocial meanings of the bonds he had established with his famous discoverer and collaborator, G. H. Hardy, a man in turn driven by his homosexual needs and his deep ambivalence towards conventional authority systems. In the process, I explore the extent to which Ramanujan's culture and his unexposure to a modern lifestyle spared him the internal conflicts of Bose, the extent to which his orthodoxy ensured his autonomy as a creative mathematician, and how his private meaning of mathematics gave him a valid personal philosophy of science so that he could live and die a functioning mathematician. The essay also includes a brief comparative discussion of the ways in which Bose and Ramanujan mediated the demands of modern science, their own motivational patterns and the traditions of their society. It ends with some theoretical speculations about the common meanings of inspiration and creativity in two men who might have been by-products of the cultural changes in their country and in the world of science.

The first chapter provides an introduction to the two essays, discussing the normative implications of these psychological and historical accounts and the theoretical concerns guiding them.

Many persons and environments have contributed to the writing of this book. I can mention here only the most important of them.

D. M. Bose, Gopal Chandra Bhattacharya, Pulin Bihari Sen, and S. N. Bose helped me with a mass of information about Bose's life and work, and Rajni Kothari, S. K. Mitra, Steven Dedijer, Avery Leiserson, Edward Shils, Lucian Pye, and D. L. Sheth commented on an earlier version of the section on Bose. Lloyd and Susanne Rudolph, Milton Singer, R. S. Das, Nihar Ranjan Ray, and Raymond Owens were some of the first to read my early draft on Bose and to encourage me in the venture. To David Edge and the anonymous referees of *Science Studies* who published a paleolithic version of the section on Bose, I owe many useful editorial suggestions.

Janaki Ramanujan, P. K. Srinivasan, J. E. Littlewood, S. Chandrasekhar, and C. P. Snow supplied me with little-known or unknown details about Ramanujan's life and about the Ramanujan–Hardy relationship. Prakash Desai wrote what virtually amounted to a review article on the Ramanujan section. His suggestions, some of which I have used in this version of the essay, also included a fascinating, comparative evaluation of Bose and Ramanujan from a psychiatrist's point of view. Once again D. L. Sheth made detailed comments, in his distinctive beatific style, on an earlier draft of the section, and C. R. M. Rao, Indukant Shukla, and C. Chintamani went with their fine editorial tooth comb through my Bengalese to turn it into tolerable English.

Section three of the essay on Ramanujan was also published in the *Psychoanalytic Review*. It owes its present shape partly to the useful criticisms of the anonymous reviewer of the journal. The Indian Council of Social Science Research provided, at very short notice, funds which permitted me to examine the Ramanujan Papers at Trinity College, Cambridge, and to interview Janaki Ramanujan, Littlewood, Snow, D. M. Bose, P. B. Sen, and S. N. Bose.

For all this generous help I am immensely grateful. But, above all, it is to the group at the Centre for the Study of Developing Societies that I owe my gratitude. By constantly confuting my position on extra-scientific determinants of science while I was writing the section on Bose and by as vehemently opposing whatever autonomy I granted to science while writing on Ramanujan (because by that time they had partly convinced me by their arguments) they may have further shaken my already-tottering belief in human self-consistency, but they helped me clarify my own concepts and sharpen my analytic tools. Though I have not been able to satisfy them fully in either of their incarnations, they have more than satisfied my need for intellectual succour.

Delhi

Ashis Nandy

Part One

Introduction

The Alien Insiders

I met Jagadis Chandra Bose accidentally. I had agreed, against my better judgement, to attend one of those typical seminars on psychology and science. It was while rueing this decision that I came upon a book of essays by Bose, republished on the occasion of his birth centenary. Written in impeccable Bengali, and often frankly autobiographical, these essays projected a distinctive concept of science and gave tantalizing clues to the personalized meaning given to science by an Indian scientist. Deeply impressed, I decided to write an essay on Bose. I was then fresh from a stretch of training and research in a psychiatric clinic, and Bose's complex personality with its articulate inner concept of science and interacting vectors of tradition, creativity, and search for new modes of intellectual self-expression captivated me. All that had to be done, it seemed, was to offset these interactions against his psychodynamics to produce a reasonably interesting conference paper. I then had no feel for the cultural and ethical problems of science. And the resulting essay, published elsewhere, reflected this.

But the subject grew on me. Mainly because, while I did something for Bose, he also did something to me. I tried to give him a new historical image which stretched beyond recognition of his virtuous, two-dimensional image, created, as it then seemed to me, by naïve biographers, credulous historians, and hypocritical journalists. Almost without trying, merely by being faithful to my discipline, I allowed the tempestuous scientist to be a little more like his real self and a little less of the play actor which he always was, but infrequently resented being. If my analysis had somehow reached Bose, he would certainly have thrown a tantrum. But perhaps he would also have been happy to have his façade pierced. After all, he had to bear alone all his life the painful, weary conflicts between the traditions of his society and the traditions of science, between a westernness associated with the culture of his country's rulers and a westernness characterizing the ruling culture of modern science, between science as an ideology and science as a gentlemanly hobby, and, above all, between an integrated but loose-ended Bose at peace with the world and himself and a troubled, authoritarian, insecure Bose who even had to overcome mental illness without professional help. (Bose's friend Girindra Shekhar Bose was India's first psychoanalyst, working next door to Bose's home and laboratory. The parallel professional life that the other Bose led, uncontaminated by and unaware of the psychological sufferings of his friend, shows how much one had to live with one's private ghosts even a few decades back.)

Jagadis Chandra, on the other hand, sensitized me to the psychological and cultural predicaments of modern science. Not through the fashionable, glib language of the so-called science of science, but by nearly succeeding and then failing as a creative scientist who hoped to delineate for Indian scientists the outlines of a possible collective identity. The identity he evolved did not work, but the effort was, to say the least, impressive. He suffered greatly as he moved from the confident innovativeness of those hopeful days when it had seemed possible to challenge successfully the western dominance of science, to the insecure, dogmatic, ideological postures that accompanied his humiliating awareness that he had failed to break this dominance, and ultimately to the even more humiliating refusal to recognize his failure. But his sufferings only showed me how much insight there was in his perception that the western culture of science was not immutable, and that the Indian search for autonomy *in* science was, actually, a variation on the age-old struggle for the autonomy *of* science.

But what is commonplace today was outside the ambit of scientific self-consciousness then. And Bose never felt that his innovations in scientific culture had any chance of survival without his success in formal science to back it up. As I moved around with him in his world, it soon became obvious that this was the most constricting of the blinkers he wore. He was not willing to accept himself as merely a creative philosopher of science. He had also to succeed as a scientist. Yet, certainly his failure as a scientist would have been forgivable. It would in fact have been surprising if he—working in isolation in a poor, colonial country—had won his battle against a science which was increasingly becoming an organized, capital-intensive, group effort—a 'big science', as many have recently begun to call it. Apart from this, it needed a man of Kepler's and Newton's abilities to end the western dominance of modern science by altering both its content and its metaphysic. Bose's gifts—his self-deceiving countrymen and western admirers notwithstanding—were much less formidable.

It was his failure to accept that he had ceased to be a creative scientist which was to have dangerous consequences for the culture of science he wanted to build. He became more authoritarian, his aggression became free-floating, and his allegiance to a science which had failed him and his society also got eroded. In middle age, he allegedly began manipulating his experimental results, advancing false claims, and encouraging exaggerated statements by influential friends and journalists about his achievements.

What were the signposts on the way from his early successes to later failures? How correctly did he read them? How responsible was his internal equipment for what he became or could not become and how much responsibility did his society and the nature of science bear? These were some of the questions that prompted me to look for a contemporary of Bose who would represent the other end of the spectrum as far as Indian responses to modern science were concerned. My choice of Srinivasa Ramanujan as a second witness was, therefore, a more deliberate and reasoned one. It was, however, a statement of G. H. Hardy that finally convinced me that Ramanujan was the scientist one should counterpoise against Bose. In his book on the Indian mathematician, Hardy says at one place that the 'solitary Hindu clerk' had pitted his brains against more than a century's accumulated knowledge of the West and that he was bound to lose. This reminded me of Bose's lifelong pursuit of a grand defeat that, by its sheer grandeur, would outdo any success he could achieve. What Bose sought so consciously and in his studied way, the Tamil Brahmin was seeking in his inarticulate, introversive, unselfconscious manner.

But Ramanujan proved to be a more intractable subject than Bose. He had the kind of modesty which the progeny of a defeated civilization rarely show. Absolutely certain about the correctness of his concept of science, he left his professional colleagues in no doubt of his certainty. He never felt called upon to justify himself, except to himself. He articulated his self-confidence in a low key, without making an issue of his philosophy of science, and without the conspicuous self-righteousness which is often the hall-mark of Indian piety. He left no autobiographical writings, few letters which did not start or end with something on mathematics, and even fewer friends who could understand both his mathematics and lifestyle. (The last is the most difficult to forgive. Not leaving an autobiography is understandable, particularly if one happens to die at the age of thirty-two. One could be impersonal or lethargic about writing letters. But not leaving behind some friends as informants for future psychologists can only be called thoughtless.)

Yet, it was not so much the scarcity of data as the wrong kind of data from friends on Ramanujan which were for me the reddest of herrings. His modernist admirers wanted him to be modern; the traditionalist ones wanted him to be magical. Between the two sets of friends, Ramanujan managed to have two implicit biographies, two career lines, and two interpretations of science.

It was while trying to reconcile these two Ramanujans that I became aware of the typical orientations to history and biography obtaining in the Indian society. And, what at first had appeared to be wrong facts, mystification, and convenient amnesia, came to acquire a new meaning as well as validity. Brought up on the orientalist belief that Indian culture was ahistorical, I had failed to notice the three distinctive attitudes to the past which characterized India's popular 'histories' and sometimes even its modern historical scholarship. Each of these attitudes, as the following discussion will make obvious, is an ideal-type by itself. But together they provide an analytic framework within which can be located the peculiar Indian attitudes to past times and persons.

The first attitude is that of the traditional minstrels or *charans*. They were wandering individuals or small nomadic troupes who sang of past events and men—giving meaning to the present by projecting its rough realities into a mythologized past so that the present became more 'livable'. Moving from village to village, singing of things the villagers would never live with but were expected to live by, they made history a folk art—a shared fantasy, if you like. While providing a capsuled world image and organized ethical criteria to the laity, they built a defensive shield which consolidated the culture through constant affirmation and renewal of its psycho-philosophical base.

The second attitude is that of the Brahminic *barots* who were genealogists and chroniclers. Using the legitimacy traditionally given to 'pure data' uncoloured by emotions, they communicated a sense of formal generational continuity by ignoring flesh-and-blood individuals. No sanctity, however, attached to the totality of facts. It was through a selective presentation of facts, including a huge load of trivia, that the genealogist made his point. His very affectlessness came in handy in this; he used it to reify all human relationships and make history an impersonal, dehumanized, abstract, tireless 'mathematics'.

Thirdly, there were the court historians and their humbler versions, the *bhats*, who sang praises of their royal employers. Such an attitude, however, need not be confined only to court historians and their royal patrons; others too created mythical, larger-than-life subjects out of the mortals who happened to be the object of their interest. Everyone, including the subjects of praise, knew this to be a game and nobody took the content of the praise seriously. It was only the form of praise that was ritually important.

All three attitudes are deeply embedded in an orientation to the past which reduces—or elevates—each social reality to a psychologically significant myth. The aim is to wipe out the historical reality altogether or supplant it by the structural realities of the mythical. It is then from the second set of realities that the 'secondary' historicized facts of a person's life are deduced.

The three attitudes have given the traditional Indian concept of the past a certain distinctiveness. The first attitude subordinates the historical reality of past individuals and individual events to the process of cultural continuity and cultural renewal. While it destroys the individuality of historical persons and events, it simultaneously invests them with the individuality that could only be given to them by their civilization. So that the present can always see a continuity between exemplary persons from the past and the perennial concerns of the society. This is how Indian society had taken care of Benedetto Croce's and R. G. Collingwood's theories of history.

Ramanujan, being a more traditional man from a more traditional background, gives one greater scope to explore this cultural individuality and its relationship with the metaphysic of science. Bose, a more modern man from a more modern subculture, seems to survive his biographers as a historical individual. In other words, contrary to what I had expected, while Ramanujan gave me new access to his culture through his life history, Bose's culture guided me to another approach to Bose's life. It is all a matter of emphasis, but this difference is reflected in the two following essays.

The second attitude to history reduces men and events to data and statistics, so as to neutralize any emotion that may be associated with them. The aim is to dissociate affect from cognition and indirectly express the former through a manifestly desiccated recital of figures and events. That is why, in traditional Indian historiography, the data produced and the statistics used are often unique. A king is mentioned as having sixty thousand children, and the heavens are mentioned as being inhabited by three hundred and thirty million gods, not only to make the point that the king is potent and the gods are many, but also to wipe out what many would consider the real data, and obviate any possibility of verification or empirical treatment. If you have sixty thousand children, no one cares to ask their names or whereabouts, not even the single-minded orientalist; and no sacred text need list the three hundred and thirty million gods, even for the priest. In fact, you are not expected to take these figures seriously. You can only counterpoise against these communications others more potent. In other words, in this type of historiography data are important only so far as they relate to the overall logic and the cultural symbols that must be communicated.

There is a remarkable isomorphism between this attitude and the scientist's attitude to the history of science.

> The more historical detail, whether of science's present or its past, or more responsibility to the historical details that are presented, could only give artificial status to human idiosyncrasy, error and confusion.... The depreciation of historical fact is deeply and probably functionally ingrained in the ideology of the scientific profession, the same profession that places the highest of all values upon factual details of other sorts.[1]

So, there were all the details of dates, degrees, and awards to Bose and Ramanujan, their genealogies, and the lists of their publications. But, in the case of Ramanujan, only one person mentioned his attempted suicide and most remained silent about his conflicted relationship with his family. In the case of Bose, none would mention the details of his 'nervous breakdown', the insomnia that dogged his adult life, or the stutter that he broke into when angry. Again, very few cared about the personal relationships of these men, or the role religion, as opposed to magic, played in their

[1] Thomas Kuhn, *The Structure of Scientific Revolution* (Chicago: University of Chicago, 1962), p. 137.

lives. Ramanujan, in this respect, was more unfortunate. His Tamil Brahmin culture was more foolproof, more confident of its answers to the enigmas of inspiration and creativity, and more contemptuous of whatever did not fit into the frame of these age-old answers. Most of his Indian biographies are, analytically, carbon copies of one another. His English friends, on the other hand, wanted him to be an ahistorical, agnostic positivist—a one-dimensional scientist, trying singlehandedly to explode the myth of the inscrutable orient.[2] Bose's *babu* environment, no less conformist in biographies, was at least more curious about the totalities of its great men.

The third attitude to history makes for the delightful exaggerations and absurd eulogies in which most Indian biographies of Ramanujan abound. For these biographers, he was a scientist as great as Newton, a man as saintly as Gandhi, and a mystic as awe-inspiring as Aurobindo. Similarly, Bose for most of his biographers, was Einstein, Houdini, and an ancient Indian *rishi* all rolled into one. Partly this is a studied style which attempts to treat individuals as symbols rather than as historical figures. Epic culture, we know, survives on such symbols. Partly this can be traced to the long colonial status of the society. Biographers are happy to stretch the reasonable statement that Ramanujan might have been the greatest mathematician of all times but for his poverty and lack of formal education. Or that Bose could have been one of the most creative plant physiologists but for his acute sensitivity to the western dominance of science and his professional isolation in India. Still suffering from some of those very handicaps which distorted the career lines of Ramanujan and Bose, these biographers like to see their eminent *alter egos* as perfect men who, in the face of heavy odds, ultimately managed to actualize their full potentialities. They fail to grasp that through such distortions they try to do the impossible, namely, simultaneously overvalue and deny the existence of the twin enemies of scientific pioneering in India, economic deprivation and political subjugation. On the one hand, they stress the

[2] India's modern scientists of course fall for the imported amnesia. I remember my long unresolved arguments with two scientists while seeking foundation support for the work on Ramanujan. Both tried to convince me that any psychological exploration into Ramanujan's personal life would be futile because Ramanujan's life was a 'short, straight line' and there was nothing to it except his mathematical career. They did not know that Littlewood, Ramanujan's friend and teacher, had made a better argument out of this. Whether Ramanujan had a private life or not, Littlewood had told an acquaintance after being interviewed by me, it was beyond the reach of a psychologist. For psychologists, he felt, could never understand mathematicians.

crushing poverty within which Ramanujan worked in his youth; on the other, they emphasize his easy victory over all the handicaps which poverty set for him. On the one hand, they mention Bose's life-long problem with the colonial situation; on the other, they presume that the impact of colonialism on Bose's science and personality was skin-deep.

In the following narratives I have tried to show that Ramanujan's poverty and his inability to get a good mathematical education were more killing than his biographers seem to realize. And colonialism subverted Bose's creativity more successfully than the nationalists seem to suspect. Poverty and colonial status become totally corroding when they enter a person's or group's self-definition and become psychological forces. In the case of Bose and Ramanujan, this internalization did take place and they had to fight their demons within as well as without.

The third attitude to history is legitimized by the indigenous theory of personality development implicit in many Indian biographies. This theory is a unique blend of inverted Freudianism and folk genetics. It presumes that the early within-family relationships of great men are not merely idyllic, but that the great qualities of the great invariably develop out of their relationships with the best of all possible parents and siblings. It is as if the Indian culture accepted the importance of early child-rearing and the primacy of a person's object relations and denied only their total content.[3] Bose and Ramanujan were two of the worst sufferers from this syndrome, partly because they themselves held the same attitude and shedding it would have meant shedding their psychological defences. Fortunately both men, while often uncommunicative in their garrulity, were always eloquent in their silence.

It was not only the silence of my protagonists' witnesses that was eloquent; that of their admirers was equally so. I never felt cheated when one of them prefaced his statement with the request that I keep to myself what he was going to say. When they narrated in hushed tones—as if speaking of some saintly pecadillo—an anecdote or a reminiscence, I had almost always at least the outlines, if not a new micro-interpretation, of an old myth. I valued

[3] There is a contradiction between this attitude and the Indian epic tradition which, like the Homeric and some other epic traditions, has an amoral, tragic sweep which confidently—almost carelessly—takes into account a person's life in its entirety. I shall avoid, for the moment, a discussion of this contradiction.

this immensely. These lapses into Indianness were the bricks of my analysis, because I was as much in search of the real lives of the two men as after the myths generated by the interactions between their lives and the large-scale psychological and historical changes taking place in their society. I believe that these two types of 'truths' and their interchanges will ultimately prove to be invaluable source material for a social psychology of Indian science.

I have been silent till now about the creative products of Bose and Ramanujan as sources of biographical insight. Presumably this silence, too, has been significant. I am neither a plant physiologist nor a pure mathematician. It was only an accident of personal history that I was able to read and understand some of Bose's scientific writings first hand. I did try to take a guided tour in the more trodden sectors of Ramanujan's as-yet-partly-charted mathematical world, but it was beyond me. Thus in the case of Ramanujan entirely, and in that of Bose partially, I had to depend on the interpretations and estimates of others. And because these interpretations and estimations were not inspired, understandably and legitimately, by the same concerns as mine, my understanding of both as scientists has remained limited.

Before proceeding further, a word about this 'dangerous' limitation. When I started work on this project, many appreciated my 'courageous' decision to study the scientists. This was their way of saying what the more outspoken of my acquaintances had bluntly asked: how could I dare write on these scientists without fully understanding their sciences? In impolite moments, I responded with a counter-question: how could a scientist hope to write about these men without fully understanding their humanity?

But all that is polemics and a product of the insecurity generated by the so-called hard sciences among social scientists. My real answer is this: the statistical probability approaches zero of someone combining in himself the skills of a psychologist and a cultural anthropologist, specialized training in one or more scientific disciplines (to understand Bose's work one would require a knowledge of sciences as disparate as physics and plant physiology) and interest in the life of scientists. To expect exactly some such combination to emerge in the case of Bose and Ramanujan would in fact be stupid. The chances are that everyone will be deficient in at least one or two of these admirable qualities. An indirect confirmation of this came when I found a number of mathematicians ignorant of Ramanujan's mathematics and a large number of physiologists admitting their ignorance and lack of interest in Bose. If even being a mathematician or a physiologist was not sufficient qualification in this age of specialization, I decided that I had done my best for my historical friends on behalf of posterity by remaining a mere psychologist.

II

I now turn to the other party involved in my encounters with these two Indian scientists: the nature of science as we have come to conceptualize it in this century. This is a notoriously protean subject, which includes today both the cultures and the histories of the natural and social sciences and their growing interlinkages. But the logic of Bose's and Ramanujan's handling of science as a medium of human self-expression lies partly in the political psychology of contemporary science. And you should know my likes and dislikes in this area too.

In the following pages I have avoided regarding science as a social process which pays off in technology and other forms of applied knowledge. Generations of social thinkers have discussed the political and ethical responsibilities of scientists at this plane. The public, too, likes to think of science as a problem-solving technology which can cure some of the world's major ills. Given this wide interest in science as technology, I felt that a few more clichés from me on this issue would not enrich existing knowledge.

I have also avoided approaching science as a system of cumulative, structured thought. Scientists like to view science as something impersonal, objective, and free from the limitations imposed by human consciousness and history. Laymen endorse this view because they find it convenient to believe that there is at least one area of life which deals only with the constants of human knowledge and rationality. Being in many ways a product of the interaction between scientists and the laity, the culture of science, too, promotes this view to impersonalize and dehistoricize science. (Note for instance, the difficulty of associating the disciplinary heroes of science, the critical individuals who build the sciences, with normal science and practising scientists. An impressive majority of astrophysicists today have probably never read even a word of Ptolemy and few would know anything about him beyond his name. If one compares with this the living presence of Thucydides in historical studies or Plato in political philosophy, it becomes obvious that science must seem to the majority of its practitioners a relatively impersonal, ahistorical vocation.) Perhaps this is one of the main attractions of science to creative scientists, who as a group seem uninterested in their human environment and tend to withdraw from interpersonal realities.[4]

The fact that I do not have anything to say about this aspect of science does not mean that I accept the concept of science as a fully cumulative, impersonal mass of knowledge. Unlike technology, science is a speculative activity and part of philosophy. Naturally, it has its cultural and psychological roots. It is the denial of these roots in the name of an impersonal reified science which, I believe, is responsible for many of the ethical problems of the contemporary culture of science and the limitations of the scientist as a human being. In the following essays too, without going into the content of Bose's and Ramanujan's science, I have tried to show how the abstract, reified structure of scientific knowledge can often act as a defensive shield against both the outside world and the alien aspects of the scientist's own self.

I prefer not to press this point to the bitter end, but it is interesting that many Indian scientists and biographers of scientists whom I consulted while writing this book seemed particularly eager to uphold the image of science as a bloodless affair. Perhaps the image of an affectless, pure science 'clicks' with some vague search for impersonal 'rational' knowledge in India's modernized literati, and particularly with the Indian scientists' search for a viable community identity. Perhaps, as Thomas Kuhn has said, this is part of the world culture of science and the search for a pure, scientific science is a characteristic of scientists as a group. But one thing seems certain: the search does somehow endorse the Brahminic concepts of uncontaminated knowledge and purity of vocation. I remember S. Chandrasekhar telling me that C. V. Raman once administered him a patriarchal rebuke for referring in a speech to Ramanujan's attempted suicide. The rebuke still rankled in his mind five thousand miles away in Chicago, and he gave me a laboured justification for this lapse. I did not then push the point that Raman, in this instance, was articulating a deeply-held belief of both the scientific estate and the Brahminic culture that by objectifying and impersonalizing knowledge and by dehistoricizing

[4] For instance Anne Roe, *The Making of a Scientist* (New York: Dodd, Mead, 1952).

the producers of knowledge one could argue away the imperfect realities of living persons and human history from the world of knowledge. It was a case of perfect fit.

To come to the point, my emphasis in the following pages has been on one particular aspect of science: its use as a creative process which allows the scientist and, through him, his society and times to impose a particular meaning on personal and social existence.

It is only recently that psychological and sociological studies have begun to yield some insights into those typical personality assets and the dynamic integration that are necessary for the creative functioning of a scientist. As time passes, one should be able to differentiate between the characteristics specifically associated with scientific functioning and scientific creativity and those predicting intellectual functioning or creativity in general. Meanwhile, in the absence of specific theories, one is forced to work on the basis of ideographic formulations which are only indirectly applicable to other similar cases.

My method was no different. I wanted to explain two persons rather than two sciences, this apologia notwithstanding. Even though my interest in the nature of science has deepened over the years, my implicit dependent phenomena were two real-life scientists rather than the developmental history of Indian or world science. I have tried to understand the latter to the extent it was relevant to my understanding of the former. But by training and exposure, I am relegated—and committed—to the study of scientists rather than sciences.

It is this specific morphogenic concern with individual psychology that made me conscious of science as a culture, with shared concepts of scientific breakthrough, creativity and originality, shared standards of verification, replication, and validation, and shared access to certain anxieties and conflicts associated with scientific functioning. It is this subjective world which makes science the peculiar institution that it is, and has given it the creative form that it has. For instance, when I closely examined the contours of euphoria in the leaders of the scientific estate—Einstein, Raleigh, Haberlandt, Thompson included—once they caught the contagion of Bose's vitalistic science, I found striking similarities between the so-called primitive or traditional science and the concepts of science lurking in the deeper layers of the modern scientific personality. Bergson, Shaw, Einstein, and Huxley—so captivated by Bose's pacifist and ethical science—were certainly not innocent admirers of Eastern mysticism, nor were they innocent of the philosophical basis of modern science. Only, all of them shared certain common anxieties about the nature of modern science and the fate of the technology-based western civilization. In Bose's identity they found elements of the new scientist that the new philosophy of science was looking for.

Thus, we arrive, via a long detour, at a predictable set of questions: Were the older concepts of science that primitive? Or are we, in ignoring them, ignoring major concerns of human destiny? Were Bergson, Einstein, Shaw, and Huxley after all right in their instinctive acceptance of some aspects of Bose's science? True, Bose's Vedantic concepts of holistic universalism and pacifism, to give an example, were defensive and ritualistic. But is that all one can say about them? Culturally, which is the more stupendous effort: to be able to allow a few persons to choose deliberately and actualize the values of integrated knowledge, universalism, and peaceful science, or to be able to turn these into ritually and magically tinted desiderata outside the compass of personal choices? Into, in other words, the institutionalized and internalized parts of a way of life? In the 1970s one cannot be too sure.

Lastly, while there is hardly much debate any longer about the existence of non-scientific determinants of scientific culture, very little intellectual effort has been expended on the process that determines the worldview and ideology of individual scientists. For example, Marxist theory was one of the first to explore the social context of the culture of science, but it has little to say about the actual process through which the social realities come to be reflected in the scientist's personality and work. As a result, when it comes to the individual scientist, orthodox Marxism makes a monstrosity of Marx's humanist interpretation of the social content of knowledge. It becomes a conspiracy theory which relates the material losses and gains of the scientist to his work on a one-to-one basis. Even the Marxist concept of false consciousness becomes for many a means of accusation rather than a technique of analysis. Again, psychoanalysis, which has given us in modern times the most influential theoretical frame for analysing the conversion of social realities into personality vectors, tends to conceive of these realities in static and narrow terms once it goes beyond the immediate interpersonal world of the individual. Its orientation to the larger social forces acting on the individual is like that of a doctor who has dealt all his life with the therapeutics of cholera and is confused when suddenly confronted with an interpretation of the disease which uses poverty as an explanatory variable. The doctor's profession is, by any standard, a legitimate one, and he knows the importance of poverty in the spread of cholera. But he knows it as a technologist to whom the patient's social condition is part of the environment of therapy, not as a scientist to whom the patient's social condition is part of his therapeutic system or scientific theory.

In my encounters with these two scientists, it is on such exchanges between individual creativity and social realities that I have concentrated. And it is the stress on these exchanges that has made the following essays psychological studies, rather than histories of science.

Admittedly, in developing these concerns, I have benefited from the growing self-reassessment of social scientists. Social sciences are called 'developing sciences' and this is as pejorative an expression as 'developing societies'. As a Third-World social scientist, working with the Third World of human knowledge, which is neither the fish of humanities nor the fowl of science, I perhaps could not avoid certain issues of dominance, control, and freedom in science. As everyone knows, living in the Third World is bad breeding; becoming a Third-World social scientist is even worse. The former is like original sin, the latter like acquired viciousness.

Thus, this exercise of looking into Bose and Ramanujan also constituted an introspective re-examination of the psychological and cultural roots of an Indian interpreter of the world, who explores the outer realities of nature and society from the vantage point of a developing science, with his slanted individual and cultural capacities, with his own attitude to authorities, orders, and pecking orders, and his own concepts of dissent and conformity. I can assure my non-Indian readers that the view from this side of the barrier is quite different.

However, I must give two warnings to those who are always tempted to analyse such self-consciousness to its vivisected death. First, this is not an attempt to support an alternative Indian model of science (as will be obvious from what I have to say about the Indian science of my subjects). I have tried to draw the right lessons from a number of Third-World analyses of social and scientific behaviour which have paid their homage to the West by striving to be the exact reverse of what a hypothetical model of western analysis is. In such cases, even in dissent, the referent is the Occident. Such dissent can be vociferous, but is predefined in such a way that it is always controllable, always on leash, and always a valued ornament of the established authority system of the world of knowledge.

Second, I am not providing a defence for a worldview for those to whom an alien culture, such as the ancient Indian or the modern Chinese, becomes important on ideological grounds. They see in such a culture not merely an alternative civilization, but also a negation of the dominant culture in their own societies. To cater to the need for such an alternative culture, I feel, is to succumb to the existing model of predictability. Take, for instance, the case of Maoist China which for a while had become a powerful symbol of dissent for many in the West. Historically sharing some of the western values of public life and orientations to politics and statehood, Maoist China rejected many of the western forms of politics, economics, and social organization. Its attraction for some sectors of the West was, therefore, understandable. Even the idea of the inscrutable Oriental contributed in the West to the Chinese mystique by hiding the common values of the cultures involved. Thus, China's dissent seemed to many to be, recognizably and comprehensively, a dissent.

Fortunately, in the case of contemporary India, such an inverse relationship between an 'Indian science' and its western counterpart is difficult to establish. The Indian 'alternative', for even the most ardent alternative-seeker, is impossibly unmanageable. It not only seems a half-dissent, it also seems inefficient, chaotic, abstruse, amorphous, and unsure of itself. Its capacity to become a dedicated opponent or even a counterplayer of any other culture is, at a level, much poorer than that of China. And, unlike China, the dominant Indian concepts of public life and collective effort have little in common with those of the dominant societies of the world. It has, therefore, very little to offer to Bertrand Russells, at one end, and Ché Guevaras at the other, men whose conformity to western values was nearly total, and the psychological denial of this fact even more so.

India's 'dissent', in this limited and peculiar sense, is less controllable. That is why Ramanujan's well-meaning English friends tried to make him predictable by remembering him as a respectable, donnish, English dissenter. But he was too much of an authentic Indian alien within the culture of science to be the surrogate of an alienated westerner. And the anxieties he generated, I am constrained to believe, were deeper than the anxieties he lived with. Bose in his innocence, on the other hand, conformed more to the style of dissent acceptable to the West. Europe understood him, and he became the rage for a while. Only, it so happened that those who were lionizing him soon found other trendy things to do. The shrewd Tamil Brahmin was a perfect match for anyone who might have wanted to make him a symbol of protest. Just when the West thought it had captured him, it opened its fist to find that he had slipped through its fingers.

Part Two

Defiance and Conformity in Science

The World of Jagadis Chandra Bose

The image of an omnipotent technology in the last two centuries has blurred the dividing lines between the products of modern science and the formal structure of scientific rationality. As a result, the mystique of science as control and power, created primarily by the Industrial Revolution but also by the certitudes that the doctrines of empiricism and positivism have sired, attaches now also to the content of scientific knowledge. In the name of the autonomy of science, this mystique has encouraged many to assume science to be a distinctive set of ideas, free from the cultural and psychological compulsions operating in other spheres of life. In the form of a lay philosophy of science which distinguishes between science and the scientist, this mystique has helped banish the person from his work and, instead of granting autonomy to the scientists, has granted it to the ideational and material products of science.

Fortunately, the Enlightenment's concept of science, from which the dominant culture of science draws sustenance, is changing and, today, the more sensitive western scientists find it impossible to accept it uncritically. But meanwhile the contagion of the vision of a fully autonomous science has spread, especially in those parts of the world that have begun to seek redemption through the science of development and, as part of that enterprise, in the development of science. There is a widespread tendency among the ruling élites of Asia and Africa to forget that every culture produces its own science as surely as each scientific achievement produces new cultural realities. The price of this forgetfulness can be heavy. As this century has shown, the tendency to see in science a mass of desiccated objective knowledge, untrammelled by human emotions, can hand over entire communities as hostage to the very emotions of which they prefer to remain ignorant. On a lesser scale, it can make the individual scientist captive to the subjectivity he is often tempted to deny and to turn his work into a constricted, defensive manoeuvre.

These are truisms. But one must remember that in communities where science carries the full burden of social hopes and individual aspirations, they remain potent threats. By conceding the cultural and psychological determination of science, in places and times when both cultural and personal systems are in flux, one exposes uncertainties that can lead to crippling anxiety and to a self-examination that can be particularly painful. Yet, when such self-confrontation takes place, it strengthens a society's capacity to use science, in its broadest sense, to creatively redefine the society's concepts of human destiny and fate.

It is in this respect that the insights of the psychology of creativity and cultural psychology have become relevant to the study of science and scientists. They help us to understand the conflicts within ancient cultures which are trying to actualize new self-definitions that would have a place for the modern scientist and, in the process, contribute something of their versions of the eternal verities to the over-professionalized, bureaucratic, technologistic culture of modern science.

A cultural psychology of scientific creativity also allows one to probe the creativity of individual scientists as a link between cultural and individual needs. Such a psychology may not reveal the entire psychosocial landscape within which science and scientists operate, but it can identify for us the type of data that has to be marshalled for such a survey. Methodologically, this has been facilitated by the shift in emphasis in psychology itself. Today the roots of creative functioning are being sought less in the absolutes of human psychosexuality and more in the individual's attempts to cope with society's prototypes within himself. With growing awareness of the cultural and historical roots of the self, the discipline of psychology has been trying to rediscover creative imagination as an interpersonal as well as psychosexual experience. It has moved away from its earlier easy emphasis on the continuities between creativity and unconscious fantasy life, and between creativity and performance on ready-made psychological tests. Instead, one can sense an uncertain shift in the discipline towards a more ethical and cross-culturally sensitive treatment of the cultural and historical processes epitomized in all creativity. As this new emphasis on an intervening, yet culturally and historically rooted, individual relegates to history the shadowy psychological man, the discipline of psychology has been forced to recognize the social content of those personal capacities it chooses to call 'scientific creativity'.

Nowhere does this social determination of scientific creativity create so much anxiety and confusion as in the societies self-consciously trying to draw up new blueprints for their futures. In such societies, science becomes a battleground where the society's new ambitions confront its 'backlogs', and the scientist becomes a microcosm where the community's adaptive capacities challenge the creativity of the individual. In the process, sometimes science itself is distorted and some scientists are destroyed. The society, too, may pay a heavy price, swinging between the extremes of total acceptance of exogenous models of science in society and a doomed search for absolute autonomy in the area of knowledge.

However, broken glass can sometimes act as a prism. The deviant cultures of science in such societies too can, through a process of refraction, give an altogether different perspective on world science, seen as an identifiable psychosocial process.

Nineteenth-century India provides a good example of such a situation. It had a well-developed indigenous scientific tradition, an elaborate entrenched theory of life, and some explicit and implicit rules that related traditional science to the traditional lifestyle. Defying the fit, a handful of men opted for modern science which, though overtly universal, had come to acquire an essentially western culture over the previous three hundred years. Some of them made this imported science their profession, others a rallying call, and still others a symbol of dissent. But in each case they had to opt for a protracted conflict between their Indianness and their professional self and they had to fight the problem of forging, out of these two components, a new oneness that would make sense of their society and to them.

The conflict was sharpened in a colonial society by the western associations of modern science—associations which were bound to make science a symbol of western intrusion. The first generation of modern scientists in India had three possible techniques of coping with the intrusion. The first was to separate the culture and the content of science and, then, fight for pluralizing the existing culture of science in such a way that it would accommodate the Indian worldview. The second was by dismantling the dominant culture of science and replacing it by a new culture more congruent with Indian values. Neither was truly practicable at a time when the difference between science and the culture of science was not a part of common sense in modern India. The first generation of Indian scientists, therefore, opted for a third device. Most of them spent their professional careers trying to build an entirely new Indian structure of science. Some gave up the task half way, finding it too onerous; they preferred to become political activists, institution-builders, or academic bureaucrats and resigned from science, if not formally, at least *de facto*. Others, a smaller group, stuck to their guns and fought a losing battle against the formidable edifice of modern science. All the responses were consistent with the logic of a colonial situation, and one must judge for oneself which was the more tragic dead end.

All three techniques of survival allow us to investigate the limits to which acculturation of a transplanted science can be taken, the extent to which elements of tradition could become functional for modern science, the nature of the legitimacy a modern scientist could hope to shore up in a traditional society where not all the social subsystems were under equal pressure to change, and the process through which cultural and personal realities become the anchors for scientific imagination and creativity. At another plane these historical attempts at transplanting knowledge give us a chance to speculate about the nature of the interdependence of the structure and culture of science.

We shall explore these problems through the life history of Jagadis Chandra Bose (1858–1937), who contributed handsomely to the development of a professional identity which, for a time, seemed capable of mediating between the needs of Indian scientists and the demands on them. His undoubted success on many fronts suggests that his creative imagination could sum up not only the drama of his personal life, but the cultural crisis of his people. A highly successful physicist and botanist, Bose gave a special Indian perspective to world science, and was also one of the first modern scientists to do interdisciplinary research in his field. He also worked out a philosophy of science which anticipated some of the major themes in the contemporary philosophy of science. Simultaneously, he was a savant and a missionary-scientist for many in the West, and a national hero in India.

Yet much of this was to prove ephemeral. Even in his life time, modern physics and botany started overtaking Bose's 'Indian science'; today, within four decades of his death, his idiom sounds flat and out-of-date even in his own country. Though the memory of his achievements survives among important sections of the Indian intelligentsia and popular versions of his life offer a role model to young Indian scientists, his scientific work has already been stripped of its glamour, and his concept of Indian science only marginally enthuses professional scientists. New currents of social change have apparently thrown up newer self-definitions in the Indian scientific community.

Nevertheless, while the struggle to find an endurable professional identity continues amongst Indian scientists, and while Bose's brain-children ambitiously continue to help science rewrite the life-plan of all Indians, his relevance to Indian science persists. The environmental dangers he faced, especially the particularist pressures to which his science ultimately succumbed, are still alive. To the extent these pressures came from his immediate social environment as well as from the larger environment of world science, the forces that made and unmade Bose are relevant not only to the 'underdeveloped' world. They may be relevant even to the technologically ill-developed societies where some of the important questions now dogging science are: How much has science lost by its mechanistic and physicalistic concepts of the universe, how much by its denial of all alternatives to the scientific culture of the industrialized world? How much has the Newtonian idea of a world machine contributed to the ethical predicament of modern science, to its role in fostering human violence, and in violence towards the non-human environment? Can the estate of science and the personality of the scientist come to reflect the common fears, anxieties or anticipations which, because they are shared, become implicit codes determining scientific activity? How much is science enriched or distorted by transcendentalism or mysticism? Bose's life story—and even his brittle self-definition—offers a chance to explore some of these issues.

But before telling the story I must make a caveat. It is, of course, obvious that while the psychosocial pressures to which Bose was subject were fairly typical, his techniques of coping with them were not. Bose by no means offered a packaged solution to the psychological problems of Indian scientists. Yet, however idiosyncratic his responses, he *was* the first distinguished Indian scientist of modern times and the first self-conscious standard bearer of the concept of Indian science. He can hardly be dismissed as a deviation from normal science or as a one-man culture of science. He may not have been an amazing genius, but neither was he a mediocrity who was lionized and blown up into a hero by Indian admirers. His western admirers were, if not more numerous, at least more influential. In fact, some Indian intellectuals sensed early on Bose's diminishing relevance to science and to the institutional growth of science in India, but were afraid of saying so because of his stature outside India. Their reaction was the obverse of that of some others in their country who became enthusiastic about Bose only after his success in the West. Bose was less parochial and less irrelevant to the culture of world science than he may seem today, and he was more typical of Indian responses to western science than Indians may wish to acknowledge. In fact, the phenomenon called Bose can be understood only with reference to certain problems in the culture of science which became central at that point of time.

II

Jagadis Chandra Bose was born in 1858 in East Bengal (now Bangla Desh) in a small, well-to-do Brahmo family.[1] The Boses were originally high status Kayasthas and had owed allegiance to the Shakti cult. Each of these details had its own psychological meaning.

Bose's forefathers came from Bikrampur near Dacca, a place the middle-aged Bose described as a 'producer' of rugged innovative frontiersmen, who crossed seas and scaled mountains 'at their mother's bidding'. Bikrampur 'was not for the weak'; like a spirited mother, she demanded of her children *bikram*—aggressive courage.[2]

[1] On Brahmoism as the first Hindu reform movement of modern times, its beginnings in Bengal in the early nineteenth century, and its attractiveness to urban, high caste, westernized, middle and upper class gentry, see R. C. Majumdar, A. K. Majumdar and D. K. Ghose (eds.), *The History and Culture of the Indian People* (Bombay: Bharatiya Vidya Bhavan: 1963), 10: *British Paramountcy and Indian Renaissance*, Part II, esp. Ch. 13. On some of the psychological sources of the movement, see Ashis Nandy, 'Sati: A Nineteenth-century Tale of Women, Violence and Protest', in *At the Edge of Psychology* (New Delhi: Oxford University Press, 1980), pp. 1–31.

[2] J. C. Bose, *Abyakto*, edited with comments and notes by Pulin Bihari Sen (Calcutta: Acharya Jagadis Chandra Bose Birth Centenary Celebration Committee, 1958), pp. 21–2.

Bikrampur was associated with two other things: first, as Bose was fond of mentioning, it had an ancient reputation as a seat of intellectual activity. It had been a place of Sanskritic and Buddhist learning in earlier times and there were even the ruins of an ancient astronomical observatory to substantiate the faith of the inhabitants of Bikrampur in their long tradition of scholarship. The community had also produced the famous thirteenth-century Buddhist theologian and monk Atish Dipankar, who had carried to Tibet the 'message' of India. This history was often invoked by the inhabitants and by Bose himself to justify their chosen status.

The second association, according to Patrick Geddes, was a certain sensitivity to matters of faith in the region.[3] In the middle ages, Bikrampur had been a centre of Buddhist learning and dissent from the orthodox Sanskritic traditions. With the decline of Buddhism in India, the place became a centre of Hindu revival, although the population of the area all around had meanwhile become Muslim. The result was that the Hindus of Bikrampur in Bose's time felt called upon to maintain, to stretch Geddes' observation, a certain alertness and heightened protectiveness towards their cultural inheritance.

These demands of Bose's birthplace did not coincide with the demands of East Bengal on his self image. If the former gave him the feeling of being chosen, the latter made him feel marked out for second-class cultural citizenship. Before a changed political geography and enforced mass exodus broke through the barriers of local lifestyles and regional identities of Bengal in 1947, the East was known as the backyard of *babu* culture—a damp, marshy, dialect-speaking nest of provincials where ugly *Bangal* ducklings dreamt of becoming elegant Calcuttan swans. In the popular imagination, Bengalis were enterprising, obstinate, and aggressive, but this did not preserve them from the disdain and sarcasm with which everywhere upwardly mobile rurals are regarded by 'polished' urbanites.

The East Bengali response to this stereotype seemed to indicate that the contempt affected them, if only partially.[4] On the one

[3] Patrick Geddes, *The Life and Works of Sir Jagadish C. Bose* (London: Longmans, 1920), p. 2.

[4] Throughout his life, Jagadis Chandra was sensitive about his East Bengali past, particularly his persistent East Bengali accent. See C. C. Bhattacharya, 'Acharyadeb Smarane', *Vasudhara*, 1958, 2, pp. 121–4; also M. Gupta, *Jagadish Chandra Bose, A Biography* (Bombay: Bharatiya Vidya Bhavan, 1964), pp. 6–7. See below an account of his first encounter with westernness and urbanity in Calcutta.

hand, they angrily reacted to such disparagement; on the other, they revealed their deeper identification with their tormentors by ruthlessly rejecting their own authenticity. By becoming second-order *babus* and, with a vengeance, first-order successes, they hoped to gain a greater acceptance of themselves. But if the contempt of others dies hard, self-contempt dies harder; and until political surgery cut off greater Calcutta so completely from the people whose economy and sense of cultural inferiority it had exploited to build its own self esteem, all good Easterners went to Calcutta when they died.

The Boses, despite some lean times, remained solvent and Bose had a comfortable childhood. His hobbies and pastimes were certainly not those of a deprived child. Some later chroniclers, encouraged probably by Bose himself, have tried to give an impression of financial hardship in his early life, but this, on closer examination, proves to be one of those log-cabin-to-White-House myths that recur in the more ambitious segments of a community.[5] It is more reasonable to conclude that, like most other nineteenth-century Bengali stalwarts, Bose had an upper middle-class upbringing. More real were the fluctuations in the family finances of the Boses, due to his father's adventures in big business which ended in near-disaster. The young Bose *was* exposed to severe economic anxiety, but it was generated more by his father's failure within a competitive, achievement-criteria-dominated, colonial political economy than by actual poverty. There is no way of finding out if it was this which first sensitized Bose to the alternative traditions of apparently stable, self-contained village communities to which he was simultaneously exposed in his childhood. The fact remains that the adult Bose consistently tried to see the attainment of a stable, orderly, simple scheme of subsistence as a specific expression of a wider search for order and simple unifying principles, in nature and in society. The search was reflected in Bose's later conversion to the new versions of Indian nationalism which sang the glories of the traditional economy and decried the horrors of 'crass western materialism'.

The Boses were Brahmos. Monotheistic, anti-idolatrous, caste-denying Brahmoism was still the most creative and intellectually alive Hindu sect. But what had started as a radical movement was

[5] For example, M. Roy and G. Bhattacharya, *Acharya Jagadish Chandra Bose* (Calcutta: Bose Research Institute, 1963), vols. 1 and 2; and Bose, *Abyakto*, pp. 22–3.

by then already showing signs of a defensive rigidity and a tendency to become cocooned within an ideological and moral purism that, within a few decades, was to destroy its ability to withstand the more aggressive Hindu reform movements. Yet Brahmoism could still inspire in its followers a sense of pride—a feeling that they were in the vanguard of social reform, and that they were obliged to 'keep up with' the expectations of some inner, as well as transcendent, authority.

Bose's father was a first-generation Brahmo and his mother never gave up her Hindu orthodoxy. The family lifestyle therefore was still strongly influenced by Shakto high cultural traditions. This may on the one hand have reduced in the family the abrasive qualities which are often associated with membership of a religious protest movement; on the other, it ensured access to some of the deepest and most powerful symbols of Brahminic traditions in Bengal. Add to these the contrast between the rural origins and exposures of the Boses and the highly westernized education and occupation of the father, and you get some flavour of the wide repertoire of cultural themes and role models available to young Jagadis.

The household consisted of Bose's parents, his paternal grandparents, and his five sisters. His brother had died at the age of ten. It appears that the family as a whole was ambivalent towards Bose: together with its adoration of him there was a latent fear that it had given him too much latitude. This could be the ambivalence of the Brahmo subculture itself. Bose was the only son and the youngest in the family, in a society which prescribed preferential treatment for sons because of their economic and ritual role. But Brahmoism built its implicit codes of child training on a rule-of-thumb synthesis of imported Victorian puritanism and indigenous high-caste asceticism.[6] The prudish strictness of Brahmo child-rearing was probably a reaction to the dominant Indian tradition of indulgence and noninterference in the process of early socialization. But not knowing itself to be a reaction, Brahmo socialization rarely freed itself from what it was reacting to, particularly so in families like Bose's in which some members continued to represent

[6] Towards the end of the eighteenth century and the beginning of the nineteenth, under British suzerainty, this Brahminic asceticism was displaced by an anomic hedonism in greater Calcutta and in the other urban areas of eastern India. Brahmoism can be read as a response to this anomie and as an attempt to reinstate the Brahminic values in a new garb. In this sense, it can be called a particular form of Sanskritization. For a brief discussion of this see Nandy, 'Sati'.

the non-Brahmo traditions within the family. A child often gauged the contradiction; deep down he knew that he had become a battleground between the old and the new, and that he would have to develop a technique of coping with the two irreconcilable but co-existing environments in his universe.

III

What was the actual content of this multiverse of Bose's?

One insight into his early interpersonal world is offered by his favourite *jatra* or folk play. Biographers have already vaguely recognized that this *jatra* draws, as a cherished myth, the outlines of an inner design against which one could examine the realities of Bose's outer world. I shall restate this awareness in my own terms.

The myth was the story of Karna in the Mahabharata. Illegitimate son of the mighty Sun-God, Karna was left to die at birth by a cruel, opportunist, all-too-human mother. He survived to become the proud, aggressive, autonomous, sun-like son of a kindly foster-father—a charioteer who humbly helped him to reach the solar stature and identity that was his by right. Bose admired the parity-seeking 'backyard man' Karna for the mix of good and evil in him, and also because, spurning all temptations, he fought fate with a courage that redeemed even his final defeat.[7] This defeat, the story goes, was ensured when Karna refused to make up with his mother before the climatic fratricidal battle of Kurukshetra. She was then in the enemy camp and trying, he felt, to placate him to save her favourite and legitimate son Arjuna, whom Karna had vowed to fight to the death before he realized his own real origin. Till the end Karna stuck to his humbler identity, in victory as in defeat, and defied the conspiracy of the gods and the original humiliation of maternal rejection by dying as his father's son in battle.[8]

[7] Roy and Bhattacharya, *Acharya*, 14.

[8] Bose's persistent fascination with the personality of Karna was also expressed in his request to Rabindranath Tagore to write about Karna. Tagore's 'Karna–Kunti Sambad' (*Rabindra Rachanabali*, Calcutta: West Bengal Government, 1962, *5*, pp. 578–82) was born in 1899. The work is an imagined dialogue in verse between Karna and his mother Kunti. It depicts Karna's intense sensitivity to the earlier betrayal by his mother, his angry refusal to make up with her even in the face of total defeat, and his mother's earnest attempts to undo the past and build their relationship anew. For two fragments of Bose's correspondence with Tagore on the subject, see his letter of 22 May 1899 in Roy and Bhattacharya, *Acharya*, p. 4, and in Gupta, *Jagadish Chandra*, p. 70.

It was in 1899 that Bose's research showed a new trend. The relation between this and changes in Bose's personality is discussed below (Section VII).

To go by the design of the myth, these cherished—and projected—themes of a grand defeat, pertinacious obstinacy, the conspiracy of fate, personal achievement, and *noblesse oblige* were tied together by the images of a heartless rejecting mother and a fiery male progenitor of all life behind a warm accepting male authority. Psychologically, the son within himself had only the choice of disowning the former and owning up the latter.

We are largely ignorant of Bose's first social relationship. While he and biographers identifying with him have written and spoken at length about his father, they have been reticent—and defensive—about his mother. We only know that her name was Bamasundari and that she remained an orthdox Hindu even after her husband had become a Brahmo. But we have no way of knowing the actual form these differences in faith took within the family.

However, two scraps of information are frequently found in biographies. The first, and the only one to find a place in Bose's own writings, describes Bamasundari's motherliness towards the child Bose and his friends. We are also told by some chroniclers that Bamasundari was severe about Bose's cruelty to animals, and imposed some restrictions on his pastimes and play in childhood. But the episode which biographers most frequently mention is the clash that took place between mother and son when she refused to let the adolescent Bose cross the seas for further studies in England. (Later she relented and even sold her ornaments so that the trip could be made, but probably not before she herself, and the constraints that she represented, had been further associated in her son's mind with traditional Hinduism.)

These scattered references suggest that Bamasundari's indulgent mothering of her only surviving son was mixed with some intervention and restraint. This mix, some informants believe, was partly a result of the stubborn, aggressive ritualism that pervaded Bamasundari's entire lifestyle. The belief is endorsed by the sensitive observations of some members of the Bose family; they help us to locate, with tolerable reliability, those crucial undercurrents of mothering which formal biographies merely hint at.[9] The episode of the sea-trip to England, they would have us believe, was typical of Bamasundasri's 'peculiar' ability to antagonize her son,

[9] Bose also had something to say about his mother: his studied silence about her was accompanied by repeated and almost obsessive references to protective and aggressive motherliness and to nurture and succour in his work—sometimes explicit, always implicit.

an ability that often elicited from the latter an angry, fiery reaction or a form of free-floating aggression that was directed not towards her but towards the world at large. It was not so much Bamasundari's 'old-fashioned ritual self', as her son once put it,[10] as the edge given to it by her crusty obstinacy that he found so exasperating.

A nephew of Bose, a distinguished scientist who was close to his uncle, also remembers Bamasundari as 'definitely neurotic', a lay diagnosis referring to the pronounced symptoms of obsession-compulsion that she reportedly showed. This, of course, was nothing uncommon in Bengal and, for that matter, India. Euphemized as *shuchibai*, or compulsive ritual cleanliness of body and mind, the symptoms were so 'popular' that they perhaps could be called a culturally sanctioned posture of certainty, to face deeper uncertainties generated by common anxieties. By turning symptoms into tolerable angularities, the society evidently institutionalized certain behaviour patterns that in some other societies would have remained a part of psychiatric symptomatology. The compulsiveness of Bamasundari, if it can be called this, could have been an accentuated form of some aspects of Bengali normality; and her kind might have been, if not quite the rule, scarcely the exception. What must have aggravated the stress was the flamboyant bouts of anger that accompanied her finicky demands. Some have linked the mother's outbursts of rage at every failure to meet her criteria of ritual performance and purity, to the perfectionist, equally finicky, scientist-son, throwing tantrums at his own and others' inability to meet his standards of excellence.

At the same time, his mother remained for Bose a symbol of indomitable will, abrasive defiance of external stimuli, succour, and fixedness of purpose.

> Man is not a servant of fate, within him there is the power by which he can become independent of the external world.... This is the means through which he will ultimately triumph over physical and mental weaknesses.... Inner power is self will!... At which stage of life is this power born?... At which stage of life does this power to fight grow?... I was thrown small and helpless into this sea of power at birth. Then outer power entered inside me to nurture my body and to help it grow. With mother's milk, affection, pity and sympathy entered my heart and the love of friends made my life flower. Power has collected inside me in response to bad days and

[10] Bose, *Abyakto*, p. 125.

external aggression and with this power I have fought against the external forces.... Life takes form due to the power struggle between the inner and the outer. At the source of both the outer and the inner lives is the same *Mahashakti* who powers the nonliving and the living, and the atom and the universe.[11]

As we know, *Mahashakti*, the great power, is also the ultimate maternal principle in Indian, particularly Bengali cosmology; it invokes mother-deities who combine traditionally the ultimate in benevolence with the ultimate in terror.[12]

It was this image of a mother, at once benevolent and terrorizing, that found expression in young Bose's favourite myths and folklore. Long afterwards it found even clearer expression in his public idiom, in his closeness to reformers and religious leaders who invoked this image as their major symbol, in his return to aspects of the Bengali projective systems presided over by a series of powerful mother-deities, and in the distinctive culture of science he tried to build around him.

We do not know how successful Bose was in handling his ambivalence towards his mother. One defence was perhaps to discover a continuity between his mother and the family tradition of mothering. The discovery might have been made possible by the presence in the household of an authoritarian grandmother, caring and restrictive at the same time.[13] Even more useful might have been the history of a quasi-mythical great-grandmother. As Bose tells the story, she was widowed at an early age and came to stay with her brother with her young son. Though an affectionate person, she was a stubborn fighter against the difficult times she was facing. One day her young son, terrorized by his teacher, came to her for protection. According to Bose, 'the affectionate mother immediately turned aggressive, tied the hands and feet of the son, and handed him over to his teacher.'[14] These imageries of a nurturing but violent mother, of a child seeking a mother's protection that is denied, transient male authorities who terrorize,

[11] Ibid., pp. 191–4.

[12] See on this subject Ashis Nandy, 'Woman Versus Womanliness in India: An Essay in Cultural and Political Psychology', in Nandy, *At the Edge of Psychology*, pp. 32–46; pp. 301–15; also Nandy, 'Sati'.

[13] 'Jagadis Chandrer Jivani', *Vasudhara*, 1958, 2, pp. 124–35, 126. Reportedly Bose's grandfather was a more accepting and indulgent figure than his grandmother. It seems that the grandparents, too, partly replicated the parents for Bose.

[14] Bose, *Abyakto*, p. 121.

and a father who cannot provide protection because he is dead or absent were to recur in Bose's later life. At the end, this imagery of a widowed mother, looking forward to her son's success, was to blend with Bose's concept of a motherland dependent upon his own success in the cruelly competitive world of science.

All this means that differentiation in the image of the mother could become, in Bose's case, the matter of a more permanent split. Mother love was to denote for him both 'nurturing kindliness' and 'annihilating power' for all time to come.[15] When used as parts of an idiom, this was to have special appeal in a culture dominated by a maternal deity who, in her multiple incarnations, represented the extremes of benevolent benignity and incorporating terror. Bose's later drift towards the world-view of pantheistic Hindu orthodoxy, which horrified many pietistic Brahmos, was, therefore, more than a considered, rational choice; it bridged the loves and hates of his infancy and the preferences of his adulthood.

Bose's mythical ego ideal Karna would have perished but for the intervention of a kindly foster-father. And the scientist's later childhood and youth were spent in a tenacious attempt to use his apparently conflict-free identification with his father as the core of his self, perhaps to disown his identification with his mother and her ritualistic, magical, domineering self.

Bose's father Bhagwanchandra was considered a cultivated man who, in Bose's younger years, was employed mainly in small towns in rural areas. To be cultivated in nineteenth-century urban Bengal had a significance which it is difficult to convey today. The idea of a general education no longer leads to aspirations of the same kind on the part of middle-class Indian parents, and professionalism and specialization have deprived work and knowledge of their earlier connotations of being conducive to the production of a rounded personality. Even Bengalis who, like the Victorians, once made a fetish of a general education, are no longer fascinated by the concept of a gentleman who by his ambidextrous qualities validates his gentility. Nothing denotes the older concept of gentility better than the fact that the elder Bose was, in addition to being a successful administrator, an entrepreneur, an amateur physicist and biologist, a promoter of technical education and part-time engineer, a devout Brahmo with an almost professional interest in the theology of Vedanta, a sportsman, and a part-time social-worker.

[15] Ibid., pp. 140–1.

He also nurtured ambitions of becoming a writer and a nationalist leader. It is evident from the admiration that this wide range of roles and interests evoked in Bhagwanchandra's contemporaries that the ideal Bengali gentleman was still a person whose multifarious talents idealized—and thus negated the anxiety of—the role confusion typical of those changing times. We shall see how this confusion, and the anxiety associated with it, later forced his son to look beyond the identification represented by the father towards the clearer self-definition offered by the mother.

Before turning to the content of Bose's relationship with his father, let me summarize what little is known about the earliest interests and pastimes of young Jagadis. These are important because they provide a clue to what he later made out of his relationship with his father. The child Bose's curiosity and enthusiasm were, we are told, unbounded. All types of growing, self-propelled, and living objects fascinated him. Together with this interest in life and life processes was also a preoccupation with violence. He played with models of battleships, cannons, and cannon shells, and trapped and killed birds (his father was permissive in this respect, his mother strict). The beginning of his lifelong interest in aggressive wild life can also be seen in his childhood practice of catching snakes and playing with them. Some of this concern with symbolic and not-so-symbolic violence was, even at that stage, linked to his creative efforts. For example, he made, with the help of unskilled labourers, the brass model of a cannon which was considered to be a remarkable feat of engineering.[16] One suspects that Bose was already using his aggressive fantasies to acquire mastery over his environment, by exploration, and experimentation.[17]

As he grew up he took to the 'manly' sports of shooting, riding, and *shikar*. The *shikar* was mainly big-game hunting and later on he would remember his tiger-hunts with some nostalgia.[18] Perhaps

[16] This model was the first intimation of Bose's superb skill at scientific instrumentation. It also provided another link between the amateur engineering of Bhagwanchandra and the applied physics and experimental physiology of his son.

[17] Phyllis Greenacre, 'The Childhood of the Artist: Libidinal Phase Development and Giftedness', *The Psychoanalytic Study of the Child* (New York: International Universities, 1957), *12*, pp. 47–52.

[18] Bose, *Abyakto*, pp. 185–6; and J. C. Bose, 'Dedicated Life in Quest of Truth', in P. K. Chatterji (ed.), *The Presidency College Magazine* (Calcutta: Presidency College, 1964), *Golden Jubilee Volume*, pp. 64–73. See also Roy and Bhattacharya, *Acharya*, pp. 18–19. Throughout his life Bose continued to decorate his drawing room with stuffed animals he had shot in his younger days. These symbols of aggression against nature

hunts were the occasion for him to externalize some of his deeper violence—by pursuing and killing wild aggressiveness, he could destroy some of those inner furies which sought an outlet in his games, pastimes, and creative products. The fact remains that the adult Bose, even when he had turned a militant pacifist, continued to feel proud of his record as a big-game hunter.

Bose's companions in these ventures were often adults and this frequently brought out his fears of being underrated and his early search for parity. A typical incident was his participation in a riding competition; though he was far behind throughout, he refused to give up and was injured badly in the process. Two similar incidents, involving his obstinate search for recognition and being successful in a competition, were a brawl with a gang of Anglo-Indian classmates and a boxing contest he won against heavy odds. Both took place in his teens in Calcutta. In each case his father openly admired Bose's exploits and, on at least one occasion, publicly congratulated him on his tenacity. One suspects that the westernization of Bhagwanchandra went beyond his 'civilized' interests, hobbies, and occupation. It had ramifications in some acceptance of aggressive competition and competitive achievement.

Bhagwanchandra also took a special interest in his son's education. It was he who introduced him to botany and physics. This direct intervention in the son's education was not common in those times in a subculture which promoted some degree of distant paternalism. But it paid dividends. The intimacy and mutual respect which grew between the father and son was to act as a fulcrum of the son's personality for a long time. Of course, there was also the relatively rare circumstance of a modernized family moving from place to place in rural and semi-rural Bengal, according to the vagaries of a transferable government job. The father may have been partly forced to intervene in the son's upbringing. But there was nothing forced about the warmth and permissive friendliness with which Bhagwanchandra handled this duty. The consequence was a deep sense of personal obligation in the son, and also a developed sense of *noblesse oblige*.

The best-known example of this has already become a popular myth among the Bengali élite. The story goes that Bhagwanchandra at one time pioneered a number of industrial ventures, which were

---

were to become rather anachronistic in his later life. See below.

to yield fabulous profits later but to him were merely a source of acute financial embarrassment.[19] This landed him deeply in debt. From this distance in history, we have no means of knowing where the decision-making went wrong; we have only the son's expressed belief that it was his father's risk-taking adventurous defiance of his safe vocation and secure income that was being punished by fate. It is evidence of Bose's idealization of his father that when he grew up he took enormous trouble to repay loans which even the creditors had written off as bad debts. Not merely that; he diligently publicized his justification for his father's business failures. In fact, his homage to Bhagwanchandra's entrepreneurship and achievement-frustrations remains one of his most maudlin public speeches.[20] He notes therein the similarity between the 'magnificent defeats' of his father and those of Karna, his favourite mythical champion of lost causes,[21] but naturally fails to see the analogous role he selected for himself, and often played, with such dramatic fervour.

Does the analogy with Karna mean that Bose unconsciously perceived his father to be, like him, a victim of a less-than-benevolent maternal authority? Was this perception endorsed by the self-willed grandmother staying with the family, or was it merely a projection of his own relationship with Bamasundari? Did this perceived victimhood seem to him to have a sacrificial content? We have no means of knowing. We only know that the image of his father as a co-victim of maternal aggression persisted. 'He was born before his time', Bose stated in his speech. 'It is on the ruins of many lives like his that the greater India of the future will be founded. I do not know why it should be so; all I know is that Mother Earth is hungering for such sacrifices.'[22]

Bhagwanchandra was an active Brahmo and Bose discovered early in life that his father's religious enthusiasm was associated with a lively interest in science and technology, an amalgam of interests that was to become a formal synthesis in the son much later. (This synthesis was sanctified in his—a 'monotheistic'

[19] According to one version, these industrial ventures involved tea and jute. It must have taken some remarkably persistent inefficiency to fail in a business involving these two goods, which within a decade or two became the two most important industries in India. Bhagwanchandra, some may conclude, was a dyed-in-the-wool Bengali gentleman.

[20] Bose, *Abyakto*, 121–34.

[21] Roy and Bhattacharya, *Acharya*, p. 8.

[22] J. C. Bose, quoted in S. P. Basu, *Nivedita Lokamata* (Calcutta: Ananda, 1968), *1*, p. 569.

Brahmo's—incongruous, life-long devotion to Vishvakarma, the second-order Hindu god of technology and scientific creativity. In particular, Bhagwanchandra was well known as a builder of instruments. This is an area in which his son too excelled, and later even the most violent critics of Jagadis Chandra's scientific theories admitted his skill in scientific instrumentation.

It was his father, again, who handed the child Bose over to two elderly servants for training, protection, and upbringing.[23] One of them, who became very friendly with Bose, had been a robber in his younger and more glorious days, and was once condemned to imprisonment by Bhagwanchandra himself. He often regaled his charge with his 'tales of bravery' and Bose was truly impressed when this retired bandit, using half-forgotten skills, saved the entire Bose family from pirates. Bose never forgot his bandit friend, and the theme of control of latent aggression, by aggressively protecting an erstwhile target of attack, was to become an important one in his life and work.

The other servant who looked after Bose was a retired army sepoy who taught Bose how to use a rifle, which, as we have seen, later came handy in his safaris.

Bose's nationalist father sent him for his early education to a *pathshala* or village school which he had himself founded. It was still possible in Bengal to combine government service with ardent nationalism and Bhagwanchandra, one may say, was one of the last to make a success of this combination. Nevertheless, his decision to send Jagadis to an indigenous school shocked many. Firstly, nobody expected him, a *babu*, to take seriously a school which he had established as a social service. Secondly, in those days children of highly-placed civil servants were invariably sent to English medium schools.

But Bhagwanchandra's decisions, when they did not relate to

[23] The role of servants in the socialization of nineteenth-century babus can be the subject of an interesting study in transitional institution-like structures. Servants represented the Bengali élite culture's new and anxious recognition that children required more supervision, control, and intimacy with adults than was provided for in the older model of socialization. By meeting some of these needs, and by validating and invalidating earlier interpersonal experiences of the children, these servants significantly influenced the transition from infancy to adulthood. And to the extent that they symbolized the parents or mediated parent–child relations, they played a vital role in the child-rearing system of the subculture. For a vivid account of the crucial role of servants in child-rearing in a modernist Bengali élite family, see Rabindranath Tagore, *Chhelebela* (Calcutta: Viswabharati, 1944).

industry and commerce, bore the stamp of pragmatism and vision. The exposure to the progeny of humble village folk and to their lifestyle that young Bose had in school was crucial to his developing self. First, his peers in school were his social inferiors and they never challenged the sense of being chosen that Bose had as an only son, in a culture which emphasized the importance of sons. On the contrary, these peers might have negated the threat to his self-esteem that Bamasundari's control represented. Second, Bose's schooling endorsed his sneaking respect for the stability and orderliness of the traditional systems. At least Bose later claimed this.[24] Perhaps it also helped him internalize the concept of a reference group to which he would at least apparently veer round, whenever threatened by criticism or neglected. Bose himself was clear about why his father had sent him to an indigenous school:

> Now I know why my father put me into a Bengali school. There I had to first learn my mother tongue, think in that language, and I got acquainted with the national culture through a national language; I also learnt to think of myself as one of the masses, and no feeling of superiority separated me from others.[25]

Despite such exposure, Bose remained a lonely child. This loneliness, his poor knowledge of English, his rustic East Bengali mannerisms, and the sudden fall from the status of being a magistrate's son to that of being an Indian amongst Anglo-Indian students and teachers, created a rather uneasy situation for him when he entered St Xavier's School at Calcutta in 1870. We have already mentioned the street brawl and the boxing contest; these incidents were the overt expression of an environment that further sensitized him to his nationality and colour, and helped him to associate his personal humiliations with the political status of his people.

Things improved when he went to St Xavier's College on a scholarship. There he developed a decisive, long-lasting intimacy with a Jesuit priest, Father Eugène Lafont (1837–1908). Lafont was the best-known professor of experimental physics of his generation in India and was one of the founders of the Science Association of Calcutta. He is still remembered as the 'father of

[24] Bose, *Abyakto*, p. 125.
[25] Ibid., 125–6.

science in Bengal'. A Belgian trained in philosophy and the natural sciences, he had arrived in Calcutta towards the end of 1865. When Bose joined St Xavier's College in 1875, Lafont was its Rector and already the Father was regarded as a pioneer in science education in India. His public exhibitions and lecture demonstrations on science were highly popular. The popularity was due not only to Lafont's personality; science was now in the air. Such was the curiosity of the *babus* of Calcutta about the new science that a contemporary report on Lafont's lecture series says:

> Notwithstanding rain and lightning, a pretty fair attendance of native gentlemen gathered around the lecture table to hear the exposition of Dalton's atomic theory and witness some experiments, illustrating the general principles of matter.... Throughout the series, the gentlemen were most assiduous and punctual in their attendance.[26]

Jagadis Chandra was inspired by Lafont's presence and this new enthusiasm for science. At first he was interested in 'natural history' and wanted to become a botanist. Lafont encouraged him to turn to physics. Bose studied physics, but combined it with Latin and Sanskrit, perhaps impressed by the mix of classics and sciences in Lafont's life. It was not only in the choice of discipline that Bose was influenced by the Jesuit. Lafont's lecture series might even have helped Bose internalize an atypical concept of a scientific audience. The series could have made him aware of the possibilities of a slightly exhibitionistic public exposition of science in a society with a strong oral tradition. Here, therefore, was another fatherly figure who combined physics with religion and metaphysics. And for Bose the experience was another stage in an unfolding intellectual identity stretching from infancy to adulthood.

Bose graduated in 1879. Like other young men of his generation and background, he started toying with the idea of becoming a civil servant. This was a highly valued occupation which, in those times, had a special attraction for the ambitious contemporaries of Bose. Also, members of the Indian Civil Service were paid well and Bose wanted to lessen his father's economic burdens. But the magistrate-father vetoed this and encouraged his son to become an academic. Instinctively, Bhagwanchandra pushed his son towards a self modelled on his—Bhagwanchandra's—idealized but partly fulfilled

[26] A. K. Biswas, 'Rev. Father Lafont of St. Xavier's College', in *Science in India* (Calcutta: Firma K. L. Mukhopadhyay, 1969), pp. 67–84.

self-definition as an intellectual, rather than on his more superficial commitment to a government job.

Bose's early role confusion, a paternal inheritance, pursued him even to England where he lived from 1880 to 1884. During 1880–1 he studied medicine but gave it up, partly because of ill health. In 1881 he joined Christ's College, Cambridge, on a scholarship to study botany, and graduated from both Cambridge and London Universities in the natural sciences. Throughout his undergraduate days, he took a variety of courses without specializing in any. However, his relations with the professors of physics and botany were decidedly deeper. In particular, his professor of physics, Lord Rayleigh, served as another Father Lafont.[27]

One does not have to be a psychologist to conclude that Bose was trying to build his self-definition, even at that stage, on his relatively conflict-free identification with his father. And, in offering him confusing and often contradictory sublimations and ego defences, that identification reveals what we have already recognized: a diffusion of identifications in the father himself. This confusion, that had dogged his father's steps all along, now picked up the son's scent too, turning careers into pastimes and pastimes into careers, as in the earlier generation.

IV

These were the assets and disadvantages with which Bose came back from England in 1884 to become an acting professor of physics at Presidency College, Calcutta. In getting the appointment, he was helped by Dr Fawcet, a benevolent elderly English educationist who was working as the Postmaster-General, and by Lord Ripon, the Viceroy of India and one of those historical figures who by their sheer personal goodness often help consolidate the oppressive systems of which they happen to be apparently unwilling parts. Both, by taking a personal interest in such a triviality, probably reconfirmed Bose's inner image of essentially benevolent public authorities.

The appointment was made despite the protests of Alfred Croft,

[27] A. Home (ed.), *Acharya Jagadis Chandra Bose* (Calcutta: Acharya Jagadis Chandra Bose Birth Centenary Committee, 1958), p. 6. Note that for the second time in his life, Bose had moved away from a subject akin to 'natural history', his first love, to physics because of his special relationship with a fatherly figure more interested in the physical sciences. He was to come back to 'natural history' again.

the Director of Public Instruction in Bengal, and C. H. Tawney, the Principal of Presidency College. Both supported the strongly-held belief of the Education Department of the Government of India, that Indians could be excellent at metaphysics and languages but not in the exact sciences. This belief was often a matter of genuine conviction, something that was ignored by the nationalists who wanted to make a *cause célèbre* out of Bose's difficulties. Thus Tawney, who so openly protested against Bose's appointment, was also a great admirer of Indian achievements in metaphysical and religious thinking and a devotee of Shri Ramakrishna, the great mystic and religious preceptor.[28]

Tawney's position was based on two typically European assumptions, both by now endorsed by sizeable sections of the Indian élite. First, there was a wide gap between the scientific achievement of the West and that of India fixated, as it appeared to many, at the level of medieval technology. Second, the natural sciences were more important than other disciplines, and in the more crucial disciplines Indians were not as good as Englishmen. The Crofts and the Tawneys looked down upon Indians only in this indirect sense. It was India's westernized middle classes which, having internalized the western concept of the primacy of science, felt humiliated because they felt they were inferior in the natural sciences and because they no longer believed in their own culture's hierarchy of knowledge.

As interesting as the process of appointment was Bose's place of work. Established in 1817 as the Hindu College, Presidency College was the first Indian college to impart western education. In Bose's time, it was by common consent India's best-known college, the most prestigious training ground for the Bengali *babus*, and their most famous gateway to the Occidental currents of thought. It was in this institution that the progeny of the Bengali aristocracy earned their spurs as modern citizens of the world exactly as their progeny, today, learn the very latest in imported theories of progress.

Unfortunately, the college at that time had practically no facilities for empirical research in science, but fortunately, this was a challenge Bose enjoyed taking up.[29] He began to devise his own instruments and laboratory aids. Bose also probably enjoyed the

[28] Basu, *Nivedita*, vol. 1, p. 571.

[29] Ibid., p. 8.

protracted quarrel with the government Education Department in which he got entangled. The quarrel was about differences in the salaries of British and Indian teachers. The obstinate East Bengali, sensitive to even the smallest slight, protested by foregoing his pay. Though he finally won when the disparity was removed after three years of unremitting struggle, his family life and personal work suffered another round of instability, brought about by the vagaries of the colonial educational system.

Bose fought his battle in a predictable fashion. Faced with a hostile authority that did not conform to his concept of what a paternal authority should do, he coped with his problem exactly as one would have expected him to: he appealed to the higher authorities, trying to arouse their sense of rationality, justice, and benevolence to grant him the parity that he had earned through hard work and skill. His success in this instance was probably the final validation that ensured the more or less cordial relations between him and the British authorities throughout his life, cemented later by that well-known token of paternal reward in British India, a knighthood.

However, the scars of the conflict may have remained, to make him rather more suspicious of western systems of education and to revive his awareness of his own deep-seated concepts of learning and vocation. And the search for personal parity that had engaged him for years, gradually began to take the shape of a search for national parity in this changed context.[30]

But Bose enjoyed his work all the same. This was his first experience of being a teacher and wielding authority. By all accounts, he was a success, friendly and egalitarian with his students.[31] Both the friendliness and egalitarianism, however, were confined to this period of his life and did not extend beyond his professional prehistory.

Till this time, Bose had not achieved any academic distinction, though some of his teachers agreed he had promise.[32] Even as a professor, he was concerned with hobbies such as photography and the building of simple laboratory instruments for his college,

[30] That he did not widen and politicize this particular version of nationalism, as he could surely have done afterwards as a national hero, only goes to show how much he preferred to, and could, keep his relationship with the authorities conflict-free.

[31] Roy and Bhattacharya, *Acharya*, p. 29; this is based on Ramananda Chatterji's description in 'Kashtipathar', *Prabashi*, November–December 1932 (Agrahayan, 1939).

[32] Ibid., p. 18.

rather than with sustained serious research. The waywardness and unfocussed passions of his youth, to which some of his biographers refer, also found expression in the aimlessness of his early professional life.

In 1887 Jagadis Chandra married; it was an arranged marriage to a woman from an orthodox and illustrious Brahmo family with a pronounced reformist and religious bent. It is said that his wife, Abala, was a particularly devout Brahmo whose insistence on regular prayers and meditation revived forgotten memories in Bamasundari's son.

Abala had studied medicine for four years before her marriage. Thanks to this exposure, she was not only able to share Bose's interest in his scientific hobbies, but also to encourage him to take up serious scholarship. Finally, when he actually did so—I shall describe the episode below—she took an active interest in his social and intellectual needs. Much light is thrown on Bose's adult personality by the nature of his conjugal relationship and the role which Abala, by all accounts, played in his life. Geddes, who knew them first hand, says:

> ...Hers has been no simple housewife's life,...not only appreciating her husband's many scientific problems and tasks, and hospitality to his students and friends, but sharing all his cares and difficulties.... For his impassioned temperament—in younger days doubtless fiery, and still excitable enough—her strong serenity and persistently cheerful courage have been an invaluable and ever active support....[33]

Bose's nephew, D. M. Bose, also speaks of Abala's calm strength and unruffled temper, and of her tact which compensated for her husband's poor interpersonal skills when dealing with important scholars.[34] Her serenity in a charged situation, Geddes says, lay in her ability to accept and modulate Bose's basic combativeness—'like the fly-wheel steadily maintaining and regulating the throbbing energies of the steam-engine'.[35] This firmness and control came overlaid with conspicuous submissiveness.

The combination was important for someone with Bose's 'prehistory': particularly the distance and ambivalence that characterized his relationship with his mother. By being motherly towards

[33] Geddes, *Life and Works*, pp. 218–19.

[34] D. M. Bose, 'Abala Bose, Her Life and Times', *Modern Review*, June 1966, pp. 441–56, esp. pp. 445–54.

[35] Geddes, *Life and Works*, p. 219. Also Roy and Bhattacharya, *Acharya*, p. 18.

Jagadis, his relatives and friends, by part seriously and part playfully assuming the role of a firm, moral authority, Abala invoked the memories of a relationship that had found its bearings in the socializing fantasies of his culture—in the rich, early tradition of mother-image-dominated Bengali myths. Here was a non-threatening, apparently controllable mother, calm, supportive and doting, and yet more convincing by virtue of being firm, independent and self-sufficient.[36] The two faces of Bose's inner mother at last showed signs of becoming one in this sensitive, humane, determined woman.

There was support for this relationship from three other sources. In a society where childlessness provoked personal and collective anxieties about the reproductive capacities of nature and the survival of the family, 'barrenness' often forced a couple to close ranks. For together they had to face a society that stigmatized them, particularly the wife, as a symbol of inauspiciousness and marital failure. Brahmos were more liberal in this respect than orthodox Hindus, but there must have been only a partial protection against the messages coming from the larger society. Second, after a decade of marriage, from 1897 onwards, continuous ill-health in her brother's family began to require Abala's presence and intervention. At first she bore partial responsibility; later she took charge almost fully. So much so that the children of the family came to look upon her as a second mother. Whether or not this long contact with an ailing family deepened her 'maternal instincts', as D. M. Bose believes,[37] it confirmed an existing pattern. Thirdly, Abala's sensitivity to, and empathy with Bose's personal insecurities increased their mutual dependence. There is a well-known anecdote that illustrates this. Bose, alwalys seeking nurture, used to ask children who visited him to declare how much love they had for him. Not till they had spread their hands out fully to indicate their total love for him would he be satisfied. Abala knew this and

[36] The maternal role played by Abala is described by almost every biographer of Bose. For a brief account see Gupta, *Bose*, pp. 85–7. As we shall see below, the pattern was confirmed by the motherly women Bose gathered around himself, particularly Ole Bull and Nivedita, two Irish women who had opted for the Indian way of life. (Geddes, *Life and Works*, Ch. 17, esp. p. 221). But it was not blind motherly love that Bose sought. Both these women as well as Abala combined nurture with power, control, understanding and acceptance. However, Abala, by adding to this combination a certain intrusive firmness, completed the image of a phallic mother. Her imposing, somewhat hairy, heavy build might have contributed to this image.

[37] D. M. Bose, 'Abala Bose', p. 445.

would encourage some of her grand-children to visit Bose by rewarding them with cookies.

The death of their only child in infancy in 1902 made Bose even more the locus of Abala's attempts to cope with her 'frustrated maternity' and made the two of them 'more completely...one'.[38] Symbolic maternity now became more critical for her, and her husband's deep need for succour became more than ever a vital necessity. In this environment, Bose's infantile fantasy of being able to appease and get love from a maternal source by compulsive orderliness and purity and by searching for an all-embracing order attained increasing importance. The gaining and holding of love through finicky neatness and order in scientific thought, imagination, and in day-to-day behaviour (for example in dress, food, work-routine, and housekeeping) now became a matter of internal order and even compulsion. The bridge between the disorganized, defiant, angry, wayward youth and the proponent of a unifying theory of life had at last been built. 'The present', Bose had said in 1894 in the first sentence of his first publication, was 'made of the past', and he often found them 'separated by an inescapable barrier'.[39] A few sentences later he corrected himself; in the fresco of a mother nurturing her baby he discovered 'the bridge between the past and the present, built on nurture and motherly love'.[40]

Absolute order, however, can be costly for a thinker, for it is only a short step from order to ritualization. The link between orderliness and compulsion in rituals, by inviting attention to the uncertainties underlying the latter, only warns one against being seduced by the pseudo-certainty of the former. One can thus trace one's steps backwards, and examine each ritual as a specific attempt to impose order and claim certainty where the forces of disorganization and uncertainty are at their most powerful and harassing. The elements of the magnificently rigid certainty that we find in the later Bose were therefore also a way of coping with a long sequence of uncertainty and deep fears of uncertainty.

V

Bose's father died in 1892, his mother in 1894. We have no record of how the son reacted to these deaths. Given the nature of the

[38] Geddes, *Life and Works*.

[39] Bose, *Abyakto*, p. 1.

[40] Ibid., p. 3.

mother–son relationship, one suspects that it was the second death that aroused intense feelings of guilt and fear of his own destructive wishes. In any case, a great change occurred in Jagadis Chandra at this time, and he started his researches in the same year. The turning point was his birthday, 30 November 1894. That day he vowed, persuaded by Abala, to take up scientific research seriously—to further knowledge by unravelling the mysteries of nature, *prakriti*, as both nature and the feminine principle are called in Bengali and Sanskrit. This marked, his nephew thinks, a more or less permanent truce with the conflicts 'which had been going on in the subconscious region of his mind.'[41]

Thus, with the help of his wife, Bose the wayward child and confused adolescent was reborn (it was his birthday) into a new life where work identification and professional selfhood could be built on a rearrangement of earlier identifications. The fight against the temptation to see science as a hobby—his father's hobby—was joined with the newly-found weapon of single-minded absorption in his scientific career. But not before a new, intimate motherliness—his wife's—had helped him partly to accept his rejected identification with his mother. He could now afford to search for evidences of 'motherliness in the steel frame of inexorable orderliness' in a ruthless *prakriti*.[42] In 1894 he wrote: 'Everybody cannot see mother's love in the heart of nature. What we perceive is only the projection of our minds. The things on which our eyes rest are merely the pretexts.'[43]

Some semblance of this search for a benevolent mother in the heart of nature continued for another five years, till another form of motherly nurture helped him to break into a new kind of research into *prakriti*. But the first breakthrough towards serious orderliness—his mother's orderliness—had been made. Though he walked for a while what he later called the safe path of research in electrical waves, he had located his personal projective medium in scientific research—a medium that would be true to him in response to his own fidelity to his deepest self.

Bose looked upon the first five years of his research as a preparatory stage—a prehistory marked by the discovery of instruments, rather than by daring theorizations. This view agrees

[41] D. M. Bose, 'Abala Bose', p. 446; Home, *Acharya Jagadis*, p. 7; Gupta, *Bose*, p. 23; Roy and Bhattacharya, *Acharya*, pp. 32–3.

[42] Bose, *Abyakto*, pp. 3, 133.

[43] Ibid., p. 4.

with the opinion of D. M. Bose and Amal Home, who have divided Bose's research career into roughly three phases:[44] 1894–1899: Production of the shortest possible electromagnetic waves (up to 5 mm) and verification of their quasi-optical properties; 1899–1902: Study of some similarity in responses in the living and the non-living; 1903–1933: Study of response phenomena in plants, the complexity of whose responses lies intermediate between those of inorganic matter and of animals.

I am not competent to evaluate Bose as a scientist, and it is difficult to get a comparative assessment of the three periods from scientists who are no longer sufficiently interested in Bose to devote themselves to all his work with equal seriousness. D. M. Bose, a rare exception, believes that the first phase has the surest scientific relevance to present-day physics and biology, followed by the third and then the second. Others make more or less similar assessments.[45] Bose himself, however, considered the second phase of work, from 1899 to 1902, the most important. After completing his *Responses in the Living and the Nonliving*, he wrote: 'My task is more or less complete; in future I shall merely have to sit idly in an atmosphere of uncertainty.'[46]

Thus while Bose himself and his Indian and western admirers valued the second, third, and first phases in that order, some of his contemporary western scientists' evaluations were not substantially different from the present-day assessments of both Indian and western scholars. The virulence of Bose's detractors notwithstanding, his belief in the anti-Indian parochialism and conspiracy of western scientists might have been based both on a realistic perception of outer hostility and on his and his society's mood. Perhaps Bose and his disciples sought, in the perceived hostility of the West, another justification of their own growing hostility to the West and of their own science.

The researches of Bose's first phase were well received. In 1896,

[44] D. M. Bose, 'Jagadish Chandra Bose (1858–1937)', *Transactions of Bose Research Institute*, 1958, *22*, v–xv; also Home, *Acharya Jagadis*, Part I.

[45] Gopal Chandra Bhattacharya, a botanist who worked under Bose for seventeen years, has a different periodization to offer. He believes that the second phase, culminating in the publication of *Responses in the Living and the Nonliving* in 1902, was the most creative period in Bose's life. Bhattacharya divides Bose's work into two stages. All the significant work according to his scheme was published before 1906; all the trivia afterwards. As Bhattacharya's periodization cuts across the others', his assessment of Bose as a scientist is not strictly comparable with that of anyone else.

[46] Roy and Bhattacharya, *Acharya*, p. 95.

the University of London awarded him a D.Sc. for his contribution to physics and the Government of India sent him to England on a lecture tour, the first Indian scientist to be so deputed. Bose did well in England. His speeches on electrical microwaves at the advanced British centres of learning were applauded by some of the best-known scientists of the time, including William Kelvin, Joseph Lister, and William Ramsay. Some of the more sedate dailies and periodicals, like *The Times* and *The Spectator*, also found his work strikingly original, even sensational.[47] The English tour was followed by lecture-demonstrations given to a number of learned societies and universities on the Continent, which were also highly praised. Bose apparently was well set to become a celebrated physicist, if not an outstandingly creative one.

But, he knew, 'success could be cheap and failure great', and his—a Brahmo's—'goddess lifted her children to her bosom only when they returned to her defeated.'[48] Failures therefore were cushioned:

> What are you afraid of? That you will not reach your goal even at the cost of your entire life? Do you not have the slightest of courage? Even a gambler stakes his life's earning on a throw of dice. Can you not stake your life for a grander game? Either you win or you lose![49]

Thus in 1899, the vision of a grand defeat and what could be the paradoxical fear of negative success,[50] made Bose cross the conventional western boundaries of scientific disciplines to enter the field of botany, a subject he had formally studied only in his undergraduate days.

A number of explanations for this shift can be suggested. One is that Bose's work on short electrical waves had till then mainly taxed his skills as an applied physicist. And instrumentation was, as we know, Bose's forte. But his researches were now leading him towards more complex mathematical work for which he had no aptitude. His students say that he dreaded mathematical details, and he himself later ascribed the change-over—great

[47] See details in Home, *Acharya Jagadis, passim*; and Roy and Bhattacharya, *Acharya*, Ch. 11–15. Also Geddes, *Life and Works*.

[48] Bose, *Abyakto*, 132–58.

[49] Ibid., p. 131.

[50] The concept of negative success is Erik Erikson's. See his *Young Man Luther* (New York: Norton, 1958), p. 44.

rationalizer that he was—to the over-mathematization of modern physics.

However, there were less mundane reasons, too. Bose had now come to believe that 'plant life was merely the shadow of human life.'[51] And he was looking for a projective medium where the objects of his inquiry would be more recognizably the living, feeling victims of the environment who needed humane intervention and protection:

> I once did not know that these trees have a life like ours, that they eat and grow. Now I can see that they also face poverty, sorrows and sufferings. This poverty may also induce them to steal and rob.... But they also help each other, develop friendships...sacrifice their lives for the sake of their children.[52]

His heightened concern with violence and its control also contributed to the change. Shankari Prasad Basu mentions Bose's reprimanding his newly-found friend Sister Nivedita (1867–1911) at about this time about her casual attitude to violence. She had told Bose of her plan to join a group of *shikaris*. This prompted Bose to hold forth on the cruelties of *shikar*. Basu asks rhetorically: 'How old was this disgust with the cruelty of *shikar* in Dr Bose?'[53] Had Basu been more cynical, he could have pointed out that Bose probably delivered this reprimand in a house decorated with a large number of stuffed animals which he had himself shot.

These reasons were probably held together by a deeper motivating force. There is a clue to this in a letter to a friend written in the following year:

> I hear, from time to time, a call from the mother. I as her servant must start by collecting the dust of her feet as a benediction. You and all my friends must bless me, so that this servant can serve the mother with all his heart and soul; and his strength for work can increase.[54]

We shall return to the implications of this 'call' later. This change in the direction of Bose's research was also brought about by his deepening relationship with an Irishwoman named Margaret Noble who adopted the name Nivedita after she became a disciple of Swami Vivekananda and came to India in 1898.[55] She came as a

[51] Bose, *Abyakto*, p. 135.

[52] Ibid.

[53] Basu, *Nivedita*, vol. 1, p. 583.

[54] J. C. Bose, Letter to R. N. Tagore, 23 June; cited in Gupta, *Jagadish Chandra*, p. 35.

[55] Vivekananda was doing in religion what Bose was doing in science. Born

social worker and immediately became active in the Ramakrishna Mission established by the Swami. Bose met her soon after her arrival and it was 'friendship at first sight'. She was then thirty-one and Bose forty.

The friendship between the nun and the scientist gradually turned into a deep platonic bond. Those were difficult days for Bose. He was not yet well known enough to have his way with the authorities, and the absence of proper research facilities at the Presidency College was beginning to demoralize him. Nivedita's strong yet supportive personality and her burning faith in a science that would reflect Indian sensitivities must have given him a new faith in his work. Bose, being a Brahmo, still did not have much patience with Nivedita's—and the Ramakrishna Mission's—version of Hinduism. But this was a minor irritant in a relationship which was quickly becoming central to Bose's life. Three developments contributed to this.

First, in 1898, Nivedita introduced Bose to Mrs Ole Bull, an American friend of India. She encouraged Bose to address Mrs Bull as 'mother' and induced Mrs Bull to accept Bose as her son, as she herself had already done metaphorically by calling him her 'bairn'. One of the major pay-offs of the Bull–Bose relationship, which Nivedita nurtured till her death, was the financial help Mrs Bull gave to Bose's research.[56]

Second, Nivedita, searching for evidence of Indian greatness in Vedantic Hinduism, could not but stumble upon the distinctive Indian concept of vitalistic, organic monism, if that is the right expression, that was implicit in some of Bose's work. Almost as soon as she came to know Bose, Nivedita took over the responsibility of editing his work.[57] Bose was neither the first nor the last

---

Narendra Nath Dutta in 1863 in Calcutta, in social circumstances roughly similar to those in which Bose was born, Vivekananda was India's first modern and nationalist Swami and missionary of Hinduism to the West. He died in 1902 when Bose was at the pinnacle of his glory.

[56] Actually, after Mrs Bull's death, her daughter began harassing Nivedita about these 'wasteful expenditures' on an Indian scientist. The other person who went with a begging bowl to rich Indians to collect money for Bose's research was Rabindra Nath Tagore. He also suffered many humiliations and attracted the hostility of other clients competing for the favours of these patrons. Particularly unpleasant was Tagore's encounter with the court of Raja Radhakishor Devanmanikya, Bose's major Indian patron.

[57] The editing was so heavy that Nivedita could legitimately be considered a junior

person to receive such editorial help from Nivedita, but he was certainly the only scientist among Nivedita's acquaintances who had something important to say and was looking for an appropriate idiom. Nivedita's basic training was in science and the areas in which Bose had specialized were, as yet, not beyond the understanding of someone with a good general education in science. She was not, therefore, shouldering an impossible task. For instance, Bose's best-known book, *Responses in the Living and the Non-living*, reported his own researches but owed its elegant style as well as structure to Nivedita. Till she died the collaboration survived. Strange though it may appear, the first articulation of Indianized science was in the language of a western woman.

Third, after his marriage Bose began undertaking a series of long sentimental trips to what he called the relics of the glory of ancient India. The trips, often undertaken in arduous, even dangerous conditions, began to have Nivedita as their constant feature after 1899. They often lasted months and brought Bose even closer to Nivedita.

The growing closeness to Nivedita introduced some changes in Bose's life. He gradually moved away from Abala's protective umbrella in professional matters. Though in other respects he continued to depend on her, in science his new motherly protector became Nivedita. This induced in him a slight sense of guilt, too. It was at about this time that Bose started making occasional private requests to his friends to praise Abala and her social work in public.

All this subtly changed Bose's research interests. However, there was nothing subtle about the results of the change, which were, if anything, dramatic. The turning from the study of the inorganic to that of organized life, as Bose described it, led to studies of the responses made by plants, animals and the nonliving to various types of mechanical and biochemical stimuli. It meant a sudden spurt in productivity too. In the five years 1894–9, Bose had published only four papers, whereas in the three years 1899–1902, he published nine papers and a book. It is an index of the radical nature of the change that during his third and last phase

---

author of some of Bose's work. According to Basu, *Nivedita*, vol. 1, p. 660, during the first ten years of her friendship with Bose, Nivedita edited about 2,500 pages and prepared about 1,000 charts and diagrams for the four books which Bose wrote during the period. This is apart from the work she put in on his large number of papers.

of work, Bose was still trying to consolidate and extend the work of his second period, rather than break new ground.

The thematic continuity in Bose's work, beginning 1899, is also reflected in the evocative titles of his papers on botanical and para-botanical researches.[58] What was a new scientific idiom, and has sometimes been explained away as only an idiom, also spilled over into his other creative work. In 1920 Bose published a collection of essays in Bengali which articulated the themes predominant in his technical papers;[59] in fact, some of the essays were actually attempts to popularize the themes.

The core of Bose's research interests was now the similarities between the living and the nonliving and a biological model that would explain physical phenomena. In 1901, for instance, he wrote:

> I have invented an instrument in which any pulsation or response created by pinching would be recorded by itself.... And just as you feel the throb of life by feeling the pulse, similarly the throb of life in the inanimate object is recorded in my instrument. I am sending to you a very astonishing record. Please observe the normal coursing of the pulse, and then how it moves under the effect of poison. The poison was applied on an inanimate object.[60]

The credo of such work was roughly this:

> There is no break in the life-processes which characterize both the animate and the inanimate world. It is difficult to draw a line between these two aspects of life. It is of course possible to delineate a number of imaginary differences, as it is possible to find out similarities in terms of certain other general criteria. The latter approach is justified by the natural tendency of science towards seeking unity in diversity.[61]

[58] A random sample: 'How the Plants React to Pain and Pleasure' (1915); 'Testing the Sensibility of Plants' (1915); 'The Unity of Life' (1927); 'Is the Plant a Sentient Being?' (1929); 'Are Plants Like Animals?' (1931); 'Injured Plants', and 'Inorganic and Organic Memory'. For a complete list see S. Bala Subramanian, 'Bibliography of Books on and by Jagadish Chandra Bose' (Calcutta: National Library, 1965), mimeographed. See also the chronology in Home, *Acharya Jagadis*, pp. 75–82.

[59] Some examples are 'Birth and Death of Plants', 'Literature in Science', 'The Mute Life', 'Injured Plants', and 'Gestures of Trees'. All the essays have been reprinted in Bose, *Abyakto*.

[60] Part of a letter probably written to Lord Rayleigh or Sir James Dewer, 3 May 1901, cited in Gupta, *Jagadish Chandra*, pp. 41–2.

[61] Bose, *Abyakto*, p. 87.

The statement underlines the paradox that was Bose. While it seems so contemporary as a statement of a personal philosophy of science, it sought to legitimize an approach which in its specifics was to prove simple-minded in the context of plant physiology within a short time.

The reaction of western scientists to such work was mixed. Some found the approach magical and mystical, and hence worthless; others found it appealing for that very reason. When Bose demonstrated, at the Royal Institute in 1901, the death agony of a poisoned tinfoil, and cured another with drugs, he merely took his biological model of physical phenomena, as both groups had expected, to its logical conclusion. After his peroration, Robert Austen, the greatest living authority of the time on metals, 'was beside himself with joy'. He reportedly said:

> I have all my life studied the properties of metals. I am happy to think that they have life.... Can you tell me whether there is future life—what will become of me after my body dies?[62]

The culture of a science may sometimes serve as a good projective medium for individual scientists and even individual societies. But the structure of scientific knowledge never has that special a weakness for any specific metaphysics or for the needs of cultural nationalism. Nor, for that matter, can it be expected to cure the anxieties of scientists at the level at which Professor Austen so innocently articulated them. As it happens, more sophisticated, though duller, interpretations of some of Bose's data are today available. Even in his lifetime, despite their apparent esotericism, the salient features of Bose's discoveries were being gradually integrated within the framework of formal science.[63] Bose, however, was never open to alternative explanations of his work. As with many pioneers, he had a hard core of dogmatism hidden by an other-worldly style. He was the obstinate mother's son who never gave in and—one must understand—could not give in. Like his ideal teacher, Ishwarchandra Vidyasagar (1820–91) and his ideal of divine creativity, Shiva, Bose felt justified in

[62] Gupta, *Jagadish Chandra*, p. 44. Austen may have sensed that Bose's work was, among other things, a remedy for—or defence against—the fear of death. See section VII for an analysis of how Bose utilized the universal human anxiety about death to organize his identity.

[63] See D. M. Bose, 'Jagadish Chandra Bose', pp. v–xv, for a brief account.

combining softness with obstinacy, protectiveness with rage.[64] For he had, he was sure, found his certitudes. His impatience with criticism was a by-word among his students and friends. And during the last twenty-five years of his life, he went on redefining and sharpening his concepts without ever substantially modifying them.

It is the middle-aged scientist that many remember. Some of his students remember him as a stout, short, impeccably dressed, energetic man—intolerably narcissistic, impatient, abstruse, and authoritarian. Satyendra Nath Bose, the most gifted and most outspoken of them, remembers him as an essentially selfish, ruthless old man who exploited rather than expressed nativistic themes. The students also remember Bose as a good orator and conversationalist, in spite of his East Bengali accent. This estimate, however, Bose would not have accepted.[65] His distrust of his orality was deep. Even in his old age, he spoke as little as he could and, when he had to lecture, took days to prepare for it. So much so that many remember his public lecture-demonstrations essentially as well-rehearsed dramatic performances, in which nothing ever went wrong: 'He would even use the same set of bricks to heighten his table every time', one of his students affirms. Abala knew this. In his last years it was she who often pressed Bose into giving his customary annual lecture to the Bose Institute.

Bose was particularly aware of his own oral aggression. Once, while appearing before the Royal Services Commission, he took along with him a memo exhorting himself: 'Do not get angry.'[66] The clearest indicator of his problems with the management of oral aggression was, however, his tendency to stammer when provoked or excited. Time has wiped out most details of the trait, but it is not impossible to guess its meaning in a person such as Bose. A classic clinical text mentions the stutterer's 'hostile or sadistic tendency to destroy his opponent by means of words', so that stuttering

---

[64] Bhattacharya, 'Acharyadeb Smarane'; Gupta, *Jagadish Chandra*, p. 94; and Bose, *Abyakto*, p. 220d. Ishwar Chandra Vidyasagar (1820–91) was an eminent Sanskritist, social reformer, and teacher. His aggressiveness, directed mostly against impersonal sources of injustice and ignorance, could not really be compared with Bose's free-floating aggression. The idealization of Vidyasagar and Shiva were rather a search by Bose for a rationalizing principle that would make his anger more acceptable to him.

[65] Gupta, *Jagadish Chandra*, p. 79.

[66] Rabindra Nath Tagore seemed to agree with Bose. See his *Chithipatra*, ed. P. B. Sen (Calcutta: Viswabharati, 1957), vol. 6, p. 107.

becomes 'both the blocking of and the punishment for this tendency.' The stutterer's hesitation often expresses his desire to kill, 'because in him speech remobilizes the infantile state when words were omnipotent.' He is a warrior who is perpetually trying to control his weapon.[67] For Bamasundari's son and one with such mixed feelings about his cultural origins and status, though, such functional disorders could symptomatize other ambivalences too:

> Occasionally, the words that should or should not be uttered have, on the deepest level, the significance of introjected objects.... The stutterer may not only unconsciously attempt to kill by means of words...his symptom also expresses the tendency to kill his words, as representing introjected objects.[68]

There was also Bose's ugly manner in classroom and laboratory. At the slightest provocation he would shout at his students and colleagues 'moron' or 'I shall whip you' ('*chabke debo*') or 'you are dismissed'. Frequently he felt sorry after his outburst and apologized, but this was hardly adequate compensation for his colleagues, already sensitized by Bose's inelegant patriarchal style. Many of them left him as his sworn enemies.

More than one of his students claim that Bose was less short-tempered when he was younger. Perhaps his aggression which in his more creative days was temporarily turned inwards had turned outwards again.[69] Perhaps the restraint once exercised by his identification with his father was now less effective. Whatever the reason, his abrasive autocratic style became in his middle years one of his major identifiers. At least one informant relates this drift towards authoritarianism to Bose's increasingly greater exposure to the *guru-sishya* concepts popularized by the Ramakrishna Mission, particularly Vivekananda and Nivedita. He now cultivated and increasingly enjoyed his public image of a distant *acharya*—a religious teacher cum preceptor. Certainly this was the image Nivedita wanted him to present to the world.

The fulcrum of the Bose–Nivedita relationship also subtly shifted. For a long time, Bose had had a Brahmo's reservation about Nivedita's faith. In a letter he had once affectionately but

[67] Otto Fenichel, *The Psychoanalytic Theory of Neurosis* (Now York: Norton, 1945), pp. 312–13.

[68] Ibid., p. 314.

[69] See the comparable dynamic in Isaac Newton in Frank E. Manuel, 'Newton as Autocrat of Science', *Daedalus*, 1968, *97*, pp. 287–319.

belligerently attacked her for her support to the caste system, Kali worship, etc.[70] On the other hand, Nivedita had never cared much for Bose's Brahmoism; nor did she take it very seriously. She had always hoped that some day Bose would move closer to her concept of Hinduism,[71] but apparently, both remained steadfast in their religious ideology till the end of their days. But while Nivedita stuck to her beliefs, Bose in fact changed under her influence in his middle years. According to Geddes, he became a celibate, which was a major plank as well as value of the Ramakrishna Mission group and which subtly balanced the scales between Abala and Nivedita.[72] Bose also physically moved close to the Advaita Ashram, Mayabati, in the foot-hills of the Himalaya. At Mayabati, he claimed, ideas rushed into his head whereas in Calcutta they dried up.[73] Young, self-confident Vivekananda had once perceptively commented to Nivedita:

> Yet that boy [Bose] almost worshipped me for 3 days—in a week's time he would be my man.... And those are always the people who make the fuss about worship of the personal. They don't understand themselves, and they hate in others what they know they are struggling against.[74]

The Swami may have been wrong in his prediction; he was not wrong in his analysis.

Bose's growing authoritarianism was also associated with diminishing self-esteem, a weakened capacity to handle professional criticism, and a growing inability to admit that he could be less than fully autonomous as a scientist. For instance, his publications gained immensely from Nivedita's editorial efforts: of Nivedita's few available letters to Bose, at least two refer to Bose's works as 'our books'. Yet, except in a stray letter he never expected to be published, Bose did not openly acknowledge Nivedita's contribution. Though he paid handsome tributes to his friend at various places, nowhere did he mention, not even in the preface to his books, the actual nature of Nivedita's help. On the contrary, he and some members of his family were reluctant to publish letters from Nivedita in which the westerner innocently mentioned the

[70] Basu, *Nivedita, 1*, pp. 594–5.

[71] Ibid., esp. pp. 585, 592n.

[72] Geddes, *Life and Works*, Ch. 17.

[73] Basu, *Nivedita*, vol. 1, pp. 594–5.

[74] Ibid., third photographic plate facing p. 592.

details of her scholarly assistance to the East.[75] Similarly, there was Bose's defensiveness about the criticisms of the famous botanist Sidney Vines. Vines had been his teacher at Cambridge and Bose often sent him his drafts for comments. But he would later carefully erase his pencilled comments, so that nobody knew the snide remarks which Vines, always considered a supporter of Bose, had in fact made about some of Bose's later work.

Nothing sealed Bose's scientific fate more completely than his inability to keep open his channels of communication with his colleagues. He never allowed anyone to contradict him in either academic or non-academic matters; he could not enjoy the company of young scientists or, for that matter, of anybody whom he considered lower in social status (even though he was considered 'jolly' company by his 'equals'); and he refused to see the experimental results his colleagues obtained if the results contradicted his own ideas. Increasingly he used his collaborators as laboratory assistants. They did the experiments and collected empirical data, having no say whatsoever in decisions regarding theory, methods, and interpretation of results. Every morning they had to attend an informal but strict roll call, after which they were assigned work for the day by their stern taskmaster. No wonder that when some scientists like R. Snow began to offer less vitalistic interpretations of some of Bose's own experimental results, he rejected their work out-of-hand.

Simultaneously, Bose worked hard to maintain the image of a humourless, puritanic Brahmo among his assistants. He was secretive about his reading habits, particularly his fondness for the best-selling middlebrow novels of Saratchandra Chattopadhyay and the humorous short stories of Rajsekhar Bose. He even cut

[75] The instrumental use made by Bose of Nivedita is also evidenced by her articulating some of his tall claims. For instance, she took Bose seriously when he said to her that he was the first to send wireless messages and that this was not admitted because of racism. This was certainly not true because wireless messages had been sent earlier in England. However, Bose had done excellent work in the area and had demonstrated his wireless equipment before G. M. Marconi did.

Incidentally, many of Bose's claims in the area of plant physiology were later to embarrass scientists at the Bose Institute after his death. A typical example was the evidence Bose claimed to have in support of his theory of a pulsating or valve activity in plants to account for the ascent of sap. He advanced this nervous theory against the theory of osmotic pressure. See also Bose's revealing letter (dated 7 October 1937) to Mr Herbert, who was planning to co-author a biography of Nivedita in Basu, *Nivedita*, vol. 1, plates 16 and 17 facing p. 592.

down on smoking, in keeping with the new puritanic posture, though his declining health too had something to do with this. He also now began to take care to hide his curiosity. He had always been an inquisitive, adventurous person as a child, but in middle age he came to hate anyone with similar qualities.

In all, one gets the impression of a harried man trying desperately to contain his feelings of inadequacy by affirming his power and uniqueness, and by posing as a larger-than-life figure. Those suspicious of the sudden emergence of well-organized character traits may see in these the evidences of a deeper self. In giving up the earlier egalitarian bonhomie with students and assistants, they may say, Bose was being true to a part of his self that had become important for him in the course of years. But by all accounts, the change was a painful process for his friends.

There were other indices, too, of the disintegration of his well-organized psychological defences. Bose had become by this time a compulsive penny pincher. He often personally visited the suppliers of his laboratory and wasted hours bargaining for small discounts. He refused to trust juniors or delegate authority in any financial transaction involving his research team. Bose's niggardliness, however, had its comic side. Overly fussy about money, he often shocked students by his gullibility. He mostly bargained for small cuts, more symbolic than substantive, and was pacified if he could convince himself that he had got a better deal than his juniors could have.

By this time he had redecorated his house in fully Indian style and given pride of place in his living room to a famous painting of Mother India or Bengal—like all true-blooded Bengalis, Bose did not, or could not, distinguish between the two—by Abanindranath Tagore. Patterned after the image of Durga, the traditional mother goddess of Bengal, the painting was another Brahmo's homage to the core archetype of his culture, one which had presided over Bose's work all through his life. He had also become obsessively finicky about food, apparently because of diabetes, blood pressure, and a 'nervous breakdown' in 1915.[76] But even earlier, his growing

[76] One wishes that something more was known about the breakdown; how for instance Bose's body, if it *was* a matter of the body, spoke the language of his inner struggles and what, other than the strain of an international journey, precipitated the symptoms. Only one biographical account provides enough material for us to guess that Bose was in an acute anxiety state and that it was at least partly a result of constantly preparing and delivering public lectures on his work during the trip. See S. C. Ganguli, *Acharya Jagadis Chandra* (Calcutta: Shri Bhoomi, pp. 141–3.) Apparently, in sickness as in health, Bose's anxieties centring around orality remained the central dynamic of his personality.

rejection of food was obvious to many (part of Abala's heroic effort towards an integrated Bose was that after her marriage she learned to cook very well).

For a short time, as a young man, Bose had a large circle of friends but, as the years went by, the radius of his interpersonal world shrank. As he grew less friendly towards his students, he distanced himself from his close friends, too. Nowhere was Bose's insecure self-image and almost paranoid fear of hostility and rejection by others as obvious as in the case of Rabindranath Tagore. The fate of this relationship deserves, therefore, a brief digression.

I have already mentioned Tagore's early support to Bose, both psychological and financial (through the patronage of the Maharaja of Tripura, Radhakishor Dev Manikya). For this, the poet even had to face the jealousy and hostility of some other protégés of the Maharaja. In other ways too, Tagore, as the acknowledged leader of Indian intellectuals, had been warm and protective towards the scientist. But the middle-aged Bose began to take Tagore's help for granted and bear him a grudge for not doing enough. He avenged this 'neglect' by refusing to help the poet in any way when the latter was trying to establish a university at Shantiniketan. And when Tagore won the Nobel Prize for literature in 1913, his friend was less than enthusiastic. Though Tagore publicly pleaded for greater recognition of Bose's work in the West and proposed him for a Nobel Prize, Bose felt unjustly neglected. His achievement concerns were always tainted by jealousy and he could never fully master his basic feelings of rejection. Moreover, he may have perceived—with the shrewdness which only a man with strong paranoid feelings is capable of—that Tagore now cared less about his science and, despite being a littérateur, that he had sensed that the future did not belong to Bose's science.

Bose now seemed to be looking for any excuse to break away from a man he had once declared was one of his best friends. The break came when Bose's nephew Aurobindo, whom Bose had himself sent to Shantiniketan, became greatly attached to Tagore and his institution. Bose was particularly fond of this nephew and possessive about him in a way only a childless man can be about a boy who would never be entirely his own.[77] He now began to fear

[77] D. M. Bose, his other nephew, mentions that in his childhood he was afraid of the enveloping, and slightly suffocating love of his uncle. Sudeb Rai Chaudhuri, '*Byakti o Byakitva*', *Desh*, 1973, *40*, pp. 751–5.

that he would lose Aurobindo to Tagore. He did his best to wean the nephew away from Shantiniketan and began a sustained but low-key private campaign against the poet among his acquaintances. Though ostensibly the poet and scientist maintained their friendship, by now both were wary of each other. It must have been singularly hard on Tagore who, out of a sense of patriotic duty, had virtually gate-crashed into Bose's life, to help him with money, encouragement, and 'propaganda'. The bitter loneliness in which he faced Bose's rejection, at a time when such personal differences could not be aired in public, can be gauged from the Bengali obituary of Bose he wrote in 1937.[78]

Gradually, Bose cooled towards Prafulla Chandra Roy (1861–1944), the illustrious professor of chemistry, and quarrelled with Devmanikya, his erstwhile patron. He also began to avoid participating in movements, large organizations, and public functions.[79] Both Mrs Bull and Nivedita were dead and recognition from the West, never complete, now became more uncertain. He had committed enemies there and his weakening grasp on his discipline made their task easier. After his mental illness, even his physical links with the West and westerners became weak.

These centripetal emotional forces may have been by-products of Bose's greater involvement in research and his attempts to find steady financial support for his work from the government, but they could also be the reflections of something deeper. He had made new and more reliable friends by then:

> In time, plants came to be his best friends. He loved them, reared them and treated them with tender care. He followed their life history and perhaps they also spoke to him. Pain and relief from pain in the plant became clear to him.[80]

No account of Bose's life can be complete without a word on the advanced research centre he established in Calcutta in 1917. The Bose Institute was an ornate, temple-like structure meant 'to search for the ultimate unity which permeates the universal order and cuts across the animal, plant and inanimate lives.'[81] Bose played a large part in the design of the building, being greatly influenced by

[78] Tagore, *Chithipatra*, pp. 6, 124–8, esp. p. 128.

[79] Roy and Bhattacharya, *Acharya*, pp. 231–2.

[80] Gupta, *Jagadish Chandra*, p. 92. Roy and Bhattacharya (*Acharya*, p. 216) also report that Bose's neighbours believed that they saw the scientist conversing with plants at night.

[81] From the inaugural speech reproduced in Bose, *Abyakto*, pp. 142–58.

Ajanta and Ellora. It is said that Nivedita before her death had discussed some of these architectural possibilities with Bose. Called Basu Vigyan Mandir (the Bose Temple of Science), the Institute had a special platform or *vedi* for its founder to sit and meditate on. In its garden were deer, peacocks, and 'talking birds'. Near the entrance to the Institute was a sculpted relief of Nivedita who had hoped and planned with Bose for such an institute and whose unconditional adoration had, to a great extent, made Bose what he was. Under the relief, Bose secretly buried a small box containing Nivedita's ashes. As emblems of the temple, Bose selected sculptured representations of the Sun-God (a symbolic pointer to the identification that had been his first bridge between *bhakti* or devotion, and knowledge), the *vajra* or thunderbolt (the weapon with which Indra fought evil in the form of demons, and a traditional symbol of legitimate fury), and *ardha amlaki*, the Buddhist symbol of total renunciation. Some of these symbols were said to be Nivedita's suggestions.

Bose's attitude to the Institute and to science as a vocation is revealed in the life-long commitment he expected from those working there. Many of his colleagues promised—or rather, if one takes into account the psychological pressures in the institution, had to promise—in writing that they would never leave the Institute.[82] Bose himself admired austerity, but never cared to live by it,[83] and yet expected total austerity in his subordinates. He also came to believe that only East Bengalis could give him the allegiance he wanted. He gave preference to them in recruitment and trusted only them in the affairs of the Institute. But his peculiar mix of self-hatred and violence affected even his treatment of them. Though he himself had a pronounced East Bengali accent, he was bitterly sarcastic towards any one in the Institute whose accent evinced an East Bengali origin.

However, Bose had the authoritarian man's special capacity to elicit and hold the loyalty of some of his subordinates. So when he began to stretch his experimental results and force his associates to do the same, presumably in the interest of the higher science he was striving towards, nobody publicly protested. And the private criticism of these associates survived only as memories of the deviation from principles and opportunism which a revolutionary

[82] The promise at first had to be given on a piece of paper. Later on, it used to be engraved on a copper plate.

[83] Geddes, *Life and Works*, p. 220.

movement cannot always avoid. For many those were the most glorious moments of their lives, and it seemed better to participate and occasionally fail than to be a mere onlooker.

The major grants towards the Institute's buildings and its research programmes came from the British Indian government. Nivedita had died in 1911 and the conduits for financing research that she had built with such care were now dry. And Bose had by then quarrelled with his Indian patrons. Fortunately, he had maintained friendly relations with the political authorities for many years. The imperial system then was run by self-confident administrators, well versed in the management of colonial societies and not prone to overreact to Bose's brand of nationalist science. Also, it had not gone unnoticed that Bose had always been in his personal life fairly attentive towards westerners and not very accessible to Indians. (Bose's nationalism was not merely tinged with a sense of inferiority, but also with a sharp awareness of where the metropolitan centres of science were located. One of his assistants mentions that he expected Abala to relate to his Indian visitors western scientists' eulogies of his work. If Abala, a more self-confident and autonomous person, forgot, Bose would take care to remind her of her duty.)

Some of his contemporaries found such links unacceptable. Prafulla Chandra Roy, an ardent nationalist, privately called Bose a *dhamadhara* or a sycophant.[84] Satyendra Nath Bose, the physicist, was harsher: Jagadis Chandra, he said, was an 'utterly selfish' man who was not merely careful to be on the right side of the British government, but also had enough political sense to build the right type of rapport with the highest authorities without hobnobbing with junior officials. Both critics failed to understand that Bose's nationalism was as real as his emotional investment in a West which was close to him by virtue of being his counterplayer; psychologically, he could not do without the West. He had after all been anti-imperialist when it was troublesome to be one—during the 1905 movement against the partition of Bengal. If he was ambivalent towards the West, it was the ambivalence of *babu* nationalism itself, a nationalism arising in response to western intrusion and binding Indians to their counterculture in a love–hate relationship. In the case of functioning scientists, the ambivalence

[84] Ray himself, however, had gone bankrupt as a researcher in middle age, trying to be a 'nationalist' chemist and becoming, in the process, mainly a patron of young scientists.

had to be deeper. The absence of knowledgeable consumers of modern scientific research in India forced them to look westwards to find such consumers and protect their self-image as scientists. Their country respected them mainly as grand successes without appreciating the content of their work. Even this success was defined in terms of bureaucratic status, degrees, wealth, and the opinion of established scientists outside India. It is to Bose's credit that despite these circumstances, he was one of the first to suggest a definition of Indianness in science and to try to integrate in the definition the role of the modern scientist. It is less important that he could not fully consolidate these gains.

But he tried all the same. Dedicating the Bose Institute 'to the feet of God for bringing honour to India and happiness to the world', the aging patriarch said:

> The excessive specialization in modern science has led to the danger of losing sight of the fundamental fact that there can be but one truth.... India through her habit of mind is peculiarly fitted to realize the idea of unity, and to see in the phenomenal world an orderly universe. It was this trend of thought that led me unconsciously to the dividing frontiers of the different sciences and shaped the course of my work in its constant alternations between the theoretical and the practical, from the investigation of the organic world to that of organized life and its multifarious activities of growth, of movement, and even of sensation.
>
> What I established today is a temple, not merely a laboratory. Truths which can be sensed are determined by experiments; but there are some great truths which can be reached only through faith.[85]

Bose died in 1937, a renowned scientist and a venerated academic, surrounded by loyal disciples. But neither the fame nor the loyalty could mask his alienation from some of the newer currents of scientific thought. Even before his death, his professional defeat was apparent, if not to him, at least to his students and co-workers, monitoring and occasionally fudging data for him. Some of these colleagues had also become secretly sympathetic to the increasingly convincing technical arguments and experimental data many non-vitalistic plant physiologists were marshalling against Bose.

This professional isolation was not merely due to Bose's

[85] For the full speech, see 'Nibedan' in Bose, *Abyakto*, pp. 142–58. The first paragraph is an English translation taken from Gupta, *Jagadish Chandra*, p. 134.

advancing age, a handicap which can be fatal in any fast-growing discipline. It was also due to three changes in the environment of science. First, as the memories of World War I faded, the first shock of seeing the other face of modern science subsided. This reduced the appeal of Bose's humane, pacifist, eco-sensitive science for other scientists. Secondly, Bose's monistic philosophy of science, which anticipated many of the concerns of the contemporary philosophy of science, was for his own time a premature development within the dominant culture of science. The manipulative, power-seeking, narrowly empirical and operationalist aspects of the dominant culture were yet to be threatened by the growing self-confidence of the critical social theories of science. Thirdly, there was a change in the state of the disciplines within which Bose worked. With the consolidation of new paradigms, these disciplines reverted to their unheroic normal activities.[86] And though they did not bypass Bose, they began to 'undramatize' his discoveries in a way which he, had he cared to know, would have found heartless in the typical western way.

VI

> *When science is universal, can there be in the world of science a place which will remain vacant without an Indian devotee? There certainly is.*[87]

To understand the identity Bose evolved as a creative Indian scientist, one must take into account three recurrent themes in his life and work. The most salient and self-conscious of these themes was pithily summarized by Bose himself as a simple principle:

> The consciousness of the scientist and the poet both go out in the search of the inexpressible one. The difference lies in that the poet ignores the means, the scientist does not.[88]

If this was an off-the-cuff reflection on his role as a scientist, the concluding remarks of the lecture-demonstration he once gave at the Royal Institute were a clearer proclamation of his professional identity as it mediated his self-concept and his concept of true Indianness:

[86] The concept of normality is of course borrowed from T. S. Kuhn, *The Structure of Scientific Revolution* (Chicago: University of Chicago, 1962).

[87] Bose, *Abyakto*, p. 150.

[88] Ibid., p. 87.

> I have shown you this evening the autographic records of the stress and strain in both the living and the non-living. How similar are the two sets of writing, so similar indeed that you cannot tell them one from the other? They show you the waxing and waning pulsations of life—and climax due to stimulants, the gradual decline in fatigue, the rapid setting in of death rigour from the toxic effect of poison. It was when I came on this mute witness of life and saw an all-pervading unity that binds together all things—it was then that for the first time I understood the message proclaimed on the banks of the Ganges thirty centuries ago—'they who behold the One, in all the changing manifoldness of the universe, unto them belongs eternal truth, unto none else, unto none else.'[89]

This must have been hard to swallow for some of his western listeners, steeped in the positivist culture of science. But it electrified the Indian élites. In this resolute attempt to obliterate the differences between the world and the self, and the living and the dead, they saw a convincing synthesis of the foreign and the indigenous. And in this synthesis, the indigenous ideals of knowledge and inquiry predominated. It not only helped them to accept their Indianness which colonialism had made a controversial inheritance, but also helped resolve their ambivalence towards western science.

For centuries the Indian imagination has used nondualist thought to impose order on diversities, contradictions, and oppositions, and a unified worldview on a fragmented society. The institutional emphasis in India on social hierarchy, plurality of norms, and segmentation of interpersonal relations has paradoxically underlined the ideological stress on the oneness of existence and the singleness of experience. The parallel attempt to tame individualism, by instilling the awareness of the unity between *brahman* (essence) and *atman* (essential reality of self) has often been a source of creativity in the Indian theory of knowledge and a rationalization of dissent.[90] The nondualist concept of an impersonal, timeless absolute gives a special meaning to the concept of scholarship. The scholar is expected to extend the perimeters of empirical knowledge while being open to its transcendental

[89] R. N. Tagore, 'Acharya Jagadisher Jaivarta', *Vasudhara*, 1957, vol. 2, pp. 107–9.

[90] At least one psychologist has felt this to be associated with easier acceptance of the new, the strange, and the different. G. Murphy, *In the Minds of Men* (New York: Basic Books, 1953), pp. 44, 268.

meaning. The idealist strands of Indian scholarship derive their primacy partly from this particular construction of the links between knowledge and reality.

Bose formulated this philosophical position into a scientific idiom and a research ideology. Once he did this, a number of compatible concepts of true knowledge, the unity of science, inter-disciplinary method, and the social obligations of a scientist became available to him. Through this culturally tinged set of concepts he constructed a positive self-image in the fluid scientific culture, generated culturally valid and personally meaningful symbols, and ensured his survival in the often-hostile Cartesian scientific culture of the modern West.

The ideology helped Bose cope with deeper diversities, too. The 'multiform unity in a single ocean of being' and 'the great pulse that beats through the universe' came to represent a personality integration he had constantly struggled towards.[91] Nothing tells the story better than a recurring motif of his life: a personal myth which became, in two senses, a concrete design. The beginning of this motif lay in Bose's early fascination with a rivulet that, springing from a hillock, flowed out from under a culvert near his childhood home and eventually merged with the Padma, the majestic easternmost branch of the Ganges, flowing towards the Bay of Bengal. This fascination with the theme of originating at an elevation, a temperamental movement or journey and final merger with a calmer but grander oneness persisted through his life. When at St Xavier's School, he made a small garden in his hostel within which was an artificial brook spanned by a bridge. Again, in two of his houses and in the Bose Institute, Bose designed artificial streams originating at a height (in a fountain, for instance) and flowing under bridges into the placidity of larger rivers. In his Darjeeling house—he called it *Mayapuri* or enchanted place, and it was reportedly the only place where he was not racked by insomnia—he did not create the motif. But he saw to it that the house was situated between two waterfalls from which two rivulets flowed noisily down to their own quieter selves a few hundred feet below.

The most famous articulation of the motif, however, was in a brief travelogue, published as an essay in 1894, the year he took the vow of fidelity to research.[92] The essay, highly personal and

[91] J. C. Bose in Ramananda Chatterji (ed.), *The Golden Book of Tagore* (Calcutta: Golden Book Committee, 1931), p. 16.

[92] Bose, *Abyakto*, pp. 73–81. For the Bose Institute he also commissioned a mural

elegantly poetic, describes his search for the origin of Bhagirathi or Ganges in a sacred fountain in the Himalaya, the shaky rope bridge over it near its source, its turbulent journey towards the plains, and its final transformation into the peaceful, creative, divine motherliness of the Ganges of the plains. He rediscovers the critical origin in the snaky, matted plaits (*jata*) of Mahadev or Shiva—the god of destruction, the mythic consort of the Mother of the Universe, and the traditional personification of phallic creativity. In the hair of the world-renouncing, austere god, Bose found the source of all life, all movement, all progress.

This fantasy of birth, beginning, and creativity, sometimes invented and sometimes discovered, had two axes: a male principle or its phallic representation as the ultimate passive, steady source of creation, creative by virtue of being able to contain its destructiveness through austerities and an active, temperamental, everchanging, feminine principle (*prakriti*) split into two.[93] The split was between a tempestuous, abrasively mobile, motive force—framed in this instance by identification with what one can only describe as a repudiated mother—and, beyond it, a secure, certain, oceanic peace, representing an ideal self and a symbiosis with the other mother within.

There was also the symbol of intervention through science in the form of the omnipresent bridge, rising above and binding 'nature', to negate or control her impulsiveness and unpredictable natural abandon. It was as if Bose had to choose his self-definition and intervene in the world while standing between 'the sly, cruel, crushing ruthlessness and the meditative affection of mother nature', two images that he knew to be 'merely the projections of one's own mind'.[94]

The fantasy of a grand fusion cannot but conceal beneath it some doubts about unity and some fears of fragmentation. Here was a person with a record of early diffusion of identifications which in youth became a protracted crisis of identity; and here was a fantasy that communicated transcendence, unity, and fusion,

---

which bore some relationship to the basic motif. It depicted, at his suggesion, the 'idol of knowledge' floating down the Ganges, with the eternal woman beside him—a representation, as a contemporary journal pointed out, of '*shakti* inspiring *purusha*'.

[93] Obviously this was compatible with the traditional Indian concept of *purusha*, the ultimate male, as a passive creator of the universe, and *prakriti* as the active participant in the process of creation.

[94] Bose, *Abyakto*, pp. 3–4.

triumphing over wild abandon and division. One suspects that the fantasy did tie together a conflicting set of identifications to tell the story of Bose's life as Bose would have liked to tell it.

Brahmoism endorsed the pattern. In it there was a built-in sanction for using *advaita* as a means of legitimizing the novel and the innovative. Rammohun Roy (1772–1833), the first Brahmo, had already shown modern India how to integrate exogenous cultural elements into Indian society with the help of Upanishadic nondualism. The technology could have been only further endorsed in a Brahmo family headed by a devout Vedantist who perhaps had sought in his new faith an antidote for his fragmented selves. The wider subcultural strain became an immediate, intimate actuality for Bose in his father. Bhagwanchandra must have been the first to combine, for himself and his son, the theory of nature with the theory of living.

However, the Brahmo concern with 'cosmic unity' was not exactly the pure monism of Vedanta. It included a conspicuous monotheistic element that showed the influence of Christianity and Islam.[95] Such a philosophy of life, by itself, could not have underwritten the 'implicit pantheism' of Bose. That pantheism had to come from the projective system of the little cultures of India—from the rituals, myths, magic, folklore, sayings, theories of nature, interpretations of ill-health, demonology, and so on. Here the abstract, universalist nondualism of the greater Sanskritic culture became a pan-psychic tendency to see the world as a living organism where the natural entities were not only endowed with life, but with the ability to manipulate human behaviour and fate. Bose's friends Vivekananda and Nivedita understood this much better than did the Brahmo leadership. Ideologically the former were more passionately committed to the philosophy of Vedanta, but in practice they constantly invoked the little culture's more dualist anthropomorphism. Understandably, their idiom reached beyond the perimeters of urban, westernized, upper-caste Bengal whereas Brahmoism slowly drowned in the blue blood of its followers. To the urban—and urbane—Brahmos, Vedanta always remained a distant Brahminical standard, legitimizing the new and the strange. The idea that it simultaneously existed as an immediate folksy theme in everyday life was too remote from the Brahmo consciousness which was trying desperately to be the vanguard in

[95] Ibid.

the running battle against Hindu orthodoxy. Bose's science cut across cultural hierarchies to draw upon both traditions of world construction.[96]

Bose's nondualism linked his creative imagination to his cultural milieu at yet another plane. It provided a frame of reference within which both Indian and western intellectuals could justify or at least explain to themselves their acceptance of Bose's science. Contrary to popular belief, western contemporaries of Bose, had they offered his type of theory or used his language, would have been totally isolated professionally. But Bose thrived, and was allowed to do so, in spite of his apparent esoterism and his highly personalized idiom. In fact, to many westerners Bose's idiom justified his science. Though he managed to collect some dedicated enemies in the West, such were the latent needs of some sections of the West at the time that he became a mouthpiece of western intellectual dissent too. Let one westerner who opted for the Indian way of life, Nivedita, speak first:

> The book on responses in living and nonliving is now triumphant. I want a far greater work, such as only this Indian man of science is capable of writing on Molecular Physics, a book in which that same great Indian mind that surveyed all human knowledge in the era of the *Upanishads* and pronounced it one, shall again survey the vast accumulations of physical phenomena which the 19th century has observed and collected, and demonstrate to the empirical, machine-worshipping, gold-seeking mind of the West that these also are one—appearing as many.[97]

Romain Rolland, himself trying to link up European intellectual dissent with Indian traditions, was equally enthusiastic.

> I hail the seer; he who by the light of his poetic and spiritual insight has penetrated into the very heart of Nature.... You have wrested from plants and stones the key of their enigma; you made us hear their incessant monologue, that perpetual stream of soul, which

[96] It has been suggested that the ability to empathize through the animation of inanimates or anthropomorphization is a basic characteristic of creative individuals. It allows them to seek and establish new relationships and a wider unity among diverse objects and is compatible with a stronger sense of gestalt (Greenacre, 'The Childhood of the Artist: Libidinal Phase Development and Giftedness', pp. 47–52). What is of interest here is the level or area of environment from which the sanction for the 'sense of actual or potential organization' is sought, and how as a result the dynamic of the latter is vitally affected.

[97] Letter to R. N. Tagore, 8 April 1903, quoted in Basu, *Nivedita*, vol. 1, pp. 627–31.

flows through all beings from the humblest to the highest.... You have boldly added to the vast domain of Indian thought a hemisphere of the Being, which the ancient intuition of your ancient sages had already recognized—these innumerable people of the vegetable and the mineral world who surround humanity.... In the course of this century India without sacrificing anything of the richness of her profound soul, of that inner world which was bequeathed to her by centuries of thought, will add thereto the intellectual weapons of Europe....[98]

Even more interesting was the comment of *The Spectator*, a publication not then known for its pro-Indian sentiment:

> The culture of thirty centuries has blossomed into a scientific brain of an order which we cannot quite duplicate in the West. He (Bose) is a prince among physiological research workers and a prophet of his age, which has brought so many new powers to life.[99]

Others backed this by a cultural theory:

> The people of the East have just the burning imagination which could extort a truth out of a mass of apparently disconnected facts; a habit of meditation without allowing the mind to dissipate itself, such as has belonged to the greater mathematicians and engineers; and a power of persistence—it is something a little different from patience—such as hardly belongs to an European.[100]

Similar panegyrics were delivered by Einstein, Shaw, Huxley, and Kropotkin. Shaw was visibly shaken when Bose demonstrated the death paroxysms of a cabbage being roasted, even as his lesser-known contemporary Massingham of *The Nation* was touched by 'the unfortunate carrot strapped to the table of an unlicensed vivisector' and by the 'feelings of so stolid a vegetable'.[101] But most revealing was the response of an anonymous westerner:

> Centuries of men may point to Bose as a conveniently identifiable point from which to date the dawn of the new thought, just as today we put our finger on Socrates when we wish to focus our

[98] Letter to J. C. Bose, September 1927, quoted in Home, *Acharya Jagadis*, pp. 71–2.
[99] Cited in Ibid., p. 13.
[100] Cited in Basu, *Nivedita*, vol. 1, pp. 573–4.
[101] Home, *Acharya Jagadis*, p. 25.

view of that new thought which inspired the West for centuries....[102]

The acute problem of ethics, and of scientific ethics, in the inter-war years had apparently induced the West to look eastwards for a plausible alternative life style—harmonious, placid, secure, and holistic. In 1919, even *The Times* of London joined the chorus:

> Whilst we in Europe were still steeped in the rude empiricism of barbaric life, the subtle Eastern had swept the whole universe into a synthesis and had seen the *one* in all its manifestations.... He is pursuing science not only for itself but for its application to the benefit of mankind.[103]

The scientists did not like to be left behind. Gottlieb Haberlandt, for instance, was, if anything, even more direct than the popular writers and the newspapers:

> We saw that there is a sleep of plants in the true sense of the term; and finally realized that a man of genius can not only *hear* the corn grow, but also see it.... In Professor Bose there lives and moves that ancient Indian spirit, which sees in every living organism a perceptive being endowed with sensitiveness.[104]

Henri Bergson also felt that while 'in Darwin's theory of natural selection, conflict is the main theme; Jagadishchandra's research has thrown light on the continuities and on the beauties of consistency in nature and life.'[105]

Evidently, some sections of the West, terrorized by the death and devastation brought about by a science gone rabid, were nostalgically looking back—through the eyes of the missionary-scientist from India—to the period in their own history when an apparently less contaminated, more humane, contemplative scientific tradition had aroused less conflict in values. Thus, like Tagore, Vivekananda, and Aurobindo, Bose too was to have his moment of glory in the West, only to be rejected after a while as counterfeit. In retrospect, the rejection was inevitable. It is mainly as a prophet that Bose was first deified and later forgotten. It was too early for anyone to realize that in a crude fashion Bose was anticipating and

[102] Cited in ibid., p. 67.
[103] Ibid., p. 67.
[104] Ibid., p. 32.
[105] Quoted in Roy and Bhattacharya, *Acharya*, p. 80.

tackling problems which within two decades would begin to erode the legitimacy of modern science itself. If Bose's philosophy of science seems less dated today than the scientism of the next generation of western intellectuals, it is mainly because the status of modern science itself has changed dramatically during the past few decades.

The West needed Bose's science on another, more mundane plane. Interdisciplinary research had not yet become common in the natural and biological sciences. Nonetheless, the growth of these sciences had brought about a recognition that such fence-breaking could lead to new theoretical breakthroughs.[106] This was the awareness that prompted J. A. Thompson to say:

> It is in accordance with the genius of India that the investigator should press further towards unity than we have yet hinted at, should seek to correlate responses and memory impressions in the living with their analogues in organic matter, and should see in anticipation the lines of physics, of physiology and of psychology converging.[107]

Bose's rejection of the conventional boundaries of disciplines, therefore, reflected a wider recognition in the sciences of some of their own methodological imperatives. It is only natural that this recognition should have found its most articulate spokesman in a scientist to whom the formalized divisions of scientific disciplines were merely so many indicators of academic factionalism.[108] Thus, Bose's philosophy of science bridged the past of a society trying to institutionalize new systems of knowledge and a science trying to integrate an emerging methodology. The philosophy became the means through which a particular Indian scientist, while trying to make sense of the modern scientific tradition, could also make sense to it.

The support which Bose received from the Indian élite confirmed these aspects of his professional self-concept. This support came in various forms. The Calcutta élite, with some of whom he

[106] Perhaps one should offset against the explosive growth of science in general the stagnation in the fields of plant physiology and biophysics then. These differential growth rates might have sharpened the sense of paradigmatic crises in these disciplines and allowed Bose to emerge as a major scientific figure of the time. See also D. M. Bose, 'Jagadis Chandra Bose'.

[107] Home, *Acharya Jagadis*, p. 30.

[108] Bose, *Abyakto*, pp. 84–5. See also Bose's letter of 5 October 1900 to R. N. Tagore on this subject, quoted in Gupta, *Jagadish Chandra*, pp. 39–40.

had abiding social ties and who constituted his immediate environment, reinforced his beliefs in public and in private. The vocal among them found in him a vindication of the Indian theory of life. They may not all have been scientists, but they spoke with the confidence of persons who knew Bose could not be wrong. For example, the Goethe-like Tagore, convinced that Bose's orderly universe justified his own universalism, affirmed:

> European science is following the way of our philosophy. This is the way of unity. One of the major obstacles which science has faced in forging this unity of experience is the differences between the living and the nonliving. Even after detailed research and experimentation, scholars like Huxley could not transcend this barrier. Venturing this excuse biology has been maintaining a wide distance from physics. Acharya Jagadis has discovered the unifying bridge between the living and the nonliving with the help of electrical waves.[109]

Subhas Chandra Bose, increasingly a symbol of aggressive nationalism, said:

> Discovery of life in inorganic matter points at the later trends in your research. Your research has provided direct empirical proof of the unity which the ancient sages of India had found in the varieties of life.... The magic touch of your genius has given life to that which seemed inert and insensate, it has generated a passion for a new awakening in the history of this country.[110]

Bose's students were no less enthusiastic:

> That inanimates have life, that plants have life, that both can be tired or excited...we find mentioned in many of the ancient texts of this country.... What we merely heard, the *acharya* has shown us.[111]

Thus, Vivekananda's criticism of the worth of an English botanist who had merely studied the life-cycle of a plant while the Bengali was making 'the very flowerpots in which the plant grows respond to impulses', reveals something more than an attempt to

[109] Tagore, 'Acharya Jagadisher Jaivarta', p. 107.

[110] J. C. Bose, quoted in Roy and Bhattacharya, *Acharya*, p. II.

[111] Hiren Dutta, 1915; reported in editorial notes, Bose, *Abyakto*, p. 234. Bose was, of course, called *acharya*. The other form of address used by his disciples was *acharyadeb*, teacher-god. Bose sometimes lived up to this image the hard way. While inaugurating the Bose Institute, he wore the saffron cloak of a religious preceptor, complete with the ritual sandalwood marks and *tilak*.

jump on to Bose's bandwagon.[112] It was an admission that Bose had done for Indian nationalism what no one expected a scientist to do. He had joined the modernizing Indian élite's desperate search for a form of self-esteem that would not be devoid of cultural roots.

VII

Bose's work was also shaped by his lifelong struggle with his own aggressiveness and the anxieties they aroused. In fact, his commitment to the Upanishadic worldview may have been partly due to the connotations it carried of impulse-control, mediation and resolution of contradictions. As he tried to reconcile through science the extremes of the living and the nonliving, the alive and the dead, aggressive active life and peaceful quiet death, and human violence and its 'natural' victims, he not only made his science a reparative or restitutive affair, but articulated one of the deepest cultural concerns of his people.[113]

Within the greater Sanskritic culture, the various taboos on expressions of instinctual and, particularly, aggressive impulses co-extend with a theory of creativity which conceptualizes creation as the control of his destructive self by the creator, and ideal knowledge as the cognition of absolute reality acquired through suppression of all desires. Towards the end of Bose's life and under Gandhi's influence,

[112] Gupta, *Jagadish Chandra*, p. 131. Such examples can be multiplied. The chorus included P. C. Roy, the foremost Indian chemist of the time; M. K. Gandhi; G. K. Gokhale, then the grand old man of Indian politics; Subhas Chandra Bose, then a stormy young politician; N. R. Sarkar, the country's best-known physician; R. C. Dutta, the eminent historian; Brajendra Nath Seal, the philosopher and educationist who saw in Bose the 'culmination of the unifying principles of traditional Indian thought'; Satyen Dutta, a well-known poet who versified his admiration for Bose's natural philosophy; Ramananda Chatterji, the doyen of Indian journalists; and Radhakishor Devmanikya, Bose's chief patron.

[113] Some of the early psychoanalytic writers thought of creativity as a form of restitution, which coped with guilt resulting from unconscious destructive fantasies. See Melanie Klein, 'Infantile Anxiety Situations Reflected in a Work of Art', *International Journal of Psychoanalysis*, 1929, *10*, pp. 436–44; Ella F. Sharpe, 'Certain Aspects of Sublimation and Delusion', *International Journal of Psychoanalysis*, 1930, *11*, pp. 22–3, and 'Similar and Divergent Unconscious Determinants underlying the Sublimations of Pure Arts and Pure Science', *Collected Papers in Psychoanalysis* (London: Hogarth Press, 1950), pp. 137–54; W. R. D. Fairbairn, 'Prolegomena to a Psychology of Art', *British* Journal of Psychology, 1938, *28*, pp. 228–303; Harry B. Lee, 'Projective Features of Contemplative Artistic Experience', *The American Journal of Orthopsychiatry*, 1949, *19*, pp. 101–11; and 'The Values of Order and Vitality in Art', in G. Roheim (ed.), *Psychoanalysis and the Social Sciences* (New York: International Universities, 1950), *2*, pp. 231–74.

even Indian anti-imperialism began translating these emphases on non-aggression into a new political idiom which frequently equated self-discipline and non-violence on the one hand, and pursuit of power, self-government, and creative social reform on the other.[114]

Research on socialization in India, mostly based on data from the more traditional sections of the society, has something to say on the subject. The data suggest that Indian non-violence is over-determined; it represents an attempt to cope with aggressive impulses that are on the whole untamed and 'do not have a chance to be patterned or shaped.'[115] The absence of social vents through which aggressive needs could be expressed in an anxiety-free manner, and the absence of slow training in child-hood which could encourage containment of aggression rather than its total denial, seems to lead to a constant fear that ego controls would fail and that violence would break out in an unpredictable, chaotic, and irrational manner, either outwards or inwards.[116]

Extrapolated into Bose's life, these insights do explain something of his scientific idiom: the emphasis on 'poisoning', 'wounding', and—to give less-than-serious examples—'pinching' and 'tickling' of plants and metal foils. Through this idiom, the ancient 'pantheistic' theme of protecting plants and the rest of apparently inanimate nature from the cruelty of humans prone to uncontrolled aggressiveness, became another link between Bose and his society. Thus, the consumers of his research became his accomplices. They helped him to contain his moral anxiety centring around aggression by seemingly sharing it.[117] The pain of a

[114] Some of these issues have been discussed in Ashis Nandy and Sudhir Kakar, 'Culture and Personality in India' in Udai Parekh (ed.), *Research in Psychology in India* (New Delhi: Indian Council of Social Science Research, 1980), Ch. 2. On the Gandhian equation between aggression control and political self-determination, see Lloyd Rudolph and Susanne Rudolph, *The Modernity of Tradition* (Chicago: University of Chicago, 1967), part 2; and Erik H. Erikson, *Gandhi's Truth* (New York: Norton, 1969).

[115] Murphy, *In the Minds of Men*, p. 51.

[116] For instance, J. T. Hitchcock and Leigh Mintern, 'The Rajputs of Khalapur', in Beatrice Whiting (ed.), *Six Cultures* (Cambridge, Mass: Harvard University Press, 1963), pp. 206–361; Rudolph and Rudolph, *The Modernity of Tradition*, Part 2.

[117] The mechanism of enlisting the consumers of creative products as accomplices by inducing them to participate in the underlying fantasy has been discussed by Fenichel, *The Psychoanalytic Theory*, p. 703; and E. Bergler, 'Psychoanalysis of Writers and of Literary Productivity', in G. Roheim (ed.), *Psychoanalysis and the Social Sciences* (New York: International Universities, 1947), *1*, pp. 247–96.

poisoned leaf, the suffering of a metal strip injured manually and cured medically—these were the data Bose worked with and the tell-tale descriptions he employed.[118] He not only personified his subjects by equipping them with animate sensitivity, he hurt them and also wanted to protect them from being hurt.

> What is the pull that removes every difference, brings the proximate nearer, makes us forget who is our own and who is not? Compassion is the pull; only the power to sympathize can reveal the real truths in our life. The ever-tolerant plant kingdom stands immovable in front of us.... They are being hurt by various powers, but no whimper rises from the wounded. I shall describe the heart-rending history of this extremely self-controlled, silent, tearless life.[119]

At another place Bose says,

> From a man's handwriting one can guess his weakness and his fatigue; I found the same signs in the responses of a machine. It was a matter of surprise that, after rest, the machine could recoup and respond again. When a stimulating drug was administered, his power to respond increased and the administration of poison made all his responses vanish.[120]

How far was this a strategy to reach the lay public, over the heads of his professional colleagues, to mobilize popular support and to secure sanction? How far was this the corollary of a deeper faith? We shall never know for sure. Some of those who knew Bose are certain that these phrases were something more than the fragments of a conscious strategy. They feel that underlying the idiom was a deep concern with anger and cruelty, survival and death. They imply that the concern had already attained a structured form when, for example, Bose showed in childhood his deep fascination with his dacoit-servant's tales of exploitation, cruelty, suffering, and death. Even at that time Bose's sympathies lay not so much with the victims as with his friend.[121] This admiration for a man who had saved his life—from death which seemed to Bose to be ever-present throughout his life—was, one suspects, something more than a transient identification. It expressed a concern that

[118] For examples see *Abyakto*, pp. 105–8, 162–81, and 206–8.
[119] Ibid., p. 162.
[120] Bose, *Abyakto*, p. 147.
[121] Roy Bhattacharya, *Acharya*, p. 10.

dominated Bose's worldview: coping with one's violence by renouncing violence, by aggressively protecting one's likely victims.

One suspects that this concern too—along with the more general values of non-violence, the unity of life, and fear of death—overlay Bose's ambivalence towards his mother, the final paradigm of a *prakriti* that held the keys to survival and mortality. The ambivalence was the frame within which Bose fought a life-long battle with his aggressiveness and made reparations to an 'apparently sly, ruthlessly cruel' *prakriti*,[122] the ultimate public target of his conflicting passions.

Studies of socialization in India have traced to the fantasy of an inconsistent, aggressive mother the Indian's modal conflicts centring round aggression and its control.[123] Whatever the final status of such studies, the consistency between Bose's inner image of motherhood and the dominant myths of his culture is underscored by a theme he borrowed openly from his culture, that of immortality.[124]

All themes of immortality are themes of mortality too, and Bose's version also contained, within it, its inverse: a primitive, infantile fear of death. To him, his creativity was not only a positive affirmation of eternity and the re-discovery of life-processes, but also a passionate denial of lifelessness. His concept of personal achievement, academic advancement and national uniqueness was powered by this denial:

> It was a woman in Vedic time, who when asked to take her choice of the wealth that would be hers for the asking, inquired whether that would win for her deathlessness. What would she do with it if it did not raise her above death? This has always been the cry of the soul of India, not for addition of material bondage, but to work out through struggle her self-chosen destiny and win immortality.... There is, however, another element which finds its incarnation in matter, yet transcends its transmutation and apparent destruction: that is the burning flame born of thought which has been handed down through fleeting generations.[125]

[122] Bose, *Abyakto*, p. 133.

[123] G. M. Carstairs, *The Twice-born* (London: Hogarth Press, 1957); Hitchcock and Mintern, 'The Rajputs of Khalapur'; Leigh Mintern and W. W. Lambert, *Mothers in Six Cultures* (New York: Wiley, 1964); Sudhir Kakar, *The Inner World: Childhood and Society in India* (New Delhi: Oxford University Press, 1979). See a review of the relevant literature in Nandy and Kakar, 'Culture and Personality in India'.

[124] Bose, *Abyakto*, pp. 13–15.

[125] J. C. Bose, cited in Home, *Acharya Jagadis*, pp. 66–7.

Behind this affirmation lay a vision of the universe as a system of power relations, within which only power or *shakti* was indestructible.[126] But for survival one needed a special kind of power:

> Every moment so many lives are being crushed, as if they were specks of dust, as if they were worms. Do you fear the threatening speed of the wheel of life?... Brighten the divine perspective within you. You will find the universe alive, not a mass of dead matter. The humblest speck of dust is not wasted, the smallest force is not destroyed; life is also possibly imperishable. Mental force represents the ultimate triumph of life. It is by power of this force that this holy land survives.[127]

The clue to survival therefore was the maintenance of intellectual potency: 'The destruction of intellectual power is real death, hopelessly final and eternal.'[128]

Tagore, it is said, was bewildered by Bose's obsession with death and the after-life when he, more or less of the same age, was much less anxious about them. The poet did not see that this fear was concerned more with the beginning than with the end, and hence, that age had little to do with it. Bose's unconscious fear of his own anger against his mother and the fear of the retaliation it might provoke, could only be bound by the reparative concern with persons, ideas, and things which were 'undecaying' and 'beyond the reach of death'. As he stated towards the end of his life, the 'efflorescence of life is the supreme gift of a place and its associations.'[129] Presumably, one could return the gift only by containing one's destructive self, and thus avoiding the wrath of the mother and her surrogates—motherland and *prakriti*, and by protecting and affirming life in the non-living.

[126] Elsewhere, Bose also expresses his belief that the 'world has no beginning and no end' (*Abyakto*, p. 7), and power is what ultimately survives in it—'power is indestructible' (ibid., p. 14; also p. 123). It is this potency which he sought for himself and his people. Particularly so because 'mother nature is unwilling to bear the burden of inefficient lives' (ibid., p. 133). Therefore, 'Our only concerns should be how we can give up the whines of the weak, effeminate touchiness and unjust demands, and how we can shape our destiny using our own power as befits men' (ibid., p. 123).

[127] Bose, *Abyakto*, p. 160.

[128] Ibid., p. 129. See also pp. 15–16, where Bose relates his concept of immortality to the traditional concept of rebirth: 'every life has two aspects. One does not age and is undying; the temporal body covers this aspect. This cover of body remains behind. The undying speck of life builds new houses in every birth.'

[129] J. C. Bose, cited in Home, *Acharya Jagadis*, p. 85.

VIII

On many an occasion, I write without thinking... On some occasions thoughts arise in my mind without effort, and I am surprised. It is my past which is pouring these messages into my ears. The root of my heart is in India.[130]

When in adulthood Bose began to build his self-definition on identifications he had earlier disowned, his past got more deeply involved with the past of his people, torn between the pulls of tradition and the demands of the culture of full-blown colonialism.

The end of the nineteenth century found the urban élite of India, particularly the *bhadralok* of greater Calcutta, searching desperately for a self-esteem that would protect them from the severe threat to their world that colonialism now posed. Participating in this search, Bose felt the need for 'equipping Bengalis with an ideal which would make the dying race confident of its own power.'[131] But for him, given his times, the confidence had to come in a special form. Sure that everyone wanted 'to see Mother Bengal on a high throne',[132] he heard in the plaudits he received from the literati of Calcutta the call of his mother: 'In the encouragement given by you all I hear my mother's voice. Behind all of you I can always see a poor, humbly clad figure. With you, I take shelter in her lap.'[133]

Bose's participation in the struggle for a collective self-image that would counter personal feelings of inferiority—and for an individual self-image that would be more than privately valid—was perhaps bound to reflect the psychological bulwarks he had built against his deeper-lying fantasies of maternal neglect and violence. Bose was perfectly willing to read his success in science as an index of the love for him of his motherland, a 'fiery mother who ruthlessly threw her children into the cruel workshop of life' and accepted them back 'only when they won in battle fame, courage and manliness.'[134] He felt he had met her standards of excellence and had earned his share of love from a mother whose ruthlessness

[130] J. C. Bose, cited in Gupta, *Jagadish Chandra*, p. 64.

[131] Discussion with D. L. Roy, reported in Roy and Bhattacharya, *Acharya*, p. 237.

[132] Bose, *Abyakto*, p. 136.

[133] Letter to R. N. Tagore, quoted in Roy and Bhattacharya, *Acharya*, pp. 233–4; also see pp. 56, 223.

[134] Bose, *Abyakto*, p. 21.

he could rationalize as essentially the protectiveness of a loving but firm mother.[135]

> After spending a long time in foreign lands, I have come back to the lap of the loving mother, drawing my courage from the hope that she has accepted my *puja*. O mother, your blessings have secured for me recognition as a servant of Bengal and India.[136]

This was not merely a way of speaking. From London Bose had written to Tagore of a 'strange unscientific event', a striking vision he had had. The vision, Bose felt, had strengthened his love for his motherland:

> All of a sudden I saw a shadowy figure, wearing the dress of a widow; I could see only one side of the face. That very sickly, very unhappy woman's shadow said, 'I have come to accept'; then, within a moment, the whole thing disappeared.[137]

Understandably, every other acceptance became to him, ultimately, secondary.

It is not clear why the search for self-esteem and parity attained salience among the Indian élite at exactly that point of time—why, for instance, Bose felt prompted to say: 'Now the time has arrived; we must spend our entire energy in glorifying our motherland.'[138] What we do know is that the scientist worked in an atmosphere in which the early Indian intellectual and élite hopes of changing Indian society through the intervention of alien ideas and instruments of power was giving way to a greater consciousness of Indian exclusiveness, Indian categories of social change, and Indian ways to political and cultural autonomy. The climate of *swadeshi*, which included all-round attempts to revalue indigenous ideas and products and which contextualized Bose's middle years, had existed well before the movement that gave it dramatic substance after 1905.[139]

As is often the case with such movements, the search for the indigenous went with a growing awareness of native inadequacies.

[135] Ibid., pp. 133–9.

[136] Ibid., p. 122; written in 1915.

[137] Roy and Bhattacharya, *Acharya*, p. 234.

[138] Bose, *Abyakto*, p. 229.

[139] See Ashis Nandy, 'The Making and Unmaking of Political Cultures in India', in Nandy, *At the Edge of Psychology*, pp. 47–69.

For Bose at least this awareness was nothing new. He had already said:

> *O abhimanini* woman.... What is his status in this world on whose glory your own glory is built?... Will he, on whom you depend, be able to save you from terrible humiliations in these bad days?... Who will strengthen his arms, keep the courage of his heart indomitable and make him fearless of death?[140]

These doubts about his compatriots were intertwined with self-doubts. 'Some day surely India will see better days, but one fails to keep this in mind constantly. Imprint on my mind that this is true. I lose my power without hope.'[141]

These intense feelings of inadequacy and the parallel search for parity were partly brought about by the widening breach between the British and their subjects. The former, impressed by the new scientific discoveries and the fast pace of industrialization in the West, had not only started perceiving Indians and particularly Bengali *babus* as an essentially inferior breed, but had begun to communicate this perception to the latter.[142] As a result the goodwill between the rulers and important sections of the Bengali élite, and the mutual accommodation that had characterized their relationship throughout much of the previous century, had begun to break down.

At the same time, the internalization of values promoted by imported institutions had begun to change the impersonal perception of Indo-British differences to more personalized feelings of Indian inferiority. Working within an increasingly westernized frame of values, as against a merely westernized form of occupation or education, many Indians found themselves splintered within. They could neither live in peace with their traditions nor disown their new-found western values.

Earlier generations of Indians, sure of their traditions and of their traditional selves, rarely sought to demonstrate the superiority of native practices or ideas over foreign ones. When they opposed westernization, they often invoked the concept of an 'equal but different' Indianness. Even the early modernists who rejected

[140] Bose, *Abyakto*, 141. The word *abhimanini* is difficult to translate. In Bengali it roughly means a woman who is angry and hurt, but retains her affection towards the cause of her anger.

[141] Letter to Tagore, quoted in Roy and Bhattacharya, *Acharya*, p. 233.

[142] Rudolph and Rudolph, *The Modernity of Tradition*; also R. C. Majumdar, *Glimpses of Bengal in the Nineteenth Century* (Calcutta: Firma K. L. Mukhopadhyay, 1960).

aspects of Indian culture and supported all-out westernization, were a self-confident lot. Men like Rammohun Roy were not afflicted by a sense of cultural or racial inferiority. It was the internalization of modern values and the growing gap between self-perception and new social ideals that sabotaged the nineteenth-century sense of competence of Indians *vis-à-vis* the West.

However, the defeat of psychological forces is rarely total. The strategy of identifying with the West by abrogating one's Indianness as a negative identification, remained an alternative to the total rejection of the West. Such abrogation of one's cultural self now required a greater psychological effort—because of snowballing Indian self-doubts and British superciliousness—but every Indian had it before him as a latent vector. The cultural conflict between the old and the new caught up with Bose through this inner strain. If exclusivism was not unknown to Bamasundari's son, Bhagwanchandra's catholicity was for him a vital experience. If struggling for parity was the cultural 'inheritance' of the backyard man from East Bengal, Brahmoism's self-confident synthetism had also been for him a crucial exposure. It would, however, seem that the reactive self-affirmation of Bose's class and the self-doubts of western intellectuals at the time (which had been communicated to Indian intellectuals, though not to British Blimps in India) combined with the changes in his personality to encourage the exclusivist response to gradually emerge as the dominant tone in his intellectual life. 'Who could be so base as to be untrue to his salt and the soil that nourished him?' Bose was to ask, particularly when that maternal presence had given meaning to his adult attainments and struggles.[143] When the choice was forced on him, Bamasundari's son found his intellectual ideals better represented by those who spoke the language of his later self than by the cultural amalgam his father exemplified.

However, in the process of adjusting his science to the climate of Indian politics and public opinion, Bose rendered two important services to western science in India.

When Bose reached adulthood, the nativist response to the West had split the intellectual culture of modern India into two. A split between traditional and modern medical systems had already

[143] Bose, 1934, cited in Home, *Acharya Jagadis*, p. 85. Talking of his journeys to the West, Bose once said: 'Nobody there waited for me with a garland of victory, rather my powerful opponents were present in a group to demonstrate my flaws. I was all alone; the only invisible help to me was the goddess of India's fate.' Ibid., p. 148.

taken place. The native system enjoying the highest status, *ayurveda*, no longer co-existed peacefully with modern medicine (though homeopathy, with its western roots but non-modern style, in practice continued to mediate between the two). Others were talking of a Hindu chemistry and an Indian mathematics that would be separate from and superior to their western counterparts. Tagore and Aurobindo had already founded institutions that imparted 'national' education, though it was conceived in universalist terms. Vivekananda had founded a Hindu church. Some politicians, too, had begun to talk of an Indian concept of nationalism and an Indian methodology of political action.

In this environment, Bose helped arrest to some extent the compartmentalization of the sciences. His was not a technology transfer or import-substitution model, for he refused to give up Indian claims to a different form of universalism. By legitimizing his work in terms of traditions and then establishing its credentials—and, as some saw it, supremacy—in the western academic world, he obviated the need for an 'Indian' natural science for Indians, as a remedy for their gnawing feelings of inferiority. India, he was fond of saying, had a contribution to make to world science, not to a special Indian science.[144] This was another way of saying that India had an alternative world science to offer, not a separate Indian science.

Thus, by demonstrating the convergence of Indian thought and the values of modern science, years before such efforts came into vogue, Bose made possible a new commitment to universal science. He believed, rightly or wrongly, that both the content and the context of science should converge. We have already discussed Bose's search for a convergence in content. The search for convergence in context is more difficult to document. But one example could be the themes of achievement and competition which run through many of his writings. Once again, he borrowed these themes from the sacred texts of India. To a majority of Indians, the achievement criteria used by western science education and organized scientific research must have seemed an arbitrary imposition. The criteria could not but seem incompatible with learning in a society where learning seemed linked to ascription, hierarchy, and self-realization. Here, too, Bose tried to build a bridge between organized world science and his society's surviving concepts of scholarship. He extended to science the model of the Indian

[144] Bose, 1917, cited in Home, *Acharya Jagadis*, p. 66.

modernizers who vaguely sensed that many aspects of traditional high culture could come in handy in the changing world, particularly in the nascent urban-industrial, colonial culture in British India.

In other words, like other nineteenth-century social reformers in general, Bose too sought to counterpoise in Indian society the older values of organized knowledge against new values borrowed from the West which were justified by more isolated traditions in well-defined, delimited areas of Indian life where these new values did not seem that new.[145] Consequently, if to his contemporaries Bose looked a representative individual trying out the role of westernized scientist within an indigenous cultural frame, his science demonstrated, to the satisfaction of most, that the trial had been successful.

Yet it is one of the lesser paradoxes of social change that a society's success does not always coincide with an individual's. First of all, Brahmo bi-culturalism carried for Bose a load of anxiety, due to his own and his father's role confusions and failures within the compass of the modern sector and the culturally more self-assertive political climate of his adulthood. He was therefore pushed towards a form of nationalism with the powerful symbols of the Bengali *shakti* cult, especially its concept of maternal authority, to create new political solidarities. This nationalism was represented not only by the Swadeshi movement, but also by movements led by Brahmabandhav Upadhyay, Vivekananda and Aurobindo. It is no accident that the slogan *Bande Mataram* or 'Praise the Mother' became the motto of the Bose Institute, in addition to being the war cry of Indian nationalism.[146]

To the symbolisms associated with this nationalism Bose was exposed overtly in adulthood, but covertly, years earlier, by his mother. Its magical, anthropomorphic overtones and its evocation of cosmic maternal principles had a special meaning for him:

> Can a son imagine a distinction between motherland and mother? The sound of the names of mother and motherland has emerged

[145] 'We must build a western society with Indians' as even Vivekananda was to describe the task. How far they were correct in formulating the society's problems in this manner is, however, a different matter.

[146] Roy and Bhattacharya, *Acharya*, pp. 231–47; Gupta, *Jagadish Chandra*, pp. 204–6, 75–8, 84–92; also see Haridas Mukherji and Uma Mukherji, *India's Fight for Freedom or the Swadeshi Movement* (Calcutta: Firma K. L. Mukhopadhyay, 1958), esp. pp. 174–234.

spontaneously from (the) heart and spread all over India. This is because that sound has touched the inner heart of India.[147]

Thus, while he scrupulously avoided conflicts with the British power and remained friendly with the more westernized section of the Bengali élite, his creative work drew upon his early identification with a feminine principle capable of dealing magically and ritually with reality and fate on the one hand, and upon his anthropomorphic and often-magical conceptualization of personal work and personal goddesses—mother, motherland, *shakti* and *prakriti*—on the other.[148]

IX

These bits, drawn from a larger historical mosaic, mark out one possible strategy available to an Indian scientist of an earlier generation to forge a workable lifestyle, as an Indian and as a scientist. Yet this was something more than a private strategy. The 'objective' scientific imagination that linked personality, culture, and the history of science in the case of Bose was part of a larger process of social adaptation. It was within that process that cultural particulars in India could find a particular scientist, and vice versa.

India, science, and Indian science—it could be claimed that Bose was needed by all. Others might wish to reverse the relationship. Bose, they may say, needed a large canvas on which to write the history of his personal crises. I hope this narrative has made it clear that such a bifurcation of perspectives is not necessary, for between the man and the canvas—and the first and the second perspective—there was a psychologically and historically determined relationship. I shall now sketch the outlines of one possible explanation of this relationship.

With the inroads made by the western economy and education into India, the confirmations that were available to older systems of socialization and personality were lost to many. The new structures rewarded skills that had a low cultural value and negated older

[147] Letter to Subhas Chandra Bose, 1937, quoted in Roy and Bhattacharya, *Acharya*, pp. 237–8.

[148] Here lies an explanation of why many Indians found Bose to be more nationalist than his participation in politics would suggest. He shared the basic symbols, values, and adaptive strategies of Indian nationalism, and the logic of his work was perfectly compatible with the logic imputed to it by a majority of those who knew something about him and his work: the world he had created made eminent sense to his compatriots.

concepts of legitimate accomplishment. The conflicts that western science generated were part of this wider confrontation. Those who accepted this new science found it advantageous, but not meaningful. When it did not seem to disrupt what was good and moral, it looked threateningly amoral and irrelevant to deep-seated concepts of goodness and rightness. Yet this new science seemed to work and was profitable—a recognition that must only have heightened anxiety by baring one's weakening faith in tradition and the temptation of joining the ranks of the deserters.

This chasm between profitable work preference and successful work identification—between acceptance and commitment—threw up into salience individuals who could help sections of the community to integrate the new science within their lifestyle as a valid medium of self-expression. The individuals, if they were creative enough, used the apparent neutrality of the new science as a screen on which to project their loves and hates. When these loves and hates turned out to be generally held, they made the new science legitimate and the new scientists eponymous.

The changing political economy of India underwrote the process—radical permutations in family and child rearing practices took place (often brought about by the nuclearization and geographical mobility of many families) and in adolescent socialization (brought about by westernized schools and colleges). Deviant individuals, carrying the impact of deviant socialization within them (including adult experiences that updated the impact), had now to find a medium of self-expression—a new mirror through which to see their own faces—in their professional life. We have seen how the content and form of Bose's research mirrored his early object relations, adult interpersonal skills, and the defensive strategies available to his self. Even his ability to combine good relations with the colonial authorities and cultural nationalism could be traced to the specifics of his own experiences, of life; and so could his later decline as a scientist.

In this case, as in others, the social forces that sought new carriers were the ones that produced the deviations in patterns of socialization. Here lay the basic significance of Bose's life. In trying to come to terms with himself, he produced for his community a possible new link between social needs and personal desires. At the same time, by rediscovering traditions through science, he helped retain a core of self-esteem in a people threatened by the patent supremacy and power of a foreign system; and by culturally domesticating a hostile science, he made it possible for a growing number of Indians to take to it. And had he not reached a dead end himself, he could be said to have offered the Indian scientist an enduring identity.

The road to this dead end was paved with two aspects of Bose's scientific self. First, he conceived of science as a means of experimentally demonstrating the truth of self-evident, axiomatic, general laws of nature enunciated in the sacred texts of India. To Bamasundari's son his revolutionary inquiries into *prakriti* were basically a revelatory experience. And like all revelations they included a principle of closure.

The hypothetico-deductive method in scientific creativity is so widely accepted today that this might at first seem absurd. Was it not true that even Newton's experiments were 'a means, not of discovery, but always of verifying what he already knew'?[149] The answer to this question, on the basis of Bose's life, will have to be different.

Creativity involves not merely the ability to use one's personal fantasies and the myths of one's culture; it is the ability to do so without being rigidly defensive and retaining a certain cognitive and emotional flexibility. Bose's obsessive-compulsive defences did not allow him to make full use of his own fantasy life and the mythic structure of his culture. He was forced by the demands of his personality to take his concept of Indian uniqueness beyond the culture and philosophy of science, into specific cut-and-dried theories of science and into actual research. No inspiration can carry that enormous load. (Perhaps a comparison with Newton would not be misplaced after all; the Renaissance man might have set an altogether different standard of creativity, but the difference between the young and the middle-aged Newton *is* comparable with the difference between the young and the middle-aged Bose.)[150]

Second, Bose's highly personalized science, combined with his later authoritarianism and promotion to the status of an *acharya*, did not allow him to develop an organizational base. So, he could not be fed back the experiences of his talented but professionally neutralized Indian disciples. The Bose Institute became a cult phenomenon in its founder's lifetime, and the patriarchy within it did not allow the growth of a community that could help his reality-testing. Neither the personalized style nor the paternalism was, by itself, anti-science. After all, there had been creative

[149] J. M. Keynes, quoted in J. E. Littlewood, *A Mathematician's Miscellany* (London: Methuen, 1957), p. 94.

[150] Ibid.; Manuel, 'Newton as Autocrat'.

scientists before the growth of impersonal organizations and the spread of democratic values. What compromised Bose's creativity was the combination of his personality and private theory of science, the colonial situation and the culture of the Bose Institute.

These two features of Bose's science had an especial meaning for the West. Both the revelatory mode and the personalized style had once been part of the western scientific tradition, but the West had been seduced away from them by the attractive promises of positivism and empiricism. The unsure gait of these philosophies of science and the conflicts they generated in Bose's time—such as the anxieties they aroused in many western intellectuals because of the violence increasingly associated with science and technology—made a section of the western élite look back guiltily towards its own past, as reflected in the scientist-savant from the East. In his worldview, the recovered past of a modern society and the cultural compulsions of a traditional society seemed to intersect. But it was also a worldview through which Bose's lay disciples in the East and the West exercised immense pressure on him to produce a science that would contain their own anxieties *vis-à-vis* modern science. Bose did not have the personality resources to resist these pressures. He went on widening his reference group to make sense simultaneously to scientists and to the larger public in the East and the West. Ultimately, what had been a strength in his struggle to achieve compatible scientific and cultural identities, became a charter for an unconditional surrender to the public demands on his science. Put simply, Bose became inauthentic as a critic of western science, too, and fell a victim to his public image.

There is another meaning behind Bose's movement from his 'clever' early works to the deeper successes and failures of his later phases. All his life he had searched for a personal identity that would be legitimate by being the prototype of an Indian scientific identity. As his early personality conflicts got resolved into a relatively stable inner man, Bose owned up parts of himself he had formerly strenuously rejected. This rejected self, with its measures against fears of one's own inner violence, its over-compensations for feelings of neglect and deprivation of nurture, its defensive orderliness and authoritarianism, was more compatible with his later science. It was at this plane that some themes in the contemporary culture of science—the stress on achievement, competition and organizational skills, hardheaded positivism, and belief in science as a value-neutral instrument of power and as a means of subjugating nature—contradicted a part of the substance of which he was made. For many years they had found a haven in the residuals of his apparently idyllic relationship with his father. But, while struggling for a personality integration where his first and deepest identification could find a place, Bose had to move from an Indian version of world science to an Indian—and paradoxically western—version of Indian science.

What then is Bose's lasting relevance to science and to India? One possible answer is that while Bose sought and found a sanction for a private experience which was recognized at that time as 'scientific creativity', he paid back his debt to a culture which had tangibly intervened in his personal science—supporting, sanctioning, and articulating it with his own needs and history. Bose's scientific universalism had to include a concept of what world science could and should do for India.

This brings us back to the central problem which Indian science faced in Bose: how to reconcile the Bose of spatial and temporal meanings with Bose the space-and-time defying scientist? It is obvious that whatever evidence of such a reconciliation one finds in Bose was only partly shaped by the formal structures of western science and Indian thought. Plant physiology, it is true, was stagnant when Bose entered the field.[151] And the diffusion of the dominant paradigms of the discipline allowed deviant scientists like Bose more elbow room and a larger audience than they would otherwise have got. It is also true that some of the ideas Bose used were straight out of his reading of the classical texts of India. But what gave him his appeal was that he could reconcile, even if temporarily, the text and the culture of modern science with the shared experiences that had been banished from consciousness by the scientists or disowned by the societies of the East and the West.

Scientific creativity, like any other form of human creativity, assumes the ability to use one's less accessible self in such a way that the primordial becomes meaningful to the community and the individual scientist. Out of this ability comes not only the creative scientist's sense of being driven, but also his distinctive approach to concepts, relationships, and operations, the order that he imposes on his data, and the limits he sets on his insights. The scientific community prescribes where and when professional assessments

[151] D. M. Bose, 'Jagadis Chandra Bose'.

begin, but it can never fully control what at any point of time is accepted as objective, impersonal, and formal scientific knowledge.

The scientific community can do worse. It can begin to collaborate with the larger society to discourage the self-examination that may accompany or follow from a creative effort. Any such examination is an inquiry into the psychological foundations of science and society and, like individuals, both have built-in resistance to self-inquiries. Science tries to build self-perpetuating paradigms and societies try to build self-validating solidarities. Both have a vested interest in establishing a link with the fears, hates, hopes, and ideals of individual scientists. Neither can afford to recognize that this search for significant solidarities can degenerate into a subtle pressure on individuals and groups to settle for palliatives which, instead of widening their awareness of their outer and inner worlds, would only sanction and sanctify their existing desires and anti-desires.

It was in this process of consolidation that Bose was so cruelly caught. It is true that his culture and the state of science *had* shaped a part of his creativity and it was an important part. But it is also true that when in the end he failed science, in a deeper sense his society and the scientific estate had failed him too.

Part Three

The Other Science of Srinivasa Ramanujan

An Essay on the Public and Private Culture of Knowledge

Towards the beginning of the twentieth century, the culture of science in India saw an all-round attempt to Indianize modern science. At one level it was an attempt to cope with the contradiction between the older concept of science, embedded in the worldview of an old civilization, and the demands of a newly dominant, alien culture of science. But at another level it was an attempt to cope with a more persistent contradiction within modern science itself. While a scientific estate survives on its faith in the universality of science, supported by a belief in the organized, disinterested, sceptical objectivity of scientists as a group,[1] a central and necessary feature of the social system of science is the scientist's faith in dominant disciplinary dogmas, euphemized in recent times as paradigms.[2] Evidently, the openness of mind expressed in universalism and rational scepticism, and the closedness nursed by scientific socialization and expressed in paradigmatic faith, contradict each other and demand psychological functioning simultaneously at two levels.[3] Evidently, too, for

[1] R. Merton, 'Science and Democratic Social Structure', in *Social Theory and Social Structure* (New York: Free Press, 1957), pp. 550–61.

[2] The best-known examples are Michael Polanyi, *Personal Knowledge* (Chicago: University of Chicago Press, 1958), and *Science, Faith and Society* (Chicago: University of Chicago Press, 1964); T. S. Kuhn, *The Structure of Scientific Revolution* (Chicago: University of Chicago Press, 1962); see also the interesting brief statement by M. Mulkay, 'Cultural Growth in Science', in B. Barnes (ed.), *The Sociology of Science* (Harmondsworth: Penguin, 1972), pp. 126–42.

[3] As is well known, Kuhn in *The Structure of Scientific Revolution* has seen this contradiction as a cultural tension within the estate of science. I speak here of the extensions of this tension within the personality of the scientist.

many Indian scientists of the time this contradiction took a particularly painful form. While western science seemed congruent with their newly internalized concept of a universal science, they had to reconcile this concept with their deeper selves and inherited concepts of science and the scientific method and, through them, with their own society's distinctive traditions and entrenched symbols.[4] It is the problems of individual creativity and professional identity posed by these contradictions in one scientist caught in the hinges of historical change that I shall discuss here.

The scientist I summon as my witness is Srinivasa Ramanujan (1887–1920), a favourite textbook example of natural genius in mathematics. I shall try to show how the two contradictions in the scientific culture became in him a part of creative tension and defined important aspects of his scientific self. In the process, I hope to identify a prototypical style of reconciling the relatively universal and rational structure of outer science and the extra-logical, culturally and psychologically bound, inner science in India.[5] This style, apparently non-rational and anti-science, has taken the culture's inner science close to the core of the objective, secular, and universal body of the outer science but—this is its strength—without disturbing the authenticity of either.

Two doubts may persist about the relevance of such an exercise. The first of these is roughly the position of Ramanujan's closest academic frriends, G. H. Hardy and J. E. Littlewood.[6] If I understand them correctly, their argument is that Ramanujan's origin in a distinctive culture and time, his religious faith, worldview, and personal motives had little bearing upon his mathematics. To these friends, Ramanujan did not seem to have

[4] On access to preconscious fantasies as a condition of creativity, and on regression at the service of the ego as a source of creativity, the pioneering works were by L. Kubie, *Neurotic Distortion of the Creative Processes* (Kansas: University of Kansas, 1952); and E. Kris. *Psychoanalytic Explorations in Art* (London: Allen and Unwin, 1953).

[5] Obviously these concepts of outer and inner sciences are related to Einstein's distinction between science as 'something existing and complete'—as the 'most objective thing known to man'—and 'science in the making, science as an end to be pursued', which is 'subjective and psychologically conditioned'. See his 'Address at Columbia University, New York, January 15', *Essays in Science* (New York: Wisdom Library, 1934), pp. 112–14, esp. p. 112. See also P. P. Wiener and A. Noland, 'Roots of Scientific Thought; A Cultural Perspective', in *Roots of Scientific Thought* (New York: Basic, 1957), p. 3.

[6] Hardy held a somewhat different view at the beginning. See G. H. Hardy, 'Notice', in G. H. Hardy, P. V. Seshu Aiyar and B. M. Wilson (eds.), *Collected Papers of Srinivasa Ramanujan* (New York: Chelsea, 1962), pp. i–xxxvi.

any serious interest outside mathematics, and his mysticism and religion 'except in a strictly material sense played no important part in his life.'[7] He was, in fact, according to one of them, an 'agnostic in its strict sense', and his conformity to his cultural traditions was determined not by any faith or commitment, but by his acute this-worldly pragmatism. From this point of view, Ramanujan's professional self could be parsimoniously explained in terms of his sane and shrewd rationality, his lack of a proper mathematical education, his killing poverty, and his 'natural' genius.

Underlying this position, I suspect, is a feeling that 'Ramanujan's mathematics was outshone by the romance of his mathematical career' and a tinge of sorrow that Ramanujan did not turn out to be a greater mathematician and a plainer man.[8] To these friends, what mattered ultimately was the content of his mathematics, the clue to which would have to be sought in the autonomous, intellectual structure of his work, the drama of his life being at worst a red herring and at best an irrelevance.

Against this we can place the observations not only of the starry-eyed Madras mathematicians and Indian friends of Ramanujan, but also of some rather hard-headed scientists who knew him well. E. H. Neville says in Ramanujan's obituary: 'He had serious interests outside mathematics; he was always ready to discuss whatever in philosophy and politics had last caught his fancy.'[9] And Prashanta Mahalanobis was convinced that, at one stage of his life at least, Ramanujan was striving towards a Vedantic mathematics and would have been happier to see his philosophy vindicated by his mathematics than in being recognized as a mere mathematician.[10] One's own view of one's work may be misleading but even B. M. Wilson, who spent some of his most creative years on Ramanujan's work, feels that the latter 'remained to the end an unorthodox mathematician. Almost everything he published bears, either in matter or the treatment, the imprint of his personality; his was highly individual work.'[11] Thus, it may not perhaps be considered

[7] G. H. Hardy, 'Introduction', *Ramanujan—Twelve Lectures Suggested by His Life and Work* (Cambridge: Cambridge University Press, 1940), pp. 4–5.

[8] J. E. Littlewood, *A Mathematician's Miscellany* (London: Methuen, 1957); and Hardy, 'Introduction'.

[9] E. H. Neville, 'The Late Srinivasa Ramanujan', *Nature*, 1920, *106*, pp. 661–62.

[10] See Section III below.

[11] B. M. Wilson, Unpublished MS on Ramanujan, Add. M.S.G. 107C, Trinity College Library, Cambridge University; hereafter Trinity Papers. Even Hardy in *Ramanujan* recognizes that the Indian was, at one level, consistently 'odd and

an instance of uncompromising psychologism if in the following narrative I seek clues to some aspects of Ramanujan's creativity and professional identity in his individuality and personal history.

The objection of Hardy and Littlewood can be met in another way. Those interested in science as a closed system of formal incremental knowledge may not perhaps find it impossible to write a history of world mathematics without mentioning Ramanujan though it will be very difficult. But to those interested in the nature of scientific creativity, it is not merely what Ramanujan added to the formal structure of mathematics which determines his importance in the history of science; it is rather the unique internal equipment he employed as an essentially self-taught genius and the opportunity he gives one to study creativity as a psycho-social process by diverting attention from the net additions to knowledge made by individuals. Like J. B. Priestley's time plays, Ramanujan's life allows one a glimpse into the alternative world of 'what could have been' without the interventions of the dominant culture of science and the dominant mode of scientific socialization.

The second objection to a psychological study of Ramanujan's life is actually a derivative of the first, but it is formulated in terms of Ramanujan's discipline rather than personality. It says in effect that pure mathematics is itself so peculiarly abstract and so far removed from the real world of events, feelings, and objects, that it is perhaps the only 'true' science with no determinants outside its own world. There is obviously some truth in this argument, but it is very partial. The pursuit of a pure science like mathematics demands not only certain cognitive skills but also an emotional apparatus that will allow, enjoy, and facilitate certain ways of problem-solving. To say that pure mathematics is, unlike most other human pursuits, culture-free and unencumbered by human emotions is to say that only some kinds of persons can become creative mathematicians.

In addition, those who stress the autonomy of the world of

---

individual'. See also Hardy's 'Notice', where he makes the point that Ramanujan 'had a passion for what was unexpected, strange and odd' and that 'all his results, new or old, right or wrong, had been arrived at by a process of mingled argument, intuition and induction, of which he was entirely unable to give any coherent account'. See also L. J. Mordell, quoted in Suresh Ram, *Srinivasa Ramanujan* (New Delhi: National Book Trust, 1972), pp. 46–7.

mathematics in connection with Ramanujan's life—predictably, they are mostly mathematicians—seem to miss an important point. Ramanujan depended very little on the existing structure of mathematics, and his work can hardly be called the logical development of the formal mathematical knowledge of his time. His exposure to modern mathematics was next to nothing, and his method was predominantly 'induction from particular cases in the crudest sense'.[12] He was an artist who was satisfied if he could convince himself.[13] Littlewood is more explicit: Ramanujan, he says,

> had no strict logical justification for his operations. He was not interested in rigour.... If a significant piece of reasoning occurred somewhere, and the mixture of evidence and intuition gave him certainty, he looked no further.[14]

Whether mathematicians like it or not, the products of such an approach have to draw upon the inner resources of the creative scientist himself and depend on his inner checks and reality testing, rather than on a standard reference group of other scientists. Anyone interested in the work of such a self-sufficient genius simply cannot avoid considering these inner resources and checks.

Also, just as Ramanujan's life tells us about the process of creativity by presenting 'alternative scenarios', his successes and failures tell us not merely about the structural growth of mathematics but also the cultural changes in science—the process through which science moves from one culture of creativity to another. At a time when science itself is examining the social and psychological factors that have led it to value its cumulative objective mass of knowledge more than its non-cumulative, non-rational, time and space-bound culture (and in the process lose its soul), a study of Ramanujan gives one the chance to speculate about a future science which might allow one to integrate the speculative, normative, and aesthetic factors with the logical, rational, and empirical ones. It permits one, at another level, to examine the living presence of the scientist within his science and the shifting relationship between observer and observed, not as something merely incidental, but as part of the essential core of science.

[12] Wilson, 'Trinity Papers'. See also note 11 above.

[13] J. E. Littlewood, Letter to Hardy, Add. MS a 94 (1–6), Trinity Papers.

[14] Littlewood, *Mathematician's Miscellany*, p. 88.

To the extent that the text and culture of modern science are moving towards greater recognition of these epistemic and methodological problems, the personal identity of Ramanujan is as relevant to science as it is to the evolving discipline of the science of science. To take a narrower view, it may also yield concepts in terms of which one could study the life histories of a number of Indian scientists of the last hundred years as records of an unconscious and daring—though mostly crude and inelegant—effort to move towards such a new science. It is as if a major civilization, in trying to meet its own problems of survival, was trying prematurely through these men to anticipate if not tackle some of the fundamental issues in the philosophy of modern science.

This point could be made in yet another way. Each phase of science has, as its correlate, a distinctive philosophy of science embodied in a congruent world image and a unique inner concept of science which gives scientific activity its subjective logic. When the Enlightenment in Europe produced a new concept of science in its attempts to give a prominent place to empircism and experimentation in scientific activity, it reduced the legitimacy of speculative and rationalist elements in the modern culture of science. The delegitimization was then necessary for the growth of modern science. But while some permanency may attach to fundamental scientific problems, none attaches to their solutions or to the contexts in which these solutions are offered. Thus, as the environment of science has continued to change, many recessive elements in the culture of science, once rejected as anti-science, have again come to the fore in response to the changed concerns of the scientific estate.

Here lies the major significance of Ramanujan in the history of world science. His professional life gives us a rare opportunity to study the survival and dissolution of cultures in the minds of scientists, and beautifully illustrates the attempt to produce a valid science with an 'anachronistic' concept of science and with the psychological and cultural equipment reportedly more suited to an earlier phase in the growth of science. Whether his specific orientation and skills can become relevant again to world science is, of course, an open question which future philosophers and historians of science may be able to answer better.

My knowledge of mathematics being what it is, I am sure that the following narrative does not explain Ramanujan's mathematics and cannot therefore deal with some of the issues raised above with even the barest sophistication.[15] But I hope that it explains something of the mathematician: the distinctive meaning his creations might have had for him and his group; the way in which his time and his society lived within him, sometimes validating and sometimes threatening his professional self; the context of outer processes and inner needs that he used in defining his own scientific identity; his attempts to solve through his science the contradictions between a long tradition of indigenous science and the felt need to participate in world science on a new footing; and finally, between the demands of the world of formal mathematics and the history of his own selfhood.

II

Srinivasa Ramanujan was born in a poor Tamil Iyengar family in 1887 in Erode in Tamilnadu, not very far from the city of Madras. Following local custom, his mother had gone to her father's home for the birth of her first child. Ramanujan was his first name. Following South Indian custom, he always wrote it second.

Only a substantial amount of piety accumulated over previous lives ensured one's birth as a Brahmin. It was even more of an achievement to obtain an Iyengarhood. Iyengars traditionally enjoyed the highest status among Tamil Brahmins, in a region where Brahminism itself, in Ramanujan's time at least, was culturally more hegemonic than in most other parts of India. In addition, the gap between Brahminic and non-Brahminic cultures was one of the widest in Tamil society. This combination of hegemony and exclusivism perhaps bound part of the anxiety associated with poverty which one expects in a family of this type in other societies. Brahminism might also have given a special meaning to the poverty by linking it to austerity. All said, Ramanujan's ritual status gave him one message, his poverty another. And he might have been forced early to learn to use the Brahminic worldview to rationalize and compensate for his poverty.

Like most gifted scientists, Ramanujan was the eldest son.[16] His

[15] Fortunately, however, excellent reviews of his mathematics and his intellectual career are available. The best known of them is naturally Hardy's *Ramanujan*.

[16] Cf. F. Galton, *English Men of Science* (London: 1874); J. M. Cattell and D. R. Brimball, *American Men of Science* (Garrison: Science, 1921); Anne Roe, 'A Psychological Study of Eminent Psychologists and Anthropologists, and a Comparison with Biological and Physical Scientists', *Psychological Monographs*, 1953, 67 (2), Whole Number; and *The Making of a Scientist* (New York: Dodd Mead, 1952).

two younger brothers were born several years after him and thus he also had the upbringing of an only son. Such experiences have a special meaning in many cultures. They are even more meaningful in a culture that is partial to sons and considers them props to the family economy, as old-age insurance, and sources of comfort in life after death because of their ritual role. Moreover, Ramanujan was born to his parents after years of childlessness. Almost by definition, one may say, he was a subject of heightened care, pride, and parental expectation.[17]

After Ramanujan's birth his mother returned to her husband's family—consisting of her husband and parents-in-law—at Kumbakonam, a small, rather typical south Indian town, midway between Madras and Cochin. It is here that the mathematician spent most of his childhood and youth. Kumbakonam was a traditional town, enjoying some status among Tamils for the alleged subtlety and refinement of its people, especially its Brahmins. However, even their fans never failed to point out that this smoothness in social style was associated with a certain sly deviousness, interpersonal distance, and insincerity. The popular perception of the town paralleled the popular perception of Iyengars who were also supposed to have a polished manner which hid shrewd ruthlessness behind a façade of traditional refinement. Stereotypes are important not for the element of truth they rarely contain, but for the feelings they invariably communicate. From these shared images of yester-years, one gets the feeling that both Kumbakonam and the Iyengars of Kumbakonam carried the connotations of tradition, élite status, and that delectable touch of decay often associated with traditional élite status.

Ramanujan's family lived in a town and though most of its members, including his mother, were educated, they were deeply conservative. What appears more remarkable—and the traditional Indian attitudes to poverty and suffering perhaps had something to do with this—is that the family, especially Ramanujan, had a certain unselfconscious confidence that was expressed in a serene acceptance of, and pride in, their own way of life. It is true that

[17] The Indian first child's world is however also vulnerable in its own special way. While his self-regard is protected by his interpersonal environment, it is also overly dependent on his ritual role and upon his being an anchor of the forces of cultural continuity within the family. As a result, he frequently becomes a battleground for different norms of social living and different expectations about his social role. See a discussion of this dynamic in J. C. Bose above.

there was Ramanujan's ordinal position among the children; his sense of competence does resemble the typical psychological profile of the first-born.[18] But his self-confidence was also protected by his family's self-confidence. His colossal success in the modern sector was eventually to shatter that confidence. So it would appear from the whining, supplicatory letters that his younger brothers wrote to his English mentors begging for trivial favours after his death.[19]

One can only guess at the emotional consequences of this combination of poverty, partial modernization, and orthodoxy. At one level it meant a combination of enforced simple living, acquired middle-class thinking, and persistent Brahminism. At another, it gave the family a distinctive ability to live off the modern sector without being swept out of their traditional ways and—which is the same thing—an ability to cope with the demands of urban living at the margins of India's expanding tertiary sector with the psychological assets and skills of an older life style.

The family was deeply devoted to the goddess Lakshmi Namagiri, Vishnu's consort in local mythology, and the goddess of worldly success and wealth. It could be that it was their poverty that induced the family to so venerate the goddess; more probably it was Namagiri's dominant status among the Kumbakonam Brahmins. Kumbakonam had a famous temple where dark granite icons of Namagiri and Narasimha were enshrined. Of the two, Namagiri was the more important deity locally; the temple was named after her, and she was considered the more powerful.

Whatever the source of this special veneration, both the two family myths that sought to explain Ramanujan's creativity to his bewildered relatives involved the goddess. The first version was that Ramanujan was born after his grandparents had fervently prayed to Namagiri for a grandson and after his grandmother had in a trance, just before her death, assured his mother that she

[18] Cf. A. Adler, *The Individual Psychology of Alfred Adler*, edited by H. L. Ansbacher and Rowena Ansbacher (New York: Basic, 1956), pp. 376–82; and Irving Harris, *The Promised Seed, A Comparative Study of Eminent First and Latter Sons* (Glencoe: Free Press, 1964).

[19] Oscar Lewis seems to suggest that the older generation, being more rooted in traditions, often do not share the sense of inadequacy of the younger ones who are no longer as secure in tradition due to their acquired modernity. Oscar Lewis, *Children of Sanchez* (New York: Random House, 1961).

would continue to speak through her grandson. According to the second, Ramanujan suddenly showed precocity after Namagiri, in one of his childhood dreams, wrote upon his tongue. An accident that must have seemed consistent with these myths was Ramanujan's noticeable physical resemblance to his mother and grandmother. His younger brother was to put it succinctly in a letter to Hardy: 'I have a corpulent mother who resembles my brother in all his physical features.'[20]

In some cultures, one could talk with some confidence about all this contributing to a diffusion of sexual identity. But in the Indian tradition, with its more complex and less differentiated distribution of gender-specific social characteristics, one can only talk cautiously of a possible heightened awareness in Ramanujan of his identification with his mother, a greater acceptance of certain feminine sensitivities and intuitive behaviour—both predictors of creativity in men—and a deeper concern with what has often been associated in many a peasant culture with primordial magical power, motherliness.[21]

Ramanujan's favourite deity, however, turned out to be Narasimha, a particularly aggressive incarnation of Vishnu, the supreme protector in the Hindu pantheon. According to popular mythology, Vishnu was once compelled to appear as Narasimha or Man-Lion to protect his earnest devotee Prahlad from the homicidal

[20] S. Lakshmi Narasimhan to G. H. Hardy, 29 April 1920, Trinity Papers. See also S. Ranganathan, *Ramanujan, the Man and the Mathematician* (Bombay: Asia, 1967), pp. 72, 126. Ranganathan's earnest and over-determined mystical explanation of Ramanujan's creativity should not blind us to the important clues that his book provides to the shared myths and fantasies in Ramanujan's environment and the meaning of his science to his community.

[21] On the likeness between Ramanujan's upbringing and early experiences of the typical homosexual in the West, see I. Bieber *et al., Homosexuality: A Psychoanalytic Study* (New York: Basic, 1962), particularly pp. 22–4, 44–53, 86–93; R. Green, *Sexual Identity: Conflict in Children and Adults* (New York: Basic, 1974), Ch. 15; and M. T. Saghir and E. Robins, *Male and Female Homosexuality* (Baltimore: Williams and Wilkins, 1973), Ch. 2. On the association between creativity and bisexuality, see for instance, Frank Barron, *Creativity and Personal Freedom* (Princeton: Van Nostrand, 1968); and *Creative Person and Creative Process* (New York: Holt, Rinehart and Winston, 1969); D. W. Mackinnon, 'The Personality Correlates of Creativity: A Study of American Architects', in P. E. Vernon (ed.), *Creativity* (Harmondsworth: Penguin, 1970), pp. 289–311. See the reviews of relevant literature in Anne Roe, 'Psychological Approaches to Creativity in Science', in M. A. Coler (ed.), *Essays on Creativity in the Sciences* (New York: New York University Press, 1963), pp. 153–82; and Frank Barron, 'The Psychological Study of Creativity', in *New Directions in Psychology* (New York: Holt, Rinehart and Winston, 1965), vol. 2, pp. 1–134.

rage of his demon-father Hiranyakashipu, and to slay the latter, tearing him to pieces. In this leonine godhead and protective male authority Ramanujan was to find later the ultimate source of his inspiration and creativity in mathematics.

One wonders why a man born as the gift of Namagiri should become a devotee of Narasimha. One possible explanation is the correlation in Tamil culture between low traditional status and an agrarian life-style on the one hand, and allegiance to feminine deities on the other;[22] so that ambitious first-generation city-dwellers often felt tempted to switch their devotion to more status-giving gods. But this explanation does not quite fit Ramanujan's unselfconscious lifestyle, and one is tempted to ask questions about his early developmental history which can never be answered fully. Was it, for instance, an expression of his deepseated ambivalence towards the family deity Namagiri and the maternal authority she represented? Or was it a denial of his feminine self, closely linked to the mother goddess through the family myths about his birth and genius? Was identification with Narasimha the symbolic expression of legitimate destructive urges in an Oedipal situation? Or was it a compensation for the absence of an authoritative male role model in the family? Against what source of threat was Narasimha's aggressive protection sought?

Let us start with what is proverbial: Ramanujan's closeness towards his mother Komalatammal. Even when he was alive, it was clear to all who knew him that Ramanujan's psychological life was primarily an unfolding of his complex relationship with his mother. That his Indian contemporaries and biographers should find this closeness striking is particularly significant, because the taboos that attached to the father–son relationship did not apply to mother–son intimacy in the Indian tradition. At a certain level of awareness, the mother in the Indian family was not merely expected to be the earliest prototype of an intimate warm authority, but also the first target of defiance. It was as if part of the Oedipal hostilities towards the father, conspicuously low in the Indian system, found expression in the Indian son's intimate ambivalence towards his mother.[23] If, after allowing for all this, some Indian contemporaries

[22] At least this is the impression one gets from H. Whitehead, *The Village Gods of South India* (Calcutta: Association Press, 1921).

[23] See a brief discussion of this in Dhirendra Narayan, *Hindu Character* (Bombay, Bombay University Press, 1957); Sudhir Kakar, *The Inner World: Childhood and Society*

found the mathematician's attachment to his mother noteworthy, it must have been either atypically deep or atypically conflictual or both.

A few facts are in any case well known. First, in all major decisions in Ramanujan's life, his mother had the last say, either directly or indirectly. Being a 'shrewd and cultured lady', she never made her authority too obvious or her 'voice' too strident. Rather, until Ramanujan's wife entered the household, she ruled the roost with a quiet firmness which, even if in some ways culturally typical, was nevertheless remarkably efficient.[24] Apparently it was a benevolent matriarchy which depended less on direct intervention in the son's affairs and more on indirect control over him through his inner concepts of authority, moral rectitude, and transgression.

Second, the son associated the mother with internal demands for performance. Perhaps it was this that some of my informants had in mind when they said that Ramanujan's mother made him what he was. Early in his life she established with him a long-term collaboration in the magical manipulation of mathematical symbols, numbers, and matrices for various occult purposes. Komalatammal was an astrologer and a numerologist herself and could recite her son's horoscope from memory.[25] She is said to have foreseen—which means she and her acquaintances thought that she had foreseen—Ramanujan's meteoric rise to greatness as well as his premature death.[26] By the time the son grew up, he had acquired the mother's

---

in India (New Delhi: Oxford University Press, 1979); and Ashis Nandy, 'Sati or a Nineteenth Century Tale of Women, Violence and Protest', in *At the Edge of Psychology: Essays in Politics and Culture* (New Delhi: Oxford University Press, 1980), pp. 1–31.

[24] Local myths would have it that this particular style of control was also typical of Ayyangar womenfolk. Although there may or may not be any substance in this, there is less doubt about the high status of women among the Ayyangars. There is even less doubt about the family tradition of this particular Ayyangar family. Ramanujan's grandmother was known for her dominant style and his grandfather for his docile submissiveness.

[25] She may have also been a part-time 'witch doctor'; Ramanujan's maternal grandmother almost certainly was. See the reminiscences of M. Anantharaman in P. K. Srinivasan (ed.), *Ramanujan, 1: Letters and Reminiscences* (Madras: Muthialpeth High School, 1967), pp. 97–8.

[26] Ramanujan's biographer P. K. Srinivasan showed his horoscope to a few astrologers without telling them whose it was. All of them predicted an early death. It is possible that both Ramanujan and his mother had made the same prediction for themselves, and it became a self-destructive, self-fulfilling prophecy.

tastes. He showed his strong identification with her not merely by claiming proficiency in astrology and precognition, but by making the crucial association throughout life between femininity and the ability to handle magically the world of sacred numbers. It was as if his joint excursions with his mother into astrology and other cognate 'sciences' marked out the design of a joint intellectual venture within which all his other collaborations had to be fitted.[27] I shall have something more to say on this later.

The mother–son collaboration also included an element of aggressive competition for control and power, though only at a symbolic level. Both Ramanujan and his mother were fond of playing an indigenous board game called the fifteen-point game, where one player has fifteen pieces standing for sheep while his opponent has three pieces symbolizing three wolves. When a sheep is surrounded by wolves, it is eaten and the player loses a piece. When a wolf is surrounded by sheep it is immobilized. It is in the nature of the game that the person playing the wolves generally wins. However, young Ramanujan mathematized the game within a few days and never again lost a single game to his mother, whether in the incarnation of a sheep or a wolf.

Lastly, an accident of genetic history—or fate, as Ramanujan and many of his contemporaries would have said—endorsed his identification with his mother. Ramanujan not only resembled his mother and grandmother in looks, he had, despite his chubbiness, a delicate and conspicuously feminine build and appearance. His velvety soft palms and long tapering fingers have been frequently commented upon. Some of the femininity had less to do with congenital physical characteristics than with acquired habits; many noticed his practice of walking with his hands out, palms down, fingers outstretched and pointing laterally, a mannerism which, in India at least, would be considered rather feminine. Young Ramanujan's aversion to outdoor sports and his manifest shyness went with this body image. They strengthened his awareness of his feminine self and powered his attempts to integrate this self as a crucial element of his self-identity.

However, one must hasten to add that a certain extroverted activism is not as clear an indicator of masculinity in India as it is in the West, for, even if the social definitions of gender roles are well

[27] The depth of this relationship was recognized by everyone, so much so that after Ramanujan's death it was his mother who was paid his pension, not his wife.

delineated in Indian culture, the psychological definitions are more confluent. Under a number of specific conditions, femininity can become an indicator of a higher form of masculinity. Not that there are no St Francises of Assissi in the West, but perhaps they are possible in many more sectors of life in India.[28]

On the other hand, Ramanujan's favourite lion godhead certainly contrasted with the diffident, retiring, male authority figure that he encountered in his father. Kuppuswamy Srinivasa Iyengar was a *gumasta* or petty accounts clerk in a cloth merchant's shop, earning a paltry salary. It is tempting to believe that the father's familiarity with numbers had something to do with the son's aptitude. But, as we have seen, there were already more powerful influences working on Ramanujan. At most, the father's profession possibly deepened the impact of the mother's passion for numbers.

Kuppuswamy Srinivasa was, by all accounts, an unassuming ineffective man who rarely got involved—or, for that matter, was involved—in his son's life. By itself, this weightlessness of the father as an immediate authority was not culturally atypical,[29] especially in a linear joint family with living grand-parents where it was customary for the father not to pay much attention to his children. This was one of the means by which the society underplayed the boundaries of nuclear units within a joint family. It was the mother's personality, I suspect, which made Kuppuswamy Srinivasa seem even more inconspicuous and non-protective than he actually was.[30] She was openly contemptuous of her husband,

[28] See on cognate issues Erik H. Erikson, *Gandhi's Truth: On the Origins of Militant Nonviolence* (New York: Norton, 1969).

[29] For instance, M. S. Gore, *The Impact of Industrialization and Urbanization on the Aggarwal Family of Delhi Area*, Ph. D. dissertation (Columbia University, 1961), University Microfilms (Ann Arbor, Michigan), pp. 2–59; G. M. Carstairs, *The Twice Born* (London: Hogarth Press, 1957); and P. Spratt, *Hindu Culture and Personality* (Bombay: Manaktalas, 1966).

[30] In fact, when counterpoised against each other, Ramanujan's parents seem to approximate Anne Roe's description of the early family environment of social scientists, rather than of mathematicians (see Roe, *The Making of a Scientist*). On the relationship between creativity in western scientists and maternal possessiveness and hostility combined with a distant father, see also B. T. Eiduson, *Scientists: Their Psychological World* (New York: Basic Books, 1962). It would, however, be hazardous to see in this combination a source of Ramanujan's concept of science as a cross between formal thinking and mystic experience. For, in this case, the crucial datum might have been not the actual content of parental models, but the extent to which they were a deviation from cultural norms.

particularly of his intelligence and, as the reader may have suspected from this narrative, tried to find in her son a substitute for her husband.

The distance between father and son was later increased by Srinivasa Iyengar's total inability to understand his son's concerns and ambitions. One gets the feeling that the pace of Ramanujan's success overawed him. But this interpretation could be overdone, for long before Ramanujan shot into fame, Komalatammal was taking an active interest in her son's mathematics and Srinivasa was a non-person in his son's life. Komalatammal might occasionally have been a trial to her son, but she was also the only intimate figure to have genuine interest in things that were central to him. Perhaps it would not be an exaggeration to say that it was she who discovered Ramanujan.

To Srinivasa the accounts clerk, on the other hand, what mattered were Ramanujan's status as the eldest son in the family and the rupee value of his numerous ill-paid jobs, stipends, and fellowships. He was a poor man with the poor man's blend of practical sense and cynicism. In any case, he had little reason to introspect or ponder over the 'finer aspects' of his relationship with his son, given that this father–son distance was not uncommon in an Indian family.

The result of all this was that the mathematician rarely, if ever, talked about his father. His biographers, too, barely mention him. Only one, almost accidentally, records the fact that he survived his son by a few months. We know nothing about how he reacted to the boy Ramanujan or to the adult; nothing even about the way he adjusted to his son's fame, and to what was, by the family's standards, prosperity.[31]

Lastly, as already mentioned, Ramanujan's brothers were much younger and this ensured him the lonely, fantasy-rich childhood of an only son. From their stray correspondence with Hardy one gets the impression that they were simple folk who tried to capitalize on their brother's fame in their own naïve fashion. It is an indication of the low ambitions of the rest of the family that they aimed no higher than at clerical posts in government departments which they hoped to get by pestering Hardy, in the ornate Indian English of an

[31] An indicator of the modern environment in which Ramanujan's illustrious contemporary, Jagadis Chandra Bose, was brought up is that his father was an active intervening figure who was, if anything, more modern than his son. See Part Two above, esp. sections III and IV.

earlier generation, for testimonials. Once they became tenured clerks, they lived out their placid lives like good Tamil Brahmins, and Ramanujan perhaps became for them, after his lonely death, one of those mythic figures in an Indian family whom one is always expected to live with but never live by.

Very little is known about Ramanujan's childhood and adolescence. Indian civilization has never made a clear distinction between the legendary and the empirical. And the former, conceptualized in terms of the primitive logic of dreams and fantasies, is frequently made to yield a hypothetical model from which the 'historical realities' of a person or a group are deduced. Such a model, I suspect, is comprehensible mainly in terms of constructs that link the group's interpretation of the person to the person's relevance for the group.

From the more concrete bits of information, one knows that Ramanujan went to school at the age of five and passed his primary school examination in 1894. He stood first in the whole district and was exempted from paying part of the tuition fees. One also knows that in common with many great mathematicians, he showed early signs of mathematical talent;[32] and that he found most of his mathematics teachers more ignorant than himself. This experience too, judging by Hardy's impression, is quite a common one for creative mathematicians.[33] However, in his relationship with these teachers he remained humble, self-effacing, and obsequious—as if he was apologetic about being so bright and knowledgeable. This, I am sure, Hardy would have found less typical. Unfortunately prophets are even less venerated in their schools than in their countries, and Ramanujan was a perpetual target of the practical jokes of his class fellows. They had little reason to like his preference for solitude and his single-minded absorption in mathematics. Moreover, he was a favourite of the teachers and the headmaster who liked his quietness and, even more so, his ability to turn out school timetables at short notice. Such situations always invite the hostility of one's classmates. In Ramanujan's case, they must have liked even less his interest in the Sanskrit classics, the sayings of saints, and the *puranas*, all of which he frequently recited in the traditional sytle of Brahmin pandits at the least provocation.

[32] C. P. Snow, 'G. H. Hardy', *Variety of Men* (New York: Scribner, 1967), pp. 21–61.

[33] G. H. Hardy, *A Mathematician's Apology* (Cambridge: Cambridge University Press, 1941).

Of these traits, the early loneliness of an only child and search for solitude in latency or pre-adolescence are particularly noteworthy. On the one hand, they are consistent with the developmental histories of a number of creative mathematicians and physicists. On the other, they seem inconsistent with the link between a dominant mother, deep involvement with social realities, and entry into the social rather than natural sciences observed in the West. Perhaps the combination was possible in the greater Sanskritic culture with its studied indifference to boundaries between the arts, the humanities and the sciences, and between the 'tougher' sciences of nature and the 'softer' sciences of society. After all, is not nature (*prakriti*) in this culture the active, mobile, feminine principle of the cosmos, to be grasped instinctively and intuitively on the basis of what one has incorporated of one's earliest and closest experiences of femininity? Is not culture itself associated with the concept of a primordial, 'passive' but authoritative maleness (*purusha*) from which one maintains a manifestly affectless distance as from one's earliest male authority? We shall have to come back to these strange questions again.

Some biographers mention young Ramanujan's fascination with zero and the startling questions he asked his school teachers. (For instance, at the age of twelve, when told that any number divided by the same number equalled one, he asked if zero divided by zero would also be one.) In his classes, he was perpetually involved in mathematical calculations and already in his latency he could give the values of $\sqrt{2}$, pi, and e to any number of decimal places. At twelve or thirteen, he is even said to have discovered the relationship between circular and exponential functions and was very disappointed to find out later that Leonhard Euler had already discovered them.

As mentioned before, this mathematical precocity co-extended with a serious interest in astrology, numerology, occult phenomena, and prescience. The simultaneous interest in modern and occult mathematics might have grown out of Ramanujan's early interpersonal relationships but now it was strengthened by his unconventional exposure to modern mathematics which he had begun to study on his own. This exposure gave him access to the text of contemporary mathematics but not to its culture. This culture might have exerted some internal pressures on him to cut himself off from the more magical systems of ideas; whereas his imperfect socialization to modern mathematics encouraged him to believe that he could enrich and extend the systems of magical mathematics through modern mathematics and make them even more powerful.

Despite his concern with 'para-mathematics' and his childhood dream of finding the 'ultimate mathematics', Ramanujan did have an uncanny sense of the significance of modern mathematics. He got exposed to it at the age of fifteen by a rather ordinary textbook he borrowed—G. S. Carr's *A Synopsis of Elementary Results in Pure and Applied Mathematics*.[34] He was then in the sixth form. The exposure came at the right moment, for a number of anecdotes suggest that numbers in general, and positive integers in particular, were already becoming, as Littlewood was later to put it, his personal friends. And in this friendship an almost feminine intuition and empathy had already started playing a prominent role.[35] There was only one problem. Not knowing Carr to be a mediocre mathematician and presuming his book was a standard mathematical work, Ramanujan once and for all modelled his style of writing on Carr's work. For the rest of his life he continued to produce what could be called the different volumes of Ramanujan's *Synopsis of Elementary Results in Pure Mathematics*.

Why did the mathematician gradually people his world with those anthropomorphic formuale and numbers, as if to contain all human relations within an affectless, formal, controllable system? The answer lies in the cultural meaning of mathematics to him.[36] Ramanujan's first exposure to mathematics (and to that branch of it in which he was later to specialize, the theory of numbers) was through his mother's astrology. This association was only strengthened by his Brahminic heritage in which mathematics and numbers had been, among other things, magical instruments for propitiating and

[34] According to Hardy and Littlewood, G. S. Carr and his book, *A Synopsis of Elementary Results in Pure and Applied Mathematics* (London: Francis Hodgson, 1880), vol. 1, and 1886, vol. 2, are now completely forgotten, except for the inspiration they gave to Ramanujan. This was the only book available to Ramanujan and the mathematical knowledge summarized in it went no further than the 1860s. See Hardy, *Ramanujan*.

[35] The best example of such intuitive powers is the story of the taxi number, too well known to be repeated. See Snow, *Hardy*.

[36] Compare the apparently affectless, anthropomorphic, obsessive-compulsive mathematics of Ramanujan with the highly emotion-laden anthropomorphic scientific world within which Jagadis Chandra Bose worked. On anthropomorphization as a characteristic of creative persons, see Phyllis Greenacre, 'The Childhood of the Artist: Libidinal Phase Development and Giftedness', *The Psychoanalytic Study of the Child* (New York: International Universities, 1957), *12*, pp. 47–52.

controlling fate or *niyati* and the nature of *prakriti*. They helped in the delineation of ritual or magical boundaries of safety (*gandis*), the choice of auspicious moments (*mahurtas, yogas, tithis, kshanas, lagnas*), the correct reading of indicators (*lakshanas*), and the identification of appropriate fetishes, magical guard plates, and protective charms (*kundalas, kavachas*, etc.). Their function was to extend some control over the two cosmic principles of *niyati* and *prakriti*, both feminine, both unpredictable, both aggressively malefic and benevolently creative at the same time. The assumption was that the maleficence could be contained through rituals, magic and mystic intervention (so that the nurtural and creative aspects of the cosmic powers could be fully released).[37] This lent a divine quality to mathematical creativity and made mathematics the 'highest truth'.[38]

Numbers and their interrelations—arithmetic, geometry, algebra—all were, therefore, parts of a cognitive and mythic order. They constituted a language, the grammar of which could not be formalized without rules that were part-sacred. One need hardly add that when not culturally sanctioned and transmitted, such an order would have seemed remarkably close to what clinicians diagnose as a delusional system. But then, by such clinical standards, every rejected theory or cosmology of science turns out to be in, in retrospect, a delusional system. Yet these are the very bricks with which the edifice of science is built.[39] The difference between magic and science lies not so much in their content, as in their internal organizational principles, methodologies, the permeability of their boundaries, and the justificatory principles they use.

Given that traditionally mathematics in India had a magical–divine connection—as chemistry had in the history of the western world—in Ramanujan's case it performed another important function. Though he knew his mathematics to be a gift of the goddess

[37] It is possible that this concept of individual control over an unpredictable feminine principle, and the aim of gaining power over powerful environmental forces to counter feelings of personal insignificance, gave such a strong push to Indian mathematics in ancient times and has made mathematics and mathematically-oriented disciplines the cutting edge of Indian scientific effort in recent times too.

[38] Ramanujan quoted by Hardy, Trinity Papers, Add. MSS a. 94 (7–10).

[39] Probably no great scientist is either wholly rational or wholly magical; see e.g. John Maynard Keynes, 'Newton the Man', *Essays in Biography* (London: Heinemann, 1961), pp. 310–23; and Michael Polanyi, 'Genius in Science', *Encounter*, 1972, *38*, pp. 43–50.

Namagiri who had blessed him by writing on his tongue, he also claimed that sometimes in his dreams the god Narasimha, in a fantastic reversal of roles, revealed his divine tongue in the form of scrolls covered by complicated mathematics superimposed on drops of blood. On these signs of oral grace Ramanujan founded his self-definition as a scholar and—perhaps more crucially at this stage—as a chosen one in whom mathematics was to become a nexus between legitimately violent, divine orality and an apparently sterilized, two-dimensional but nonetheless nonviolent representation of it; between a powerful, cosmic, feminine principle—represented by a magical mother who was so by virtue of being an exponent of magical mathematics—and the grace of a benevolent god representing protective violence.

None of this should be construed to mean that Ramanujan had any sense of a grand mission or a religious calling at that stage. If he had any such ideas, we do not know of them. On the contrary, it appears that he was still a bright village boy trying to do well in areas in which a poor but educated Brahmin's son should try to do well. He was a good student and, on the basis of his high school performance—he got a first class—secured a scholarship in 1903 for studying F. A. at the Government College, Kumbakonam.

What happened during the next year we do not know. But the teen-aged Ramanujan now began, even more than formerly, to see his mathematics as a transcendental abstraction and as a means of isolating his affect, and ultimately himself. Perhaps his adolescent asceticism—serving as a defence against the surging instinctual, notably aggressive and sexual, impulses—had something to do with this. He may have sought in mathematics a disembodied counterpoint to knowledge that related to things physical, interpersonal, and empirical. One indication was his singular horror of physiology which, of the subjects he studied, was the only one concerned with the functions of the body and the biological self.[40] The subject also aroused his deepest anxieties about aggression. Ramanujan hated dissection, particularly the anaesthetization and destruction of experimental animals, and there are accounts of how, shedding his customary shyness, he would sneer at a science that forced one to vivisect in order to learn.

Not unnaturally, Ramanujan failed in the first year examination

[40] Suresh Ram, *Srinivasa Ramanujan* (New Delhi: National Book Trust, 1972). Apart from physiology, Ramanujan's subjects were English, Greek and Roman history, mathematics and Sanskrit.

of his college. A popular Indian myth would have it that he failed in mathematics, but this has now been proved wrong—he actually scored 100 per cent in mathematics. (Perhaps the myth-builders wanted to make his victory over modern mathematics total, but it now appears that he failed in English and physiology.) In any case, he lost his scholarship and wandered about for a couple of months in the neighbouring state of Andhra Pradesh with his notebook full of mathematical work. According to one account, Ramanujan ran away from home at the 'instigation' of a friend, but the details have been washed away by time. Another mentions a six-month-long 'mental aberration'. Again there are no details.

The second possibility must be seriously considered. On two other occasions, Ramanujan showed the same peculiar form of amnesia marked by a sudden loss of contact with the immediate environment and a tendency to 'walk away from it all' as if in a trance. It reminds one of the story by H. G. Wells in which the hero was haunted by the vision of a door in a wall through which he was called into an enthralling Eden, away from the realities of the world of competition, ambition, achievement, and success. Wells' hero lost the road to this alternative world in the welter of his myriad transactions with day-to-day existence and finally paid with his life to regain his utopia. Ramanujan perhaps found a partial clue to it in his mathematics, which promised an alternative gateway to this lost world.

To continue: Ramanujan after a while returned home and rejoined the Kumbakonam College. But he could not make up, it is said, for his poor attendance at college and failed to get his F. A. certificate. Still eager to get a degree and prodded by the anxiety of his lower middle-class parents, Ramanujan then joined a well-known college at Madras. The change did not help. He failed again at the Madras University examination in 1907. He now abandoned formal studies altogether, and devoted himself entirely to the private study of mathematics.

For three years he lived in total obscurity and filled up his now-famous ledger-like notebooks, which he had maintained since the age of fourteen, with a mass of mathematical formulae, based mainly on intuition and crude induction and almost invariably without any proof. This stretch of intense activity was interrupted only by his marriage in 1909.

Ramanujan's failure to get a degree and his 'futile' absorption in mathematics had deeply disappointed his parents and, to cure their own 'depression' and the son's 'waywardness', they had recourse to that time-tested Indian psychotherapy: an arranged marriage. The son's lack of employment rarely discouraged fond Indian parents from fulfilling their parental duties in this area and in Ramanujan's case too, his mother soon enough found a bride in Janaki Devi. Since it was an arranged marriage Ramanujan had not even seen Janaki before she landed in his life as his bride. Apparently her cultural background was roughly similar to Ramanujan's.[41]

Janaki was only nine at the time of her marriage. Her parents exercised the option, which Tamil custom gave them, of keeping her with them until puberty. Perhaps Ramanujan's joblessness had something to do with the decision; he was then partly earning his living by coaching students. There was also reportedly some unpleasantness at the time of the marriage; it might have prompted Janaki's father to refuse to formalize the marriage for a while. All we know is that, until 1913, Janaki paid only occasional visits to her husband at Kumbakonam.

Strange though it may seem in view of Ramanujan's ambivalent relationship with his mother, the marriage worked out well. Not only was the husband–wife relationship close by all accounts, which might have been a remnant of the emotional cross-investment between Ramanujan and his mother, but the scientist also developed with his wife—whom he called his 'house'—a low-key, shy but, by the standards of their culture and time, a romantic relationship. That his wife did not stay with him for more than three years in all might have contributed to this. For she was—and is—in many ways a formidable woman. One cannot rule out the possibility that, had they lived together longer she would have triggered some of the same anxieties in her husband that his mother frequently did.

As it happened, Janaki permitted her obsessive husband a lot of room for rumination and isolation and tried to provide him with non-demanding, non-controlling succour. She also perhaps helped him cope more successfully with his ambivalent strivings for autonomy, by taking care of his dependency needs which the partial separation from his mother due to marriage may have heightened. On the other hand, by openly resenting Komalatammal's dominance over her son, Janaki disrupted her mother-in-law's low-

[41] However, in one respect, Janaki belonged to a more conservative family. At the time of marriage she was totally illiterate, whereas even Ramanujan's mother had some education.

key authoritarian control over the household. This might have threatened the defences of her husband, bringing out his latent ambivalence towards his mother. It might also have mobilized the other second-class citizens in the household to identify with Janaki. Srinivasa Iyengar, according to some, became extremely fond of her.

The kind of husband–wife relationship Ramanujan and Janaki developed is thrown into relief by their cultural background. This background demanded undemonstrative conjugality, under-emphasis on sexuality in marriage, and stress on nurture and succour. The underlying institutional need was to discourage within-family fissures developing along the boundaries of nuclear units within joint households. But Ramanujan's relationship with his wife seemed to take on, even while conforming to the institutional demands of an Indian family, the features of a genuine person-to-person relationship. And this within the steel frame of a subculture which had made, in this one area at least, the rules of family-living foolproof over the centuries.

The Ramanujans were a childless couple. Soon after his marriage, Ramanujan was operated upon for hydrocele at Kumbakonam. Given the state of the medical sciences and the medical advice available in those parts, it is not surprising that a short while after the operation Ramanujan started bleeding from his surgical wounds; so the couple were forbidden to have physical relations for about a year. After that Ramanujan went abroad and came back a very ill man to stay with Janaki for only about a year. Thus, it was a case of enforced childlessness. Nonetheless, it is doubtful if the couple could have avoided the repercussions of it. They lived in one of the most conservative sections of Indian society in which the inability to reproduce arouses not only deep feelings of inadequacy and guilt, but also the pity and hostility of others. Pity, because infertility could not but be one of the worst afflictions in an agrarian worldview in which fertility had been historically a powerful cultural motif; hostility, because in a culture with an over-determined concern with the production, preservation, and loss of potency,[42] it sets off one's deepest anxieties about one's own generativity and about the fecundity of nature or of the land that sustains one. The situation is worse for the childless in a linear joint family. The older generation invariably makes clear what it thinks of the couple's, particularly the wife's, inability to

[42] E.g., Carstairs, *The Twice Born*.

supply it with a grandson to perpetuate the lineage and perform the rituals that ensure comforts in after-life. Where life is short and living tough, childlessness deprives the parents and grandparents of even the hope of the pleasures of after-life.

The family, close friends and relatives knew about the operation; others did not. But India's folk wisdom almost always assumes the wife to be the cause of childlessness, unless proof is supplied to the contrary. The family may not have been hostile to Janaki on this score but, to many others, her apparent barrenness may have made her a bad omen and her presence on religious and other festive occasions a source of resentment. It is true that the Iyengar subculture did not openly stigmatize a childless wife as many other Indian subcultures did; nevertheless, in a tradition which valued a woman primarily as a mother, barrenness was seen to be an abdication of womanliness itself.

In such a context, it is not surprising that there were frequent conflicts between the young wife and the centre of power in the family, the mother-in-law. To some extent, the conflicts were inherent in a culture where a major access to social status was through the son. The childlessness of the Ramanujans induced Janaki to make her husband even more the focus of her attention.[43] But the more Janaki tried to find in her husband a compensation for her childlessness and to protect him from the intrusiveness of his mother, the more Komalatammal felt that her son was slipping away from her. As we know, Komalatammal, too, had a history of childlessness. She might have seen in the childlessness of her daughter-in-law reflections of her own past when her own long period of barrenness had made her a target of self-hatred and the hostility of others. Their common history, however, did not lead to any abiding empathy. Instead, both these possessive, powerful and yet insecure women started trying to gain control over the person they had been trying to use as an extension of their selves. Ramanujan contributed to the crisis by trying to remain close simultaneously to his mother and his wife, and in the process arousing the jealousy of both.

Notwithstanding the distractions of marriage and post-marital conflicts, the years 1907–11 were some of Ramanujan's most

[43] See a comparable situation in the life of Jagadis Chandra Bose in Part Two, Section III above.

productive.[44] By the end of the period, he had attained the necessary self-esteem as a mathematician. He told one or two people that he was doing something worthwhile and that Narasimha was personally interested in his work—the first such direct statement of sacred involvement in his mathematics.[45] Some of his acquaintances, too, although not sharing the wide interests of Narasimha, could sense that Ramanujan was on to something important and conveyed their appreciation to him.

But the absence of a proper scholarly setting made his work a risky affair. It was rendered more risky by Ramanujan's belief in private research and meditative mathematics. As a result, most of his discoveries of this period later turned out to be rediscoveries of the work of European mathematicians of the previous century. Being an amateur, he was 'beginning every investigation at the point from which the European mathematicians had started 150 years before him, and not at the point which they had reached in 1913.'[46] Unknowingly, he had pitted himself, as Hardy pointed out, against the accumulated mathematical knowledge of the West and he was bound to lose. However, it was typical of Ramanujan to have independently rediscovered the discoveries of mathematicians of the stature of Euler, Bauer, Georg Riemann, von Staudt, and Adrien Legendre. The Brahmin's mind was a choosy one.

Ramanujan himself found all this out later, when he had built other props to his self-esteem and could shakily cope with his disappointments about his wasted efforts. By that time, in the process of learning about the extent of his wasted efforts, he learnt something about his achievements too. After all, as E. H. Neville and Hardy often said, in areas that interested him, Ramanujan was 'abreast, and often ahead, of contemporary mathematical knowledge'. But, on the whole, by 1911, his early poverty and isolation had already done the damage and he was never able to make up for the loss.[47]

[44] One wishes that more was known about this crucial period 1907–11. Unfortunately, Ramanujan's shy reclusiveness did not allow him to share his experiences of this period with any one.

[45] Radhakrishna Ayyar, quoted in Ranganathan, *Ramanujan*, p. 73. According to this account, Ramanujan believed that Narasimha had directed him in a dream not to publish his results at that stage, because better opportunities would come his way in a short while.

[46] E. H. Neville, quoted in Ram, *Ramanujan*, pp. 25–6.

[47] Hardy always claimed that it was not Ramanujan's early death which was the greatest tragedy of his career—it was rather his inability to get a good mathematical education in the most formative years of his life.

At the end of this period, in 1911, Ramanujan published his first paper.[48] He was then twenty-three. Scholarship of any kind was *ipso facto* valued by the Brahminic literati, and especially by its Tamil variety, and Ramanujan became a slightly better-known figure in the scientific circles of Madras. Within a year he published two more papers in the same journal. He also found a job in the office of Madras Harbour as a petty clerk in 1912. This ensured him a paltry but stable income of twenty-five rupees a month and he continued his mathematics as a hobby for another year. However, he still had to write his notes on packing paper or in red ink across papers already written upon in blue ink.

He also found a kindred spirit in the manager of the Madras Port Trust, Narayana Iyer, who had formerly taught mathematics in a college. He encouraged Ramanujan in his academic ventures, but also injected him with the fear that westerners would plagiarize his work, specially if he gave the proofs of the theorems he was producing. From then on, Ramanujan paled whenever any westerner so much as opened his notebooks and he later carried a part of this suspiciousness to England. As a result, a large part of his earlier work remained a jigsaw puzzle to mathematicians for many years.

By this time he had come in touch with a large number of people and many of the early first-hand impressions of Ramanujan were collected during this period of his life. Most people remembered him as short, plump, light brown in complexion with a high forehead and a big head. On these were fitted a square face, broad nose, and a pair of small ears. A thick growth of hair brushed sideways and the occasional ritual white and red marks put on his forehead completed the picture. Some acquaintances found him uncouth, unshaven, and dirty, and with a stiffer and more feminine version of a Chaplinesque gait. The dirtiness and unkemptness could have been due to poverty, because he made a somewhat different impression on some of his English friends later on.

Two features of his physical appearance seem to have impressed his acquaintances most. The first was his captivating, almost bewitching, eyes. They were the eyes of a mystic and a fanatic, made the more striking by his otherwise shy, withdrawn, rustic appearance and manner. At first meeting he also seemed insensitive and callous to many. But once he turned to his favourite

[48] This and four other papers published by Ramanujan in the *Journal of the Indian Mathematical Society* before he left for England have been reproduced in Hardy, Seshu Aiyar and Wilson, *Collected Papers*.

subject, the mystic significance of mathematics, he emerged from his private world, shedding his customary shyness. His eyes then burnt with an unmistakable fire. Often, in his most intense moments, only the white of his eyes could be seen. His prodigious single-minded industriousness fed into this image of a privileged fanatic. Ramanujan made clear to everyone who came in touch with him that mathematics was the centre of his life. It was not a matter of professional choice or of nationalism or a step to worldly status, but an end in itself and a part of his self.[49]

III

The real break for Ramanujan came at the beginning of 1913 when he was twenty-five. That year, encouraged by two of his Indian patrons, he sent the 'bare statements' of some 120 theorems, mainly formal identities, to the well-known Cambridge mathematician, G. H. Hardy (1877–1947). This was the first step towards the now legendary collaboration between the two mathematicians and perhaps the most remarkable East–West scientific collaboration we have known.[50]

At the time he wrote to Hardy, Ramanujan was still working for the Port Trust in Madras and his salary was still a redoubtable twenty-five rupees per month. But he was no longer an unknown, half-educated villager obsessed with mathematics. His papers had already been published in the *Journal of the Indian Mathematical Society*, and people had begun to call him a genius. However, this estimate of his work in his new social circle had not yet seeped into Ramanujan. Though he had the self-assurance born of a deep faith in the mystic significance of his mathematical work and his 'chosen' status, he felt diffident and insecure confronting the world of academic mathematics.

So he sent his work to Cambridge with a covering note tinged with both obsequiousness and bravado.[51] The mix was dangerous.

[49] The one informant who spoke of nationalism as a major inspiration of Ramanujan actually seemed to have in mind the collectivity of the Indian scientists of the period, rather than Ramanujan alone.

[50] Hardy was the third person to receive samples of Ramanujan's work; two English mathematicians had earlier returned them without comment. Littlewood says with some relish that these two mathematicians, whom he identifies only as Baker and Popson, felt rather foolish afterwards. For a lively description of the discovery of Ramanujan, see Snow, *Hardy*.

[51] The entire letter has been reproduced in Ram, *Ramanujan*, pp. 22–30. It is

It was bound to make mathematicians suspicious, particularly someone like Hardy who was, by nature as well as by conviction, a sceptic. In 1913, he was thirty-seven, famous and cynical. As a professional, he was only too aware of the mathematical cranks who abound in all parts of the world and pester famous mathematicians. Moreover, Ramanujan's talents were not so obvious as they were to appear to Hardy and others in retrospect. It is now known that two accomplished Oxbridge mathematicians, E. W. Hobson and H. F. Baker, had previously returned Ramanujan's works without comment.

Thus it is not surprising that Hardy was at first suspicious. Rather, it testifies to his personality resources and intellectual acumen that despite his initial doubts he assessed his Indian correspondent's worth correctly within a day. That momentous day has been described by many. Here is the argument which helped Hardy finally to make up his mind:

> I should like you to begin by trying to reconstruct the immediate reactions of an ordinary professional mathematician who receives a letter like this from an unknown Hindu clerk.... (some of the theorems Ramanujan sent) defeated me completely; I had never seen anything in the least like them before. A single look at them is enough to show that they could only be written down by a mathematician of the highest class. They must be true because, if they were not true, no one would have had the imagination to invent them. Finally (you must remember that I knew nothing whatever about Ramanujan and had to think of every possibility), the writer must be completely honest, because great mathematicians are commoner than thieves or humbugs of such incredible skill.[52]

Immediately afterwards, Hardy began trying to bring Ramanujan to England with the help of Neville, mathematician and Fellow of Trinity College, who was on a visit to Madras at the time. Others in India, too, were trying to get Ramanujan a fellowship and some money to visit Cambridge. As a result of these efforts, he received

---

noteworthy that Ramanujan in his first letter to Hardy claimed to be 23 years old, when he was actually 25; only a few weeks afterwards Gilbert Walker, a mathematician visiting Madras, was told that Ramanujan was 22 years old; ibid., p. 27. It is not known whether Ramanujan's friends encouraged him to misrepresent his age or whether he himself thought of this ploy to impress his prospective patrons.

[52] Hardy, *Ramanujan*, pp. 1–3.

within a year both a fellowship tenable in England from Madras University and an invitation from Cambridge. However, his first response to the invitation was a disappointment to his patrons. He refused to leave India because of his caste prejudices. Crossing the seas was considered polluting by many conservative Hindus and Ramanujan on such issues was a conservative.[53]

His mother's adamant opposition to the idea, based on fears of pollution, was another source of external—and internal—resistance.[54] Fortunately, she withdrew her objections later, after most appropriately dreaming that Namagiri, the family goddess, had interceded in favour of her son's journey to the West. The event was less esoteric than it may seem at first. Convenient dreams had played a major role in Ramanujan's life. As in the case of many of India's major folk heroes, his dreams, too, often sanctioned his participation in things that were novel or implied the defiance of conventional authority.[55] There was also another development within the family which might have had something to do with the dream. Ramanujan's teen-aged wife, Janaki, had come to stay with her in-laws permanently a few months earlier. Perhaps the prospect of her son being away from her daughter-in-law cum rival Janaki helped bind Komalatammal's anxiety about being separated from her son.

Ramanujan reached Cambridge in April 1914 and stayed the first two months with Neville. He must have been the oddest of arrivals at the university, with his ill-fitting clothes, newly cropped hair—he had cried like a child in Madras when his sacred tuft was removed before his departure for England—and fiercely tight new shoes. And his discomfort showed. Long after, some of his English acquaintances were bitter about his being made to suffer all this merely to look more like an English gentleman. But in 1914 Victorian England was still a living reality. And the insistence on formal dress was certainly not diminished by the heightened nationalism that was to plunge Europe, within a few months, into another massive orgy of violence.

A place was found for Ramanujan at Trinity College and the

[53] Perhaps there was also the painful memory of his first 'departure from home' for Madras.

[54] Characteristically, Ramanujan's father did not interfere in the matter at all, nor was he a party to the decision.

[55] Ibid. It is possible that these convenient dreams in Indian life and mythology are homologues of what Freud called 'obliging dreams'. See Sigmund Freud, 'Psychogenesis of a Case of Homosexuality in a Woman', in James Strachey (ed.), *The Standard Edition of the Complete Works of Sigmund Freud* (London: Hogarth, 1955), *18*, pp. 165–6.

task of educating him fell to Hardy and Littlewood. They were conscious that this re-education had to proceed without destroying the self-esteem of their ward which the latter's extreme modesty suggested was fairly vulnerable. But the Indian was less fragile than he looked: the inner strength that had seen him through his Madras days was very much a part of his personality. His English patrons, one suspects, were taken in by his diffident manner. Littlewood today admits this indirectly; Ramanujan, he says, was too engrossed in his own work to learn much. Even Hardy, at one level, knew this. In retrospect, he felt he had learnt more from Ramanujan than Ramanujan from him.[56]

It did not take the strange Indian long to become a great academic sensation and a legend in Cambridge. In 1916 he received an honorary B. A. degree from the university, and in 1918, at the age of thirty, he was made a Fellow of the Royal Society and of Trinity College. It is doubtful if these formal rewards helped him gauge his new position in the world of science. Socially, he remained as reclusive and oblivious of his environment as ever. And he continued to shock and embarrass his friends by deciding to apply for undergraduate prizes at a time when he was already being compared to Euler and Karl Jacobi. The attitudes evident in the pathetic applications he wrote in India during 1910–13, seeking a job and soliciting some attention for his mathematical work, had persisted in spite of acclaim and success. One would imagine that though Ramanujan knew the value of his work, he did not know its price. At least, he scarcely understood the academic status system of which he had become a formidable if innocent part.

The most remarkable aspect of Ramanujan's encounter with the West was however his relationship with Hardy. Neither of them were the same after meeing the other, particularly Ramanujan, who had for the first time the chance of living the life of a creative mathematician in his own right, rather than remaining a cute example of a prodigiously endowed natural genius in mathematics. Hardy gave him exactly what he needed: non-intrusive nurture and 'unemotional' support. No other break Ramanujan had had could compare with this. Littlewood is right in saying that his 'genius had this one opportunity worthy of it'.[57]

[56] Quoted by Wilson, Trinity Papers, unnumbered.

[57] Littlewood, *A Mathematician's Miscellany*, esp. p. 90.

Were the bonds between Ramanujan and Hardy solely intellectual and scientific ones? How did the differences in their cultural backgrounds and personalities influence their relationship? Did the fact that one of them belonged to a subject society and the other to a powerful imperial power at the peak of its glory matter to either of them?

Their mathematical gifts were certainly to some extent complementary. I can only refer the reader to Littlewood's fascinating account of the way a joint paper was written by Hardy and Ramanujan.[58] It is more difficult to speculate, from this side of history, on the type of interpersonal dyad built by the two collaborators coming from two antipodal cultures. But a few guesses can yet be made.

The son of a modest middle-class family of teachers, Hardy always felt an outsider within the British élite culture of which Oxbridge was the ultimate academic symbol. Contemporaries recall his partiality for non-white students and colleagues, and his shyness and diffidence in dealing with the progeny of the English upper class who these universities were crowded with.[59] He probably saw in Ramanujan aspects of his own self: a marginal man fighting tremendous odds and promising to upset the steady apple-cart of British academia. The Indian provincial, a colonial subject and, like him, a shy, introverted outsider and an underdog, was the mightiest weapon Hardy could have discovered to attack the Establishment with.

The awe-inspiring commitment of Ramanujan to mathematics must have inspired a special respect in Hardy. Hardy, his autobiography explicitly states, never had any intrinsic commitment to mathematics to start with.[60] Along with the advantage of 'mathematically minded' parents, what he grew up with was a substantial quantum of mathematical talent. This was shaped to perfection by his socialization as a scientist and his own sharp perception of the differential advantages of a mathematical career. It is this calculated occupational choice that helped Hardy develop his abiding

[58] Ibid.

[59] This only apparently contradicts Snow's description of Hardy as a scintillating conversationalist. His conversations were hardly expressions of interpersonal warmth or attempts to relate to people. Characterized by a 'grammar' derived from cricket, and tinged by a tendency to shock, they were virtuoso performances which appear to have been desperate attempts to formalize and bind anxiety, even depression.

[60] Hardy, *A Mathematician's Apology*.

allegiance to the discipline. However, this was the allegiance of a professional. On the other hand, Ramanujan had the commitment of a man possessed. Even within his own world, he saw himself as a mystic and a *yogi*, not as a Brahminic preceptor or *acharya*. Such self-transcendence through knowledge a self-conscious rationalist like Hardy could only admire but never duplicate.

Hardy and Ramanujan shared another marginality which I can indicate only imperfectly. One of the distinctions between pure mathematics and the other sciences is the 'restrictions' that pure mathematical creativity imposes on the culture of the discipline. A mathematician can himself subscribe to the dominant style of science in the modern West with its positivist emphases on manipulation, control, prediction and power. But such a style is essentially incompatible with the 'natural' of pure mathematics, which perforce stresses intuitive gestalts and certain aesthetics of form—what Poincairé calls 'the beauty of equations' in another context. Hardy, on the other hand, 'had no faith in intuitions, his or anyone else's.' Yet his writings give one the feeling that at some plane he was sensitive to the importance of the other culture of mathematics with which Ramanujan was linked and which had become recessive at the time.[61]

I doubt if this sensitivity made Hardy conscious of the analogous stylistic differences between the western and the eastern sciences. For Hardy, there was no 'Indian science'. For all his marginality, for him the only science was the one to which he was socialized. Nor could he distinguish between the culture of science, as something that could be parochial and ideologically coloured, and the formal text of science, as something more universal and objective. Nonetheless, Hardy perhaps saw in Ramanujan a personification of the speculative, intuitive, and aesthetic elements which, although recessive in the ultra-positivist culture of western science, were the very stuff of pure mathematics. Hardy's whole upbringing, his professional identity and the scientific norms he had internalized, must all have protested against any admission that

[61] To give an example, he, like Littlewood, sensed that Ramanujan was a mathematical anachronism for two reasons. First, Ramanujan's *forte* was equations and the day of equations, Hardy felt, was over. Second, Ramanujan's weakness was the technology of proof, which had become central to the discipline in his time, and which, as Hardy knew and said, was a relatively inferior and mechanical part of pure mathematics. One suspects that Hardy had at least an intuitive awareness of Ramanujan's self-confident loyalty to the other tradition of mathematics.

such a philosophy of science was possible or legitimate. But he could pay symbolic homage to this philosophy by cultivating and nurturing Ramanujan.

Apart from the fact that his style was closer to the culture of natural philosophy than to that of the experimental sciences, Ramanujan also represented a third culture of science. Early in life he had learnt to use mathematics as an instrument of magical power, extra-sensory perception, and astrological prediction. This use of mathematics could not but arouse anxiety in many scientists because, as they liked to believe, it was on the ruins of this third culture that the modern sciences had been built. Hardy at least consistently denied that Ramanujan had any tendency to equate mathematics with magical intervention in nature and society. One guesses that Ramanujan's 'superstitions' unnerved the aggressively positivist Hardy because they made Ramanujan look irrational—Hardy's identification with his friend was too deep for him to allow that the Indian was anything less than totally rational—and seemed to affirm that the world of mathematics was not as sterilized as the mathematicians would like it to be. In addition to those non-demanding, controllable, and compulsively rule-bound numbers and symbols, Ramanujan's eccentricities seemed to say, that world, too, had its passionate demons.

Thus, through an involved process of intellectualization, Hardy developed a blind spot which, instead of weakening, cemented his bonds with Ramanujan. Hardy was an atheist in a society which was not only puritanic but also conformist. He gradually came to believe that his protégé was an agnostic too. This belief was based on a single statement of Ramanujan's, which Hardy recounted. 'I remember well his telling me (much to my surprise) that all religions seemed to him more or less equally true.'[62] From this one statement, which is actually part of the prescribed daily prayer of a Brahmin, Hardy concluded that Ramanujan had no definite religious beliefs and that he 'saw no particular good, and no particular harm, in Hinduism or any other religion.'[63]

Anyone with even a superficial acquaintance with Hinduism would immediately see the absurdity of this conclusion. Today, the available social anthropology of the Indian civilization has made it unnecessary to stress that the greater Sanskritic culture, while institutionally one of the most rigid, has always been ideologically

[62] Hardy, *Ramanujan*, p. 4.

[63] Ibid. To get a feel of this Hardy, see his *A Mathematician's Apology*.

one of the most tolerant; that it has always rejected the idea of a chosen people with exclusive claims to revealed truth and always disavowed any monopoly of the technology of personal salvation. These were at the time much less obvious. The possibility that a religion could regard other religions, including various forms of atheism, to be different ways towards the same goal, and could even forswear its claims to a superior revealed truth would have been totally incredible to a down-to-earth western sceptic and anti-cleric like Hardy; he would have rejected the idea outright. It is therefore a reasonable guess that Hardy projected his Judaeo-Christian concepts of religion and religiosity into Hinduism and arrived at an image of his protégé that was more congruent with his own needs. On his part, Ramanujan apparently practised with his naïve collaborator what the latter thought Ramanujan to be practising with his Indian friends: 'a quite harmless, and probably necessary, economy of truth'.[64]

Hardy was an outsider in yet another sense; he had strong homosexual needs. Since this is Ramanujan's story, not Hardy's, I shall provide only a brief outline of the personality background Hardy brought to his relationship with his Indian friend.

Margins are meaningful only with reference to the centres to which they are marginal and every marginality respects its corresponding centrality by carrying within it intimations of the latter. Hardy was a marginal man with a strong touch of strangeness about him. But the strangeness, paradoxically, was of a predictable variety; one might even hazard the guess that it was in some ways promoted by aspects of his society and by his upbringing. His early socialization in a middle-class family—his father was a bursar, his mother a teacher—and in a rough, all-male, typical public school, which he deeply hated and where he once almost died, were later on continuously endorsed by the ready-made, over-defined masculinity and the highly compartmentalized sexual identities of the élite culture of Edwardian England. Perhaps this by itself would have been adequate to gradually ease him into the homoerotic culture that thrived in the British public schools, Oxbridge and Bloomsbury, and received part of its sanction from the neo-Hellenism then in vogue. This culture, though not blatant homosexuality of the type that led to the trial and sentence of Oscar

[64] Hardy, *Ramanujan*, p. 4.

Wilde at the turn of the century, had become, in a sexually repressive society, a major organizing principle of intellectual life. Those living the life of the mind, in turn, accepted the homosexual personality type if not as a preferred model of total dissent, at least as a mode of predictable deviation.[65]

To start with, Hardy's homosexual needs might have found expression mainly in the aesthetism of a remarkably handsome man trying to live up to his self-image of an Adonis blessed with perennial youth. Such a self-image might also have received some indirect validation from the culture of Hardy's discipline, the very essence of which, according to one historian of mathematics, is its 'eternal youth'.[66] But as C. P. Snow's sensitive account makes obvious, Hardy was not merely an individualist trying to get through his overt eccentricity and conventional brilliance what he could not get through his mathematics. He was also a lonely man, shy, deeply self-conscious and fearful of company. He never married and never made any significant emotional investment in any woman except for his sister in his middle age. As far as deep relationships were concerned, he lived in a virtually all-male world. His apparently platonic friendship with Littlewood possibly only hid its libidinal content by being seemingly aphysical.

At the same time, Hardy was a person desperately fighting his loneliness and self-consciousness through smart conversation and self-assertiveness, and a narcissist not at peace with his narcissism. He did not like to be photographed, did not tolerate mirrors at home, and whenever he went to a hotel his first move was to cover up the mirrors. He also was a depressive with strong self-destructive tendencies who never forgot that a mathematician was relatively old by the time he was thirty. The culture of homosexuality at Cambridge and the Bloomsbury 'traditions of higher sodomy', as some have called it,[67] gave him only partial protection against the potency-driven tough-mindedness of the outer society and his own complex, tortured self.

A part of Ramanujan's attractiveness to Hardy lay exactly here.

[65] See for instance Michael Holroyd, *Lytton Strachey* (London: Heinemann, 1967), vol. 1. Holroyd's book provides excellent material on the dominant interpersonal style at Oxbridge at that time.

[66] T. Bell, quoted in Ram, *Ramanujan*, pp. 82–3. For identifying the pattern of Hardy's interpersonal relationships, I have partly depended upon our interviews with people who knew him. Some hints are also available in Leonard Woolf, *Sowing* (London: Hogarth, 1961), pp. 110–13.

[67] P. Levy quoted in D. E. Moggridge, *John Maynard Keynes* (Harmondsworth: Penguin, 1976), pp. 10–11.

It was probably not merely the Indian's self-transcendence that impressed Hardy, but also his remarkably integrated self. It was as if Ramanujan, taking advantage of his own history and culture, had found an identity in which femininity, as defined by the western culture, was a valued part. Here was a shy, withdrawn man of 'feminine' build and ways, who knew he conspicuously resembled his mother and grandmother in looks and who shared the family myth that he was a reincarnation of his grandmother. Yet, he retained in him a self-acceptance and serenity which Hardy lacked. True, Hardy perhaps found in his collaborator's personality a classic instance of the phallic woman, the ultimate love object underlying the homosexual's search for feminine men. Being a narcissistic homosexual, he probably also found in the Indian a love object similar to himself, by loving whom he could symbolically get love himself.[68] But the main strength of the relationship was, I suspect, Hardy's discovery in Ramanujan, for the first time, a comfortable, non-threatening figure who did not share the insecure, overly masculinized self of the English social élites of the time. Ramanujan, on his part, with his ambivalent feelings towards an interfering and possessive maternal authority and his emotional distance from his father, found in Hardy for the first time an intervening, caring, close male authority who did not trigger his ambivalence towards all combinations of intervention, care, and proximity.

One area of life where Hardy openly showed his femininity was his intense, uncompromising pacifism.[69] Pacifism was not a proof of his homosexuality but an expression of some of those gender-specific identifications his culture and times had forced him to drive underground. It is nearly impossible to convey today the extent to which pacifism and femininity were psychologically intertwined in Edwardian England. Even a casual knowledge of the lifestyle of the English gentry of the time would suggest that the extroversive jingoism and chauvinism that World War I spawned could be negated, at least at one plane, by aggressively affirming one's 'effete' and 'effeminate' intellectual self and by being a militant pacifist. As if, by being a 'queer' professor in a protected

[68] Otto Fenichel, *The Psychoanalytic Theory of Neurosis* (New York: Norton, 1945), pp. 331, 332.

[69] Snow, *Hardy*. Hardy did not join the British war effort and stayed back at Cambridge because of his pacifist views. This made him unpopular in certain circles, but also enabled him to spend the entire 1914–18 period with Ramanujan when almost all important Cambridge mathematicians were away from the university.

environment like that of Cambridge, one earned the right to defy both the English élite identity, crudely summarised in the image of John Bull, and the plebeian's alternative identity of the Tommy.

Thus, Ramanujan's apparently 'ultra-radical' pacifism, as Hardy called it, gave Hardy's dissent some much-needed psychological support. The Indian's pacifism may or may not have had its ideological roots in the deep fears of aggression and the defensive demands for its total unconditional control which characterize child-rearing in even some of the 'martial' communities in India. But it had its practical ramification in Ramanujan's steadfast refusal to work on any problem connected with the war, even when requested to do so by Littlewood.

This linking of homosexuality, aesthetism, femininity, and pacifism also influenced Hardy's attitude to mathematics. He found applied mathematics a 'useful science', and hence, 'repulsively ugly and intolerably dull'.[70] Many defensive mathematicians considered this attitude to be a form of sickening 'cloistral clowning'—an admission of shock which must have pleased Hardy no end. Others tried to blunt the sharper edge of his dissenting views—and the anxiety they provoked—by accepting Hardy as a 'strange' eccentric whose opinions and prejudices were deliberately assumed poses. They read him as a 'predictably odd' professor on show in an academic reservation. (None of these critics grasped that Hardy had somehow sensed the increasing instrumental use of science to gain power and control over man and nature and to express one's destructive impulses.) As it happened, the ideas of science as play and science as self-exploration were not unknown to Ramanujan. His Brahminic world-view refused to overvalue practical knowledge and knowledge not accompanied by introspection.

Behind all this was Hardy's regard for a certain cultural strength that Ramanujan carried with ease and elegance. Ramanujan belonged to a society that demarcated sexual roles much less rigidly than did the modern West. In many situations his society shuffled or switched the culturally-defined gender-role-specific qualities across gender boundaries. It accepted and even valued Ramanujan's pronounced femininity. Such femininity was after all one of the traditional manifests of spirituality, particularly yogic powers and godliness. The man of religion in India was expected to

[70] Hardy, cited in E. C. Titchmarsh, 'Obituary of G. H. Hardy', *The Journal of the Royal Mathematical Society*, April 1950, pp. 81–8.

be rather more bisexual and rather less concerned with maintaining the this-wordly boundary between the sexes. Ramanujan's self-esteem was born of an awareness of this acceptance of his feminine self. To this extent he served as Hardy's target of conflict-free identification, perhaps even as an ego-ideal. Hardy once wrote, 'I owe more to him [Ramanujan] than to anyone else in the world with one exception, and my association with him is the one romantic incident in my life.'[71] He was perhaps not speaking here of a person with whom he had acted out his passions, but of one who had brought adventure and high drama as well as care, responsibility and tenderness into his life.[72] He was indeed paying homage to a person who had seemingly redeemed his troubled sexual identity.

In this congenial, cosy environment Ramanujan's creativity blossomed. His finest papers were written jointly with Hardy at Cambridge, and he seemed well set to lead the serene life of a Cambridge don. Cambridge, particularly Trinity, was tolerant of all kinds of eccentricities and that helped. Ramanujan managed to live there the life of a devout Brahmin without much difficulty, though not without grumbling. He continued to hate the ways of the heathens and, more understandably, the English weather and English food. Even the bedrooms posed problems. Ramanujan once complained to Prashanta Mahalanobis that the extreme cold forced him to sleep in his overcoat, with a shawl wrapped around him. Mahalanobis went to his bedroom to see whether he had enough blankets, and found that the bed had a number of them but all tucked in tightly, with a bedcover spread over them. Ramanujan did not know that he should turn back the blankets and get into the bed. The bedcover was loose, and he was sleeping under it wearing his overcoat and shawl.

In his spare time, Ramanujan read the *puranas* and all sorts of mystical, theosophical, and astrological stuff, attended popular lectures on the Ramayana and the Mahabharata and, despite the English winter, often wore his cotton *dhoti* and shirt, avoiding shoes and socks. He also cooked his own food, convinced that even

[71] Hardy, *Ramanujan*, p. 2.

[72] The other role perhaps only Littlewood could have played in his life. Whether he played it or not will remain a matter of conjecture. Another of those lonely, brilliant bachelors at Cambridge, Littlewood was a more hardy, masculine specimen who reportedly had even had an illegitimate child.

vegetarian food, when ordered from the college kitchen, was polluted. The one place he enjoyed visiting was the London zoo. He talked about it at great length on his return to India.

He also wrote regularly to his parents, assuring them that he continued to observe orthodox practices. But an even better index of his conformism was his explanation of a bombing raid on Liverpool in which he was caught during the war; he considered it to be God's punishment for drinking a glass of Ovaltine, a beverage he subsequently found contains a small measure of powdered egg. He immediately packed up and left for Cambridge to avoid further temptations.

Ramanujan in Cambridge also apparently became more sensitive to any kind of personal rejection—more touchy, as some of his friends were to describe it later. This touchiness was not new in him and some of his older friends at Madras knew about it, but in England it became more pronounced. He was always socially withdrawn; now he became something of a recluse in his rooms in college. However, one need not read too much into this behaviour; first, he had always tried to isolate himself, to immerse himself in his own orderly world of numbers, and to sterilize his inner world peopled by those for whom he carried conflicting feelings. Secondly, what to outward appearances was a search for solitude in a strange place might also have been the fear of a sociality that presumed new norms and ways of social life. There is some evidence in his letters that Ramanujan tended to make emotional investments in a few relationships, mostly with Indians, and to abstract and reify the rest. In fact, goaded by his loneliness, he later began to have excessive expectations of these Indian friends. For instance, some Indian contemporaries recount how at a dinner given by Ramanujan they suddenly found their host missing. He had actually walked straight out of the house and away from Cambridge as he felt that his guests had not been sufficiently appreciative of his cooking.[73] It is not easy to reconcile such sensitivity with the sturdy ego strength he showed as a lonely discoverer in Madras. He survived on a controlled, ego-syntonic split, which allowed him self-confidence

[73] This is the fourth instance of that peculiar tendency to 'walk out' suddenly on a confusing, and perhaps painful, interpersonal world. Apart from the Andhra Pradesh trip and the Liverpool incident, once, in Madras, he had happened to see a man buying a ticket and boarding a train, and as if in a trance, followed suit. Only after a while did he come back to his senses, wondered what he was doing alone in a train, and returned home.

in one sector and self-doubt in others.[74] Perhaps mathematics was his one conflict-free sphere which remained relatively unaffected by the anxieties he lived with.

The perimeter of Ramanujan's interpersonal world shrank not only due to his fear of being hurt. He had no time for any of the facilities available in the college which could have brought him in touch with other scholars. He did not teach, was not interested in sports (Hardy, for instance, was not able to infect Ramanujan with his passion for cricket), and there is no evidence of his ever having gone to plays and shows (except once when he saw and immensely enjoyed the comedy *Charlie's Aunt*) or interesting himself in the activities of the Indian Majlis (that delightful little club where succeeding generations of scions of the Indian aristocracy picked up their nationalism and radicalism, and imported these, along with their English accents, degrees and blazers, to the seller's market called India). What surely cut off Ramanujan most effectively from other scholars were his food habits. He never dined in college, where he would have encountered other Fellows.[75]

Only in one respect did Ramanujan try to move out of his loneliness and flout his 'culture'. He tried exchanging letters with his wife. Unfortunately, this adventurous assertion of autonomy proved costly. One of those routine quarrels was on between Janaki and her mother-in-law, and Ramanujan's letters, as well as Janaki's to him, were intercepted and destroyed by Komalatammal. South India fifty years ago was not renowned for respecting the privacy of conjugal communication. Nevertheless, even by the standards of that society, a wife could rightfully share with her inlaws letters received from her husband, and a husband too had the right of access to his wife's letters. Yet nobody in the family, certainly not Ramanujan, protested against the manner in which Komalatammal's authority was exercised in this instance. One can only construe it as yet more evidence of the mother's immense power in the family and the son's relapse into conformism after the defiant gesture of writing to his wife.

[74] On segmentalization as a characteristic adaptive mode in the Indian personality, see e.g., Milton Singer, *When a Great Tradition Modernizes* (New York: Praeger, 1972).

[75] This however had its brighter side too. Littlewood has said in another context, 'the thing to avoid, for doing creative work, is above all Cambridge life, with the constant bright conversation of the clever, the wrong sort of mental stimulus'. Littlewood, *A Mathematician's Miscellany*, pp. 69–75.

But Ramanujan suffered all the same. Probably his strong defences against his latent anger towards his mother were now to some extent breached, arousing guilt and self-hatred. What his friends noticed were touches of depression and even melancholia. For many of them this was evidence of homesickness;[76] they had no reason to guess that, in a person so clearly a mother's son, such depression was likely, at some point, to find expression in self-destructive behaviour.[77] They did not know that the thought of death had exercised an eerie fascination over Ramanujan from an early age and that he had shared the astrological 'knowledge' with his mother that he would die young—a prophecy which was, as it turned out, a self-fulfilling one. Nor were these friends sensitive to the fact that in his culture one of the time-worn techniques of expressing anger against one's 'significant others'—and a defence against the moral anxiety generated by such anger—had been to turn upon one's own self.

Other things too may have happened during the year. Circumstantial evidence suggests that it was during the years 1916–17 that Ramanujan came to appreciate for the first time the full magnitude of his wasted efforts.[78] It had gradually become clear to him, mainly due to his exposure in Cambridge, that it was not a matter of a theorem here or an equation there, but that about three-fourths of his earlier work done in India had been a mere rediscovery. He also probably guessed that, given the relationship between physical age and mathematical gifts, he stood no chance whatsoever of making up the lost time. His early poverty had already done its bit. It is true that in most transcendental theories of knowledge, glory attaches as much to those who go through an experience and enrich themselves as to those who cull from the experience externally valued, objective discoveries. It is also true that Ramanujan's culture frequently valued a thing because it was produced by someone in particular, and not a person because he had produced something

[76] Hardy knew better; there is indirect evidence that he tried to mitigate Ramanujan's anxieties by bringing about a rapprochment between Ramanujan and his family. See his letter to S. M. Subramanian, 20 September 1977, in Srinivasan, *Ramanujan*, pp. 69–75.

[77] Moreover, one unconscious motivation for suicide is said to be the suicide's mystical oceanic longing for union with the mother. See Fenichel, *The Psychoanalytic Theory*, pp. 400–1.

[78] The first inkling had come during 1914–15. See, for instance, his letter to Krishna Rao, S. M. Subramanian and S. Narayana Iyer, in Srinivasan, *Ramanujan*, pp. 13–27, 29, 32–3.

in particular. Nonetheless, it must have been painful for him to know that partly he was being adored as a grand eccentric rather than as a person whose work was a benchmark in the history of world mathematics.

All this resulted in a deep personal crisis, and some time in the second half of 1917 Ramanujan attempted suicide by jumping on the path of a train on the London Underground.[79] He escaped death narrowly, but was badly injured. An attempt to commit suicide was a penal offence under British law and Ramanujan was duly picked up for questioning. It was the shy, retiring Hardy who saved him from gaol by bluffing the investigating police officer.[80] Hardy himself had strong suicidal tendencies, expressed later in an unsuccessful and pathetic attempt at suicide and one can well understand the empathy between him and the lonely Indian fighting depression. Ramanujan too confided in Hardy some of the personal problems which had prompted the attempt. Neither his friends nor his family came to know anything of the incident.[81] Hardy was now persuaded that his friend's family had a role, however trivial, to play in the history of mathematics. He began taking a more active interest in the family quarrels of the Iyengars, and once even agreed to act as arbiter.

The attempted suicide should not blind us to the working relationship Ramanujan developed between his worldview and his science. His problem was not with the text of his mathematics, with its philosophical implications, or with the relationship between his field of knowledge and the world in which he lived. And he knew this. After all his greatest professional tragedy, namely his lack of a sound mathematical education, was 'external' to him, according to both Hardy and Littlewood. He was deeply unhappy that much of his work consisted of what could only be called rediscoveries, but it was not the unhappiness of a person who had lost in professional competition. He had a philosophy of life, and the mathematics he

[79] The attempted suicide was first mentioned in public in India fifty years after the event. And the mention immediately provoked protests. See a brief discussion of Indian attitudes to history in the 'Introduction'.

[80] Hardy told him that Ramanujan was an FRS; the officer seemed duly impressed. The fellowship actually came to Ramanujan after some weeks. Years later Hardy learnt that the officer knew this all along, but nonetheless had wanted to be helpful.

[81] Years after the death of Ramanujan, S. Chandrasekhar, the astrophysicist, told Janaki Devi for the first time the cause of the marks on Ramanujan's knee about which she had been worried throughout his life.

knew and the mathematics to which he had exposed himself formed an integrated whole from the point of view of that philosophy. He even knew his priorities. His friend P. C. Mahalanobis once said, 'He [Ramanujan] would have been better pleased to have succeeded in establishing his philosophical theories than in supplying rigorous proofs of his mathematical conjectures.'[82]

What was the content of the self-sufficient relationship Ramanujan forged between his work and environment? Mahalanobis' reminiscences are again pertinent, not only because he knew Ramanujan at Cambridge, but also because as an agnostic, Marxist, mathematical statistician, he can be expected to ignore the magical interpretations which adulatory biographers like Ranganathan try so hard to foist on us. This is what Mahalanobis, the Indian modernist, says about the mathematician, against Hardy's testimony:

> He was eager to work out a theory of reality which would be based on the fundamental concepts of 'zero', 'infinity' and the set of finite numbers.... He sometimes spoke of 'zero' as the symbol of the absolute (*Nirguna Brahman*) of the extreme monistic school of Hindu philosophy, that is, the reality to which no qualities can be attributed, which cannot be defined or described by words and is completely beyond the reach of the human mind; according to Ramanujan, the appropriate symbol was the number 'zero', which is the absolute negation of all attributes. He looked on the number 'infinity' as the totality of all possibilities which was capable of becoming manifest in reality and which was inexhaustible. According to Ramanujan, the product of infinity and zero would supply the whole set of finite numbers. Each act of creation...could be symbolised as a particular product of infinity and zero, and from each such product would emerge a particular individual of which [the] appropriate symbol was a particular finite number.[83]

The social anthropologist may call this only another instance of the ritual neutralization of western science, but it does not need much imagination to guess that, in Ramanujan's life, this also was a search for a state which reduced persons and social relationships to abstractions and contained them within an obsessively ordered universe of ideas. It was an attempt to use mathematical abilities to symbolically freeze the living universe of people into a semi-magically controlled world of numbers.

[82] P. C. Mahalanobis quoted in Ranganathan, *Ramanujan*, p. 80.

[83] Ibid., pp. 82–3.

In May 1917, while still in England, Ramanujan was found to have tuberculosis. Probably the early symptoms had been neglected, for it became obvious after the diagnosis that the illness was at an advanced stage and, given his Brahminic food habits and the existing state of medical knowledge, incurable. At best, drugs, nursing, a careful diet, and change of climate could buy him some time. But even this seemed unlikely because he was unwilling to live in a suitable environment under proper treatment.[84] He placed more reliance on a *kavacha*, a magical guard plate, to protect himself.

His diet was another problem. He had always been finicky about food and dismissive about western food. The illness made things worse. His correspondence with some Indian friends, particularly letters he never expected to be shown to others, reveals that it was not merely a matter of abjuring animal proteins or an inability to adjust to English cooking. It was not even austerity; Ramanujan apparently enjoyed good Indian food, whereas he could not even eat vegetarian western food, such as cheese, bread, butter or jam (in spite of his misleading pet name in Cambridge, 'Dear Jam'). One suspects that, as with the western lifestyle as a whole, English cuisine too was entirely outside his frame of reference.[85] He was a culturally self-sufficient man with strong psychological defences and neither his environment nor any form of rationality except his own had easy entry into his life. On the other hand, though he did not seem to recognize it, his culinary skills were less formidable than his mathematical ones. The price he paid for his failure to realize this, even after he had tuberculosis, proved heavy.

[84] On how difficult a patient Ramanujan was, see Francis Dewsbury's letter to G. H. Hardy, 22 December 1919, Trinity Papers. Hardy suffered too. Once in a London hospital, when cucumbers were not in season, Ramanujan wanted cucumbers, of all things, to eat. Hardy got him some, nobody knows from where.

[85] See Ramanujan's letter to his friend A. S. Ramalingam, 19 June 1918 and Ramalingam's reply of 23 June 1918, MSS a 94 (1–6), Trinity Papers. Also see Ramalingam's letter to Hardy of 23 June 1918, ibid., which suggests that Ramanujan would eat plain boiled rice sprinkled with red pepper or hot pickles rather than any English vegetarian food.

One should, however, remember that if Ramanujan's fads tell us something about the distinctive pattern of his orality because they centred round food, they also underline Ramanujan's obsessional and compulsive defences. True, they were included by his culture within the range of normal adaptive responses; but the fact that certain behaviour patterns are considered normal in some cultures and abnormal in others does not, by itself, deprive these patterns of their psychodynamic content.

It was pointless now to linger on in England. Ramanujan himself, his friends and doctors, all agreed that he should return to India. At some level they all knew that the death sentence had been passed and it was better to be close to one's relatives and to one's 'home'.

Did he during his last days in England regret having to leave? Or ponder over the question which hounds his biographers even now, whether his trip to England was justified? Hardy was sure that the trip was necessary and Ramanujan would have died an unhappier death if he had not moved out of India.[86] Perhaps he was right. But did Ramanujan look at it that way? It is true that he had vaguely thought of returning to England and left behind some of his personal belongings. But must he not have felt in his lonelier moments that the uterine warmth within which he had pursued his mathematics during the early part of his life was, if not more rewarding, at least more real than the alien world of Cambridge? The answer may well be 'yes'.

The semi-rural Kumbakonam, after producing the only great man in its long history, has relapsed into somnolence, assimilating Ramanujan into a local legend only partly tainted by life. Similarly, to the shy, provincial Brahmin who had made good in the company of the great and was now on his death bed, his five years in England must have seemed as ephemeral and mythical as any memory of grandeur. His English sojourn had merely torn him asunder from his gods, his way of life, and his simplicity and autonomy. In the process, science may have gained, but he had certainly lost.

IV

Ramanujan returned to Madras in March 1919. At first he was happy to be back with his wife, his relatives and friends, and his beloved Tamil food. Though bed-ridden, he regularly received

[86] I doubt if one can say as confidently as Hardy did that Ramanujan's English trip made him, professionally, what he was. One wonders if it ever struck Ramanujan that out of the roughly eight areas in which he worked (hypergeometric series, partitions, definite integrals, elliptical integrals, highly composite numbers, fractional differentiation, and number theory) it was his work on fractional differentiation which perhaps came closest to being a major breakthrough in mathematics. This work was done entirely in India, before he left for England. Most mathematicians claim that Ramanujan's weak point was his work on number theory, despite his image of being mainly a number theorist.

visitors and friends and tried to enliven his company by a form of grim wit or black humour. But soon he had to face a new personal crisis, which also happened to be one of his last. It started with Komalatammal's efforts to send away Janaki to her parents' home. According to the mother's reading of the wife's horoscope, at least a temporary separation of the couple was necessary for the scientist to survive. The reading may have been a cover for the Indian folk wisdom which forbade sexual intercourse for those suffering from tuberculosis. But Ramanujan was, we have seen, a particularly sensitive person. He might not have been able to diagnose his mother's behaviour for what it perhaps also was: an attempt to express her latent jealous wish to possess the son all by herself, without feeling guilty about eliminating her rival. But he must have sensed, through the subtle communication that goes on in such close-knit relationships, that something more than his health was involved in the horoscope-reading: that his mother was trying to monopolize him by removing Janaki from the scene.

One does not know if there was any anger and if it triggered off the repressed anger that he had once turned against himself in the London Underground. After all, with his blind faith in astrology and expertise in palmistry, he may have seen in his mother's reading of the future the crueller hand of fate speaking through a temporal authority. He may even have felt guilty about resenting his mother's prescription. There is circumstantial evidence that Ramanujan's reaction was a mixture of all three. In any case, Komalatammal had not reckoned with her son's hidden strengths. This time, Ramanujan refused to send Janaki away to her parents.

Apparently, despite his adoration of his mother—even during his illness in England it was her that he mainly missed—and his sense of duty towards his brother Lakshmi Narasimhan, his patience with them was wearing thin. His wife at least feels that he wanted them to go away to Kumbakonam where his father, youngest brother, and grandfather were living. Janaki is a biased witness, but in this instance she may not be entirely wrong. Ramanujan always feared interpersonal conflicts and the chances of such conflict increased enormously with not only the two self-willed women but also the flamboyant Lakshmi Narasimhan living under the same roof. Moreover, Ramanujan's English period might not have made him a modern man, but it had exposed him to norms that legitimized some of his deeper inclinations. He was now freer with his wife in the presence of others, would constantly call her by ringing his bedside bell, and occasionally pull her towards him with the crook of the walking stick which he kept near his bed. He would even sometimes say that had he taken Janaki with him to England, he would not have contracted tuberculosis. In other ways too, he became less inhibited with his wife. He began teaching her the elements of science and using her as a secretary. Her job was to remind him of his various unfinished mathematical problems by using simple verbal tags which he provided her with.

In January 1920, Ramanujan was taken to Chetpeth, a suburb of Madras. His condition was deteriorating fast and it was felt that the air at Chetpeth would be beneficial. Others in the entourage were Janaki, his mother, grandmother, and Lakshmi Narasimhan. According to several accounts, it was now a withdrawn, depressed, and sullen Ramanujan who faced death. His black humour persisted, but the intense and penetrating look in his eyes betrayed the acute mental suffering and impotent rage of a man living under sentence of death, convinced that fate was against him. 'Namagiri sent me to England', he sometimes said, 'but she did not give me good health.' His anger, usually directed inwards, now became more outer-directed and free-floating. It set the emotional tone of his life and his strongest defences against it crumbled. Once in a while he would chew the thermometer put into his mouth or stealthily walk down to the kitchen and mix up or scatter the provisions on the floor. If Janaki stood at a distance, he would burst with anger and begin to throw things at her. He also often lost his temper with his mother and Lakshmi Narasimhan.

His last days were not happy. Poverty had dogged his steps all his life. Now he had money, but the culture of poverty stayed with him. He would get irritated with his brother for squandering his money or for being too stingy with it, and get agitated if he felt that he was not getting a proper account of the family's expenditure. Sometimes he said that, according to his own reading of his horoscope, if the family could somehow gift gold sovereigns equivalent to his weight, he would be cured; sometimes he assured Janaki that whether he lived or died, she would never again be short of money. The traditional image of tuberculosis did not help matters. It was called a *rajroga*, the disease of kings, and it required expensive treatment befitting its kingly nature; the emphasis was on rich food, change of air, and long stays in expensive sanatoria.

If Ramanujan was anxious about money, so was his family. Perhaps some of them were eager to make the best of the last few good days given to the family. While Ramanujan lay dying, they began to remove the few pieces of furniture and valuables from the house, anticipating his death. At one point, Janaki says, her brother had to call in the police to stop this.

Ramanujan's religious beliefs no longer provided complete protection against this collapsing world and the long, painful and, at times, ugly process of dying. One friend suggests that he even partly lost his faith in his favourite deities and considered them devils. His wife, too, feels that his faith in Namagiri wavered in his last days.[87]

Yet, one must hasten to add, Ramanujan simultaneously showed evidence of serene resignation and acceptance of 'fate'. As if, at one plane, he was still convinced that he should be tolerant of the force that had once given him success, but was now working against him. Until the end, he remained steadfast to his principles, showing the same single-minded, purposive unity of life-style that had characterized his whole career. As during his illness in England, he refused to take non-vegetarian protein food in spite of medical advice. His interest in psychic phenomena, astrology, precognition, and mystic mathematics was undiminished. And to the very end he remained an active mathematician—exploring, speculating, innovating. He would often work, against his doctors' advice, until one or two at night, trying to complete as many things as possible before he died. His free-floating aggression, which made him unwelcoming towards his friends in his last days, also helped him to snatch time to produce some of his finest creative work.[88]

Srinivasa Ramanujan died on 26 April 1920. He was then thirty-two, a ripe old age in a country which at the time had a life expectancy of less than thirty. Mathematicians too, Hardy affirms, are quite old at thirty. But not everyone is an Indian or a mathematician; in that case one might say he died rather young.

[87] It is possible that Hardy's faith in Ramanujan's rational agnosticism was partly the result of some comment made by the latter along these lines from his sick-bed. But in some systems of faith, anger against specific gods and goddesses does not signify loss of faith. After all, even in England, Ramanujan had tried to cure his tuberculosis with a *kavacha*.

[88] G. N. Watson, for instance, says (Valedictory address to the London Mathematical Society, quoted in Ram, *Srinivasa Ramanujan*, p. 72), 'Ramanujan's discovery of the mock-theta functions makes it obvious that his skill and ingenuity did not desert him at the oncoming of his untimely end. As much as any of his earlier works, the mock-theta functions are an achievement sufficient to cause his name to be held in lasting remembrance.'

V

Srinivasa Ramanujan did not live the life of a torn genius trying to reconcile science and culture, fighting the spectre of alienation, or desperately protecting a modern self against a traditional environment. His is the story of a conservative but integrated scientist, for whom ancient meanings and modern knowledge were one. I do not deny the psychological conflicts that dogged him throughout life, but they only marginally involved the content of his work. In fact, one marvels at the remarkably consistent way in which Ramanujan used mathematics to symbolize his inner states, without either damaging his mathematics or getting pre-occupied with the political or social implications of his success.[89] There were a number of reasons for this.

In the first place, Ramanujan's inner conflicts arose mainly from his attempts to cope with an unkind world outside, not with an alien self. He never internalized the Enlightenment culture of science;[90] traditions, whether expressed in strange customs or in mystic mathematics, were part of his innermost experience; he did not have to be apologetic about them. Nor did he seriously try to prove the modernity of his religious ideas, to Indianize western science, or to use his professional success to counter feelings of inadequacy.[91] Ramanujan was no conflicted proselytizer like Jagadis Chandra Bose, who tried to replicate in science the attempts of Swami Vivekananda and Shri Aurobindo to 'carry the message' of India to the West and that of the West to India. All these eastern Indians were sensitive to the West's political and cultural dominance, and their missionary zeal grew out of their sense of humiliation. Ramanujan was truer to Hindu orthodoxy; he neither sought any place in the metropolitan culture of knowledge nor showed any missionary passion.

This self-confidence was expressed in various ways. G. H. Hardy and J. E. Littlewood, when they said that Ramanujan had no

[89] Even Suresh Ram, in his otherwise naïve biography, recognizes that the 'majesty' of Ramanujan's search for self-definition 'lay in the harmony of his inner and outer beings', Ram, *Srinivasa Ramanujan*, p. 76.

[90] Ramanujan never said so, but seemed to draw a line between the content and the context of modern science. The former to him was part of the eternal verities; the latter peripheral to his concerns.

[91] He was not oblivious of the political and social changes taking place in India. But he kept his mathematics unburdened by his political or social beliefs. As if religion was the only load his work could carry.

clear concept of proof and showed little interest in its methodology, had in mind not merely the intellectual limitations of their Indian friend. They were also vaguely aware of Ramanujan's sturdy reliance on his own intuitive powers and insights.[92] For example, Ramanujan at Cambridge must have come to know that the days of formulae were more or less over and that his style of mathematics had become *passé*.[93] His friends in the university also tried to acquaint him with the new concerns of the discipline. But in success as in failure he remained true to his own version of mathematics. Though he made half-hearted attempts to adapt his style to the culture of modern mathematics, it was obvious to all who knew him that he could be neither easily taught nor formally educated. At most, he would learn on his own the things that interested him and were of value to him.

Ramanujan once reportedly said—and this would have deeply hurt his agnostic benefactor Hardy—'An equation has no meaning for me unless it expresses a thought of God.'[94] The statement, if his, was less a criterion of self-assessment than an acknowledgement of his God-given gifts. All his life he lived with a serene faith in his own supernatural precognitive powers and in the sacred origin of his mathematics. He was exposed early to his family's appraisal of him as a mystic genius, and his Indian friends mostly validated this estimate. His later exposure to western and Indian sceptics did not alter the self-image, which remained the traditional image of a *yogi*. He did not fancy himself to be an *acharya*, a Brahminic preceptor, but a man of superlative extra-sensory powers—a man possessed.[95]

There was also Ramanujan's strange love–hate relationship with the culture of modern science itself. Overtly, he did not fight the culture; he bypassed it. Covertly, he refused to collaborate with it.

[92] For instance, Hardy, *Ramanujan*, pp. 4–5. See the section on Ramanujan in Littlewood, *A Mathematician's Miscellany*, esp. pp. 86–88.

[93] See his letter to S. M. Subramanian, 7 January 1915, quoted in Srinivasan, *Ramanujan*, vol. 1, p. 21.

[94] R. Srinivasan, quoted in Ranganathan, *Ramanujan*, p. 88. Many western scientists have claimed that God is a mathematician; in the world of Ramanujan, mathematics was a system which integrated God, nature, and man.

[95] It must already have become obvious to clinically minded readers that Ramanujan's ego ideal was the mystic union with divinity often sought after by, apart from mystics, schizophrenic patients. This is significant in the context of his early object relations which also were, in many ways, consistent with the family dynamics of schizophrenics. However, more important was the manner in which this dynamic was integrated within the range of a particular, slightly esoteric, form of normality in his community.

This ambivalence deserves a digression on two differences between the modern western and the traditional Indian attitudes to science. First, a word on the more obvious of them.

The Indian tradition of science may be on the whole less positivist than its modern counterpart. But the tradition has been more open to certain empirical realities that Baconian science has come to acknowledge only reluctantly in recent years. Thus, many schools of Indian thought admit freely that science can be a product of a person's intuitive, infantile, non-rational self, and that the problems of the social responsibility of scientists can intrude into the very text of science. On the other hand, in Ramanujan's time, the operational principles of scientific creativity and the mainstream philosophy of science had become disjunctive. Creative science was often hypothetico-deductive, coloured by aesthetics and speculative thinking, and demanded personality resources compatible with these characteristics. The dominant philosophy of science, however, feared the cultural and psychological determination of science and favoured a crude form of inductive empiricism.

Hence, when exposed to western science for the first time as an adult, Ramanujan was caught between two powerful sets of attitudes. One agreed with what most scientists were saying but only a few were doing; the other agreed with what very few scientists were saying but at least the creative ones were doing. He therefore borrowed his philosophy of science from his inherited world-view to legitimize his work. Otherwise there was little in the mainstream philosophy to give meaning to his mathematics. (Threatened by the 'odd' way his Indian friend resolved this issue, Hardy re-read Ramanujan, as we know, as a self-consistent, agnostic English don. In his own case, the same manoeuvre did not help the troubled English mathematician overmuch. Facing the same contradiction, Hardy assumed the style of dissent of a modern European intellectual. Yet many of his 'saner' contemporaries promptly decided that he was an eccentric clown.)

Second, pure mathematics is unashamedly non-empirical, and the 'operative philosophy' of pure mathematics is comfortable with a rationalist attitude. With the growth of experimental science and empiricism, this rationalism was to some extent marginalized in the West. On the other hand, the Indian theories of knowledge, for whatever reason, maintained some openness to such rationalism, and at least, allowed some scepticism towards the positivist emphases on application, experimentation, control, prediction and testability in the 'real' world of the senses. Such openness might have crippled the hard sciences, but it certainly nurtured mathematical talents.

Naturally, Ramanujan's science did not try to be socially useful. Nor did it involve anything as non-Brahminic as experimentation, observation and proof. His was rather the clean, speculative non-dualism that has dominated Indian thought since about the eighth century. Two beliefs associated with this philosophy—the belief that contradictions represent aspects of the same indivisible truth, and the belief that 'true' knowledge would reveal the entire universe to be a unified living system—justified the mystical feelings of uterine, cosmic oneness frequently associated with scientific creativity, particularly with the *satori* experience of creative moments. Such feelings and such moments were not unknown to Ramanujan.

That is what gave Ramanujan the esoteric touch that seemed so attractive to the scientists of the inter-war years. Even his hard-headed collaborators could not remain immune to this charm. In his later years a slightly embarrassed Hardy rejected as unjustified sentimentalism the following paean to his friend's exotic appeal.

> It [Ramanujan's work] has not the simplicity and the inevitableness of the very greatest work; it would be greater if it were less strange. One gift it has which no one can deny, profound and invincible originality. He would probably have been a greater mathematician if he had been caught and tamed a little in his youth; he would have discovered more that was new, and that, no doubt, of greater importance. On the other hand, he would have been less of a Ramanujan, and more a European professor, and the loss might have been greater than the gain.[96]

However, as long as Ramanujan lived, Hardy had not recanted. It was the earlier, 'sentimental' Hardy who validated Ramanujan's self-identity and personal faith.

These issues of self-definition, autonomy, and creativity can be approached from another vantage point. That approach is summed up in two specific questions. Why did Ramanujan's orthodoxy

[96] G. H. Hardy, 'Notice'. It is possible to argue that the younger Hardy was more perceptive; the later Hardy was merely trying to make Ramanujan look a fully rational man, just as the latter's Indian admirers tried to make him look an occult magician.

never interfere with his creativity, while the modern idea systems like nationalism and Brahmoism could not check the intellectual disintegration of Jagadis Chandra Bose? Does the difference between the two men tell us something about the individual adaptations to the culture of modern science which individual scientists have attempted in India?

Seemingly, the answer to the first question is simple. Ramanujan died young; he could not grow into an entrenched symbol of Indian supremacy over the West or become a public attraction in his country. He did not get involved in organizational activities, remained outside the academic bureaucracy, and bypassed the ornate status hierarchy of the Indian educational system that engulfed many of his contemporaries. But all this, while obviously true, is only part of the story. One must look deeper for a full answer to this question. I shall try to do so by comparing his self-definition with that of Bose.

One difference between the two men was their area of study; the content of pure mathematics is patently less influenced by cultural and personal forces than most others and is less open to defensive projections. Its abstract, non-empirical structure is so formidable, and its ready-made delibidinized form so severe, that most cultural or personal themes lose their particularist edge when they enter the text of mathematics. It is literally the purest of sciences.

This purity has another source. Both modern physics and biology share with the social sciences the problem of 'contamination' from observation: the more detailed and intensive the study of a scientific phenomenon, the greater the likelihood of its being altered in the process of investigation. Particle physics, which among the hard sciences has most explicitly recognized this relationship between the observer and the observed, also suggests something else: that it is possible partly to transcend this indeterminacy only in the mathematical theory of a phenomenon.[97] In this respect, pure mathematics may be the closest to an observer-free science.

As a corollary there are certain specific demands which pure mathematics makes on the scientist's personality. Evidence has it that creative mathematicians and mathematical physicists have comparatively more impersonal identifications and tend to use withdrawal as a solution to their interpersonal problems.[98] In this respect, there is a fit

[97] Max Born, 'Man and the Atom', in Morton Grodzins and Eugene Rabinowitch (eds.), *The Atomic Age* (New York: Basic, 1963), pp. 590–601.

[98] For example, Roe, *The Making of a Scientist*; also D. C. McClelland, 'The

between the early environment that produces pure mathematicians and a Brahminic socialization. The latter, too, promotes a certain diffusion of identifications, encourages the use of the defences of isolation, denial, and intellectualization, and glorifies withdrawal from the profane world of real persons and events as a spiritual achievement.[99] Here is at least one reason why the traditional Indian ideal of mastery over self and the struggle to abstract oneself from worldly goods, instinctual needs, emotions, and social relationships, have found their supreme expression in mathematical creativity.[100]

This was one of Ramanujan's main advantages. Bose was working in what was then the unsure and inchoate disciplinary contexts of plant physiology and biophysics. He did not sense that while his vitalistic concept of science, rooted in the Upanishadic theory of life, could provide a valid philosophy of science, it could neither furnish ready-made scientific theories nor foreclose on alternative explanatory models.

Ramanujan's other advantage was his self-contained Brahminism which did not make overbearing demands on the content of his mathematics. Such demands were mainly confined to his personal life. The traditional Brahminic worldview had its own concept of science and it cared little for any other. Confident of itself, it also permitted a person to segment his life and maintain a certain distance from the non-traditional roles he might have had to take on for reasons of survival. Bose's semiticized Brahmoism could not permit this distance between what a person did and what he valued. Brahmoism was, after all, a rebellion against exactly this role diffusion and 'amoral' segmentation of life in India's modern sector.

In addition, the ideological intensity of Bengali high culture induced Bose to see the old and the new, the indigenous and the borrowed, as directly in opposition. The Bengali upper castes had always been aware of their peripheral status in India and they

---

Calculated Risk: An Aspect of Scientific Performance', in C. W. Taylor and F. Barron (eds.), *Scientific Creativity: Its Recognition and Development* (New York: Wiley, 1963).

[99] Spratt, *High Culture*; Carstairs, *The Twice Born*; Gardner Murphy, *In the Minds of Men* (New York: Basic, 1953).

[100] I have in mind here not only the mathematical achievements of ancient Indians, but also the comparative performances in contemporary India of, say, the mathematically-oriented scientist, on the one hand, and the applied scientist, on the other.

sought to consolidate their new salience, acquired through the colonial connection, by being belligerently Brahminic and modern. The efforts of the Bengali élite, the *bhadralok*, to define nationalism as essentially a modernist movement, rooted in rediscovered traditions, was a part of the same story.[101] The Bengali version of Indian nationalism was in more direct touch with modernity and was more aware of modern science. Its demands were personal *and* scientific, and it insisted on greater consistency between the private and the public. All these influences—Brahmoism, Bengali high culture, and nationalism—forced on Bose a more clear-cut decision between the traditional and the modern than on Ramanujan.

Finally, the absence of pronounced feelings of national and personal inadequacy allowed Ramanujan to use his fluid, unself-conscious, projective animism for the purpose of self-transcendence. Mathematics to him *was* a personal medium and he was very definitely concerned with his country's fate. But the former did not become the expression of the other. Bose's science, on the other hand, was coloured by the psychology of subjecthood and feelings of personal inadequacy. It allowed him neither enough autonomy nor flexibility. Unlike the European scientists of the age of faith and other Indian scientists more immersed in traditions, Bose in his science could not take advantage of the integrative strengths and range of his personality. Ramanujan was narrower in his politics and personal concerns but enjoyed the advantage of a less encumbered personality which had a wider range of fantasy life and symbolizing capacity.

This was unavoidable. For the very sensitivities that made Bose creative also made him sensitive to his colonial status. If his nationalism was a straitjacket, it was one he could not help wearing. One could even speculate that it was this sensitivity to issues of dominance and submission, and not any actual interference in the processes of research, which was often the main contribution of colonialism to intellectual decay. Ramanujan, less aggressively nationalistic and yet confident in his orthodoxy, escaped this double bind. And, if one could define intellectual autonomy as indifference to issues of dominance and submission, he was certainly the more autonomous of the two. Bose's modern

[101] For a brief discussion of some of the sociopolitical reasons of the sharper opposition, see Ashis Nandy, 'The Making and Unmaking of Political Cultures in India', *At the Edge of Psychology* (Delhi: Oxford University Press, 1979), pp. 47–69.

nationalism bound him too closely to the West, both in admiration and in hatred.

However, one could also define intellectual autonomy as a continuous search for new elements of identity which could be integrated within an indigenous frame, without humiliating the recipients, to allow the pursuit of a culture's distinctive version of universal knowledge. Perhaps at that plane, Bose, in his defeat, is a more relevant seeker of autonomy in the history of Indian science.

VI

A society survives by ensuring some consistency between the early developmental profile and the adult experiences of its members. In fact, its strength is this consistency in the life cycle of a large number of people. On the other hand, it is by stretching this consistency that a person gives meaning to whatever is new or disturbing to him and his society. If by using the symbolic repertoire of the culture, he succeeds in making this meaning authoritative or, at least, acceptable, he is recognized as creative. If he fails to do so, he is identified as an outsider.

So, when one discusses Ramanujan's response to his culture's definitions of authority, knowledge, inquiry and uniqueness, one must also refer to the new meaning he gave to science in his culture by stretching these definitions. This involved using the symbols and fantasies that were available to him as source materials for creative science in the twilight zone of his personality.

I have already said that the conflict between old and new in his society only marginally affected Ramanujan's developmental history. His adult experiences did sometimes contradict his early learning and selfhood. But the contradiction never deeply touched the core of his self. Perhaps the conflicts he suffered from did not require public resolution through ideological formalization. They demanded a re-enactment of early relationships through a more private rearrangement of his armoury of defences. Ramanujan's first authorities were a weak, passive, aloof father who threw into relief a possessive, overprotective, seductive mother. And he learnt early to cope with the passions these twin authorities aroused—by reifying, isolating, and systematizing the microcosm so as to be totally absorbed in the macrocosm. It was this crypto-schizoid dynamic that remained the fulcrum of his personality, in conformity and in defiance.[102] In his peak experiences he consistently used the symbols associated with motherhood and cognate ideas of unity, benevolence and magical power.

As in much of India, the experience of the mother as the most intimate authority figure, and of the father as a distant, intruding stranger were not unknown in Tamil culture. In it, critical sectors of life were presided over by female deities; and concepts of power, survival, nurture, and nature were inextricably linked with mothering. Much of the richness of one's fantasy life also derived from one's first object relation. And any access to one's deeper self or any regression at the service of the ego—as some psychoanalysts may like to describe the process—also led to the nuclear conflicts involving one's initial womanly authority. Creativity in such a world had to presume the capacity to exploit one's first projective identification with a cosmic maternal principle, one's feminine self, and one's concepts of defiance of a feminine authority and the reparation that had to be made for the defiance.

This play of authority, dissent and atonement was also a matter of psycho-ecological balance. In a culture where power seemed to reside outside the individual and nature often appeared as an absolute but fickle tyrant, the overlap between the individual's experiences of mothering and the community's experiences of nature's mothering was up to a point unavoidable. This overlap gave a different kind of sanction to the Indian man who sought to exploit his feminine self for creative purposes. It allowed him to defend himself against his fears of maternal vengefulness, and his basic distrust of the world of emotions and senses, through reified two-dimensional thinking.[103] It was mainly his mother's meta-science that gave meaning to Ramanujan's work. His 'insane vision' of creativity bypassed the world of modern science and mobilized his deepest and most androgynous self, for he had to master an animistic environment magically, to be in peace with and make

[102] Note that despite Ramanujan's pronounced obsessive traits, his personal experiences look remarkably similar to the family environment often found associated with schizophrenia in the West. See for example some of the papers in G. Handel (ed.), *The Psychosocial Interior of the Family* (London: Allen and Unwin, 1968). Yet, his family was not particularly atypical. This may be an indicator not of the society's obsessive or schizoid character, but of its ability to integrate certain obsessive and schizoid responses within its range of normality.

[103] Carstairs, *The Twice Born*, has dealt indirectly with this issue.

sense to himself. It is in this odd sense that Ramanujan's philosophy of science was unitary and he was one of the last representatives of the age of faith in science.[104]

[104] Interestingly, the same fantasies had parochialized Bose's science. For that matter, even the conflicts of Newton as he stood between the older magical science and the new science, and between two ages were, apart from the altogether different standards of creativity that he set, not very different. For a brief analysis of Newton from this point of view, see L. S. Feuer, *The Scientific, Intellectual and Sociological Origins of Modern Science* (New York: Basic, 1963).

Index

THE ILLEGITIMACY OF NATIONALISM

Rabindranath Tagore and the Politics of Self

Contents

Preface

This essay is a product of my interest in the psychological biography of the modern nation-state in India. It was while working on various contemporary constructions of the state in the minds of Indians that I first became aware of the crucial role Indian nationalism has played in these constructions.

The idea of the modern nation-state entered Indian society in the second half of the nineteenth century, riding piggy-back on the western ideology of nationalism. Most nationalist leaders in India, as in other such societies, were then convinced that the absence of a proper nation-state and proper nationalist sentiments were major lacunae in Indian society and indices of its backwardness. To those leaders, India's earlier experiences with large indigenous state-systems were, if not a liability in the contemporary world, at least irrelevant.

According to Sudipta Kaviraj, Bhudev Mukhopadhyaya (1827–1894), a political thinker and educationist from Calcutta, was the first to formally identify this 'fatal flaw' in Indian civilization. Bhudev was not merely a staunch nationalist, he was one of the first aggressive national-integrationists of India. Like many of his generation, he wanted to make 'constructive' use of the British presence in India and he saw English education as the principal means by which Indians would be freed of their irrationalities and be knit into a single cohesive political and cultural community. Being a Bhadralok from Calcutta, Mukhopadhyaya was a direct product and the indirect beneficiary of the colonial culture of the mid-nineteenth century which had taken a clear stand on the ability of Indians—mired in their village society, devious and, when not greedy and corrupt, impractical and otherworldly—to run a proper modern state. He was unlikely to feel close to the memory of the large states which had often dotted the Indian landscape. He would have learned to look upon such states as hopelessly feudal and terribly oppressive in comparison with the British-Indian state.

Perhaps such a view was bound to emerge and gain strength in a subjugated society confronting a highly successful imperial power and trying to discover the secret of its success. Yet, strangely enough, by the early 1920s a semblance of ambivalence towards the idea of a monocultural nation-state and towards nationalism itself had appeared within the Indian freedom movement. And this ambivalence was often expressed by some of the most important figures in the movement, by those very persons who could be considered the major builders of India's national identity. Evidently, by then, some of them had found out—having acquired the confidence to do so—the cultural and moral impact of nationalism, not only on its opponents but even on its champions. These sceptics also began to associate nationalism with modern colonialism's record of violence and, while they continued to view an anti-imperialist stand as being an almost sacred responsibility, they refused to accept the western idea of nationalism as being the inevitable universal of our times. Some Indian thinkers, political activists, and public opinion-makers sought to marginalize such critics by treating them either as sophisticated but apolitical traditionalists, bewildered by disturbing social and political changes, or as ideologues who had borrowed an odd version of universalism from western radical thought. Either way, any reservations about nationalism were regarded by many as a deliberate or unwitting compromise both with western imperialism and native obscurantism.

On the other hand, those who took a position against nationalism were themselves divided. To a majority of them nationalism appeared to be a premodern concept that had re-appeared as a pathological by-product of global capitalism. Once humanity overcame the seductive charms of this vestigial medievalism and owned up the Enlightenment concept of freedom, they expected this form of self-expression of nationalities to wither away. In its place they expected a new, enlightened, secular universalism to emerge as the cultural basis for a future One World, which would be free of all ethnic and territorial loyalties. A small minority of Indians, however, became what can only be called dissenters among dissenters. They regarded nationalism as a by-product of the western nation-state system and of the forces of homogenization let loose by the western worldview. To them, a homogenized universalism, itself a product of the uprootedness and deculturation brought about by British colonialism in India, could not provide an alternative to nationalism. Their alternative was a distinctive civilizational concept of universalism embedded in the tolerance encoded in various traditional ways of life in a highly diverse, plural society.

This essay tells the story of one such dissenter among dissenters, Rabindranath Tagore (1861–1941), whose reservations about nationalism led him to take up a public position against it, and who built his resistance on India's cultural heritage and plural ways of life. I also touch upon similar ambivalences in two other nationalist thinkers of India, to show that Tagore's dissent was not idiosyncratic; it was latent in others, too. In fact, it was based on a certain reading of Indian civilization and actual political processes in India, and on a particular native meaning given to the political struggle against imperialism.

Tagore's dissent, the reader will find out, did not develop in a unilinear fashion: he went through contradictions and loops within loops in his voyage towards ideological clarity. He did not, after all, claim to be a systematic political thinker; he was a poet, articulating some of the unspoken concerns of Indian public consciousness at that time. I suggest that these contradictions and digressions can be partly understood by viewing Tagore in the context of the politics of culture in his times.

One methodological point: this essay is written in the form of a simple narrative. Despite many temptations, I have tried to avoid as far as possible what could be called technical interpretations of texts as well as—this was the more difficult part—personalities. I hope that young Indians confronting and perhaps resisting the violent emergence of a steam-rolling modern nation-state in their country will discover in the essay an useful construction of the past.

This study has grown out of a paper written for a conference held at Karachi, 14–18 January 1989. It was sponsored by the World Institute of Development Economics Research of the United Nations University and organized by Tariq Banuri and Frédérique and Stephen Marglin. I am beholden to the participants for their suggestions and criticisms, particularly to Carol Breckenridge for her detailed comments. Subsequently, very useful suggestions came in from Tariq Banuri, Girdhar Rathi, Sisir Das, Meenakshi Mukherji, T.N. Madan, and Punam Zutshi. They, too, have shaped the present version of the essay significantly.

This work could not have been done but for the research assistance given to me by Heather Harlan, Amit Das and Roshna

Kapadia during 1987–9. I also gratefully acknowledge the help of Veena Das, with whom the first half of Section IV was first written; Sajal Basu, who introduced me to a number of sources not previously known to me; Frédérique and Stephen Marglin, who persuaded me to do the essay in the first place; and Sujit Deb, who gave me excellent biblographic help.

A part of the work was done at the Woodrow Wilson International Centre for Scholars, Washington. The Centre of course is not responsible for the views expressed herein. Another part of the essay was presented at the Delhi Group of Psychoanalysis and gained much from the comments of Shib Kumar Mitra, Ashok Guha, Ashok Nagpal and, especially, Indrani Guha.

Three conventions regarding the spelling of proper names in the essay should be explained here. First, to distinguish between persons with the same surname, first names have occasionally been used, as is commonly done in India and occasionally in the West, as with Galileo and Leonardo. Second, wherever a person is widely known by a certain English form of his or her name I have retained it. Elsewhere, standard conventions have been followed: thus, Tagore and not Thakur; but Bankimchandra Chattopadhyay, not Bankim Chandra Chatterji. Third, for wider communicability, diacritic marks have been avoided and Bengali proper names and their phonetics have been only partially Sanskritized. Thus Bimala, not Vimala; Baradasundari, not Borodasundori.

A. N.

One
The Ideology

Nationalism *versus* Patriotism

During the last hundred and fifty years, Afro-Asian reformers and thinkers have tried to reconcile three basic sets of contradictions or oppositions: that between the East and the West; that between tradition and modernity; and that between the past and the present. For some, the contradictions overlap; for others, they are orthogonal. To many, traditions and the past seem synonymous; to others, surrounded by tradition, they are very much a part of the present, politically cornered but nonetheless alive and kicking. To some, the East is by definition traditional; to others, important aspects of eastern traditions seem more compatible with the modern western personality and culture.

The attempts to reconcile these contradictions have produced many modes of negotiating the three sets. For contemporary India, the ultimate prototypes for such modes have been provided by two persons: Mohandas Karamchand Gandhi (1869–1948) and Rabindranath Tagore (1861–1941). Each deeply respected the other —Tagore was the first person to call Gandhi a *mahatma*, Gandhi was the first to call Tagore *gurudev*—and they shared many basic values. However, they differed significantly in their worldviews. These differences, often articulated publicly and with some bitterness, can be traced to the ways in which they handled the three sets of oppositions. To Tagore, the oppositions could best be handled within the format of India's 'high' culture, within her classical Sanskritic traditions, leavened on the one hand by elements of European classicism, including aspects of the European Renaissance, and on the other by India's own diverse folk or little traditions. In his world, modernity had a place. To Gandhi, on the other hand, resolution of the contradictions was possible primarily within the little traditions of India and the West, with occasional inputs from Indian and western classicism, but almost entirely outside modernity. Consequently, there were often sharp debates in public as well as private discomfort about what the other represented politically.

When closely examined, however, these differences turn out to be a matter of emphasis. Few Indians have used the folk within the classical more creatively than Tagore. And few Indians have used the classical within the format of the non-classical more effectively than Gandhi. Also, despite being a modernist, Tagore began to make less and less sense to the modern world in his lifetime. He ended as a critic of the modern West and, by implication, of modernity. Gandhi, despite being a counter-modernist, re-emerged for the moderns as a major critic of modernity whose defence of traditions carried the intimations of a post-modern consciousness. It should also be recognized that the two appreciated, and were fascinated by, each other's enterprise, and between them they offered post-Independence India a spectrum of choices in the matter of coping with India's diverse pasts and linking them to her future. However, on the whole, we can stick to our proposition that Tagore sought to resolve these contradictions at the level of high culture, Gandhi at the level of the 'low'. It is fitting that independent India's first prime minister claimed to be an heir to both traditions. Being a practised politician, Jawaharlal Nehru was aware that a durable basis of political legitimacy could be built only by simultaneously drawing upon both.

In one area, however, Tagore and Gandhi's endeavours overlapped and ideologically reinforced each other. Both recognized the need for a 'national' ideology of India as a means of cultural survival and both recognized that, for the same reason, India would either have to make a break with the post-medieval western concept of nationalism or give the concept a new content.[1] As a result, for Tagore, nationalism itself became gradually illegitimate; for Gandhi, nationalism began to include a critique of nationalism. For both, over time, the Indian freedom movement ceased to be an expression of only nationalist consolidation; it came to acquire a

[1] An excellent introduction to the ideological content of Indian nationalism as it developed in the second half of the nineteenth century, is provided in Partha Chatterjee, *Nationalist Thought and the Colonial World: A Derivative Discourse?* (London: Zed, 1986). On the social basis of Indian nationalism, the most useful work remains A.R. Desai, *Social Background of Indian Nationalism* (Bombay: Popular Prakashan, 1946).

new stature as a symbol of the universal struggle for political justice and cultural dignity. It was as if they recognized unself-critical Indian nationalism to be primarily a response to western imperialism and, like all such responses, shaped by what it was responding to. Such a version of nationalism could not but be limited by its time and its origin.

This fear of nationalism in the two most influential theorists of Indianness of our times was not an expression of the easy internationalism that became popular among the Indian middle classes in the inter-war years, thanks to the intellectual bridgeheads already established in the country by some schools of liberalism and radicalism. In both Tagore and Gandhi, the fear of nationalism grew out of their experience of the record of anti-imperialism in India, and their attempt to link their concepts of Indianness with their understanding of a world where the language of progress had already established complete dominance. They did not want their society to be caught in a situation where the idea of the Indian nation would supersede that of the Indian civilization, and where the actual ways of life of Indians would be assessed solely in terms of the needs of an imaginary nation-state called India. They did not want the Indic civilization and lifestyle, to protect which the idea of the nation-state had supposedly been imported, to become pliable targets of social engineering guided by a theory of progress which, years later, made the economist Joan Robinson remark that the only thing that was worse than being colonized was not being colonized.

This essay explores, mainly through an analysis of the three explicitly political novels Tagore wrote, the political passions and philosophical awareness which pushed him towards a dissident concept of national ideology. This concept could survive for a while as an ideological strand in India's political culture, thanks to Gandhi's leadership of the national movement. But the dissent was doomed. For in this ideology, of patriotism rather than of nationalism, there was a built-in critique of nationalism and refusal to recognize the nation-state as the organizing principle of the Indian civilization and as the last word in the country's political life.

In examining this critique, the essay follows Tagore in his intellectual and emotional journey from the Hindu nationalism of his youth and the Brahmanic-liberal humanism of his adulthood to the more radical, anti-statist, almost Gandhian social criticism of his last years. It was a journey made by one who had been a builder of modern consciousness in India, one who ended up—against his own instincts, as we shall see—almost a counter-modernist critic of the imperial West.

Tagore's 'Nationalism'

Humayun Kabir claims that the principles of non-alignment and federalism were Tagore's contributions to Indian foreign policy and the Indian constitution, respectively.[2] He was the first great Indian, according to Kabir, who defied the Eurocentrism introduced by colonialism into India and revived India's ancient ties with Asia and Africa. As for federalism, Kabir says, it was Tagore who had first declared, towards the beginning of this century, that 'if God had so wished, he could have made all Indians speak one language ... the unity of India has been and shall always be a unity in diversity.'[3]

Neither non-alignment nor federalism are solely Tagore's contribution to the culture of Indian politics. Both principles have been supported by Indian traditions, by a galaxy of influential anti-imperialist Indian political thinkers, and by the process of participatory politics in a multi-ethnic society. But few gave non-alignment and federalism greater legitimacy than Tagore did within the modern sector, for not even Gandhi could ram down the throat of the Indian literati his particular awareness of Indian traditions as Tagore did. Any modern Indian who claims that nationalism and the principles of the nation-state are universal has to take, willy nilly, a position against both Gandhi and Tagore. And taking a position against the latter is often more painful. Gandhi was an outsider to modern India, Tagore an insider. Tagore participated in shaping the modern consciousness in India; his voice counted. When Jawaharlal Nehru claimed that he had two *gurus*—Gandhi and Tagore—what he left unsaid was that the former was his political *guru*, the latter the intellectual. In rejecting Tagore, one rejects an important part of the modern consciousness in India.

[2] Humayun Kabir, 'Tagore Was No Obscurantist', *Calcutta Municipal Gazette* 1961, Tagore Birth Centenary Number, pp. 122–5.

[3] Ibid., p. 125.

Nationalism Against Civilization

What was Tagore's starting point in the matter of nationalism? In his brief, well-argued—though at places uncomfortably purple—book on nationalism, he distinguishes between government by kings and human races (his term for civilizations) and government by nations (his term for nation-states). He believes that 'government by the Nation is neither British nor anything else; it is an applied science.'[4] It is universal, impersonal and for that reason completely effective.[5]

> Before the Nation came to rule over us (under British colonial rule) we had other governments which were foreign, and these, like all governments, had some elements of the machine in them. But the difference between them and the government by the Nation is like the difference between the hand-loom and the powerloom. In the products of the hand-loom the magic of man's living fingers finds its expression, and its hum harmonizes with the music of life. But the powerloom is relentlessly lifeless and accurate and monotonous in its production.[6]

Tagore admits that India's former governments were 'woefully lacking in many advantages of the modern governments'. However, they were not nation-states—'their texture was loosely woven, leaving gaps through which our own life sent its threads and imposed its designs.'[7] Squarely confronting the popular belief in the backwardness of pre-colonial India, Tagore says,

> I am quite sure in those days we had things that were extremely distasteful to us. But we know that when we walk barefooted upon ground strewn with gravel, our feet come gradually to adjust themselves to the caprices of the inhospitable earth; while if the tiniest particle of gravel finds its lodgment inside our shoes we can never forget and forgive its intrusion. And these shoes are the government by the Nation—it is tight, it regulates our steps with a closed-up system, within which our feet have only the slightest liberty to make their own adjustments. Therefore, when you produce statistics to compare the number of gravels which our feet had to encounter in the former days with the paucity in the present regime, they hardly touch the real

[4] Rabindranath Tagore, *Nationalism* (1917) (reprint, Madras: Macmillan, 1985), p. 10.
[5] Ibid. [6] Ibid. [7] Ibid., p. 14.

> points.... The Nation of the West forges its iron chains of organization which are the most relentless and unbreakable that have ever been manufactured in the whole history of man.[8]

Does this relate only to colonial India? Will the analysis hold true even for an independent society ruled by its own nation-state? Tagore answers these questions, too. He says, to his non-Indian audience:

> Not merely the subject races, but you who live under the delusion that you are free, are every day sacrificing your freedom and humanity to this fetish of nationalism.... It is no consolation to us to know that the weakening of humanity from which the present age is suffering is not limited to the subject races, and that its ravages are even more radical because insidious and voluntary in peoples who are hypnotized into believing that they are free.[9]

He recognizes that the standard advice to India will be: 'Form yourself into a nation, and resist this encroachment of the Nation.'[10] He rejects the advice because it assumes that human salvation lies in the 'dead rhythm of wheels and counterwheels' and on 'mutual protection, based on a conspiracy of fear'.[11] Instead, he looks back to what he sees as the real tradition of India, which is to work for 'an adjustment of races, to acknowledge the real differences between them, and yet seek some basis of unity.'[12] The basis for this tradition has been built in India at the social level, not the political, through saints like Nanak, Kabir, Chaitanya, and others. It is this solution—unity through acknowledgement of differences—that India has to offer to the world.[13] Tagore believes that India 'has never had a real sense of nationalism' and it would do India 'no good to compete with western civilization in its own field.'[14] India's ideals have evolved through her own history and if she desires to compete in political nationalism with other countries, it would be like Switzerland trying to compete with England in building a navy.[15]

Yet the educated Indian was trying 'to absorb some lessons from history contrary to the lessons of their ancestors'. To Tagore it was part of a larger problem: the entire East was 'attempting to take into itself a history, which [was] not the outcome of its own living.'[16] India, he believed, would have to pause and think before buying the more dazzling, transient products of contemporary history and paying for them by selling its own inheritance.[17]

[8] Ibid., pp. 15–16. [9] Ibid., p. 18. [10] Ibid., pp. 18–19.
[11] Ibid., p. 59. [12] Ibid. [13] Ibid., p. 64. [14] Ibid.
[15] Ibid., p. 65. [16] Ibid., p. 64. [17] Ibid., p. 65.

The author of India's national anthem, one who had so deeply influenced Indian nationalism through his poetry, songs and active political participation, was outspoken in his views. Years earlier, he had spoken of nationalism as a *bhougalik apadevata*, a geographical demon, and Shantiniketan, his alternative university, as a temple dedicated to exorcise the demon.[18] He now declared even more directly that he was 'against the general idea of all nations'. For nationalism had become 'a great menace'.[19] Tagore recognized the sanctity of the anti-colonial movement and the futility of the method of 'begging' for 'scraps' used by the early Indian National Congress, at the time a liberal institution. But he also rejected the ideals of the 'extremists' which were based on western history.[20] Tagore sought a political freedom which would not be only the freedom to be powerful, for he knew,

> Those people who have got their political freedom are not necessarily free, they are merely powerful. The passions which are unbridled in them are creating huge organizations of slavery in the disguise of freedom.[21]

Strong words indeed; spoken at a time when the spirit of nationalism had already made a place for itself in the Indian public consciousness and when some like Sri Aurobindo (1872–1950) had already located their nationalist passions in a theory of transcendence that made sense to many Indians:

> Nationalism is an *avatar* (incarnation of divinity) and cannot be slain. Nationalism is a divinely appointed *shakti* of the Eternal and must do its God-given work before it returns to the bosom of the Universal Energy from which it came.[22]

Tagore was probably encouraged by the entry into Indian politics of a person who openly declared that his nationalism was 'intense internationalism', that it was 'not exclusive' because it recognized the eternal truth '*sic utere tuo ut alienum non laedas*'.[23] This new entrant, Mohandas Karamchand Gandhi, was not afraid

[18] Letter to Jagadananda Roy, quoted in Seema Bandopadhyaya, *Rabindrasangite Swadeshchetana* (Calcutta: National Book Agency, 1986), p. 22.

[19] Tagore, *Nationalism*, pp. 66–7.

[20] Ibid., p. 68. [21] Ibid., p. 73.

[22] Sri Aurobindo, 'The Life of Nationalism', in *On Nationalism, First Series* (Pondicherry: Sri Aurobindo Ashram, 1965), pp. 33–9; see p. 39.

[23] M. K. Gandhi, *Collected Works* (New Delhi: Publications Division, Government of India, 1969), Vol. 32, p. 45; and *Collected Works*, 1971, Vol. 45, p. 343.

to say, even if it meant disowning one important strand of anti-imperialism in India, 'Violent nationalism, otherwise known as imperialism, is the curse. Non-violent nationalism is a necessary condition of corporate or civilized life.'[24] And the Indian freedom movement, therefore, was 'India's contribution to peace'.[25]

[24] Gandhi, *Collected Works*, Vol. 25, p. 369.
[25] Ibid., Vol. 48, pp. 226–7.

Two
The Novels

The Home and the World

Against the stated political ideology of Tagore, we shall now examine the three explicitly political novels he wrote, treating them as vital psychological and cultural clues to his concept of politics and his political selfhood. We shall do so with the awareness that some of his other novels—for instance two early works, *Bouthakuranir Hat* and *Rajarshi*—also have clear political messages;[1] the vicissitudes of power and the corruption brought about by it were amongst Tagore's favourite themes. However, the novels analysed here are ones which give a central place to the political debates taking place in India over the methods of the Swadeshi movement and social reform in general.

Of the three novels, *Gora* is technically closest to the nineteenth-century idea of a proper novel. But it has the worst English translation of the three and almost invariably disappoints the English-speaking reader. There have, however, been excellent translations of the novel into the Indian languages and its reputation and influence are built on them. *Gora* was written in 1909, when the poet was forty-eight.[2] It was Tagore's sixth novel, counting his unfinished first novel, *Karuna*.

The second novel considered here is *Ghare-Baire*, available in English as *The Home and the World*.[3] Published in 1916, it was

[1] Rabindranath Tagore, *Bouthakuranir Hat* and *Rajarshi*, in *Rabindra-Rachanabali* (reprint, Calcutta: Vishwabharati, 1988), Vol. 1, pp. 607–98, 703–83.

[2] Rabindranath Tagore, *Gora*, in *Rabindra-Rachanabali* (reprint, Calcutta: West Bengal Government, 1961), Vol. 9, pp. 1–350. English tr. Anon. (Calcutta: Macmillan, 1924, reprint 1965). All quotations are from the English translation.

[3] Rabindranath Tagore, *Ghare-Baire*, in *Rabindra-Rachanabali* (Calcutta: West Bengal Government, 1961), Vol. 9, pp. 405–550. English tr. S. N. Tagore, *The Home and the World* (Madras: Macmillan, 1919). All quotations are from the English translation.

Tagore's eighth novel. The third is *Char Adhyay*, translated slightly more competently into English as *Four Chapters*.[4] It was Tagore's thirteenth and last novel. When published in 1934, it immediately sparked off a first-class public controversy because of its theme.

As we shall see, Tagore's political concerns in the three novels were roughly the same; they did not change over the twenty-five years of his life that the writing of the three novels spanned. This analysis therefore will not follow the historical order in which a problem that is primarily political–psychological in *Gora* becomes predominantly political–sociological in *Ghare-Baire* and political–ethical in *Char Adhyay*. Instead, the analysis imposes a psychological sequence on the historical order by tracing the political sociology of *Ghare-Baire* and the problem of political ethics in *Char Adhyay* to the political psychology of *Gora*.

Bimala's Choice

The story of *Ghare-Baire* is simply told. Bimala is a highly intelligent, fiery girl whose very name conveys both everyday plainness and transcendent power. She marries into a rich, aristocratic family proud of the beauty of its women and equally of its dissipated, self-destructive men. However, her husband Nikhilesh or Nikhil, she finds out, has broken with family tradition. Not only has he married in her a girl who is not beautiful; he is a well-educated, modern man, given to scholarship and social work.

Bimala's main support in Nikhil's family turns out to be his grandmother, who adores Nikhil and believes Bimala provides an auspicious presence in the house. The grandmother is the one who vehemently defends Nikhil when he founds a bank to give easy, unsecured loans to poor peasants in his area, and loses a fortune through it. She considers it a small price to pay for Nikhil's refusal to be drawn into the 'normal' lifestyle of the men of his family.

Nikhil adores his wife who is happily absorbed in her domestic life, but has other ambitions for her. A liberal humanist, he wants her to enter the modern world by learning the English language and English manners and he engages an English governess, Miss Gilby, to instruct her. Gradually, Bimala gains acquaintance with the outer world through Miss Gilby who virtually becomes a member of the household.

[4] Rabindranath Tagore, *Char Adhyay*, in *Rabindra-Rachanabali* (Calcutta: Viswabharati, 1986), Vol. 7, pp. 375–418. To bear comparasion with the quotations from *Pather Dabi*, all quotations have been translated from the Bengali version.

There are also two widowed sisters-in-law of Nikhil in the household—in the English version only one of the characters is retained—who provide the counterpoint to Bimala. They are uneducated and petty-minded, but Nikhil does not seem concerned with their education or exposure to the world. To some readers, though, they may emerge as self-willed women outside the control of the hero, what Bimala herself might have become, had she been less sensitive, impassioned, or alert.

It is the era of the Swadeshi movement, and one day a friend of Nikhil's, Sandip, comes to the house. Sandip, true to his name, is a fiery nationalist leader. Nikhil has been supporting him financially, much against his wife's wishes. Bimala had seen Sandip's splendid features in photographs but has never quite liked him, feeling that he lacked character, that 'too much of base alloy had gone into (the) making' of his handsome face and 'the light in his eyes somehow did not shine true.' However, when Bimala hears him speak in public she is thrilled, and inspired by his ideas; he appears like a conqueror of Bengal who deserved 'the consecration of a woman's benediction'.[5] For the first time Bimala feels unhappy at not being 'surpassingly beautiful', since she wants Indian men to 'realize the country's goddess in its womanhood'. Above all, she wants Sandip to find the *shakti* or divine power of the motherland manifest in her.[6] She invites him to dinner at home.

Over dinner, Bimala and Sandip discuss the national movement. Sandip makes a show of being impressed by her and invites her to rise above her diffidence and become 'the Queen Bee' of the movement. He promises that his associates would rally around her, that she would be their centre as well as inspiration.[7] As for himself, he is more direct: 'The blessing of the country must be voiced by its goddess.'[8]

Bimala is carried away by all this. She starts meeting Sandip regularly and Sandip begins to consult her on every aspect of the nationalist movement. As Bimala recounts it,

> I who was plain before had suddenly become beautiful. I who before had been of no account now felt in myself all the splendour of Bengal itself.... My relations with all the world underwent a change. Sandip babu made it clear how all the country was in need of me.[9]

[5] Tagore, *The Home and the World*, p. 34.
[6] Ibid., p. 24. [7] Ibid., p. 37.
[8] Ibid., p. 26. [9] Ibid., p. 43.

This change acquires for Bimala transcendental features. She would later remember the experience in almost mystical terms—'Divine strength had come to me, it was something which I had never felt before, which was beyond myself.'[10] Sandip nurses her new-found sense of magical power and is quick to establish an equation between his political mission and the 'natural' politics of women, as opposed to the socially-learned politics of men.

> In the heart of a woman Truth takes flesh and blood. Woman knows how to be cruel.... It is our women who will save the country.... Men can only think, but you women have a way of understanding without thinking. Woman was created out of God's own fancy. Man, he had to hammer into shape.[11]

Bimala now goes all out to help Sandip in his work, neglecting her husband, home and friends. She even 'takes' from the household money to give to the movement. Her love for Sandip has, however, a tragic end; Bimala loses both the home and the world, for Sandip runs away once large-scale violence, instigated by his speeches, breaks out and he is shown to be merely a shallow and callous manipulator; and Nikhil dies trying to quell the violence born of Sandip's version of nationalism. The angry, bitter outburst of one of Nikhil's sisters-in-law at his death reveals the deeper conviction of the family: it is a death brought about by Bimala, by her cannibalistic impulses.

It also becomes clear that the tragedy is not merely a personal one, for the social divide brought about by nationalism is more permanent than the political movement it spawns. Bimala's identification with the country becomes a literal one; the destruction of her home and her world foreshadows the destruction of the society.

The story of *Ghare-Baire* is told through the first-person narratives of the three main characters. But there is no Roshomon effect; it is the same story, fleshed out by all three in their own ways. The aim is to reveal differences in personality through differences in perspective, not the plural nature of reality itself. The issues and personalities of the main protagonists do not change from narrative to narrative. There is, in effect, a single, straight narrative from the point of view of Bimala, symbolizing Bengal, who is shown confronting the choice between two forms of patriotism. Though the background is the Swadeshi movement, in

[10] Ibid. [11] Ibid., pp. 31, 43–4.

which Tagore himself had actively participated and for which he had written some of his finest poetry and songs, the novel's message is clear: nationalism has enormous hidden costs. To make this point, the British remain a shadowy presence in the novel, which is essentially an exploration of the Indian consciousness as it confronts, grapples with and resists the colonial experience. The author splits this consciousness into two parts: one finds expression in the contrast between the hero and the villain, the other in the conflicts within the heroine.

As for the contrast between the hero and the villain, one gradually learns from the narrative that the aristocratic landowner Nikhil is no less a patriot than the demagogue Sandip. But Nikhil's patriotism is not as dazzling or strained as his friend's. Sandip believes that God is manifest in one's own country and it must be worshipped. Nikhil believes that, in that case, God must be manifest in other countries, too, and there is no scope for hatred of them. He believes that countries which live by oppressing others have to answer for it; their history has not yet ended.[12] Sandip and, under his spell Bimala, hold that one has the right to be humanly covetous on behalf of one's country, while Nikhil feels that as a human one should avoid projecting individual evil into the self-definition of a country. To Sandip, Nikhil's position is staid, unimaginative and unfeeling;[13] to Nikhil, Sandip's nationalism is only another form of covetous self love.[14] It is easy to guess which ideology wins in the short run: Sandip becomes a successful political leader who invades and overruns Nikhil's family life.

Bimala's first instincts were right. Sandip *is* inauthentic, both as a patriot and as a lover. He is only a professional politician. Bimala's love for him, however, is genuine, though it is of a special kind. Though there is a physical component to it, the love is not entirely blind infatuation: she is shrewd enough to sense Sandip's shallowness but considers it her patriotic duty to ignore it. Fired by the spirit of nationalism and a search for freedom which demands no deep political vision and partly stems from the defiant idealism of youth, Bimala finds in Sandip both a heroic role model and a love-object which she cannot break away from.

Nikhil, in contrast, is low-key and unheroic both as a lover and patriot, and he is outshone by Sandip's flamboyance till a tragic,

[12] Ibid., pp. 28–9.

[13] Ibid., p. 29.

[14] Ibid., p 35.

irreversible sequence of political, social, and personal events reveals his true heroism to Bimala.

Bimala, therefore, is the link between the two forms of patriotism the men represent. Not only is she the symbol for which Sandip and Nikhil fight, but her personality incorporates the contesting selves of the two protagonists and becomes the battlefield on which the two forms of patriotism fight for supremacy. In this inner battle, Nikhil's form of patriotism eventually wins, but at enormous social and personal cost.

There is another, less consequential, link between the protagonists: Amulya, an idealistic young student, with whom Bimala has a special relationship. Amulya works closely with Sandip and as a result, finds out quite early Sandip's instrumental concept of patriotism. Caught between his affection and respect for Bimala and his awareness of what Sandip is, Amulya turns out to be the real victim of Bimala's politics, and Bimala knows this. His death at the end of the story foreshadows Tagore's later anxiety about the nature of the violence let loose by nationalism.

The violence, a full-fledged Hindu–Muslim riot, is the inevitable corollary of Sandip's nationalism, Tagore suggests. The riot that kills Nikhil—his fate is left unclear in the novel, though in Satyajit Ray's film he dies—is set off by the ruin that poor Muslim traders face due to the nationalist attempts to boycott foreign goods immediately and unconditionally.

The violence is a natural by-product of the strategy of mobilization employed by Sandip and his enthusiastic followers. Such a mobilization requires, Tagore implies, symbols embedded in an exclusivist cultural–religious idiom. *Ghare-Baire* does not say why it should be so, but there are hints that, for Tagore, this form of populism combines mob politics with *realpolitik*. It is this combination which Tagore holds responsible for the growth of communalism, not religious differences, not even the representation of these differences in the political arena. Sandip precipitates a communal conflagration not merely by refusing to accommodate the interests of the Muslims as a community, and by imposing on them glaringly unequal suffering and unequal sacrifice for the nationalist cause, but also by depending on a form of political stridency which requires primeval sentiments to be mobilized and acted out.

One remarkable aspect of the novel is Tagore's brief but prescient reconstruction of the process by which a communal divide takes place in Nikhil's world. As Tagore tells the story, the image of the Mussalman in Bengali upper-caste Hindu minds emerges as that of a primal force, representing untempered, unmediated 'primitive' impulses. However, Mussalmans are also part of the 'natural' scene in Bengal and are in communion with similar primordial forces within Hinduism which, by common consent, have to be contained. Thus, beef-eating among Muslims is balanced by buffalo-sacrifice among the predominantly *shakto*, upper-caste Hindus of the area. But once Sandip's nationalism reaches down to find roots in the primordial, to give nationalism a base in the deepest of passions, it induces a similar regression in Muslims. On Nikhil's estate, Muslims who had more or less given up eating beef turn to it now on ideological grounds. To them, too, religion becomes less a faith or a way of life than an ideology.[15]

Lukacs' Choice

How incommunicable such an approach to anti-colonialism can sometimes be is best evidenced by Georg Lukacs' caustic review, published in 1922, of *The Home and the World*.[16] It is true that the novel in translation fails to convey the subtlety of the original and Tagore's magical power over words, notably his poetic use of prose. Also, Tagore comes off in the English version as moralistic and 'consciously attitudinizing' in his narrative.[17] Yet one suspects that behind Lukacs' critical judgement there are specific political barriers erected by the European critical consciousness which Tagore could not penetrate. Lukacs, given his Eurocentric Marxism, would find it difficult to admit the extent to which his critical apparatus was designed to maintain a hegemonic cultural discourse. For, if Lukacs is right and Tagore cannot but fail to

[15] Ibid., pp. 156–9. For further discussion of the split between religion-as-ideology and religion-as-faith, see Ashis Nandy, 'The Politics of Secularism and the Recovery of Religious Tolerance', *Alternatives*, 1988, *13(3)*, pp. 171–94.

[16] Georg Lukacs, 'Tagore's Gandhi Novel: Review of Rabindranath Tagore, *The Home and the World*', in *Reviews and Articles*, tr. Peter Palmer (London: Merlin, 1983), pp. 8–11.

[17] Kalyan K. Chatterjee, 'Lukacs on Tagore: Ideology and Literary Criticism', *Indian Literature*, 1988, 31(3), pp. 153–60; see p. 158. This paper is a fascinating attempt to place Tagore's novel within its cultural context and to separate the novel as a socio-political document from its more time-and-space bound stylistic elements.

communicate with Europe, Satyajit Ray's reasonably faithful film version of *The Home and the World* should make little sense to the modern world fifty years after the novel was first written. Certainly Ray's work does not raise doubts about Tagore's anti-imperialism either in India or in Europe.

Lukacs notes with great sarcasm that Tagore's hero is an aristocrat. He ignores that Nikhil, even if by default, stands with a religious minority which is also the poorest section of the society, and confronts boldly a middle-class-dominated, avowedly majoritarian formation that, modelling itself on India's colonial rulers, is dismissive towards the peripheries of the society. Lukacs says:

> Tagore himself is—as imaginative writer and as thinker—a wholly insignificant figure. His creative powers are non-existent; his characters pale stereotypes; his stories thread-bare and uninteresting; and his sensibility is meagre, insubstantial....
>
> The intellectual conflict in the novel is concerned with the use of violence.... The hypothesis is that India is an oppressed, enslaved country, yet Mr Tagore shows no interest in this question....
>
> ... A pamphlet—and one resorting to the lowest tools of libel—is what Tagore's novel is, in spite of its tediousness and want of spirit.
>
> This stance represents nothing less than the *ideology of the eternal subjection of India....*
>
> This propagandistic, demagogically one-sided stance renders the novel completely worthless from the artistic angle....
>
> But Tagore's creative powers do not stretch to a decent pamphlet.... The 'spiritual' aspects of his story, separated from the nuggets of Indian wisdom into which it is tricked out, is a petty bourgeois yarn of the shoddiest kind ... (his) 'wisdom' was put at the intellectual service of the British police.[18]

Lukacs gives a number of reasons for his distaste for the novel. Three of them are obvious. First, Tagore raises the issue of violence in the context of nationalism and ventures a moral—according to Lukacs, spiritual—critique of the anti-colonial struggle. Second, Tagore glorifies conventionality, family life and one-sidedly turns the nationalist leader Sandip into a 'romantic adventurer'. The extent of Lukacs' knowledge of Indian politics can be gauged from his belief that Sandip is a caricature of Gandhi. For some strange reason, this alleged attack on Gandhi goes against Tagore, because Lukacs seems naïvely unaware that he has neatly displaced on to

[18] Ibid., pp. 8–11.

Tagore the Comintern's evaluation of Gandhi ventured two years earlier in September 1920, at its first congress in Moscow. That evaluation (which Lukacs did not contest), states: 'Tendencies like Gandhism, thoroughly imbued with religious conceptions, idealize the most backward and economically most reactionary forms of social life, preach passivity and repudiate the class struggle, and in the process of the development of the revolution become transformed into an openly reactionary force.'[19] Third, Lukacs thinks that Tagore has failed to write a proper novel with detailed development of characters. The characters in *Ghare-Baire* are almost caricatures, the plot is a trivial one and the tone partisan.

Ghare-Baire is a nineteenth-century novel, written in a nineteenth-century style. It is only chronologically a product of this century. The novel's English translation, whatever its other demerits, is fortunately not designed to introduce somewhat provincial European intellectuals to the plural traditions of the Indian freedom movement and the debates within it. Lukacs, having read *The Home and the World* second or third-hand and living in what he believed to be the middle kingdom of world literature, is naturally willing to believe that, to Tagore, Gandhi in the form of Sandip is the rabble-rouser, seducing India in the form of Bimala from a gentle colonial figure, Nikhil, who is keen to introduce her to the modern world.

As we shall see, Tagore provides a slightly more nuanced approach to the interconnected problems of violence, anti-imperialism and nationalism. But to understand where Lukacs goes wrong, we must look beyond his Eurocentrism and his absolute faith in his culture's critical apparatus, into the nature of the enterprise which Tagore's political novels are.

The concept of the novel entered South Asian societies in the nineteenth century as part of the colonial experience. There are many descriptions of this process of assimilation, which first took place in eastern India. The process itself is not particularly relevant to our concerns, though its end-products are. The genre quickly became popular and entered the interstices of the Indian literary world; Bankimchandra Chattopadhyay (1838–94) was already India's first established novelist when the novel as a literary form entered other Asian and African societies.

Bankimchandra was influenced by a number of English nove-

[19] Quoted in Chatterjee, 'Lukacs on Tagore', p. 156.

lists. Of them, for some reason, he found Walter Scott to be the most congenial. Many contemporary critics were to call Bankim the Scott of India. Yet Bankim's concerns and worldview were fundamentally different; he only borrowed from Scott something of his narrative method.[20] These influences and the subsequent popularity of the novel form in India should not blind one to the sophisticated narrative traditions that predated the novel in the region and which, once the genre was established, entered it as if through the back door. *Upanyasa*, the Bengali term for the novel, itself indicates that the novel was expected partly to serve the purposes of—and to seek legitimacy and sustenance from—the older tradition of *upakathas*, fairy-story-like narratives surviving in the public memory, often as morality tales. This tradition is alive in *Ghare-Baire* and it dominates *Char Adhyay* in many ways.

At first, the novel served as a residual category for many South Asian thinkers. Individual novelists gave it a more personalized form, before such liberties became common in Europe: after all, the reason for the popularity of the novel form in South Asia was its ability to take up issues and themes that were peripheral to traditional forms of literature. For instance, the novel could be directly used, Indian writers found out, for political, polemical, and satirical purposes. Tagore himself used it mostly as an extended short story. Once he had written his early novels—*Gora* being one of them—he chose to move from the prose form of a conventional novel to a poeticized form more suited to allegorical tales of the kind which were to appear on the English and French literary scene much later. In the Indian context, one could say that he started writing contemporary *upakathas* or *puranas* rather than *upanyasas*.

This specific cultural experience with the novel was alien to Lukacs to whom the categories of literary criticism could not but be universal, which in his case meant exclusively European. Hence his two devastating errors of political judgement which no Indian social analyst can ignore, for the errors arise from an ethnocentrism that verges on racism.

The first of these errors is a ludicrous one and only some one like Lukacs could have made it. The 'villain' in *Ghare-Baire* is not a caricature of Gandhi. (Gandhi was hardly a part of the Indian

[20] For an analysis of some of these concerns see Sudipta Kaviraj's as-yet-untitled work on Bankimchandra Chattopadhyay (New Delhi: Nehru Memorial Museum and Library, 1988), mimeo.

political scene when Sandip was created in 1915–16. Tagore had observed from a distance Gandhi's South African *satyagraha*, and the two had met in March 1915; this limited acquaintance made him an admirer of Gandhi. His reservations about important aspects of Gandhi's politics and counter-modernism came later.) Sandip is, if anything, anti-Gandhi and criticism of him is an oblique defence of Gandhian politics before such a politics had taken shape, besides being a bitter criticism of sectarian Hindu nationalism, which at the time was a powerful component of Indian anti-imperialism. Creating a character like Sandip at that time would actually have deeply offended many Bengali revolutionaries who would have seen in him an attack on their own ideology, as well as character.

Second, *Ghare-Baire* offers a critique of nationalism but also a perspective on the form anti-imperialism should take in a multi-ethnic, multi-religious society where a colonial political economy encourages the growth of a complex set of dependencies. In such a society, the politically and economically weak and the culturally less westernized might be sometimes more dependent on the colonial system than the privileged and the enculturated. The novel suggests that a nationalism which steam-rollers society into making a uniform stand against colonialism, ignoring the unequal sacrifices imposed thereby on the poorer and the weaker, will tear apart the social fabric of the country, even if it helps to formally decolonize the country.

Lukacs does, however, get the title of his review right. *Ghare-Baire* is Tagore's Gandhi novel. It anticipates the low-key, unheroic, consensual nationalism which Gandhi wanted a multi-ethnic society like India to follow. For it was on such a consensus that Gandhi sought to build his more complex critique of the West and the western—that is, modern—civilization.

The Politics of New Violence

Char Adhyay begins by recognizing that the propagation of violent revolt against colonialism in India was an 'appropriate' transition to the violence associated with the modern scientific worldview—from the language of sacrifice and feud that a traditional society uses, to the language of vivisection or scientized violence.[21] From the time of the Boer War Tagore had been sensitive to the growing role of violence in human affairs. Some of his poems in *Naivedya*, published in 1901, reflect that sensitivity. One even knows that when he wrote *Char Adhyay*, Tagore had already become aware of the new forms of violence let loose on the world by modern technology. In the travelogue *Parasye*, based on his experiences on the way to Iran in 1932, he had commented on the special form of sanitized violence increasingly available in the modern world, thanks to the discovery of new means of 'distant violence' such as aerial bombing. Such forms reified not merely the individual humanity of their targets but also the reality of violence itself.[22]

Colonialism had a special role to play in the growth and legitimation of this sanitized violence, both as a source of such violence and as a system that encouraged its victims to mimic the style of violence practised by their oppressors. Colonialism, after all, was not merely the product of a theory of progress that hierarchized races, cultures, and civilizations; it was also a by-product of the Baconian theory of objective, scientific, 'true' knowledge which strictly partitioned off the observer from the observed, the subject from the object of knowledge, the enlightened agents of history from the passive ahistorical laity, the rational from the nonrational.[23] For the theory of progress grounded the right to rule oneself not so much in democratic principles as in the ability to run a modern nation-state objectively, rationally or scientifically—all defined according to the Baconian worldview.

The underlying evolutionist assumptions of colonialism did not leave the colonized cultures untouched. Many living in these cultures sensed that they were victims of a worldview which saw the alien human beings inhabiting Africa, Asia, and South America as closer to nature and therefore, given the growing objectification of nature, as things. In turn, many of these victims began to re-interpret their alien rulers and to see them, through a complex

[21] The first part of this section is almost entirely based on a part of Veena Das and Ashis Nandy, 'Violence, Victimhood and the Language of Silence', *Contributions to Indian Sociology*, 1985, *19*, pp. 177–95.

[22] Rabindranath Tagore, '*Parasye*', *Rabindra-Rachanabali* (Calcutta: West Bengal Government, 1961), Vol. 10, pp. 747–802; see pp. 749–56. For a discussion of the cultural context in which the awareness of the new scientized violence emerged see Ashis Nandy, 'Science, Authoritarianism and Violence: On the Scope and Limits of Isolation Outside the Clinic', in *Traditions, Tyranny, and Utopias* (New Delhi: Oxford University Press, 1987; reprint, 1992), pp. 95–126.

[23] Ashis Nandy, *The Intimate Ennemy: Loss and Recovery of Self Under Colonialism* (New Delhi: Oxford University Press, 1983; reprint, 1992).

process of identification with the aggressor, as closer to things. Among the first to diagnose this process and to identify the new language of violence emerging in the Indian political culture was Tagore, by then an admirer of Gandhi even though he had already rejected important aspects of the Gandhian worldview.

When in 1934 Tagore wrote *Char Adhyay*, one of his slighter novels according to most critics, he chose to set it even more explicitly within a political context. This novel, too, grapples with the dual encounter between East and West, and between politics and ethics, against a colonial background. However, unlike *Ghare-Baire*, *Char Adhyay* specifically introduces and deals with the changing nature of violence in contemporary politics. For it was written after World War I, the Nazi take-over in Germany, and the growing violence in Indian public life despite the by then predominant presence of Gandhi.

Through the development of characters rather than the plot, and the depiction of the characters' inner struggle, Tagore's own critique of terrorist violence is set out. The preface to *Char Adhyay* states that the inspiration for the novel was the life of Brahmabandhab Upadhyay (1861–1907), a Catholic theologian and Vedantist scholar, editor, social worker and nationalist revolutionary, who had been a pioneer in the use of terror as a political weapon. Tagore, according to the preface, was attracted by the personality as well as work of Upadhyay, who was one of the first critics to recognize his literary worth. The preface then goes on to describe Upadhyay's last visit to Tagore:

> At the time I had not met him for a long time. I thought, having sensed my difference with him on the method (*pranali*) of the nationalist movement, he had become hostile and contemptuous towards me.
>
> ... In those days of blinding madness, one day when I was sitting alone in a third floor room at Jorasanko, suddenly came Upadhyay. In our conversation we recapitulated some of the issues we had discussed earlier. After the chat he bid me goodbye and got up. He went up to the door, turned towards me and stood. Then said, 'Rabibabu, I have fallen very low.' After this he did not wait any longer. I clearly understood that it was only to say these heart-rending words that he had come in the first place. But by then he had been caught in the web of his actions (*karmajal*), there was no means of escape.
>
> That was my last meeting and last words with him.

> At the beginning of the novel this event needed to be recounted.[24]

Following the outcry over the novel in Bengali nationalist circles who were still fired by the ideal of a violent revolution led by a few exemplary revolutionaries, Tagore withdrew the preface from later editions and claimed that the novel was mainly a love story. It does seem, however, that whatever Tagore may have thought later, at the time of writing he was more concerned with the exploration of the inner world of political extremists and especially the loss of self in Atin, a young revolutionary caught in the violence. Despite this concern though, the characters in the novel remain primarily symbols or mouthpieces rather than complex many-faceted persons.

Ela's Choice

Char Adhyay is the story of a group of Bengali revolutionaries who are under pressure from the colonial police. Early in the novel we are told that informers have begun to take an unusual interest in some members of the group who outwardly lead a conventional, apolitical life. As the pressure mounts not only does the group begin to disintegrate, so do its members. Under stress, the psychological and moral costs of living the life of a terrorist are bared and the cultural rootlessness of the movement is underscored. So that what begins as a struggle for freedom becomes, by the end of the story, an invitation to a new form of bondage.

The story of *Char Adhyay* revolves around three persons: Indranath, a revolutionary leader; Atindra or Atin, scion of an impoverished aristocratic family and a young recruit to the revolutionary cause; and Ela, an attractive girl who is also a member of Indranath's group and in love with Atin. The plot is simple: it is woven around the course of Ela and Atin's relationship. Attracted by Ela, Atin joins the revolutionary group led by Indranath, a revolutionary trained in Europe, a brilliant student of science and languages and also skilled at armed and unarmed combat. But Indranath's most striking trait is a dispassionate, fully scientific, ruthless commitment to what can only be called instrumental rationality. Under Indranath's tutelage, Atin becomes competent at his revolutionary tasks but also begins to lose his humanity. Atin's love for Ela provides him with a partial escape from this dehumanization, but the situation is complicated by the fact that though Ela

[24] Suddhasatva Bosu, *Rabindranather Char Adhyay* (Calcutta: Bharati Publications, 1979), pp. 6–7.

takes the initiative in establishing a relationship with him, she refuses to marry him because of her vow to remain a celibate in the service of the country.

Finally, Ela herself becomes a liability to the group. The task of eliminating her falls on Atin, and in a moving last chapter, there is a confrontation between Atin and Ela. Both are aware that the meeting must end in Ela's execution. Ela is a willing victim; she refuses the anaesthesia that Atin offers her not only because she wants to die fully self-aware but because to die at Atin's hand has an erotic significance for her. Further, she has a sense of guilt over Atin's penury and devastated health. Though roughly of the same age, she had occasionally claimed to be older than him and felt responsible for him.

For Atin this is the final revelation that he has fallen from his own distinctive *svadharma* (code of conduct) and *svabhava* (individual specificity). He recognizes that Ela is willing to be sacrificed not because she accepts the meaning given to it by Indranath's modern nationalism but because of a privatized meaning, derived from her relationship with him, Atin.

It is necessary to describe briefly the structure of the novel. The four chapters which give the novel its title are preceded by a prologue, which is purely narrative. It gives us the life-history of Ela, and we learn that she has had an unhappy childhood, seeing throughout her early years her mother tyrannizing over her submissive father, a professor of psychology. Later, in her uncle's home, she found a similar situation: her aunt turned out to be petty, jealous, and narrow-minded. These experiences left Ela with a distaste for marriage and encouraged her to live the life of an independent woman.

This life story is not provided for other characters in the novel. It is as if Tagore had again chosen to make his heroine the battleground where different political ideologies and moralities were being tested out and as if Ela, as a woman and symbol of her society, needed to be given more substance than the various competing social engineers.

Each of the four chapters begins with a brief narrative that provides the context for the dialogues that follow. The narrator, rather like a camera-man, records a series of nearly static interpersonal situations. The first chapter is in the form of a dialogue between Ela and Indranath in a cafe, from which the reader gathers that Indranath takes pride in using his followers as instruments for furthering the nationalist cause. He repeatedly uses the language of sacrifice and compares himself to Krishna, who advised Arjuna to kill his kinsmen in the service of *kshatradharma*, the warrior's code of conduct. Yet the difference between the two is also established by Indranath's clinical attitude toward his own followers. Ela is obviously recruited for her ability to attract young men like Atin to the revolutionary group.

The second chapter establishes the growing attraction between Ela and Atin through a conversation that takes place in Ela's bedroom. Though Ela admits she loves Atin, she refuses to marry him for she has vowed to remain celibate. In the third chapter Ela goes to Atin's hide-out and sees the utter penury to which he has been reduced. She offers then to marry him but it is a futile reparative gesture from a puppet attempting to be an autonomous being. In the final chapter Atin goes to Ela's home to execute her. As the two converse, Atin reflects upon the journey he has completed to reach this stage in his life. Again, the characters reveal themselves through their conversation; nothing is allowed to intervene between the characters and the reader, as if the experiential reality of violence could be understood only through an intellectual discourse.

It is obvious from the above that Tagore allotted the personal traits of Upadhyay to both Indranath and Atin. Indranath is the theologian of the new violence and the Gita is his bible. He is the *mantradata*, the giver of *mantra*, in Tagore's words. The transformation of self and the inner experience of violence is projected on to Atin. At this plane, Indranath as the prototype of Upadhyay and Atin as his disciple are caught in an ambivalent relationship. Indranath senses Atin's imperfect commitment to nationalism; Atin discovers Indranath's betrayal of his civilization. Yet, neither can disown the other, for each is the other's double.[25]

The author makes clear that Indranath's training of Atin—who is not fully amenable to the training, being not only a revolutionary, but a poet, and a lover too—also represents a ruthless training of Indranath's own self; and that Ela's death signifies not only the final destruction of Atin's selfhood but also the final defeat and fall of Indranath. Through this defeat and fall Tagore tries to convey something of the meaning of Upadhyay's anguished reference to his having fallen very low.

The fact that the novel begins with the story of Ela's life suggests

[25] I have in mind here the clinical picture drawn by the likes of Otto Rank. See his *The Double: A Psychoanalytic Study* (tr. and ed.) H. Tucker, Jr. (University of North Carolina Press, 1971).

two points. First, it is into Ela's world that Indranath and Atin are to enter and not the other way round. Second, Atin comes face to face with his own loss of humanity only as it may be registered with regard to Ela, recalling the confession of Upadhyay to the poet himself. In the final encounter Atin describes himself as *svadharma-bhrasta* (fallen from his own *dharma*) and *svabhavachyuta* (fallen from natural inclination). His own relation to Indranath, his revolutionary leader and teacher, is movingly summarised:

> The theoretician (*mantradata*) said, 'All of you collectively tug at a thick rope (of the juggernaut) closing your eyes—this is your only work.' Thousands of boys began doing so. Many fell under the wheels, many were maimed for life. Suddenly the theory changed; the order came to pull in a reverse direction. The chariot (*ratha*) turned the other way. Those whose bones were broken (as a result) could not be put back to health. The invalids were swept away into the dust heaps on the roadside. The faith in one's own strength was destroyed so fully that everyone proudly agreed to mould oneself after the official ideal of the robot. When in response to the strings pulled by the leader everyone began to dance the same dance, strangely enough everyone thought it to be a dance of power. The moment the puppeteer loosened his strings, thousands became superfluous.[26]

The question that remains to be asked is whether, in Tagore's view, violence always led to loss of self or whether there was something specific in the way in which violence was used in the freedom movement in Bengal that was under criticism? One has to remember that the concept of necessary and legitimate violence was present in Indian society; that legitimate violence *was* linked to the

[26] Tagore, *Char Adhyay,* p. 398. The tacit assumption here is that the theory of dissent developed by the likes of Indranath represents the internalization of the new language of the state that the colonial power has brought into India's political discourse. It also emphasizes the control and technological manipulation of subject populations and the total impersonalization of the public realm.

It would be interesting to compare the discourse on violent resistance in *Char Adhyay* with both Bankimchandra Chattopadhyay's *Anandamath* and Saratchandra Chattopadhyay's *Pather Dabi* which are partly the ideological counterparts of Tagore's novel. *Pather Dabi* tries to bypass the issue of 'thingification'—as Aimé Césaire calls it in his *Discourse on Colonialism* (New York: Monthly Review Press, 1972)—by either legitimizing counter-violence as resistance or by using the language of feud. Saratchandra in this respect might be read as Indranath's self-justification outside the bounds of *Char Adhyay*. However, as we shall see below, the heroine of *Pather Dabi* defies its author to reproblematize the issue.

notion of sacrificial renunciation.[27] It is no accident that *dharmayuddha* and *yajnayuddha* (just war or war as sacrifice) were the operative concepts borrowed from the Gita. Much of the available folklore on just wars also counterpoises the fight for *dharma* against the fight for gain. One must fight to the last for a just cause, they seem to say, regardless of the strategy or victory. Were the revolutionaries continuing this tradition of legitimate violence or had they in fact reversed it?

It does seem that Tagore had sensed the basic difference between sacrificial violence and the new political violence which made instrumental use of people. Sacrificial violence is justified only if it involves self-sacrifice, that is, if sacrifice *to* god is balanced by sacrifice *of* god,[28] and this necessarily demands the consent of those sacrificed within the meaning-world of the sacrifice. Sacrifice loses its sanctity if awareness of the subjectivity, both of those who are compelled to be victims and of those others who identify themselves with them in the community, is lost. As Indranath trains himself to become 'ruthless', 'impersonal', and 'scientific', it becomes necessary for him to snap the emotional link between him and his followers, now being used as so many puppets. He has to manipulate the inner world of his followers and empty it of moral autonomy.

Franz Fanon's defence of exorcism through violence was that the only way victims could recover their subjectivity was by 'objectifying', in their turn, the violent oppressors. Tagore, on the other hand, seems to have been persuaded that a ruthless, clinical theology of violence must inevitably lead to a loss of self and of signification. To him, the continuity with the language of the Gita, used so frequently by Indian votaries of the new violence, only masked a discontinuity in concepts. In this respect, *Char Adhyay* represented a break in the structure of ideas within which violence was being understood in India. The novel recognized that the consciousness and political culture of the Indian people was being irreversibly altered by new modes of resistance which took the worldview of the colonizers for granted; that the revolutionaries' ability to find legitimacy for their actions in ancient texts only showed that real disjunctions in consciousness could often be hidden by the use of traditional language.

[27] Das and Nandy, 'Violence, Victimhood and the Language of Silence'.

[28] Veena Das, 'The Language of Sacrifice', *Man* (n. s.), 1983, *18*, pp. 445–62.

Bharati's Choice

Char Adhyay includes an impassioned critique of Indranath's politics, but not a full critique of his personality. Though Tagore hints at the possibility of such a critique, he does not make Indranath a rounded, flesh-and-blood character—it is only Ela, the heroine, who has the nuances of her personality delineated and to some extent contextualized. So, to get an idea of how Indranath as a type may have fitted into the political culture of the Bengal of the time and Tagore's implicit assessment of that culture, I shall have to go outside Tagore's world and re-enter it through a well-known nationalist novel of the post-Swadeshi period, *Pather Dabi*.[29] Written by Saratchandra Chattopadhyay (1876–1938), by far the most popular novelist India has produced and a major influence on Indian middle-class consciousness during the first half of the twentieth century, *Pather Dabi* was published in 1926, eight years before *Char Adhyay*, and was almost immediately banned by the British Indian government. The first edition of *Pather Dabi*, though, was entirely sold out in less than a week, before the police could move in to pick up the copies. The ban was lifted in 1939, a year after the author's death.

Saratchandra requested Tagore to join in the widespread protest against the ban. The poet refused, not on the grounds of political ideology, an issue he deftly bypassed, but on the grounds of Saratchandra's undoubted literary gifts. He wrote:

> ... What a writer like you tells in the form of a story will have permanent influence.... From immature boys and girls to the elderly, all will come under its influence. Under the circumstances, if the English did not stop the circulation of your book, it would have shown their total contempt and ignorance about your literary powers and your status in this country.[30]

Tagore, however, gratuitously chose to add that, everything considered, the British regime was, comparatively, the most tolerant regime in the world. Saratchandra was furious. In his response, which he did not finally send or publish, he asserted that if the regime had the right to ban the book, the subjugated Indian had at least the right to protest.[31]

[29] Saratchandra Chattopadhyay, *Pather Dabi*, in Sukumar Sen (ed.), *Sarat Sahitya Samagra* (Calcutta: Ananda Publishers, 1986), pp. 1130–1266.

[30] Sarojmohan Mitra, *Saratsahitye Samajchetana* (Calcutta: Granthalaya, 1981), pp. 153–4.

[31] Ibid., p. 154. The bitterness was deep and persistent. See Saratchandra Chat-

After the publication of *Pather Dabi*, its hero Savyasachi quickly became the ideal of many Bengali freedom-fighters. A number of memoirs of post-Swadeshi freedom-fighters mention how they took enormous risks and sometimes faced police prosecution to possess or even read the novel and how greatly they admired Savyasachi. It is against this background that one must take note of the remarkable similarities between him and Indranath, including the similarity in names. Savyasachi is another name of Arjuna; Indranath means, among other things, one whose lord or father is Indra. It can therefore also mean Arjuna. Anyone interested in literary sleuthing would be tempted to hypothesize that the character of Indranath was inspired by Savyasachi and was an attempt to develop—and define the limits of—some aspects of Savyasachi's self-definition. These are the aspects widely admired in the modernized sections of the non-western world as markers of political rationality and the ideal political personality.

Savyasachi is a Bengali Brahman who brings to his Kshatriya vocation the full power of Brahmanic cerebral potency. As a Bengali police officer pursuing Savyasachi says, with sardonic respect, Savyasachi is a *mahapurush*, a great man, who has rebelled against the king and deserves to be called *svanamadhanya*, a person true to his name. Not merely is he ambidexterous, all his ten senses, *dashendriya*, are equally powerful. A superb shot, he can swim across torrential tropical rivers and simultaneously take on half-a-dozen policemen in single combat.[32] He is a master of disguise, too.

These abilities are matched by his mental powers. Savyasachi knows at least ten languages (at one point he claims that he 'knows' all the languages of the world) and he has been educated (like all good Indian, middle-class ultra-nationalists) in Europe and North America. He is a man of dazzling virtuosity and versatility. He has studied medicine in Germany, engineering in France, law in England and an unmentioned discipline in the United States.[33] The reader may remember that Indranath, too, lived in Europe for many years and studied science there. Equipped with excellent

topadhyay's letters to Radharani Debi, 10 October 1927, and to Umapradas Mukhopadhyay, 10 Bhadra 1334 (1927), reproduced in Gopalchandra Roy, *Saratchandrer Patrabali* (Calcutta: Bharati, 1986), pp. 291–3, 320.

[32] Chattopadhyay, *Pather Dabi*, pp. 1149–74.

[33] Ibid., p. 1149.

testimonials from his European professors, Indranath has taught French, German, botany, and geology, and is also a trained doctor, besides being an expert at armed and unarmed combat.[34] And Savyasachi, too, despite being an agnostic, seeks support for his work from the Gita.

Savyasachi's attainments were not chosen at random. Among those who contributed to Saratchandra's conceptualization of his hero were well-known, gifted revolutionaries like Jatindranath Mukherjee (1879–1915), Jadugopal Mukherjee (1886–1976), Rashbehari Bose (1886–1945), M.N. Roy (1887–1954), Bhupendranath Dutta (1880–1961), Taraknath Das (1884–1958), and Satish Chandra Chakravarti (1889–1968).[35] Thus the combination of extraordinary physical strength and courage and the capacity to be forgiving and caring came from Jatindranath; the skill at disguise from Jadugopal; organizational ability, particularly the ability to build international networks, from Bose and Roy; western education from Dutta and Das; and ambidexterousness from Chakravarti.[36] There were indirect influences from figures such as Aurobindo, though it is pretty obvious from the narratives that both Saratchandra and Tagore had sensed the break that had already taken place between the transcendental theories of nationalism ventured by the likes of Aurobindo and the new, secularized nationalism increasingly backed by a theory of 'scientized violence'. Within that new nationalism, even the Gita had acquired a paradoxical status; it had become a cultural sanction for the primacy of desacralized nationalist politics and for the separation of politics from morality. (The text of course had a completely different set of meanings in Gandhian politics.)

With Savyasachi's wide repertoire of skills go other 'attainments' which aroused deep ambivalence in his creator. Savyasachi is 'passionless like a stone' and callous.[37] Through single-minded, rigorous training, he has acquired extraordinary control over every part of his body and mind.[38] This is the kind of control which Indranath, too, so conspicuously displays.

> We ... have given up kindness and charity, otherwise we would have hated ourselves for being sentimental. This is what Sri Krishna has taught Arjun. Do not be cruel but, when duty is

[34] Tagore, *Char Adhyay*, pp. 381, 385.

[35] Saratchandra Chattopadhyay. quoted in Mitra, *Sarastsahitye Samajchetana*, p. 155.

[36] Ibid.

[37] Chattopadhyay, *Pather Dabi*, p. 1172.

[38] Ibid., pp. 1223, 1232–3.

> involved, be ruthless.... My nature is impersonal.... I accept with the illusionless mind of a scientist that one who is will die.... If one seeks to do one's duty out of anger, one is more likely to do that which is not one's duty.[39]

As Savyasachi puts it,

> ... I am a revolutionary. I have no attachment, no mercy, no sense of nurture—both sins and good deeds are nonsense to me. India's freedom is my only goal, only *sadhana* ... except for it in this life I have nothing nowhere.[40]

Predictably, Savyasachi is a secular rationalist. To him all traditions are lies, 'primitive superstitions'; the human race has no greater enemy than them.[41] This faith gives his calculations about human life and sacrifice almost mathematical precision. With all this apparent objectivity and rationalism, however, the precision includes an erotic fascination with violence. Savyasachi believes that the sins of man-made suffering can only be washed away by the blood of its rebellious victims.[42] For him, the poison in the heart of the victimized is the real capital of revolution, the base on which he would have to build his rebellion. All talk of peace, he declares, is mere rhetoric and a conspiracy of the exploiters.[43]

Savyasachi, therefore, is psychologically and culturally ambidexterous, too. He is equally accomplished as Kshatriya and as Brahman, he has internalized both the East and the West, and he is at home both with modern instrumental rationality and the primitive, passionate love for his motherland that drives him from country to country 'like a wild animal'. In addition, he oscillates between fulfilling the traditional Bengali concept of the ideal person and the modern European concept of the ideal person he has chosen for himself.

But, within all this, there is a schism: Savyasachi's worldview is hyper-masculine. In political ideology, strategies, and in the stereotypes he has of his own Bengali community, he is openly potency-driven. At the same time, he cannot fully disown those personality traits that rebel against his self-definition. These contradictory pulls imbue him with some of the qualities of

[39] Tagore, *Char Adhyay*, pp. 385, 388–9.
[40] Chattopadhyay, *Pather Dabi*, p. 1234.
[41] Ibid., p. 1249.
[42] Ibid., pp. 1232–3. [43] Ibid., p. 1233.

Saratchandra's other heroes, who are always conspicuously androgynous. It is as if Savyasachi were hiding this other bipolarity—his ability to be almost maternal in some situations, defying his own overly masculinized concept of the ideal male. The dynamics of this self-defiance, which Tagore chose to ignore, unfolds in the course of Savyasachi's interpersonal experiences narrated in the novel.

The story of *Pather Dabi* is set entirely in Burma, at that time a part of British India. It revolves around Apurba, a young, orthodox, middle-class Bengali Brahman who comes to Rangoon to work as a petty official in a Dutch company. Apurba is the son of a district magistrate under the Raj, and has a master's degree in science. He confesses to being a physical coward, has a touch of misogyny born of fears of pollution, and is a docile colonial subject, a maudlin, conventional mother's boy. He is accompanied by a Brahman cook-bearer, Tiwari, who is as cowardly and fearful of the whites as Apurba is. In Rangoon, they come to know Bharati, the daughter of a Bengali Brahman woman who defied her family to marry an aggressive, boorish, hard-drinking South Indian Christian. Apurba's first encounter with Bharati is unpleasant, but they draw close to each other when Bharati nurses Tiwari through an attack of small-pox.

Meanwhile, Apurba becomes friendly with a spirited Maharashtrian Brahman called Ramdas Talvarkar. Through Talvarkar and Bharati, Apurba is introduced to a nationalist secret society called Pather Dabi (literally, The Demand of the Road) and its leader, Savyasachi, whom everyone in the group calls 'Doctor'. The president of the Rangoon branch of Pather Dabi is Sumitra, an intelligent, self-assured, attractive woman, half-Jewish and half-Bengali-Brahman, whom Savyasachi has rescued from 'a life of indignity'. Sumitra is in love with Savyasachi.

After a while, Apurba's courage fails him and he informs on the secret society. He is captured by members of the society and condemned to death. Partly from pity and partly for Bharati's sake, Savyasachi spares Apurba's life, against the wishes of the majority of the group. Savyasachi then has to repair the damage done by Apurba's betrayal and deal with at least one member who finds in Savyasachi's kindness towards Apurba a new excuse for liquidating Savyasachi himself. The novel ends on a melancholy but dramatic note, with the revolutionary leaving Rangoon on a stormy night to rebuild his shattered organization in Asia.

Much of the second half of *Pather Dabi* consists of long conversations between Bharati and Savyasachi, following Savyasachi's magnanimous gesture to Apurba. From these conversations one comes to suspect towards the end that the author's identification with his hero is not total, that he identifies partly with Bharati whose worldview is at variance with her leader's.

While a cursory reading of the novel reveals the similarities between Savyasachi and Indranath, one must read it more carefully to notice the differences. For these are based on qualities that enter the narrative despite the author's obvious sympathy with his hero. Saratchandra shares much of Savyasachi's political wisdom, such as his diagnosis of 'Europe's world-engulfing hunger from which no weak nation has ever been able to protect itself'; the belief, obviously borrowed from nineteenth-century European radicalism, that 'peasants never risk life for ideas, for they do not want freedom, they want peace—the peace of the incompetent and the impotent'; and the conviction that it is wrong to believe that 'lies need to be created while truth is permanent and uncreated' because 'truth is constantly recreated by mankind, for truth also lives and dies.'[44] Saratchandra even makes his hero mouth a defence of the Bengali middle classes as a creative and potentially revolutionary formation,[45] as if to compensate for the negative portrayal of Apurba's personality.

But once again—one is tempted to say, despite himself—the author introduces into the novel another form of patriotism. This is a patriotism which his hero selfconsciously rejects but at times unwittingly lives out. It has two main elements.

First, Savyasachi does not turn out to have as clear-cut a personality and ideology as he appears to have at first. His ambivalence towards Bengal and the Bengalis, for example, is deep. He believes that Bengalis are cowardly and selfish but also confidently states that, of all the languages in the world, Bengali is the sweetest.[46] As for his instrumental rationality and the primacy he gives to the goal of freedom, he acknowledges at one place, 'Independence is not the end of independence. *Dharma*, peace, poetry—these are even greater. It is for their unique development that one needs independence.'[47]

[44] Ibid., pp. 1239, 1241, 1247.
[45] Ibid., p. 1261.
[46] Ibid., pp. 1248–9.
[47] Ibid., p. 1237.

Second, the novel subtly suggests that Savyasachi's *dharma* is actually *apatdharma*, codes of conduct that can be followed in exceptional circumstances, in this instance in a situation where his motherland is being violated and he, as a freedom fighter and dutiful son of India, has to live in a liminal world inhabited by marginal individuals. Almost all the characters of *Pather Dabi* are from or live on the periphery of Bengali middle-class Brahmanism. Even their secret society, though it extends over much of Asia, is poorly linked with the mainstream of Indian political activity. Savyasachi claims he has chosen Burma as the headquarters of Pather Dabi because women in Burma are freer and he expects women to make his revolution.[48] Yet the role of the Burmese ends with that statement. The novel has no notable local character. The cultural and physical characteristics of Burma, usually the latter, merely act as the backdrop for a clutch of marginal Bengalis and their few non-Bengali associates playing out their political and historical roles. The writer's final warning to his own hero, delivered through Bharati talking in her sleep, is thus of significance.

> You are a superman; for you my respect, adoration and affection will ever remain immovable. But I shall never accept your intellectual judgement (*vicharbuddhi*). Let freedom come to our country through your hands, but never give the immoral the shape of the moral.... If you give necessity the highest priority and thus create for the weak-hearted the impression that *adharma* is *dharma*, your sorrow will never end.[49]

This could be Ela speaking to Indranath, not in her sleep but in her most alert, self-conscious moments. And we are left with the question: could Bharati repeat her criticism of her hero when fully awake? Perhaps what Tagore says directly in *Char Adhyay*, Saratchandra can only say indirectly, almost despite himself in *Pather Dabi*. Yet, the continuity cannot be ignored. In both cases, the authors express their moral doubts through their heroines and assume that their heroes have compromised, at least partly, with the forces of *adharma* and impersonal, instrumental violence.

In other words, resisting his actual political ideology, Saratchandra's identification with his hero is less than complete, and his differences with Tagore less sharp than the poet might have cared to admit. Saratchandra *was* an ardent nationalist, he *did* write

[48] Ibid., p. 1221. [49] Ibid., p. 1251.

Pather Dabi as a political act, and he *did* conceive of Savyasachi as a national hero. But a narrative in the hands of a creative writer acquires an impulse and momentum of its own. Saratchandra's novel acquires this autonomy through the author's residual identification with Bharati.

Tagore all but misses this identification when modelling Indrajit on Savyasachi. He makes an anti-hero of Savyasachi in the form of Indranath. The 'ruthless, firm-hearted, fearless, unpitying' revolutionary of *Pather Dabi* becomes in *Char Adhyay* something more—a passionless, calculating industrialist of violence, to whom violence is a matter of assembly-line deaths, geared to the production of political results.[50] At this plane, Tagore is less than sensitive to the subtleties of Saratchandra's response to the problem of scientized violence. At another plane, however, Tagore's creative self, too, acquires an autonomy of its own. It senses his colleague's latent identification with his half-caste, crypto-Gandhian heroine. Bharati's political philosophy finds voice and her moral anxieties concrete shape in *Char Adhyay*'s Ela.

Loss and Recovery of Self

That which is mainly a matter of social choice in *Ghare-Baire*—between two political ideologies represented by two different persons with distinct personalities—becomes primarily a problem of inner choice in *Gora*. The continuity between Bimala and Gora is maintained in *Char Adhyay* through Ela, for whom morality and politics—also moral and political action, the private and the public, and the home and the world—gradually become inseparable. At this plane, the three characters can be seen as extensions of each other and the novels constitute a single narrative, one continuing story of a divided self in which two antagonistic social forces are represented by two persons, who first constitute a latent (Nikhil and Sandip), then a manifest double (Atin and Indranath), and finally a split self (Gora).

However, there are clear breaks in the narrative. The choice for

[50] Ibid., p. 1257.

Bimala and the reader of *Ghare-Baire*—as Lukacs points out—is made easier because of Sandip's flawed character. In *Char Adhyay*, too, Atin faces internal choices which are almost entirely moral and, for some reason, deliberately located in a two-dimensional fairy-tale world. It is not surprising that once Tagore withdrew his preface from later editions of the novel, *Char Adhyay* could quickly be absorbed into the mainstream of Bengali literature as aa mythic statement on political morality, far less controversial and ques--tionable than Tagore intended it to be.

In *Gora*, the choice, which remains political, takes a psychological form. Whereas in *Ghare-Baire* the conflict over political morality is shown to be external to the two main antagonists, who remain close to ideal-typical representations, *Gora*, like *Char Adhyay*, projects the problem of public morality into the personality of Gora himself, into his self-definition. The moral and political contradictions are almost entirely within him; it is Gora who learns to evaluate or pass judgement on himself. Here there is no Indranath to share the blame. As we shall see, even those who side with Gora's political superego cannot share his pain as he works through his older political–psychological self to acquire a new moral vision.

The characters in the novel play out their roles against the background of an ideological debate which makes no sense to the non-Bengali reader or to Bengalis of later generations. This debate, between orthodox Hinduism and the Brahmo reform movement, gradually turns out to be more than an intellectual encounter between two sects or faiths. Shorn of its denominational meaning, it is seen to be a clash between two structures of consciousness. By the end of the novel, the author virtually repudiates the two manifest planes of Hinduism and Brahmoism along which he places the characters at the beginning; he now places the characters along the two orthogonal structures of consciousness, serving as two latent, political–ethical planes in Indian public life.

Gora's Choice

Though written during the period of the Swadeshi movement, *Gora* is set at the fag end of the 1870s. The chief protagonist is a young, passionate, but scholarly social reformer who has turned ultra-Hindu, and believes that the humiliation of being colonized can only be overcome by a tough protectiveness towards everything indigenous. Gora is familiar with the common arguments against his position and he has well-thought-out, powerful counter-arguments. Thus, when he decides to bathe at Triveni, it is not in search of purity or piety; he knows there will be pilgrims there; he will have to shed his diffidence and stand with the common people.[51] As he says, 'when the whole world has forsaken India and heaps insults upon her, I for my part wish to share her seat of dishonour—this caste-ridden, this superstitious, this idolatrous India of mine.'[52] In this respect, Gora has a touch of Swami Vivekananda (1863–1902) and Sister Nivedita in him:

> Those who *you* call illiterate are those to whose party *I* belong. What *you* call superstition, that is *my* faith.... Reform? ... More important than reform are love and respect. Reform will come of itself from within after we are an united people...[53]
>
> ... The goddess of my worship does not come to me enshrined in beauty. I see her where there is poverty and famine, pain and insult.[54]

Predictably, Gora is not apologetic about being oriented to the past. He believes that one kills the past by talking about it as if it were dead and gone.[55]

His exclusivism pushes Gora towards a strain of nationalism that was not then a political force in India. Originally inspired by the 'nativism' of Bankimchandra Chattopadhyay and Vivekananda, this strain only became a significant political movement after the partition of Bengal in 1905. However, it was already showing signs of its future shape. As it grew into a movement, it brazenly embraced western concepts of the nation, state, statecraft, technology, and history as the unavoidable universals of contemporary politics. This reactive westernization subsumed under the western category of nationalism—he called it the internalization of western history—prompted Tagore to avoid grappling with the issue of imperialism directly and instead to focus on the two conflicting forms of response to imperialism.

[51] Tagore, *Gora*, p. 29.

[52] Ibid., p. 267. [53] Ibid., pp. 50–1.

[54] Ibid., p. 71. A critic has suggested on the basis of biographical details that the inspiration for the character of Gora, for much of his life an Indian ultra-nationalist of Irish origin, was primarily Nivedita. Bimanbehari Majumdar, *The Heroines Of Tagore; A Study in the Transformation of Indian Society, 1875–1941* (Calcutta: Firma K. L. Mukhopadhyay, 1968), p. 225. [55] Ibid., p. 88.

The novel is organized around a series of events that constitute an attack on Gora's nationalism and self-definition. These events goad him to search for more authentic forms of patriotism and faith, grounded in a more authentic self. In the course of the search, Gora's inner divide comes to acquire a sharpness greater than that in some of the real-life characters on whom he might have been modelled. But there are continuities, too. They bridge the divide and make his personality change believable. The most important of these continuities is Gora's initial reluctance to mimic the West. 'If we have the mistaken notion', he says at one place, 'that because the English are strong we can never become strong unless we become exactly like them, then that impossibility will never be achieved, for by mere imitation we shall eventually be neither one thing nor the other.'[56] On this belief is built Gora's self-discovery towards the end of the novel.

Gora is the son of a retired government official who, in retirement and after living a rather naughty life, has turned to orthodoxy with a vengeance. Anandamayi, his superbly composed, insightful wife, has a matter-of-fact, pragmatic morality which helps her negotiate both the fiery Gora and her other son Mahim, who is perfectly 'normal' and, hence, 'realistic' and cynical. Anandamayi's primary concern, though, is the 'abnormal', idealistic Gora, and her life is organized around him. Unlike her husband, Anandamayi is at peace with tradition and therefore more open to cultural differences and dissent. There are hints that her liberal vision stems from her deep roots in tradition. We are told that her father died in her infancy; she was brought up by her grandfather, a pandit at Varanasi.

The novel begins with Binay, Gora's friend, accidentally meeting a reformist Brahmo family headed by a philosophical, ideologically open, doting father, Pareshchandra Bhattacharya, known as Pareshbabu. Pareshbabu's reformism is 'natural' and derives more from his personal morality and spiritual sensitivity than from any ideology. However, though Paresh dominates his family morally, his comically-Anglicized wife Baradasundari dominates its political thinking. Barada is as particular about maintaining the purity of Brahmoism as Gora is of Hinduism.

Gora resents the encounter between Binay and Pareshbabu's family. He fears that his friend will be influenced by the family and

[56] Ibid., p. 102.

lose his ideological purity. He has no inkling that the main attraction the family has for Binay is its ability to satisfy his growing rebelliousness against Gora's idea of India as 'negation incarnate'.[57] As it happens, Gora himself is gradually sucked into Paresh's social orbit, if only for occasional testy exchanges with the family and their prim, self-certain guests, including a pillar of Brahmo orthodoxy, Haranbabu. So it is in front of Gora's unbelieving eyes that Binay ultimately falls in love with a daughter of the family, Lalita.

A spirited, defiant girl with a mind of her own, Lalita is jealous of Binay's emotional dependence on Gora. An accident suddenly alters the context of this grudge. Lalita wants to avoid taking part in a dramatic performance organized by her mother in honour of an English commissioner who had sentenced Gora to imprisonment a few days earlier for championing the cause of oppressed villagers. She precipitates a first-class scandal by running away from home and joining Binay on his journey back to Calcutta. Binay now finds his allegiance to Gora's ideology pitted against Lalita's direct moral reaction to the injustice done to him.

Meanwhile, Gora's concept of India is severely shaken by his experiences in rural Bengal and, particularly, from his encounter with the resistance offered by a predominantly Muslim village. Especially impressive to him is the more open Hinduism of the village barber who lives in solidarity with the Muslims rather than with their Hindu oppressors.

Ultimately, Gora himself gets emotionally involved with another girl of the Brahmo family, Sucharita, an adopted daughter of Pareshbabu. At one time, 'the fact that there were women in India hardly entered Gora's mind'; now he makes 'a new discovery of this truth through Sucharita ...' and this shakes him.[58] He comes to regard Sucharita not as a special individual, but as a special idea, a representation of Indian womanhood.[59] He becomes aware that women do not merely symbolize the motherland; they are the motherland and it is the indifference to the humiliation of women-as-motherland which explains the Indian male's insecurity about his loss of manhood.[60] Gora is now torn between the attraction he feels for Sucharita—at first, he is unable to own up his love for

[57] Ibid., p. 30.
[58] Ibid., p. 271.
[59] Ibid., p. 272.
[60] Ibid., pp. 272–3.

her—and his political–religious ideology. More so since, to go by Pareshbabu's reading, 'Gora is too high-handed.... The simple and assured peace which clothes the thought and word and deed of those who are the bearers of truth, [is] not one of Gora's possessions.... '[61]

The dénouement—a rather contrived one—comes when Gora finds out that he himself, though he has tried to live the life of a pure, ascetic Brahman, is actually the orphaned child of an Irish couple, abandoned during the Sepoy Mutiny in 1857. He is reduced overnight to an untouchable and a non-Indian. Traumatic though it is, the revelation does not, however, destroy Gora as a person. Instead, he acquires the courage to confront the fact that Pareshbabu's religious consciousness is superior to his and so is Anandamayi's practical morality. Once he has acquired this awareness, his first symbolic act is to own up the Christian—and hence presumably untouchable—domestic help, Lachmi, who was once his nurse-maid.

Although the novel is roughly twice the length of *Ghare-Baire* and *Char Adhyay*, its plot is not particularly complex. However, the characters in *Gora* are more fully developed than in *Char Adhyay*, and the ideological confrontations in it are filigreed with detail. Indeed, one can make out a case that the basic theme of *Gora* is the changes in personality and ideology that are brought about by interpersonal and cognitive encounters. Tagore's own political ideology, his ideas of 'true' patriotism and desirable modes of social change, enter the narrative less directly and aggressively than in the other two novels. Gora at the end is not a mere vehicle of Tagore's political philosophy.

Central to the narrative is Gora's patriotism. When it finds expression in nationalism, this patriotism has a number of distinct features. First, Gora has no awareness that his nationalism, his idea that Hindus should become a single homogeneous nation,[62] is borrowed from the West; and that therefore it has no cultural roots. When he goes to a village as a political and social activist, he encounters another form of political community, culturally more rooted in the moral codes of the civilization. The experience does not free him from his ideology; it merely plants some doubts in his mind. Only towards the end does Gora discover that his national-

[61] Ibid., p. 89.
[62] Ibid., p. 294.

ism and cultural exclusivism are reactions to his own uncertain cultural moorings and are, therefore, doubly purist.

Second, Gora's nationalism reifies the idea of the nation. Those forming a part of the Indian nation or serving as the beneficiaries of nationalist ideology have some sanctity for him but, ideologically, they are political and cultural abstractions. It is only much later that the reality of rural Bengal—the oppression and violence it contains—confronts him with a choice between the empiricism of life and that of books. This ability of nationalism (as of any theory) to reify its prospective beneficiaries—that is, the citizens of the nation that it idealizes—is a constant theme in Tagore's work; in *Gora* he explores its consequences in contemporary politics for the first time.

Third, Gora's nationalism assumes that the indigenous is intrinsically and fundamentally different from the exogenous and that the Indian or Hindu self can be fully defended on its own terms. So even Hindu catholicity and tolerance become arguments to prove the catholicity and tolerance of a superior civilization. Gora's parentage is used by Tagore as the ultimate symbolic proof that such a concept of national identity is itself exogenous and violates the fundamental principles of Indianness and Hinduism.

One should note that in 1909, when he wrote *Gora*, Tagore was already trying to move away from the conventional structure of the western novel, introducing elements from the Indian epic tradition into it. We have seen how this approach also led Tagore to write *Char Adhyay* almost in the form of a fairy tale. *Gora* allows one a glimpse of the other side of the coin—of some of the possible reasons for the success of the new form in India: the novel can explore aspects of the self in ways that are simultaneously psychological, moral, and spiritual.

Gora's changing concept of nationalism is a consequence of the changing contours of his self-knowledge, acquired through a painful process of self-confrontation. The secret of his birth does not clinch the issue. The reader knows the secret, Gora does not, and when it comes out at the end, it only gives a certain poignancy to the self-awareness that has already been arrived at.

Four persons play crucial roles in this self-confrontation—Binay, Paresh, Anandamayi and Sucharita. Of the four, Paresh provides the metaphysical and moral fulcrum for the story and is the main agent of change in Gora's personality. But it is Anandamayi who emerges as the most powerful presence in the narrative.

Forced to choose between the India of Gora and India as Anandamayi, Gora's closest friend and double, Binay, chooses Anandamayi. The choice is 'passive' and 'intuitive'. Later, Gora himself makes the same choice more self-consciously when he senses that Anandamayi represents in her womanliness the spirit of India more truly than his pure, disinfected, masculine version of Indianness and Hinduism.

One guesses that Anandamayi is the prototype of the character that in the later novels develops into the splintered personalities of Bimala and Ela. It is Anandamayi's authenticity that is being engineered, by Sandip in one instance and Indranath in another, in the cause of nationalism. This engineering seeks to break down the barrier between the private and the public by giving absolute priority to conjugality over maternity, and erects a new barrier between the home and the world: one which does not permit feminine values in the domestic space to invade or spill over into public life. To ensure that the maternal selves of Bimala and Ela are not entirely overshadowed by their conjugal selves or sexuality, Tagore introduces in *Ghare-Baire* and *Char Adhyay* the characters of Amulya and Akhil.[63] They underscore the continuity between Anandamayi, Bimala and Ela and the threat to the authenticity and authority of the feminine self which serves as an organizing principle of the Indic civilization.

The other central issue in *Gora* is that of purity, both as a cultural value and as an aspect of personal morality. Gora starts with a fixed concept of pure Hinduism and tries to be true to it. To him, Pareshbabu's family is contaminated and Anandamayi compromised. By the end of the novel, Gora's original concept of purity has disintegrated and he sees Paresh and Anandamayi as more truly pure than his own father and Haranbabu. Paradoxically, Paresh and Anandamayi acquire this new status in Gora's eyes by their willingness to sacrifice their purity to reaffirm a moral universe which Gora finds that, despite all his efforts, he cannot disown.

That shared moral universe, Tagore suggests, is a universal one and, if Anandamayi can so effortlessly make it her own and defend it, it is in continuity with Indian traditions. What Paresh has acquired through self-discipline, Anandamayi has acquired through everyday womanliness, by being herself. This is what

[63] Suddhasatva Bosu, *Rabindranather Char Adhaya* (Calcutta: Bharati Publications, 1979), p. 36.

Bimala in *Ghare-Baire* tragically fails to recognize. It is also what Ela in *Char Adhyay* refuses to acknowledge till the end, once again with tragic consequences. Bimala and Ela, under the influence of Sandip and Indranath, are as much *svabhavachyuta* as Atin is, for they try to become equals in a man's world by choosing values derived from that world. Their personal tragedies come from the pursuit of values embedded in the masculinized world of nationalism and nation-state—from what could be called the principle of egalitarian patriarchy—rather than from any genuine reaffirmation of feminine values.

To locate the moral fulcrum in femininity in this fashion is to repudiate the aggressively phallo-centric, 'fierce self-idolatory of nation-worship' (of which Indranath represents the sophisticated form and Sandip a more street-smart version) and 'the colourless vagueness of cosmopolitanism' (depicted in *Gora* through the pathetically comic imitative modernity of Baradasundari).[64] India's history, Tagore believed, was the 'history of continual social adjustment and not that of organized power for defence and aggression.'[65] Hence, when voluntary and self-imposed, such masculine nationalism in India can be even more devastating.[66]

Of the three novels discussed here, *Gora* is the only one to end on a happy note. It was as if, after establishing the illegitimate birth of Hindu nationalism, Tagore could afford to allow his hero to live with himself. The new awareness of his origins and his 'genetic untouchability' saves Gora from his narrow nationalism and brings him closer to his mother and, by implication, motherland. It was as if a self overly well defined and exclusive could not, by definition, be an authentic Indian self capable of serious relationships with other Indians and Indianness. Once the point was made, Tagore's other political novels followed; they were the logical corollary of the political psychology of *Gora*.

Kipling's Choice

To understand the politics of self in *Gora* more fully, it may be useful briefly to compare its hero with that of Rudyard Kipling's

[64] Rabindranath Tagore, *Nationalism* (reprint, Madras: Macmillan, 1985), p. 2.

[65] Ibid.

[66] Ibid.

well-known and influential novel, *Kim*.[67] I shall attempt the comparison here keeping in mind a recent paper by Kalyan Kumar Chatterjee,[68] where Gora is seen not as an Indian who is finally shown to have alien roots but as an outsider who has come to stay as an insider.

Kim was published in 1901, nine years before *Gora*, and was an immediate success. It is possible that Tagore had at least heard of the major concerns of *Kim*. Even if he had not, his own novel provides a counterpart to Kipling's. Both deal with the loss and recovery of selves, and the anxieties and pain associated with that.

Kipling's novel, at first sight consistent with his other work, turns out to have some unique features. Kipling had been away from India for about a decade when he wrote *Kim*, and his painful, tense ambivalence towards the country and its inhabitants had partly worn off by the time it was completed. The novel has an uncharacteristic mellowness and an evocative, nostalgic tone, as if it was an attempt to capture the fleeting spirit of eternal India as reflected in her contemporary absurdities and social contradictions. These qualities do not fully fit the Kipling one is familiar with, who usually shows such sensitivity only when dealing with the flora and fauna of India, for instance in the *Jungle Books*, not when dealing with the human beings who inhabit the country's hot and dusty plains. Some critics have recognized this break with the past. One has called *Kim* Kipling's valedictory address to India and the most genuine interpretation of everyday Indian life written by an Englishman.[69]

The hero, Kim, is a white child lost in the wilderness of urban India, cruelly tanned by the Indian sun and speaking an Indian tongue. Kim's parents, like Gora's, were Irish,[70] but are now dead and Kim lives like any other Indian street child in Lahore. The

[67] Rudyard Kipling, *Kim* (reprint, New York: Dell, 1974).

[68] Kalyan Kumar Chatterjee, 'Incognitos and Secret Sharers: Patterns of Identity, Tagore, Kipling and Foster', *Indian Literature*, May–June 1989, No. 131, pp. 11–130.

[69] K. Bhaskara Rao, *Rudyard Kipling's India* (Norman: University of Oklahoma Press, 1967).

[70] The psychological significance of being of Irish blood in a British–Indian relationship remains underexplored in fiction as well as social analysis. *Ex facie* Irishness represented a form of liminality. It marked out a westernness which seemed culturally more accessible, being non-dominant and non-mainstream; it marked out a territoriality which seemed to be a co-victim of British imperialism; and carried associations with a form of Christianity, Catholicism, which was obviously not the religion of the empire and which was explicitly more open to the cultural styles and traditional religious beliefs of Indians (see Ch. 3, pp. 55–6 below).

novel describes how he recaptures his 'true' identity through a series of adventures which link him to the colonial government and make him a protector of its security interests. The story begins at the Lahore Museum, which is presided over by an English Curator modelled on Kipling's father, where Kim accidentally meets a 'strange' Tibetan Lama on a pilgrimage. Kim befriends the other-worldly, lovable Lama and becomes his disciple or *chela*.

Much of the novel consists of a description of the adventurous journey the two undertake along the Grand Trunk Road. In the course of it, they meet a variety of people and Kim gets more enmeshed in unravelling and resisting a conspiracy against the Raj. In this unravelling and resistance, Kim's Indian self comes in handy. He can lie like an Oriental and all hours of the day are the same to him, he can give and take bribes like any Asiatic, and he can passive-aggressively ensure his own and his *guru*'s survival. Thus, he begs skilfully, exploits the superstitions of the natives to negotiate difficult social situations, and even—V.S. Naipaul would enjoy this—chews *pan* and spits on the floor of the compartment he is travelling in to blend with his environment.[71]

Gradually it becomes clear to the reader that Kim and the Lama constitute not merely a social but also a psychological dyad. They serve as each other's double and, in the process, come to symbolize forces larger than themselves. They are bound together by their latent common Other—the India which the Lama has transcended and which Kim uses instrumentally as a camouflage. To put it simplistically, Kim represents Kipling's self as it might have been, a self which can suspend its suspicion of the diversity, rawness and violence of India mixed with the country's seductive, androgynous charm. The Lama, on the other hand, is what one critic calls 'the triumphant achievement of an anti-self' by Kipling, so powerful that it becomes the 'touchstone for everything else'.[72] The Lama in his childlike otherworldliness is a negation of everything Kipling politically stands for. The character was for Kipling a once-in-a-lifetime break with his painfully-constructed imperial self.

Kim can be read as an interplay of the two selves, a play in which neither wins; both are finally subjugated to a third self serving the conventional state. But, in the meanwhile, the novel provides a moving justification for the two abrogated selves—one located in

[71] Kipling, *Kim*, pp. 27, 30–1, 36.

[72] Mark Kinkead-Weeks, quoted in Lord Birkenhead, *Rudyard Kipling* (London: Weidenfeld and Nicolson, 1978), p. 222.

Kipling's lost past, and the other in the disowned present of the Orient. It is this empathy with the defeated which makes *Kim* different from the majority of Kipling's works. Kipling was never to show the same cultural and psychological sensitivity or the same moral courage again. He was a person who feared identifying with victims, especially when they defied authority, and he always found some sanction for authorized violence. Elsewhere I have associated this fear with Kipling's deeper fear of looking within, of baring his latent awareness of what he actually was—an insecure bicultural whose sources of creativity lay in his biculturality rather than in his unicultural self. For this was artificially constructed with the help of current theories of progress and social Darwinism to avoid facing the moral demand to identify with the subjugated and the weak.[73]

In the boy Kim can be found Kipling as he appeared to many of his fellow Anglo-Saxons in India—ill-mannered, under-socialized, unruly and, even, overly tanned.[74] Like Gora, Kim comes from the outside to become part of the Indian world. What marginalizes him in Anglo-India brands him as an insider for Indian society. What could be a handicap in a 'civilized' society is an asset in the 'native quarters of Lahore'. He can merge with the Indian environment easily and with uninhibited grace.

Gora, on the other hand, comes in like a storm into a conventional Bengali family and manages to lay bare not merely his own but also his family's latent contradictions and hypocrisy. He is the mythical Englishman who, as Tagore had written in 1898, had been sent by destiny as an envoy 'to burst through our rickety door and enter into the very interior of our house.'[75] Despite being brought up as an Indian, Gora's character retains elements of his western self, physical as well as psychological. He 'roars' when he speaks, is needlessly assertive, and he lives in a world which does not admit any shade of grey.

Whereas Gora's voice and assertiveness give the lie to his copper-coloured skin, and set him apart in Indian society, Kim's sensitivity to the local scene reflects the consciousness of an insider. Unlike Gora, Kim does not have to affirm his Indianness as a psychological defence; he uses it naturally as part of his social

[73] Nandy, *The Intimate Enemy*, pp. 35–9, 64–73.
[74] Birkenhead, *Kipling*, pp. 62–3.
[75] Rabindranath Tagore, quoted in Chatterjee, 'Incognitos and Secret Sharers', p. 113.

armour. He is what Kipling could have been or felt he had been in his earlier life.

Underlying these differences is a deeper parallel. Tagore in *Gora* tries to integrate a part of his Indian self modelled on the western man; Kipling in *Kim* tries to own up the Indian part of his western self. The struggle is more intense and painful in Kipling. He has to grapple with his fears of Indianness which he can neither own up nor jettison; he clings to his English selfhood with a desperation which his overdone commitment to the Raj and notions of racial superiority cannot hide.[76]

Hence the dramatically different endings of the two novels. In *Gora* the hero acquires a wider self-definition where his western self is not disowned but finds a place in a larger philosophy of life:

> The significant note here is of re-birth. At the very moment of being caught in a limbo, of having nowhere to go, he (Gora) finds a new habitation through a new baptism. At the same time as Hindu sanctums closed their doors against him, the vast country with its diversity is thrown open before him for a new quest, a new career, a new victory possibly.[77]

In *Kim*, there is no re-birth. Its Mowgli-like hero already has an everyday philosophy of life that embeds him in his culture. At the end, Kipling does provide a bureaucratic link with the Raj for Kim, but that is a somewhat contrived ending shaped by Kipling's private anxieties and his inner need to give an acceptable meaning and legitimacy to Kim's Indian self. In what must be one of the great anti-climaxes of literature, Kim narrows down his self-definition to become a member of the security services of the empire. He has to become an outsider to his own cultural self to be acceptable to the world of his creator.[78]

[76] Nandy, *The Intimate Enemy*. See also Edmund Wilson, 'The Kipling that Nobody Read', in Andrew Rutherford (ed.), *Kipling's Mind and Art* (Stanford University Press, 1964), pp. 17–69.

[77] Chatterji, 'Incognitos and Secret Sharers', p. 118.

[78] Angus Wilson seeks to explain away this narrowing of self by arguing that the regime or state to which Kim gives his allegiance protects the innocence of both Kim and the Lama. 'The two higher values in the book—the richness and variety of Indian life and the divine and spiritual idiocy of the Lama—can only be preserved from destruction by anarchic chaos or from despotic tyranny by that [British] rule.' Angus Wilson, *The Strange Ride of Rudyard Kipling, His Life and Works* (London: Secker and Warburg, 1977), p. 130. Wilson fails to notice that Kim's acute sense of survival and repertoire of defensive skills come from his Indian self and the Lama is protected not so much by the Raj as by Kim. Wilson himself remarks four paragraphs earlier, Kim 'unites

The Politics of Dissent

Let us pause for a moment and take stock. All three of Tagore's novels deal with the fragility and resilience of political authority and the birth, survival, and death of moral dissent. All show how the division between the public and the private—and, by implication, the secular and non-secular—domains of morality are not ultimately sustainable. The subversion of morality in the public sphere after a while distorts primary human relationships and the very core of one's cultural selfhood.

What gives the three novels their complexity—and their politics of self its depth—is the author's plural concepts of authority and dissent. Political authority for Tagore has three distinct strands. There are the standardized, routine structures of authority, a new set of claimants to authority trying to usurp the moral space created by the rebellious victims of the first set, and a third category, cutting across these two, consisting of those committed to their traditions and to the victims as living, suffering, real human beings rather than as categories in an abstract ideology of dissent. The third set carries the seeds of a genuine rebellion in the future, against the oppressive aspects of the past and an intolerable present. For it includes those in deeper touch with traditions who are, for that very reason, more open to the new and the exogenous. Nikhil's grandmother, Gora's mother and Pareshbabu exemplify the inner strengths of the Indian tradition far better than those aggressively defending the tradition.

The existing structure of authority against which rebellion begins, is weak, compromising, doomed to defeat. The claimants to authority are arrogant, totalizing, efficiently violent, and confident in their new-found power and legitimacy derived from history. It is as if, after demystifying the power of a coercive paternal authority—Indian social orthodoxy on the one hand, and the illegitimate colonial power on the other—one was suddenly confronted with a new fraternal counter-authority claiming total allegiance on the grounds that the other rebels were neither adequately oppositional nor versed in the intricacies of dissent.[79] Tagore's own attack is directed mainly against this new counter-authority. He feels that

the knowingness, the cunning, the humour and the appeal of the Dodger, with the gentleness and goodness of Oliver Twist, a seemingly impossible task' (ibid., p. 129).

[79] Cf. Erik Erikson, 'The Legend of Hitler's Childhood', in *Childhood and Society* (New York: Norton, 1961), 2nd ed., Ch. 9.

the moral bankruptcy of the establishment, native as well as foreign, has already been revealed and need not be re-emphasized.

Of the two powers in recession, social orthodoxy and colonialism, the latter remains mostly in the wings. An occasional English magistrate, police officer or informer are all that there is by way of a direct encounter with the Raj. But the presence of colonialism is everywhere felt and it shapes the narrative at every stage. Each major contradiction in the novels involves the entry of western ideas of the nation-state, history, and progress, into the Indian life style, as a means of reorganizing the culture's self-definition. These ideas set the terms of political discourse even among Indians. This success of colonialism is matched by the ambitions of a nationalism which, after faithfully swallowing the colonial worldview hook, line, and sinker, is willing to sacrifice Indians at the altar of a brand-new, imported, progressivist history of the Indian nation-state in the making.

In contrast, the hollow paternal authorities representing Hindu social orthodoxy who might have set the tone for the heroes of *Ghare-Baire* and *Char Adhyay*, are all dead and their self-destructive, feudal traditions are easy to break. More difficult it is to defy the new breed of robust dissenters who fight these decrepit, collapsing authorities on the one hand, and British imperialism on the other. Both Sandip and Indranath find Indian orthodoxy insufficiently rebellious against the Raj but, in an Oedipal twist, they are themselves tied to their target, the colonial authorities. This is not merely on account of their general conceptual grid but also through the specific theory of political morality and scientized violence borrowed from modern Europe. Ultimately, the followers of Sandip and Indranath get caught in the same trap. Politics, they discover, can be liberating, but it can also mask a form of self-deception that helps hide less obvious bondage.

Nikhil, who rebels against the first set of authorities, social orthodoxy and colonialism, also rebels against the second. But he comes to realize that the second battle, the one against the emerging counter-authorities, will have to be fought out primarily in the minds of the victims. For him the battleground turns out to be both the local community and his wife. Bimala reaches the same intellectual position, but only after a tortuous and self-destructive journey.

Likewise, Ela sees through the empty power of her domineering mother and the self-castration of her academic father soon enough.

She creates for herself an independent professional existence outside her unhappy parental home with relative ease. But the moral totalism of Indranath turns out to be both alluring and suffocating. Atin, like Nikhil, finds it easy to despise the meaningless luxury of his aristocratic family home, but is unable to fight Indranath's authority and its fatal charm, and that inability destroys him. Ultimately Indranath, the brilliant self-possessed strategist, loses the battle for Ela's mind to Atin, the weak self-doubting poet. But the victory is more Ela's than Atin's, for it is she who breaks Indranath's spell, he cannot.

In *Gora*, this new authority is internalized; it is part of the hero's fractured self. He sees through the emptiness of his father's authority and his return to faith in his old age. It is more painful for Gora to disown his self-imposed nationalism and the psychological defences that go with it. That nationalism colonizes his self more successfully than any imperial power could have done. This victory of nationalism, Tagore implies, is ultimately a victory of the West over Indian civilization.

A final word. The apparent robustness of Sandip, Indranath, and the Hindu nationalist in Gora derives from their denial of aspects of their culture and self that are identified with effeminacy, especially maternity. The strongest resistance to them, too, finally turns out to come from women; they are the psychological barricade that the culture puts up to protect its *svadharma*. Hence, when women conform or collaborate, they become mere caricatures of conformity and collaboration. Baradasundari is only the most absurd of such caricatures.

Of the women who resist the contesting ideologies of conventionality, collaboration and defensive neo-conservatism, it is Anandamayi whose resistance is the deepest and most 'natural'. She fathoms the inauthenticity of Gora's nationalism from the beginning, while Bimala, despite her initial scepticism about Sandip as a person, is disillusioned with him and his ideology only when destruction has already stared her in the face. Ela lacks even that initial doubt. Both become aware of the psychopathology of nationalism through their relationships with the two men they love. In Tagore's world, motherliness questions the dominant consciousness and resists it more radically and effectively than does conjugality. Hence, when Gora goes through his climactic transformation to arrive at a political position that anticipates the

Gandhian worldview in significant ways, his first reconciliation is with his mother and his childhood nurse.

That resistance is the obverse of the seductive unstated claim of nationalism that it is a tested Oedipal remedy—against the anxieties aroused by an indigenous paternal authority, who is perceived to be impotent. Nationalism offers the hope that, by adopting aspects of an exogenous authority that has already laid bare the impotency of the indigenous authority, it is possible to defeat both forms of authority. These aspects include a clearly territorialized concept of the nation-state as the first identifier of a people, a sharp sense of history that reconstructs the past as a unilinear narrative or unfolding of an amoral cross-national zero-sum game, and a theory of progress that sanctions the increasing impersonalization of violence as a mode of cultural self-engineering and self-preservation. The male ancestors of Nikhil and Atin, and even Gora's father, despite their dissipated life style that suggests sexual promiscuity, invoke anxieties about self-castration and social retreat. Nationalism sets up against them rebel claimants to authority who convey a different, more potent, cosmopolitan image of male authority. Sandip, Indranath, and the nationalist self of Gora are violent intrusions into the Indian cultural scene. These claimants act out their imperial paternity, both in rebellion and in conformity. All are caught in a painful Oedipal situation intensified by the presence of two sets of paternal authority, one eastern, the other western. As against them, the biculturality of Nikhil and the 'reborn' Gora represents a new mode of cultural continuity. They have been through and emerged relatively intact from the humiliation of the colonial experience; and the even greater humiliation of fighting colonialism with the help of methods and ideologies imported through the colonial connection.

Three

The Lives

Brahmabandhab Upadhyay: Tagore's Political Double

The three novels can be read in many ways. We have read them as a testament of Tagore's political beliefs. We can also read them as a record of Tagore's attempt to grapple with his ambivalence toward the complex, melodramatic personality of Brahmabandhab Upadhyay (1861–1907), a contemporary who served as Tagore's other self in matters of nationalist politics. In the process, I shall explore the form of patriotism which Tagore finally endorsed, superficially opposed to the one Upadhyay upheld but actually in alliance with what Tagore saw as the other self of Upadhyay.

Brahmabandhab Upadhyay was one of the most colourful figures of late nineteenth-century India. Tagore found him 'spirited, fearless, self-sacrificing ... and extraordinarily gifted', and recognized that it was in *Sandhya*, a journal founded and edited by Upadhyay, that 'the first subtle hints of the beginnings of terrorism in Bengal appeared.'[1] Tagore may have sensed that these 'beginnings' were not an accidental by-product of Upadhyay's politics but the direct result of Upadhyay's efforts to work through some of the inner conflicts with which Tagore himself had struggled for much of his life.

[1] Rabindranath Tagore, quoted in Suddhasatva Bosu, *Rabindranather Char Adhyay* (Calcutta: Bharati Publications, 1979), pp. 6–7. Julius Lipner argues that contrary to Tagore's belief, Upadhyay never explicitly advocated violence as the means of expelling the British from India but on occasion came close to doing so. It is, of course, not important whether Upadhyay really said what Tagore thought he was saying, but whether Tagore read Upadhyay's political writings in a particular way. Julius Lipner, 'A Case-Study in "Hindu Catholicism": Brahmabandhab Upadhyay (1861–1907)', *Zeitschrift fur Missionswissenschaft und Religionswissenschaft*, January 1988, pp. 33–54.

Brahmabandhab was born the same year Tagore was, 1861, in a village called Khanyan, thirty-five miles north of Calcutta, in Hooghly district. He was the youngest of three brothers. His real name was Bhavanicharan Bandopadhyay; at home he was called Bhedo. It was a high-status Kulin Brahman family, proudly Shakto. One marker of Kulin status was hypergamy. Bhavani's great-grandfather, Madanmohan Bandopadhyay, had as a matter of fact established his kulinhood the hard way, by marrying fifty-four times.

Madanmohan's son, Bhavani's grandfather Harachandra, was said to be opposed to polygamy, for he had considerately married only twice. Perhaps this had something to do with the fact that Harachandra was the first in the family to be exposed to the expanding world of British India and the opportunities it presented to educated, upper-caste Bengalis. He was a police inspector working with Sleeman to eliminate thuggee. Bhavani's father Debicharan, a less colourful upholder of the family tradition, was also a police inspector and had a transferable job which took him to all parts of India. We presume that he was as much a pillar of the Raj as his father had been.

Details of Bhavani's childhood and family are scanty. We know next to nothing about his brothers and nothing about his relationship with them. We know that his mother died when he was less than a year old and that he was brought up by his grandmother, Chandramoni. Though an orthodox Brahman, Chandramoni had travelled in India, thanks to her husband's job as Sleeman's assistant. She introduced to Bhavani not only the vividness of his cultural traditions but also something of her own disjunctive experiences. Despite being a 'formidable' presence in the household, Chandramoni was particularly fond of her motherless grandson and often protected him from the ire of her stern, disciplinarian son. Despite the tact of Bhavani's biographer, Brahmachari Animananda, Debicharan comes through as an 'autocrat' and 'a man with an iron will' who faithfully followed the imported Victorian adage of never sparing the rod and spoiling his son.[2] However, Debicharan was often not at home and it was Chandramoni who defined much of Bhavani's early social environment for him. Animananda sums up his *guru*'s early interpersonal world as follows:

[2] Brahmachari Animananda, *The Blade: Life and Work of Brahmabandhab Upadhyay* (Calcutta: Roy and Son, n. d., estimated 1940), pp. 10–11.

> There, right under his nose, were two cultures .... Inside the house too it was not all the old system.... in Chandramoni ... lived all the spirit of affectionate self-sacrifice that belonged to old *Bharat*. It is on her lap that he learned the language of the Bengali village. She was the source of the sparkling touches, the beautiful homely expressions that brightened domestic topics in the *Sandhya*. She it was who gave him an eye for things Indian, —the mossy tank, the trees, shrill birds, and the sacred river Sarasvati.... Her pious devotions, her sacred stories, her very life was an embodiment of the old Hindu ideal; Bhavani would never forget it.[3]

The family deity of the Bandopadhyays was the goddess Kali. 'This could not have been', Julius Lipner points out, 'the mild, sensuous figure the sage Ramakrishna popularized later in Bengal, but the awesome deity current in popular devotion—of frightful countenance, terrible to her enemies but beneficent to her devotees.'[4] Many years later, Lipner adds, Upadhyay would invoke 'Kali-the-Terrible' in graphic Bengali, 'as the mediatrix of India's freedom'[5]—perhaps to legitimize the violent, sacrificial element he sought to introduce into Indian nationalism. It was to remain a major cultural innovation in Indian nationalism, an innovation which built upon Bankimchandra's more nuanced invocation of Bengal's dominant mother deities, to provide the symbolic and paradigmatic frame for the invocation of the sacredness of mother India.

Bhavani's early education in a village school probably only confirmed his interpersonal stereotypes. In the school, discipline was strict and physical punishment common. There was only a single teacher; decades later, Bhavani was bitter enough to remember him as Pitambara the Lame and to call him 'a veritable *yama-raj*', God of Death.[6] Bhavani probably suffered more than other students from the culture of his school, for he was a particularly rebellious boy. The fact that he was an excellent student did not help much. One is left with the impression that, between them, Debicharan and Pitambara succeeded in shaping for Bhavani the concept of a terrorizing male authority.

At the age of thirteen, Bhavani had his sacred-thread ceremony and within a year he also took a vow not to eat meat or fish and not to taste alcohol. It was a strange vow to take in a Shakto family and

[3] Ibid., pp. 9–10. [4] Lipner, 'Hindu Catholicism', p. 38.
[5] Ibid. [6] Ibid.

one can only hazard the guess that young Bhavani chose unconsciously to identify with his widowed grandmother rather than with the men in the family; that he already felt some discomfort with the lifestyle associated in his mind with his male elders and was trying to move closer to the mix of the old and the new his grandmother represented. Also, Bhavani's mother Radhakumari might have been a Vaishnava. At least Lipner guesses so from her name.[7] Her faith might have underscored the association young Bhavani could have sensed between being abstemious and moving away from the available male role models in the family.

In keeping with his new ascetic commitments, the adolescent Bhavani also took to physical culture and traditional learning with a vengeance. He joined an indigenous gymnasium, *akhada*, to learn wrestling, picked up ju-jitsu, and became a favourite student of the well-known wrestler, Ambika Guha. Bhavani also turned out to be an excellent cricketer. As for traditional learning, he joined a Sanskrit school, *tol*, to study Sanskritic texts from the famous pandits of Bhatpara. According to one of his biographers, at this age Bhavani also showed qualities of leadership.[8]

Bhavani was not unhappy when, at about this time, his father was transferred to Chinsura, a small city west of Calcutta, where he was admitted to a less oppressive school. But he did even better when, after another transfer, he was sent to a school at Hooghly. There he became a great favourite of Robert Thwaytes, the school's English principal, and Yajnesvara Ghose, the headmaster. When Debicharan was transferred yet again, Bhavani was admitted to the General Assembly Institution which, despite its odd name, was a well-known school in Calcutta. Vivekananda, then known as Narendranath Datta, was his class-fellow.

These rapid moves exposed Bhavani to the invigorating atmosphere of the late-nineteenth century urban culture of the Bengali babus, many of them trying to bring about major changes in their traditional way of life in response to the colonial impact. The stirrings of Indian nationalism which were visible by the mid-1840s had now acquired momentum. By the 1860s, metropolitan Calcutta and the surrounding areas were seething with new ideas about—and experiments with—lifestyles, faiths and ideologies.

There was one expression in particular of this adventure of ideas and reformist zeal which acquired a special meaning in Bhavani's

[7] Lipner, 'Hindu Catholicism', p. 38.
[8] Animananda, *The Blade*, p. 11.

life. His uncle, Kalicharan Banerjea (1847–1907) had become a convert to Christianity when Bhavani was three, and was something of a pillar of the Bengali Christian community. Kalicharan was an educationist, political thinker, and close associate of liberals and nationalist leaders like Surendranath Banerjea (1848–1925) and Ananda Mohan Bose (1847–1906).[9] Though his conversion had shaken the family, social links with him were not severed; he used to visit Khanyan at week-ends. During his visits, he helped Bhavani with his lessons and told him stories from the Mahabharata, which quickly became a favourite with the boy. From the accounts available, one suspects that it was Kalicharan who, of all the father figures Bhavani encountered in his early life, maintained some continuity with Chandramoni's magical world of maternal nurture. One wonders if, through his uncle, Christianity too did not get identified for the young boy as a possible link to that world.

The attraction of Christianity for young, well-placed, upper-caste reformist Hindus in Bengal had many aspects which we need not go into here. However, in the context of Upadhyay's life the comments of Bhupendranath Dutta (1880–1961)—who knew Upadhyay and his family well, was himself a respected freedom fighter of the Swadeshi era, and a believer in the use of violence in the anti-imperialist struggle—are particularly relevant. He diagnoses the attraction of Christianity in late nineteenth-century Bengal to be the result of the all-too-manifest glamour and power of western civilization. This glamour and power dazzled many young Indians exposed to the modern sector and Christian missionaries often rubbed this in. They 'equated the new western civilization with Christianity to establish the superiority of their civilization and religion.... Consequently, seeing the poor state of their own religion and race, many Hindus were attracted to Christianity....'[10]

We shall have to come back to this issue in the context of Bhavani's life, but should mention here that by the time Kalicharan embraced Christianity, Christian missions in India had developed two sharply contrasted attitudes to Indian culture: one was 'strong-

[9] Kalicharan Bandopadhyay also played an interesting role in Gandhi's life. See Mohandas K. Gandhi, *The Message of Jesus Christ* (reprint, Bombay: Bharatiya Vidya Bhavan, 1986), p. 9.

[10] Bhupendranath Dutta, 'Bhumika', in Haridas Mukhopadhyay and Uma Mukhopadhyay, *Upadhyay Brahmabandhaba* (Calcutta: Firma K.L. Mukhopadhyay, 1961), pp. v–xix.

ly evangelical in tone, viewed human nature as utterly corrupted by the Fall', and was uncompromisingly confrontational towards Hinduism and Indian traditions; the other, more conciliatory, refused to condemn non-Christian religions *a priori* and, therefore, was less keen on prosellytization and more open to Hindu categories.[11] Broadly speaking, the first attitude was mainly associated with the Protestants, especially the Baptists, the second with the Catholics.[12] There were unexpected consequences: from the time of Rammohun Roy, the urban upper-caste Bengalis regarded Protestantism as a protest against the amoral hedonism emerging among the babus exposed to colonial rule, while Catholicism was regarded as a culturally more tolerant—and thus less critical—faith. Strange though it may seem in retrospect, this made Catholicism less attractive to the social critics and reformists among the babus who were searching for new bases for social criticism and for new uses of aspects of western culture in India. The number of urban *bhadralok* who turned to Catholicism remained small. We shall return to this point.

At the age of fifteen, Bhavanicharan completed his schooling and was admitted to the Hooghly Mohsin College. The next phase of his life is best described in a delightfully witty, tongue-in-cheek autobiographical essay written by him many years later and, in the next few paragraphs, I shall broadly follow that essay in narrating his story.

The life of a regular student could hold Bhavani only for a year or so (1876–7). Impressed by the nationalist fervour of some of his uncle Kalicharan's mentors, mainly Surendranath Banerjea, he decided to devote all his time to the freedom struggle. Beyond a point, however, the constitutionalist approach of the liberal nationalists failed to satisfy him. It struck him as ineffective, futile posturing. Though he was deeply moved by the public lectures of Banerjea and Ananda Mohan Bose and was later to compare his condition at the time to that of the *gopis* after they had heard Krishna's flute,[13] Bhavani was also influenced by his grandmother's caustic comment: 'Lectures have finished the country.'[14]

[11] Lipner, 'Hindu Catholicism', p. 37.

[12] Ibid.

[13] Animananda, *The Blade*, p. 13.

[14] Brahmabandhab Upadhyay, '*Amar Bharat Uddhar*', *Swaraj*, 26 May and 2 June 1907. For an English translation of this essay I have mainly depended on the extracts translated in Animananda's *The Blade*, pp. 13–22.

At the same time, the idea of the ascetic warrior that had become a part of *bhadralok* folklore since the publication of Bankimchandra's *Anandamath*, was re-emerging in Bhavani's imagination as a practical proposition, probably sanctified by his reading of *Gita* as a political text. Finally, a year later, he decided to give up his studies and join the army of the Maharaja of Gwalior to learn *yuddhavidya*, the science of war. (He also attempted to join the British Indian army so as to fight the Zulus, through a step-uncle of his who worked for the commissioner of recruitment. The uncle did not want his nephew to choose such a risky job; he made sure that the application was shelved on the grounds of Bhavani being a minor.)

Bhavani set off for Gwalior with ten rupees in his pocket, the money for two months' college fees. Three of his friends who joined him were roughly in the same financial state. As a result, the journey turned out to be particularly eventful. They managed to travel up to Etawah in western Uttar Pradesh by train, but Gwalior was another seventy-two miles away. They finally walked it.

The adventure did not last long, for there were three families looking for them. The boys were soon found and brought back to Calcutta. This time Bhavani was put into another college, the Metropolitan Institute, where Surendranath Banerjea himself taught English. But not even the privilege of studying under one of his political idols helped and Bhavani went into a kind of depression for a while, and it appears, even took to drugs.

But he was not one to remain in this condition for long—within a year he had given up taking drugs. His romance with Gwalior was not yet over; the city still beckoned the prospective revolutionary. Soon Bhavani ran away from home again, this time on his own. He was now eighteen and had the princely sum of thirty rupees with him. On it, he reached Gwalior via Agra and Dholepur and even had a dietary adventure on the way. He had turned vegetarian but,on the way to Gwalior, in his enthusiasm to prove himself truly a member of a martial race, he broke his vow and ate meat at the home of a Bengali family. He even persuaded himself that he had enjoyed his return to meat-eating as part of his return to a martial lifestyle, *kshatradharma*.[15] Like many other social reformers and political leaders of his time, Bhavanicharan believed that there was a direct relationship between the cultural practices

[15] Ibid., p. 19.

of the British and their political success; that if Indians could somehow model themselves on the British, political success would automatically follow. And like Vivekananda and unlike Gandhi, he never quite grew out of the belief.

But the Gwalior Army remained an unattainable dream, though for an altogether different reason this time. On arriving at Gwalior, Bhavani first took to teaching English to make a living—he had been an excellent student of English in his school days—and then found the courage to go and meet an elderly general of the Scindia army and tell him straight out, 'Make me a soldier.' The general was, as his interlocutor was to recount many years later, a remarkably impressive, kindly, calm and humble man whom Bhavani immediately respected. He patiently explained to the young nationalist the state of affairs in British protectorates, pointing out that though he was called a general, he did not have any power at all. Even more painful to Bhavani was the reason the general gave for his loss of power. Apparently, once, during exercises, the maharaja and the general were heading two opposing forces. Some English guests were also present. When the maharaja felt hungry, he ordered a path to be cleared for breakfast to be brought in; the general sent word that meals would not be given safe conduct. The maharaja, given his priorities, quickly acknowledged defeat and the relationship between the two soured.[16] After hearing this story, Bhavani could no longer avoid facing the fact that the Scindia of Gwalior was already a toothless vassal of British India. He came back heart-broken to Calcutta in 1880–1.

As with many of his contemporaries, Bhavani's martial nationalism was parallelled by his religious quest. For a while he did odd jobs at a couple of places and went, somewhat aimlessly, on one pilgrimage after another. He also drew close to the mystic philosopher–teacher Ramakrishna Paramhamsa (1836–86) and to Keshabchandra Sen (1838–84) of the Nababidhan Brahmo Samaj, who led at the time one of the most prominent social reform movements in India. By the end of 1881 Bhavani had become a devotee of Sen whom he now considered the greatest Indian of his time.[17] He even enthusiastically joined Sen's bible classes. Though he met the seer Ramakrishna through Sen and admired him greatly, he remained primarily Sen's disciple. It was through Sen and his

[16] Ibid., p. 22.

[17] Mukhopadhyay and Mukhopadhyay, *Upadhyay Brahmabandhab*, p. 15.

uncle Kalicharan that Upadhyay began to move towards Christianity.

When Sen died in 1884 Bhavani found his successor, Pratap Chunder Majumdar, impressive as well as inspiring. As a result, in 1887 Bhavani became a Brahmo and formally joined the Nababidhan movement. Meanwhile there was another development. In 1883 a few graduate students of Calcutta University had established a discussion group called the Eagle's Nest which Bhavani had joined as a teacher of Sanskrit. Among the founders of the Nest was a young Sindhi student, Hiranand, later to become famous as Sadhu Hiranand. After obtaining his B. A. from Calcutta University, Hiranand had returned to Sind, and in 1888, he asked Bhavani to help him in running a school he had founded in Hyderabad, Sind. Bhavani agreed and joined the school as a teacher of Sanskrit.

By all accounts, Bhavani was extremely popular with his students. Certainly he was an uncommon classics teacher at a time when teachers of Sanskrit were stereotyped as being totally cut off from the contemporary world. He played cricket and football with the students, swam, went kite-flying with them, and was as much their friend as their teacher. In addition, he delivered public lectures, worked as a Brahmo missionary, and even officiated at a Brahmo wedding. His integration into the local community was apparently complete. Animananda goes so far as to describe him in Sind as an influential Sindhi among Sindhis.[18]

By now it must be fairly obvious that Bhavani's relationship with his peers always tended to be happier than that with male authorities: the traces of his relationship with Debicharan were probably not dead in him. Now that Bhavani was acquiring the trappings of authority himself, he may have taken special care to see that he remained the first-among-peers rather than become a feared authority.

It must have appeared to many of his well-wishers that at last Bhavani was a happily settled man. They were soon to be proved wrong. He was a person constantly searching, a person for whom a stable external environment only brought into the open new questions and unknown inner passions. This time it was the sudden illness of his father, who had been transferred to Multan in west

[18] Animananda, *The Blade*, p. 33.

Punjab that provided the occasion. Bhavani rushed to Multan and nursed him devotedly, but Debicharan died.

It was while nursing his sick father that Bhavani read Joseph Faa-di Bruno's *Catholic Faith* which exposed him to a new world. He had always been interested in Christianity; the Brahmoism Keshab-chandra represented was itself heavily influenced by Christianity. According to Animananda, 'Bhavani had been attached to Jesus Christ from his early boyhood. He looked upon him as a personal friend.'[19] Now the exposure to Bruno pushed Bhavani onto a more adventurous religious path. He had encountered what to him must have seemed a version of Christianity unconnected with the Raj and more open to the Indian style of spirituality. He was not unduly perturbed by the Catholic connection with imperialism in Africa and South America.

Hiranand, who had some indication of the way his friend's mind was working, wrote to Bhavani's elder brother, warning him of Bhavani's intentions, and was asked to dissuade Bhavani from becoming a Christian. Bhavani dutifully agreed to postpone his conversion by a fortnight. But the die was cast. After the fortnight was over, on 26 February 1891, he joined the Protestant church in which his uncle Kalicharan was already an important figure. Six months later, on 1 September, he became a Catholic and moved to Karachi.

During his ten years in Sind, Bhavani was successful as a social worker and he took an active interest in a number of religious traditions. Prominent among them were Sikhism and Islam, particularly the Islamic tradition of Latif. It was in Karachi in 1893 that Bhavani adopted the name Brahmabandhab Upadhyay, a name which invokes the informal title 'Brahmananda' given to his hero Keshabchandra Sen by his admirers, and also hints both at Bhavani's Brahmanic origins and his lifelong efforts to establish a less hierarchical relationship with the patriarchal theistic authority common to both Brahmoism and Christianity.

The name also invoked that part of his hereditary vocation which never failed to excite him—teaching.

> I have adopted the life of Bhikshu (i.e. mendicant) Sannyasi. The practice prevalent in our country is to adopt a new name along with the adoption of a religious life. Accordingly, I have adopted a new name. My family surname is Vandya (i.e. praised) Upadhyay (i.e. teacher, lit. sub-teacher), and my baptismal name

[19] Ibid., p. 31.

> is Brahmabandhu (Theophilus). I have abandoned that first portion of my family surname, because I am a disciple of Jesus Christ, the Man of Sorrows, the Despised Man. So my new name is Upadhyay Brahmabandhu.[20]

Later, as it was felt that 'Brahmabandhu' could be considered not adequately respectful, a slight change was made in the last name without altering its meaning.[21] More confident of himself now, in 1894 Upadhyay started *Sofia*, a Catholic journal, wanting to make it not merely a mouthpiece of Catholicism but a journal that would cover comparative, critical theology and attempt to search for truth. He also declared that politics would not be discussed in the journal.[22]

It must be obvious by now that Upadhyay had cast himself in the heroic mould and his experiences in Sind had not allowed him much chance to prove himself. The only half-chance that came his way was late in 1896 when Annie Besant (1847–1933) came to Karachi and Upadhyay was drawn into a public debate with her on, of all things, the nature of God. A public debate has a logic of its own: the fireworks and excitement generated by two learned, well-motivated but highly-charged and self-righteous persons could not but lead to each being convinced that he or she had won the debate. The last word on the subject, though, was certainly said by Mrs Besant and it must have hurt the thirty-five-year old, saffron-clad Catholic. On 14 December 1896, she wrote to him:

> Dear Sir.... I trust that some day you also may feel that God is an object of adoration rather than a subject for debate, and that He is better served by truth and good-will than by the stirring up of strife.[23]

What Paresh says about Gora applied as much to Upadhyay: simple, assured peace of mind was not one of his possessions. But Mrs Besant's admonition might have gone home. When plague broke out in Karachi in January 1897, Upadhyay and his disciples, with extraordinary courage and dedication, nursed the abandoned, plague-stricken poor of Karachi; they lived amongst them and cooked for them. One of his devoted disciples, Daulatsing

[20] Editorial in *Sofia*, December 1894, quoted in Lipner, 'Hindu Catholicism', p. 43.

[21] Ibid.

[22] *Sophia*, January 1894, pp. 1–2, quoted in Mukhopadhyay and Mukhopadhyay, *Upadhyay Brahmabandhaba*, p. 34.

[23] Annie Besant, quoted in Animananda, *The Blade*, p. 4.

Ramsingh, died of the plague; it was a miracle that in Upadhyay's circle the toll was so slight.

Despite his own beliefs Upadhyay's Catholicism was in fact a unique statement of faith which he hoped would become part of the Indian culture. On the basis of his study of the neo-Thomists and others, he seemed to take the position that while Hinduism was a natural religion, Christianity was a supernatural one and hence one could simultaneously be both Hindu and Christian. That is, an Indian could be a Christian without needing to renounce or vilify Hinduism or deculturizing himself. A religion that seeks to go beyond reason, he argued, destroys its own basis when it attacks a religion based on nature and reason such as Hinduism. One suspects that Upadhyay wanted to remain a Hindu as far as everyday practices were concerned and make Catholicism the vehicle for his personal spiritual quest, perhaps with Jesus Christ as his *ishthadevata* or personal god.[24] But he was clear in his mind about his religious beliefs: 'Let us be called by any name. We mean to preach the reconcilation of all religions in Christ whom we believe to be perfectly divine and perfectly human.'[25]

Also, the politics of culture always remained a latent passion of Upadhyay's. Even his definition of his new-found faith was contaminated by this passion:

> By birth we are Hindus and shall remain *Hindus* till death.... But as *dvija* (twice-born) by virtue of our sacramental rebirth, we are *Catholic*: we are Hindus as far as our physical and mental constitution is concerned, but in regard to our immortal souls we are Catholics. We are Hindu-Catholics.[26]

Such a view of the relationship between Hinduism and Chris-

[24] Lipner, 'Hindu Catholicism'. For a discussion of the environment within which this response arose, see Julius Lipner, 'A Modern Indian Christian Response', in H.G. Coward (ed.), *Modern Indian Responses to Religious Pluralism* (The State University of New York Press, 1987),,, pp. 291–314.

It seems that while Upadhyay's theology has had a direct impact on the Indian church only recently, his basic philosophical position established a continuity with Indian practices, *lokachara*, early enough. I learn from Jyoti Shahi that in Madras the proportion of those who accept Christ as their *isthadevata* is more than five times the proportion of Christians.

[25] Animananda, *The Blade*, pp. 39.

[26] Brahmabandhab Upadhyay, in *Sophia*, July 1898. Quoted in Chaturvedi Badrinath, *Dharma, India and the World Order: Twenty Essays* (New Delhi: Centre for Policy Research, 1991).

tianity contrasted strongly with the confrontational style of the missionaries of the period and, even more important, with the attitude of Bengali converts to Christianity. One of the main attractions of Christianity for upper-caste Bengalis was the uncompromising hostility shown to Hindu traditions by most missionaries, specially the Protestant denominations chief of whom were the Baptists. Since the days of Rammohun Roy, the Bengali youth had been searching for faiths and ideologies which would take a clear position on the growing hedonism and anomie among the urban Bengalis brought about by the large-scale social disruptions caused by the colonial political economy. Many of these rebels saw no possibility of Hinduism being reformed from within. Catholicism often seemed to such youth, despite the efforts of a number of Catholic missionaries, to be 'soft' on rituals, icons, a plurality of gods, and worldy pleasures. The severity of Protestantism with its sternly monotheistic beliefs and puritan ethic seemed to offer a more appropriate remedy for the social problems of the Bengali middle classes.

The Catholic Church of the time, perhaps sensitive to the same issue, was unlikely to be sympathetic towards Brahmabandhab's venture, especially since there was a heavy dose of Vedanta in Brahmabandhab's version of Christianity. The Church soon stopped the circulation of *Sofia* among Catholics and the journal had to close down in 1900. When Brahmabandhab restarted *Sofia* as a monthly, the Church again expressed its displeasure with some vehemence, for the journal now had a clear political line. The journal finally closed the same year.

It was while editing *Sofia* that Upadhyay first acknowledged the presence of Tagore as a major literary figure in the world. In 1901, as the co-founder and editor of the *Twentieth Century*, one of the first things he did was publish an appreciative review of a book of Tagore's. Tagore remarks in the preface to *Char Adhyay* that that was the first 'unhesitant' critical praise he had ever received. At about this time Tagore started his rural university at Shantiniketan, and in this he sought the help of his new-found friend who had earlier experimented with similar educational ideas.

Upadhyay did help Tagore but did not stay at Shantiniketan for long. He moved to Calcutta and became an ardent preacher of

Vedanta and, in his new incarnation, a passionate apologist of the *varnashrama dharma*, the caste codes. He also undertook a trip to England in 1902–3 to lecture on Hindu philosophy and society. His childhood friend, Vivekananda, had just died and partly the inspiration to spread the philosophy of Vedanta in the West came from Vivekananda's earlier success there. At one time Upadhyay had criticised Vivekananda and his version of the Vedanta; now, deeply moved by Vivekananda's death, he took upon himself his friend's unfinished task, at least partly motivated by what he saw as his friend's real mission: *firingijaivrata*, literally 'the rite of conquering the whites'.[27]

Upadhyay started for England with twenty-seven rupees in his pocket. He was later to describe the visit in his typically self-deprecating manner as an attempt to get from the fair-skinned the same applause that he had received in Calcutta, Bombay and Madras.[28] He was more than successful. Both at Oxford and Cambridge his lectures were highly thought of and Cambridge University not only requested him to recommend a traditional Vedantic scholar as a lecturer at the University but also to find the money to finance a chair in Vedantic studies. However, Upadhyay himself disliked what he saw of the western lifestyle—its rampant consumerism, its self-interest based competitiveness and, above all, its 'liberated' women.

Upadhyay's reaction to the western woman was, to say the least, surprising. He had a Brahmo past and was still a Christian. Both these religious movements had eagerly taken up in Bengal the cause of women. Perhaps, as a *brahmachari* and *sannyasi*, having struggled long with his sexuality, he found the man–woman relationship in England overly eroticized and, hence, painfully anxiety-provoking. Perhaps he missed in England the manner in which both Brahmoism and Christianity in nineteenth-century Bengal linked the cause of women and sexual puritanism. He did write on what he described as the English over-concern with *prakriti* (the common Sanskrit and Bengali word for women as well as nature, including human nature), and the English inability to

[27] Mukhopadhyay and Mukhopadhyay, *Upadhyay Brahmabandhbab*, pp.75–6. In later life, Lipner says ('Hindu Catholicism', p. 48), Upadhyay used the pejorative term *Firingi* for the European.

[28] Mukhopadhyay and Mukhopadhyay, *Upadhyay Brahmabandhab*, p. 78.

understand the Hindu ideals of *nivritti* or abstinence, and *nishkama* or desireless autonomy from *prakriti*. He was probably already unwittingly moving towards the position that Gandhi was to formalize later as an attempt to transcend patriarchy through celibacy.[29]

On his return from England in 1904, Upadhyay started a new daily in Bengali, called the *Sandhya*. When Bengal was partitioned in 1905, *Sandhya* was at the forefront of the struggle against partition and its policy became increasingly supportive of the idea of violent resistance to British rule. It is said that at this time he repeatedly faced and was deeply hurt by the hostility of some Hindu nationalists partly because of his Brahmo and Protestant past but primarily because he was still a practising Catholic. To finally allay their misgivings, Upadhyay performed *prayashchitta* (penitential rite or penance) under the *mitakshara* system of social codes to become a Hindu again. According to his Christian disciple Rebachand, Pandit Panchanan Tarkaratna gave Upadhyay the *vidhan* or injunction for this form of penance. But even before he had performed the rite, Bhupendranath Dutta says, Upadhyay had begun to move towards Hinduism, somewhat in the manner in which the Spanish nationalist El Cid had moved towards Christianity.[30]

In 1907, Upadhyay started a weekly to supplement *Sandhya*. Among other things, the weekly attempted to discover the native culture of the Aryans and attack Nordism in its various guises, particularly its aesthetics. Even a cursory look at Upadhyay's writings of the time makes it clear that he was moving towards a total rejection of the West and a redefinition of the Indian self in such clear-cut, well-bounded, native terms that it could not but lead to the idea of violent resistance and terrorism to drive the British out of India. When Dutta told him in 1907 of an instance of passive resistance by the early Christians, Upadhyay told him straightaway, 'That will not do for us.'[31]

Predictably, Upadhyay was soon picked up and tried for sedition. He refused to appear in court, saying:

[29] Brahmabandhab Upadhyay, '*Bilat-Jatri Sannyasir Chithi*', 1906, quoted in Mukhopadhyay and Mukhopadhyay, *Upadhyay Brahmabandhaba*, pp. 82–4; also see Pat Caplan, 'Celibacy as a Solution? Mahatma Gandhi and *Brahmacharya*', in Pat Caplan (ed.), *The Cultural Construction of Sexuality* (London: Tavistock, 1987), pp. 271–95.

[30] Dutta, 'Bhumika', pp. xiii–xiv, xvii.

[31] Ibid., p. xvii.

> I do not want to take part in the trial because I do not believe that in carrying out my humble share of the God-appointed mission of Swaraj I am in any way accountable to the alien people who happen to rule over us.[32]

While the trial was on, Upadhyay suddenly fell ill and was taken to the Campbell Medical College, Calcutta, where, on account of a tetanus infection after a hernia operation, he died in pain on 27 October 1907.

The hospital authorities, perhaps because they were government officials, did not even wait for his relatives and friends to come and take the body; it was put out in the street, in the sun, outside the hospital.[33] But his admirers by now were legion; they picked up the body and, spontaneously forming a procession in which about 10,000 persons participated, took it to the cremation grounds.

The British-Indian press could hardly hide their relief at Upadhyay's death. The Indians were heart-broken. Many talked of his death as *ichchha-mrityu*, self-chosen death, to avoid being tried by the British.

My brief account of Brahmabandhab Upadhyay's life cannot begin to convey its drama and passions. (Fortunately, there are a few biographies which do some justice to him, particularly the ones by Swami Animananda and Haridas and Uma Mukhopadhyay.[34]) However, I hope I have conveyed some of its richness and complexity, and shown how, since he represented some of the major streams of the nationalist and social reform movements, debates or exchanges over these were not a matter of external encounters for him but became internal confrontations.

In coping with social and political cross-currents as inner vectors Upadhyay was not unique. His friend Vivekananda's brief life was equally stormy, dramatic, and characterized by deep internal

[32] Brahmabandhab Upadhyay, quoted in Jogeshchandra Bagal, *National Biography* (New Delhi: Government of India, 1974), Vol. 4, pp. 372–4.

[33] Dutta, 'Bhumika', p. xiv.

[34] The latter also includes a fascinating foreword by Bhupendranath Datta. We have already used them in this account. Julius Lipner and George Gispert-Sauch are working on a new anthology of Upadhyay's writings which promises to deal with the unique worldview and theology Upadhyay developed. Lipner's two published papers, which we have also used in this account, provide an excellent introduction to Upadhyay's life and work and the reasons which have made him a cult figure for contemporary Christian theologians in India.

contradictions.[35] Similarly, the Gujarati poet, Narmadashanker Lalshanker Dave (1833–86), known as Narmad, had, unknown to Upadhyay, internalized and then given flamboyant, personalized expression to the public issues of his time.[36] However, the social currents in Bengal in Upadhyay's time were more sharply opposed and, as we have already seen, Upadhyay was prone to seek his solutions to private and public problems in a heroic and extravagant fashion. This made his shifts of belief and vocation all the more spectacular and his failures, as Tagore might have put it, more heart-rending. This was fit material for a novelist and Tagore did not waste it.

In all three political novels, Upadhyay is the model for the hero as well as the 'villain'; in two of them, *Char Adhyay* and *Gora*, the heroes, being anti-heroes, can also be seen as the villains. It is possible to contend that Sandip's distorted personality cannot possibly represent Upadhyay's but it is equally possible to answer that, to Tagore, Sandip was the inevitable pathological end-product of the political forces released by the likes of Upadhyay in his later life, and should be construed as Upadhyay's brain child. Nikhil, on the other hand, could be read as the socially creative other self of Upadhyay or as Rabindranath himself, identifying with the earlier, pre-Swadeshi self of Upadhyay. There is little scope for debate about the other two novels. In both, the social conflicts around culture and selfhood are presented in a poignant fashion and, as part of the exercise, nationalism itself is analyzed with a ruthlessness which only a self-confident theorist and builder of Indian self-definition like Tagore could have the courage to do. Had they been written by anyone else, all three novels would have seemed collaborationist to Indians, as at least one of them seemed to Lukacs. (Though a part of Tagore's self-confidence, as we shall suggest below, might have been powered by the morally discomforting awareness that he had within himself something of both Sandip and the earlier Gora.)

[35] Sudhir Kakar, *The Inner World: Childhood and Society in India* (New Delhi: Oxford University Press, 1979; reprint, 1981), pp. 160–81; Krishna Prakash Gupta, 'The Role-Playing of a Religious Tradition: Vivekananda's Reconstruction of Hinduism', in D.L. Sheth and Ashis Nandy (ed.), *The Hindu Vision: Heritage, Challenge and Redefinitions* (New Delhi: Sage, forthcoming).

[36] Navalram Lakshmiram Pandeya, *Kavijivan*, ed. Mohanbhai Shankarbhai Patel (Ahmedabad: Gujarat Vidyapeeth, 1955); Gulabdas Broker, *Narmadashankar* (New Delhi: Sahitya Academy, 1977).

Authority and Defiance: The Artist as Autobiographer

What attracted the romantic, anti-imperialist poet to the heroic nationalist revolutionary? This question is only a variation of one which neither Tagore nor we have posed directly in connection with his three political novels: what attracted Atin to Indranath and Binay to Gora? Or, even more pertinently, what bonded Nikhil to Sandip? Nikhil, after all, knew Sandip well and sensed the seductive pull he might exert over Bimala. Where did innocence end and collusion begin?

Part of the answer can be gleaned from the complex story of Tagore's life, and from his personality as it intermeshed with Upadhyay's. That is a subject too vast for the scope of this essay, but I shall nevertheless permit myself a brief digression on Tagore's early exposure to various forms of social and political authority, with the help of Tagore's two autobiographical works, *Jivansmriti* and *Chhelebela*. I shall suggest that Tagore's relationship with authorities in his childhood was never as conflicted as Upadhyay's and, more crucially, that Tagore often sensed the fragility and transience of such authorities. His rebelliousness, therefore, was tempered as well as deepened by a stronger sense of filial responsibility and personal efficaciousness.

It is as well to remember that the poet himself had little time for biographies and historical empiricism. According to him, a life history has no relevance to a poet's life or selfhood. In 1901 he reviewed a two-volume work on Alfred Tennyson, produced by Tennyson's son, and stated in the review that a poet does not compose his own life the way he composes poetry.[37] Unlike the biographies of *karmaviras*, successful social activists who intervene in life to re-define it and thus lend a touch of poetry and greatness to their own lives, the life of a poet may consist of trivial and routine details.[38] While curious about the lives of the poets of ancient India, he is therefore not unhappy that there is no biography of any of them. 'No one will accept as history the stories that are current about Valmiki. But we feel that they constitute the observed reality about the poet.'[39] Defying this warning however,

[37] Rabindranath Tagore, '*Kavijivani*', in *Rabindra-Rachanabali*, Vol. 4, pp. 688–90.
[38] Ibid., p. 688. [39] Ibid., p. 689.

we shall try to enter the personal life of Tagore, not to define him by the 'hard' realities of his early life, but to set a context to his construction of his own past as it interacted with his times.

There were remarkable differences between the life-experiences of Rabindranath Tagore and Bhavanicharan Bandopadhyay turned Brahmabandhab Upadhyay. Tagore was born in the same year Bhavani was, at Calcutta, thirty-five miles away from the village where Bhavani spent his early years. He too was the youngest child of his parents. Here the similarities end, for Tagore was born into an aristocratic, wealthy, Brahmo family, already well-known for its contribution to the political, economic and cultural life of India. His grandfather, Dwarakanath Tagore (1794–1846), was considered one of the greatest Indians of the nineteenth century. A close associate of the scholar, social reformer and religious leader, Rammohun Roy (1772–1833), and one of the first to embrace Brahmoism, Dwarakanath started life as an official of the British East India Company and ended as a successful entrepreneur, a pioneer in the mining industry, shipping and banking in India, and as a noted social reformer.

Socially at ease with the British community in India, Dwarakanath remained, despite his reformist zeal, a pillar of Bengali society till the end of his life. He was in the forefront of the movement against the practice of *sati* and worked throughout his adult life for the spread of western education, especially the modern system of medicine, in India. Like his hero, Rammohun Roy, he spent his last days in Englannd and died in Surrey.[40]

Dwarakanath's son and Rabindranath's father, Debendranath Tagore (1817–1905), suffered huge financial losses. But the loss was compensated by his enormous stature as a pious man and a social reformer. Debendranath became an ascetic early in life—to judge by his fascinating autobiography, mainly as a reaction to his father's hedonism—and remained so deeply involved in spiritual pursuits that he came to be known in later life as a *maharshi*, a great seer.[41] Such was his commitment that even Benjamin Franklin's 'wordly-wise' religiosity, otherwise clearly impregnated with puri-

[40] The Tagores were *Pirali* Brahmans with a lower status than ordinary Brahmans. Two generations earlier, a forefather had reportedly accepted meat from a Muslim and invited the censure of the community. This marginality, it can be argued, made them fit candidates for new vocations and ventures which would allow them to redeem their lost social status. And the new political economy in eastern India, introduced by the Raj, opened up such a possibility for them.

[41] Debendranath Tagore, *Atmajivani*.

tan ethics, disturbed him by its worldliness.[42] Asceticism, however, did not interfere with Debendranath's organizational skills and it was he who did the most to give a sustainable structure to the Brahmo Samaj movement. Even after Keshabchandra Sen (who was to fire the imagination of the young Bhavani) parted company with him in 1864, Debendranath continued to head a major faction of the Brahmos.

By the 1870s, the Tagores were even more heavily influenced by western intellectual traditions and social mores. There was obviously some legitimacy for this bicultural existence in urban, upper-caste Bengali society; it must have met a widely-felt social need. The *babus* perhaps sensed that such experiments in bicultural living were important and, contrary to popular belief, they did not view the Tagores' western ways as an attack on native society. Certainly the Tagores, despite their cultural and religious heterodoxy, dominated the Bengali cultural scene for about one hundred years, not only in the world of literature, music and the fine arts, but also in fashions and lifestyle. They remained till the 1940s the most important of the families trying to set the standards by which urban upper-caste Bengalis decided what should or should not be borrowed from the culture of their rulers, and what could or could not constitute the necessary new forms of pan-Indian contemporaneity. (There is no better illustration of this than the now-dominant style of wearing the sari which the Tagore women evolved. Influenced by the traditional Bengali and some south Indian ways of wearing a sari, the new style evolved by the Tagores quickly became for most urban Indians the formal, pan-Indian, 'traditional' Bengali way of tying the sari. The only comparable 'invention of tradition' I can think of is the Gandhian *charkha*, which was a version of the traditional *charkha* developed by an urban Parsi technician with Gandhi's encouragement.)

Rabindranath claims in his autobiography—and most knowledgeable Bengalis would agree with him—that though his family adopted many western practices or *prathas*, the Tagores always retained their pride in their own country.[43] This pride found expression in a somewhat adolescent, romantic defiance of the British authorities, which the authorities were mature enough not

[42] Rabindranath Tagore, '*Jivansmriti*', *Rabindra-Rachnabali*, Vol. 10, pp. 3–125; see p. 45.

[43] Ibid., p. 66.

to take seriously or attempt to suppress. In *Jivansmriti* Tagore comments, with a mixture of sarcasm, self-deprecation, and admiration for the finesse of the colonial power, that no one had written to the London *Times* complaining about the casual attitude of the British-Indian government to the arrogance of a defiant young poet and the danger he posed to the Raj.[44]

Tagore relates in *Jivansmriti* how he attended a number of adventurous secret meetings organized by his cousin Jyotirindranath Tagore or Jyoti. These were held, appropriately enough, in an abandoned house in a Calcutta lane. The only thing dangerous about the meetings was their secrecy.[45] Tagore constructs the moral of the story thus:

> Courage may be comforting or discomforting but it always invokes respect; a way must be kept open in any state for the expression of heroism. In the absence of such an opening, it finds expression in peculiar ways and its consequences become unthinkable.[46]

Rabindranath perspicaciously adds that if the government had suspected real danger, the farce would have become a tragedy.[47] He goes on to describe Jyoti's introduction of a rather comic form of national dress that was a cross between *dhoti* and pyjama, and his attempts to establish an indigenous match-box factory and a textile mill. Both were fiascos and it was only the entry of a couple of realistic, 'sane' persons into the group that brought it down to earth.[48] But not before Tagore had internalized the image of Jyotirindranath as a possible model for a patriotic hero—romantic, to the extent of being comically so, but also courageous, moral and supportive. Almost, one is tempted to add, an early prototype of Nikhil in *Ghare-Baire*.

Jyoti and his kind may not have left a mark on the political history of Indian nationalism, but they did provide for Tagore another model of patriotism. In this model, patriotism had touches of aristocratic amateurishness, of a game that was serious, but not serious enough to be turned into a combat with no scope for chivalry, romance, or fun. The casual comments in Abanindranath Tagore's autobiography on Jyoti's nationalism endorse Rabindranath's memories in every important respect, besides indicating why, to the Tagores, the tense nationalistic spirit of the post-

[44] Ibid., p. 67. [45] Ibid.
[46] Ibid. [47] Ibid. [48] Ibid., pp. 68–9.

Swadeshi period was to seem a betrayal of the youthful innocence and authenticity of truly Indian nationalism.[49]

In Abanindranath's reconstruction of the spirit of that nationalism, there was no intense pain or conflict, no gory heroism; there were only lovable successes and forgivable failures. Rabindranath led the younger Tagores into adventurous business ventures which invariably failed, reaffirmations of Bengali culture, dress and language which sometimes succeeded, and into the collection of funds for nationalist work through organizing processions and demonstrations which, whether they were successful or not, ended as noisy, festive events. Few feared such nationalism, certainly not the whites. Abanindranath even recounts one episode where some English residents of Calcutta waved their hats and shouted nationalist slogans like 'Bande Mataram'. When Abanindranath's mother took to the *charkha*, a Mr Havell (presumably the principal of the Government Art College, Calcutta) imported a *charkha* from England for her.[50]

'One's memories of one's life', Tagore says at the beginning of *Jivansmriti*, 'is not the same as the history of one's own life'; 'the invisible artist who draws one's life on one's memory paints a picture and is not interested in a mirror image.'[51] If the story of one's life is not the same as a life history or a formal autobiography, if such a story is ultimately a matter of creative fantasy, it should bear a relationship with one's literary works and perhaps even with the organizing principles of one's creative imagination. We shall briefly introduce here only one of the threads of continuity running through Rabindranath's story of his own life, his political novels, and his complex ambivalence towards Upadhyay's nationalist politics. This continuity is the nature of the male authority Rabindranath encountered in his early years, the means he developed to cope with it, and the strengths and weaknesses which eventually informed his concept of a political leader. The discovery of Jyoti as a model might not have been an accident.

Rabindranath's father, we learn from *Jivansmriti*, was frequently away from home during the poet's childhood. At home, Debendranath's authority was unquestioned; when he was absent, a huge staff of servants constituted the immediate authority for the young

[49] Abanindranath Tagore and Rani Chanda, *Gharoa* (Calcutta: Visvabharati, 1971).

[50] Ibid. See especially pp. 24–34.

[51] Ibid., p. 5.

Rabindranath. His mother, with her large brood of children, always remained for him something of a distant source of love and care.

The urban, upper middle-class Bengali world had already developed in Calcutta a culture which was to play a significant social role over the next hundred years. This culture gave servants an important place in child-rearing and pre-adolescent socialization, a function that survived till after the end of World War II. One important aspect of the function was the disciplinary powers the servants exercised over the children, perhaps as a partial compensation for the monetization of their work culture and social relationships with employers. Holding such authority over the children was probably a mutually acceptable means of reaffirming the non-contractual nature of social relations between employer and employee. In *Jivansmriti*, Rabindranath calls the system *bhrityarajak tantra*, and compares its presiding authorities with the slave dynasty which had ruled India in medieval times.[52]

Certainly in Tagore's family, to judge by a number of memoirs, the servants wielded enormous authority.[53] They supervised the food, dress and play of the children and their power, though only a delegated one, seemed to the children quite awesome. It was this second-order, fragile but oppressive immediate authority that Tagore first learnt to negotiate in life. He quickly found out that

[52] Ibid., pp. 16–17. Cf. the role of the servants in the life of another great Calcuttan, a physicist turned plant physiologist, Jagadis Chandra Bose (1857–1937), in Ashis Nandy, 'Defiance and Conformity in Science: The World of Jagadis Chandra Bose', in *Alternative Sciences: Creativity and Authenticity in Two Indian Scientists* (revised edition, New Delhi: Oxford University Press, forthcoming 1993), Part 2.

In later life, in one of his most moving short stories, Tagore was to reverse the relationship he describes with such wit in *Jivansmriti*. See Rabindranath Tagore, '*Khokababur Pratyavartan*', *Rabindra-Rachanabali*, Vol. 8, pp. 514–19. The story indicates that underlying the tense relationship between servants and children of the Tagore family lay an awareness of the loyalty, affection and, what Takie Lebra calls self–other exchange which bound the two sides together. See note 53 below.

[53] See for instance the two classic general descriptions of the Tagore family environment in Tagore and Chanda, *Gharoa*; and *Jorasankor Dhare* (Calcutta: Visvabharati, 1960). Cf., for instance, Takie S. Lebra, 'Socialization of Aristocratic Children by Commoners: Recalled Experiences of the Hereditary Elite in Modern Japan', *Cultural Anthropology*, in press; and 'Migawari: The Cultural Idiom of Self–Other Exchange in Japan', presented at the International Conference on Perceptions of Self in China, India and Japan, Honolulu, 14–18 August 1989. Interestingly, Lebra presumes her observations, very similar to ones available about the Tagore family, to be unique to Japan.

while physical punishment was frequently given, it could, with some adroitness be avoided. For if a child preferred to have simpler (and cheaper) snacks than the parents had provided for, it allowed the servants to make money on the children's food. If a servant was addicted to opium and, needing extra nourishment, did not press the children unduly to drink their milk, a child very soon learnt—as Rabindranath did—to make a fuss about drinking milk.[54]

This created space for manoeuvre went with a latent perception of the feebleness of the servants' hold over them. The final authority vested in the adult members of the family, who were a varied lot, mostly unconcerned with the children's day-to-day life, and lived in their own world, a world to which the children had only limited access.[55] Certainly nowhere in Rabindranath's childhood memories does one find the tense, passionate bitterness towards authority that is revealed in Upadhyay's reconstruction of his childhood. Both in *Jivansmriti* and *Chhelebela*, there are references to oppressively strict schools and unimaginative teachers but the happier memories of affectionate, highly creative authorities soften them and convert them into half-serious half-comic experiences. At least the two autobiographical accounts suggest that Debendranath never seriously interfered with Rabindranath's autonomy, not even when assertion of that autonomy involved defiance of Debendranath's tastes and opinions.[56] The only thing Debendranath seemed uncompromising about was cold baths; Rabindranath says that even at Dalhousie, the Himalayan hill resort, he had to bathe in icy water.[57]

While young Rabindranath was discovering for himself the secret of controlling his immediate authorities, his family was introducing him to the secret of new forms of dissent from the established and the authoritative. In this, Jyotirindranath again played an important part. Jyoti was the first to offer young Rabindranath not merely a model of dissent but also a model of male authority which was both ardently patriotic and gifted with an intense capacity for artistic expression together with a style of creativity which borrowed uninhibitedly from both the East and the West. Rabindranath says:

[54] *Jivansmriti*, pp. 16–17.
[55] Tagore, *Gharoa*, pp. 103–4.
[56] Ibid., p. 47. [57] Ibid.

> In studying literature, in the cultivation of the arts, from childhood onwards, my main support was Jyotidada.... I uninhibitedly joined him in discussions of things emotional and cognitive; he did not ignore me as a mere child.
>
> He gave me a certain large-sized freedom; in his company I lost my inner inhibitions. Nobody else would have dared to give that kind of freedom.... If I had not been freed from fetters at the time, I would have been crippled for the rest of my life.[58]

It was Jyoti who was the formative influence in developing Rabindranath's basic ambivalence towards the idea of social evolution and human engineering. Discussing the role Jyoti played in his life Rabindranath says:

> The powerful always seek to limit freedom by talking of the misuse of freedom, but freedom cannot be called freedom unless one has the right to misuse it.... Only Jyotidada, without any inhibition and through all good and evil, has pushed me towards my self-realization.... From this experience I have learnt to fear the menace of the good-that-comes-in-the-form-of-improving-others more than evil itself.[59]

There have been many rumours about Rabindranath's love for, or even affair with, Jyoti's wife, Kadambari Devi. The rumours, even if they have no basis, serve to underscore the intense relationship Rabindranath had with his sister-in-law. If it was Jyoti who introduced Rabindranath to the world of politics and the arts, she was the first of the Tagores and their family friends to recognize Rabindranath's immense creative talent. Certainly she was the first to give the young Rabindranath, deeply unsure of his writing, confidence in himself.

Kadambari Devi killed herself a few months after Rabindranath's marriage. The suicide probably had more to do with Jyoti and his association with the world of the threatre than with Rabindranath, but it was nevertheless a trauma for the young poet. He was certainly haunted till the end of his life by painful memories of one who represented a mix of protective care, and the spirit of intellectual adventure and social commitment. In his seventies, when he took to painting, the face of Kadambari Debi became a leitmotif in his work. It is probably no accident that in some of his important novels, including *Ghare-Baire*, there are

[58] Ibid., p. 61. [59] Ibid.

situations where wives guiltily recognize that they have fallen in love with talented, spirited poetic figures—men who were sometimes inspired, like the young Rabindranath, by passionate, violent forms of nationalism—thus betraying the trust of their less flamboyant husbands who were equally noble, public-spirited, courageous beings.[60] In Tagore's novels, such husbands are often men who are open to other cultures, and their affirmation of Indianness is often affirmation of a more catholic form of cultural selfhood. Jyoti might have provided the inspiration for Nikhil and it is easy to interpret Nikhil and Sandip as being two aspects of Brahmabandhab; but at another plane both Nikhil and Sandip can be read as aspects of Rabindranath himself, with the 'guilty' self 'villainized' and projected counter-phobically into Sandip.

Jivansmriti underscores another sharp contrast between the life experiences of Upadhyay and Rabindranath Tagore. To Tagore, thanks to his early exposure to the West, the West was never a forbidding presence.[61] He perceived the social and cultural diversity of the West, including the poor, the humble and idealistic. In *Jivansmriti* he remembers his Latin teacher in England—shy, badly-dressed, undernourished, prematurely old, and vulnerable.[62] He remembers his English school as a place where he was the subject of friendly curiosity and where his fellow-students would often shyly push apples and oranges into his pocket and run away.[63] He was also exposed early in his stay to the less-than-imperial self of an England brutalized by the industrial revolution. In his second letter from England he mentioned, with a clear touch of disgust, the dirty, pathologically violent, sub-human existence of the lower classes in England.[64] He noticed the cultural barrenness of everyday life in England as well as the inferior position of women and the empty lives they led.[65] It was unlikely that he would ever be in awe of England: to him the country would be like any other, a mix of good and evil. Tagore, like Gandhi, could not but feel that there was an acceptable, in fact, a lovable West, and that this other West was waiting to be rediscovered.

In comparison, Tagore's sensitivity to the India beyond Bengal is

[60] See especially Rabindranath Tagore, '*Nastanir*', in *Rabindra-Rachanabali*, Vol. 9, pp. 337–70. Also accessible in film form as Satyajit Ray's classic film *Charulata*.

[61] Tagore, '*Jivansmriti*', see particularly pp. 73–88.

[62] Ibid., p. 75. [63] Ibid., p. 74.

[64] Rabindranath Tagore, 'Europe-*Pravasir Patra*', in *Rabindra-Rachanabali*, Vol. 10 pp. 242–6. [65] Ibid.

somewhat obtuse. His description of his days at Ahmedabad is culturally empty, and though the city inspired him to write one of his finest stories, *Kshudita Pashan*, the inspiration came primarily from the palace in which his elder brother, an official of the Raj, stayed. There is nothing of Gujarat in the story. Likewise, the little cultures of the Himalaya are hardly noticed in the *Jivansmriti*, even though he writes with great feeling about his days at Dalhousie. The closest Rabindranath comes to acknowledging the other traditions of India is when he mentions his father's participation in the singing of *gurvani* at the Golden Temple in Amritsar.[66]

Here, too, one notices the contrast with Upadhyay, who—despite his deep commitment to the greater Sanskritic culture, and his occasional crude harangues against the little cultures of India—was deeply influenced by his experiences in Gwalior and Sind. Tagore's catholicity, on the other hand, had little place for the little cultures of India outside eastern India; he presumably identified them as minor local variations of the greater Sanskritic tradition. On the whole, however, for both Tagore and Upadhyay—or for that matter almost all the major political and intellectual actors of their age—Vedantic Hinduism was the real core of Hinduism and the basis of all social and political activism. Few were sensitive to the élitism and defensiveness implicit in such Vedanticism. It was only after the entry of Gandhi into Indian public life that a new awareness arose of the politics of cultures which was turning the little cultures of India into the society's last line of defence against the colonizing West. They became a major source of resistance against what Tagore identified as the pathologies of nationalism and the organized violence increasingly associated with the modernization of India. Gandhi was willing to build upon the contradiction between the nationalism which entered India as an imperial category and the nationalism which sprang out of democratic aspirations, hoping that the latter would some day supersede the former. For the former had established clear links with the classical tradition and the Brahmanic order, the latter with the noncanonical and the local. The Mahatma might not have shared Tagore's hostility to the very idea of nationalism but he did share the poet's moral concerns.

Presumably they were the same moral concerns that moved

[66] Tagore, '*Jivansmriti*', p. 43.

Upadhyay. Or so at least Tagore believed when he described his last encounter with his revolutionary friend a short while before he died in 1907. To the extent Tagore saw Upadhyay as rooted in his culture, he also saw him as sharing his concerns with resisting the scientization and impersonalization of violence in the name of nationalism. At the least, the poet must have presumed, there was a painful and intense struggle within the revolutionary to reconcile his culture with his own political methodology.

The encounter between the two derived its moral tension and tragic grandeur from Tagore's faith that Upadhyay in his authenticity could not but rebel against the other Upadhyay who gave priority to nationalist allegiance over cultural selfhood.

Underlying the tension was, however, Tagore's deep ambivalence towards Upadhyay as a nationalist actor. The ambivalence was generated by something more than the purely moral concerns we have spelt out. We have already hinted that during his younger, Hindu *mela* days, Tagore had agreed with many elements of Upadhyay's culturally exclusivist ideology. Tagore's image of India at that stage, at least one commentator has noticed, excluded not merely Muslims and Christians but also the low-brow pagan India of the epics.[67] We have already noted that Tagore's sensitivity to the little cultures of India was less than impressive. As late as 1902, Tagore wrote authoritatively that the Brahmavidyalaya at Shantiniketan would not allow anything which went against the Hindu society;[68] his concept of Hinduism at that time was not as catholic as it was to become later.

It is even possible to argue that for Tagore, before the turn of the century, only a Brahmanic India could be India.[69] It was after 1905 that he became open to an inclusive concept of India, and capable of writing the three political novels we have analysed in this essay.

To this second Tagore, Upadhyay was a psychological threat. At one time, Upadhyay had summed up for Tagore Indian attempts to resolve the contradictions between East and West, and between Hindu and non-Hindu. Upadhyay had achieved in personal terms what Tagore was only now struggling to do. Yet, for reasons which were not very clear, Upadhyay was not merely willing to retreat

[67] Surajit Dasgupta, '*Desh o Dharma Prasange Rabindrachetanar Vivartan*', in Premendra Mitra and Amyakumar Majumdar (ed.), *Rabindra Prasanga* (Calcutta: Baitanik, 1976), pp. 36–40.

[68] Ibid., p. 38.

[69] Ibid., pp. 37–9.

—from inclusiveness and tolerance to exclusivism and intolerance —he seemed on the verge of acting out his new-found ideology. What must have disturbed Tagore even more was his realization that it was not a new ideology; Upadhyay was merely reverting to Tagore's earlier nationalist stance, which the poet had—perhaps painfully—transcended.

Four

Conclusion

The Larger Crisis

Many of my observations on Tagore's attitude to nationalism may sound strange to Indians whose own nationalism has been significantly shaped by Tagore and his creative works. Many former freedom fighters recall how they faced police violence during the freedom movement singing Tagore songs. Jogendranath Gupta mentions how in 1906 the aging freedom fighter Bipin Chandra Pal once caught hold of the horse of a Superintendent Kemp, at the head of a baton-wielding police posse, and tremulously sang these lines from a Tagore song:

> The more they tighten their knots
> The weaker will our knots be ...[1]

What is the nature of this consciousness to which Tagore was trying to give shape, while rejecting nationalism?

One obvious answer would be that Tagore rejected the idea of nationalism but practised anti-imperialist politics all his life. But this only leads to the further question: how did he arrive at this position at a time when nationalism, patriotism and anti-imperialism were a single concept for most Indians? One suggestion, already given, was that to Tagore, Indian unity was primarily a social fact, not a political agenda. From the days of the ninth Hindu Mela in 1875, when at the age of 14 he was first exposed to public life, to the day he resigned his knighthood in protest against the Jallianwalla Bagh massacre in 1919, Tagore refused to grant primacy to politics even while sometimes participating in politics. Here lay his basic difference with Gandhi, to whom politics was a

[1] Jogendranath Gupta, '*Rabindranath o Swadeshi Andolan*', in *Rabindra Shatabarshiki Smarak Grantha, Calcutta Municipal Gazette*, 1961, pp. 35–41.

means of testing the ethics appropriate to our times and was therefore crucial to one's moral life. Everyone did not have to be an active politician, but everyone, Gandhi felt, had to work within a framework in which politics had a special place.

What linked the two was, however, their continuing attempts to reaffirm a moral universe within which one's politics and social ideology could be located. This is a concept of politics which had begun to recede a little more than two hundred years ago. For the global system of nation-states—which, according to Tagore, had made a science out of statecraft—did not recognize any link between politics and morality, unless morality was willing to articulate itself as a political force, so that it could not be ignored as a significant presence in political calculation. Gandhi understood this and was perfectly willing to politicize his moral stance, though on moral grounds, not political. He was willing to live, to borrow an expression from Arnold Toynbee's tribute to him, in 'the slum of politics'. Tagore respected Gandhi's worldview up to a point but lived in a different world.

A central theme in Tagore's reaffirmation of a moral universe was an universalism that denied moral and cultural relativism and endorsed a large, plural concept of India. He said so directly:

> Because we have missed the character of India as one related to the whole world, we have in our action and thought given a description of India which is narrow and faded; that description has given primacy to our calculativeness, out of which nothing great can be created.[2]

This universalism of Tagore was not an entirely new contribution to Indian politics. (The terms Arabindo Poddar and some others use to describe the concept of patriotism that underpins this universalism are apt: *Bharatchinta* or *swadeshchinta*, literally 'thinking about or concern with India or one's own country'. Both terms convey the idea of patriotism without nationalism.) From the very beginning of the growth of Indian 'nationalism', there had been a conscious effort on the part of many Indian social reformers and political activists to develop a *Bharatchinta* which would project a self-definition transcending the geographical barriers of India. The first serious political thinker of modern India, Rammohun Roy, had refused to view the problems of India in isolation from the world, and this tradition was even more alive in Tagore's time.

[2] Arabindo Poddar, '*Rabindranather Bharatchinta*', *Calcutta Municipal* [illegible] Tagore Birth Centenary Number, 1961, pp. 86–9.

Despite occasional attempts to base Indian nationalism on unalloyed self-interest, 'pure' nationalism had never been able to mobilize even the Indian middle classes fully. Indian nationalism still vaguely reflected, in however distorted a form, what could be called the ultimate civilizational ambition of India: to be the cultural epitome of the world and to redefine or convert all passionate self–other debates into self–self debates.

In Tagore's case, this ambition was sharpened by his attempt to locate the problem of India in the crisis of the global civilization. He was to diagnose this crisis in a moving testament he published on his 80th birthday, a few weeks before his death.[3] It is an appropriate text with which to end this essay.

In the testament Tagore points out that India has always been open to other civilizations and particularly to Europe, since an unique conjunction of events had fastened India's fate to England's history. As a result, even in their struggle for national freedom, Indian faith in the English people was not completely extinguished.[4] Not merely the declamations of Burke and Macaulay, but the poetry of Shakespeare and Byron, and the English openness to political refugees from other countries contributed to the survival of this faith.[5] Tagore mentions that, as a boy in England, he had heard John Bright speak and his 'large-hearted, radical liberalism' had left such a deep impression on him that it had not faded even at the age of 80. He mentions that since the *sadachara* of Manu (the concept corresponding to civilization in Sanskrit), appeared to many young Indians of that time to have degenerated into a 'socialized tyranny' of 'set codes of conduct', they had preferred the ideal of 'civilization' represented by the English term.[6]

Slowly, however, came a 'painful parting of ways' and disillusion. Tagore began to discover 'how easily those who accepted the highest truths of civilization disowned them with impunity whenever questions of national self-interest were involved.'[7]

> There came a time when perforce I had to snatch myself away from mere appreciation of literature.... I began to realize that

[3] Rabindranath Tagore, *Crisis in Civilization* (Bombay: International Book House, 1941).

[4] Ibid., p. 2. [5] Ibid.

[6] Ibid., pp. 2–3. [7] Ibid., p. 4.

> perhaps in no other modern state was there such a hopeless dearth of the most elementary needs of existence. And yet it was this country whose resources had fed for so long the wealth and magnificence of the British people. While I was lost in the contemplation of the world of civilization, I could never have remotely imagined that the great ideals of humanity would end in such ruthless travesty. But today a glaring example of it stares me in the face in the utter and contemptuous indifference of a so-called civilized race to the well-being of scores of Indian people.[8]

This political awareness brought about Tagore's 'gradual loss of faith in the claims of the European nations to civilization.'[9]

> The spirit of violence which perhaps lay dormant in the psychology of the West, has at last roused itself and desecrates the spirit of man. I had at one time believed that the springs of civilization would issue out of the heart of Europe, but today when I am about to quit the world that hope has gone bankrupt altogether....
>
> As I look around I see the crumbling ruins of a proud civilization. Any yet I shall not commit the grievous sin of losing faith in Man. I would rather look forward to the opening of a new chapter in history....[10]

Perhaps this was merely the rambling despair of an elderly pacifist confronted with two world wars within his lifetime. Or perhaps Tagore had come full circle to Gandhi's position that Indian nationalism as well as universalism had to be built on a critique of the modern West. We only know that this indictment of the West was the context within which Tagore sought to locate his new politics.

On the other hand, it is doubtful if he had much hope of Indian nationalism either. Once he had dreamt, like Gandhi, that India's national self-definition would some day provide a critique of western nationalism, that Indian civilization with its demonstrated capacity to live with and creatively use contradictions and inconsistencies would produce a 'national' ideology that would transcend nationalism. However, even before his death, nationalism in India proved itself to be not only more universal but also more resilient than it had been thought. Today, fifty years after Tagore's death and forty years after Gandhi's, their version of patriotism has almost ceased to exist, even in India, and for most modern Indi

[8] Ibid., pp. 4–5. [9] Ibid., p. 8. [10] Ibid., pp. 10–11.

this is not a matter of sorrow but of pride. Only a few Indians, who have begun to sense the decline of the present global system of nation-states, perceive that the decline of that distinctive tradition of political self-awareness means the loss of an alternative basis for human and political orders.

Writing of nationalist thought, Ernest Gellner comments that the precise doctrines of nationalist thinkers

> are hardly worth analyzing. This is because we seem to be in the presence of a phenomenon which springs directly and inevitably from basic changes in our shared social condition, from changes in the overall relation between society, culture and polity. The precise appearance and local form of this phenomenon no doubt depends a very great deal on local circumstances which deserve study; but I doubt whether the nuances of nationalist doctrine played much part in modifying these circumstances.[11]

Maybe Gellner is right. But the question still remains: how were Tagore or, for that matter, Gandhi able to defy the universal sociology of nationalism? And how were they able to institutionalize their scepticism of the clenched-teeth European version of nationalism in the Indian national movement itself? Was there something in Indian culture, as Tagore believed, which allowed such play, even if it was only a temporary phase?

This essay has not answered these questions adequately. Yet, to round off the picture and to add to the part-answers, I shall briefly consider here the possibility that questions about nationalism can be posed on an altogether different plane. On that plane, cultural and psychological issues are less inconsequential and human ingenuity is more significant. To give random examples, attempts to pose the question thus have been made by Erik Erikson in his study of Adolf Hilter's younger years; Sudhir Kakar in his study of Swami Vivekananda's childhood; Susanne and Lloyd Rudolph and Victor Wolfenstein in their essays on Gandhi.[12] In this way of looking at nationalism, individual thinkers and their thoughts become crucial in ways which Gellner may not approve of.

[11] Ernest Gellner, *Nations and Nationalism* (Ithaca: Cornell University Press, 1983), p. 124.

[12] Erik Erikson, *Childhood and Society*; Susanne Rudolph and Lloyd Rudolph, *The Modernity of Tradition: Political Development in India* (Chicago University Press, 1967); Kakar, *The Inner World*, pp. 160–81; E. Victor Wolfenstein, *The Revolutionary Personality* (Princeton University Press, 1967).

A simple-minded book formulates the issue plainly: Richard A. Koenigsberg argues in *The Psychoanalysis of Racism, Revolution and Nationalism* that faith in the absolute reality of the nation is constituted of three interrelated core fantasies: the fantasy of the nation as a suffering mother, the fantasy of the nation as omnipotent mother, and that of the nation as a projection of infantile narcissism.[13] The wish to save the nation is the 'projective equivalent of the wish to restore the omnipotence of the mother',[14] Koenigsberg argues, and he goes on to use, among others, the example of Sri Aurobindo's invocation of the mother:

> Insofar as the nation is experienced by the nationalist as a projection of the omnipotent mother, the nationalist tends to feel that, as long as he is contained within the boundaries of the nation, he shall be shielded from the external world: the nation shall act as a 'buffer', standing between the individual and the harshness of reality....[15]

It is this projection which helps the religious impulse to find expression in the ideology of nationalism.

Koenigsberg is supported in the Indian context, and specificially in the case of Aurobindo, by others suggesting a roughly similar interpretation.[16] But something more might have been involved for persons like Gandhi and Tagore. They saw themselves as belonging to a civilization that refused to view politics only as a secularized arena of human initiative. While associating the country with maternity and sacredness, they insisted that the association imposed a responsibility on the individual to maintain that sacredness. Certainly in both there was not only a built-in critique of nationalism but also that of the social and cultural realities of the nation. It is significant that Gandhi, who dismissed Catherine Mayo's racist criticism of India in *Mother India* as a drain inspector's report, nevertheless advised every Indian to read the book.[17]

Thus, at one plane, Tagore may be read as a perfect instance of Koenigsberg's thesis; his uninhibited use of the symbolism of the

[13] Richard A. Koenigsberg, *The Psychoanalysis of Racism, Revolution and Nationalism* (New York: The Library of Social Science, 1977), p. 2.

[14] Ibid., p. 6.

[15] Ibid., pp. 8–9.

[16] Philip Spratt, *Hindu Culture and Personality* (Bombay: Manaktalas, 1966); on Aurobindo see specially Nandy, *The Intimate Enemy*, pp. 85–100.

[17] Catherine Mayo, *Mother India* (New York: Blue Ribbon Books, 1927).

country-as-mother in many of his patriotic songs and poems gives them intense emotional vibrancy. However, this symbolism of the country as mother also invokes something of a peasant's or tribe's traditional, ecologically sensitive, ego-syntonic fantasy of a nurturing mother who can any moment turn less benevolent. The omnipotence of the mother is recognized but feared; it is not romanticized or defensively glorified. Nor is it used merely as a means of restoring one's infantile narcissism through identification with a nation, as probably happens in societies that have clearly broken away from or repressed or lost touch—through disasters like large-scale uprooting–with their pre-modern pasts.

So while Tagore wrote with great sensitivity and felicity about the nation as suffering mother, he also took a position against nationalism. Even the national anthems he wrote (he posthumously flouted the first canon of exclusivist nationalism by authoring the national anthems of two independent nation-states which are not always on the best of terms and one of which is the only Islamic state ever to have a national anthem written by a non-Muslim) are remarkably free of any parochialism. They celebrate the contemplation of the Earth Mother in one case and the ruler of the hearts of the people on the other. But then, perhaps only in South Asia would they be chosen as national anthems.

One should not underestimate the hostility Tagore's concept of nationalism aroused in the expanding middle-class culture of Indian politics. The modern Indian, I have already indicated, has never been happy with Tagore's idea of patriotism. For instance, controversy has dogged the national anthem, *Janaganamana*, and claims have occasionally been made that the song was written in honour of King George V when he visited India. There is a particularly touching letter of Tagore to the literary critic Pulinbihari Sen that expresses the poet's distress on that score, for Tagore *did* sense that many Indians, unable directly to question his patriotism, were focusing on the supposed origins of the song. In the letter to Sen, written in 1937, Tagore says,

> You have asked if I have written the song *Janaganamana* for any particular occasion. I can sense that the question has arisen in your mind because of the controversy in some circles of the country about the song... I am responding to your letter not to stoke the fire of the controversy but to satisfy your curiosity....
>
> ...That year arrangements were being made for the arrival of

the emperor of India. A friend of mine well-established in the government made an earnest request to me to compose a song of victory (*jayagana*) for the emperor. I was shocked and with the shock there rose in me anger, too. In a strong reaction, I announced in the song *Janaganamana* the victory of that creator of India's destiny (*bharatabhagyavidhata*), who is the eternal charioteer (*chira sarathi*) of travellers walking eon after eon on the uneven road of declines and ascents (*patana abhyudaya bandhur-panthay yuga-yuga dhabita yatri*), a charioteer who knows the heart of the people and can show them the way (*antarayami patha parichayaka*). That that eternal charioteer of human fate (*yugayugantarer manavabhagyarathachalaka*) could not be the fifth, sixth or any George even the loyalist friend of mine understood. For however firm he might have been in his loyalty, he did not lack intelligence....[18]

Tagore never defended himself publicly over this issue:

> I should only insult myself if I care to answer those who consider me capable of such unbounded stupidity as to sing in praise of George the Fourth or George the Fifth as the Eternal Charioteer leading the pilgrims on their journey through countless ages of the timeless history of mankind.[19]

But he was bitter about the controversy all the same, for he knew that it was a no-win situation. He could never satisfy his detractors, as their accusations did not stem from genuine suspicions about the origins of the song but were partly a product of middle-class dissatisfaction with the 'insufficient nationalism' the song expressed, and partly a response to what seemed to them to be Tagore's own 'peculiar' version of patriotism. To the chagrin of Tagore's critics, his version of patriotism rejected the violence propagated by terrorists and revolutionaries, it rejected the concept of a single-ethnic Hindu *rashtra* as anti-Indian, and even anti-Hindu, and it dismissed the idea of the nation-state as being the main actor in Indian political life. His critics guessed correctly that *Janagana-*

[18] Rabindranath Tagore, Letter to Pulinbihari Sen, 10 November 1937, quoted by Chinmohan Sehanabis, in '*Janaganamana Adhinayaka Sangita Prasange Rabindranath*', *Parichay*, May–June 1986, pp. 20–2.

[19] Rabindranath Tagore, Letter of 29 March 1939. Quoted in Prabodhchandra Sen *India's National Anthem* (Calcutta: Visvabharati, 1972), p. 7. Sen's book covers the whole controversy reasonably thoroughly.

ıld only be the anthem of a state rooted in the Indian ...n, not of an Indian nation-state trying to be the heir to the British-Indian empire. They also probably sensed that *Janagana-mana* was possibly the poet's attempt to moderate his earlier deep allegiance to *Bande Mataram* because of the fierce associations the latter had acquired in the course of the growth of post-Swadeshi extremism.

There might even have been some guilty recognition on Tagore's part that, despite his long record of anti-imperialist activity and his attempts to shape the Indian cultural resistance to imperialism, he *had* for a long time avoided the responsibility of providing a developed cultural critique of the modern West. In the name of cultural syncretism, he had chosen to believe that knowledge and creativity could be neatly separated from political passions and interests, that he had pushed the line that while knowledge and the arts were universal, politics was parochial. Blinkered by that belief, he had even accepted a knighthood from the British government soon after he won the Nobel Prize in literature, presumably on the grounds that it was a reward for artistic achievement, not political loyalty. (Tagore's acceptance of the knighthood saddened many freedom fighters. Saratchandra Chattopadhyay mentions that Chittaranjan Das (1870–1925), a respected leader of the freedom struggle, broke down on hearing that Tagore had accepted the award.[20] People like Das were mollified only when Tagore returned the knighthood in 1919.) I have already suggested that, exposed to the tumultuous events of the 1920s and 1930s, Tagore later began to move towards somewhat different concepts of creativity, intellectual responsibility and universalism. They were no longer located in a facile synthesis of India's civilizational categories and the values of the Enlightenment but in an awareness of the global politics of cultures. As he put it in a letter to Amal Home soon after the Jallianwalla episode, 'We also needed this [the massacre] to get out of our illusions.'[21]

Under the circumstances, Tagore could do little beyond accept philosophically the stray criticisms of *Janaganamana*. Towards the end of his letter to Sen, he says with a touch of resignation, 'In this connection I remember an advice of Bhagwan Manu which goes, "treat honour like poison, accusations like nectar."'[22]

[20] Mitra, *Saratsahitye Samajchetana*, p. 110.

[21] Ibid., p. 109.

[22] Tagore, quoted in Sehanabis, '*Janaganamana Adhinayaka Sangita Prasange*', p. 22.

Fortunately for Tagore, middle-class, modernized India never was nor is it now the whole of India.[23] The public space created by him and, even more, by Mohandas Karamchand Gandhi for a distinctive Indian concept of a public realm and state were never fully occupied by the nascent Indian nation-state. Some of their concerns have returned after about half a century, to haunt Indian nationalists and statists from time to time.

This is a story of divided selves, in confrontation and in dialogue. It has been told at three planes: ideological, mythic and biographical. The story tells how British colonialism in India released cultural forces which fractured the personality of every sensitive exposed Indian and set up the West as a crucial vector within the Indian self. The endorsement that was earlier available to the Indian self from the precolonial culture of public life was thus irrevocably lost.

Nationalism, being a direct product of the western past and thus an imported category, was caught in this inner tension. It consolidated the western presence on the cultural plane, while it nurtured the rebellion against the West on the political plane. This schism led to further conflicts. In a small minority, nationalism triggered off a resistance to itself. This minority distinguished nationalism from anti-imperialism and patriotism; for them it was an imposition, an attempt to mould the Indian concept of the public realm to the requirement of standardized western categories. They sensed that Indian nationalism did not merely mean internalization of an alien history, it was also an exteriorization of India's inner conflicts triggered by the colonial political economy.

Was the separation of nationalism from both patriotism and anti-imperialism viable in India? Was it a viable alternative for any Third World society which had been a victim of the West?

This question has not been answered here. Which does not mean that the alternative to nationalism which Tagore and Gandhi hinted at was too ephemeral or fragile to withstand the turbulence of mass politics. It means that they foresaw some of the problems that are now emerging in the political culture of nation-states in

[23] The only opinion survey of the three possibilities for India's national anthem was conducted in Bombay. The results of the survey show that while on some criteria *Bandemataram* was found a superior anthem, the respondents rated *Janaganamana* to have the strongest 'national characteristics' (Sen, *India's National Anthem*, pp. 55–7). Tagore did not live to see the survey. *Janaganamana* remained the last patriotic song he wrote, although he lived thirty years longer.

both the West and the East. Perhaps the time has come to take stock of the costs of the nation-state system and the nationalism that sustains it. Such stock-taking may not alter the past but it may lead towards a redefinition of the concept and functions of the state, at least in this part of the globe.

Many years ago, at the time of World War I, a person as manifestly apolitical as Sigmund Freud claimed that the state had forbidden to the individual the practice of 'wrong-doing' not because of a desire to abolish it but because of a desire to monopolize it. Gandhi and Tagore may never have read Freud, but they pushed this awareness into the political culture of India. That the awareness did not survive the harsh realities of international relations and the early stages of nation-building and state-formation in the southern world has no bearing on the viability of their dissent. And we, at the end of the twentieth century, may be in a position to affirm that eighteenth- and early nineteenth-century Europe did not say the last word on the subject. Time may still vindicate the vision of the two dissenters.

Index

THE SAVAGE FREUD

and Other Essays
on Possible and Retrievable Selves

Contents

Preface

I would have titled this book *Textual Politics* but for the touch of fashion and stylization associated with the terms in these reportedly post-modern days. For while this collection of essays deals with texts and has its politics, it is far removed from the world of formal analysis of texts.

My main aim in the following essays became clear to me only after I had assembled some of them for publication in this volume. The effort is to develop a critique of the dominant, quasi-global consciousness that now frames the culture of commonsense for all debates on public issues in modern India. This consciousness has concocted, out of the various forms of conventionality available in the global mass culture, what is believed to be a tough, realistic, historically rooted, masculine Indianness that would reportedly stand the strains of the present global system of nation-states and the global development regime.

There *were* criticisms of middle-class consciousness—by which I mainly mean criticisms of the political worldview of the urban, quasi-westernized, upper-caste Indian—in the latter half of the nineteenth century. In my part of India, Michael Madhusudan Dutt's *Buḍo Sāliker Ghāḍe Ro*, Pyarichand Mitra's *Ālāler Gharer Dulāl*, Bankimchandra Chattopadhyay's *Kamalākānter Daphtar* and 'Babu' are obvious examples. Such critiques had a certain verve till, in the 1920s, the Indian middle classes began to lose their political confidence due to the new sociological profile the freedom movement had started acquiring. Social criticism now meant something different to a class threatened by its diminishing political power, even though the social and cultural power of the class was growing, thanks to the expansion of the modern sector in the country.

By the 1930s, with new versions of the theory of progress

flooding the Indian market from the West, all such criticisms of modern India projected, as it were, a split personality. At one plane, the criticisms continued to be directed at the hypocrisy, greed and contradictions of the bourgeois life, but less and less at the cognitive categories that sustained and gave meaning to the life and justified the disproportionate power and privileges of the class being criticized. At another, such criticisms regarded the 'little' traditions of India as the bastions of violence and irrationality—and as the ultimate source of the pathologies of the middle class—and refused to take seriously the categories of these little traditions unless they tallied with the categories being popularized in modernizing India. As a result, what these criticisms offered with one hand, they took away with the other. After all, moral criticisms of hypocrisy and greed are merely moral criticisms; they can be safely forgotten when the mean but unavoidable principles of realpolitik and economic interests come into play.

The national movement on the other hand, despite the now-commanding presence of Mohandas Karamchand Gandhi, gradually developed at its upper echelons an ideology that was in tune with the globally dominant idiom of the nation-state. This idiom survived intact after India became independent and established a centrality in Indian public life that would have been unthinkable even two decades earlier. It endorsed the relaxing self-reflexibility of the middle classes.

This language of public life, which has now begun to preside over the culture of Indian politics, has one marked strength: it leaves ample scope for in-house dissent—from Gandhian to Marxist to Liberal. It has the strength and elasticity to rephrase such dissent in its own terms and to nurture and comfortably live with their tamed domesticated versions. This strength allows it to claim for itself a superordinate presence in Indian public life; for it has the alleged ability to subsume all other idioms, or at least the saner parts of the idioms. The editorials of the country's national dailies, the values projected by the newly popular video news magazines, and the language of debate in Parliament are good instances of this openness of the dominant idiom to what it believes to be sane alternatives to it. One thing, however, the ideology does not allow one to do: to challenge or remove any of the components that constitute its core.

These core components cannot be defined exactly in a brief preface, mainly because in many cases they have been indigenized out of recognition. But they can be roughly represented by a series of concepts that have become central to all public discourse in modern India. Among them are the state (by which is meant the nation-state); nationalism (defined as allegiance to a steamrolling monocultural concept of India, composed of the nineteenth-century European concept of nationality); secularism (used not as one possible way of containing religious strife but as a synonym for the promotion of supra-religious allegiances to the now-dominant idea of the Indian state); development (which has now fully colonized the idea of social change); history (paradoxically seen as an ahistorical, linear, scientific enterprise); rationality (as an allegedly non-partisan, contemporary embodiment of the post-Enlightenment theories of progress) and a totally romanticized concept of *realpolitik* that is neither realistic nor truly political in its content.

These essays try to look at aspects of Indian public life while avoiding the loving embrace of these scaffolds of the culture of the Indian state. Some of the essays, in fact, can be read as attempts to demystify these scaffolds and provide a glimpse of the principles of dominance that sustain them politically. In the process, the essays also act as pointers to some of the categories that have been marginalized by the culture of the Indian state, though not necessarily by the culture of Indian politics. The assumption is that these marginalized categories still make sense to Indians not fully socialized to modern political institutions and they give Indian political life its distinctiveness. They are categories which confuse and exasperate metropolitan Indians who would like to consider themselves the sane, rational, tough-minded political analysts of India's public culture. This book celebrates that ability to confuse and exasperate.

One final comment. The author of these essays is not the offspring of village India. Nor is he a Gandhian social activist or a fanatic environmentalist who finds the tinsel glitter of the city an immoral, seductive presence. He is a child of modern India, looking for a language of social criticism that will not be entirely alien to a majority of Indians who have been increasingly empowered by an open political process, however imperfect that openness. Those who would prefer to read the following pages as a romantic invocation of Indian culture will do well to remember that such accusations of 'romanticization' are never directed against the return to Hellenic culture in any history of the emergence of modern science during the Enlightenment. Yet, it is fairly obvious that the Greek science the Enlightenment rediscovered was not the whole of Greek science; nor were the medieval traditions of European science that disjunctive with the modern.

These essays are not historical reconstructions of the past; they are part of a political preface to a plural human future. My source of inspiration in this enterprise are those Asian, African and South American intellectuals who, whether they know it or not, are trying to ensure that the pasts and the presents of their cultures do not survive in the interstices of the contemporary world as merely a set of esoterica. These intellectuals implicitly recognize that for the moderns the South is already, definitionally, only the past of the contemporary West and the future of the South is only a glorified term for the present of the West. Only the past remains unconquered. Despite the painstaking efforts of modern historians, at least the remembered pasts of the savage world have not yet been fully appropriated by the North. Hence the desperate and often-pathetic attempts to return to the past in the southern world, not only to time-travel or locate one's utopia in the past, but also to discover possible alternative bases for social criticisms of the existing order.

'The Discreet Charms of Indian Terrorism' has grown out of the Gandhi Memorial Lecture, 1987, delivered at the Raman Research Institute, Bangalore, and published in *The Journal of Commonwealth and Comparative Politics*, March 1990. It was also presented at the Department of South Asian Studies, the University of Pennsylvania, in 1988. The present version owes much to the issues raised by the listeners and to informal discussions with scholars, activists and friends, particularly Sivraj Ramaseshan, Satish Dhawan, S. Radhakrishnan, R. L. Kumar, and Girdhar Rathi.

'Sati as Profit Versus Sati as a Spectacle' was first published in *The Illustrated Weekly of India* on 17 January 1988. The present version was prepared for John S. Hawley (ed.), *Sati, The Blessing and the Curse* (New York: Oxford University Press, 1994). It has gained immensely from Hawley's detailed suggestions and criticisms.

'The Other Within' was given as a lecture at the Commonwealth Centre for Literary and Cultural Change of the University of Virginia, Charlottesville, in April 1990. Later on, it was presented at the Institute for Advanced Study in Humanities at Edinburgh and published in *New Literary History*, February 1992. I am grateful to these institutions and to R. S. Khare, Ralph Cohen, Peter Jones, C. Douglas Lummis and Richard Falk, for providing the facilities and help without which the paper could not have been written. I am also grateful to some members of the family of Radhabinod Pal—Balai Pal, Lakshmirani Pal, Prashanta Kumar Pal, and Debi Prasad Pal—and to Masao Kunihiro, Girdhar Rathi, Sarvani Sarkar, Savita Singh and Sujit Deb for their comments and help. Nearly a decade before this essay was written, M. J. Knottenbelt had sent me unsolicited papers and data, some of which I accidentally rediscovered recently and found immensely useful while revising the essay.

'The Savage Freud' was first presented at a conference at Karachi sponsored by the World Institute of Development Economic Research and the UN University in 1989. It was rewritten for Frédérique Apffel Marglin's *Decolonizing Knowledge* (Oxford: Clarendon Press). Work on the paper began when I was a Fellow at the Woodrow Wilson International Centre for Scholars, Washington, in 1988 and was completed at the Department of Politics, University of Hull, when I was Charles Wallace Fellow there in 1990. I am grateful to these institutions for the facilities they provided. They are not, however, responsible in any way for the contents of the paper. I am also beholden to the participants in the Karachi conference, especially Durre Ahmed and Frédérique Marglin, and to Alan Roland for their extensive criticisms and suggestions. The present version of the paper owes much to Roland's detailed comments. It has also gained from discussions with Debiprasad Chattopadhyay, Bijayketu Bose, Bhupen Desai, Charuchandra Bhattacharya and from the help given by Tarit Chatterji, Hiranmay Ghosal, Heather Harlan, Amit Das, and Sajal Basu. A section of the paper was presented at the Delhi Group for Psychoanalysis in 1990, where it benefited from the comments of Shib K. Mitra, Indrani and Ashok Guha, Ashok Nagpal, and

Veena Das. I would not perhaps have used the idea of the secret self as an organizing principle in this essay but for a long discussion on the subject with Noel O'Sullivan.

'Modern Medicine and its Nonmodern Critics' has grown out of Shiv Visvanathan's and my participation in a project sponsored by WIDER and first appeared in *Dominating Knowledge*, edited by Frédérique Apffel Marglin and Stephen Marglin (Oxford: Clarendon Press, 1990). It has benefited much from the suggestions given by the participants in the project, especially Francis Zimmerman, Tariq Banuri, and Stephen and Frédérique Marglin.

An earlier version of 'The Intelligent Critic's Guide to Indian Cinema' was serialized in *Deep Focus*, 1987–8 and parts of it were published in *The Illustrated Weekly of India.* It has benefited from my long discussions with Chidananda Dasgupta and Iqbal Masud and from the criticisms and comments offered by two young activists, R. L. Kumar and George Kutty.

A section of 'Satyajit Ray's Secret Guide to Exquisite Murders' borrows from an essay published in *The Illustrated Weekly of India*. It was written for the International Conference on Perceptions of Self: China, India, and Japan, held at Honolulu in August 1989 and published in *Films, East and West*, June 1990. I am grateful to the participants at the conference, Wimal Dissanayake in particular, and to Punam Zutshi for their comments. I am also indebted to Bijoylakshmi and Kajal Bose and to Sujit Deb for helping me with some not-so-easily available books. My grateful thanks to Chavi Bhargava for doing the index.

Finally a comment on the style of spelling. Sanskritized spellings of Indian names and titles and diacritical marks have been used in this book only when English versions of such names or titles have not been used by the persons or authors themselves and when they are not in common use. When used, the diacriticals and the spellings seek to retain the flavour of vernacular usage. As with a number of my recent works, Surabhi Sheth has helped me with this part of the story.

A. N.

The Discreet Charms of Indian Terrorism

According to the poet Umashankar Joshi, Arnold Toynbee said after Gandhi's death, 'Henceforth, mankind will have to ask its prophets, "Are you willing to live in the slum of politics?"' This is a compliment Gandhi would have accepted, for he had always held that morality took different forms at different times and that in our time it took the form of politics.[1] For the right kind of politics not only allowed one to test out the *yugadharma*, ethics appropriate to an age, it also allowed one to confront the multi-layered realities of cultures and personalities.

After this one comment, it will be for the reader to decide whether the events related here have anything to do with the Gandhian vision: with its simultaneous emphases on cultural traditions as a reaffirmation of a moral universe, and on politics as a dialogical encounter which, set within that moral universe, can reduce the area of human violence.

II

At 5.50 p.m. on 5 July 1984, a group of Sikh terrorists hijacked an Indian Airlines flight, IC 405, flying from Srinagar to Delhi. The hijackers struck soon after the plane, an airbus, took off, and directed it to Lahore. There they gave a six-hour ultimatum to the Indian government to meet their demands, which were: a ransom of about Rs 300 million as compensation for the damage done to the Golden Temple complex during the army action

[1] See for instance Bhikhu Parekh, *Gandhi's Political Philosophy* (London: Macmillan, 1989).

there in June 1984, the return of the cash and valuables seized by the army, and the release of all Sikhs arrested following the action.

Pakistan had at first refused to permit the plane to land and blocked the Lahore runway. But the hijackers, claiming to be a suicide squad consisting of the family of some of those killed during the action at the Golden Temple a month earlier, threatened to blow up the plane if permission was not given. However, once the plane landed at Lahore, the Pakistanis did not concede the hijackers' demands, which were to offload the passengers, refuel the plane, and leave for another country.

There were 149 men, 72 women, 19 children and 15 infants on board the plane. Two persons suffered injuries when the plane was seized—one allegedly from a bullet, the other from a penknife. Airhostess Kuldeep Kaur Gujral had resisted the attack by banging the cockpit door on the hijackers. She had now to cool their ire by revealing that she was a Sikh. The ploy worked. The hijacker who had threatened her earlier called her 'sister', touched her feet and asked for forgiveness.[2]

Soon other details began to come in. Mohan Ram, a veteran journalist caught in the hijacking, wrote his story in the *Indian Express*.[3] According to him, after the plane took off from Srinagar, half a dozen Sikhs jumped out of their seats shouting slogans and brandishing knives, pistols and an iron bar ripped off the plane. There were three clean-shaven Sikhs among them. They now put on yellow and blue turbans. All of them looked very young, the youngest no more than fifteen, or so it seemed to Ajay Bose, another journalist in the plane. 'One of them rushed towards our row', says Ram, and told the panic-stricken passengers, *'Mere pās do pistol aur grenade hai'*—'I have two pistols and a grenade'.[4]

Despite their youth, the hijackers looked rather fearsome to some of the passengers and the crew. Flight Steward D. K. Mehta, who had experienced an earlier hijacking in 1981, said

---

[2] *The Times of India*, 8 July 1984.

[3] *Indian Express*, 7 July 1984.

[4] Ibid. According to later accounts, there were eight or nine hijackers in all. All Hindi and Punjabi expressions used in this paper are quotations from newspapers. Hence the occasional odd spelling, grammar, and inconsistency.

that this group of hijackers was more ruthless than the earlier one.[5] He had reason to say so; during the take-over, amidst the confusion, Mehta had resisted the hijackers and was stabbed. One of his colleagues, Flight Engineer Pran Mahajan, too, was injured.[6] A more fearsome account of the take-over was given by Bose in a first-person story soon afterwards; according to him, the hijackers had said, 'Our leader Sant Bhindranwale is alive and we are taking you to him in Khalistan which is situated in Pakistan. There your fate would be decided'.[7] They also, Bose added, mercilessly beat up the passengers and the crew, and one of the hijackers 'took particular pleasure in walloping the Hindus in the cabin and humiliating them'.[8] Bose did not explain how the hijackers so quickly identified the Hindus from among so many non-Sikh passengers.

There was also much pushing and scrambling after the take-over. The hijackers went after two uniformed army men, one a major and the other a colonel, stripped them of their rank, and tore their clothes, Bose saw the major 'severely beaten' and lying 'bleeding with his hand fractured'. At one point it seemed to Bose that the hijackers would kill the officers.[9] The major himself later gave a less dramatic version of the event. He did not mention his fracture but said that the leader of the hijackers gave him a bandage and some cotton to tie over his swollen right hand after the assault.[10] Most of the passengers sat still during the take-over and watched the goings-on in 'grim silence', for the hijackers had told them, 'Fasten your seat belts and don't move or we will shoot'.[11]

On reaching Lahore, the plane landed amidst full-throated slogan-shouting by the hijackers. From the testimony of passenger Shama Kohli, 25, one surmises that slogan-shouting was the main occupation of the hijackers during the flight to Lahore and subsequently during the night at Lahore airport.[12] One

---

[5] *The Times of India*, 7 July 1984.

[6] Ibid.

[7] *The Sunday Observer*, 8 July 1984.

[8] Ibid.

[9] Ibid.

[10] *The Times of India*, 7 July 1984.

[11] *Indian Express*, 7 July 1984.

[12] *The Times of India*, 7 July 1984.

passenger was allegedly roughed up because he did not shout slogans along with the hijackers.

At Lahore, the hijackers waited with transistor radios to hear the news from All India Radio and Radio Pakistan. They also participated in half a dozen impassioned recitals of Sikh religious texts. The passengers were told not to disturb them. Pistols were pointed at those who moved or even fidgeted. It was very stuffy in the plane and many passengers wanted to go to the toilet. They were allowed to do so after being frisked. 'In the beginning the hijackers tried to terrorize the passengers', Ram says in his article but adds, 'one or two of them seemed decent—they provided the infants with baby food and milk'.[13] The process of normalization was helped by Pinkha Singh, a well-behaved hijacker nicknamed 'Jolly' by the passengers, assuming leadership.[14]

At night, the hijackers took over from the airhostesses and served the passengers. Next morning, the airhostesses were back at work. The hijackers then checked the passengers' tickets and divided them into four groups: Indians, Muslims, Sikhs, and foreigners. This may have been a formality. For passenger Dilmohan Singh claims that there was no discrimination among the communities and everybody was treated equally well.[15] There was now considerable activity and much discussion among the hijackers. Mohan Ram got the feeling that they were divided over their next move.[16] But they took one joint decision; they released seven passengers on the grounds of health during the wait at Lahore.

The children on the flight were at ease with developments. Ram heard a child tell a hijacker, 'Uncle, toilet *jānā hai*'—'Uncle, I have to go to the toilet'. Some of the youngsters, according to Ram, were even building up their appetite for a good meal. One of them told his mother, '*Main āj ālu baigan khāungā*'—'Today I shall eat potatoes and eggplant'.[17] The children had probably sensed what passenger Bhavana Kilam later told the press—that

[13] *Indian Express*, 7 July 1984.
[14] *The Sunday Observer*, 8 July 1984.
[15] *The Statesman*, 7 July 1984.
[16] *Indian Express*, 7 July 1984.
[17] Ibid.

the hijackers gave 'top priority' to the children and 'saved water and fruits for them'.[18]

Other passengers complete this picture. Ritu Murgai says that the hijackers 'kept saying that the passengers should not worry as they would be released'.[19] Mushtaq Ahmad remembers the hijackers saying that their quarrel was with the Central Government, not with the passengers, who would not be harmed.[20] André Goldstein, an American student, felt that the hijackers were mostly 'very nice' with the passengers.[21] But the hijackers did say that if their demands were not met, the plane would be blown up.

Sophia Bamu gives a more precise account of the happenings. She said to the press that one of the hijackers was 'very kind' and offered the passengers milk and cakes; another looked 'very tough' and beat up anyone who argued with him. She also guessed that one of the hijackers was no more than fifteen or sixteen.[22] This does not seem to tally with Flight Steward Mehta's impression that the hijackers were a ruthless lot but does tally with the evidence of passenger Har Prem Singh Longman that one of the hijackers had fainted during the hijacking and another had cried.[23]

However, at 10 a.m. the following day, the hijackers threw a bombshell and announced that they had finally decided to blow up the plane in five minutes. 'You can all say your last prayers now', they said and proceeded to force the passengers to say '*Vāi Guru Satya Nām*'.[24] Few disbelieved their threat and some women began to cry. According to Kilam, some of the hijackers, too, were now in tears and they said '*Ab choḍ dete hain*'—'Now let us release them'.[25] But everyone was not equally impressed by the sentiments expressed, Mohan Ram says, 'We all thought that it was now all over. Everyone sat in mournful silence'.[26]

---

[18] *The Statesman*, 7 July 1984.

[19] Ibid.

[20] Ibid.

[21] Ibid.

[22] *The Times of India*, 7 July 1984.

[23] Ibid.

[24] Ibid.

[25] *The Statesman*, 7 July 1984.

[26] *Indian Express*, 7 July 1984.

However, a flurry of activity followed and Ram sensed that the hijackers were divided on whether or not to blow up the plane.[27] Eventually, wiser counsels prevailed. The hijackers told the passengers that Prime Minister Indira Gandhi had rejected their demands but that the passengers would be released in any case. 'We are against the tyranny of the government. We are releasing you all on humanitarian grounds. We don't want to hurt innocents.'[28] The passengers were asked to leave the aircraft about 38 hours after the drama began. The hijackers stayed back. According to *The Times of India*, 'They surrendered to the authorities with tears in their eyes and many of the passengers also broke down. They said that if they had caused any inconvenience to anyone, they were sorry for that'.[29] They also said that they did not want another Harmandar Sahib.[30]

Young journalist Ajay Bose, who had earlier assumed the tone of a war correspondent, was by now thoroughly perplexed. He had to locate his experience beyond the range of normality and sanity.

> Suddenly passengers and hijackers were in each others' arms, crying like children as the tension of the past twenty hours visibly melted away. It was a crazy scene I shall not forget. Passengers who were hijacked, humiliated and beaten up by these nine desperadoes were actually jostling with each other to get the hijackers' autographs on the back of their air tickets. Conversely all the aggression and mental resolve of the Sikh extremists seemed to be cracking up. The fearsome Sikh with an axe ran round hugging passengers while Pinkha Singh made it a point to shake hands individually with everyone in the cabin and the fifteen-year-old boy hijacker just sat down on the floor and cried his heart out.[31]

Within a day, analyses of the hijacking began to appear. Two of the first were by G. K. Reddy, in *The Hindu*, and K. Gopalakrishnan of *The Week* who, as a passenger of the pirated plane, spoke to the press. Reddy pointed out that the Government of

---

[27] Ibid.

[28] *The Times of India*, 7 July 1984.

[29] Ibid.

[30] That is, a bloodbath of the kind that took place at the Golden Temple. Dilmohan Singh, quoted in *The Statesman*, 7 July 1984.

[31] *The Sunday Observer*, 8 July 1984.

Pakistan had acted adroitly and handled the hijackers well; that the hijackers, finding the Indian and Pakistan governments equally firm, became nervous and started changing their demands frequently and this was fully exploited by the officials at Lahore. In the end, the gamble paid off.[32] Gopalakrishnan in his brief comments said that 'Security at the Srinagar airport had been very tight'.[33]

Already however the press, especially the editorial writers and political analysts, were building up the hijacking as the act of a group of well-trained, well-armed, merciless commandos let loose on Indian soil by enemy countries and traitors, taking advantage of the poor security at Indian airports. Thus, Reddy, who was not on the plane, pointed out—as did *The Times of India* editorial of the same day–the security lapses at Srinagar airport which allowed terrorists to board the plane with pistols, hand grenades and iron bars. Neither was unduly perturbed by what Gopalakrishnan had said on the subject to the *Times*. Nor was Reddy's style, or that of the *Times*, cramped by the statement of the bruised major of the pirated plane, published the same day in *The Times of India*, that he thought the hijackers only carried toy pistols, that the only deadly weapon they seemed to have was the pickaxe picked up from the plane itself.

The major was also aware that he had been attacked because he was in uniform, for there was much resentment amongst Sikhs about the army action at the Golden Temple. The captain of the hijacked plane, C. S. P. Singh, also did not see much planning in the piracy. He told *The Times of India* that six of the nine hijackers had looked like amateurs.[34] The *Indian Express*, too, pointed out that the hijackers seemed to have been youthful novices acting on a passing impulse or whim. They were 'desperate youth with no clear idea of what they wanted to do apart from embarrassing the Government of India'.[35] The Pakistanis who dealt with the hijackers had the same impression.[36]

The Times of India also mentioned the hijackers' youthfulness,

---

[32] *The Hindu*, 7 July 1984.
[33] *The Times of India*, 7 July 1984.
[34] Ibid., 8 July 1984.
[35] *Indian Express*, 7 July 1984.
[36] Pran Chopra, ibid., 12 July 1984.

but did not stress it. Instead the paper took to a logical conclusion the security concerns of the popular press, and extolled El Al as the ideal airline because it was virtually piracy-proof.[37] And, though the paper had itself reported that the Minister of State for Civil Aviation had praised the Pakistani authorities for their co-operation and although the Government of India had formally thanked the Government of Pakistan, it now claimed that the very fact that on four occasions pirated Indian planes had been taken to Pakistan indicated that the Pakistanis encouraged such hijacking.[38] The same point was made by *The Tribune* in its editorial.[39] *The Times of India* added that preliminary official inquiries had shown that the hijackers had been trained in hijacking and commando tactics at training camps for Sikh extremists in Pakistan. Inexplicably, the newspaper considerately added that all hijackings of Indian planes to Pakistan had ended happily.[40]

The Patriot, The Hindu, The Tribune and, more guardedly, the *Indian Express* joined the chorus.[41] All blamed the security arrangements at Srinagar, saying that the arrangements should have been better, particularly after the duly elected government of Jammu and Kashmir, led by Farooq Abdullah, had been dismissed by the Premier and Governor Jagmohan. The *Indian Express* however added that it would be fatuous to blame Abdullah, given that the Congress-I had rewarded an erstwhile hijacker of an Indian plane with an elective office already. The new chief minister of Jammu and Kashmir, Abdullah's brother-in-law G. M. Shah, was not restrained by such arguments. He claimed that Abdullah had organized the hijacking and that one of the hijackers was a member of Abdullah's party.[42] Abdullah himself thought that the federal intelligence agencies had organized the hijacking to malign him.[43]

The Statesman was the only newspaper to hint that the

[37] *The Times of India*, 9 July 1984.
[38] Ibid., 7 and 9 July 1984.
[39] *The Tribune*, 7 July 1984.
[40] *The Times of India*, 9 July 1984.
[41] *The Patriot*, 7 July 1984; *The Hindu*, 9 July 1984; *The Tribune*, 7 July 1984; *Indian Express*, 9 July 1984.
[42] *The Times of India*, 14 July 1984.
[43] Ibid., 13 July 1984.

passengers and their relatives were in many cases treated worse at Delhi than when the plane was hijacked. The paper also commented on the contradiction between talk about the hijackers having had commando training in Pakistan and their apparent amateurishness. But even *The Statesman* thought the magnanimity of the hijackers and the 'tame ending' of the episode suspicious.[44]

III

On the morning of 24 August 1984, another Indian Airlines plane, this time a Boeing 737, was hijacked after it took off from Chandigarh. The plane was on its way to Srinagar, and it was once again taken to—where else?—Lahore. Pilot V. K. Mehta, captaining the flight, later said that compared to the earlier hijacking, this one was done by a group which 'meant business'.[45] Let us examine what the business was.

According to one of the passengers, Jitender Gurmeet Singh, the eighty-seven passengers in the plane were drinking tea after take-off when they heard footsteps thumping off in different directions. One passenger, Rabindra Kaur Khandari, thought that some men were heading towards the toilets. Things became clearer a few seconds later. Co-pilot B. L. Ghai was pulled out of the cockpit, roughed up and tied to a chair with a turban. Ghai later said that one of the hijackers, Sandhu, sat down in his chair in the cockpit and said that he had always wanted to be a pilot.[46]

There was now an announcement that the plane had been hijacked and that no one should move. The flight number was changed from IC 421 to Khalistan 125. There was even some talk of changing it to Khalistan 125,000 or *'sawa lakh'*. Airhostess Rita Singh, who made the announcement to the startled passengers, had already sufficiently recovered her wits to ask one of the hijackers, 'Now that we have inaugurated the new airlines, would you make me your chief airhostess?'[47] The plane was

[44] *The Statesman*, 7 July 1984, and 10 July 1984.
[45] *The Times of India*, 27 August 1984.
[46] Ibid.
[47] Quoted by K. Subrahmanyam, *Indian Express*, 29 August 1984.

thereafter ordered first to circle the Golden Temple for a while and then proceed to Lahore.

Four of the hijackers were turbaned and four clean-shaven. One passenger guessed they were in their teens and at least three of them were indeed found to be no more than eighteen.[48] At first, the hijackers held nothing in their hands but said they were armed with time bombs. Scared out of their wits, none of the passengers dared move. Later, Mrs Khandari noticed one of the hijackers carrying a pickaxe (picked up from, of all places, the cockpit), and another carrying a round object covered with paper which he claimed was an explosive. Another had a camera which he said was a time bomb.[49] Frequent deep-throated chanting of the religious slogan, '*Jo bole so nihāl, Sat Śri Ākāl*', rent the air. In between, the hijackers spoke among themselves in Punjabi with some English thrown in. From their conversation, the passengers came to know that one hijacker's name was Shanty, another's Tintoo, and a third was called Kissie. Their demands were Rs 500,000 per passenger, eviction of the army from the Golden Temple, and safe passage for themselves to the United States via Bahrain.

As the nervous passengers waited, the plane circled over Lahore for 45 minutes before the reluctant Pakistanis allowed it to land at 10.35 a.m. While the plane was circling Lahore, the pantry was ransacked by the teenagers and chocolates and biscuits were distributed to all.[50] For the next ten hours the passengers had to sweat it out in the plane. They were given water but there was no food, and tension mounted when the hijackers began a debate among themselves and started noisily chalking out their course of action. (Later, it was found that while there was no proper food in the plane, a few remaining biscuits were distributed.)

This time, too, the children assessed the situation in their own way; they went on playing cards.[51] A few of the adults, however, succumbed to the pressure. Mrs Khandari, a heart patient, complained of palpitations. At first, one of the hijackers cour-

[48] *The Statesman*, 26 August 1984; *Indian Express*, 26 August 1984.

[49] *The Statesman*, 26 August 1984.

[50] Subrahmanyam, *Indian Express*, 29 August 1984.

[51] *The Hindustan Times*, 29 August 1984.

teously told her '*Mātāji beth jāo*' ('Respected mother, sit down'). But when a doctor on board confirmed her condition, she was released. She later said, 'There was no violence on any of the passengers and the hijackers were quite polite to those who took ill.'[52]

Mr M. K. Dhar, a polio victim, told the hijackers that he was not feeling well. He was not allowed to contact a doctor among the passengers. However, when he became semi-conscious and a doctor confirmed that he was suffering from shock, he was released. The shock could not have been severe, for Mr Dhar suddenly woke up and refused to disembark without his wife and son. So, they too were released. Mrs Dhar later said that the hijackers talked 'nicely' to the passengers and 'kept assuring them that they would come to no harm as long as they co-operated'.[53]

Another passenger, Gurmeet Singh, though married to an Indian army officer, was allowed to go because she was suffering from dehydration. She said later that the passengers were quite cheerful as long as they were at Lahore. 'They had the feeling that like all earlier hijacking attempts, this one will also pass off peacefully.'[54]

When the heat became oppressive, the captain was allowed to switch on the airconditioner for a while. After that it was switched on and off at short intervals. The hijackers also kept opening the doors of the aircraft and filling flasks of water for the passengers. Such courtesies paid; all the passengers later spoke well of their captors. Mrs Singh claimed that the hijackers were 'mild mannered and did not harm any passenger', and that six of them had behaved 'very well', especially with the children.[55] Sanjay Malik found them 'extremely polite' and Mrs Khandari agreed with him. So did Mr Dhar, adding that the hijackers 'sang to their heart's fill'.[56]

Even those who did not comment on the hijackers' behaviour gave no impression of being terribly scarred by their experience. Their reaction was summed up by airhostess Sumbul Hasan who

---

[52] *The Statesman*, 26 August 1984.

[53] Ibid.

[54] Ibid.

[55] *The Hindustan Times*, 26 August 1984; *The Statesman*, 26 August 1984.

[56] Ibid.

said on her return to Delhi that she had had some of the most exciting moments of her life.[57] Evidently some of the passengers shared her attitude; after their release, they returned to Delhi from Dubai with duty-free purchases such as VCRs and 'two-in-ones'.[58]

However, we have jumped ahead of our story. Let us get back to the stranded passengers at Lahore. As the night at Lahore airport became a long-drawn-out one and the passengers got increasingly tense and bored, a young hijacker, the one called Kissie, began to sing melancholy love songs from Hindi films. The songs included old favourites like '*Ham choḍ cale hai mehfil ko, yād aye kabhi to mat ronā*' and '*Mile na phul to kānton se dostī kar lī*'. Kissie also sang a classical *tappā*.[59] Though it was past 1 a.m., the passengers pressed Kissie to sing more.[60] A colleague of his also joined in with a political number, '*Bhindrānwāle sanch sipāhī*'.

After about ten hours' wait at Lahore, the plane was refuelled and left for the United Arab Emirates via Karachi, where it was refuelled again. On reaching Dubai, the plane circled above the airport for a while, for the authorities there had switched off the runway lights. When fuel was running low and the crew were thinking of ditching the plane, the UAE authorities relented at the request of the Indian government.

The plane landed at 6.25 a.m. It must have been rather nerve-racking for the captors as well as their passengers, and they all spontaneously applauded and shouted, 'Captain Mehta, hip hip hurray!' Though described by *The Hindustan Times* as an 'expert group with good knowledge of piloting', the hijackers were obviously shaken and frightened. One of them actually had to be consoled by an airhostess.[61] Once when Mehta came out of the cockpit, the leader of the hijackers clasped both his hands and said, 'If Captain Mehta wants whiskey, we shall get it for him'.[62]

Fifteen hours after the plane had landed at Dubai and after eight hours of negotiations, at 8.30 p.m. on 25 August the

---

[57] *The Hindustan Times*, 26 August 1984.

[58] *The Times of India*, 27 August 1984.

[59] *The Statesman*, 27 August 1984.

[60] *The Times of India*, 27 August 1984.

[61] *The Hindustan Times*, 25 August 1984; *The Times of India*, 15 September 1984.

[62] Quoted by Subrahmanyam, *The Times of India*, 27 August 1984.

hijackers surrendered to the authorities of the United Arab Emirates; the UAE did not grant the hijackers asylum but assured them of onward passage to the USA. The passengers were permitted to leave the aircraft soon after the understanding was reached. While they were getting down, they noticed that the hijackers had written pro-Khalistani slogans all over the inside of the plane using the airhostesses' lipsticks, eyebrow pencils and nail polish.

When the passengers were leaving, Shanty tried out a few political slogans which elicited a lukewarm response. He then shouted the first line of the religious slogan, '*Jo bole so nihāl*'. This time the passengers, Sikhs and non-Sikhs, spontaneously and vociferously responded, '*Sat Śri Ākāl*'. One of the passengers now thanked the hijackers for their good behaviour with their captives.[63] The leader of the hijackers then apologized to the passengers for the trouble he and his group had caused. Mr Ghai heard this and complained that he had been beaten up. The hijacker embraced him.[64]

Once again, reactions to the hijacking began to get standardized within a day or two. Mr K. Subrahmanyam, who fancies himself as India's most tough-minded defence analyst and is a severe critic of Indian softness in matters of the state, was in the hijacked plane. He published his account in *The Times of India* on 27 August, saying that, against his expectations, the airhostesses of flight IC 421 were calm as well as courageous. Like many ardent Third World nationalists, Mr Subrahmanyam does not expect natives to live up to his norms of public performance. He was, therefore, most impressed by the way the airhostesses, when the plane was about to be ditched over the sea near Dubai, coolly instructed passengers in the use of safety devices and even disciplined the hijackers. Subrahmanyam also noticed that the fear of ditching had dissolved the tension and hostility between captors and captives, and that the former showed a new respect and admiration for the crew.

At one point in Pakistan, the hijackers had been requested to

[63] Subrahmanyam, *Indian Express*, 29 August 1984.
[64] *The Tribune*, 28 August 1984.

provide insulin shots and food to Mr Subrahmanyam, who is diabetic. The hijackers agreed and their leader went to the hospital with him. But in the process they also came to know who he was, an important bureaucrat of the defence ministry. Later, during negotiations, when the hijackers threatened to shoot one passenger every half-hour, they latched on to Subrahmanyam and announced that he would be the first to be shot. This was duly broadcast to the world. It went virtually unnoticed that the hijackers had whispered to him that it was all a drama to put pressure on the authorities and that he would not be harmed. Subrahmanyam, not one to be impressed by the softer side of life, was neither assuaged nor amused.

Subrahmanyam also wrote a three-part article on the hijacking, published in the *Indian Express*, avowedly as a defence expert and specialist on air piracy. In it he said that he had realized quite early that the hijacking was a 'highly professional operation', that whatever else it might have been, it was 'not amateurish'.[65] He also noted that the hijackers had 'very lethal instruments like a time-device-equipped explosive or petroleum bomb'.[66] Yet, in the same article, he indicated how clever he was in seeing so easily through the unbelievably clumsy attempts of the 'highly professional' hijackers to pass off a newspaper packet as a bomb. Nor would he tell his readers why, if the hijackers were so professional and had such powerful weapons, they had to arm themselves, according to his own account, with a less-than-fearsome needle of the kind the Sikhs use to comb their beards.[67]

It was an indicator of the public mood that it was the innocent 'realism' of the Subrahmanyams that caught the public imagination, not the more nuanced details of the actual piracy. Thus, the *National Herald* did not question the presence of liquid bombs on board the pirated plane and said in an editorial that the government would have to find ways of detecting liquid bombs which eluded metal detectors, as if that was the main issue in the hijacking.[68] Others, too, wrote eloquently on the shortcomings of Indian Airlines and the security agencies. An

---

[65] *Indian Express*, 28 August 1984.

[66] Ibid.

[67] Ibid.

[68] *National Herald*, 26 August 1984.

editorial in *The Statesman* focused on security lapses; another in the *Indian Express* demanded a ban on the open carrying of ritual *kirpāns* in flight, though the Dubai authorities said the same day that the knives had been concealed by the hijackers under their turbans and not carried as *kirpāns*.[69] *The Hindu* wrote about what other countries did when their planes were hijacked; *The Hindustan Times* and *The Sunday Observer* reported that there was an official proposal, obviously inspired by Israeli practice, to post armed commandos in all Indian Airlines flights.[70] Subrahmanyam had already written from the security angle and there was much editorial advice to the government and the public not to underestimate such hijackings.[71] At least one newspaper—predictably the *Indian Express*—advised the government to resign.[72]

The politicians did not want to be left behind. The pro-Congress-I *National Herald* claimed that the hijackers had met the erstwhile chief minister of Jammu and Kashmir, Farooq Abdullah, before their venture.[73] The Bharatiya Janata Party leader, Atal Behari Vajpayee, now pointed out that the Centre seemed more interested in blaming the hijackers and Abdullah than in taking steps to stop such hijackings.[74] Suresh Kalmadi, a Congress-S Member of Parliament, took an entirely different line. He charged in the Rajya Sabha that the plane had been hijacked to divert people's attention from Andhra Pradesh, where a duly elected government was being unseated by Prime Minister Indira Gandhi with the help of an unscrupulous and corrupt governor. Kalmadi's suspicions about the government's aims were shared by many in the Opposition because two Congress-I workers who had hijacked an Indian Airlines plane earlier, during Janata rule, had been rewarded on Mrs Gandhi's return to power; they were now members of the Uttar Pradesh Legislature.

---

69 *The Statesman*, 26 August 1984; *Indian Express*, 7 August 1984; *The Times of India*, 27 August 1984.

70 *The Hindu*, 2 September 1984; *The Hindustan Times*, 28 August 1984; *The Sunday Observer*, 26 August 1984.

71 E.g., *The Tribune*, 25 August 1984; *The Times of India*, 27 August 1984.

72 *Indian Express*, 25 August 1984.

73 *National Herald*, 25 August 1984.

74 *The Statesman*, 26 August 1984.

The Government of India responded to the criticisms by promptly blaming Pakistan. A government spokesman claimed that one of the hijackers had displayed a pistol only after the plane reached Lahore. Two British passengers confirmed this. As a result, the security staff at Chandigarh avoided the fate of the security staff at Srinagar after the previous hijacking; they escaped wholesale suspension.[75] Some Congress-I and Opposition MPs soon joined the anti-Pakistan chorus. Pakistani officials of course denied the allegations. Two of them said that they did not use force against the hijackers because that would have jeopardized the lives of the passengers; later on, the hijackers when questioned by the Dubai police admitted that they had boarded the plane with pistols.[76] According to *The Hindu*, however, the Government of India was sore with Pakistan, while *The Tribune* felt that Pakistan had indirectly encouraged the hijackers by giving them shelter.[77] *The Times of India* thought that the Government of Pakistan was less helpful to India this time, for the plane had been refuelled.[78] Only *The Sunday Observer* in its editorial said, without any qualification, 'Of all the people drawn into this episode, Pakistan comes off best, showing exemplary conduct'.[79]

To crown it all, the *Indian Express* told its readers that the terrorists had planned to hijack two planes but the two groups set up for the purpose landed in the same plane by mistake.[80] At this point, some of the passengers of the pirated IC 421 denied earlier reports and claimed that no one had been hit with any weapon. One said that the hijackers were 'very jovial and sang songs'; another insisted that the hijackers 'took good care of the passengers'.[81] The hijacker who had regaled the passengers with his singing was later found to be one Tejinder Singh, a second-year student at Chandigarh. His family had reported him

[75] *The Hindustan Times*, 28 August 1984.

[76] *The Times of India*, 28 August 1984. The hijackers were to again change their version under questioning by the Indian authorities to whom they were subsequently handed over for trial.

[77] *The Hindu*, 27 August 1984; *The Tribune*, 27 August 1984.

[78] *The Times of India*, 26 August 1984.

[79] *The Sunday Observer*, 8 July 1984.

[80] *Indian Express*, 26 August 1984.

[81] Ibid.

missing since he had gone out with friends on a 'singing assignment'.[82]

The *Indian Express* also revealed that it had been contacted by a youth who had walked into its New Delhi office with a press note from the All-India Sikh Students Federation and said that, though the hijackers had had enough ammunition to blow up the plane, they had no plan to kill anyone. 'We will not do that', the youth had said.[83] The Dubai police chief also spoilt some of the fun by confirming that there was no bomb in the plane, only two .22 pistols.[84] The Government of India, too, soon took some of the drama out of the episode by trying desperately to forget its statement in Parliament that the pilot and co-pilot had been drugged during the take-over.[85]

IV

Why have I chosen to recount these curious details of two minor air piracies? Am I trying to show that in an underdeveloped society, even a plane cannot be hijacked efficiently? Or to say that in such societies public life is shaped by the idiom and melodrama of the commercial cinema? That the Indian press is inconsistent and security forces incompetent?

The conclusions I draw from these two events are more modest. Before listing them, however, I have first to point out a few common features of the two events which strike me as being psychologically relevant.

First, in both cases, the hijackers, crew and passengers established and maintained a dialogue among themselves. Not once did they try to place themselves outside each other's interpersonal world. Nor did they presume any incommensurability between their worldview and that of the others. As a result, despite some low-level violence, the social world of the pirated IC 405 and IC 421 did not become a free-for-all or an amoral Hobbesian jungle. Later on, attempts were made to explain the piracies in terms of the standard categories of international

[82] *The Times of India*, 28 August 1984.
[83] *Indian Express*, 28 August 1984.
[84] *The Hindustan Times*, 26 August 1984.
[85] *The Statesman*, 25 August 1984.

terrorism. But these attempts could not obscure the genuine humaneness which had informed the behaviour of the crew, the passengers and the hijackers.

Of course, the events narrated here can be interpreted in other ways. Reading between the lines of Subrahmanyam's articles, one can easily construct another, realpolitik-based interpretation of the same events. There are other clues, too. One hostess claimed that she had been taught, as part of anti-hijacking training, to be friendly with hijackers and to ask them questions about their families and their personal lives. That was why she had been so friendly to them and it had helped.[86] The Pakistani authorities, too, saw in the softness of the hijackers evidence of 'low morale'.[87] In such 'realistic' interpretations, hijackings become a zero-sum game. Each gesture to the passengers becomes a concession extracted through adroit bargaining, and clear-headed, dispassionate politics. Nor can there be any doubt about which of the two interpretations will fit better with the paramount models in the world of knowledge. Any graduate student in a respectable university would be well advised to assume Subrahmanyam's tone rather than mine.

I claim that neither of the two interpretations is more 'true' than the other. While to some, my account of the hijackings will make them appear maudlin or mystifying, to others, Subrahmanyam's account will seem unrealistic and based on a romanticization of realpolitik. They will find anti-empirical his assumption that the odds did not favour the hijackers and hence their ploy of good behaviour.[88] For the success rates of hijackers in seizing hostages, escaping punishment and gaining major publicity have ranged between 79 to nearly 100 per cent.[89] That is to say, the hijackers did not have to behave the way they did merely to hedge their bets or save their skins on a possibly doomed mission. Ultimately, the interpretation is a matter of choice, and the choice is both political and moral.

---

[86] It is easy to guess in which part of the world the training manual must have been prepared, and the influence on it of the image of the sentimental, family-loving, Asian terrorist.

[87] *Indian Express*, 12 July 1984.

[88] Ibid., 28 August 1984.

[89] R. Kupperman and D. Trent (eds.), *Terrorism: Threat, Reality, Response* (Stanford: Stanford University Press, 1979), p. 21.

Second, captors and captives collaborated, perhaps unwittingly, to re-establish a moral order in an extreme situation. In this order there was a place for the children and the ill, for the disabled and the injured, for the basic needs of passengers, and for music, humour, and pathos. The child who called a hijacker 'uncle', the airhostess who retained her wits in a crisis, the hijacker who called a passenger '*mātāji*' or the hijacker who sang to the tired, nervous passengers were not merely forging temporary kinship ties. They were refusing to move into the standardized world of international terrorism typified by, say, the Munich massacre, the Tel Aviv airport killings or by our own Mukteshwar bus massacre.

Of course, there is no guarantee that terrorist acts such as the ones I have described will not give place to more ruthless, gory violence. India has perhaps already graduated to the second stage of terrorism and the 1984 hijackings perhaps belong to another age; the hijackings took place before the assassination of prime minister Indira Gandhi by two of her Sikh security guards, and the large-scale slaughter of Sikhs at Delhi, virtually organized by the ruling party under the patronage of the Indian state. Yet the fact remains that when the hijackings took place, they did so within the limits imposed by another moral order, and this order kept in check the desperate youths even when they were cornered and faced total defeat.

Third, though the language of international terrorism was sometimes used, it was explicitly even if indirectly conveyed that the usage was merely a matter of form, not substance. Thus, when the outside world was told that one passenger would be shot every thirty minutes, the passenger chosen as the first victim was told the threat was a sham. The hard-boiled journalists and strategic analysts in the plane may not have got the message but the other passengers and crew did. That is why the hijackers responded so easily to the discipline of the young airhostesses when the need arose, and the hostesses could so effortlessly assume authority over them. That is why, till the end, the crew and passengers retained their faith in the humanity of their captors and the captors also tried to live up to the image of courageous, self-sacrificing, moral rebels fighting for a just cause.

This compact among passengers, hijackers and crew was not

lost on the Indian mouthpieces of the universal language of statecraft, who knowingly or not tried to erase detailed memories of the hijackings. Not only did this leave ordinary newspaper readers with only a vague sketch of the events but it reduced all the moral gestures made in circumstances of great physical and psychological stress to spicy or comic incidents involving the 'unthinking Sikhs' of popular *sardārjī* jokes. On the basis of these filtered memories, a set of standard slogans about terrorism was devised for the consumption of the Indian middle classes. (There was at least one rumour after the second hijacking that, when a passenger on her return to Delhi said something positive about the hijackers to the press at the airport, the interview was cut short and she was whisked away by the security agencies.) The army major caught in the first hijacking, sensing the mood of the authorities, refused to give his full name to the press and called himself only Vijay. He might have suspected that his views would be considered unpatriotic.

Fourth, all three parties—hijackers, crew and passengers—refused to raise the stakes during the hijackings. (Even the AISSF participated in the refusal.) Their actions were not equally palatable to all, but they were nevertheless located in a shared moral universe. The leader of the hijackers who brought out bandages and cotton after roughing up the army major, and the major who, despite being ill-treated, never lost his realism and refused to take the assault as a personal affront, illustrate this point neatly.

There is a set of cultural questions relevant to this issue which I shall not try to answer. These questions involve the touches of reparation or atonement in some of the hijackers' actions. What was the source of this atonement in an avowedly martial community, in a context which could be interpreted to be a just war? Did the traditional Sikh concept of just warfare, with its built-in protection for children, women and non-combatants, come into play? Did the non-Sikh passengers and crew share that concept of warfare, so that the hijackers had to protect their self-esteem and the purity of their struggle by making reparative gestures to undo their deviations from the traditional Sikh principles of warfare? I leave the subject to those who are more competent to handle it.

It is, however, clear that the hijackers refused to absolutize the difference between their politics and that of the passengers and crew. If one goes by Gandhi's belief that such absolutization is essential to terrorism,[90] the distinctive nature of these terrorist acts would be obvious. The hijackings of IC 405 and IC 421 were the ninth and tenth in a series. All the earlier ones had ended reasonably peacefully and with little bloodshed. The passengers, especially the women and children, were treated well and, despite melodramatic touches—in one instance, the hijackers ostentatiously ate apples stuck onto knives[91]—in no case was there real panic. As a non-Indian passenger said after one of these occasions, he had experienced a hijacking with a difference.

Fifth, the maudlin and comic aspects—which are certain to jar on the sophisticated sensitivity of the Indian *haute bourgeoisie*—were exactly those that helped to establish the bonds among the three parties involved. These sentimental and comic aspects were vestigial elements of a dialect which everyone had half forgotten but which everyone recognized at crucial moments of crisis and/or truth. The passengers, crew and air pirates played for very high stakes indeed: their own liberty and lives. They had to back their actions with something more than learnt, scientific-rational interpretations—they had to fall back on their real convictions about the nature of their interpersonal world and draw on their deepest private theories about what might work in an extreme situation in their society. That to articulate these convictions they chose to borrow sentiments from Hindi commercial movies, rather than from the editorial pages of the national English dailies, suggests that the sentiments reflected something more than the half-digested global mass culture these movies are supposed to typify. One suspects that in trying to cater to the lowest common denominator of popular taste, the popular movies of the subcontinent have established a complex relationship with some of the deep but increasingly cornered elements of Indian culture.

The inefficiency, nervousness and amateurishness of the

[90] Bhikhu Parekh, 'Gandhi's Theory of Non-violence: His Reply to the Terrorists', in Noel O'Sullivan (ed.), *Terrorism, Ideology and Revolution* (Brighton: Wheatsheaf Books, 1986), pp. 178–202.

[91] *The Times of India*, 1 October 1981.

hijackers were also part of the same half-forgotten dialect; they were in fact an indication of another moral universe not known to the world of international terrorism and its cut-and-dried, expert analysts. That this dialect borrowed so heavily from the world of low-brow commercial films is unfortunate from the point of view of the Indian intelligentsia; but it appears that this dialect, despite all the efforts of modern secular India, cannot be entirely driven out of the culture of Indian politics. It manages to return, like Freud's unconscious, to haunt our public life.

Paradoxically, while the hijackers and their victims spoke the language of the fantasy world of commercial films, nevertheless they remained throughout in better touch with ground realities than the outside world of what Kupperman and Trent term 'counter-theatrics'.[92] It was in fact the Indian press, the airlines' bureaucracy, the foreign office, the security machinery and defence experts who appeared to be living in an unreal, mythical world created by the western experience with terrorism. When these outsiders talked of the hijackers, foreign involvement and security lapses in reified terms, they seemed to be totally out of touch with the real world of air piracy as it had been experienced by real persons uninitiated in sophisticated academic theories of terrorism.

A crucial element in this academic, objectivist approach was the pathetic faith in the technology of anti-terrorism. I have mentioned the demand for means of identifying liquid bombs which eluded conventional x-rays. But the two hijackings did not depend on the hijackers' weapons. They were the products of the ingenuity and power to bluff of teenagers whose strength—as well as weakness—was their inexperience. No technological device on earth can identify liquid bombs that do not exist, nor could such a device have given confidence to the crew and passengers to call the bluff at the right moment. They would have had to take the hijackers at their word.

Lastly, a methodological point. The narratives here can be read as studies in mass media and popular culture. I have depended entirely on the national English press and have avoided, for the moment, drawing upon direct interviews with

---

[92] Kupperman and Trent, *Terrorism*, p. 92.

the hijacked passengers and crew. I have tried to show that the data I have marshalled can be cast in either of the two languages I have identified—the universal language of the modern nation-state, which shapes so much of the available theories of terrorism, and the vernacular in which the majority of those in the hijacked IC 405 and IC 421 spoke. In the process, I have tried to create some space for the latter in our contemporary understanding of South Asian politics. For my argument is that there is a semi-articulate public awareness in these societies which has a place for the vernacular. I have called it a dialect earlier to indicate that it does not enjoy the status of a language. Modern political analysis has already successfully discredited it as soft, effeminate, immature, and irrational.

V

Finally, a few comments on the subject of terrorism in South Asia. It is possible to argue that modern terrorism and counter-terrorism have become, in some cases, consumption items for the middle classes. Terrorism, too, can now be advertised, sold and purchased as a political spectacle and as a commodity through the TV, the newspapers, the radio and commercial films. Some well-known experts on terrorism have, in fact, said that terrorism thrives on media exposure and cannot survive without publicity.[93] Perhaps this link between terror and the media has helped the Indian middle classes to internalize, rather quickly, a simplistic theory of terrorism and encouraged the Indian journalist, a self-conscious dealer in middle-class opinion, to assume the role of an expert on the subject overnight. Both groups confront the experience of terrorism second-hand, without any scope to reflect on its long-term meaning, political or cultural.

The theory and the expertise converge, in that they both overlie deep ambivalences triggered by the problems of living with a modern nation-state in a traditional, post-colonial society. In such a society, the westernized middle classes see themselves as guardians or custodians, trying desperately to protect the rest

---

[93] For instance, Yonah Alexander, 'Terrorism, The Media and The Police', in Kupperman and Trent, *Terrorism*, pp. 331–48.

of the society—seen as inefficient, anarchic and irrational—through a hard-boiled law-and-order approach and the technology of the state, which is viewed as the major instrument of modern rationality. The expertise that the modernizing middle classes and journalists claim to have follows directly from their perception of the rest of the society.

Opposed to this potent combination of an almost blind faith in the rationality of the state and ambivalence towards the ordinary Indian's unpredictable, non-modern Indianness, are the observed realities of hijacking as they unfold within the culture of everyday life in India.

Existing theoretical and empirical studies stress two differentiae of contemporary terrorism. First, terrorism is primarily a psychological weapon: 'its purpose is to instill fear in an attempt to reach specific objectives.'[94] Second, terrorism is 'essentially indiscriminate' and its choice of victims is arbitrary or random.[95] 'The lack of discrimination helps to spread fear, for if no one in particular is the target, no one can be safe.'[96]

By both criteria, the hijackings described here fail to qualify as terrorism. After the first clumsy attempts to instil some fear in the victims, the hijackers of IC 405 and IC 421 consistently attempted to bring down the level of that fear. Not only by the restraint of their behaviour, but also by caring for the captives and reassuring those whom they should have terrorized according to all the books. As we have seen, many 'victims' specifically told the press that there was no panic in the aircraft. Likewise, while the choice of aircraft was random, the terrorization of vicitims was not. Elaborate South Asian concepts of fair play and duty towards non-combatants determined and made predictable the hijackers' behaviour.

The clash between middle-class faith in the state, its technology and expertise, on the one hand, and the 'imperfect terrorism' shaped by traditional morality and restraints on violence, on the other, has its counterpart in the latent clash between the

---

[94] Paul Wapner, 'Problems of U.S. Counter-Terrorism', *Alternatives*, 1988, 13(2), pp. 271–8.

[95] Anthony Arblaster and Michael Walzer, quoted in Wapner, 'Problems of U.S. Counter-Terrorism'.

[96] Raymond Aron, quoted in Wapner, 'Problems of U.S. Counter-Terrorism'.

dominant language of the nation-state system and the residual traditional language of rebellion, now virtually inaccessible to those who speak the first language. I have argued here that the persistence of the second language allows one a different kind of political play in some societies. However, I have not over-emphasized the last point and I have not argued away international power politics and the security aspects of hijacking. I have merely tried to hint at the possibility—alas, being a product of the Indian middle-class culture myself, I can only call it a possibility—that there may be ways of dealing with one's counter-players and enemies which recognize the multilayered nature of human personality and social relationships.

Some will call this absurd, maudlin moralism; to others it is the heart of politics.

VI

Only a postscript remains. I have said at one place that the culture of the two air piracies covered in this essay might now be a thing of the past and India might already have entered an era where such hijackings could no longer afford to have the same mix of the pathetic, the funny and the fearsome. In general, the use of political terror in South Asia *is* becoming more professional, hard-eyed and 'world class'. But cultures and culturally embedded cognitive orders and interpersonal styles are notoriously resistant to change, and this end-of-a-phase comment might be a trifle premature. This postscript is designed to warn the reader that the increasingly violent culture of Indian politics, including the assassination of two of the country's prime ministers during the last ten years, has not entirely wiped out either the form or the substance of the older culture of Indian politics. The old and the new coexist, even if somewhat more uncomfortably now.

Two air piracies that took place while this book was going to press tell the story of that mixed heritage.

On 27 March 1993, Hari Singh of Jhajjar, Haryana, hijacked a Madras-bound airbus of the Indian Airlines. Singh was about forty years old, married, with two children aged seven and one, and stayed in a modest government residential colony. He had worked as a drawing teacher in a school once run by the step-father of Jagdish Tytler, the Union Minister of Surface Transport. For a few years he had also worked for DHL, the speed-post firm, and so he knew something about aircraft. Singh spoke chaste Hindi, wore kurta pyjama, and carried an Indian flag with the picture of a dove symbolizing peace. His kurta carried some telling caricatures of Prime Minister P. V. Narasimha Rao and two well-known Hindu extremist leaders, L. K. Advani and Bal Thackeray.

The flight to Madras left Delhi at 6 a.m. with 192 passengers and a crew of eleven. When it was flying over Bhopal, Singh sent a note to the pilot, Captain M. V. V. Rao, saying that he would blow up the plane with the explosives wrapped around his waist if it was not taken to Islamabad. He claimed he was a human bomb and had been trained by the LTTE, the Sri Lankan militant outfit. He used a hidden air dryer under his belt to convince everyone that he was serious.[97] The captain invited him to the cockpit and tried to dissuade him, but Singh was adamant.

Subsequent details get a little blurred. It seems that the captain got in touch with Delhi Airport and the intelligence agencies, and then flew the plane to Lahore. The airport

[97] Singh's choice of weapon might have been inspired by two earlier air piracies. The 1990s began with a young man from Coimbatore trying to hijack an Indian Airlines flight when it was landing at Bangalore in September 1990. He was armed with a 'bomb', actually a cake of soap wrapped in a handkerchief. He wanted to take the plane to Australia to seek employment there but was easily overpowered by the crew of the plane (*The Times of India*, 28 March 1993). The following year, a twenty-four-year-old Bengali student of commerce from Berhampur tried to pirate a plane, to settle some 'issues' with the government. The issues included demands to strip the former prime minister, Morarji Desai, of the highest national award, the Bharat Ratna, and to repeal President's rule in Assam and Tamil Nadu. His 'bombs' were an apple and a pomegranate wrapped in cloth (ibid.).

In January 1993, twenty-two-year-old Satish Chandra Pandey of Sultanpur, a small town in Uttar Pradesh, hijacked an Indian Airlines plane flying from Lucknow to Delhi with 48 passengers, including two union ministers. He was trying to impress his mother, he admitted (ibid.). The opposition leader, Atal Bihari Vajpayee of the Bharatiya Janata Party, intervened to persuade the 'earnest young' supporter of his party to surrender, securing the hijacker's safety, 'which was probably more endangered than the passengers' (ibid.). Pandey was armed with a 'bomb' made of wheatflour wrapped up in thread; others say it was a cricket ball.

authorities at Lahore, given past experience, refused him permission to land and blocked the runways by parking vehicles across them. The plane circled over the airport for a while. The hijacker was then told that, since the aircraft was running out of fuel, it had to be flown to Amritsar which was barely five minutes' flying distance from Lahore. The hijacker agreed, with the apparently inexplicable proviso that the plane had to be later flown to Delhi for a news conference.

As the passengers were not told of the hijacking till they landed at Amritsar, some of them at first thought that they were at Hyderabad. But when the captain announced that they had been hijacked and appealed for calm,[98] it was it seems unnecessary. Almost all the passengers, including the half-a-dozen foreigners, were later to tell the press that there had been no panic whatsoever;[99] evidently because the hijacker spoke to them over the intercom and then met them personally. He shook hands with some of them and assured them that he did not mean them any harm.[100]

One by-product of this relaxed atmosphere was mentioned by only one newspaper subsequently. According to *The Times of India*, a foreign traveller, James G. Rayan, Director of the International Crop Research Institute for Semi-Arid Tropics (ICRISAT), claimed that a letter drafted by some of the passengers and signed by all of them might have been the turning point in the whole episode.

> The passengers were calm and cool and decided to pass the hijacker a note signed by all. The moment he read the letter and realized that the passengers were empathetic towards him, he picked up the microphone and informed the authorities that he was prepared to surrender.[101]

When negotiating with K. P. S. Gill, the high-profile Director-General of Punjab Police and expert in counter-terrorism, the hijacker was first insistent that the plane be refuelled and taken to Delhi but later agreed to surrender if a news conference was

---

[98] *Indian Express*, 28 March 1993.
[99] Ibid.; also *The Hindustan Times*, 28 March 1993.
[100] Ibid.
[101] *The Times of India*, 29 March 1993.

organized for him at Amritsar. Assured by the police that journalists were listening to him in the control room, Singh enthusiastically read out a four-page memorandum. After that he surrendered and was taken away by the security forces and the hostages were released.

It was obvious at the end that the passengers as well as crew did not have any ill-feeling towards Singh.[102] Not only did 'the passengers including women and children looked relaxed and poised',

> most of them had ... developed a soft corner for their tormentor .... He, according to them, was very well-behaved and after surrendering, touched the feet of many elderly passengers and apologized to them for the inconvenience and harassment.[103]

According to one hostage, M. K. Singh, after surrendering, Singh shook hands with all his hostages and when he was being whisked away, he received 'tremendous applause' from them.[104] Another, K. Rajanna, noted that many took the hijacker's autograph;[105] they seemed to share Singh's anxiety about the state of India's politics and governance. All this was not lost on Singh. After the whole thing was over, during an interview with journalist Ritu Sarin, he said, 'You are talking about the difficulties the passengers faced. They all cooperated with me'.[106]

The result was that while Gill earned kudos from the passengers, their highest respect was reserved for Captain Rao; Rao had not lost his grip on all aspects of reality despite every provocation and temptation.[107] But even in Gill, the hard-boiled specialist in counter-terrorism, there was an awareness that everything had not gone according to the textbooks. Speaking to a newspaper and recalling the events with a touch of perplexity, he said, 'Whenever I spoke to him he would say it was not possible. Finally, he came up saying, "You are like my father."'

---

[102] *The Statesman*, 28 March 1993.

[103] *The Hindustan Times*, 28 March 1993.

[104] *Economic Times*, 28 March 1993.

[105] *The Hindustan Times*, 28 March 1993.

[106] Ritu Sarin, 'I Did it for Peace, Love and Harmony', *The Pioneer*, 28 March 1993.

[107] Ibid.

This was when it was suggested to Singh, the newspaper adds, that he should give up and to everyone's surprise, he agreed.[108]

At the end of the episode, while surrendering, Singh described himself as a nationalist Hindu. His intention, he said, was to address a press conference at Lahore on the demolition of the disputed mosque at Ayodhya on 6 December 1992. He said he was not a terrorist but 'a citizen of secular India'.[109] 'I am not a terrorist. I have done this to convey a definite message because I feel the country is going to the dogs.'[110]

He lashed out at politicians, particularly Rao and Advani. He felt that Rao was weak and old, and 'instead of restoring dignity of the Indians, the PM along with the Finance Minister were going to other countries begging for alms'.[111] Advani on the other hand, Singh felt, had taken the country to the brink of civil war.[112] 'The minority communities in the country were totally unsafe', Singh said, and this he traced to the BJP's 'policy of communalism'.[113] He also added that he wished Advani had been in the pirated plane to watch his protest; he had hijacked the plane under the impression that Advani was to travel by it.[114]

Singh also said that he was not sorry for his deed and knew the punishment for it. He also considerately promised to use some other method to voice his protest next time.

If hijackers and their victims have not changed much, neither have the security community and the media. Once again, there was much talk about security lapses and, of course, a Pakistani connection. *The Times of India* reported that the senior police officers interrogating the hijacker at the Joint Interrogation Centre had already revealed that there were possible links between Singh and Pakistan's intelligence agencies. The officers claimed that Singh had visited the Pakistan High Commission once between 18 January and 4 February 1993 and the air piracy had been planned around that time.[115] The nonviolent,

---

[108] 'Hijacker Gives in After High Drama', *The Pioneer*, 28 March 1993.
[109] *Indian Express*, 28 March 1993.
[110] *The Times of India*, 28 March 1993.
[111] *The Hindustan Times*, 28 March 1993.
[112] *Indian Express*, 28 March 1993.
[113] Ibid. [114] Ibid.
[115] *The Times of India*, 29 March 1993.

comical aspects of the hijacking infuriated some sections of the press: *The Hindustan Times*, for instance, was not thankful for the absence of bloodshed. Describing the hijacking as 'bizarre', 'crazy' and 'weird', it said in an editorial, 'No mercy should be shown to the hijacker just because the worst fears his criminal act generated in the country did not materialize'.[116] Some academics were equally unhappy with the way things had gone. A few of them resurrected the old ghost of the Stockholm syndrome (crudely, the tendency of a hostage to identify with his or her tormentor); others talked of the trampled human rights of the passengers. Belatedly sensing the dominant mood, one of the passengers of the hijacked plane, a retired army officer turned businessman, broke ranks and wondered why, like Israel, India could not have two commandos in each flight.

The prime minister, accused of being weak and old, was probably waiting to score a point against the hijacker, who had been a worker of his own party for ten years. He promptly praised the police and the administration. The other butt of the hijacker's barbs, Advani, claimed as promptly that the hijacking highlighted the 'frail and vulnerable security environment' of the country.[117] On that the last word was said by Kalyan Majumdar, the airport manager of Indian Airlines at Calcutta: airport security is so tight now, he claimed, 'that the only thing left to make it fool proof is to stop people from travelling'.[118]

On 24 April the same year, another Indian Airlines plane was pirated, while flying from Delhi to Srinagar. The episode turned out to be nasty, brutish and short.

After take-off a young man who called himself Syed Jalaluddin—he was later to change it to Muhammad Yusuf Shah—took out two handguns from the plaster cast on his leg, *à la* Frederick Forsyth's *Day of the Jackal*, and declared the plane hijacked. This time the guns were real. Shah was said to be high up in the Hizbul Mujahideen and tried to live up to his role and status the hard way. Obviously tense, he talked tough not merely with the negotiating authorities but also with the crew and passengers.

---

[116] *The Hindustan Times*, 29 March 1993; also *The Statesman*, 28 March 1993.
[117] *Indian Express*, 28 March 1993.
[118] *The Times of India*, 28 March 1993.

Thus, when told by some of the passengers that the children in the plane were suffering, Shah offered to shoot them one by one to put them out of their misery.[119] Though he later ordered medicine and other supplies for the hostages, that early impression of him as a hard-core killer persisted.

The élite commandos of the National Security Guard, the Black Cats, were ready this time; they made a swoop, captured the hijacker and released the passengers. They then took Shah out of the plane and shot him in cold blood.[120] Hardly anyone bothered or protested. One newspaper described the expertise and technical skill with which the killing was done—apparently a .22 pistol fitted with a silencer was used[121]—and another said,

> Senior officers of various security agencies confided that experience has shown that not much can be found out about the motive of the crime by prolonging the interrogation of a political murderer or hijacker.[122]

The officers considerately added that lengthy, unnecessary, public trials of such hijackers wasted a lot of public funds and created fresh security problems.[123]

---

[119] *The Observer*, 28 April 1993.

[120] There were some half-hearted attempts to contest this version, at first accepted by Gill, by other government spokespersons who either claimed that Shah had died while trying to escape or that he died in the cockpit of the hijacked plane during the commando raid.

[121] *The Statesman*, 10 May 1993.

[122] *The Observer*, 28 April 1993.

[123] Ibid.

Sati in *Kali Yuga*: The Public Debate on Roop Kanwar's Death

The peculiar mix of fascination, fear, theatrics, self-righteousness, and anger with which India's westernized middle classes reacted to the sati committed by Roop Kanwar at Deorala in Rajasthan in 1987 would have delighted a psychologist. Evidently, the very idea of suicide on the funeral pyre of one's husband—or the possibility that this ancient rite could be exploited to hide the murder of a young widow—had its own strange fascination for the modern mind. However, for a small minority, the reactions to the sati only deepened the tragedy of the death of a teenage widow.

The minority could not forget that during the previous decade, a number of such instances of sati had taken place in Rajasthan without arousing the same passions in urban India. Some remembered their discomfort at the unconcern with which most social activists and journalists had greeted instances of sati only a few years earlier. Such events were almost invariably reported in the inside pages of the English language dailies, usually as a form of esoterica that had survived the juggernaut of progress. A large majority of those who were ready to throw epileptic fits at the mention of the word 'sati' after Roop's death, did not care to write even a few standard letters to the editor when, for instance, the last-known sati took place only a year earlier, even though that case, too, was duly mentioned in the English language press.[1]

---

[1] For instance, Chinu Panchal, '1,500 Witness "Sati" Ritual', *The Times of India*, 6 October 1986.

Were the passions aroused at Roop's death caused by a sharply heightened moral awareness or was there something more to it? Why did this instance of sati at this point of time so inflame the urban intelligentsia?

Both questions relate to the politics of public consciousness in contemporary urban India. To that extent, one would think, journalists, social scientists, and activists should find them relatively easy to handle. Other important questions about the incident demand answers that have to be teased out of a mass of tangled data and from a world that is more unfamiliar to modern India. What motivated those who organized, witnessed, or applauded the rite? What is the symbolic meaning of sati in contemporary times? And what structure of self-interests fuelled it?

Strangely, while answers to the latter questions have been attempted, the first two questions about the role of the Deorala sati in the politics of public consciousness have been little discussed either in India's English press or in scholarly journals. Does this tell us, urban, westernized Indians, something about ourselves? This is the first question to which we must give an answer, however imperfect, before proceeding any further.

My tentative answer to the question would be: I suspect that two contradictory social-psychological forces are operating in India's middle-class culture of politics. On one side is the growing political power of the mass culture through which the urban, middle-class Indian has begun to influence the political process. This pan-Indian mass culture, now closely linked to the global mass culture, is strengthened by a number of social forces, among which are the growing reach of the media, urbanization, industrialization, physical mobility brought about by changing occupational patterns, and technological growth. On the other side is the democratic process, threatening to consolidate further the political presence of non-modern India in the public sphere. In an open system, in however distorted a form, numbers count.

In such a system, the only way the 'moderns' can retain the legitimacy of their social and political dominance is by setting themselves up as the bastions of rationality and in the vanguard of social change. They have to seek a sanction for their disproportionate political power from what they regard as the symbols of their superior knowledge and morality. Thus it is not surprising that in recent years, the westernized and semi-westernized middle classes have tended to justify their political power by playing up in the media the spectacular technological and organizational achievements of the Indian state and the modern sector—or the equally spectacular evidence of backwardness and irrationality in non-modern India. Together the two sets of spectacles endorse the culture of modern India and its status in the higher reaches of Indian public life. Hence the feigned panic and hyperbole that followed the Deorala sati; they are an attempt to confirm the status of this sati as the clinching evidence of the need to give modern India a disproportionate access to political power, even if it meant bypassing the democratic process. Hence also the remarkable claim, as part of the same hyperbole, made by India's Harvard-trained Minister of State for Home Affairs at the time, that hundreds and thousands of Roop Kanwars have been killed in India. In so claiming, P. Chidambaram ignored the fact that in the last fifty years cases of sati have been confined mainly to one state, and within that state to one region. Naturally, he neglected to point out that the figures involved do not match the rate of homicide in even the smallest Indian town.[2]

One suspects that it is this search for grand spectacles of evil that has shaped much of the middle-classes' response to Roop's sati and caused them to avoid some of the basic issues raised by her death. For only this search for evidence of the inferiority of the other India can explain the paradox in the public debate on the subject: those who declared the Deorala sati to be a 'pure case of murder' attacked, in the same breath, Indian traditions, village superstitions, even the Mahabharata and the Ramayana. As if a pure case of murder could not involve greed, pure and simple, and could not be handled under the existing Indian penal code, without reference to the larger cultural factors.[3]

---

[2] P. Chidambaram, quoted in Tavleen Singh, *Indian Express*, 29 May 1988. On the broad sociology and 'epidemiology' of sati, see the special issue of *Seminar*, February 1988 (342).

[3] In the context of Deorala, only one paper comes close to recognizing the nature of this problem. See Madhu Kishwar and Ruth Vanita, 'The Burning of Roop Kanwar', *Race and Class*, July–September 1988, 30(1), pp. 59–67, esp. pp. 66–7.

This ambivalent response, depicting sati as simple murder, yet as something more than murder, has already created strange anomalies in Indian public life. First, thanks to the supposed legal reforms brought about by anti-sati activists—the new statute relating to the glorification of sati and prosecution of those involved in a sati—there can now be systematic attempts to pass off cases of sati as cases of murder, since cases of murder now give the accused and the police more room for manœuvring than cases of sati.[4] For instance, abetment to murder does not invite the death penalty, but abetment to sati now does.[5] Second, this draconian law, rushed through Parliament as a public gesture against a social pathology, is now available to the state for misuse against political opponents, or even for the simpler purpose of extorting money by the lower levels of the law-enforcing agencies.

In the following pages, I shall try to rescue four such 'un-discussable' issues that have fallen victim to the new mystifications produced by the public debate on sati in metropolitan India. The issues I have chosen to reproblematize are: the nature of coercion in sati, the glorification of sati, the roots of sati in the traditional role of women, and the use of the state to stop the practice of sati.

II

First, the matter of coercion. The earliest reports on the Deorala sati did not mention any coercion. Some people, including Roop Kanwar's parents and their relatives staying at Deorala, seemed sure that none was used. (As one knows from cases of wives killed by their in-laws for failure to bring satisfactory amounts of dowry from their parents, the victim's parental family are usually the first to challenge the suicide theory floated by the in-laws.) In

---

[4] See the case of Shakuntala Yadav, reported in Rahul Pathak, 'Confess to Murder, Cops Tell Family', *Indian Express*, 13 January 1988; Minu Jain, 'Sati or Murder', *The Sunday Observer*, 18 January 1988; also 'Sati or Suicide', *Indian Express*, 12 January 1988; and 'Another Sati Reported in U.P. Village', *The Statesman*, 12 January 1988.

[5] Maja Daruwala, 'Overkill of Sati Bill', *The Statesman*, 21 January 1988. For the text of the new sati legislation, see *The Commission of Sati (Prevention) Act, 1987 [Act No. 3 of 1988] with Short Notes* (Lucknow: Eastern Book Co., n. d.).

the second week stray reports of coercion came in, but the majority still did not mention force.[6] By the end of the third week the large majority of journalists were fully convinced that Roop's death was a clear case of cold-blooded murder. One newspaper gave lurid details of how she had run away and hidden in a barn and was pulled out from there to be burnt.[7] Nine months later, coercion was so obvious an element that at least one reporter in a major national newspaper—and some policemen—had reached the point of lamenting that torture could not be used to extract information from some of the witnesses.[8]

I believe that the possibility of coercion having been exercised exists in all cases of sati. I say so not merely because I am a sceptic in such matters, but also because I once studied the epidemic of sati in eastern India in the early years of British rule.[9] Nearly all the cases of sati for which there were data suggested direct or indirect coercion; something that is difficult to forget. For the moment, however, I am concerned not with the empirical reality of the sati at Deorala but with the certitudes of middle-class commentators on that reality.

I believe it was naïve on the part of journalists and social workers to assume at the beginning that there had been no coercion. In the main, their information came from the same villagers who had applauded the rite in the first place. It was

---

[6] For instance, Shabnam Virmani, 'The Spirit of Sati Lives On', *The Times of India*, 12 September 1987. According to her, it was 'unlikely that Roop Kunwar was coerced into it by relatives', and that the villagers were 'tight-lipped and wary of press reporters and the public'. Within two weeks the same newspaper published Sunil Menon's 'Roop Kunwar's Act was Not Voluntary', *The Times of India*, 25 September 1987. Roop Kanwar's parents have till now maintained that she was not coerced. See Sanjeev Srivastava, 'Deorala Revisited', *The Illustrated Weekly of India*, 22 May 1988, pp. 20–3.

[7] 'Dragged to Pyre for Sati', *The Statesman*, 21 October 1988.

[8] Sanjeev Srivastava, 'Doctor Elusive about Deorala Incident', *The Times of India*, 4 June 1988. Srivastava wrote wistfully, 'Some of the police officials associated with the investigation of the case also feel handicapped in their efforts to extract more information as no "third degree methods" could be used during the interrogation of Dr Singh'.

[9] Ashis Nandy, 'Sati: A Nineteenth Century Tale of Women, Violence and Protest', *At the Edge of Psychology: Essays in Politics and Culture* (New Delhi: Oxford University Press, 1980, reprint 1989), pp. 1–31.

equally naïve for others, who later came to believe that the Deorala sati was a clear case of homicide, to trust the same villagers who had earlier denied any coercion. In both cases, there being no outside observers when the sati took place, a little healthy scepticism about the constructions of the villagers would have done no harm. Villagers, when dealing with their urban compatriots, can be remarkably devious, cautious, and secretive, and display a sharp sense of survival. Many of the same Rajput youth who bared their swords at Deorala in 1987 to defend the sacred place of sati against its opponents were later seen hedging their bets, after the state had reaffirmed the illegality of sati. To depend upon such defenders of the faith as informants may reveal one's trust in human nature, but is no indication of one's political acuity.

In any event, direct physical coercion was hardly the central issue—unless those claiming that Roop's death was a case of murder really meant that had force not been used, the rite would have been justified. If they did, theirs was essentially the position of the Shankaracharya of Puri and local politicians such as the Janata Party chieftain in Rajasthan, Kalyan Singh Kalvi. They too said that sati was unjustified when force was used, but concluded that since force had not been used in this instance, Roop's sati was justifiable. There may have been disagreement about the fact of coercion but, at least in the public debate, there was perfect agreement between most supporters and opponents of sati as to the principle involved. Few raised the crucial question: could sati be justified if no direct physical coercion was used?

The answer to this question must be based on an awareness that no religious event of this kind can any more remain uncontaminated by our times. Nothing is safe from the secular cost-calculations and market morality which have now entered the interstices of Indian society. (Many Rajputs protesting against the new anti-sati legislation refuse to acknowledge that triumph of secularism and modernity. Some of them are convinced that the rest of society is merely trying to get them. In reaction, they are trying to defend a rite which now only theoretically remains part of the traditional religious worldview. In practice, that rite is already outside the compass of tradition and has become part of the modern business culture that has already engulfed most religious spectacles, festivals, pilgrimages, and religious family endowments and trusts.)

Thus it is possible to argue that today, even when a widow independently decides to commit suicide, her independence in doing so cannot but be imperfect. One can never be sure that her family, her village, and her caste, motivated by common greed and the hunt for higher status, have not pushed her into it. They need not even be self-consciously greedy or status-hungry. It is possible to push a person to self-destruction by creating the right atmosphere, often without being aware of doing so.

In any case, even if no force was used in Roop's case, it is clear that the family and village did nothing to persuade her against her 'impetuous' decision. Nor did they help her come out of the depression caused by her husband's death; rather, they colluded with her self-destructive impulses. The sati was organized within a few hours, before Roop's parents could even talk to her, and there is no record of any serious effort by her in-laws to dissuade her from self-immolation. Roop's own family behaved no better: after being confronted with a *fait accompli* they evidently decided not to create a fuss. But this proves their pragmatism, not the authenticity of the sati. Both sides of the family knew that the sati would pay them—the relatives, the villagers, and the caste—handsome, long-term dividends. It is pointless to argue that they did not know beforehand the full extent to which they would profit. Living in the *kali yuga*–the final, fallen age in the Indian version of the human time cycle–they should have known.

The second question is: how far can or should glorification of sati go? A recent act proscribing all glorification of sati may seem *prima facie* justified to many but cannot stand up to critical scrutiny. Does the new law mean that children will not read about or admire Queen Padmini's self-chosen death in medieval times? Does it mean that that part of the Mahabharata which describes Mādrī's sati will now be censored? What about Rabindranath Tagore's awe-inspiring, respectful depiction of sati and Abanindranath Tagore's brilliant invocation of the courage, idealism, and tragedy of sati in medieval Rajasthan?[10]

---

[10] For instance, Rabindranath Tagore, '*Vivāhā*', *Kathā o Kāhini*, in *Racanābalī* (Calcutta: Vishwabharati, 1987), *4*, pp. 71–3; and '*Mā Bhaiḥ*', *Racanābalī*, *3*, pp. 676–9; Abanindranath Tagore, *Rājkāhinī* (Calcutta: Signet Press, 1956).

Do we proscribe their works, too, forgetting that the Tagores had been in the forefront of the movement against sati during the colonial period? What about Kabir, who, over the last four centuries, has remained the ultimate symbol of spiritual achievement and interreligious tolerance in this country? After all, as Coomaraswamy points out, Kabir constantly uses 'the impulse to sati' as an image of surrendering one's ego to God.[11]

Finally, what does one do with the original Sati? Does one ban the celebration of Durgā Pujā or, for that matter, the reading of Kālidāsa's *Kumārasambhava*, because both celebrate the goddess who committed sati? Do we follow the logic of the two young activists who were keen to get the Ramayana declared unconstitutional, so that the epic could not be shown on India's state-owned television? What does one do with the faith of millions of Indians that the soil that received the divided body of Sati constitutes the sacred land of India? That these questions may not in the future remain merely theoretical or hypothetical is made obvious by the fact that the Indian History Congress felt obliged to adopt a statement critical of the TV Ramayana in its 1988 convention.[12]

One possible response to such questions is to *presume* that in the mythical past sati was a rare, fearsome, but moving ritual which symbolized the reaffirmation of the purity, self-sacrifice, power, and dignity of women and the superiority of the feminine principle in the cosmos. Those decultured, ill-informed Indians who view classical or mythological instances of sati as instances of the degradation of women would do well to read what is probably the twentieth century's most spirited defence of the philosophy of sati, the one offered by Ananda K. Coomaraswamy. It questions the artificial line drawn between self-immolation for trendy, secular causes like revolution and nationalism, and self-immolation for low-brow, old-fashioned religious or cultural causes.

---

[11] Ananda K. Coomaraswamy, 'Status of Indian Women', *The Dance of Shiva: Fourteen Indian Essays* (Delhi: Munshiram Manoharlal, 1982), pp. 115–39. See p. 128.

[12] Only one scholar has critically assessed the modern discomfort with the TV Ramayana, arguing that the discomfort comes from the moderns' lack of access to the epics and inability to use them creatively. See G.P. Deshpande, 'The Riddle of the Sagar Ramayana', *Economic and Political Weekly*, 22 October 1988, pp. 2215–16.

> The criticism we make on the institution of Sati and woman's blind devotion is similar to the final judgment we are about to pass on patriotism. We do not, as pragmatists may, resent the denial of the ego for the sake of an absolute, or attach an undue importance to mere life; on the contrary we see clearly that the reckless and useless sacrifice of the 'suttee' and the patriot is spiritually significant. And what remains perpetually clear is the superiority of the reckless sacrifice to the calculating assertion of rights.[13]

This asymmetric public perception of sacrifices for secular and non-secular causes, to which Coomaraswamy drew our attention, persists. It is now being systematically propagated through the Indian media as the last word on the subject. In the third week of November 1987, when the debate on sati was at its height, the self-immolation of a DMK party worker in Tamilnadu for the cause of Sri Lankan Tamils was mentioned without any fanfare in the inside pages of virtually all the national dailies. It is no surprise that there was not even a murmur of discomfiture from the newspaper-reading public.[14]

However, whatever one may presume about the nobility of sati in the mythic past, its status now—in deep *kali yuga*—is a different story. In practice the rite has been corrupted by modern market forces and by the idea of negotiable social status. In historic times, as opposed to the mythic, it is safer to presume that sati is a perverted form of sacrifice, if not homicide. Therefore, to borrow a phrase from criminal law, it is better to prevent a hundred authentic satis than to allow one inauthentic sati to occur.

This differentiation between sati in mythical times and sati in historical times, between sati as an event (*ghatanā*) and sati as a system (*prathā*), between the authentic sati and its inauthentic offspring, between those who respect it and those who organize it in our times, is not my contribution to the understanding of the rite. These distinctions were already implicit, for instance, in the writings of Rabindranath Tagore, who was an aggressive

[13] Coomaraswamy, 'Status of Indian Women', p. 127.

[14] The reaction of modern India to the self-immolation of a Jain man of religion at about the same time was also minimal. The death was viewed as the foolish self-destruction of a slightly senile religious enthusiast. The reaction to the self-chosen death of Vinoba Bhave some years earlier did not differ greatly.

opponent of sati as practised in contemporary times, yet respectful towards the ideas behind it. It is implicit in folk culture in many parts of India. It is also implicit in the difference between the simple faith of the pilgrims who thronged to Deorala after the sati of Roop Kanwar, and the actions of the organizers of the event, who profited from it.[15] And certainly it is implicit in the contrast between the monuments that have attended some of the satis in west and south India and the absence of such monuments in the wake of the largest epidemic of sati ever witnessed, namely the one that occurred in eighteenth- and nineteenth-century Bengal.

While there are more than a hundred sati temples and hundreds of *chhatris* spread over large parts of India, to the best of my knowledge there is no such temple or *chhatri* in honour of any one of the thousands of women who committed sati in the eastern Indian epidemic. There are a few sati temples in Bengal,

---

[15] When I first made a distinction between sati as a *ghatanā* (event) and sati as a *prathā* (system or practice) in this and an earlier essay ('Sati in Kaliyuga', *Indian Express*, November 1987), there were howls of protest in some journals and news weeklies. It was read as directly supporting sati and some, not knowing that I was not a Hindu, even found in it indicators of Hindu fanaticism. One called it a *dhārmic* support to sati (Sudhir Chandra, 'Sati: The *Dhārmic* Fallacy', *New Quest*, March–April 1988 (68), pp. 111–14). Another found in the use of the 'Hindu' fourfold division of *yugas* itself clinching evidence of my real self (Kumkum Sangari, 'Perpetuating the Myth', *Seminar*, February 1988 (342), pp. 24–30). It restored my faith in the practical wisdom imposed by involvement in the politics of social reform when two women activists, troubled by the sati bill, subsequently wrote: 'The bill assumes sati is a practice, whereas it could be described as a kind of rare and frightful event which reveals, in a flash, several of the problems of our time. In other words, we might do well to consider whether it is now being given the sanctity of tradition and practice, and if so by whom and with what motives. In order to do this, we must first distinguish between sati as an act, sati as an ideology, and sati as a source of political and financial profit.

'There is ... a difference between those who organise the event of sati, ... those who eulogise the principle of sati underlying one particular incident hundreds of years ago but repudiate the act of sati today, ... and those who glorify the act in self-interest, be it practical or financial' (Latika Sarkar and Radha Kumar, 'Flaws in New Sati Bill', *The Times of India*, 15 December 1987).

The only thing I might add is that Sarkar and Kumar do not seem to be aware here that sati is being associated with 'the sanctity of tradition and practice' not merely by religious fanatics but also by a large section of India's modern literati, with a different set of motives and interests. Cf. S. Sahay, 'Perspective on Sati', *The Telegraph*, 26 January 1988.

set up mainly by Rajasthanis, and someone may discover one or two of them to have developed a connection with mythologized satis from the early years of colonialism. Yet the paucity of temples commemorating late eighteenth- and early nineteenth-century satis and the inability of Bengalis to find even a few satis to honour among the five per day or so that took place at the height of the epidemic, tell us something. As does the comment of the priest in one of the few existing sati temples in Bengal that true sati is impossible in our times. Evidently, at some level, there is an awareness that the satis in colonial Bengal were not authentic and therefore did not deserve to be honoured. It is not all a matter of superstition and blind faith. Traditional Indians do discriminate; they do make moral choices.

However, one acquires the right to talk of the inauthenticity of satis in the *kali yuga* only after respectfully admitting the authenticity of the values that speak through the acts of sati recorded in epic and myth or through mythologized accounts of satis in historical times, such as those recounted by the balladeers and folk-singers of Rajasthan. The two Tagores, Rabindranath and Abanindranath, showed us how to do it, by writing with great sensitivity and a touch of tragedy about sati in mythologized history, even though they were proud that their own family had been at the forefront of the struggle for the abolition of sati in their own time.

If such discrimination is not shown, modernist criticisms of sati are likely to have the same impact that criticism of child-marriage has had so far on village India—none at all. For obviously, the ideas represented in the myth of the original sati, as reaffirmed in epics, folk-tales, and ballads, continue to live in the hearts of millions of Indians. These ideas constitute part of the basic substratum of Indian culture. They cannot be wiped away by angry letters to newspapers.

Once one shows respect for the idea of sati at the mythological level, one paradoxically acquires the right to criticize all individual instances of sati, even those put forward in the myths themselves. One can even say Mādrī in the Mahabharata or, for that matter, Pārvatī should not have committed sati, and that what took place at Deorala was not sati but murder. Such criticism will make sense to many of the 300,000 pilgrims to Deorala, in the same way that similar criticism by reformers made sense to earlier generations. After all, the criticism of sati that began many centuries ago in a traditional context has continued to resonate up to now, even if not in a tone audible to modernists.[16]

In this respect sati is part of a larger picture. Rammohun Roy was listened to when he ridiculed Kṛṣṇa for killing Putanā; and Tagore when he criticized the way Sumitrā was treated in the Ramayana or when he made Karṇa, not Arjuna, the hero of a verse-play based on part of the Mahabharata. Both had precedents in premodern times. Madhusudan Dutt made Rama the villain of his epic and Meghnād the hero, and he too was said to have been inspired by lesser-known, earlier texts: a Tamil and a Jain Ramayana. These great Indians viciously attacked aspects of traditions that did not fit in with their concept of *yugadharma*, ethics appropriate to their age, and few challenged their right to do so. Because they understood and respected the values enshrined in tradition, they were listened to with respect when they attacked or reinterpreted certain figures in the Indian epics or even made fun of them. Only a few illegitimate children of the British Raj—the comic-strip warlords of Hindutva—whose feelings of cultural inferiority made them semiticize and masculinize Hinduism—have challenged this traditional right to dissent in recent years, and got away with it. And only in metropolitan India at that.

Third, there is the question of the alleged degradation of women in the ideology of sati. The existing literature on sati in some Indic traditions—sati was not endemic to them all nor was it unknown in non-Indic traditions—indicates that the traditional concept of sati was associated with ideas of the sacred and magical powers of woman, of both the straightforward right-handed and potentially sinister left-handed kinds. These associations went with fear of woman, her power, and her special status in the cosmos. As the carrier of the ultimate principle of nature and representative of the cosmic feminine principle, a woman was thought to be the natural protector of her man. It was taken for granted that a man could not match her in piety, power, and

[16] Cf. Arvind Sharma, *Sati* (Delhi: Motilal Banarsidass, 1988), pp. 15–17; and Romila Thapar, 'In History', *Seminar*, February 1988, (342), pp. 14–19.

will. To moderns, the mythology of the rite seems an insult to women mainly because these meanings are lost to us. While we blame traditional India for being organized around religion we claim in the same breath that the sacred power women enjoyed in Indian society was meaningless.

What has happened in recent times is that these non-economic powers of women have both declined and been devalued. Like men, women in India, too, are assessed more and more in terms of their productive capacity and the market value of that capacity. Wherever that market value is low and market morality enters social relationships, the chances of sati—now more appropriately called widow-burning—increase.[17] They also increase when women have access to economic power within families in which social relationships become brittle or interest-based due to cultural changes.

It was such a combination of circumstances—and the one-dimensional valuation of women that it produced—that precipitated the one large-scale epidemic of sati we have witnessed in the last three hundred years. The Bengal epidemic of sati was the logical culmination of rational, secular cost-calculation in a society convulsed by massive disruption of traditional values.

Fourth and finally, there is the question of social intervention through the state. V. N. Datta in a recent book has tried to sum up the attitudes of the Muslim rulers of India, specially the Mughal emperors, towards sati.[18] The Mughals were hostile to sati and some of them saw it as a by-product of Hindu idolatry. But they did not use the might of the state to suppress it. Instead, they insisted on prior government permission for the performance of sati as an insurance against coercion. By delaying such permission, supposedly to screen the genuine sati from the inauthentic one, they placed obstacles in the way of the prospective sati. The aim, Bernier says, was to tire out the patience of the widows. That this usually worked is surely indicated by Jean de Thevenot's remark that the relatives of prospective satis sometimes sought to bribe Mughal officers. Women with children were in any case not allowed by the Mughals to burn themselves, because

---

[17] Nandy, 'Sati'.

[18] V. N. Datta, *Sati: Widow Burning in India* (New Delhi: Manohar, 1987), esp. pp. 13–14.

they were expected to look after and educate their children. One emperor, Jahangir, required those wishing to commit sati in regions near the capital to appear before him personally to obtain permission. Promises of gifts and land were made to them to dissuade them from the act.

Such tactics probably worked because, paradoxically, the Mughal hostility to sati accompanied the deep respect of the Mughal state towards the values represented by the rite. Coomaraswamy reminds his modern readers of the poem of Muhammad Riza Nau'i, written in the reign of Akbar, upon the sati of a Hindu girl whose betrothed was killed on the day of their marriage.

> This Musulman poet, to whom the Hindus were 'idolaters', does not relate his story in any spirit of religious intolerance or ethical condescension.... He does not wonder at the wickedness of men, but at the generosity of women....
>
> This Hindu bride refused to be comforted and wished to be burnt on the pyre of her dead betrothed. When Akbar was informed of this, he called the girl before him and offered wealth and protection, but she rejected all his persuasion....
>
> Akbar was forced, though reluctantly, to give his consent to the sacrifice, but sent with her his son Prince Daniyal who continued to dissuade her. Even from within the flames, she replied to his remonstrances, 'Do not annoy, do not annoy, do not annoy.'[19]

The last word of Nau'i on the subject is:

> Teach me, O God, the Way of Love,
> and enflame my heart with this maiden's Fire.[20]

As for the colonial period, it is not widely known that Rammohun Roy (1772–1833), the social reformer whose name is most closely associated with the struggle against sati in historical times, was himself ambivalent towards a legal ban on sati; according to some, he opposed such a ban.[21] Moreover, he showed respect to the values underlying the mythology of sati by pointing out that the rite presumed the superiority in the cosmos

[19] Coomaraswamy, 'The Status of Indian Women', pp. 128–9.

[20] Ibid., p. 129.

[21] Ramesh Chandra Majumdar, *Glimpses of Bengal in the Nineteenth Century* (Calcutta: Firma K. L. Mukhopadhyay, 1960).

of the feminine principle over the masculine, and recognized the woman's greater firmness of spirit, loyalty, and courage.[22] Perhaps he wanted the reform movement he had initiated from within the society, and not the colonial state, to be the main instrument of social change. Given that he also saw the values constituting the philosophy of sati to be an endorsement of the superiority of the feminine principle over the masculine, it could even be hypothesized that he saw his society as perfectly capable of handling the pathology of sati with the help of its own cultural resources. He had certainly sensed that the epidemic of sati all around him was a product of colonialism, not of India's own traditions; and that the epidemic affected exactly that section of society—the westernizing, culturally uprooted, urban and semi-urban Indians—which was often dismissive towards the rest of the society, regarding it as a swamp of superstition and atavism.[23]

Interestingly, many contemporaries of Rammohun Roy acknowledged the modern, colonial links with sati. Some of them were aggressively anti-Hindu and would have loved to blame Indian tradition for the outbreak of sati in Bengal—for instance, the Baptist missionary Joshua Marshman. Even those who were unable to see the direct colonial connection often identified the distorted remnant of tradition as the main culprit, and saw that sati became a social problem only when such traditions were under attack.[24]

One can end by saying that, even if one takes a consistently modernist view, sati, when it was a *ghatanā* or an event, was an instance of individual pathology and thus remained primarily in the domain of clinical psychology and psychiatry; when it became a *prathā* or system, it became primarily a social problem and entered the domain of social psychology and social psychiatry. The state comes in as an important actor mainly in the second case.

Blurring the two categories—sati as an event and sati as a custom or epidemic—is an essential device for those who seek to adapt the colonial discourse on sati for internal use, both as a political

[22] Nandy, 'Sati'.
[23] Ibid.
[24] Ibid.

strategy and as a psychological defence. It is remarkable how since the Deorala event there has been a revival of efforts by Anglophile, psychologically uprooted Indians (exactly the sector which produced the last epidemic of sati in eastern India) to vend sati as a stigma primarily of Hinduism, and not as one of the by-products of the entry of modern values–especially the absolutization of impersonal human relationships, the productivity principle, and market morality—into the interstices of Indian society. At one time, most of these efforts were closely associated with attempts to justify British rule in India. Now, as the cultural projection of a new form of internal colonialism, such efforts are primarily associated with the rootless, westernized, Indian bourgeoisie that controls the media, either directly or through the state. Only one scholar has so far expressed her distress that the criticisms of sati since the Deorala event have borrowed so heavily from colonial discourse.[25]

Actually, such borrowing is to be expected. Colonialism has to try to discredit the culture of the colonized to validate the colonial or quasi-colonial social relationships that it itself creates. The persistence of culture is a form of resistance, and those seeking hegemony in the realm of political economy cannot afford to leave culture alone. Those who see themselves as social engineers in the southern world and their supporters within the western knowledge industry know this fully. It is an indicator of that awareness in India today that Roop's tragically unnecessary death has become for the urban, uprooted, Indian bourgeoisie another marker of the backwardness of the traditional Indian, even though responsibility for the death should be shared by the social forces that these westernized Indians have supported handsomely. These forces constitute the kind of attack on traditional lifestyles that has resulted in epidemics of sati in the past.

Middle-class progressivism reveals itself most clearly in its intolerance towards the values that prompted Indians to venerate the remembered premodern satis that took place over the centuries. These values cut across Indian society, across the barriers of caste, class, gender, age, and even religion. Available data show

[25] Veena Das, 'Strange Response', *The Illustrated Weekly of India*, 8 February 1988.

that the veneration of sati continues to be a characteristic of the society as a whole.[26] Many middle-class social critics and radicals call such respect 'glorification of sati' and want it to be banned. They believe it contributes directly to the practice of sati in contemporary times. Many who hold this view style themselves historical materialists; yet when it comes to sati and village India, they conveniently forget the socioeconomic determination of social pathologies. They speak as if the ideology of sati itself produced sati.[27]

---

[26] 'Roop Kanwar did the Right Thing', *The Times of India*, 11 December 1987. This survey showed that 63.4 per cent of the respondents (63 per cent of women and 41.5 per cent in the age group 25–40) supported sati and 50.8 per cent refused to accept it as a crime. This is 160 years after sati was legally banned.

[27] In much that I have said, I have compared contemporary middle-class and earlier colonial reactions to sati. There is an even closer comparison in the reaction of the urban bourgeoisie to the Muslim Women's Bill of 1986—the Shah Bano affair—and in a not-so-widely-known plea that some well-known Bengali intellectuals made to the West Bengal government at about the same time to suppress Santhal witch-doctors. As the agitation against the Muslim Women's Bill is likely to be better known than the Santhal case to my readers, I shall confine my comments to it.

The protest against the Muslim Women's Bill, like that against sati, too, was meant to resist the victimization of women and was justified as such. But those who made a public issue out of the victimization of the likes of Shah Bano (who had been divorced and left in penury by her well-to-do Muslim husband), ignored or tried to whitewash the larger victimization of the community involved. They pretended that the Shah Bano case which triggered the Bill, and the Bill itself, could be discussed without taking into account the fact that a sizeable proportion of the Muslims had been discriminated against, subjected to violence, and pushed increasingly into urban ghettos by a series of riots. They behaved as if one could ignore that in this discrimination and violence, the Indian state and its law-enforcing agencies—two main actors in the Shah Bano case and professed agents of social change within Muslim society—had played a growing role, both deliberately and by default. (Cf. Bhikhu Parekh, 'Between Holy Text and Moral Void', *The New Statesman*, 24 March 1989, pp. 29–33.)

In their insecurity, fear, and sense of being cornered, a large section of Muslims were bound to see the Supreme Court's decision in favour of Shah Bano, specially in view of the homilies on Islam included in the judgment, as another attack by the same state machinery on their identity and culture, which had already become their last line of defence. No wonder they closed ranks, supporting even the more obscurantist and fanatic elements among them. This closing of ranks perfectly suited the westernized middle-class Indians who opposed the bill; as if they were waiting for just that. The moment some of the more atavistic elements in Muslim society joined the protest, it was interpreted by

III

Let me conclude by admitting a central problem that every critic of modernity must face up to. Every culture has a dark side. Sati in the *kali yuga* is an actualization of some of the possibilities inherent in the darker side of India's traditional culture, even if this actualization has been made possible by the forces of modernity impinging on and seeking to subvert the culture. After all, the tradition of sati exists only in some cultures, not in all; the kind of pathological self-expression displayed by some cultures in South Asia is not found in other parts of the world.

It is not easy to acknowledge the complicity of either the underside of traditions or of South Asian modernity. For modern academics it is the reference group of professional colleagues and the fear of being shamed in the metropolitan centres of intellectual life; for nonmoderns, there are the loyalties to one community and the pathetic attempts to reaffirm a faith that has become shaky within. Particularly in Roop's case, the moderns suspect that it was a matter not only of blind superstition but of rational cost-calculation superimposed on nonrational faith. They are horrified by villagers using secular, instrumental rationality to profit from their traditions. Many angry interpreters of the case probably see their own faces, distorted by the 'strange customs' of village India, in those of Roop's in-laws.

It is perhaps the absence of that particular mix of the rational and nonrational which makes the middle classes relatively indifferent towards dowry deaths in urban India. Dowry deaths—in which a young wife is torched, usually by her in-laws because she has brought them less dowry than they expected—are the result of rational cost-calculation and profiteering through and through. Though the greed for dowry does hang on the peg of what is allegedly a pan-Indian custom—I say allegedly because it

---

a drove of excited social analysts as the final proof of the moral and cultural decadence of the Muslims—in fact, as another of the stigmata of Islam itself. Notorious Muslim-baiters shed copious tears over the plight of Muslim women in much the same way that some well-furnished drawing rooms in urban India later reverberated with lamentations about the plight of rural Rajasthani women after the Deorala event.

is known that bride-price was more widespread in India than dowry until the earlier decades of this century—no scope for mystery is left by the practice. That is why the hundreds of dowry deaths (the average for New Delhi in the mid-1980s was roughly 150 deaths per year) cannot match the impact of one sati. As a letter to the editor of *The Times of India* pointed out soon after the Deorala event:

> On November 1, *The Times of India* reported the death of five women by burning. All the incidents were from Delhi. What is shocking is that it is almost a daily feature now, with only the numbers varying.
>
> The sati incident at Deorala pales into insignificance before this phenomenon.... These are not mishaps; these are planned deaths.... When will women's welfare organisations and the Central and State governments wake up?[28]

The letter draws attention to the asymmetry which is not obvious to many urban westernized Indians but was all too obvious to some of the Deorala women, who sarcastically pointed out to visiting women journalists that burning to death in a West Delhi lower-middle-class concrete slum was no less painful than burning to death in a Rajasthani village; that they, the Deorala women, were not accustomed to burning their daughters-in-law to death the way urban women did.[29]

In sociological terms, dowry deaths are clear cases of murder, for no one justifies them, not even the neighbours. Sati is different. It arouses anxieties which moderns—Indians as well as non-Indians—are unable to cope with. The very idea of self-immolation is deeply disturbing in a world where self-interest is the ultimate currency of public life. That is why, after saying that sati is nothing but unalloyed murder, moderns worry not about the nearly three thousand people getting murdered every year in Bihar's countryside in land-related disputes but about the

---

[28] Satish Gogia, Letter to the Editor, *The Times of India*, 5 November 1987. Also see Pradeep S. Mehta, Letter to the Editor, *The Times of India*, 5 December 1988.

[29] Perhaps I should also add here that if Roop's death was a case of murder through burning, there is no dearth of modern Indians who either kept silent or colluded with the burning of thousands of Sikhs on the streets of Delhi in 1984. Some national dailies, which published the most strident condemnations of the Deorala sati, were then busy censoring news of the anti-Sikh pogrom lest the role of the Indian state and the ruling Congress Party in it became apparent.

few cases of sati in Rajasthan. Moderns can understand the use of sati for profit, but they nervously remember the 300,000 people who went to Deorala on pilgrimage after Roop's death, with no interest in profit at all. Their faith was real and not feigned; that faith tells something to modern Indians they do not like to hear.

For modern societies do not lack their own rituals of self-imposed or forced self-immolation. Why is it not troubling to see teenaged soldiers goose-stepping to their death in war? Or seeing one's own country getting increasingly militarized? Instead of opium, soldiers are given alcohol; instead of fears of the widow going back on her decision to commit sati, in their case there is fear of desertion. Modern Indians have even argued that any mention of conjugal loyalty in the context of sati is sexist, because men do not immolate themselves at the death of their wives. But just because self-immolation in war is largely a male preserve, does that mean that women are incapable of loyalty to the nation? As in sati, so in war, there is the charged atmosphere and ritual fervour that makes all self-immolation seem justified; there are even the priests, secular and non-secular, to ease one's journey to the other world. Above all, there is profit to be made from the self-immolations of wars; in fact the magnitude of the profits made through modern warfare could put to shame both Roop's in-laws and their political supporters. Is the comic anti-hero in *Monsieur Verdoux* correct when he insists that if one kills a few one is a murderer, but if one kills a million, one is a hero, for number sanctifies? Can it be that war is acceptable because it does not prove the superstitions of the defeated cultures of Asia and Africa but is a respectable instrument of diplomacy and a profession on which the modern world is built?[30]

---

[30] In the entire debate on sati during 1987–8 in the English press, probably only Bill Aitken in his 'Abomination (Private) Limited', *The Statesman*, 30 March 1988, had the honesty to confront the issue of priorities, which was first raised by Ananda Coomaraswamy in the 1930s. Aitken, being a mere intellectual and not an academic, raised the issue in response to the shallow, crypto-racist, bogus anthropology of George L. Hart in 'Sati Just a Form of Human Sacrifice', *The Statesman*, 29 March 1988. There have been more human sacrifices in this century, Aitken says in response to Hart, than in the 2000 years leading up to it.

Aitken also recognized that Hart's article was a crude attempt to placate India's

What is the sickness of soul that numbs social sensitivities thus? Is it the same that blinded the apologists of sati to Roop Kanwar being an eighteen-year-old girl, traumatized by her husband's death and unable to take responsible decisions? Is it the same that prevented 'her people' from helping her out of her depression and made them push her into self-immolation even before her parents could meet her?

---

westernized élite, provoked by his protégé Patrick D. Harrigan's two articles: 'Tyranny of the Elect?' (*The Statesman*, 5 November 1987) and 'Is Tradition Ridiculed by Western Values?' (*The Statesman*, 5 March 1988). Both dissented from the views popular among India's modern élites, though the dissent was steeped in innocence about the political sociology of traditions in contemporary India.

The Other Within: The Strange Case of Radhabinod Pal's Judgment of Culpability

This essay has two beginnings, one mythical and one personal. Let me start with the mythical.

Towards the end of the Mahabharata, there is a well-known story about one of the last political acts of Kṛṣṇa. Some modern commentators—mainly historically minded, westernized, reformed Hindus, deeply embarrassed by the paganism that informs their faith—consider the story *prakṣipta*, a later interpolation into the original epic. Even if it is so, for centuries millions of ordinary Indians have lived and died with the story.

The story goes that after the defeat of the ungodly in the climactic battle of Kurukṣetra, the evil king Duryodhana hides in a lake. The Pāṇdavas find him there, and Bhīma, the Pāṇdava who has vowed to kill him for his past misdeeds, engages Duryodhana in a duel with maces. But the battle refuses to go Bhīma's way. It is then that Lord Kṛṣṇa, standing among the onlookers, directs Bhīma by a gesture to strike his evil cousin on the thigh. Accordingly, against the canons of Kṣatriya duel, Bhīma fells Duryodhana. As Duryodhana lies dying, he delivers a majestic admonition to Kṛṣṇa for participating in dishonourable conduct in war. Even though a god, Kṛṣṇa is embarrassed. And when Duryodhana dies, the heavens shower flower petals on him for dying as a true Kṣatriya and as the victim of an unjust duel.

In the Indian epics, as in most pagan worldviews, no one is all perfect, not even the gods. Nor is anyone entirely evil either; everyone is both flawed and has redeeming features. If there is a touch of the amoral politician in Kṛṣṇa, there is also a touch of the courageous but misguided warrior in Duryodhana. One must make one's moral choices in an imperfect world in which heroes and villains partly incorporate each other. The hero is only primarily a hero; the villain only primarily a villain. In such a world the rules of combat have priority over the demands of vengeance, for only such rules can have moral constancy in a worldview that shuns binary oppositions. We shall return to this story towards the end of the essay.

Now the personal, which is much less important and by way of a minor autobiographical footnote. I used occasionally to see Radhabinod Pal (1886–1967), whose name figures in the title, in my childhood and teens. Pal is now almost entirely forgotten, even in his own country, but he was an important figure forty years ago. He was a retired judge of the Calcutta High Court, a former Vice Chancellor of Calcutta University, and member of a number of important judicial commissions, national as well as international. Though some twenty years older than my father, Pal was friendly with our family and occasionally he would chair public meetings or grace small discussion groups at the invitation of my father. He also visited our home once or twice. He lived a retired life, but was active in the public sphere.

As I remember him, Pal was a tall, dark, slim man, polite and soft-spoken. Though his photographs usually show him in western dress, I always saw him dressed in a dhoti. In winter he sometimes put on a shawl and wore, as many Bengalis of his generation did, shoes and socks along with his Bengali dress, a combination that was already becoming rare. He looked very grandfatherly then.

Pal lived the last twenty years of his life in independent India. His services were occasionally used by the young nation-state. But he was already being overshadowed by younger and more flamboyant legal luminaries. In any case, those were tumultuous years in the life of Bengal and the city of Calcutta. Apart from the consequences of Partition, there were religious massacres, the first elections of independent India, the initiation of five-year plans, and many such exciting events. Pal was bound to be forgotten.

Even as a child, however, I knew of Pal's one brush with destiny. We knew that whatever people might say of him while introducing him at public meetings, his main claim to fame was his membership of the International Military Tribunal for the Far East. The Tribunal conducted the war crimes trial at Tokyo from 1946 to 1948 and was the eastern and less audible counterpart of the Nuremberg trials in post-war Germany. Most Calcuttans I knew admired Pal for his 'unconventional' views and dissenting judgment at Tokyo. But that was not a large capital with which to enter the public memory.

Years afterwards, I found out that even during his lifetime few people outside India and Japan had taken him seriously—not even at the time of his brush with history in 1949, when after a long, highly publicized trial at Tokyo,[1] Radhabinod Pal delivered his judgment on the culpability of the Japanese leaders accused of war crimes:

> For the reasons given in the foregoing pages, I would hold that each and every one of the accused must be found not guilty of each and every one of the charges in the indictment and should be acquitted of all those charges.... As a judicial tribunal we cannot behave in any manner which may justify the feeling that the setting up of the tribunal was only for the attainment of an objective which was essentially political, though cloaked by a juridical appearance.
>
> The name of Justice should not be allowed to be invoked only for the prolongation of the pursuit of vindictive retaliation.[2]

Few took the judgment seriously, partly because it acquitted all the accused on all counts. Newspaper-reading Indians, however, were pleased with Pal. Many were happy simply because an Indian had been in the company of the famous at a historic moment; they were prouder of Pal's participation in an international tribunal than of the legal-philosophical content of his judgment. Other Indians, when they applauded the judgment, did so because, as they saw it, a worthy son of India had

---

[1] The trial began on 3 May 1946 and lasted two and a half years. There were 818 court sessions spread over 417 days. It went through the testimony of 419 witnesses and examined 779 affidavits.

[2] Radhabinod Pal, *Crimes in International Relations* (Calcutta: University of Calcutta, 1955), pp. 193–4. For the full text of the judgment, running to some 700-odd pages, see Radhabinod Pal, *International Military Tribunal for the Far East* (Calcutta: Sanyal, 1953).

repaid the Japanese warlords for their support of the Indian freedom movement, especially the Indian National Army of Subhas Chandra Bose, which had fought alongside the Japanese army during World War II. Only a small minority took a serious interest in the nature of the judgment, and that was mainly because it was delivered by an Indian and published from Calcutta.

In Japan the judgment was taken more seriously. It was viewed by the nationalists as a vindication of the wartime behaviour of the Japanese army and the militarism of the Japanese élite.[3] Some Japanese saw it as the first step towards restoration of the dignity of the Japanese war dead. The wartime prime minister, Hideki Tojo, hanged as a war criminal after the Tokyo trial, even left a *haiku*, a brief poem, written in Pal's honour before going to the gallows. On the other hand, the Pal–Shimonaka Memorial Hall at Hakone, near Tokyo—which serves as a temple and memorial to both Pal and the famous Japanese publisher Yasaburo Shimonaka—is witness to the links that Japanese pacifism established with Pal's judgment. The temple, according to an inscription on it, seeks to advance the influence of the 'teachings of that great sage of the twentieth century, Mahatma Gandhi'.

Outside India and Japan the judgment was mostly viewed as an expression of woolly Gandhian sentiments. John Appleman, for instance, writing five years after the event, says of Pal's judgment: it 'seems to be a translation of Ghandi's [sic] theory of passive resistance or of no resistance into judicial terminology.'[4]

---

[3] Ienaga Saburo, 'The Historical Significance of the Tokyo Trial', C. Hosoya, N. Ando, Y. Onuma, and R. Minear (eds.), *The Tokyo War Crimes Trial: An International Symposium* (Tokyo: Kodansha, 1986), pp. 165–70; see esp. p. 169: 'If I seem obsessed with the [sic] Pal's opinion, it is because . . . it is inextricably linked to the movement to assert the injustice of the Tokyo trial and to affirm the "Greater East Asia War", and that it is being used ultimately in the service of a wholesale negation of Japan's postwar pacifism and democracy.'

Also see the comment of Onuma Yasuaki (ibid., pp. 200–1): '. . . even Judge Pal's minority opinion, like Professor Minear's *Victor's Justice*, has been made use of in Japan, most unfortunately, as an argument for "Japan's innocence", as an argument affirming wholesale Japan's actions in the past.'

[4] John Appleman, *Military Tribunals and International Crimes* (Indianapolis: Bobbes-Merrill, 1954), pp. 263–4. Quoted in Richard Minear, *Victor's Justice: The Tokyo War Crimes Trial* (Princeton University Press, 1973), p. 32.

In no case was there any serious comment on the legal and moral issues raised by Pal's verdict. His judgment was included in the official records but these were never published in full. In Tokyo, at the end of the trial, only the majority judgment was read out in the open court, and that occupied public awareness in the western world. As Richard Minear points out, only a very diligent reader would find it mentioned, on p. 1212, that the judgment was not a unanimous one.[5]

In any case, the two judges from colonized Asia on the Tribunal—Pal and Delfin Jaranilla from the Philippines—had been an afterthought, included in the Tribunal a few months after it had started functioning for fear the Tokyo trials would look like a trial of Japan by mainly white powers who had no business to be in Asia in the first place.

In those days the memories of a fierce and brutalizing war—particularly of the Japanese army's record in the Far East and South East Asia–were still fresh. By the end of World War II, a large number of writings had been spawned that were both prosecutory and judgmental, and which predictably apportioned much, if not all, the blame for the Pacific war to Japan and her wartime leaders. In that charged intellectual atmosphere, Pal's judgment could only be seen as an aberration.

First, the judgment presumed that the accused were prisoners of war who enjoyed protection under international law against arbitrary acts of revenge. 'Prisoners can be tried', Pal repeatedly said, 'only for breach of recognized laws of war'; the victors could not establish new crimes and new definitions and punish prisoners according to them.[6] As it happened the Australian President of the Tribunal, William Webb, expressed some indirect sympathy with Pal's position without agreeing with it. So did another judge of the Tribunal, B. V. A. Röling, in the 1960s though, according to one observer, he was Pal's 'most venomous opponent' at the time of the trial.[7] The following comment makes Pal's argument clear.

---

[5] Minear, *Victor's Justice.*

[6] Pal, *Crimes in International Relations*, pp. 53, 64, 68, 215.

[7] Personal communication and papers provided by M. J. Knottenbelt (especially, Memo 2 on the IMTFE, Judgment; Signature Pages, Rotterdam, 26 April 1979, mimeo). These papers, various other communications from Knottenbelt

> Mr Justice Jackson of the United States in his report as Chief of Council for the United States in prosecuting the principal war criminals of the European Axis observed: 'We could execute or otherwise punish them without a hearing. But indiscriminate execution or punishments without definite findings of guilt, fairly arrived at, would violate pledges repeatedly given, and would not sit easily on the American conscience or be remembered by our children with pride.'
>
> It is indeed surprising that no less a person than Mr Justice Jackson, in his considered report to no less an authority than the President of the United States, could insert these lines in the Twentieth Century. On what authority, one feels inclined to ask, could a victor execute enemy prisoners without a hearing?... I do not think that during recent centuries any victor has enjoyed any such right as is declared by Mr Justice Jackson in his 'report'.[8]

Pal's final verdict on this part of the story was:

> The so-called trial held according to the definition of crime now given by the victors obliterates the centuries of civilization which stretch between us and the summary slaying of the defeated in a war.[9]

Second, there are scattered hints in Pal's judgment that he knew or thought he knew what his fellow judges' verdict was going to be.[10] His judgment reads, to a lay person, not merely as

---

and a copy of his 'monograph', *The Röling Gang*, were some of the early sources of my curiosity in the less-than-honourable politics of the Tokyo trial.

[8] Ibid., p. 225.

[9] Ibid., p. 187.

[10] Daisaku Ikeda, *The Human Revolution* (New York and Tokyo: Weatherhill, 1974), vol. 2, p. 101. See also the comments of Tanaka Masaki on Pal's belief that the trial was imposed on Japan by the judges and that more severe punishments were given to Japanese war criminals than to the Nazis (p. 63 below).

That the questions Pal raised were not legally as toothless as is made out is shown by the modalities of handling the dissenting judgment. First, a sixty-three-word passage, signed by ten of the judges, was inserted into the judgment denying the validity of Pal's position; then, to avoid the embarrassment of signing the denial, this signed interpolation was deleted from the judgment and an updated page was again signed by the judges endorsing the judgment 'as read in the open court'. The qualification 'as read in the open court' was subsequently omitted from the ratification of the judgment by the United Nations (Knottenbelt, Memo 2, p. 4).

a verdict on the accused but also on the 'impartial' judges ostensibly speaking on behalf of the innocent victims of aggression. Pal felt he was speaking for the other, judicial-moral self of his fellow judges in his verdict. He himself had been pressurized, through Rama Rao, the Indian ambassador to Japan at the time, not to damage the international relations of his newly independent country by breaking ranks in his judgment, and he suspected that other judges might not have been in a position to resist such pressures. In addition there might have been, for other judges, the fear of public opinion at home; Justice Röling's attitude towards the accused, for instance, softened noticeably with the passage of time. In the 1960s, his dissent from the majority judgment could no longer be called cautious, though he was still possibly engaged, as one commentator charges, in whitewashing his past. To a lesser extent, a similar change took place in Justice Webb.

There is also in Pal's judgment a touch of surprise that his brother judges knew no better. (Obviously Pal had not read Roger Money-Kyrle's psychoanalytic interpretation of war as a regression to the infant's earliest psychic situation—to the paranoid-schizoid position—in order to locate the unacceptable parts of the self, the bad objects, outside.[11]) Yet there is in Pal's dissenting judgment an implicit invitation, not so much to the accused to ponder on their guilt as to the plaintiffs, and perhaps also the judges, to discover the accused in them. Pal was speaking of the symbiosis of adversaries; he could have said, in the voice of someone who was to write in another context:

> The enemy, who we are certain is a despicable 'other', is in fact endowed and littered with parts cast out from the self. The 'enemy' is ... *an inner representation become flesh.* The 'boundary' is thus a sacred illusion and delusion.... By directing all of our respective acuity *outward*, we can avoid the painful look inward.[12]

Speaking crudely, Pal's judgment was contextualized by the nature of the crimes of the accused, by the tribunal that was set

---

[11] Roger Money-Kyrle, *Psychoanalysis and Politics: A Contribution to the Psychology of Politics and Morals*, 2nd ed. (Westport, Conn.: Greenwood, 1973).

[12] Howard Stein (ed.), *Developmental Time, Cultural Space: Studies in Psychogeography* (Norman: University of Oklahama, 1987), p. 193.

up to try them, by the accused, and by the international law brought to bear upon the cases.

The Tokyo trial was conducted on the basis of a charter drawn up by the American chief prosecutor, Joseph Keenan. The fifty-five crimes for which the Japanese were tried could be classified under three headings: conspiracy to commit aggression, aggression, and conventional war crimes. Of these, conspiracy to commit aggression did not exist in international law as a crime; it was 'created' *ex post facto* by the Tribunal. The case for the defence was further damaged by the Tribunal's refusal to admit any evidence that showed such conspiracy—indicated by, say, military build-up—to be a realistic response to similar steps taken by the victorious power. As for aggression, the principal charge in the Tokyo trial, till 1944 France, Great Britain and the United States had agreed that aggression was not a crime in international law. Officially, the reason was that war in self-defence could not be prohibited and each state retained, in the language of the Pact of Paris (28 August 1928), 'the prerogative of judging for itself what action the right of self-defence covered and when it came into play'. The unofficial reasons included, one suspects, the eagerness of some of the western powers to protect the fruits of aggression that were being gathered in the colonies in the southern hemisphere.

Legally, according to Pal, the Japanese could be tried only for conventional war crimes. To do otherwise might itself violate international law.

> The Instrument of Surrender which provides that the Declaration of Potsdam will be given effect imposes the condition that conventional War Crimes, as recognized by international law at the date of the Declaration (26th July 1945) would be the only crime prosecuted....[13]
>
> Under international law, as it now stands, a victor nation or a union of victor nations would have the authority to establish a tribunal for the trial of war criminals, but no authority to legislate or promulgate a new law of war crimes.[14]

Worse,

---

[13] Pal, *Crimes in International Relations*, pp. 170–1.

[14] Ibid., p. 188.

> As the law now stands, it will be 'war crime' *stricto sensu* on the part of the victor nations if they would 'execute' these prisoners otherwise than under a due process of international law, though, of course, there may not be anyone to bring them to book for that crime at present.[15]

The prosecution's case had been further weakened, Pal felt, by the inability of the Allied powers to bring to book criminals on their own side. He was convinced that the fire-bombing of Japanese cities—over 100,000 civilians had died in the very first attack on Tokyo—and atomic bombing of Hiroshima and Nagasaki should have been brought within the purview of the Tokyo Tribunal as instances of subversion of the Geneva Convention. He quotes from a letter Kaiser Wilhelm II of Germany wrote to the Austrian Kaiser Franz Joseph:

> My soul is torn, but everything must be put to fire and sword; men, women and children and old men must be slaughtered and not a tree or house be left standing. With these methods of terrorism, which are alone capable of affecting a people as degenerate as the French, the war will be over in two months, whereas if I admit considerations of humanity it will be prolonged for years. In spite of my repugnance I have therefore been obliged to choose the former system.[16]

Pal goes on to add:

> In the Pacific war under our consideration if there was anything approaching what is indicated in the above letter of the German emperor, it is the decision coming from the allied powers to use the ATOM BOMB[17]

By not including such considered decisions, taken at the highest levels of a government, into consideration at the Tokyo trial, its judicial status was impaired, Pal felt. Hence his wry comment towards the end of his judgment that, after eliminating the Nazis and imprisoning the Japanese conspirators against peace, people still had to be warned (as part of the Cold War rhetoric) that 'never before in history has the world situation

---

[15] Ibid., p. 189.

[16] Pal, *International Military Tribunal*, p. 620.

[17] Ibid.

been more threatening' to the 'ideals and interests' of those holding the Tokyo trial.[18]

This part of Pal's judgment has been the least palatable. Even those who do not share Appleman's contempt for Pal resent the line the latter draws between the random atrocities of local commanders and state-organized atrocities. Yet those who explicitly reject Pal's position, as Philip R. Piccigallo does, cannot but admit that the Japanese atrocities were 'perhaps not the result of an organized governmental plan' and have to grant that the ultimate instance of a state-organized, centrally controlled atrocity on civilians in the eastern theatre of war was the atomic bombing of Hiroshima and Nagasaki.[19] (Neither Pal nor Piccigallo knew the full magnitude of the horror. Hiroshima was chosen for bombing because it was *not* a military target and had therefore escaped Allied bombing earlier in the war. The city allowed the destructive capacity of the new weapon to be accurately measured. Hiroshima was chosen by hawkish scientists, despite some half-hearted protests by army officers, as a perfect experimental subject for nuclear weapons research.[20])

As for the nature of the accused in the Tokyo trial, there were twenty-five defendants, though at first there were charges against twenty-eight. Seven of the twenty-five were sentenced to death, sixteen to life imprisonment, and two to shorter terms. From the beginning, the attitude towards the Japanese differed significantly from that towards the German war criminals. There

---

[18] Ibid., p. 700.

[19] Philip R. Piccigallo, *The Japanese on Trial: Allied War Crimes Operation in the East 1945–1951* (Austin and London: University of Texas, 1979), p. 209.

[20] See for this *Half Life: A Parable for the Nuclear Age* (documentary film), dir. Dennis O'Rourke. Also, Ashis Nandy, 'The Bomb', *The Illustrated Weekly of India*, 8 August 1985. Forty years later Justice Röling was to say: 'Admiral Leahy, who was chairman of the Joint Chiefs of Staff under Roosevelt, was opposed to dropping the atomic bombs. He was no mere admiral in the navy, no mere fleet admiral, but the chairman of the Joint Chiefs, and he left exact memoranda. In fact, they are cited by the English historian Liddel Hart in his history of World War II—that kind of record.'

B.V.A. Röling, 'The Tokyo Trial and the Quest for Peace', in C. Hosoya, N. Ando, Y. Onuma, and R. Minear (eds.), *The Tokyo War Crimes Trial: An International Symposium* (Tokyo: Kodansha, 1986), pp. 125–45; see pp. 138–9. See also Gar Alperovitz, 'Did the U.S. Need to Drop the Bomb on Japan? Evidently Not', *International Herald Tribune*, 4 August 1989.

was a casualness about legal niceties that was endorsed by the same racial and cultural differences that had made the Pacific war a particularly bitter memory. For instance, the American prosecutor said, when asked why the Russian defiance of its non-aggression treaty with Japan was not being considered, 'The recipe for rabbit stew is first to catch the rabbit'.[21] Given such an attitude, the result of the trial was a foregone conclusion. By the time the various war crimes trials in Germany and Japan had ended, 927 Japanese were executed. The comparable figure for Germans was less than 100, if one ignores the Dachau trials.[22]

As for the judicial process, the Tribunal was established on 19 January 1946, and it consisted of eleven judges. The trial lasted from 3 May 1946 to 4 November 1948 and its official languages were English and Japanese. As it happened, the Soviet judge understood neither language.[23] That did not burden his conscience overmuch. Nor did it cramp his judicial style. He continued to function as a judge self-confidently. The first American judge appointed to the Tribunal soon resigned—in disgust, according to Minear.[24] Another person was quickly appointed in his place. Justice William O. Douglas, in his usual forthright manner, later gave short shrift to the pretence of being a supplier of impartial western justice to savage Orientals. The Tokyo trial, he claimed, acted as an instrument of the military and of the executive branches of government. 'It took its law from its creator and did not act as a free and independent tribunal to adjudge the rights of petitioners under international law.'[25]

---

[21] Richard Minear, 'War Crimes Trial', *Kodansha Encyclopedia of Japan* (Tokyo: Kodansha, 1983), pp. 223–5; see p. 223.

[22] Ibid., p. 225. For a fascinating set of essays that seek to contextualize the moral questions involved in war crimes, including the racial and colonial issues raised by the Tokyo trial, see Richard A. Falk, Gabriel Kolko, and Robert J. Lifton (eds.), *Crimes of War: A Legal, Political-Documentary, and Psychological Enquiry into the Responsibility of Leaders, Citizens, and Societies for Criminal Acts in War* (New York: Random House, 1971).

[23] Ibid., p. 223.

[24] Ibid., p. 225.

[25] William O. Douglas, quoted in Minear, 'War Crimes Trial', p. 225. Cf. Pal's judgment: '. . . this right which . . . a state might have over its prisoners of war is not a right derivative of its sovereignty but is a right *conferred on it* as a member of the international society *by the* international law' (Pal, *International Military Tribunal*, p. 26). Italics in the original.

All this was not unknown even to Justice Jackson, the enthusiastic American legal scholar and reportedly the main author of the charter for the Tribunal. During an argument he once said, with a touch of naïvété, 'One of the reasons this was a military tribunal, instead of an ordinary court of law, was in order to avoid precedent-creating effect of what is done here on our own law.'[26]

As things stood, the Tribunal was not constituted to bring cheer to the Japanese, least of all to the defence lawyers. Eight judges represented countries which were direct victims of Japanese militarism, and one was a victim of the infamous Bataan march in the Philippines. Years later Minear, himself a professor of international law, summed up his assessment of the judges in the Tokyo War Crimes Trial in the following words:

> All eleven justices shared the disability of being citizens of the victor nations. Five justices were vulnerable to a more specific challenge: that they had prior involvement in the issues to come before the tribunal; that they lacked the necessary languages; that they were not judges. All five supported the majority judgment, if not all of the sentences.... what of positive qualifications? How many of the men appointed to this international military tribunal had any background in international law? The answer is one: Justice Pal.[27]

Minear's view had the support of persons such as Takayanagi Kenzo and Viscount Hankey who insisted that Pal was indeed the only one who knew international law. Apart from this, Pal appeared to have one other advantage. He came from a country which had suffered the least from the Japanese army. In absolute terms, the Indian involvement in World War II was deep; the number of Indian combatants killed in the fighting exceeded that of most countries more directly involved in the war: India lost 24,338 combatants compared to Australia's 23,365, New Zealand's 10,033, and the Netherlands' 6235. The peak strength of the Indian army fighting in the war was 2,150,000, as

[26] Justice Jackson quoted in Pal, *Crimes in International Relations*, p. 407.

[27] Minear, *Victor's Justice*, pp. 85–6. Minear does not mention that subsequently there were to be accusations from the Japanese side and hints in one of the dissenting judgments that seven of the judges constituted what amounted to a clique to corner the possible dissenters—Webb, Röling, Bernard, and Pal.

opposed to 650,000 in Belgium and 500,000 in Yugoslavia. But then, India was a country of four hundred and forty million at the time. In proportional terms Indian war casualties were low and had less impact on the Indian public consciousness than those in other countries. Also, unlike the other judges, Pal did not have to struggle with his personal bitterness against Japanese occupation or the memories of national humiliation at the hands of imperial Japan.

Indeed, Pal was a nationalist of sorts, and that went in favour of the Japanese. As we have already mentioned, there was a Japanese connection with some strands of anti-imperialism in India. This connection was strongest in Pal's home state, Bengal. Nowhere in the southern hemisphere was the naval victory of Japan over Czarist Russia at Tsushima Straits in 1905 as widely celebrated as in colonial Bengal. Literate Bengalis called it the first Asian victory over a European imperial power. Also, some years before World War II, Rashbehari Bose (1880/6–1945), a Bengali freedom fighter, had escaped to Japan from India and founded the Indian National Army there. Having married a Japanese woman, he settled in the country (neither of them a mean achievement in those times). The Army was later led by Subhas Chandra Bose, a former president of the Indian National Congress who had broken ideologically with Gandhi. Bose had escaped dramatically from India in 1941 to Germany and then to Japan. The army he led was composed largely of Indian prisoners of war, captured by the Japanese while fighting the British Indian Army in South East Asia, which naturally remained in close touch with the Japanese. In 1946, at about the time Pal was appointed to the International Tribunal, some officers of the Indian National Army were tried in India, giving rise to widespread public protests and demonstrations. In a dramatic gesture, Jawaharlal Nehru even donned his barrister's gown after nearly three decades to defend three of these officers in the trial held at the Red Fort in Delhi.

There was also, for Pal, the larger Afro-Asian context of Indian nationalism. He belonged to a generation for which Asian solidarity had not become an empty slogan. His message at the dedication of the Pal–Shimonaka Memorial Hall, engraved there in Bengali and English, says: 'For the peace of those departed souls who took upon themselves the solemn vow (*mantradīkṣita*) at the salvation ceremony (*muktiyajña*) of oppressed Asia.' The inscription includes a quotation from a classical Sanskrit text: *Tvayā Hṛṣīkeśa hṛdisthitena yathā niyukto'smi tathā karomi* (O Lord, Thou being in my heart, I do as appointed by thee).

All this served as a backdrop to Pal's judicial verdict. It is pointless to deny that there might have been latent private politics in his judgment too. But then the break between the morality of politics and the politics of morality can never be total. To an Indian, Appleman's dismissive comment, however misconceived, has to serve as a clue to the politics of Pal's juridical morality.

II

Pal was born in 1886, in the high noon of both Victorian England and the British empire, which, we are told by Jan Morris, immortalized the nineteenth century. He came of a poor family from Shalimpur, a small and sleepy village in Nadia (now in Bangladesh). The Pals were Kumbhakaras, traditionally low-caste potters. Radhabinod was the only son of his parents. He had two sisters.

The Pals were never well off and the economic worries of the family were compounded when Radhabinod's father renounced the world and deserted the family when Radhabinod was three years old.[28] His mother began to work at a relation's home, virtually as a housemaid, to support the family. However, while Pal never quite forgot the early experience of poverty, financial anxieties did not shape his personality in any significant way. What left a more lasting mark on him was the awareness that his mother had reared him and his sisters single-handed, bearing enormous physical strain and making much personal sacrifice. She became for him the final authority and source of moral legitimacy. She

---

[28] Regrettably, there is no usable biography of Pal. I have depended on a brief biographical note, prepared in the form of a pamphlet by a member of his family after Pal's death, on the occasion of his obsequies or *shrāddha*, probably in 1967—*Samkṣipta Jīvanī* (Calcutta: Express Printers, n. d.). I have also been helped by my discussions with some members of the Pal family over the last few years.

on her part depended heavily on her children to give meaning to her life, splintered by her husband's conspicuous moralism and other-worldliness. Perhaps in reaction her own morality and ambitions remained severely this-worldly. Her ambition and confidence in her only son were unbounded, as if she was determined to prove correct Sigmund Freud's belief that such ambition and confidence contributed to the success and creativity of sons.

That early intense relationship with his mother defined much of his emotional and intellectual life, Pal believed. All through life, he retained an acute sensitivity to the interrelationships of morality, vocation, and tradition. The representation of colonized India as a victimized, widowed mother—he used the expression *ciraduḥkhinī* or ever-suffering, recurrent in the politics and arts of Bengal by the middle of the nineteenth century—became an important image in his cognitive repertoire.

Radhabinod never knew a well-defined, continuous, paternal authority, though technically he continued to live in a joint family with a number of adult males. He grew up, it seems, with a diffused concept of paternal authority, composed of the distant, world-renouncing and quasi-mythical image of his father on the one hand, and the protective but overly practical, unimaginative, fleeting authority of his uncles. The two were bridged by the authoritative, stable, nurturing presence of his mother, the fulcrum of his world. (One by-product of this dynamic of an absent father and an ever-present mother might have been Pal's vegetarianism. Though he came from a low-caste, Bengali meat-eating family, he became vegetarian in later life—perhaps in identification with his mother, widowed for all practical purposes, perhaps in homage to the truant asceticism of his father.)

As if to compensate for his absent father, during Pal's early life there was a series of encounters with a variety of male authorities apart from his uncles. To start with, his grandfather was a source of care and practical help. He was the founder of the village school where Radhabinod's education began. When he finished his studies at this school, doing well enough in the lower primary examination to win a modest scholarship of two rupees per month, he moved to an aunt's home in another village for further study. However, as he had to help in the grocery store of an uncle in another village, he was late for school every day. The uncles themselves after a while began to pressurize Radhabinod to give up his studies and take a job in the grocery shop for a salary of four rupees per month. At this point his mother, according to one of Pal's daughters, advised him to run away from home and continue his education.

As it happened Radhabinod did not have to take such a drastic step. On his mother's advice, he wrote to a number of schools asking for an opportunity to study further. The kind-hearted teacher of a school at Kumdi responded. Accepting the offer meant losing the protection of a doting mother and starting a new life in a strange place. But the son, as determined as the mother, went.

Radhabinod successfully passed his minor examinations at Kumdi, and joined a high school at Kusthia, a small town nearby, where he was given free accommodation by a kindly landlord. From Kusthia Pal went to Dubalhati, where the local raja's family took the financial responsibility for his studies. Soon the family grew fond of Pal and even began to feed him as part of their daily ritual of feeding the poor.

Pal sat for his entrance examination from the Dubalhati Raja Haranath High School in 1903 and went to college at Rajshahi on a scholarship. Once again a series of father figures came forward to take care of him, first at Rajshahi and then at Calcutta, when he joined the mathematics (honours) course at Presidency College. Thanks to them, he was able to send most of the money he got through scholarships to his mother in the village. Pal took a first class bachelor's degree in 1907. The following year he took his master's in mathematics from Calcutta University, once again doing well.

Radhabinod married Nalinibala when he was in Presidency College. The Pals were to have nine children, four of them daughters. The children remember Nalinibala as a highly intelligent, strong, supportive person who in many ways replicated for Radhabinod his mother's formidable presence. Though she married very young, she played a crucial part in all the hard decisions her husband had to take in his professional life. She died in 1949, when her husband was at the zenith of his fame.

Having lived in poverty for so long, Pal joined the Accountant-General's office at Allahabad as a small-time functionary immediately after passing his examinations. It was while working at

Allahabad that he took his first degree in law. Soon afterwards he found a job at Anandamohan College, Mymensingh, as a mathematics teacher, this time at a respectable salary of 150 rupees a month. This gave him a chance to pay off some of the debts he had incurred. Pal also began to repay, in the traditional manner, some of his other obligations. Many poor students ate daily at his place; Nalinibala cooked for them. He also started financing the education of a large number of them, which he continued to do all his life.

Pal duly got his master's degree in law in 1920, performing brilliantly as usual. In 1923 he began teaching law at Calcutta University and did so continuously for the next thirteen years. Once again, when he was showing signs of settling down into a comfortable job, his mother pushed him towards a more risky but ambitious legal career. It was her hope that her son would one day become an eminent judge. Though virtually illiterate herself, she said to him occasionally, 'Our needs are few. Can you not become someone like Sir Gurudas?' (Sir Gurudas Bannerji was a distinguished jurist and judge of the Calcutta High Court). She was to see her son fulfil most of her dreams: she died when Pal was a judge at the Calcutta High Court.

In 1924 Pal received his doctorate in law, a rare honour in those days. The degree came the hard way. There was much politics which, encouraged by Nalinibala, Pal defied. It is said that he was pressed to delay the submission of his dissertation so that a politically influential candidate could get the degree first. In addition, Pal found he did not have the money to print his dissertation, a university requirement in those days. The money had to be borrowed. At the prompting of the Vice-Chancellor, Ashutosh Mukhopadhyay, however, the university later purchased all the copies of the dissertation to lessen Pal's burden.

Pal's doctoral work was on traditional Hindu law, based on a study of the ancient texts, most of them in Sanskrit. One of his examiners was P. V. Kane, the distinguished scholar. Kane's appreciative comments on the dissertation heightened Pal's confidence; his knowledge of Sanskrit came from a traditional school (*tol*) where he had studied in his childhood under a Muslim pandit. Later on, when he was invited by Calcutta University to deliver the Tagore Lectures in law, he chose to speak on the same subject. The doctoral dissertation and the

Tagore Lectures grew into comprehensive volumes on Hindu law—one on its philosophy, the other on its history. In 1951, when he was invited again to deliver the postponed Tagore Lectures for 1938, he spoke on crimes in international relations.[29] By this time, he was well known in the field of international law. His full Tokyo judgment had not been published but its gist was widely known, and he used the lectures to review the judgment and its legal and philosophical justifications. These justifications, in fact, often come out more sharply in the lectures than in the judgment. This essay uses the two texts interchangeably.

The reader may have noticed that, left to himself, Pal's continuous intellectual concern was with cultural continuities rather than the disjunctions of social change. That concern with continuities had already survived his vigorous efforts during his formative years to enter and succeed in a westernized educational system which was Victorian in culture and social-evolutionary in idiom. It was also to survive the dominant language of Indian public life in which he was to become adept—the language of Nehruvian socialism and secular morality with its built-in suspicion of tradition and of those who lived with tradition.

Pal was appointed a judge of Calcutta High Court at the beginning of 1941. The rest, as the cliché goes, is history.

III

This brief sketch of Pal's life tells us little about his emotional life and self-definition. However, it reveals one astonishing fact about which his detractors were not entirely wrong and the likes of Hankey, Minear, and the Japanese defence lawyers at the Tokyo trials were not entirely correct. Pal had no formal training in international law. He only had a general though superb knowledge of law and a specialized knowledge of the traditional laws of India. Though later in life he impressed many scholars of international law and served as an expert on the subject to a number of world bodies, notably the United Nations, he pro-

[29] Pal, *Crimes in International Relations*.

bably acquired much of his command of international law only after he was appointed a judge at Tokyo. At least this is the impression of his own family which is dominated by a galaxy of well-known lawyers.

This is another way of saying that the emotional and moral background of Pal's judgment at Tokyo was provided not by the culture of modern international law, but by his long exposure to the traditional laws of India. In spite of his modern idiom, Pal never fully broke away from the moral tenor of his early work on the meaning of justice in different phases of the growth of law in India. But the times were not propitious; he was fighting on too many fronts to open up a new one. The closest he came to owning up to his true inspiration was with the following words from Hankey's book, *Politics, Trials and Errors* (1950), which he quoted twice:

> I shall once again quote what Lord Hankey says is a Pagan Pronouncement [note the capitals], but sets a standard that the Allies never even approached in the Second World War. The pronouncement is: 'For the purpose with which good men wage wars is not the destruction and annihilation of the wrongdoers, but the reformation and alteration of the wrongful acts. Nor is it their object to involve the innocent in the destruction of the guilty, but rather to see that those who are held to be guilty should share in the preservation and elevation of the guiltless.
>
> The standard set in this pronouncement has perhaps been too high for the modern nations since the First World War.[30]

Prior to World War I, Pal adds, it was the custom for belligerents to insert in their peace treaties an amnesty clause, giving immunity to all those who had committed wrongful acts on behalf of the belligerents in the course of the war. Even in the absence of a treaty, an amnesty was one of the legal consequences of the termination of war. With the Treaty of Versailles 'a striking exception to the customary law' was made in the clauses providing for the trial and punishment of the German Kaiser and some members of the German army.[31] While for the latter the measures prescribed were legal rather than political, for the Kaiser a new offence, not cognizable according to existing law,

---

[30] Ibid., p. 399.
[31] Ibid.

was created; he had to be tried for 'a supreme offence against international morality and the sanctity of treaties'.[32]

In other words, Hankey's comments helped Pal to relocate an aspect of Indian tradition in the western past. Pal did not have to contaminate his critique of the modern attitude to international law with precedents drawn from the strange laws of strange lands. His criticism could be based on the norms professed by the modern world and could pass as an internal rather than external critique of contemporary international law.

However, it is not impossible to bypass Pal's defensiveness to have a fuller idea of the influences that framed his concept of culpability. To do so, we shall have to look at his deeper concepts of justice, order, and law.

Pal's works on traditional Hindu law are identifiably products of colonial times. They are, like all such products, fractured by the conflicting claims of the indigenous and the exogenous. As a result, they too have their manifest and latent selves.

Outwardly, the works are mainly narrations of who said what and when, with a rather pallid attempt to cast the narrative in a social-evolutionist frame. They follow the style of the scholarship of nineteenth-century Europe as modernizing India adopted it. There is in them the same overdone dependence on western scholars writing on India to justify one's position, the same overdone attempt to provide a comparative picture and to explain India in western terms, and even the same protectiveness about Indian classicism and embarrassment about the little cultures of India. At places, Pal's narratives meander into India's past in a way that to the more self-confident native scholars of this generation looks hopelessly if charmingly dated.

Behind this conventional façade, however, one can catch glimpses of Pal's latent moral and analytic concerns in his occasional comments on the texts. I shall focus on a single issue—the connection between Pal's judgment and his concept of law. I shall briefly examine this connection in the limited context of Pal's interpenetrating concepts of the culpability of others and that of the self. It is my belief that it was this

[32] Ibid.

connection that made Pal not only a dissenter among the judges of the Tokyo Tribunal but also a dissenter among dissenters like Minear. As a dissenter among the judges, Pal functioned on the basis of his formal knowledge of international law and, in the established language of legal scholars, as a strict constructionist who went by the letter of the law. That was his manifest or public self. As a dissenter among dissenters, Pal functioned on the basis of a cultural concept of justice, camouflaged by his self-taught knowledge of international law. That cultural concept was the core of his secret self, a self he could never fully own up to.

The History of Hindu Law is based on a series of lectures Pal delivered in 1932.[33] It makes clear at the very beginning Pal's attitude to law. In the preface he says,

> The modern practical jurists understand by the word 'law' generally only legal provisions.... On the other hand, those who centre their attention, not on legal provisions, but on the social order, would be sure to observe and emphasize the common element in the midst of this variety. This social order is among civilized states and peoples similar in its main outlines.[34]

Pal goes on to defend this common or universal social order as something resting on fundamental social institutions such as marriage, family, possession, contract, and succession.[35] Because 'law' in his scheme of things stands for legal order, the study of law must take the inner ordering of the society as the historical starting point.[36] This ordering comes from *ṛta*—'which is at once the organized principle of the universe and the divine ordering of earthly life'.[37] According to the *ṛṣis* or seers, 'before there could be any society, before there could be any social ideality, rita [*ṛta*] evolved'.[38]

Pal marks out the contours of this inner order by drawing an evolutionary profile of Hindu law based on the works of seventeen *ṛṣis*, including Viśvāmitra, Vaśiṣṭha, Parāśara, Gautama,

---

[33] Radhabinod Pal, *The History of Hindu Law in the Vedic Age and Post-Vedic Times Down to the Institutes of Manu* (Calcutta University, 1959), p. 447.

[34] Ibid., p. iii.

[35] Ibid.

[36] Ibid., p. iv.

[37] Ibid.

[38] Ibid., p. vi.

and Manu. Fearing that he will be open to the charge that his concept of law is transcendental and cannot cope with the mundane, secular problems of the day, he hastens to add:

> This view of human society however did not ignore what we now call the material context of law,—law affiliated with human purpose and human benefit. According to these Vedic Rishis, even the primal cause of this universe, the creator, God, has a purposive existence. Indeed these Rishis, while viewing law as of divine origin, conceive of it as the product not of 'divine will' but of 'divine reason', divine essence. 'Divine will' might present itself as inscrutable, as arbitrary and beyond human understanding. 'Divine reason' is not so.[39]

Pal acknowledges the diverse positions Hindus have traditionally taken over the origin of law. For instance, unlike the Ṛg-Veda *ṛṣis*, the sages of the Upaniṣads conceive of law as less 'primal', originating after the crystallization of social diversity, and as purposive.

> Indeed the aim of creation, the end of all was to ensure security of the whole. When it was felt that the creation of 'wisdom', 'might', 'the people', and 'the nourisher' did not suffice to secure this end, then He created still further 'the most excellent law': *tatśreyorūpa-matyasṛjat dharmam.*[40]

But in neither case can law be separated from the sacred, even though the nature of the sacred in India, not being based solely on the idea of the divine will, is not what it is in some other cultures.

Pal himself, however, does not care for this divine connection. The trouble with the Vedic *ṛṣis*, he says at one place, is that they confused the problems of the Vedic society with those of religion.[41] Nevertheless, despite some discomfort, he appropriates this tradition to resacralize law. He does so by resurrecting the common concept of law that underlies the diverse interpretations of the origins and specificities of law in ancient India. Probably here lies the final source of his judicial morality and his answer to a world in which he feels the economic, social,

---

[39] Ibid., pp. vi, 259–60.
[40] Ibid., p. vii.
[41] Ibid., p. 27.

and international arrangements have all come to be based on lovelessness. 'All the world's organizations in relation to Nature, in regard to art, concerning human beings, reveal this lovelessness.'[42] Law can contribute, Pal feels, to the ongoing struggle against lovelessness.

Pal's concept of law derives its moral power also from his rejection of instrumentalism. Whether it is prior or subsequent to social differentiation, law in Indian culture is not a mere social component, designed to contain or control Hobbesian human beings. Nor is it, Pal feels, an expression of the social contract or a form of socially sanctioned revenge, even though at an early stage criminal justice remained in the hands of those who wronged.[43]

The Hindu Philosophy of Law uses a historical–evolutionary frame to develop this line of argument further.[44] In this book Pal rejects utilitarianism, which he reads as a form of hedonism, on the grounds that it cannot act responsibly towards the future.

> The so-called theory of utility could not satisfy a Hindu mind which was always so much alive to the relativity of pleasure and pain. Besides this, however, there remains the unresolved question of accounting, by the theory of utility, for law and right in those cases in which the advantage of a future period is antagonistic to that of the living generation, and where it must be bought by some sacrifice on the part of the latter.[45]

Once again, however, Pal hastens to stress the role of reason. He quotes Gautama to suggest that, as the ultimate source of law, reason is not discarded by the Vedas themselves.[46]

Neither such reason nor the law grounded in it, however, is culturally empty. Indeed, the growing institutionalization of cultural diversity defines the context of all law. Pal does pay the usual tribute of his generation to the nineteenth-century vision of one world towards which human society is supposedly moving. But his deeper concerns push him towards a position that is exactly the reverse—towards a plural concept of the

---

[42] Ibid.

[43] Ibid., p. 355.

[44] Radhabinod Pal, *The Hindu Philosophy of Law* (Calcutta: Biswa Bhandar, n.d.).

[45] Ibid., p. 173. Also Pal, *The History of Hindu Law*, pp. 260–1.

[46] Pal, *The Hindu Philosophy of Law*, p. 143.

human future. Given this plural future, law has to take into account cultural diversities and, presumably, cultural rights. For cultural diversity rather than cultural unity represents a higher stage of social development. Mixing the metaphors of cultural relativism and social evolutionism, he says:

> the development of society would consist in the establishment of new psychological relations under the influence of which the community, as well as its surroundings, become transformed by passing from the condition of relatively indefinite and disconnected uniformity, into that of relatively determinate and connected diversity, the constituent elements of the community becoming more and more decidedly individualized.[47]

Finally there is in *The Hindu Philosophy of Law* Pal's construction of the ends of law as they emerge from his reading of traditional texts. He has already argued in *The History of Hindu Law* that law means the rejection of 'mere indiscriminate revenge',[48] and he has identified the Brahmana period of the development of law in India as a more primitive period because criminal justice remained in the hands of those who wronged.[49] He now appears to favour the Buddhist Dhammapada position which sees law as virtually a substitute for violence.[50]

Those observations are set within a conceptual frame deeply ambivalent towards linear concepts of time and stage-oriented historical theories of the growth of law. Apparently, Pal accepts the theory of progress, but he builds into it important checks and counterchecks. Thus even Vico's theory, according to him, 'represents the line of evolution as a Periplus, a Cycloid, a line which returns by a circle to its beginning, thence to start once more over the same path'.[51] In the same context Pal also speaks of regressions and hurdles in progress and evolution much more easily than one would expect from a person who uncritically accepts the theory of progress.

[47] Ibid., pp. 173–4.

[48] Ibid., pp. 134–5.

[49] Pal, *The History of Hindu Law*, p. 330.

[50] Ibid., p. 355.

[51] Pal, *The Hindu Philosophy of Law*, r .36.

IV

This rough sketch of the cognitive and moral map on which Pal plotted his reading of Japanese war crimes is also an incomplete one, mainly because, like many other South Asian scholars of that generation—P. V. Kane immediately comes to mind—Pal writes primarily a simple, linear narrative on Hindu law and legal thought. His own opinions, likes, dislikes and even his own interpretations emerge either indirectly or accidentally. Nevertheless, I hope some parts of his moral framework have now become clearer. The rest is for us a matter of political choice, as it was for Pal at Tokyo.

That choice is well summarized in the story of Duryodhana and Kṛṣṇa I told at the beginning. Duryodhana was evil. He had even fought the battle of Kurukṣetra without consistently conforming to moral norms. Bhīma had the right to kill him. But as the supreme symbol and protector of *dharma* Kṛṣṇa was not free to flout or betray *kṣātradharma*, the Kṣatriya *bushido*. His responsibility was not merely to administer justice but also to be subject to it. Kṛṣṇa failed in this instance because he sought a purely political solution to a problem of morality. He became captive for a moment to the forces he was fighting. He sought to play Duryodhana's game in order to defeat Duryodhana.

One suspects Kṛṣṇa knew his own lapse. He bore the last admonition of Duryodhana quietly and was not surprised when the gods sprinkled flowers from heaven on Duryodhana at the moment of his death. The evil king in his last speech had even succeeded in reminding him, Lord Kṛṣṇa, of his *svadharma*. That was no mean achievement. No wonder that generations of Indians have treated the story as an authentic part of the Mahabharata, not as an interpolation. The story captures something of the essential spirit of their moral world.

There is also in the story a partial—some may say un-Indian—decontextualization of the moral frame within which organized violence takes place. The story suggests that the personality and past record of Duryodhana, including his past acts, are not fully relevant to the judgment passed on the actions of Bhīma and Kṛṣṇa. It suggests that the moral codes of battle cannot be contextualized.

For Pal the moral of the story must have been obvious. The

Japanese warlords and other defendants at the Tokyo trial could have been seeking endorsement of their past actions in Pal's judgment and *ex post facto* legitimacy for Japan's imperial past and militarism. The Japanese admiration for Pal might have been merely instrumental. The trial itself, in spite of specific public denials at the time, also might have been only a political trial for the Allied powers.

All this was not unknown to Pal. And as a liberal social democrat speaking a progressivist language he took public positions on each of these issues. Daisaku Ikeda points out that the scholar-judge never justified the Pacific war waged by the Japanese but had his own point of view about it.

> The war the Japanese waged *differed essentially* from the. one conducted by the Nazis who, over a long period, consistently and deliberately conspired for the conquest of the world. He *admitted* the overwhelming evidence of atrocities committed by members of the Japanese armed forces, but asserted that, unlike the Nazi leaders, the so-called Class A Japanese war criminals had not been proved guilty of giving either permission or command to commit acts of barbarity....[52]

Yet the Japanese wartime leaders had to experience this travesty of justice at Tokyo, because of the same racism of the West that prompted the western powers to be counterphobically harsh on Japanese racism towards other Asians and the West. Pal was 'the only one among the eleven judges who openly criticized western racism in Asia'.[53]

---

[52] Ikeda, *The Human Revolution*, 2, p. 99. Pal distinguished between international delinquencies and international crimes, the latter defined as crimes against or crimes under international law. It is possible that he felt imperial Japan's behaviour could be classified as delinquency rather than crime, given the existing international laws. See, for instance, Pal, *Crimes in International Relations*, p. 107. See also the comments of Tanaka Masaaki: 'Pal was by no means suggesting that Japan was right. He did not say that. He questioned whether it was right to impose such a trial on Japan one-sidedly.' Hosoya, Ando, Onuma, and Minear, *The Tokyo War Crimes Trial*, p. 186. For a similar conclusion, see Yukiko Koshiro, 'Japan's Racial Arrogance on Trial', unpublished MS.

[53] Koshiro, 'Japan's Racial Arrogance'. Later discoveries about Japanese atrocities, particularly those relating to the use of enslaved Asian women from countries occupied by Japan in Japanese military brothels and medical experiments and medicalized killings and torture by Japanese doctors in occupied Asian lands, were not known to Pal. But that might not have changed the overall tenor of his argument.

Behind Pal's liberal conviction lay, however, another cultural world with its own ethics. Pal also had to establish the continuity between the culpability of the accused and that of the plaintiffs, as persons and as nation-states. His judgment had to establish that the responsibility for the war in the East was not one-sided. That responsibility had to be shared by both sides. That even though the war had to be fought as if *dharma* was on one side and *adharma* on the other, exactly as the war in the Mahabharata was fought, victory imposed other responsibilities, including those relating to the interpretation of the origins or sources of the war itself.[54]

Hence Pal's judgment at Tokyo refers to the use of nuclear weapons and the fire-bombing of Japanese cities by the Allied powers and offsets these acts against the accusations of immoral disregard for civilian lives in the Japanese wartime leadership. Pal points out the larger political and economic forces released by the nation-state system, by modern warfare, by the dominant philosophy of international diplomacy, and by the West's racist attitude to Japan, all of which helped produce the political response of the Japanese. The West had to acknowledge that wartime Japan wanted to beat the West at its own game, that a significant part of Japanese imperialism was only a reflection of the West's disowned self. Like Aimé Césaire, who traced Nazi racism and violence to attempts to try out within Europe what Europe's colonial experiments in the non-European world had 'legitimately' done over the centuries to its colonial subjects, Radhabinod Pal set the Japanese imperial guilt in this century in a larger global context. If the accused were guilty, so were the plaintiffs.[55]

---

[54] Cf. Falk, Kolko, and Lifton, *Crimes of War*, which implicitly comes close to this position through another route more accessible to the contemporary world.

[55] On this plane, perhaps the only moral position on culpability at Tokyo that Pal would have endorsed is that of a person who did not belong to his cultural world—that of Kinoshita Junji in his play on the Tokyo trial, *Between God and Man: A Judgment on War Crimes*, tr. Eric J. Gangloff (Tokyo: University of Tokyo, 1979). Prima facie the argument in Kinoshita's play is exactly the reverse of Pal's. If the plaintiffs were guilty, Kinoshita seems to say, the accused were guilty, too. Not because they were proven guilty in the court, but because they were morally responsible. The play judges culpability and apportions guilt not by defending the trial which, Kinoshita admits, was ethically flawed, but through a

This was Pal's way of coping with the nineteenth-century dialectic between the culpability of the individual and society. Elsewhere I have tried to show that the concept of culpability in the Victorian consciousness was defined by two co-ordinates.[56] Along one of them, the individual bore the main responsibility for social pathologies and society could be corrected primarily by eliminating or reforming the culpable individual. (This part of Victorian culture found expression in some aspects of criminal jurisprudence, in most forms of Christian evangelism, and in popular constructions of crime; probably its clearest articulation is in the Sherlock Holmes stories.) Along the other co-ordinate, the individual was seen as a mirror of society, perfectly rectifiable through social engineering and, thus, perfectly unresponsible for his or her actions. (The clearest articulation of this position is, of course, in the socialist and anarchist literatures.) Emphasis on the idea of individual responsibility showed one's moral stature and, sometimes, social class; emphasis on the idea of social responsiblity showed one's intellectual brilliance but irresponsibility and absence of good breeding.

When Pal granted himself the right to judge, he was being both an Indian and a Victorian trying to transcend the moral dichotomy of the age. Like Andrei Sakharov, he believed every crime to be in its orgin social as well as individual. Culpability, Pal sought to argue in his Tokyo judgment, could never be divisible and responsibility, even when individual, could paradoxically be fully individual only when seen as collective and, in fact, global.

---

process of self-judgment brought about by the hero's encounter with a victimhood that is savage by virtue of not being able to defend itself. That attempt to establish a continuity between the plaintiff and accused Pal would have endorsed as moral; he would have recognized that, being a Japanese, Kinoshita has to start from the other end of the continuum.

[56] Ashis Nandy, *The Tao of Cricket: On Games of Destiny and the Destiny of Games* (New Delhi: Viking/Penguin, 1988), Part I.

The Savage Freud: The First Non-Western Psychoanalyst and the Politics of Secret Selves in Colonial India

Of the nineteenth-century European schools of thought that have shaped our self-definition in this century, the two most influential 'in-house' critiques of the modern West are those offered by Marxism and psychoanalysis. Both are deeply ambivalent towards their culture of origin. They seek to bare the normative and institutional anomalies of the Enlightenment and to demystify the bourgeois culture that has inherited the anomalies, but they do so in terms of the values of the Enlightenment itself. This is what makes the schools internal, rather than external critiques of the modern West.

The other aspect of this ambivalence is the tendency of both schools to own up their cultural roots by building into their theoretical frames aggressive Eurocentric critiques of non-western cultures. For both, the primitive world, especially the Orient, is an anachronistic presence and represents an earlier stage of cultural order that social evolution has rendered obsolete. Through this second criticism, that of the non-West, the schools pay homage to their first target of criticism, the West, and atone for being dissenting children of the Enlightenment.

Both schools, it is true, have their self-doubts, expressed through their lurking nostalgia towards the very cultures they try to relegate to the dustbin of history or the wastepaper basket of the clinic. Apart from the fascination the Orient exercised over their founders—the Orient viewed as a victim of impe
Europe or as an anthropological field populated by the 'natu

the antiquated, and the exotic—both schools have produced ideas such as those of primitive communism and regression at the service of ego as latent reparative gestures, to correct for or work through the arrogant social evolutionism that structures their theories of progress. It is the obverse of Albert Schweitzer's famous reparative gesture towards the West, to disabuse all those who thought that his medical mission to Africa was a homage to human dignity or an atonement for colonial violence. The African was his brother, the intrepid missionary agreed, but a younger brother.

When Marxism and psychoanalysis were imported into the savage world in the high noon of imperialism, this racial arrogance was not obvious to their native converts. For the main attraction of these schools of thought in the tropics was their bi-directional criticism—of the contemporary European society *and* of the savage world. Afro-Asian scholars and activists found these schools excellent instruments of self-criticism. In fact, when it came to the native way of life, such scholars and activists rejected or undervalued ideas that softened the critical thrust of the two schools. Thus, psychoanalysts such as Carl Jung, who were especially open to the Indian worldview, found few adherents in India; Marxist scholars such as Ernst Bloch, who sought to establish a continuity between the Marxist vision and the older religious worldviews, never enjoyed a vogue in non-European societies organized around religion. Such 'returns to tradition' were considered legitimate attempts to enrich social criticism in the modern West, not in societies bogged down in tradition.

Marxism was to have a more lasting impact on intellectual and political life in the South than psychoanalysis, which, after an early flurry of activity in a few societies—after as it were a late spring lasting about two decades—gradually became peripheral to the culture of public life in the South. Was this because Marxism became a political movement in Asia and Africa at a time when politics was about to become the most important sector of these societies? Or were there other reasons that had to do with the culture of psychoanalysis, such as the torn personalities of those who tended it in its new habitat and the persisting indigenous theories of the mind that, like a chronic illness, resisted western remedies prescribed for the problems of living in Asian and African backwaters?

This essay pursues the second set of questions. It does so by focusing on the cultural meanings psychoanalysis acquired in its early years in India where it first established a bridgehead in the 1920s. The essay examines these meanings through the prism of the personal experiences, intellectual concerns, and metapsychology of the first non-western psychoanalyst, Girindrasekhar Bose (1886–1953), who pioneered the discipline in India.

Bose began trying out psychoanalytic concepts and methods in his clinical practice towards the end of the 1910s when, following the partition of Bengal in 1905, the Swadeshi movement had become a significant political presence; and he founded the Indian Psychoanalytic Society in 1921, when the non-cooperation movement had started and Gandhi had become the leader of India's freedom struggle. Both these political events had their cultural counterparts, such as renewed efforts to revalue indigenous systems of knowledge and growing awareness that the West's intellectual domination depended greatly on the philosophy of science and analytic categories popularized by the European culture of knowledge.

Psychoanalysis in its early years reflected these changes in India's intellectual climate. The discipline came to represent something more than a therapeutic technique that could be adapted to the mental health problems of India's burgeoning, partly decultured, urban bourgeoisie, even though that is how Bose often viewed it, especially when writing for his international audience. Psychoanalysis also had to serve as a new instrument of social criticism, as a means of demystifying aspects of Indian culture that seemed anachronistic or pathological to the articulate middle classes, and as a dissenting western school of thought that could be turned against the West itself.

The following story tells how Bose's unique response to Freud's theories was shaped by the psychological contradictions that had arisen in Indian culture due to the colonial impact and by the cultural contradictions within psychoanalysis itself. As a result, the usual encounter between an ancient culture with its distinctive culture of science and an exogenous science with its own distinctive culture fractured the self-definitions not only of Bose but of many others involved in similar enterprises. At the same time, the encounter initiated a play of secret selves which widened as well as narrowed the interpretations of both Indian culture and the culture of psychoanalysis. The story suggests that the more speculative, political, cultural-critical aspects of the young science—its disreputable 'secret self'—gave greater 'play' to non-western psychoanalysis in the early years and might even have given it a stronger creative 'push' under another kind of political-intellectual dispensation.

PART ONE: THE PSYCHOLOGY OF MORALITY

I *Śarvilaka's Gita*

In ancient Magadha in eastern India, there lived a powerful, learned, highly respected, rich Brahmin called Śarvilaka. Disciples came to him from distant lands and his house resonated with the recital of and discussions on sacred texts.

Śarvilaka had a gifted son called Puṇḍarīka. Though young, Puṇḍarīka had already mastered the religious texts. When Puṇḍarīka reached the age of sixteen, Śarvilaka told him, 'Son, today is an auspicious day. Fast for the entire day and maintain your purity by following the right practices. At 2 o'clock tonight, when the moonless night begins, I shall initiate you into our *kaulika prathā* or family custom. From evening onwards stay in seclusion and meditate.'

At 2 a.m. Puṇḍarīka was still reciting the name of God when, suddenly, the doors of his room opened. In the faint light of a lamp, he saw a huge man entering the room. The intruder wore a loin-cloth, his body shone with oil, and he held an axe on each shoulder. With a shock Puṇḍarīka recognized that the stranger was his father. Śarvilaka said, 'Son, do not be afraid. The time for your initiation has come. Come, dress yourself like me, take one of these axes, and follow me.' Puṇḍarīka followed as if mesmerized.

Through a maze of streets, Śarvilaka led his son to the highway connecting Magadha to Varanasi and stood under a banyan tree. He then said, 'Puṇḍarīka, stand quietly in the dark, so that nobody can see you.' Puṇḍarīka stood trembling with fear, shock, and the strain of the long walk.

A rich merchant was travelling from the palace of Magadha to Varanasi in a horse-drawn carriage. He was carrying with him 10,000 gold coins. The route being dangerous, he had eight armed guards escorting the vehicle. As soon as the carriage reached the banyan tree, Śarvilaka attacked it with a mighty roar. In the faint light, he looked even more fearsome. The driver and guards immediately ran off. Śarvilaka decapitated the merchant with his axe, picked up the heavy bag containing the gold coins on his shoulders, and came back to the banyan tree. Puṇḍarīka by then was shaking with terror; his axe had fallen from his hand. Śarvilaka picked up the axe and led Puṇḍarīka by the hand towards home. He then pushed his son into his room and latched the door from outside.

After a long while, Puṇḍarīka regained some of his composure. By now, his mind was churning with contempt, anger and hurt. He decided not to stay at his father's home for even one moment. In this state of high tension, he fell asleep. When he woke up in the morning, he found the sun's rays shining into his room. His father was standing near the bed, his usual serene self, wearing his usual dress. For a moment Puṇḍarīka felt that his memories of the previous night were part of a nightmare. But his own oily body and loin-cloth showed otherwise. Śarvilaka broke the silence to say, 'Son, do not be unnecessarily perturbed. Nothing has happened which should cause you heart-burning.' Puṇḍarīka said, 'I don't want to stay in your house even for a moment.' His father responded, 'You are not in the right state of mind because you haven't eaten or slept properly, and you are tense. Have a bath, eat and rest. Then I shall tell you about our family custom. If after hearing me out you still want to leave, I shall not stop you.'

Śarvilaka returned in the afternoon and had a long conversation with his son. He first narrated how the family had followed the same *kaulika prathā* from the time of the Mahabharata and how he himself was initiated into the custom by his father. He said he knew he seemed a hypocrite, robber and murderer to his son. But he also had faith in his son's intellect and knowledge of the sacred texts. Śarvilaka then went on to justify every act of his by the tenets of the Gita, for he felt that Puṇḍarīka's moral anxieties were similar to those of Arjuna before the battle of Kurukṣetra; they were born of *moha*, attachment. Arjuna, too, had felt like living on alms rather than killing his own relatives for material gain.

Śarvilaka's arguments were sophisticated and they could be summed up by three broad propositions. First, Śarvilaka agreed, he did not openly talk of his *kulācāra* (family practices) because he feared public censure and harassment. He followed *lokācāra* (customary practices) by day and *kulācāra* at night. As a result, he now appeared to be a hypocrite to his own son. Yet no one could survive in the world by being totally truthful. All human beings were weak to a degree; to defend themselves they had to lie. Even Lord Kṛṣṇa had to hide his intentions when he killed the demon Jarāsandha. Otherwise, too, untruth was of divine origin. The creator of the universe had equipped some of his creatures with the capacity to lie and cheat; even animals like lions and tigers resorted to stealth when stalking their prey. Human beings were too insignificant a species to invent on their own the idea of falsehood.

Second, everyone was to some extent a robber. When one ate fruit, one deprived the trees of their fruit or perhaps animals of their lives. Living itself meant living off other lives. Moreover, God had not sent anyone to earth with property or riches. One won worldly success by depriving others. *Vasundharā vīrabhogyā* —the earth was for the enjoyment of the brave.

Third, one had to overcome the fear of being called a murderer. Arjuna feared the epithet when the battle of Kurukṣetra was imminent and the correct response to that fear, Śarvilaka felt, was best given in Kṛṣṇa's sermon to Arjuna in the Gita. The oppressor and the victim, the Gita said, were both unreal because *ātman* (soul) was the sole reality and it was indestructible—*na hantā na hanyate*. None should rue the loss of a destructible, transient body. The prosperous merchant killed on the road to Varanasi was aged and yet attached to his worldly goods. The destruction of his body had actually done him good. If Śarvilaka had forsaken his *kuladharma* or family's code of conduct to spare the traveller, that would have been far more sinful. Human beings were mere agents of divinity—*nimittamātra.*

Puṇḍarīka listened to this discourse with rapt attention. The doubts and contradictions in his mind rapidly dissolved. At the end of the discourse, he touched his father's feet to pledge undying loyalty to their family custom.

With this story of homicide, secret selves, a seductive 'immoral' father, his vulnerable 'moral' son, and their final Oedipal compact after an aborted rebellion, the world's first non-western psychoanalyst, Girindrasekhar Bose, begins in 1931 his interpretation of the Gita in the pages of *Pravāsī*, the influential Bengali journal of the pre-Independence years.[1] Bose was already a famous psychiatrist and had founded the Indian Psychoanalytic Society. By the time he began his work on the Gita, he had been exposed to psychoanalysis for nearly two decades. Yet there are odd anomalies. Though it has been called 'perhaps his most significant work' and a pioneering attempt 'to correlate Hindu philosophy to western psychology',[2] the interpretation is more social-philosophical than psychoanalytic. Though Bose claims to be motivated by psychological curiosity rather than religious faith,[3] in many places psychology enters the interpretation almost inadvertently, even diffidently.

Was Śarvilaka's interpretation of the Gita correct? Did the Gita permit him the interpretation he offered? And if he was wrong, on what grounds was his interpretation flawed? What were the real meanings of the *ślokas* Śarvilaka cited? Bose interprets the Gita in response to these questions.[4] In a society where texts survive as living texts mainly through interpretation and reinterpretation, Bose could create a space for his new science of interpretation only by enunciating and demonstrating its principles. Yet he ventures his interpretation of the Gita without any open reference to a psychoanalytic concept.

To find out how Bose relates his interpretation to his own

---

[1] Girindrasekhar Bose, 'Gita', *Pravasi*, 1931, *31*, Part 2(1), pp. 9–16.

[2] Jagdish Bhatia, 'Pioneer Who Explored the Psyche of India', *Far Eastern Economic Review*, 13 August 1987.

[3] Bose, 'Gita', p. 15.

[4] Ibid., p. 13. Bose's commentary is based on the following principles he enunciates in the opening paragraphs of his work on the Gita: 'Wherever more than one meaning of a *śloka* is possible, the simpler and more easily comprehensible meaning is taken. Gita, it is presumed, is meant for the ordinary people and the author of Gita did not lack the skill to write lucidly.'

'If an interpretation of a *śloka* contradicts other *ślokas*, it is rejected. So are all internally inconsistent interpretations. Also rejected are all supernatural meanings. As a general principle, the commentary also tries to be impartial and non-sectarian.' Ibid., p.15.

theories of consciousness, especially psychoanalysis, we shall therefore have to go to some of his other writings. Before we do that, however, we should be aware of the broad outlines of the personal and social background he brought into psychoanalysis. For we must remember that while the story of Śarvilaka affirms the emergence of a new exegetic voice, that of an Indian psychoanalyst, it also enforces on Bose strange silences. It remains unexplained why Bose has nothing to say about the passive resolution of the Oedipal encounter that takes place in the story or about the inverted relationship between a weak son personifying his father's manifest moral self and a powerful father personifying moral seduction and the amoral rationality latent in the son. Was Bose's psychoanalysis a negation of Puṇḍarīka's weak, transient rebellion against a strong, amoral, paternal authority? Did that defiance of defiance make Bose's cognitive venture an ethical statement? Why does Bose refuse to consider the possibility that Śarvilaka's secret self, the one that his son finally owns up, represents unmediated primitive impulses of the kind that psychoanalysis subsumes under the category of the id? Is it because there is in Śarvilaka a complex structure of rationalization, including an element of controlled, dispassionate violence, that defies the conventional definition of the id and the primary processes?

Nor does Bose explain why his partiality for Puṇḍarīka's early Oedipal dissent is justified not in the language of the ego but that of the superego, whereas Puṇḍarīka's moral seduction by Śarvilaka is cast not in the language of the superego but that of the ego. It was as if the triumph of the therapeutic in South Asia heralded not so much a new bridgehead of the ego in the realm of the id as an empowerment of the superego through an abridgement of the sphere of the unencumbered, psychopathic ego. The rest of this essay can be read as an attempt to work out the full implications of these abstract and somewhat opaque formulations.

II *The Rediscovery*

Girindrasekhar Bose was probably born on 30 January 1886, the youngest of four sons and five daughters. He often described to his students and trainees, with great relish, two details about his early years: first, he was a breech baby. As he loved to put it, he was born feet first, holding his head high. He paid dearly for the privilege; injury at birth left him with one foot slightly shorter than the other. Second, he was breast-fed till he was five. Defying psychoanalytic wisdom, Bose claimed that the prolonged breast-feeding had not heightened his oral dependency needs; rather it had contributed to his psychological well-being and optimism.

The Boses came from Nadia in West Bengal. Girindrasekhar's father Chandrasekhar had worked for an English landlord early in his life, but was the Maharaja of Darbhanga's Diwan when his youngest son was born. As a result, the son spent most of his formative years outside Bengal, in north Bihar. His childhood memories of Bihar occasionally emerged in later years in the form of rustic wisdom laced with wit, and provided a part-comic but robust counterpoint to urbane babus in his works of fantasy.

Chandrasekhar conformed to the Bengali urban élite's ideal of a gentleman: he was known for his managerial efficiency, financial probity, and Vedantic scholarship. By the time he reached middle age, the Boses were established as a rather successful Kayastha family—respected, prosperous, and committed to learning. Chandrasekhar himself, however, despite his social status, was regarded with some ambivalence by the local Brahmins on account of his attempts to break into traditional scholarship. That might explain why the family, despite their orthodoxy, moved in the social world of reformist Brahmos after they moved to Calcutta. Many actually mistook the Boses for Brahmos. That did not improve matters much; the Brahmos now began to make fun of the orthodox ways of the Boses, especially their faith in gurus, *purohitas*, *kuladevatās*, *iṣṭadevīs*, etc.

Chandrasekhar's first two wives had died young. A daughter by his first wife had also died early. In middle age, he remarried yet again, this time a young girl 22 years younger than him called Lakshmimani, who bore him all his nine surviving children. If Chandrasekhar was a scholar, Lakshmimani had imagination. Superbly well read, especially in the *purāṇas*, she was also a poetess who had a lively intellectual curiosity. The two provided for their children a potent intellectual atmosphere, enlivened by stories from the Ramayana and the Mahabharata. Two of Chandrasekhar's sons were to become well-known writers. Rajsekhar, the most successful of the siblings, became famous as a satirist, classical scholar, translator, grammarian and, perhaps reflecting Chandrasekhar's range of interests, an applied chemist and industrial manager, He was also an early patron of the Indian Psychoanalytic Society; the first psychoanalytic clinic in South Asia, probably the first in the non-western world, was established on a piece of land donated by him.

Of the siblings, Rajsekhar remained the closest to Girindrasekhar. His literary work resembled in style the self-articulation Girindrasekhar assumed in his scientific discourse. There was a combination of rigour and robust directness, on the one hand, and a dependence on the idiom of the epics and the philosophical visions of the classical Sanskritic heritage, on the other. Both brothers strove for the nearly-unattainable—an austere, rationalist discourse that would reflect the moral urgency and poetry of the classics. Both, one suspects, were searching for culturally rooted moral codes appropriate for their times, away from the puritanic moralism of the reformist Brahmo and the defensiveness of the orthodox Hindu.

We know little else about Girindrasekhar Bose's childhood. Though a psychoanalyst, he showed a certain reticence about his own personal life, born partly from a sense of defensive privacy and partly from an indifference to history. Even his own comments about himself, of the kind I mentioned earlier, were off-the-cuff, casual ones; they served mainly as capsuled, psychoanalytic witticisms. They were also gulped down as such by his students, trainees, and admirers. As a result, even today, an enterprising clinician cannot easily produce a psychoanalytic case history of the southern world's first psychoanalyst. The reader will have noticed that one cannot be absolutely certain even about the exact date of Bose's birth. By way of a life history, one is mainly left with the memories of a few surviving contemporaries and the biographical notes of some of his students and trainees, notably those of psychoanalyst Tarun Chandra Sinha, his closest associate.[5] In addition, there are the outlines of Bose's

[5] Tarun Chandra Sinha, 'A Short Life Sketch of Girindrasekhar Bose', *Samiksha*, Bose Special No., ed., Nagendranath Dey, 1954, pp. 62–74.

educational career, which followed a course somewhat resembling that of his chosen guru, Sigmund Freud.

According to Sinha, Chandrasekhar was a 'true' father who exercised 'full authority and control'.[6] He was a strict disciplinarian and a conservative who conformed to family traditions 'fairly rigidly'.[7] Though Sinha hastens to add that Chandrasekhar was no autocrat, as if apprehensive that he was hinting at a classical Oedipal situation, something of the father's style rubbed off on the son. Girindrasekhar, it seems, was domineering even as a child and he enjoyed exercising his authority.[8] This was probably tolerated by the family because of his physical handicap and his fragile health, caused by an attack of blood dysentery in the first year of his life. The child despot was taken to school in a palanquin, we are told.[9]

Girindrasekhar's early schooling took place in Darbhanga. As a result he had a good command of Hindi. He was also well-versed in Sanskrit, thanks to his father. However, Girindrasekhar later claimed, in some Bengali essays, that his knowledge of the language was inadequate and that he depended on the help of traditional Sanskrit scholars in his serious work. (Perhaps he felt intimidated by Rajsekhar's superb Sanskrit and highly creative use of Hindi.) We also know that Girindrasekhar was a handsome, self-confident child despite his physical handicap, and was, perhaps because of the handicap, protected by and close to his mother. This self-confidence must have been an asset when, having been brought up in an environment alien to the world of Bengali babus, he later entered Calcutta's intellectual life.

In 1904, at the age of seventeen, Girindrasekhar was married off to Indumati, a girl of ten. They had two daughters, one born in 1908, the other four years later. From the beginning, it seems, Bose kept family life separate from his academic life. The former was private, the latter public. Except on a few rare occasions, Bose's students and trainees never had a glimpse of his family; many of them never ever met or even saw his wife or daughters.

---

[6] Ibid., p. 62.

[7] Ibid.

[8] Ibid.

[9] Ibid.

This may or may not have anything to do with his attitude to women. His brother and ego-ideal, Rajsekhar, who was a bachelor, maintained a similar, if not stricter, separation between his private and public lives.

After finishing school, Girindrasekhar joined the Presidency College, Calcutta's foremost educational institution and intellectual hub, where he studied chemistry, a discipline that was Rajsekhar's vocation, too. After graduating in 1905, Girindrasekhar joined the Medical College in Calcutta. At about this time his father retired and the entire family moved to Calcutta, purchasing a house in north Calcutta (14 Parsibagan Street), and settled down there. The house was to become famous afterwards as a citadel of psychoanalysis in India. In 1910 Girindrasekhar got his medical degree and started private practice.

Bose's earliest passion was yoga and a focus of scholarly curiosity in his teens was Patañjali's *Yogasūtra*. Bose's nephew Bijayketu Bose, a psychoanalyst himself, believes that his uncle was basically searching at this point of time for supernatural or magical powers, *alaukika kṣamatā*.[10] Later on, at the age of fourteen or so, Bose developed a keen interest in magic and hypnotism, and became an amateur magician and hypnotist. This was not particularly uncommon in Calcutta at the time. Many middle-class Bengalis had begun to take an interest in these pursuits, perhaps attracted by their liminal status. In Bose's case, if we accept his nephew's interpretation, there was also a direct continuity between the choice of magic as a vehicle of self-expression and the earlier search for magical powers.

Bose made a success of this venture. While still a medical student, he gave occasional public performances, and even won a prize for an original article in a journal of magic.He went still further with hypnosis. Encouraged by some of his teachers, he used hypnotic therapy with partial success in cases of insomnia, nausea in pregnancy, and, more dramatically, in an instance of cardiac asthma. This was while he was still an adolescent (1902–7). Later, when he came to know more about psychoanalysis, he did

[10] Psychoanalyst Bhupen Desai believes that an analogous search for magical powers explains the choice of psychoanalysis as a career by many Indians. Desai says that he himself was motivated by the search for omniscience and gives the examples of others whose unconscious goals were similar.

not entirely give up hypnotism in deference to the psychoanalytic belief in the absolute superiority of free association.[11] He retained, as part of his analytic technique, hypnotic suggestion as an occasional therapeutic tool. He even made good use of the differences between two types of hypnosis: the father-type and the mother-type. One was didactic; the other persuasion-based.[12]

After taking his medical degree, Bose quickly established himself as a general practitioner, and became within a decade one of Calcutta's leading doctors with a large private practice. When in 1926–7 he decided to restrict his general practice and concentrate on cases of mental illness, he was barely forty.[13]

Bose's fascination with Freud's new science began with casual encounters. Though he might have heard of psychoanalysis as early as 1905–6, his interest in it was first stimulated around 1909 by articles published in various periodicals. At the time only Brill's translation of a selection of Freud's papers was available in English. (Bose began to learn German only in his middle years.) The preface to *Concept of Repression* suggests that Bose, when he started psychoanalytic work, had not even read Brill.[14] The preface, in fact, reveals that some of the concepts Bose thought he had developed he found had already been developed by Freud when translations of Freud began to reach India after the world war ended in 1918. He was not defensive about the discovery; he accepted the superiority of the psychoanalytic concepts and began to use them in his work. He was actually better off in this respect than his more famous Tamil contemporary, the untutored mathematical genius, Srinivasa Ramanujan (1887–1920). A large proportion of Ramanujan's discoveries later turned out to be rediscoveries; he had to

---

[11] See a brief discussion of Bose's long-term interest in hypnosis later in this essay.

[12] The classification was borrowed from Sandor Ferenczi. See Girindrasekhar Bose, *Concept of Repression* (Calcutta: Sri Gauranga Press, 1921, and London: Kegan Paul, Trench, Troubner and Co., 1921), pp. 140–1.

[13] This account of Bijayketu Bose is not consistent with Sinha's claim that Bose had to undergo financial hardships in his early years as a doctor. Perhaps Sinha had in mind the fact that when Bose concentrated on psychiatry, his average income declined dramatically to about Rs 100 a month. Sinha, 'A Short Life Sketch', p. 64.

[14] Bose, *Concept of Repression*, pp. v–viii.

reconcile himself to being an immortal in the world of mathematics on the basis of the remainder.

Over the next five years, three more translations of Freud's books were published: *The Three Lectures on Sexuality* (1910), the lectures at the Clark University in the United States, published as *Five Lectures on Psychoanalysis* (1910), and the *Interpretation of Dreams* (1913). By that time Bose was committed to the new science. One suspects from the sequence of events that the reasons for his decision to switch from conventional psychiatry were not purely intellectual ones, that he gave his allegiance to Freud even before he had read him systematically. Something in the framework and concerns of psychoanalysis had deeply touched the young doctor. The strange, new-fangled ideas of the controversial Viennese physician *did* have something to say about Bose's own world.

Bose's 'conversion' did not signify much to his community, for few people in India had heard of Freud. Rabindranath Tagore (1861–1940) relates in a letter that a Bengali admirer of Freud, while speaking to Tagore about psychoanalysis, consistently pronounced 'Freud' as if it rhymed with 'fruit'. Bose, however, found in Freud a kindred soul and saw immense possibilities in psychoanalysis. He eagerly read everything available on the subject and began to apply the method in his psychiatric work; he appears to have been satisfied with the results. At any rate, given his background and the intellectual position he had been moving towards before discovering psychoanalysis, he did not have to make too many modifications in his therapeutic style.

Bose's new passion heightened his curiosity about the discipline of psychology in general. From his early years, he had been an orderly person and, in many respects, a perfectionist. Once his interest in psychology was aroused, he began to feel handicapped by his limited knowledge of abnormal psychology. Whatever he knew was derived from the undergraduate courses in medicine he had attended, inadequate grounding for a practitioner especially interested in the theory and practice of psychiatry.

When the Calcutta University opened a new department of psychology in 1915, Bose enrolled as a student, and got his master's degree in two years, once again doing well in the examinations. He was immediately appointed a lecturer in the department. One of the first things he did was make courses in psychoanalysis compulsory for all students of psychology, making the department one of the first academic establishments in the world to do so.[15] He was then thirty-one.

After four years, Bose completed his doctoral thesis which was published as the *Concept of Repression*.[16] Though fascinating in many ways, it is a clumsy work, made still clumsier by Bose's awkward and cluttered English. Despite this, it was well received. The thesis was reportedly dictated to a stenographer in a week, in response to a bet taken with a fellow member of the Utkendra Samiti or Eccentric Club that Bose and some of his friends had founded at his Parsibagan residence. His friends had ragged him, claiming that his disregard for degrees and formal qualifications was a pose, meant to hide his incapacity to get a doctorate.[17] Bose's dissertation was to remain the only doctoral thesis in psychology completed in an Indian university during the 1920s, and this further underwrote the pre-eminence of psychoanalysis in Indian academic psychology. Perhaps in no other country was psychoanalysis to register such easy dominance as in India.

When his thesis was published, Girindrasekhar sent a copy of the book to Freud. It bore the inscription: 'from a warm admirer of your theory and science'. Freud was pleasantly surprised and wrote back almost immediately.The old dissenter was not used to easy acceptance; he was genuinely intrigued that in far-off India psychoanalysis should have met with so much interest and recognition so early in its career. Thus began an intermittent correspondence between the two which lasted nearly two decades.[18] Bose never met Freud. Going to the West for an education and 'proper' recognition of one's worth was popular among the westernized élites of colonial India and this irritated Bose. Despite an invitation from his guru, he refused to go

---

[15] Christiane Hartnack, 'Psychoanalysis and Colonialism in British India', Ph.D dissertation, Berlin, Freie Universität, 1988, p. 85.

[16] Bose, *Concept of Repression*.

[17] Sinha, 'A Short Life Sketch', p. 64.

[18] Sigmund Freud to Girindrasekhar Bose, 29 May 1921, in 'Correspondence Regarding Psychoanalysis', *Samiksha*, 1956, *10*, pp. 104–10; *10*, pp. 155–66.

abroad because that would be 'more of a fashion than need'.[19] There were also, according to Ernest Jones who invited Bose to Europe several times, Bose's numerous duties in India and 'perhaps a certain shyness'.[20]

In 1922, barely three years after the British Psychoanalytic Society was formed, Bose founded the Indian Psychoanalytic Society in Calcutta at his own residence. Of the fifteen founding members of the group, nine were college lecturers of psychology and philosophy, five were doctors, and one a business executive who also happened to be a generous patron of the Society. Of the thirteen Indian members, twelve were upper-caste Bengalis; the two remaining members were whites. The social origin of the thirteenth Indian member is not apparent from his name. Of the five doctors, two were British, one a relatively nondescript doctor in the colonial health service. The other was Owen A. R. Berkeley-Hill (1879–1944), also a member of the health service but already famous as the psychiatrist who had made the Ranchi Mental Hospital one of the best known in the East. Berkeley-Hill's name is inextricably linked to the history of modern psychiatry and psychoanalysis in India, and he epitomized in many ways some of the central problems in the culture of the two disciplines in South Asia. He was the first westerner to attempt a psychoanalytic study of the Hindu modal personality and the first westerner to use psychoanalysis as a form of cultural critique in India. A word on him will provide a counterpoint to Bose's philosophy of knowledge.

Berkeley-Hill was no ordinary migratory bird in India. Son of a wealthy and famous English physician, he was educated at Rugby, Göttingen, the University of Nancy, and Oxford, from where he received his medical degree. Berkeley-Hill entered the Indian Medical Service in 1907 and, except for a four-year stretch during World War I, spent the rest of his life in India, complaining all the while about living conditions in the colony. He married a Hindu, despite his preoccupation with the dis-

---

[19] Bhatia, 'Pioneer'. Also Freud to Bose, 1 March 1922, 'Correspondence', *Samiksha*, 1956, *10*, p. 108.

[20] Ernest Jones, 'Foreword', *Samiksha*, 1954, Bose Sp. No., p. 1.

torted personality and culture of the Hindus. The marriage and its Eurasian offspring were an almost certain indicator, during the period we are talking about, both of social defiance and uncertain social status among the whites. Neither defiance nor uncertainty was lacking in Berkeley-Hill. Christiane Hartnack points out that in Berkeley-Hill's autobiography, which includes an open discussion of his premarital sex life and ends with 'a detailed description of the character and look of his horses, there is less mention of his wife than of [his] extra-marital affairs.'[21]

Perhaps as a result of his liminal stature, Berkeley-Hill showed in many of his papers an aggressive psychoanalysism. Given his fractured self, simultaneously repelled and seduced by imperial England and Brahminic India, this analysism took necessarily a particular form. As befitted an Edwardian gentleman educated at an English public school and Oxford, he showed a deep concern with the vicissitudes of anal eroticism and found in its patterning among the Hindus *the* clue to their cultural pathology and moral depravity. He passed judgment on their character, on behalf of all other cultures, in the following words:

> It is not unlikely that the strange antipathy that is felt for the Hindus by most, if indeed not all, the races of the world is nothing more than an expression of an unconscious feeling of antagonism brought about by some of the peculiarities of the manifestations of anal eroticism as met with among the Hindus. It is certainly a fact that wherever the Hindu may go, no matter whether it be in Asia, Africa or Europe, he is to the inhabitants of that country a veritable Dr. Fell. We must therefore assume that this obscure but nevertheless very real dislike which is shared by all races of mankind for the Hindu, must, from its very nature, have its roots in some deeply buried source of feeling. Books on India teem with references to this singular 'otherness', if I may use the term, of the Hindu as compared, for instance, with the Muslim or Christian Indian.[22]

---

[21] Hartnack, 'Psychoanalysis and Colonialism', pp. 28–9. Most of the biographical material on Berkeley-Hill used in this paper is from Hartnack's comprehensive work on the shadow cast by colonialism on the work of the first psychoanalysts in India.

[22] Owen A. R. Berkeley-Hill, 'The Anal-Erotic Factor in the Religion, Philosophy and Character of the Hindus', in *Collected Papers* (Calcutta: The Book Co., 1933), pp. 75–112; first published in the *International Journal of Psycho-Analysis*, 1921, *2*, pp. 306–38.

On the basis of the theoretical work of his mentor, Ernest Jones, Berkeley-Hill then goes on to identify, rather charmingly and with the confidence of one advancing a dispassionate scientific thesis, the two effects of anal eroticism.[23] The valuable qualities thrown up by anal eroticism are:

> individualism. determination, persistence, love of order and power of organisation, competency, reliability and thoroughness, generosity, the bent towards art and good taste, the capacity for unusual tenderness, and the general ability to deal with concrete objects of the material world.[24]

The despicable ones are the obverse of the above:

> incapacity for happiness, irritability and bad temper, hypochondria, miserliness, meanness and pettyness, slow-mindedness and proneness to bore, the bent for tyrannising and dictating and obstinacy.[25]

Predictably, the Hindus suffered from a 'metapsychosis' featuring the second set of traits. On the other hand, 'the character traits of the English people as a whole belong for the greater part to the first of the two groups distinguished by Ernest Jones'.[26]

Berkeley-Hill's views were, however, not as one-sided as these extracts from his papers suggest or as Hartnack would have us believe. On occasion, his defiance overcame his social insecurities and he could be remarkably incisive in his cultural analysis. Nearly twenty-five years before James Baldwin made such ideas a part of American folklore, Berkeley-Hill suggested that colour prejudice among the whites sprang from a deep fear of the perceived greater potency of the blacks and from the fear that the whites would lose their womenfolk to the blacks.[27]

The aggressive psychoanalysism was, however, the dominant tone. Like Kipling's imperialist stance, it reads today like an exaggerated gesture of allegiance by a marginal man to the culture of the ruling community, though at one time it must

---

[23] Ibid., p. 107.

[24] Ibid., pp. 108–9.

[25] Ibid.

[26] Ibid., p. 111.

[27] Berkeley-Hill, 'The "Colour Question" From a Psychoanalytic Standpoint' (1923), *Collected Papers*, pp. 139–48.

have appeared to be a pungent exercise in social criticism and demystification. Berkeley-Hill, like Kipling, was both fascinated and repelled by India, and the fascination was more painful to bear. It cut him off from his own kind and tainted him as culturally impure. His writings make it obvious that to him India was a living negation of the Victorian ideal of a moral self, and the seductive appeal of Indian culture had to be fiercely resisted.

For Berkeley-Hill to pursue the cultural-critical aspect of psychoanalysis to its logical conclusion would have meant taking a political position against a part of himself and against the social evolutionism that underpinned Victorian morality and sanctioned colonialism. He could not afford to own up that responsibility. He had to defend himself by turning the tools of his new-found critical apparatus against the Indian culture itself, both with a vengeance and an immense effort of will, the way Kipling had earlier turned against that part of himself which constituted his Indianness.[28]

Berkeley-Hill began his personal analysis at London with the well-known Welsh psychoanalyst, Ernest Jones, and he probably completed his training with Bose at Calcutta. Along with his lesser-known compatriot Claud Dangar Daly, another protégé of Jones and subsequently an analysand of Freud and Ferenczi, Berkeley-Hill defined for his generation of psychoanalysts the domain of psychoanalytic studies of modal personality or national character in India.[29] We have already told a part of that story. The political psychology of that pioneering effort—especially the links between psychoanalysis, colonialism, and the culture of science in the inter-war years—is neatly summed up in Christiane Hartnack's verdict on the two British psychoanalysts. After analysing their work and interpretive styles, she concludes:

---

[28] For a brief sketch of Kipling from this point of view, see Ashis Nandy, *The Intimate Enemy: Loss and Recovery of Self Under Colonialism* (New Delhi: Oxford University Press, 1983).

[29] For example, Owen A. R. Berkeley-Hill, 'A Report of Two Cases Successfully Treated by Psychoanalysis', *The Indian Medical Gazette*, 1913, *48*, pp. 97–9; and 'The Psychology of the Anus', ibid., pp. 301–3; also 'The Anal Erotic Factor'. One wonders after reading the last paper if its diagnosis was not partly influenced by Berkeley-Hill's long personal acqaintance with Bose. Also Claud Dangar Daly, 'Hindu-Mythologie und Kastrationkomplex', tr. Peter Mandelsohn, *Imago*, 1927, *13*, pp. 145–98.

> There is an unquestionable tendency in both writers to find in psychoanalysis a new scientific tool for getting a grip on problems of public order that were getting out of control.... This explicitly political appropriation of psychoanalytic theory...coincided in the 'twenties and 'thirties with the first successes of the newly formed Indian independence movement. In line with European thought at the time, Berkeley-Hill and Daly conceptualized a moral hierarchy with white men at the top and dependent people, women, infants, so-called primitives, and neurotics at or near the bottom.[30]

Thus

> Berkeley-Hill's and Daly's writings on Indians had in common that they...both failed to note any achievement or positive aspect of the Indian culture....Both men identified themselves fully with British colonialism. For them, Indians were a source of threat and had thus to be combatted, and resistance had to be smashed not only on a military but also on a cultural level. Unlike Orwell, who left colonial India in order not to cope with the dual identity of a colonial bureaucrat by day and a questioning and critical human being by night, Daly and Berkeley-Hill worked to...contribute to a properly functioning colonial world.
>
> Contemporary psychoanalytical thought offered them models to legitimize their...separation from Indians. If one was not a British (i.e., Christian) adult healthy male, one was in trouble.... Victorian women, Anglo-Indians, Irish, Moselms, children, sick and old people could to some extent still be accepted, as there were some common denominators between them and the British ideal. But women who did not obey the Victorian mores, mentally disturbed British subjects, Hindus and people of colour...were not only perceived as entirely different and thus inferior, but were also considered to be dangerous. They were not only in the majority, but there was the potential of hysteria, violence, revolution, sexual seduction and other supposedly irrational acts, which would be difficult to control. Therefore, it was the 'white man's burden' to keep them under surveillance....[31]

One should not be too harsh on the two well-meaning, simple-hearted practitioners of the young science of psychoanalytic psychiatry when the dominant culture of the now fully grown science has not done much better and when all around them the

[30] Hartnack, 'Psychoanalysis and Colonialism', p. 5.

[31] Ibid., p. 73.

two could find even Indians lovingly embracing the same overall perspective. It is fairly obvious that both British psychoanalysts were strictly allegiant to a transfer-of-technology model that had already become popular on the Indian scene and would remain paramount in Indian intellectual life four decades after formal decolonization. Berkeley-Hill and Daly, like many before them and after, saw psychoanalysis as a state-of-the-art therapeutic device and hoped to introduce it with minor modifications into India as a partial cure for the worst affliction Indians suffered from—Indianness. The exclusive universality imputed to most systems of modern scientific knowledge was a function, then as now, of the political privileges such a transfer created for specific individuals and groups.

With hindsight, is it fair to ask if the early Indian analysts were adequately aware that they were caught in a colonial grid of knowledge? Did they sense that analytic responsibility in the hot and dusty tropics had to own up a new political responsibility? They both did not and did.

Manifestly, they did not react at all to the colonial psychology of Berkeley-Hill and Daly. To the first generation of Indian psychoanalysts, such politically loaded cultural interpretations were not uncommon and they blended with the dominant tone of the humanities and social sciences at Indian universities; Berkeley-Hill and Daly would not have appeared particularly vicious or scathing. Also, the Indians attracted to analysis were themselves searching for new modes of social criticism that would make sense to their community; they were themselves given to provocative and arrogant psychoanalytic summary trials of the Indian culture and personality. To them their British colleagues were probably merely two slightly overenthusiastic white associates of Bose having their fling at the psychoanalysis of Indian culture. After all, in Bose's circle their formal status though high was not formidable.

But psychoanalysts, too, have their unconscious. During the early years of the Indian Psychoanalytic Society, one member of the Society did an imaginary portrait of Freud, not having seen the master nor even a photograph of him. This portrait, a near-perfect test of projection, was, appropriately enough, gifted to Freud. Freud was pleased, but complained in a letter that he looked a perfect Englishman in the portrait.[32] None pointed out

[32] Sigmund Freud to Lou Andreas-Salome, 13 March 1922, in Ernst Pfeiffer

to the ageing pâtriarch the analytic implications of his casual remark and the political tragedy that lay unarticulated in it.

Some questions, however, still remain unanswered. Were Berkeley-Hill and Daly merely tropical extensions of the arrogantly international, 'universal' culture of knowledge of which psychoanalysis was trying to be a part? Or were they adapting to the stress induced by the colonial situation with the help of existing psychoanalytic categories and by seeking sanction from the acceptance of psychoanalysis by some 'learned Hindus', as Freud described them?[33] Were Bose's attempts to locate psychoanalysis in the Vedantic tradition and giving it a distinct non-progressivist language an unintended response to the colonial psychoanalysis of his two white colleagues and the social evolutionism implicit in the dominant culture of psychoanalysis?[34] Is it coincidental that some methodological comments in his *Purāṇa Praveśa* read like a direct response to Berkeley-Hill's interpretive style? Was it significant that both British psychoanalysts had a record of mental illness and therapy under Jones? Were they both 'infected' with the hard-boiled social evolutionism and positivism of Jones and the 'imperious', 'opinionated', 'spiteful' aspects of his self?[35] Did they pick up from Jones his fear of ideas, metaphysics and, above all, the fear of a reading of psychoanalysis that would allow one to turn the discipline upon itself? Or was the problem deeper and did it begin with Freud himself? I shall attempt an indirect answer to a few of these questions later in this essay.

Berkeley-Hill and Daly did not define entirely the culture of psychoanalysis in India. Other psychoanalysts were also to leave their mark on the history of psychiatry and psychology, though in different ways. Tarun Chandra Sinha was one of the pioneers of psychoanalytic anthropology in India; Haripada Maiti and

---

(ed.), *Sigmund Freud and Lou Andreas-Salome Letters*, trs. W. Robson-Scott and E. Robson Scott (New York: Harcourt, Brace and Jovanovich, 1972), p. 114, quoted in Hartnack, *Psychoanalysis and Colonialism*, p. 1. One wonders if this is the same portrait that the well-known illustrator Jatindra Kumar Sen did of Freud.

[33] Ibid.

[34] Bose claimed to be a Vedantist, even though he reportedly helped his wife in her *pujā* or worship, Sinha, 'A Short Life Sketch', p. 69.

[35] Paul Roazen, *Freud and His Followers* (London: Allen Lane, 1976), pp. 345–6.

Pars Ram were to be associated with the founding of major institutions of psychoanalysis and psychology at Patna, Ahmedabad and Lahore; Bhupen Desai contributed handsomely to the growth of psychoanalysis in Bombay; Suhrit C. Mitra and S. K. Bose became central to the growth of professional psychology in the country. Two of the most important pioneering figures in the Indian social sciences and humanities were also in the psychoanalytic movement: Nirmal Kumar Bose, in later life the doyen of social anthropology in the country, and Debiprasad Chattopadhyay, who was to make signal contributions to the philosophy and history of science in India. Others like Rangin Halder and Sarasilal Sarkar made crucial inputs into Bengali cultural life. Many of them were not merely Bose's students, the imprint of Bose's intellectual and clinical concerns carried over into their work, including some of the limitations of Bose's distinctive style of psychoanalysis. Of his students and trainees, Sinha, who had had psychological problems and had been Bose's analysand, was to prove particularly dynamic organizationally. He used his therapeutic experience creatively to become a talented psychoanalyst and a gifted institution-builder, enabling psychoanalysis to be a continuing presence in Bengali social life after Bose's death.

Through Freud and Ernest Jones, then the president of the International Psychoanalytic Association, the Indian Society soon got affiliated to the international brotherhood of psychoanalysis. And Bose joined two others, Freud himself and August Aichhorn, as one of the only three psychoanalysts ever to be recognized as psychoanalysts on the basis of his self-analyses. Bose remained president of the Indian Psychoanalytic Society till his death in 1953.

It is not easy to judge Bose's contribution as the founding father of the Indian Psychoanalytic Society. One gets differing assessments of him as an ideologue, organizational man and as a person. Some say he was indiscriminate in his admissions policy and overeager to spread psychoanalysis to all corners of India. Others point out that he never had many trainees, and that many dropped out in any case. However, there are two things about which one can be more certain.

First, the formal requirements of psychoanalysis were often diluted for organizational and logistic reasons in India, so that the technical aspects of psychoanalysis remained underdeveloped. This may not have been entirely a tragedy. The underemphasis on technique allowed psychoanalysis to retain the potentiality (never actually realized) of becoming something more than an Indian subsidiary of a multinational professional corporation.

Second, as a pioneer in matters of the mind and as an organizational innovator, Bose showed remarkable ideological tolerance. He was a difficult person and, according to one of his students, a relatively self-contained man of knowledge. It is doubtful if for him psychoanalysis was an ideological movement with a core of inviolable dogma. He used to say, an associate remembers, that psychoanalysis was a medical system like ayurveda or homeopathy; it worked with some people, while other systems worked better with others. Others mention that Bose never pushed psychoanalysis with his students of psychology and his own psychological theories with his analytic trainees or colleagues.

This non-ideological stance was mirrored in Bose's politics, or non-politics. Psychoanalysis became established in India at politically tumultuous times, when Gandhi was emerging as the new leader of the anti-imperialist movement, displacing both moderate and extremist leaders. Among those being threatened by such displacement and facing political demise were the entire old leadership of Bengal, with their base mainly among the Hindu middle classes and the cities. Before their very eyes politics had become mass politics, bypassing them to reach into India's sleepy villages. Even in the metropolitan cities, the political atmosphere was no longer what it had been only five years earlier. Though there is some controversy among those who knew Bose about his response to Gandhi, he probably did believe that Gandhi represented the 'well-sublimated', rational, healthy personality.[36] Otherwise, but for a vague patriotism,

---

[36] Debiprasad Chattopadhyay believes that Bose was a *nisthāvāna* or loyal Gandhian; others like Bijayketu Bose and Charuchandra Bhattacharya strongly disagree. An indirect but important clue to Girindrasekhar's attitude to Gandhi is in Rajsekhar Bose's futuristic, comic fantasy, '*Gāmāṇus Jātir Kathā*', in *Galpakalpa* (Calcutta: M.C. Sarkar,1950), pp. 1–19. The fantasy lends indirect support to Chattopadhyay, rather than to Bose and Bhattacharya. On the other hand,

Bose remained quite apolitical throughout his life. Even that patriotism was, according to some, methodologically open. He was never particularly enamoured of political movements or the nitty-gritty of politics.

This apolitical attitude might have underwritten the low salience of the cultural-critical aspects of the new science in India, but it allowed Bose to hold the loyalty of a wide variety of young enthusiasts belonging to diverse ideological strains, ranging from Indra Sen, one of the first transpersonal psychologists of our times and later on a prominent mystic at the Pondicherry Ashram, to Debiprasad Chattopadhyay, then a budding radical philosopher of science, apart from being a practising psychoanalyst. The latter, however, did have to bear Bose's aggressive interpretation of the Oedipal roots of Marxism.[37] Probably Bose's belief that psychoanalysis was primarily a method helped him to be ideologically open; he expected methods to have limitations and to be controversial. (Apparently the Indian Psychoanalytic Society failed to retain its intellectual catholicity after Bose's death. Chattopadhyay was excommunicated soon after his mentor died as his Bengali book, *Freud Prasange*, an early Marxist interpretation influenced by the likes of John Somerville and Joseph Needham, was found too critical of Freud, though it was less so than many works produced later by pillars of the psychoanalytic establishment. *Freud Prasange* paid handsome tribute to Freud's method and accepted it fully but faulted the master on his philosophical assumptions. The tribute did not help Chattopadhyay; he was expelled all the same. After Bose's death, a stylistic similarity appears to have developed between the psychoanalytic movements in India and the West.

Bhupen Desai, himself a Gandhian and from a family of Gandhian freedom fighters that has made major sacrifices for the Gandhian cause, remembers the touch of sarcasm with which Bose once talked about Gandhian asceticism. Desai believes that Bose, though he admired Gandhi, rejected the Gandhian attitudes to sexuality and the *varna* system.

[37] Chattopadhyay recounts his debate with Bose on the subject. It seems he once asked Bose why, if Bose was so keen on an Oedipal explanation of communism and the indigenous 'terrorist' movement, he exempted Gandhi from it, even though Gandhi also had risen against authority. Bose's reply was that Gandhi had been effective because of his rationality and his cool, dispassionate, efficacious politics. This conversation seemingly confutes Bijayketu Bose's belief in the methodological openness of his uncle's politics.

Both shared the same internal contradiction when it came to dissent—limited theoretical tolerance with unlimited organizational intolerance.)

It says something about Bose's organizational skills that, unlike its western counterparts, the Indian Psychoanalytic Society quickly acquired a sound financial base. Once when the parent body was in financial trouble, the Indian branch sent it some money as a contribution. It is not known how his friend Berkeley-Hill reacted to such evidence of organizational ability, whether he attributed the trait to Bose's deviation from Hindu culture through self-analysis or to the persistence in him of Hindu anal-erotic style.

Bose himself, however, changed in the process of becoming a psychoanalyst and institutionalizing the new discipline, at least according to his wife. From being an 'energetic' and 'jolly' person he became a 'thoughtful' one.[38] He also, it appears, had different styles of management for the Indian Psychoanalytic Society and the Department of Applied Psychology of the Calcutta University, which he had headed since it was established in 1937. In the Society he was easy and egalitarian; in the university more paternalistic, socially withdrawn, and unwilling to share power. When Sinha says in his biographical note that Bose was considered stingy, impersonal and aloof, he was probably speaking of Bose in the university setting.[39] Some who knew him in the university find similarities between his style and that of his friends J. C. Bose, whom we have already mentioned, and P. C. Mahalanobis (1893–1972), the pioneer of modern statistics and development planning.

However, it was not the Society or the Department which ensured the early success of psychoanalysis in the metropolitan culture of India. It was Bose's own intellectual presence and, later, that of some of his talented students and admirers such as Tarun Chandra Sinha, Haripada Maiti, Pars Ram, Rangin Halder, Indra Sen. Bose's own intellectual range was formidable: he was chemist, Sanskritist, historian of ideas, experimental psychologist, doctor, teacher, artist, translator, and man of letters. In addition he wrote scholarly commentaries on sacred

---

[38] Sinha, 'A Short Life Sketch', p. 68.

[39] Ibid.

texts and was the author of a highly popular children's tale, *Lāl Kālo*, which included some lively poems and a drawing that could have adorned a Gothic horror story.[40] His very personality attracted some of the better young minds of metropolitan India. (Bose had a ready Freudian explanation of the careerism which did not allow the brightest of the Bengali youth, with a few exceptions, to come to psychoanalysis.)

This intellectual presence was underscored when the Indian Psychoanalytic Society belatedly brought out its journal, *Samiksha*, in 1947. The journal was an immediate success and its early days were the last few golden years of Indian psychoanalysis. Apart from Indians, the contributors included Geiza Roheim, David Rapaport, Clara Thompson, George Devereaux, Edmund Bergler, K. R. Eissler, Jules Masserman, and Fritz Wittels. Moving evidence of how seriously the journal was taken is a contribution by James Clark Moloney, who wrote from aboard a warship approaching Okinawa before one of the climactic battles of World War II.[41]

Bose was a gifted therapist, too, effecting cures that were nothing less than spectacular. His writings give the impression that he was overly didactic, in the sense in which the same expression is used by some of Erich Fromm's erstwhile colleagues to describe Fromm's therapeutic style. Such directness is said to have been not entirely alien to Freud's own therapeutic style, either.[42] It has also been said that Bose reinvoked the *guru–śiṣya* relationship in his analytic encounters.[43] Perhaps he did, but the result was dramatic therapeutic successes. As a

[40] Girindrasekhar Bose, *Lāl Kālo* (Calcutta: Indian Associated Publishing Co., 1956).

[41] James Clark Moloney, 'The Biospheric Aspects of Japanese Death by Suicide', *Samiksha*, 1949, *3*, pp. 104–24.

[42] Marie Jahoda, *Freud and the Dilemmas of Psychology* (London: Hogarth, 1977), p. 10.

[43] Sudhir Kakar, 'Stories From Indian Psychoanalysis: Context and Text', in James W. Stigler, Richard A. Shweder, and Gilbert Herdt (eds.), *Cultural Psychology* (New York: Cambridge University, 1990), pp. 427–45. On the *guru–sīṣya* relationship as a possible model for therapeutic work, the best-known paper is J. S. Neki's 'Guru-Chela Relationship: The Possibility of a Therapeutic Paradigm', *American Journal of Orthopsychiatry*, 1973, *43*, pp. 755–66.

result, by the time he was in his late forties, he had become for the urban Indian a legendary doctor of the mind.

This directness, however, also introduced into Indian psychoanalysis a theoretical twist. Therapy was viewed primarily as a cognitive venture, involving the acquisition of knowledge or information, and only secondarily as a matter of rearrangement or reinterpretation of emotions. His success as a therapist suggests that he may have deviated from this view in practice, but the view did influence and, according to some, lowered the standard of analytic training in India.

As a person, Bose was, like many successful clinicians, a bundle of contradictions. Since many of those who knew him belonged to the fraternity of psychoanalysts, he also comes off as a depot of neurotic symptoms. Some remember his pronounced orality—his love for food, cooking and the spoken word; his language skills; and his emphasis on the core fantasy of the split mother, what Sudhir Kakar calls the 'hegemonic myth' of Indian culture. Others remember Bose's long struggle with the hypertension that finally killed him. (The concern with the fantasy of the split mother has proved particularly resilient. From Berkeley-Hill, Daly, Philip Spratt and G. Morris Carstairs, to John Hitchcock, Leigh Mintern, Monisha Roy, Susan Wadley, Kakar, and Alan Roland—a wide range of social scientists influenced by psychoanalysis, including this writer, have returned to the myth with the feeling of making a new and important discovery.[44] They have been strengthened in their belief by a galaxy of Indian writers and artists, myth-makers in general,

---

[44] Berkeley-Hill, 'The "Colour Question"'; Claud D. Daly, 'Hindu Treatise on Kali', *Samiksha*, 1947, 1(2), pp. 191–6; Philip Spratt, *Hindu Culture and Personality* (Bombay: Manaktalas, 1966); G. Morris Carstairs, *The Twice Born: Study of a Community of High-Caste Hindus* (London: Hogarth, 1957); J. Hitchcock and Leigh Mintern, 'The Rajputs of Khalapur', in Beatrice Whiting (ed.), *Six Cultures* (New York: John Wiley, 1963), pp. 203–361; Monisha Roy, *Bengali Woman* (Chicago: University of Chicago, 1975); Susan Wadley, *Shakti: Power in the Conceptual Structure of Karimpur Religion* (Chicago: University of Chicago, 1975); Sudhir Kakar, *The Inner World: A Psychoanalytic Study of Childhood and Society in India* (Delhi: Oxford University Press, 1978); Alan Roland, *In Search of Self in India and Japan: Toward a Cross-Cultural Psychology* (Princeton, N.J.: Princeton University, 1988); Ashis Nandy, *At the Edge of Psychology: Essays in Politics and Creativity and Authenticity in Two Indian Scientists* (New Delhi: Oxford University Press, 1995).

who have regularly reinvoked the fantasy of a partitioned mother in their creative works and autobiographies.[45])

Most remember Bose's obsessive-compulsive ways—the meticulous records, the orderly minutes, the spotlessly white, immaculately starched Bengali dress that was virtually his uniform, the frugality and—as with many nineteenth-century Indians exposed to the western concept of time and seeking to overcorrect for the perceived Indian overemphasis on 'timelessness'—the fanatic devotion to punctuality. The frugality was of a special kind; it went with much wasteful expenditure to ensure order and cleanliness. For his small family he had a retinue of twelve to fourteen domestic servants and his wardrobe included, one student claims, at least eighty dhotis. His orderliness influenced his taste in music: he liked *dhrupada* with its austere, orderly, rigid frame and not the flamboyant *khayāl* with its greater emphasis on fluidity and imagination.[46] He recognized these traits in himself; he once bluntly told his trainee Desai, 'I am obsessive-compulsive'.

Whether the orderliness interfered with his own creativity or not, he retained a sharp sensitivity throughout his life to the obsessive-compulsive traits of his students and analysands. Remarkable stories are told about how he would leave coins scattered about on his desk and draw diagnostic conclusions from the way some of his visitors and students handled them. Indian psychoanalysis inherited this sensitivity; some of the most fascinating work on individual cases and cultural patterns in India centres around the analysis of the same psychopathology.

Others remember livelier scenes. Debiprasad Chattopadhyay remembers Bose washing with an antiseptic lotion the goat to be eaten at his daughter's wedding. Charuchandra Bhattacharya remembers how he went, armed with a stop-watch, from Bose's home to the Howrah railway station on two successive days, once without and once with luggage, as a rehearsal for Bose's planned

---

[45] Kakar has recently related this myth to the difference between Bose and Freud on gender psychology. Bose believed that the acceptance of the maternal–feminine component by Indian males in themselves made them less prone to castration anxiety and hence psychologically healthier. Sudhir Kakar, *Intimate Relations: Exploring Indian Sexuality* (New Delhi: Viking, 1989), Ch. 7.

[46] Sinha, 'A Short Life Sketch', pp. 68–9.

train journey the following day. Desai remembers Bose saying once that for his holidays at Deoghar in Bihar, he had calculated beforehand all the possible expenses, including that of the wear and tear of his car tyres. Many speak of the twelve goats that Bose purchased for his nephew Bijayketu's marriage feast being fed on gram to make their meat more tender. Though he planned the marriage and marriage reception with meticulous care, he could not attend the actual ceremony, because he had to go to bed at his usual hour, at exactly 8 p.m. All this contributed to the myth.

There might have been a weightier reason, too, for Bose's emergence as an important cultural figure in Bengal. Bose turned to psychoanalysis at a time when the traditional social relationships that took care of most of the everyday problems of living—the neuroses and less acute forms of psychosis—were breaking down in urban India. These relationships and the worldview that informed them were being replaced by a new network of social relationships sanctioning a new set of 'superstitions'—constructions of mental illness derived from remnants of traditional ideas of lunacy and available scraps of modern psychiatric knowledge. The first victims of this change were the psychologically afflicted; they were no longer seen as aberrant individuals deserving a place within the family and the community, but as diseased and potentially dangerous waste products of the society. As Bijayketu Bose puts it, the shock-absorbing capacities of the society had declined considerably at the time. And as a Michel Foucault or a Ronald Laing might have said, the dialogue between sanity and insanity had broken down; the society was now dominated by a monologue of sanity.

Girindrasekhar Bose took it upon himself to attack these perceptions and to offer the mentally ill a more humane treatment and voice. In 1933, he established India's first psychiatric out-patient clinic in Calcutta's Carmichael Medical College and Hospital. In 1948, on the initiative of Sinha and partly financed by Rajsekhar Bose, the Indian Psychoanalytic Society established a hospital and research centre at Calcutta's Lumbini Park. In 1949, Bose founded a school for small children organized on psychoanalytic lines.

A word on the early impact of psychoanalysis on urban India

in contrast to that on Europe and North America, may be appropriate at this point. Freud's explosive emergence on the European intellectual scene had shattered the Victorian world image. That image, as Carl Jung once pointed out, was not merely a feature of Anglo-Saxon societies but of much of Protestant Europe, though on the continent 'it never received such an appropriate epithet'. Along with that image went a concept of bourgeois respectability built on attempts to artificially keep alive through repression a set of anaemic ideals. These ideals were, Jung felt, remnants of the collective ideals of the middle ages, badly damaged by the French Enlightenment.[47]

When Freud challenged this respectability, he seemed to flout the basic tenets of social decency and challenge the moral universe of nineteenth-century Europe that framed and 'stabilized' everyday culture after the disruptions and uprooting brought about by the industrial revolution. In this stabilization, along with the concepts of the nation-state and progress, a central role had been played by the concept of scientific rationality, viewed as a tool of knowledge and power but serving in fact as a moral fulcrum. The concept might have been thrown up by the Enlightenment but ensured now, independently, a certain moral continuity and social sanction. By invoking this concept of rationality and hitching it to the newly dominant philosophy of individualism, Freud sought to legitimize a new concept of self that would accommodate a rediscovered, previously disowned underside of the self—a 'more real self' operating according to principles the 'apparent self' knew nothing about or rejected as immoral.[48] The Victorians could neither ignore nor swallow them.

Freud's ideas were much less controversial in India. He might have viewed himself as one of those who disturbed the sleep of the world, but he did not disturb many Indians even in their waking hours. Only small sections of the Indian middle classes had deeply internalized Victorian moral codes. Even fewer were exposed to the Victorian social norms relating to sexuality—

---

[47] C. G. Jung, 'Sigmund Freud in His Historical Setting', in Frank Cioffi (ed.), *Freud: Modern Judgement* (London: Macmillan, 1973), pp. 49–56; see pp. 49–50.

[48] Cf. Roland, *In Search of Self*, esp. Chs. 1 and 2, for insights into the comparative impact of psychoanalysis in India, Japan, and the West.

among them, objections to psychoanalysis were often strong and impassioned. Many of them saw Bose's love for psychoanalysis as a moral betrayal and the content of psychoanalysis as dirty. (For instance, one well-known Bengali writer, Saradindu Bandopadhyaya, in one of his plays compared the Freudian to a pig enjoying itself in a sewer. And Debiprasad Chattopadhyay's father stopped sending money to Debiprasad when he found that his college-going son had purchased Freud's works with this money. Such hostility was not widespread. Only a Marxist outfit named after Ivan Pavlov kept up the barrage till the late 1950s by rejecting psychoanalysis as being bourgeois and pornographic.)

Otherwise, Indian academics did not find Freud's ideas particularly wicked. Psychoanalysis might not have made much headway in India as a discipline, but the opposition to it could hardly be called frenzied. Most Indians, perhaps even most Indian psychoanalysts, would have been perplexed by Freud's famous statement to Jung on their way to Clark University as their ship approached New York harbour in 1909, 'They don't realize we're bringing them the plague'.[49] Why this indifference?

The easy answer is that there was both a casual unconcern with the content of the discipline and a widely felt need for an updated, reasonably holistic theory of mental illness in urban India. The need was strong enough for many to ignore the actual content of psychoanalysis. While this might on the whole be true, there is also a less pleasant answer. The bourgeois respectability that Freud attacked and which paradoxically defined him–the way industrial capitalism defines trade unionism—came to colonial India as part of the West's cultural baggage, intertwined with other forms of respectability. But these other forms—colonialism itself, secularization, scientism, individualism and impersonalization of social relationships are four examples that immediately come to mind—were rarely targets of the social criticism psychoanalysis offered in the southern world. As a result, psychoanalysis was bound gradually to look like another tame professional enterprise, another of those many new sciences being imported by westernized Indians, rather than as a critical, subversive presence. For a discipline that

---

[49] Douglas Kirsner, 'Is there a Future for American Psychoanalysis?', *The Psychoanalytic Review*, 1990, 77, pp. 176–200, see p. 197.

was 'double-edged'—both a means of exploring the human mind and a means of avoiding such exploration—this could not but lead to loss of selfhood.[50] Let me spell out the first and easier answer here because it relates directly to Bose's life. I shall return to the second answer at the end.

It was from Bengal that the British empire had started expanding after the Battle of Plassey in 1757. Bengal was the region where colonial intrusion was the deepest and the most disruptive in South Asia. Calcutta was not only the capital of British India, it was the second largest city in the empire and probably the liveliest marketplace of ideas from the East and the West in the world. Already some modern institutions—such as those providing western education and law—had entered the interstices of Bengali society and created a flourishing westernized middle class that sustained a variety of cultural forms, neither exclusively western nor Indian. From theatre to food, from family dynamics to sports, and from dress to style of scholarship, every area of middle-class life in Bengal carried the imprint of the West.

Living in two worlds is never easy, and the new middle class in Bengal had lived for decades with deculturation, the breakdown of older social ties, and disruption of traditional morality. In response to these, the class had even produced a series of highly creative social thinkers and reformers who sought to design new worldviews and new moral visions for fellow-Indians.

As it happened, none of these reformers had directly addressed the psychological problems thrown up by the breakdown of social ties and cultural uprooting. There had been indirect efforts to grapple with such problems in literature, social criticism and theology; there were even the rudiments of new social and political theories sensitive to them. But there was as yet no new theory of consciousness, no new culturally rooted, self-assured theory of modern individuality and subjectivity. Modern Bengal and for that matter urban India, were waiting for a theory of personality and selfhood to explain the psychological forces by which they were being buffeted.

This was the need Bose attempted to meet with the help of

---

[50] Ibid.

psychoanalysis. There might also have been a vague awareness in him that the sectoral, one-dimensional approach of the various schools of conventional academic psychology could not really cope with the psychological problems of Indian society or establish a durable link with Indian traditions. Psychoanalysis with its complex, holistic approach to the human personality—with its invocation of the person as a thinking, feeling, driven individual—at least allowed one to reinterpret its interpretations and to adapt them to the complexities of Indian society. To turn the discipline on itself, psychoanalysis could allow itself to be used as a projective medium for parts of Indian society, while being simultaneously used as a critique of that society.

It was this possibility of the young discipline that Bose exploited, and it was this possibility that gave it its early start in India. Even Freud, no stranger to theoretical speculations, was impressed by the vivacity and intellectual power of the first Indian psychoanalyst and recognized the Indian's philosophical acumen. On receiving *Concept of Repression*, he wrote:

> It was a great and pleasant surprise that the first book on a psychoanalytic subject which came to us from that part of the world should display so good a knowledge of psychoanalysis, so deep an insight into its difficulties and so much deep going original thought ... [the author] is aiming at a philosophical evolution ... of our crude, practical concepts, and I can only wish psychoanalysis should soon reach upto the level to which he [Bose] strives to raise it.[51]

Of course, there was a touch of politics in Freud's enthusiasm and, later, that of Ernest Jones, who reviewed Bose's book in the *International Journal of Psychoanalysis.*[52] Both were happy to see psychoanalysis spread to India when it was still beleaguered in Europe and North America. Hence also Freud's emphasis, in a letter to Lou Andreas-Salome, on the fact that most members of the newly founded Indian Psychoanalytic Society were 'learned Hindus', not white expatriates or semi-literate native dilettantes.[53] Its cultivated Indian converts gave psychoanalysis, apart from ethnic colour, the semblance of cross-cultural validity.

---

[51] Freud to Bose, 20 February 1922, in 'Correspondence', *10*, p. 108.

[52] Ernest Jones, 'Review of *Concept of Repression*', *International Journal of Psychoanalysis*, 1921, *2*, p. 453.

[53] Freud to Andreas-Salome, p. 1.

However, there might also have been in Freud's and Jones's views a mix of awe and ambivalence that Bose spanned so effortlessly the worlds of psychoanalysis, philosophy, and cultural tradition. Certainly Jones, nurtured in the heady atmosphere of Anglo-Saxon positivism, might have found Bose's speculative bent of mind a bit of a trial. Jones needed, he himself said, 'the sense of security which the pursuit of truth gives'—in this instance, the certitudes produced by science—and he lived in an intellectual atmosphere in which Bertrand Russell was soon to call J. B. Watson the greatest scientist after Aristotle and compare the ultra-behaviourist with Charles Darwin.[54] For Jones, as for James Strachey, even Freud's cultural origins were an 'eccentricity' rather than a 'living factor in his life' and all religions were superstitions.[55] But then, Jones also had a more mundane reason to tolerate Bose's flirtation with philosophy. In another few years, he would want to make the British Society the regulating psychoanalytic body for the British empire, with the societies in the colonies functioning as subordinate groups. Bose's support in this venture might have been seen as vital.[56]

Freud, on the other hand, was brought up in an intellectual culture in which the pedagogic split between philosophy and science had not ossified. It was typical of the 'temperamental differences' between Jones and Freud, Roazen says, 'that whereas the former feared religion's anti-naturalism, the latter was more afraid of the dangers of medicine's scientific materialism'.[57] Freud could not but be intrigued by Bose's daring. Though he claimed to steer clear of philosophy, Freud was nevertheless impressed by it; it was with some difficulty that he kept his interest in metapsychology in check.[58]

Neither this support from Freud nor its precocious growth and cultural distinctiveness saved Indian psychoanalysis from

---

[54] Ernest Jones, *Free Associations: Memories of a Psychoanalyst* (London: Hogarth, 1959), p. 63; also David Cohen, *J. B. Watson—The Founder of Behaviourism: A Biography* (London: Routledge, 1979).

[55] Roazen, *Freud and His Followers*, p. 347.

[56] Ibid., p. 346.

[57] Ibid., pp. 354–5. Roazen bases himself on a letter of Ernest Jones to Sigmund Freud, 10 January 1933 (Jones Archives).

[58] On Freud's ambivalent attempts to distance himself from philosophy, see Section IV below.

exhaustion within a few decades. So much so that Alan Roland has recently asked why psychoanalysis developed so early in India, and why it has not grown there as it has, for instance, in America or even France since the late 1960s.[59] Roland gives the answer at two planes. He notes the ease with which a theory of the unconscious can be integrated within a culture demanding 'extraordinary interpersonal sensitivity' from those living in extended families and other traditional groupings as well as the 'highly particularistic emphasis on a person's development through the combination of their qualities (*gunas*), power (*śakti*), effects of familial and individual actions (*karma*), and attachments (*samaskāras*) carried over from past lives'.[60] Roland's answer to the second part of the question is sociocultural and it supplements what has already been said about the non-controversial impact of psychoanalysis on Indian society. Comparing India with the western developed societies, Roland speaks of the 'deconversion' that has taken place from the belief systems and symbols of the traditional communities in the West and of the shift to a culturally less integrated society that shares only the symbols of science and where each individual must create his worldview of symbols and meaning.[61] The individual has been thrown back upon himself or herself in the West; not in India.

In other words, the factors which gave vibrancy to psychoanalysis in its early years in India may also have handicapped it as a vocation. The individuation that has taken place in the West remains in India the characteristic of a small proportion of the society. Psychoanalysis as a therapeutic technique in such circumstances has to remain a matter of cognitive choice; it cannot resonate with the private search for self-definition or a theory of life for the majority of Indians. In a paper on the early years of psychoanalysis, Kakar says: 'Cut off from the thrust and parry of debate, controversy and ferment of the psychoanalytic centres in Europe, dependent upon not easily available books and journals for outside intellectual sustenance, Indian psychoanalysis was nurtured through its infancy primarily by the enthusiasm and intellectual passion of its progenitor.'[62]

---

[59] Roland, *In Search of Self*, p. 57.

[60] Ibid. [61] Ibid., p. 58.

[62] Kakar, *Stories From Indian Psychoanalysis*.

Probably it was. Probably, for the same reason, psychoanalysis in India never grew spectacularly as a clinical discipline. In a culture in which complex, often ornate, theories of consciousness of both right- and left-handed kinds were an important component, psychoanalysis had neither enough philosophical punch as a theory of the person threatening to supersede all other theories of the person, nor did it carry a strong enough impress of the evil and the smutty (in a society that treated the *Kāmasūtra* as a sacred text) to become the subject of a highly charged moral debate on the nature of the human mind. Psychoanalysis rather quietly became the best-known school of western psychology in India, controversial but not particularly live politically.

Christiane Hartnack says that 'the reception of psychoanalysis in British India varied from outright rejections of Freud's concepts as inappropriate for Indian conditions to unquestioned transfers.'[63] Actually, the 'outright rejections' here means in most cases nothing more dramatic than a certain unconcern. Only a few pages later, Hartnack is surprised at the public response to Rangin Halder's paper on the Oedipus complex in Rabindranath Tagore's poetry:

> Halder's attempt[s] to demystify the writings of this celebrity, the first Indian Nobel prize winner, who was seen as a kind of national hero in his country, do not seem to have caused any negative reaction from the Bengali side.[64]

So much so that Halder presented the same paper a few years later to a wider audience at the Indian Science Congress—this time in English.

One reason for such 'tolerance' was public ignorance about Bose's worldview. Bose was not popularly known to the urban middle classes of India as a psychoanalyst, though that is usually what he called himself. Most Indians knew him as a doctor of the mind. They were relatively unconcerned (*udāsīna* is the expression Bijayketu uses) about psychoanalysis. Girindrasekhar himself, as we shall see below, may have been obsessive about many things, but not about the purity of psychoanalytic concepts, their philosophical roots in western thought, or about the therapeutic

[63] Hartnack, 'Psychoanalysis and Colonialism', p. 151.

[64] Ibid., pp. 161–2.

tradition being built in Europe by the Freudian movement. Nor did he stress that psychoanalysis was unique as a school of psychology.

Was psychoanalysis, then, merely an artefact in urban India's attempts to explore its own soul? Was it severely refracted through and, hence, incidental to Bose's personal quest for selfhood as a healer? That, too, is doubtful. It says something about the science that Bose, already exposed to a wide range of eastern and western options—from Patañjali's *Yogasūtra* to academic psychiatry to behaviourism and experimental psychology—should have chosen to call himself a psychoanalyst. Somewhere, at some plane, the discipline's concerns and implicit social-critical thrust had crossed the boundaries of culture, though not in the sense in which its Viennese founder's Eurocentric worldview would have it.

On the other hand, one must hasten to add that Freud's Eurocentrism, too, had its in-built checks. The most conspicuous of them was his concern with the future of psychoanalysis. He did want the discipline to cross cultural barriers and become a truly international movement; when faced with a choice, therefore, the old war-horse did try to create a space for Bose's concerns within the mainstream of psychoanalysis. Perhaps in the case of Bose he was spared some of the anxieties that dogged his relationships with his European followers. Certainly in his treatment of Bose's work there was no reflection of the 'tragic flaw' in Freud's personality to which Peter Rudnytsky has again recently drawn our attention.[65] But that tolerance of Bose by the founding father of psychoanalysis had its own limits:

> After corresponding with Bose and confronting his publications,... Freud could no longer easily defend his claims for the universality of his concepts. Confronted with Bose's deviant theory, Freud considered working aspects of Bose's concepts into his system. He evidently intended to functionalize Bose's contribution like some kind of intellectual raw material, and to incorporate them into his own theory, not realizing that these were based on an entirely different conceptual system.[66]

---

[65] Peter L. Rudnytsky, 'A Psychoanalytic Weltanschauung', *The Psychoanalytic Quarterly*, 1992, *79*, pp. 289–305.

[66] Hartnack, 'Psychoanalysis and Colonialism', p. 192.

PART TWO: THE MORALITY OF PSYCHOLOGY

III *The Relegitimation*

The compliment from Freud notwithstanding, Bose's English papers on the range and concerns of psychology, especially psychoanalysis, lack something of the philosophical imagination and elegance of his Bengali papers on the same subject. The reasons for this are not clear. Perhaps he was less at ease in English than in Bengali, being more self-conscious and aware of an international audience when he wrote in English. It is even possible that in Bengali he could more openly reconcile Indian classical traditions and the science of psychoanalysis, not as two distinct cognitive orders but as two aspects of his own self. Thus, while 'The Aim and Scope of Psychology' (1932) and 'A New Theory of Mental Life' (1933) are both competent and fresh, one misses in them the touches of theoretical daring born of cultural self-confidence that one finds in some of his Bengali papers.[1]

Both papers introduce the reader to the broad disciplinary framework within which he, the first non-western psychoanalyst, worked and the conceptual boundaries of his depth psychology. 'The Aim and the Scope' specifically seeks to create a legitimate place for psychology in the world of knowledge by anticipating and resisting attacks on the infant discipline on three fronts. First, the paper rejects as invalid the behaviourist approach in psychology, for behaviourists deny the existence of mind on the grounds that mind cannot be perceived without the intervention of matter. Bose considers the denial analogous to a physicist's rejection of the existence of matter on the grounds that matter cannot be 'seen' without the intervention of mind.[2] Second, the paper tries to reclaim from physiology terrain that rightfully belongs to psychology. Bose rejects attempts to reduce psychology to the functioning of the brain and the nervous system:

[1]Girindrasekhar Bose. 'The Aim and Scope of Psychology', *Indian Journal of Psychology*, July–Aug. 1932, *9*, pp. 11–29; and 'A New Theory of Mental Life', *Indian Journal of Psychology*, 1933, *10*, pp. 37–157.

[2] Bose, 'The Aim and Scope', p. 13.

using the same arguments, one could then claim endocrinology was a branch of psychology. If changes in psychological states follow changes in the brain, glandular changes also follow from psychological changes. The paper obviously does not suffer from the positivist modesty which sometimes afflicted Freud. It does not even hint that in some distant future psychology would in effect become the biology of the mind.[3] Finally, the paper takes on 'the oldest claimant to the psychological terrain', philosophy. Here Bose is more tolerant, given his own bent of mind, and he makes his point with qualifications. 'I am quite willing to admit that philosophical studies afford an excellent discipline to the science students but I cannot understand why it should be tacked on to psychology alone and not to any other science such as physics.'[4]

The second paper recapitulates Girindrasekhar's once-popular theory of pan-psychic psychophysical parallelism, first propounded in *Concept of Repression*. Now entirely forgotten, the theory was at one time taken seriously in many circles. It also subtly influenced the course of his friend Jagadis Chandra Bose's vitalistic biophysics, which took the world of knowledge by storm in the inter-war years.[5] The theory has parallels with Freud's belief in his student days that 'the physiological processes of the brain and the psychological processes of the mind were not parallel and causally linked but, rather, were identical. They were one and the same thing apprehended by the scientist in two different ways: through external observation in the natural sciences and through inner perception in psychological investigation.'[6] 'A New Theory' is unlikely to impress even a sympathetic psychologist reading it in the 1990s; it is likely to interest only the historians of science. For though it is the work of a psychologist well-versed in and committed to the non-dualist Vedantic tradition, it can be read as only a plea for a dualist psychology rooted in the Vedanta. The dualism, however, is a

---

[3] Ibid., p. 14.

[4] Ibid., p. 16.

[5] See Nandy, *Alternative Sciences*, Part II.

[6] William J. McGrawth, *Freud's Discovery of Psychoanalysis: The Politics of Hysteria* (Ithaca and London: Cornell University Press, 1986), p. 18.

qualified one; it is set within the frame of a non-dualist vision and idiom.

In sum, while neither of the two papers reveals Bose's hand fully, both show that, unlike Freud and some of the early analysts, Bose made no attempt to underplay the philosophical and social meaning of the new science. Nor did he share Freud's belief that psychoanalytic therapy 'would be overtaken within half a century by biochemical therapies'.[7] On the contrary, he was not hesitant about making large claims for his discipline. 'We can look forward to the day', he grandly says at the end of 'The Aim and Scope', 'when Psychology [note the capital] will establish itself as our guide, friend and philosopher in all human affairs, and will be looked upon as the greatest of sciences.'[8]

In Bengali, Girindrasekhar Bose wrote voluminously and with enormous intellectual energy. (Most of these writings are now out of print and not easily available; some of his essays and important letters are lost.) The most remarkable feature of his Bengali writings is that, when on India's sacred texts and epics, they were often surprisingly unencumbered by his disciplinary faith. Thus, his *Purāṇa Praveśa*, a three-hundred-page tome on the Indian epics, is mainly a meticulous—some may say Teutonic—study of genealogy, a chronological dynastic history of the *purāṇas*, not a study of fantasies or defences.[9] There are, however, in the book fascinating comments on the politics of scholarship and the responsibility imposed on Indian commentators on the *purāṇas*. We shall touch on this later. Similarly, there is the low-key presence of psychoanalysis in his commentary on the Gita, as we have already noted. All this 'restraint' was observed at a time when the analysis of myths and religious texts had already become, thanks to Freud himself and to younger psychoanalysts like Ernest Jones and Geiza Roheim, an important and fashionable part of psychoanalysis and even in distant India some had experimented with such analysis.

---

[7] *Psychoanalysis and Faith: The Letters of Sigmund Freud and Oscar Pfister* (London: Hogarth, 1963), quoted in Jahoda, *Freud and the Dilemmas*, p. 10.

[8] Bose, 'The Aim and Scope', p. 29.

[9] Girindrasekhar Bose, *Purāṇa Praveśa* (Calcutta: M. C. Sarkar, 1934).

However, Bose did write a few perceptive essays in Bengali which help to link his reading of Indian culture to the Freudian theory of mental life. Unlike Berkeley-Hill and others who followed him, in these essays Bose did not use psychoanalysis solely to demystify Indian culture and everyday life or to bare the pathologies of western middle-class culture in the colonies. He also used Indian cultural categories to domesticate psychoanalysis for Indians. From this point of view, his two most important papers are: '*Sattva, Rajaḥ, Tamaḥ*' and '*Mānuṣer Mana*', both written in Bengali and published in 1930.[10] Some of the ideas in the essays were later included in his English works but they lacked the same directness. The first essay offers an understanding and justification of psychological knowledge in native terms, leading up to the Freudian tenet that the ego should ultimately supplant or supersede the id. The second extends the argument further and defines psychology as a science of persons, a personology, as Henry A. Murray might have described the venture.

Both papers depend on Indian classical texts and on a particular reading of India's past. The second dependence has however to be gleaned from Bose's other Bengali writings. Thus, from *Purāṇa Praveśa*, also written in 1933 though only published the following year, we come to know of Bose's conviction that foreign—read western—historians of India are bound to be partial. They cannot be fair to the Indian texts because they think of themselves as a superior race. To expect an impartial history of India from the *videśīs* or foreigners is, Bose says, the same as expecting the British to protect Indian self-interests in politics.[11] Bose tries to correct for such racist interpretations by proposing that the *purāṇas* are supported both by reason and empirical data.[12] There is no need to study the history of these epics, for they themselves are the Indian equivalent of history.[13]

Then, responding as it were to Berkeley-Hill, Bose mentions

---

[10] Girindrasekhar Bose, '*Sattva, Rajaḥ Tamaḥ*', *Pravāsī*, 1930, *30*, part 2(1), pp. 1–5; Girindrasekhar Bose, '*Mānuṣer Mana*', *Pravāsī*, Āsāḍ 1337 (1930), *30*, part 1(3), pp. 339–53.

[11] Ibid., p. 212.

[12] Ibid., pp. 1, 3.

[13] Ibid., p. 179.

the two kinds of exaggeration to which Hindus are allegedly given: the fantastic exaggerations in the *purāṇas* (*atiranjana*) and the exaggeration of the past achievements of their culture. As for the former, Bose believes that the stylized exaggerations of the *purāṇas* can be handled through *atyukti vicāra*, analysis of overstatement. It is a question of appropriate and empathetic reading of texts. Bose's response to the second issue is more political. He traces the hostility of western scholars to things Indian to two main causes. First, Indians, unlike the ancient Babylonians or Egyptians, have survived to flaunt their glorious past against their inglorious present status as colonial subjects.[14] This cannot but infuriate many westerners. Second, western scholars project into the Indian situation the enmity between Church and State existing in Europe. This makes them hostile to Hinduism and virulently anti-Brahminic.[15] Under such circumstances, given that the organizing principle of Indian culture has always been religion, any serious consideration of India's past cultural achievements is bound to look like an exaggeration.

'*Sattva, Rajaḥ, Tamaḥ*' discusses *guṇa*s (traits, attributes or qualities) in *prakṛti* or nature. The concept of *guṇa* is notoriously complicated and, some may say, slippery. The essay mentions in a footnote that even Max Müller found it difficult to understand the concept, but found Indian philosophers so clear about it that no explanation was needed.[16] The essay suggests that these qualities are of two kinds: *guṇa*s that control *ajñāna* or the absence of knowledge (in a person) and *aprakāśa* or the non-manifest (in nature) are classified as *tamaḥ*.

The second kind of *guṇa* controls *jñāna* or knowledge (in human personality) and the manifest (in nature). These *guṇa*s can, in turn, be of two types: *bahirmukha*, literally outer-directed or extroversive and *antarmukha*, inner-directed or introversive. The essay identifies the former as *rajaḥ*; and the latter as *sattva*.[17] Bose summarized his argument in the following manner:

---

[14] Ibid., pp. 212–13.

[15] Ibid.

[16] Max Müller, quoted in Bose, '*Sattva, Rajaḥ, Tamaḥ*', p. 3.

[17] Bose, '*Sattva, Rajaḥ, Tamaḥ*', p. 3.

Guṇas (attributes of nature)

↓

↓	↓
Which control knowledge (*jñāna*) and the manifested (*prakāśa*)	Which control ignorance (*ajñāna*) and the non-manifested (*aprakāśa*)
↓	↓

↓	↓	
introversive (*sattva*)	extroversive (*rajaḥ*)	(*tamaḥ*)

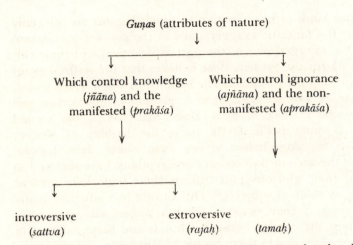

It is not clear whether Bose borrows the second-order dichotomy—between extroversion and introversion—from Carl Jung, who had published his work on personality types in 1923.[18] The work should have reached Calcutta by the time Bose wrote his essay in 1930. On the other hand, the impact of Jung on the first generation of Indian psychoanalysts was limited, despite the overlap between his theories and aspects of traditional Indian thought. This is surprising when one remembers that Bose and some of his associates were well-versed in traditional philosophy and should have found Jung especially attractive. As inexplicable seems the fact that, though Jung visited India in 1938 and it was a triumphant visit, Bose probably did not meet him.[19]

Were these measures of the loyalty of the Indian group to psychoanalytic orthodoxy, as Hartnack assumes?[20] Were Indian psychoanalysts repelled by Jung's inadequate knowledge of Indian traditions, as some of them were to later claim? Or did Freud meet some deeper needs in Indians, who were searching at the time not so much for in-house criticisms as for a critical theory adequately discontinuous with a psychologically minded culture and able to serve as a radical critique of it? Probably the latter; Jung probably was too close to India to serve as a base for

---

[18] Carl G. Jung, *Psychological Types* (New York: Harcourt Brace, 1923).

[19] Hartnack, 'Psychoanalysis and Colonialism', p. 93; Bose's student Charuchandra Bhattacharya says that Bose probably met Jung but did not have any extended exchange with him.

[20] Ibid.

social criticism or to avoid cultural incorporation of the kind Bose nearly brought off in the case of Freud. We shall come back to this point.

What emerges clearly is the hierarchy Bose imposes on the entire set of *guṇa*s. Like Freud, he believes that the unconscious and the non-manifest (together constituting the *tamaḥ*) represent an inferior level of personality functioning. Unlike Freud and Jung but like a true Hindu, Bose extends this hierarchy to extroversion and introversion. In his model, the extroverted or *rājasika* becomes inferior to the introverted, seen as definitionally more *sāttvika*.[21] However, the hierarchy has no social-evolutionist thrust, of the kind that permeates the work of psychologists such as Abraham Maslow. Nowhere does Bose imply that only after the basic needs of a person have been met can he or she graduate to introversion as part of a developmental profile.[22] As in Jung, the hierarchy remains in essence a classificatory scheme.

Bose goes on to say that the *ātmā* or self is *bhūmā* or all-pervasive; it pervades all nature.[23] Compared to *ātmā*, nature is narrower and more limited. And it is not so much the knowledge of self but the relationship between self and nature that is the stuff of genuine knowledge. The *śāstrakāra*s or writers of sacred texts in India were primarily concerned, according to Bose, with this relationship. For the knowledge of this relationship can be truly emancipatory.[24] I should emphasize that the few concepts verging on technical psychoanalytic terms in the paragraphs above are mine, not Bose's. The entire essay, though it provides an excellent indirect comparison between some aspects of the traditional Indian theory of the person and psychoanalysis, seems strangely oblivious of its own range. There is no direct mention of any psychoanalytic concept in the essay.

Bose offsets his typology of *guṇa*s with the proposition that

---

[21] Bose, '*Sattva, Rajaḥ, Tamaḥ*', p. 3.

[22] See a discussion of this issue in Ashis Nandy, 'The Idea of Development: The Experience of Modern Psychology as a Cautionary Tale', in Carlos Mallmann and Oscar Nudler (eds.), *Human Development in Its Social Context: A Collective Exploration* (London: Hodder and Stoughton, 1986), pp. 248–59.

[23] Bose, '*Sattva, Rajaḥ, Tamaḥ*', p. 3.

[24] Ibid.

awareness of—or encounter with—the self is the same as the awareness of the ultimate reality of being and God. In his scheme, the *ātmasākṣātkārī*, one who encounters one's own self, is automatically a *brahmasākṣātkārī*, one who encounters/confronts the absolute, and *atmajñāna* (self-knowledge) is *brahmajñāna* (knowledge of the absolute). One must, therefore, know *ātmā*; *ātmānam viddhi*, know thyself.[25]

Further, *antarmukha jñāna* or inner-directed knowledge is the knowledge of pure experience or awareness, whereas *bahirmukha jñāna* is material knowledge. 'From pure experience gradually grows pure knowledge.... In pure knowledge there is no plurality (*nānātva*). *Na iha nānāsti kiñcana*.'[26] This pure knowledge is self-knowledge and, therefore, knowledge of the absolute. It defines the nature of the soul. So the non-duality that is sacrificed for the sake of the mind–body duality in Bose's concept of psychology is restored at another plane. (Elsewhere, Bose equates pure consciousness with the state of *samādhi* as described in Patañjali's *Yogasūtra*.[27])

Obviously, Bose is here trying to locate contemporary psychology in the Indian experience and to legitimize the discipline as a natural outgrowth of traditional knowledge. As it happens, the space thus created for psychology also accommodates a heavily textual version of Advaita as the core of Indian consciousness. The psychologist is the ultimate scientist because he or she tries to look within. Psychology is *sāttvika*; so is the psychologist's work. The work of the psychiatrist and the psychotherapist, like that of the physicist and the chemist, is applied or instrumental and, hence, *rājasika*.[28] When counterpoised against Bose's formal emphasis on the therapeutics of psychoanalysis, this proposition makes strange reading. It is as if, after justifying psychoanalysis in terms of its *sāttvika* content, Bose is pleading for a less exalted *rājasika* role for it.

The second proposition of the essay is to define the individual

[25] Ibid.

[26] Ibid., pp. 3–4.

[27] Girindrasekhar Bose, quoted in Hartnack, 'Psychoanalysis and Colonialism', p. 98.

[28] Bose, '*Sattva, Rajaḥ, Tamaḥ*', p. 5.

as the ultimate unit of intellectual and, presumably, social analysis. Bose quotes from the *Kauṣītaki Upaniṣad:*

> Do not try to understand speech; try to understand the speaker. Do not try to know smell; try to know the smeller. Do not try to know beauty; try to know the beautician; do not try to understand words; try to understand the listener.... do not try to know the deed (*karma*); try to know the doer (*kartā*). Do not try to understand the mind; try to understand the thinker.[29]

As opposed to the first proposition, which is clearly identifiable with aspects of Vedantic thought, the second goes directly against some of the most influential readings of the Vedanta. For Bose does not emphasize essence or platonic quality; he emphasizes the carrier of the essence. One suspects that he needed this sanction for using the individual as the basic unit of analysis both as a psychologist and as an urban Indian being constantly exposed to a wide variety of new institutions ideologically wedded to individualism.

A few other propositions emerge from '*Mānuṣer Mana*' as by-products of Bose's unselfconscious attempt to break out of the regime of the positive sciences. Science has become a fashionable word, Bose says, and it is invoked as an 'explanation' even for magical episodes in the Indian epics and rituals by Indians defensively seeking to give the episodes some respectability in contemporary times. This is natural, Bose feels, for whenever a science becomes popular, it produces its counterpoint, an *apavijñana* (false or bad science).[30] To avoid the pitfalls of such cheap scientism, he justifies psychoanalysis, and psychology in general, in larger philosophical terms.

To Bose it is natural that psychology is a new science, the last science to crystallize as a separate discipline, for human beings are more interested in the outside world than in the inner.[31] According to the *Kaṭhopaniṣad*, God has created human beings as *bahirmukha*: our sense organs are oriented to externalities. A

---

[29] *Kauṣītaki Upaniṣad*, tr. Sitānāth Tattvabhuśaṇa, quoted in Bose, '*Sattva, Rajaḥ, Tamaḥ*', p. 4.

[30] Bose, '*Mānuṣer Mana*', pp. 339, 349.

[31] Ibid., p. 339.

few serene persons (*dhīravyakti*) very occasionally cross the barrier of attachment to the outside world, to face and examine the self. From the wishes of this minority arises the need for *ātmadarśana*. According to the sacred texts *ātmajñana* or self-knowledge is impossible unless the mind becomes inner-directed.[32]

> *Parāñcikhāni vyatṛnat svayambhūḥ*
> *Tasmāt parāk paśyati nāntarātman*
> *Kaściddhīrāḥ pratyagātmānamaikṣa-*
> *dāvṛtta cakṣuramṛtattvamicchan*

Hence the small number of psychologists in the world. Bose implies that most people, being extroverted, are driven by emotions like anger and fear; when angry and fearful, we do not examine the internal changes in us.[33]

In other words, from the point of view of the Hindu *śāstras*, psychology is the highest of the sciences.[34] The growth of psychology is not merely an expression of the intrinsic power of the Indian civilization but also a marker of the intellectual and cultural maturity of Indians. This growth has a disciplinary meaning, too. Bose believes that as a science develops, its boundaries are better defined. By defining the boundaries of psychology more clearly, he is helping the science to grow.[35]

'*Mānuṣer Mana*', a slighter essay, makes three other points. First, it relates psychological awareness to the study of sensibility and draws the readers' attention to the scientific works of Jagadis Chandra Bose which show that there can be sensibility even in inert objects. After Jagadis Chandra, to assert the presence of such sensibility is no longer a form of mysticism, the essay claims.[36] Second, there is an untearable (*acchedya*) chain of causality which ties together the entire material world.[37] This makes causality—presumably a scientific category—a special case of and intrinsic to the monistic vision of life. Third, at a more practical level, the essay affirms that the idea of the

---

[32] Ibid.

[33] Ibid.

[34] Ibid., p. 340.

[35] Ibid.

[36] Ibid., pp. 346–7.

[37] Ibid., p. 347.

unconscious unburdens the individual of the need to believe in superstitions such as ghosts. Acceptance of the unconscious does not secularize one's world, for the unconscious is not particularly incompatible with spirituality, but it cures one of pseudo-spirituality:

> Human beings usually try to attain happiness by extending their control over the external world. All the material sciences help men in this endeavour. The Hindu *śāstras* advise that there is no permanent happiness in external objects; genuine happiness comes from restraint over mind (*manaḥsanyama*). The serene person (*dhīraprajña*) is happy under all circumstances. To keep the mind under control, many advices/suggestions are given for rituals, institutions and asceticisms. Reduction of ignorance [unconscious?] is a way of attaining happiness and peace. The scientist of the unconscious (*nirjñānvit*) assures us that when the dammed instincts subside, the conflicts of mind dissolve and all sorrows are eliminated. Till now, the source of peace for the disturbed mind, tortured by mourning, anxiety, tiredness, lay in the moral lessons given by the religions. In this respect, the material scientist had to admit defeat at the hands of the religious preachers. Today, psychology, by offering human beings words of assurance and peace, has moved ahead to establish the dignity of science.[38]

Thus, the fate of the science of the unconscious, human happiness, and the dignity of science converge in the step-wise unravelling and transcendence of the *guṇa*s. According to the *śāstra*s, Bose acknowledges, all three *guṇa*s are hindrances to self-realization but, of the three, inner-directedness poses the least problem.[39] Ultimately though, he says, one must rise above one's attachment to the way—even when it is inner-directedness and even when it goes with the analytic attitude—to reach one's destination.[40] But, in the meanwhile, unravelling the *tāmasika guṇa*s by focusing on inner experiences must become an important part of the agenda of any worthwhile theory of consciousness. Psychology, when it establishes the dignity of science, is presumably no longer a positivist science, but science as a

[38] Ibid., p. 353.
[39] Ibid., p. 5.
[40] Ibid.

philosophy of consciousness. It emancipates science from its own strait-jacket, as Jagadis Chandra Bose's plant physiology has done.

Apparently the latent critical-moral stance of early psychoanalysis in India came from this tacit equation between the *tāmasika guṇas* and the instinctual impulses. Analytic interpretation became not merely a cognitive venture or an instrument of therapy, but also a moral statement and a form of social criticism. Freud did not like to view his infant science as a philosophy of life and he would have shuddered to think of it as a moral statement—Philip Rieff or no.[41] Some of Freud's first patients were even made to feel that 'he was not at all interested in politics, ethics or philosophy of life'.[42] And the admiring Fritz Wittels, despite his belief that the master was 'too profound a person not to grasp the need for a *weltanschauung*',[43] could not avoid confronting Freud's own statement made in 1926: 'I must confess I am not at all partial to the fabrication of *weltanschauungen*. Such activities may be left to philosophers.'[44]

Bose had no such inhibitions when writing in the vernacular. His attempts to limit the critical–moral role of psychoanalysis and his stress on the therapeutic role of the discipline were not evidently the whole story. Nor, for that matter, was Freud's avoidance of philosophy and worldviews. I like to believe that the work of Berkeley-Hill and Daly had shown Bose that the declared value-neutrality of psychoanalysis was no guarantee against latent moral judgments tilted in favour of the powerful. But one can never be sure that the Indian read his British colleagues that way. What we know for certain is that at least one part of Bose, a part that was a not-too-secret self either, would

[41] Philip Rieff, *Freud: The Mind of the Moralist* (New York: Doubleday, 1959).

[42] Roazen, *Freud and His Followers*, p. 512.

[43] Fritz Wittels, *Freud and His Time: The Influence of the Master Psychologist on the Emotional Problems of Our Lives* (London: Peter Owen, 1956), p. 52.

[44] Sigmund Freud, 'Inhibitions, Symptoms and Anxiety' (1925), in James Strachey (ed.), *The Standard Edition of the Complete Psychological Works of Sigmund Freud* (London: Hogarth, 1959), *20*, pp. 75–175; see p. 96. Freud had already declared a year earlier, 'even where I refrained from observation, I carefully avoided approach to actual philosophy. Constitutional incapacity rendered such self-restraint easy for me.' Sigmund Freud (1925), quoted in Wittels, *Freud and His Time*, p. 50.

have ceased to be what it was if it gave up its philosophical and ethical moorings. Like early analysts such as Wilhelm Reich and Karen Horney who sought an element of social criticism in their therapeutics even at the cost of therapeutic 'finesse' and methodological 'sanity', Bose would have found psychoanalytic ego psychology in particular and the highly professionalized psychoanalysis of the Anglo-Saxon world in general, anti-analytic. This despite the subsequent career of the discipline in his own country, a career that he himself helped to shape.

IV *The Fate of Psychology*

Girindrasekhar Bose was not the only person to create a space for western psychology in Indian public life and the culture of healing. Nor were his works, especially his English works, free of inelegance, crudity and simplification. But he was certainly the most colourful and robust figure to emerge in the world of Indian psychology in the first half of this century. No one since his time has moved back and forth so daringly and freely between the implicit psychology of traditional Indian thought, academic psychology, and psychoanalysis.

He obtained this freedom by operating at two levels: by emphasizing the organizational needs and the therapeutic role of psychoanalysis for his western and westernizing pan-Indian audience and by disembedding the discipline from its cultural moorings in the West to relocate it in Indian high culture and in the bicultural lifestyle of the urban middle classes in colonial India.

The first was by design, and it made him into yet another high priest of the-transfer-of-technology model that reigned supreme in the academic circles of India at the time. The latter was by default and that unintended dissent gave him his intellectual robustness. But the dissent, by the logic of his life experiences and personality, had to remain partial. Bose did believe the Sanskritic tradition to be the core of Indianness and, his exposure to and assessment of the little traditions of India being what they were, he could not help looking at the world of knowledge through the eyes of the babu. On the other hand even this partial dissent paid him rich dividends. Though he often was 'too logical' and 'mechanical'–the judgment was Freud's—when writing in English, he wrote in Bengali as if he had anticipated the adage of Christopher Lasch that, in an age that had forgotten theory, 'theory had to begin in remembrance'.[45]

As this narrative has shown, the memories Bose chose to excavate were not random ones. They were selected and shaped by his personality, which in turn mirrored the experiences of a civilization and the anguish of an age and a class. Naturally, the memories had their own half-life. While they let modern psychology go native and acquire a moral standing in local terms, they also narrowed the discipline's social base. This base sustained the young discipline as a sectarian profession and therapeutic technique, not as a cultural critique. Like many other imported systems of knowledge and some of the new theologies, reform movements, and refurbished cults in South Asia that began spectacularly and then withered away, psychology, too, gradually lost its sense of adventure and wider social appeal to become a 'proper' vocation.

'During his lifetime, however, Bose did manage to keep it a significant presence in Indian intellectual life. That would have been a harder task had he not been living in Calcutta in near-total isolation from the day-to-day culture of psychoanalysis in Europe and North America. For the isolation allowed Bose to take advantage of a contradiction in the European culture of science which got telescoped into Freud's self-definition and which the late nineteenth-century Viennese medicine man was never able to reconcile in his life or work. It was this contradiction that made Freud's vision a Shakespearian one for some like Lionel Trilling.

The contradiction was defined by a number of polarities, not all of them orthogonal: the metaphysical versus the applied or the narrowly empirical; the clinical versus the experimental; the intuitive and aesthetic versus the tough-minded and the objective; and, above all, between Freud the holistic healer and social critic inspired by the romantic tradition of science versus Freud

[45] Christopher Lasch, 'Introduction', in Russell Jacoby, *Social Amnesia: A Critique of Conformist Psychology from Adler to Laing* (Hassock, U.K.: Harvester, 1975), pp. vii–xv; see p. vii.

the heroic, masculine scientist-engineer and pioneer of a new theoretical school, self-consciously speaking the language of hard-eyed positivism.[46] Some of these polarities were to survive in a few of his followers and in the disciplinary culture they built, though they had to drive underground the culturally less acceptable ends of the polarities, for fear of the social and professional costs of their dissenting philosophy and politics.[47]

But first a word on Freud's self-definition as a scientist. Freud was the product of a culture of science within which German romanticism was not quite dead. For though he lived well into the twentieth century, he really belonged to the previous one. By his own admission, he decided to study medicine after reading Goethe's evocative essay on nature, and he was exposed through his friend Wilhelm Fliess to romantic medicine, many of the assumptions of which came from the *naturphilosophie* of Schelling.[48] The exposure was deep enough for Robert Holt to trace to it one entire genre of Freud's work. Holt calls the genre 'phylogenetic theory' and includes in it books such as *Totem and Taboo, Beyond the Pleasure Principle, Group Psychology and the Analysis of the Ego, The Future of an Illusion, Civilization and its Discontents*, and *Moses and Monotheism*.

Holt's paper was published in 1963 and there is in the author, as in Freud, a clear touch of ambivalence towards such speculative stuff. Within ten years, Iago Gladston is already less apologetic on behalf of Freud and considers the romantic

---

[46] A roughly comparable dichotomy is between critical and professionalized psychoanalysis used by Kirsner in 'Is There a Future?' Kirsner's dichotomy hinges on his understanding of where Freud's real interest lay. He quotes Freud's statement that the analytic relationship is based on 'a love of truth' and the prime interest of psychoanalysis is to find out what resistances this love of truth meets and the 'mental, theoretical and institutional formations based on our need to *avoid* the truth' (ibid., p. 181). Professionalized psychoanalysis, on the other hand, is heavily dependent on what Freud calls 'therapeutic ambition', which he sees as 'only halfway useful for science'. For such ambition is 'too tendentious' (ibid., p. 182).

[47] See, e.g., Russell Jacoby, *The Repression of Psychoanalysis: Otto Fenichel and the Political Freudians* (New York: Basic Books, 1983).

[48] Robert R. Holt, 'Two Influences on Freud's Scientific Thought: A Fragment of Intellectual Biography', in Robert W. White (ed.), *The Study of Lives: Essays in Honour of Henry A. Murray* (New York: Atherton, 1963), pp. 364–87.

tradition so central to Freud as to call him 'an ethologist and ecological and holistic scientist'.[49]

The culture of science that sustained Freud as a holistic scientist was, however, one into which the experimental method and the idiom of positivism had made heavy inroads. George Rosen succinctly evokes the changing culture of science when Freud was a student and a young researcher, especially the way four young experimentalists—Ernst Brucke, Emil du Bois-Reymond, Hermann Helmholtz, and Carl Ludwig—came to set the tone of late nineteenth-century German science.[50] Within twenty-five years these four men had realized their youthful dream: they had not merely become the leaders of scientific physiology in the German language area, they and their students were a major influence in the entire western community of medical researchers. As it happened, it was in Brucke's laboratory that young Freud honed his self-concept as a scientist. Holt, in fact, considers it ironic that the 'attraction to a poetic, metaphysical, grandiosely encompassing approach to nature led Freud into medicine and thus into the University of Vienna Medical School, a hotbed of physicalistic physiology'.[51]

The heart of the project of the four researchers was their tough-minded experimentalism. They had prised out the disciplines of physiology and pathology from the clinic and relocated them in the laboratory. These were now independent basic sciences which employed the precise methods of the natural sciences. Clinical observations were now at a discount. Rosen writes:

> Brucke and his friends were in the forefront of a generational movement. They were members of a generation of young physicians who insisted that medical problems receive scientific treatment based more on laboratory experimentation and less on clinical observation....
>
> Underpinning this mode of thought was a philosophical posi-

---

[49] Iago Gladston, 'Freud and Romantic Medicine', in Cioffi, *Freud*, pp. 103–23; see pp. 109–10.

[50] George Rosen, 'Freud and Medicine', in Jonathan Miller (ed.), *Freud: The Man, His World, His Influence* (London: Weidenfeld and Nicolson, 1972), pp. 21–39; see esp. pp. 27–9.

[51] Holt, 'Two Influences on Freud's Scientific Thought', p. 370.

> tion.... Life was equated with matter and energy, so that their genesis and development had to be studied and explained in material terms, that is, in terms of the chemical and physical forces that determine these processes, and thus ultimately on the basis of the impersonal, objective laws of nature. Intention and purpose had no place in such an approach to biological phenomena. This doctrine, comprising positivism, mechanism and materialism, was the philosophy to which Freud was exposed during his formative years as a medical student and young physician. Transmitted to him by those with whom he had chosen to identify, it was a major factor in the formation of his mode of thought and his self-image as a scientist.[52]

Beyond these exposures lay Freud's own need for social recognition and self-acceptance. Recent work suggests that his family background was one of East European Jews exposed to Hassidic influence. Later his family moved from eastern Europe to Germanic countries, first Czechoslovakia and then Austria. But the earlier exposures did not entirely wear off; he had a much more traditional upbringing than he ever publicly admitted. As a result he struggled not merely with his Jewish self as denigrated by the gentile world but also with his non-Germanic self which was looked down on by German Jews as open to non-rational mystical influences.[53]

The basic contradiction in Freud, therefore, was between the inner logic of clinical work which demanded a set of categories that came from myths, fantasies, and self-analysis, and a philosophy of science which demanded a different language of self-expression. The conflict between his emotions and reason sharpened the contradiction. Billa Zanuso goes so far as to suggest that 'there is not a single trait of his character, not a decision he made nor an incident in his life, that cannot be interpreted in two different ways' due to this conflict.[54]

For an outsider to the western world, these fissures within

---

[52] Rosen, 'Freud and Medicine', pp. 28–9.

[53] Yosef Hayim Yerushalmi, *Freud's Moses: Judaism Terminable and Interminable* (New Haven: Yale University Press, 1991). I am grateful to Alan Roland for drawing my attention to this part of the story.

[54] Billa Zanuso, *The Young Freud: The Origins of Psychoanalysis in Late Nineteenth-Century Viennese Culture* (Oxford: Basil Blackwell, 1986), pp. 64–86, esp. pp. 73–5.

Freud opened up immense possibilities, some of them invisible to those close to Freud culturally. The most important was the scope to construct a Freud who could be used as a radical critic of the savage world and, at the same time, a subverter of the imperial structures of thought that had turned the South into a dumping ground for dead and moribund categories of the Victorian era. Whether the possibility was fully explored by the likes of Bose or not is, of course, another issue.

Before we deal with that issue, let me spell out the nature of the conflict within Freud himself in some more detail.

As a school of thought, psychoanalysis acquired its political thrust from being part of the western critical tradition. It was a tradition to which a galaxy of thinkers from Giovanni Vico to Frederich Nieztsche to Karl Marx had contributed. As part of the tradition, Freud expanded the Enlightenment vision of a desirable society and sharpened its major methodological weapon, demystification.

However, this participation in the Enlightenment project was overlaid by certain insecurities and ambivalences in Freud towards the relationship between science and philosophy. Even a person as blinkered as Jones, who spent all his life reading and defending Freud as a hard-boiled positivist, admitted that as a young man, Freud had an early but 'thoroughly checked tendency to philosophize'.[55] Only after a decade-long détour by way of the medical-biological sciences had Freud been able, at an advanced age, to return to the problems of philosophy and religious psychology.[56] Holt is truer to the grain of psychoanalysis when he turns to the problem. He points to the

> many indications that Freud's earlier inclination towards speculative psychology was something against which he felt a very strong need to defend himself.... [The] involvement of conflict and defence is perhaps more convincing when one reflects that Freud took no less that five courses in philosophy... during his

---

[55] Ernest Jones, quoted in Roazen, *Freud and His Followers*, p. 24.

[56] Sigmund Freud to Frederich Eckstein, quoted in McGrath, *Freud's Discovery*, p. 94.

eight years in the university, when he was supposedly studying medicine.[57]

Others have contextualized this defensiveness by identifying cultural influences on Freud that had an older, 'less respectable' pedigree, against which, too, he had to defend himself. David Bakan, for instance, has made an impressive case that Jewish mystical traditions found identifiable, if convoluted, expression in the master's work.[58] Still others have discovered in Freud the negation of at least some aspects of the Enlightenment culture of science. Some of them have used the discovery to denigrate psychoanalysis as anti-positivist and counter-modernist.[59] However, as the nineteenth-century concept of science itself has suffered a decline, scholars in recent decades have been more tolerant of these 'disreputable' aspects of psychoanalysis. Thus, unlike his forebears, Gladston is neither derisive nor defensive when he says:

> Freud has been compared to Darwin, to Newton, and to Copernicus. I concur in these comparisons. Yet, to my mind there is one man he truly resembles—not in any other respect—but in the signature of his personality—that man is Paracelsus.[60]

Nor is Friederich Heer hesitant to admit that Freud's tragic vision implied a rejection of 'the simplest Anglo-American belief in the virtues of progress'.[61]

Freud himself, however, having driven underground his other self, worked hard to retain and use the idiom of tough-minded psychology. He was always fearful that psychoanalysis might otherwise be accepted not as a positive science but as a cultural artefact or philosophical speculation. One suspects that he avoided developing a worldview because he feared the outlines of the worldview he sensed within himself, 'Is Freud... a meta-

---

[57] Holt, 'Two Influences on Freud's Scientific Thought', p. 371.

[58] David Bakan, *Sigmund Freud and the Jewish Mystical Tradition* (Princeton, N.J.: Van Nostrand, 1958).

[59] For example, Hans J. Eysenck, *Fact and Fiction in Psychology* (Baltimore: Penguin, 1965); and *The Decline and Fall of the Freudian Empire* (London: Viking, 1985).

[60] Gladston, 'Freud and Romantic Medicine', p. 121.

[61] Friedrich Heer, 'Freud, the Viennese Jew', tr. W. A. Littlewood, in Miller, *Freud*, pp. 22–39; see p. 24.

physician?', Egon Friedell asks and goes on to answer, 'Yes, but he does not know it'.[62] Perhaps Freud knew but feared the knowledge.

The worldview Freud disowned was 'rooted in the culture of the late German Enlightenment with its interest in the exploration of dreams, emotions, and other mysterious phenomena in man's inner world'.[63] To the first psychoanalyst, seeking academic credibility, that worldview must have looked overly open to the culture of science associated with the German romantic tradition. He could warmly endorse Bose's work, blatantly philosophical though it was, because that was what the Hindus were known for and could get away with. He himself had to be more circumspect.

This other—and according to Bruno Bettelheim, more mature and humanistic—Freud, who emerged from the shadows only when he was in his late fifties, was unknown in the popular cultures of the West and the East during the days psychoanalysis was spreading to distant corners of the globe.[64] To most western-educated Indians, as to much of the Anglo-American world, what mattered were the comparisons being made between Freud, on the one hand, and Copernicus, Newton, and Darwin, on the other. These comparisons invoked connections that made psychoanalysis a positive science, an exportable technology, and an index of progress. They tied mainstream psychoanalysis not merely to the European Enlightenment, but also to the triumphalism of nineteenth-century European science. The other psychoanalysis survived, as did the other Freud, in the cracks of the modern consciousness, as reminders of an underside of the discipline that, regrettably, existed but should not be owned up.

As it happened, the Enlightenment vision, of which the dominant culture of psychoanalysis and the positivist sciences

---

[62] Egon Friedell, quoted in Rosen, 'Freud and Medicine', pp. 23–4.

[63] McGrath, *Freud's Discovery*, p. 93.

[64] According to Bettelheim, this was mainly due to the destruction of the European traditions of psychoanalysis by the rise of the Nazis and shift in the locus of psychoanalytic activities to the Anglo-Saxon cultures and the faulty English translations through which Freud's works came to be known in large parts of the world. Bruno Bettelheim, *Freud and Man's Soul* (London: Fontana, 1985).

were now valued parts, came to India neither through apolitical cognitive choices nor through 'natural' cultural diffusion. They came to India through colonialism, riding piggy-back on Baconian science, the utilitarian theory of progress, evangelical Christianity, and their practical extension, the British colonial theory of a civilizing mission. Together they sought to systematically subvert a way of life and devalue all surviving native systems of knowledge. When the vision won over sections of the Indian middle classes, it also won over people who, however creative in other ways, were to constitute an emerging class of intellectual compradors. As if the new psychological man in India had to be, by definition, a colonial subject. As if psychology had to be, by definition again, the latest in a series of techniques of retooling Indians into a prescribed version of the nineteenth-century European.

Bose's vernacular self tried to find a way out of the predicament by rediscovering an older version of psychological man in a traditionally psychologically minded society. He probably hoped that this discovery would anchor the new discipline outside the colonial progressivist discourse. It did not. In his own professional life, there were signs that the culture of Indian psychology was being integrated within the dominant global culture of psychology, its 'fangs' safely removed. By the time Bose died in 1953, he was already being seen both in India and abroad as a pioneer whose days were past. It is not insignificant that when he died many of the major international journals of psychoanalysis did not publish obituaries. Such slights did not burden Indian psychoanalysts overmuch. Even in Calcutta, where it all began, any 'critical engagement with received theory' was soon almost to disappear.[65]

For the moment, let us not ask whether or not such a colonial connection was inevitable for Enlightenment values, given their links with three processes that were to ensure the creation and substantiation of the concept of the Third World as a territorial and cultural category in the post-colonial dispensation—the search for the absolute secularization and objectification of the world and for total control of nature, including human nature,

[65] Kakar, 'Stories From Psychoanalysis', p. 433.

through science; the primacy given to history as a form of consciousness and as a way of constructing the past; and the hierarchy of cultures and social evolutionism written into the bond the Enlightenment forged between power and knowledge. The fact remains that the Enlightenment vision—especially its progeny, the Baconian philosophy of science—did systematically underwrite in Asia and Africa colonial theories of progress and the stratarchy of cultures and races.[66] Granting the emancipatory role this vision might have played in Europe, it was impossible to ignore its racist content and oppressive associations for the southern world.

Any serious critique of cultures in British India had to take into account this anomaly. Even when accepting psychoanalysis as emancipatory in principle, such a critique had to turn it into a means of concurrently criticizing the native culture and the packaged progressivist discourse available as a legitimating ideology for colonial domination. That is, the analytic attitude, which Philip Rieff believes lies at the heart of the Freudian project,[67] had to bear a dual responsibility in India. It had to be self-critical at two planes: it had to demystify aspects of Indian culture and it had to demystify the proxy-West, constituted by the interlocking cultures of the colonial state and westernized middle-class Indians.

Many psychoanalysts—and social critics—chose the easy way out. Their 'self criticism' was directed against nonmodern India, as if they were an organic part of it, and they exempted every category dear to westernized, middle-class India from criticism. As against them, Girindrasekhar Bose unwittingly—probably against himself—owned up this dual responsibility of the Indian psychoanalyst. This may be the other reason for his urgent attempt to re-read psychoanalysis as a revised version or logical conclusion of some of the older theories of consciousness in India.

---

[66] Jatinder K. Bajaj, 'Francis Bacon, The First Philosopher of Modern Science: A Non-Western View', in Ashis Nandy (ed.), *Science, Hegemony and Violence: A Requiem for Modernity* (New Delhi: Oxford University Press, 1988), pp. 24–67.

[67] Philip Rieff, *The Triumph of the Therapeutic: Uses of Faith After Freud* (New York: Harper, 1968).

Bose's re-reading was backed by two methodological deviations from mainstream psychoanalysis, both prompted by the need to situate the new science in an old cultural milieu.

Freud was fond of saying that he had not discovered the unconscious; it had been discovered by some of the great minds of antiquity. All he had done was invent a method of studying it. He had in mind the technique of free association, which evolved in response to two felt needs. One was the need to venture beyond the limits of the method of hypnosis with which he had started his career; the second was the need to go beyond the method of introspection developed by experimental psychologists such as Wilhelm Wundt and E. B. Titchener towards the end of the nineteenth century. This method, European academic circles now felt, had run its course. Freud himself said,

> It is . . . an illusion to expect anything from intuition and introspection; they can give us nothing but particulars about our own mental life, which are hard to interpret, never any information about the questions which religious doctrine finds it so easy to answer.[68]

Bose did not feel burdened by either of the two needs. He never felt called upon to transcend the techniques of either hypnosis or introspection. He was not fully exposed to the culture of academic psychology in the West, and such tides and ebbs in methodological fashion might have looked to him, undersocialized to the modern academe, as sectarian ones. He had been a hypnotist himself and, to him, free association did not supersede hypnosis, but built on it. Most psychoanalysts believed, following Freud, that hypnosis disguised, psychoanalysis revealed.[69] Wittels acts as their spokesman when he says:

---

[68] Sigmund Freud, 'The Future of an Illusion' (1929), *Standard Edition, 21*, pp. 5–58. This statement of Freud flatly contradicts Bettelheim's claim that psychoanalysis is an introspective psychology wrongly converted into a behavioural one in the United States (*Freud and Man's Soul*, p. 54). But the contradiction is only apparent, for the introspection that Bettelheim talks about is not the kind Freud had in mind when he rejected introspection but of the kind that Freud endorsed in the case of Bose.

[69] Sigmund Freud, 'Lecture XXVIII: Analytic Therapy', *Standard Edition*, 1963, *16*, pp. 448–53.

> Hypnosis is one of the states in which the secondary function is put out of action. The secondary function is delivered over to the hypnotist. He assumes the testing of reality, decides between fantasy and actuality, logical and ethical problems, and precisely in the degree in which the medium renounces his own use of the secondary function.[70]

It is difficult to believe that Bose, a practising psychoanalyst and one of the editors of the *International Journal of Psychoanalysis*, was not aware of Wittels' argument. More likely, Bose sensed the presence of, and was impressed by, Freud's other, less socialized self, more open to methodological adventures. As early as 1905, emphasizing the ancient origins of psychotherapy, Freud had said, 'There are many ways and means of practising psychotherapy. All that lead to recovery is good.'[71] Fourteen years afterwards, he was to restate that faith in a context that must have sounded strikingly familiar to Bose:

> It is possible to foresee that at some time or other the conscience of society will awake and remind it that the poor man should have just as much right to assistance for his mind....
>
> We shall then be forced by the task of adapting our technique to the new conditions.... It is very probable, too, that the large-scale application of our therapy will compel us to alloy the pure gold of analysis freely with the copper of direct suggestion; and hypnotic influence, too, might find a place in it again....[72]

As for introspection, Bose never disowned it. To him, to view introspection as only a method of psychology was a trivialization. Introspection had behind it the authority of at least two thou-

---

[70] Wittels, *Freud and His Time*, p. 302.

[71] Sigmund Freud, 'On Psychotherapy' (1905), *Standard Edition*, 7, p. 259. In any case, there were probably limits to Freud's enthusiasm for psychoanalytic *therapy*. At least on one occasion he is said to have remarked, 'Neurotics are a rabble (*Gesindel*), good only to support us financially and to allow us to learn from their cases: psychoanalysis as a therapy may be worthless'. J. Dupont (ed.), *The Clinical Diary of Sandor Ferenczi*, trs. M. Balint and N. Z. Jackson (Cambridge, Mass.: Harvard University Press, 1988), quoted in Rudnytsky, 'A Psychoanalytic Weltanschauung', p. 291.

[72] Sigmund Freud, 'Lines of Advance in Psychoanalytic Therapy' (1919), *Standard Edition*, *17*, pp. 157–68; see pp. 167–8. Jahoda in *Freud and the Dilemmas*, p. 26, adds that, after Freud's death, 'some psychoanalysts reverted to hypnosis and could overcome its disadvantages, even its boredom'.

sand years of India's past, besides the association with some European philosophers found relevant by Indians (such as David Hume, George Berkeley and John Stuart Mill). It was a method that had shown its possibilities over and over again. Fifty years of academic psychology in one cultural region of the world could not wipe out those possibilities.

Hartnack notes Bose's commitment to introspection, but fails to gauge its full meaning. When Bose said in 1938, surveying the work done in psychology in India during the previous twenty-five years, 'psychological truth can *only* be discovered through introspection',[73] he was in effect conveying four messages: that he was unaware that the free-associative method had grown partly in reaction to introspection in western psychology and he saw free association mainly as an extension of introspection; that to him, the discipline of psychology was inextricably associated with introspection, which in turn represented insight in its grandest philosophical sense; that, as a trained academic psychologist, he was aware of but uninterested in the transient western academic debates on method; that though he casually used the language of progressivism he had acquired from his western education, he judged all techniques in terms of the philosophical quest that had continued unbroken in his society over the centuries, unimpeded by the rise and fall of dynasties and regimes. To Bose, 'India's ancient learned men had a genius for introspective meditation and the Indian psychologist has that heritage. In this respect, he enjoys an advantage over his colleagues in the West.'[74]

It is facile to call this merely an expression of nationalism. It should rather be read partly as a statement of intent, a construction of the past oriented to a preferred future and serving as a critique of an imperfect present.

Was the tradition of introspection so dominant in Indian civili-

---

[73] Girindrasekhar Bose, 'Progress in Psychology in India During the Past Twenty-Five Years', in B. Prasad (ed.), *The Progress of Science in India During the Past Twenty-Five Years* (Calcutta: Indian Science Congress Association, 1938), pp. 336–52; see p. 345. Quoted in Hartnack, 'Psychoanalysis and Colonialism', pp. 97–8. Italics mine.

[74] Ibid.

zation? Was traditional India that psychologically minded and was colonized India its true heir? When Bose opted for psychoanalysis, was it psychoanalysis he opted for? When he anticipated the other Freud whom historians of ideas identified only some three decades later, what empirical and conceptual clues did he use? Or was he reading Freud, too, as a classical text open to diverse interpretations, because he had more freedom as a *bhāsyakāra*, a traditional commentator on texts partly cut off from the modern West, than an a formal psychoanalyst?

These questions remain unanswered in this essay. The issues they raise, I am aware, are debatable ones. Without prejudging the issues or foreclosing the debates, however, it is still possible to propose that, at one level of the intellectual culture Bose created, such questions were less than important. Bose, at this level, true to his vocation, was not concerned with unearthing the objective past, but with working through the remembered past. He seemed to know that, as with the individual, in some societies at some points of time the past flows out of the present as easily as in other societies, at other points of time, the present flows out of the past.

Modern Medicine and its Nonmodern Critics: A Study in Discourse*

I *Development, Medicine and Language*

The idea of development has served many purposes in our times. It has served as a reason of state, as a legitimizer of regimes, as a component of visions of a good society and, above all, as a shorthand term for the needs of the poor and the needy. It has produced a new expertise and created a new community of scholars, policy-makers, development journalists, readers of development news, development managers and activists–who together can be said to constitute the development community.[1]

There is one purpose, however, that development has served rather less conspicuously: it has endorsed the claims to power over the human body, as a domain of social knowledge and social intervention, ventured by organized centres of power in a society. These are centres inaccessible to the citizen and often even to the community to which he belongs. Taken away from the individual and handed over to the organized centres of power in the society, the body politically becomes and is redefined as either a carrier of hedonistic pleasures or as a vehicle of diseases and suffering.

If the body can be separated from a person's selfhood and

---

* Written with Shiv Visvanathan.

[1] Readers will of course notice the similarity between Henry Kissinger's concept of the foreign policy community and our concept of the development community. This is not accidental. Both communities perform roughly analogous functions.

controlled, it can also be corrected and improved. Also, the body can be controlled only if it can be corrected and improved. Either way, another area of supposedly individual choice becomes a part of public life, directly subject to the society's power–knowledge nexus and to the typical format of expertise which goes with the nexus. What was once a matter of personal suffering and personalized healing becomes thus subject to the demands of large-scale engineering, planning and intervention. Medicine becomes a proper theme in development.

Development in its halcyon days was mainly economic development. Other disciplines entered the area apologetically or stealthily—as the supplementary knowledge of social structures facilitating or hindering economic growth, as insights into the psychological factors motivating or discouraging economic growth, as information about the political factors influencing economic decisions. As the idea of development has expanded, development has become a larger area: not merely is there now a science of development but also a development of science; not merely the technology of development but also the development of technology.

As a consequence of such reversals in speech, development no longer is the mere treatment of the economic ills of a society; the development of healing as a science has become an important plank in the ideology of development. Development is no more development unless it takes the benefits of modern medicine to the traditional, underdeveloped parts of the society, unless diseases and pestilences are removed by modern knowledge from the lives of the citizens, and unless the entire population of a country is brought within the ambit of modern medicine and taken out of the dominion of folk wisdom, domestic remedies and non-modern healers.

Such a dénouement was probably inescapable. Since the 1950s, when the social sciences came into their own after World War II, the language of modern medicine has contributed handsomely to the language of development. Pathology, sickness, treatment, diagnosis, and cure have all been important terms in that part of the language of the body politic which has constituted the main discourse on development. Thus the now-recessive enthusiasm for the psychological sources of economic growth has often used the language of *injecting* the entrepreneurial spirit in underdeveloped cultures and of *curing* the pathology of non-entrepreneurial persons by introducing the *virus* of the achievement motive into them under quasi-therapeutic conditions.[2] The non-enterprising person has been seen, regularly enough, as falling short of full psychological health and negating the organizing principles of the fully functioning personality, at least in the popular culture of development studies.[3] Development is good, the argument goes, because it brings true health to everyone; development is health because healthiness takes you towards or gives you development; and finally, development is healthy because the language of development extends the modern language of healing not only to the individual but also to the society.

Well before Michel Foucault and Ivan Illich became eponymous figures in contemporary social criticisms of modern medicine, traditional systems of thought and ways of life displayed a certain scepticism not only towards foreign or non-rooted systems of healing, including what is called modern medicine or allopathy, but also towards traditional systems, including the ones to which the sceptics gave their allegiance. It was this element of 'self-criticism' which gave the traditional systems of medicine part of their resilience and humanness.

It is possible to argue that modern medicine, one of the last sciences to grow out of the traditional sciences in Europe and consolidate itself as a 'proper' science in the nineteenth century, was the first major system of healing to try to do away with this element of scepticism and self-criticism. Some of the scepticism and criticism survived in the popular culture, but did not translate into philosophical doubt within the system. The Popperian principle of falsifiability, so central to the positivist self-

---

[2] See, for instance, the description of the group therapy-like situations in which achievement motive was sought to be introduced in Third World societies in David C. McClelland and David G. Winter, *Motivating Economic Achievement* (New York: Free Press, 1969).

[3] If one offsets against this Everett Hagen's description of the non-enterprising person as the authoritarian person *à la* Theodor Adorno and his associates, one is left with little doubt that the problem of development was sought to be medicalized by some. E. Hagen, *On the Theory of Social Change* (Homewood, Ill.: Dorsey, 1963).

image of modern science, does not include within its scope any scepticism about the basic philosophical assumptions or culture of post-seventeenth-century science. Once medicine became a positivist science, it also became philosophically and culturally less self-critical.

The self-doubt of the modern doctor is essentially a personal self-doubt; so is the doubt of the patient expressed through medical litigation, or in the relationship the patient enters with the doctors. The doubt almost always centres on the doctor's skills or around empirical medical knowledge, rarely around the philosophical and cultural assumptions of modern medicine.

In fact, it is possible to argue that the principle of falsifiability itself has suppressed many forms of critical consciousness within modern medicine. Certainly the principle has not allowed the kind of folk wisdom which many traditional systems of healing have often used as a baseline of criticism (expressed for instance in the often-quoted quasi-Sanskritic saying in many parts of India, of which a free translation is 'one who kills a hundred becomes an ordinary doctor, one who kills a thousand becomes a great physician') or the kind of folk wisdom which holds medicine rather than the doctor in awe.[4] Clifford Geertz has talked of commonsense as a cultural system.[5] By disconnecting itself from the community life which organizes commonsense as a culture, modern medicine has disconnected itself from the commonsense which endorses scepticism in many traditional cultures of medicine.

In this essay we review the implicit visions of health and knowledge which scaffold modern medicine in South Asia, and in the process provide an outline of the worldview and the concerns of some of the more explicit criticisms of modern medicine produced in the region. We provide this stock-taking with the awareness that the intellectual debate on modern medicine in South Asia is organized around two philosophical positions.[6] For the first, a critique of modern medicine has to be

---

[4] See discussion of this scepticism in Sudhir Kakar, 'Doctor at Large', *The Illustrated Weekly of India*, 6 July 1986, pp. 18–21.

[5] Clifford Geertz, 'Commonsense as a Cultural System', *Local Knowledge: Further Essays in Interpretive Anthropology* (New York: Basic Books, 1983), pp. 73–93.

[6] This position is associated with groups such as Medico Friends Circle, the

primarily contextual; for the second, it has to be both contextual *and* textual.[7] We locate our analysis in the space defined by these two groups and try to expand the scope of the debate by reconstructing some of the debates on the subject which took place earlier in this century.

We are aware of the excellent work done on traditional systems of Indian medicine by academics such as Charles Leslie, Paul Brass, Roger Jefferey and Francis Zimmermann. But they bypass intellectual attempts in India, often from outside academia, to grapple with the social relations and political content of modern medicine in contemporary India. And we, living in a post-Bhopal world, are forced to define our intellectual responsibility mainly in terms of the politics of knowledge with which live the social critics and political activists working in the domain of health in India today.

Manifest critiques

There are some identifiable foci in the public debate on modern

---

Delhi Science Forum, Kerala Sashtra Sahitya Parishad, Consumer Education and Research Centre, and some others associated with the Drug Action Network as well as by activist-scholars like Abhay Bang, Anil Sadgopal, Narendra Mehrotra, Dhruv Mankad and even probably the redoubtable Zafrulla Chaudhuri. See, for instance, Kama Jayarao and Ashvin Patel (eds.), *Under the Lens, Health and Medicine* (New Delhi: MFC, 1986); Abhay Bang and Ashvin Patel (eds.), *Health Care, Which Way to Go* (New Delhi: MFC, 1985); C. Sathyamala, Nirmala Sundharam, and Nalini Bhanot, *Taking Sides: The Choices Before the Health Worker* (Madras: ANITRA, 1986).

[7] This position is associated with activist-scholars like Ziauddin Sardar, Claude Alvares, and Mira Shiva of the Voluntary Health Association of India and many in the PPST group. Manu Kothari and Lopa Mehta, two of the best-known social critics of medicine in this part of the world, take a more eclectic position though they are obviously more in sympathy with the second position philosophically. See, for instance, Ziauddin Sardar, 'Medicine and Metaphysics: The Struggle for Healthy Life-Styles', *Afkar Inquiry*, October 1986, *3*, pp. 40–7; Madras Group, 'What is the Role of Indigenous Medical Sciences in Our Health Care System?', *PPST Bulletin*, June 1984, *4*, pp. 64–95; Claude Alvares, 'Science, Colonialism and Violence', in A. Nandy (ed.), *Science, Hegemony and Violence: A Requiem for Modernity* (Tokyo: United Nations University Press and New Delhi: Oxford University Press, 1989), pp. 68–112; Manu L. Kothari and Lopa Mehta, *The Nature of Cancer* (Bombay: Kothari Medical Publications, 1973); and *Cancer, Myths and Realities* (London: Marion Boyars, 1979); also various issues of *Information*, the newsletter of the Voluntary Health Association of India, the *PPST Bulletin*.

medicine the world over. And both sides in the debate, the external and internal critics, have their own distinctive approach to them. The dominant idiom is that of the internal critics who stress implementation—the social responsibility of the modern doctor, the inequity in medical delivery systems and the pros and cons of socializing medicine. The external critics try to bring the *content* of modern medicine under critical scrutiny. Their baseline of criticism is outside modern medicine, often outside the modern worldview.

Thus, external critics give the example of the major killers in human history—pestilences ranging from plague to cholera—which have been eliminated from many countries not by modern drugs but by improved public health systems. Plague died out in Europe well before its nature was identified and a medical antidote was found for it.

> The study of the evolution of disease patterns provides evidence that during the last century doctors have affected epidemics no more profoundly than did priests during earlier times....
>
> The infections that prevailed at the outset of the industrial age illustrate how medicine came by its reputation. Tuberculosis, for instance, reached a peak over two generations. In New York in 1812, the death rate was estimated to be higher than 700 per 10,000; by 1882, when Koch first isolated and cultured the bacillus, it had already declined to 370 per 10,000. The rate was down to 180 when the first sanatorium was opened in 1910, even though 'consumption' still held second place in the mortality tables. After World War II, but before antibiotics became routine it had dropped into eleventh place with a rate of 48. Cholera, dysentery, and typhoid similarly peaked and dwindled outside the physician's control.... nearly 90 per cent of the total decline in mortality between 1860 and 1965 had occurred before the introduction of antibiotics and widespread immunization.[8]

---

[8] Ivan Illich, *Medical Nemesis*: *The Expropriation of Health* (New York: Pantheon, 1976), pp. 15–16; '12 Years After, Ivan Illich Revisits Medical Nemesis', *IFDA Dossier*, July–August 1988 (54), pp. 3–8. The only apparent exception to the rule has been smallpox. This exception can be viewed in many ways. For instance, one may argue that the 'irrational' resistance to smallpox vaccination in many societies is partly a result of a 'rational' generalization made by the public from their experience with other epidemics. Whereas the use of the example of smallpox by the élites and the westernized middle classes of the Third World to illustrate irrational resistance to modern health care can be seen as an interested attempt

Even if one does not fully accept such arguments, it is possible to see the major elements in the present crisis in medicine as the points of convergence of both contextual and textual—external and internal—problems. As the 'hard realities' of this crisis are not our concern here—this is a study in discourse, not an empirical stock-taking of modern medicine—we shall enumerate the problems only to set the stage for our analysis.

The first is the much-discussed problem of clinical iatrogenesis. There are now societies where nearly one-third of all medical referrals are reportedly iatrogenic. In specific areas the data could look even more disturbing. For instance, in Massachusetts, the number of children disabled by the treatment of cardiac non-disease exceeds the number of children under effective treatment for cardiac disease.[9] The situation attains a certain poignancy in many African and Asian societies where entire populations are often herded like cattle, through coercive legislation or with the help of massive propaganda by state-owned media, towards accepting medical or surgical interventions or drugs which are unacceptable to many rich societies. Millions of plastic loops distributed for contraception without proper medical supervision, the heavy use of harmful yet useless chloroquinol-based anti-diarrhoeal agents, indiscriminate prescription of concentrated vitamin preparations (which have dramatically improved the health of ants and earthworms in many societies because they are excreted by the human body within a few hours), useless surgery ranging from unnecessary tonsilectomy and removal of impacted molars to cardiac bypass and Caesarean section, over-intervention in cases of cancer—they can all lead to forms of suffering against which there is usually little check—medical, social or legal—in Third World societies.

Second, there are the mutant organisms or the drug-resistant

---

to generalize from a single exception. It is also doubtful if the theory of smallpox-as-an-exception can be fully sustained, for traditional methods for combating the disease were effective but were politically eliminated, often through the use of coercion. See Frédérique Apffel Marglin, 'Smallpox in Two Systems of Knowledge', in Frédérique Apffel and Stephen Marglin (eds.), *Dominating Knowledge: Development, Culture, and Resistance* (Oxford: Clarendon Press, 1990), pp. 102–44.

[9] Illich, *Medical Nemesis*, p. 24.

strains of bacteria which have 'learnt' to live with drugs. As the drugs multiply, so do the strains of common organisms. These new strains are often more virulent and less manageable than the original organisms with which humans have learnt to live for thousands of years. Typhoid vaccination, according to some, is now effective in less than fifty per cent of cases; the Widal test, till recently a reasonable laboratory 'proof' of typhoid, is effective in fewer and fewer cases. Meanwhile, typhoid has become more difficult to identify through clinical observation, for the contours of the disease have changed in many countries, and chloramphenicol, the antibiotic routinely used in typhoid, now refuses to give results in a large proportion of typhoid patients, due to its heavy and indiscriminate use over the last three decades for even minor ailments.

Third, there is the growing cost of treatment. Medical research now costs more not merely because of inflationary pressures, but also because of the growing demands on the medical R&D systems to produce drugs to cope with iatrogenic complications and mutant organisms. The average American now spends more on his health bill every year than on food or shelter. This cost becomes prohibitive for the poorer parts of the world which are often unable to keep up with modern medical R&D but have to bear a major share of the burden by paying high prices for drugs and new medical technology. Not only have the new drugs begun to reflect galloping R&D costs; just when some Third World societies acquire the technology for a wonder drug and can bring down its price through mass production, the effectiveness of the drug begins to decline. Thus by the time penicillin was made cheap and easily accessible to Indians, its effectivity had declined from 92 per cent in the 1950s to 8 per cent in the early 1980s, and doctors were forced to resort to costlier and more effective alternatives.

Fourth, there are now health problems created and sustained by the urban–industrial lifestyle. Modern medicine finds it difficult to cope with environmentally induced health disasters because it operates on the basis of Baconian inductionism, somewhat in the fashion of the detective in a Victorian crime thriller pursuing a single criminal who seemingly has nothing to do with the rest of the society and whose elimination leaves the society healthy and whole. One example will suffice:

Some years ago, large quantities of DDT were used by the World Health Organisation in a programme of mosquito control in Borneo. Soon the local people, spared a mosquito plague, began to suffer a plague of caterpillars, which devoured the thatched roofs of their houses, causing them to fall in. The habits of the caterpillars limited their exposure to DDT, but predatory wasps that had formerly controlled the caterpillars were devastated.

Further spraying was done indoors to get rid of houseflies. The local gecko lizards which previously had controlled the flies, continued to gobble their corpses—now full of DDT. As a result, the geckos were poisoned, and the dying geckos were caught and eaten by house cats. The cats received massive doses of DDT, which had been concentrated as it passed from fly to gecko to cat and the cats died. This led to another plague, now of rats.

They not only devoured the people's food but also threatened them with yet another plague—this time the genuine article, bubonic plague. The government of Borneo became so concerned that cats were parachuted into the area in an attempt to restore the balance.[10]

Finally, giving these four elements of the crisis a sharp edge is what Mira Shiva infelicitously calls the pharmaceuticalization of health.[11] In societies where modern medical technology is available only in a few pockets, where the number of modern doctors and hospital beds are few, and where the capacity to pay for modern medical facilities is poor, medicalization has built-in limits. But the penetration of drugs into all spheres of life, including medicine, becomes for the same reasons deeper and more dangerous. Often one finds in such societies that drugs with their easy and wide reach are expected to take over the responsibility for public health from the doctor and health care agencies, in fact from society itself. And the drugs, in the context of these expectations, become an end in themselves. According to at least one estimate, the proportion of useless drugs in India is as high as 70 per cent and there are 4000 drugs in circulation

[10] Anne Ehrlich and Paul Ehrlich, *Extinction* (London: Victor Gollancz, 1982), quoted in Edward Goldsmith and N. Hildyard, *The Social and Environmental Effects of Large Dams* (Powys, Wales; Wadebridge Ecological Centre, 1984), vol. 1, p. 79.

[11] Mira Shiva, 'Towards a Healthy Use of Pharmaceuticals: An Indian Perspective', *Development Dialogue*, 1985 (2), pp. 69–93.

in the country which are banned or could be banned in other countries.[12]

These five crises of modern medicine can be studied in many ways—as problems of medical R&D, as problems of medical training and hospital management, and even as indicators of a paradigmatic crisis in modern medicine. Here we seek to grapple with the crises at the plane on which the dominant philosophy of healing constructs the patient as a scientific reality and defines the doctor and his therapeutics as a scientific enterprise.

Latent critique

Underlying the manifest crises of modern medicine are two basic and related issues: first, the reconstruction of the reality of the patient through standardization of the two-person relationship within which a therapeutic encounter takes place, including the specific forms the principles of experimentation and operationalization assume within modern medicine; and second, the reconstruction of the doctor as a specialist or professional and the redefinition of the doctor as an applied scientist rather than a healer. Those providing a critique of modern medicine with an awareness of these latent issues assume that the core of medical practice is not the cumulative knowledge of physiology and drugs but the dyadic interpersonal relationship between doctor and patient.

The relationship between the modern doctor and his patient, one part of the critique says, is increasingly characterized by attempts made by modern medicine to methodologically decompose the patient as a person. True to the traditions of the positivist sciences, medicine tries to change the patient from an experiential reality to an experimental one, move him from his life world to the laboratory, reduce him from a molar to a molecular reality, and reinterpret his disease as somatic or psychological rather than psychosomatic.

The expression 'experimental' here does not mean that doctors experiment on the patient, though some doctors do and most doctors unwittingly endorse the vivisectionist base on which the consciousness—and the unconsciousness—of the

[12] Ibid.; also Claude Alvares, 'The Dangerous, the Useless and the Needy', *Afkar Inquiry*, October 1986, *3*, pp. 26–33.

experimental machine is built. 'Experimental' also does not mean that the patient ceases to be human to the doctor, though something of that too is involved in the change.[13] The expression refers to the reconstruction of the patient and his suffering into a set of variables and readings as in a laboratory process. It means that modern medical practice, even if temporarily and for the purposes of the clinic, *has* to give primacy to the laboratory reality of the person in preference to his personal and, as it happens, clinical realities. It is by suppressing the last two realities that the scientific enterprise called medical practice can be sustained. The process of suppression could be called depersonalization but for the fact that the term depersonalization is associated with a specific personality process in schizophrenia which, in its full-blown form, is independent of its social environment. We are here referring to what could be called a temporary depersonalization, socially imposed by a particular form of expertise which bases itself on the dualist worldview of modern science.[14]

To give an example of another kind of reductionism involved here, the transformation of a psychosomatic reality to either a purely somatic case or a purely psychiatric (usually the former) does not mean that modern medicine does not have any space for the psychosomatic. It has; however, this space is reserved for a specialization. In modern medicine, there are three forms of illness—somatic, psychological and psychomatic, each one requiring a different kind of professional expertise, whereas for some other visions of health there is only one form of illness—the psychosomatic. Some of them, such as homeopathy, are discerning enough to add that while all illnesses are psychosomatic, some tend towards the somatic and others towards the psychological. That which is a classification in one system becomes a scale in others.

---

[13] See, for instance, Robert Lifton's deeply disturbing study of concentration camp doctors, 'Medicalized Killing in Auschwitz', *Psychiatry*, November 1982, *4*, pp. 283–97. Also, *The Nazi Doctors* (New York: Basic Books, 1986).

[14] On this dualist worldview, involving a transition from objectivity to objectification, see Ashis Nandy, 'Science, Authoritarianism and Culture: On the Scope and Limits of Isolation Outside the Clinic', in *Traditions, Tyranny and Utopias: Essays in the Politics of Awareness* (New Delhi: Oxford University Press, 1987), pp. 95–126.

The main point is that the doctor who trusts the voice of the patient more than pathological test results in his own clinical work is perceived as less scientific in his practice, even though he may be perceived as a more gifted healer and more respected as a practitioner. He may be respected as a doctor but not as a scientist and, though he may be considered successful by his community, professional honours and fame are likely to pass him by.[15]

This is because laboratory test results provide a series of readings from which it is possible to reconstruct the patient as a clinical body in which the doctor therapeutically intervenes. The readings, when seen as operational definitions of the reality of the patient, must have priority over the doctor's personal impression of the patient as a person and the doctor's clinical impressions of the patient as a patient. The latter are parts of a trans-science, as defined by Alvin Weinberg; their vicissitudes fall outside the science of modern medicine and the whole area is sometimes dismissively termed 'bedside manners'.[16] The former allow for control and prediction and are therefore seen as the heart of the science of medicine.

This shadow patient, the patient reconstructed from pathological test results, acquires a medical reality and autonomy of his or her own; it is with that shadow that the modern hospital is primarily concerned. The rest, that is the patient's personal and clinical realities, are seen by the medical system as variables that induce compromises—often major and necessary compromises—with the science (as opposed to the art) of medicine. They are not seen as variables having intrinsic scientific status. And because modern medicine is constantly trying to be a better science rather than a better art, the logic of the process pushes the discipline yet further towards viewing the human body as a complex machine.

---

[15] There is a shift in this respect from the earlier phases of modern medicine in India, dominated by larger-than-life physicians like Nilratan Sarkar (1861–1943) and Bidhan Chandra Roy (1882–1962), to the present phase when the most prominent figures in the world of western medicine in India are primarily researchers. See also the plague episode and Haffkinism discussed below.

[16] Alvin Weinberg, 'Science and Trans-Science', *Minerva*, 1972, *10*, pp. 209–22.

The second part of the critique says that modern medicine has to conceptualize the patient as the sum of a finite set of subsystems which, in turn, have to be seen, for therapeutic purposes, as relatively and functionally autonomous of each other. Each of these subsystems, when affected by disease, have to be separately treated according to the demands of the disease—a process which is seen as an external encroachment into one or more subsystems.[17] The treatment usually consists in entering the affected subsystem(s) with a 'counter-agent' or in intervening in the subsystem surgically. If in the course of this battle against ill-health–the metaphor of warfare is common in the modern medical discourse—other subsystems are affected, they are handled through another set of interventions, in the form of another set of drugs or another form of surgery. Previously such effects used to be called side-effects; now they are called clinical iatrogeny.

It is possible to argue that the entire range of specializations in modern medicine is the direct outcome of such a perception of the patient. Specialists are increasingly regarded not as a tangential development or deviation from the primary agent of medicine in action, the general practitioner. The general practitioner is seen as a residual category–that which is left behind after the specialists and the specializations are taken out of the field. In the medical utopia, therefore, there is no place for the GP. He or she is there today as a stop-gap measure. For truly scientific and fully developed medicine is viewed as definitionally the sum of medical specializations. Ideally such a medicine should not have any place for the generalist.

Obviously this way of looking at things is a far cry from the work cultures of many non-modern medical systems in which, because the patient/client is seen in holistic terms, the doctor is also expected to be a generalist first and specialist second. In fact the specialist, when operating in a non-modern system (for instance, the osteopath in Ayurveda), often enjoys a lower status than the generalist.

---

[17] This view of disease as an external process finding a habitat in the body could itself be an interesting subject of enquiry, because many other systems see disease as a basically internal process triggered by external factors. See Section IV for an example.

The obverse of this issue is the problem of operationalism. If the patient's scientific reality is coterminous with the patient's operational reality, as modern medicine seems to assume, then it is only this operational reality which allows the doctor—and through him, society—'true', controlled intervention. The individual patient's health becomes assessable mainly from the central tendencies of a series of statistical distributions, on the basis of which the doctor predicts (prognosis), tests the prediction, reformulates the diagnosis, and alters the course of intervention. Thus the dialogue between doctor and patient is redefined as another input into a quasi-man-machine system constituted by the doctor and the laboratory. The limits to the system are set by the existing level of medical technology and the 'contract' between doctor and patient.

This gives scope in the medical discourse only for a monologue from the doctor and for either silence from the patient (the best patient is probably the one who considerately allows the doctor to do a *post mortem*) or for 'noise' (the language of suffering used by the patient during consultation, a language only fit to be interpreted with the help of standardized categories of medical symptomatology).

In such a world, the doctor's sense of security no longer depends on his clinical, empathetic understanding of two sets of data, one derived from clinical examination of the social reality of the person and the other derived from the operational measures of the patient's body functions or disfunctions. The doctor's sense of security begins to depend almost exclusively on the latter. Thus, for those interested in the art of medicine or in a holistic understanding of healing, cholera is caused by two sets of facts—(1) by poverty and the associated collapse of public health measures and (2) by the cholera germs finding a habitat in an individual's body. For those seeing medicine from the worldview of modern science, cholera is caused only by germs and can be eliminated by vaccination or, after one has been stricken by the disease, through rehydration and maintenance of the body's fluid composition. The social context enters only the epidemiology, not the therapeutics. In the first case, the 'voice' of the victim is important; in the second case it is not.

Three languages of criticism

There are two ways of taking stock intellectually of the criticisms of the modern medical system in the savage world. The first is through empirical analysis, cataloguing its efficiency through an audit of births, deaths and health. Such analysis allows one to uphold some criticisms and reject others on 'scientific' grounds. However, such analysis also tends to become 'internal' and focus on the political economy of medicine, on the sociology of hospitals or on the medical profession. The second approach to the task of stock-taking is by way of what may be called an ecology of knowledge. In this approach the modern medical system as a collective representation is made to confront the possibility of its 'other'. To make this simple point in the most complex manner, we shall now shift our focus to the dialectic between the 'self' of modern medicine and its 'other', laying particular stress on the availability of alternative imaginations within which the dialectic works.

More specifically we shall examine the intellectual critiques of modern western medicine within the Indian national movement. The period we shall consider is the post-Swadeshi period, but our analysis will be a free-wheeling description drawn from mainly four 'archives': the feminist–theosophist–occult writings of Helena Blavatsky (1831–91), Lind-Af-Hageby and Annie Besant (1847–1933), the neo-vitalist biology of Patrick Geddes, Gandhi's *Hind Swaraj* and G. Srinivasmurthi's construction of an ayurvedic critique of allopathy. These constitute what we shall call the archives of dissenting western imagination in alliance with indigenous knowledge systems in India.[18]

We choose such a period and its archives for three reasons.

[18] The most important element in these archives is theosophy. Theosophy played a significant role in the Indian national movement. Allan Octavian Hume, generally regarded as the founder of the Indian National Congress, was a theosophist. Annie Besant (1847–1933), President of the Theosophical Society, was elected President of the Indian National Congress. She was also, as we know, a leader of the Home Rule Movement. Patrick Geddes (1854–1932), the Scottish biologist, came to India in 1914 to prepare a town planner's report on Madras. He was the first professor of sociology at Bombay University and the first English biographer of botanist J. C. Bose (1858–1937). Maria Montessori (1870–1952), who played such an important role in shaping the nationalist education policy in India, also had strong theosophical leanings.

The debates in this era were pluralist. Parallel to the opposition between black and white, the colonized and the colonizer, was a deeper encounter in which western participants saw in India a possibility to be lived out. India to them was a place within which the other West of William Blake and Paracelsus could be revived. India in turn, seeking liberation from the West, nevertheless saw in the West an addition to the pool of alternatives in knowledge available within India.

Second, the era anticipated the disrepute in which later critiques of western science sometimes fell. Today, such critiques are often seen as being associated either with passing fads or with obscurantism and authoritarianism. The possibilities of alternative medicine or science immediately bring to mind the years of Lysenko, the fact that Adolf Hitler was a great advocate of nature cures, that Mussolini was an anti-vivisectionist. We shall however argue that, instead of being the eclectic fads which some critiques of modern medicine are today, the debates of the post-Swadeshi era had a civilizational tenor to them. Also, there was in the debates a certain naïveté, a nakedness of intentions which makes it easier for us to identify that tenor and elaborate their core concerns, strategies and consequences.

Third, we feel that in any reconstruction of a critique of a knowledge system, emphasis on only the nature of power encoded in the system is inadequate. One must concentrate on the content and strategies of dissent. All too often dissenting groups have sought the replacement of those in power without challenging the nature of the discourse. The critics become contextual and emphasize the social misuse of medical science; they fail to grasp the intrinsic nature of the science as a mode of cognition. The exoteric history of science, too, has concentrated on such overt processes, failing to show how esoteric critiques have provided ethical spaces from within which one can confront the hegemony of modern science.

II *The Theosophy of Alternatives*

One of the most obvious illustrations of this is the feminist movement and its critique of medicine. Official feminism has often stressed equality, without an adequate, built-in cultural critique of uniformity and standardization. It has not been a celebration of difference, of reciprocity. Such a feminism has basically left unchallenged the official medical discourse. As a result, such externalist critiques have merely enlarged the scope of the scientific gaze. We shall make this point by taking the reader through the works of Lorna Duffin and Jacques Donzelot, then contrasting them with the efforts of occult feminism in the works of theosophically inclined writers who influenced the Indian national movement.

Duffin's 'The Conspicuous Consumptive: Woman as an Invalid' is a remarkable study which shows that the perfect lady in upper-class Victorian England was a perpetual invalid.[19] Duffin argues that the social construction of woman-as-the-perpetually-invalid could not have been maintained without the aid of the medical profession. Using issues of the *Lancet* from 1850 to 1890, Duffin describes the different strategies by which the medical profession, through the scientific definition and control of the woman's body, helped maintain the social inequality of women.

The picture that emerges is one of a classic double bind. First women were regarded as ill because they were women and, second, women became ill when they attempted to do anything outside the conventionally accepted feminine role. Both nature and culture were conscripted to maintain the status of the woman as invalid.

By defining the woman as ill, all specifically female functions were treated as pathological. Puberty, menstruation, pregnancy, labour, lactation and menopause, all became conditions that 'invalidated' the woman, rendering her incapable of mental or physical labour. 'The entire animal economy of woman', as one doctor put it, 'is linked to the gigantic power and influence of the ovaries.'[20] There was a corollary to this. All nervous disorders of women were linked to disturbances in the reproductive system. Robert Barnes in his Lumleian lectures of 1878 claimed that the convulsions of childbirth were indistinguishable from those of

---

[19] Lorna Duffin, 'The Conspicuous Consumptive: Woman as an Invalid', in Sarah Belamont and Lorna Duffin (eds.), *The Nineteenth Century Woman* (London: Croom Helm, 1978), pp. 26–56.

[20] Ibid., p. 34.

epilepsy. He added, 'at menopause, the nervous force no longer finding useful function goes astray in every direction'.[21]

Duffin notes that by defining all normal female functions as pathological, doctors also removed the control and management of pregnancy and childbirth from the hands of women and midwives, and placed them in the hands of male medical practitioners. It is thus easy to understand the responses of the medical profession to the entry of women. It involved another double bind. If women themselves become ill by transgressing the boundaries of the feminine role, protecting women from the hazards of the medical profession was a medical responsibility. Neurasthenia, Duffin shows, became a women's disease because it was allegedly caused by increased mental activity; she notes the increase of clitoridectomy and overectomy as cures for epilepsy, hysteria, sterility and insanity in woman. Herbert Spencer in his *Principles of Biology* claimed that 'flat chested girls, who survive the high pressure of education' would be unable to bear a well developed infant or feed it.[22] On the other hand, reverting to the pristine purity of womanhood was reverting to illness, too.

The history of the feminist movement chronicles the various attempts by women to liberate themselves from the bounded sexuality that medicine imposed on them. Particularly important were the efforts of Marie Stopes, Margaret Sanger and Annie Besant in her pre-theosophy days. Yet one senses that while they allowed for a greater role for women in the economic and political systems, they left the content of medical science intact. One could go further and say with Donzelot that the redefinition of the mother–child bond, so central to the feminist movement, was extracted at a heavy price.[23] For the new medical sciences like eugenics and psychotherapy used the feminist movements to widen the power of the scientific gaze. As a result, psychology escaped 'from the insane asylum' and established tutelage over the grid of social health that has now become central to contemporary medical hegemony. The process is similar to what Foucault describes in *The Birth of The Clinic*.[24] Foucault argues

[21] Ibid., p. 36.
[22] Ibid., p. 33.
[23] Jacques Donzelot, *The Policing of Families* (London: Hutchinson, 1979).
[24] Michel Foucault, *The Birth of The Clinic* (London: Tavistock, 1963).

that the patient, particularly the poor patient, could avail himself of medical facilities only by opening himself up to scientific observation and intervention, by becoming the object of the new science of medicine.

In sum, the possibility of a feminist style in science was ignored in these attempts. Geddes and Thomson make this point clearly. They emphasize the need to make the most of the complementary qualities of women.

> It is important that medical schools and medical posts should be open to women of special aptitude. But from our general biological point of view, it seems that the most promising line of experiment would be that of providing specialized education for medical women—not 'easier' or 'lower' or any nonsense of that sort, but different—so that there might arise not duplication of one type of medical servant in the state but two distinct types of medical servant. It must be urgently emphasized, however, that the fittest medical education is not likely to be that which men in their wisdom prescribe, but that which women with a free hand, work out for themselves.... As Ellen Key has declared, 'to put women to do men's work is as foolish as to set Beethoven or a Wagner to do engine driving.'[25]

Geddes did not specifically talk of an alternative feminist science of medicine but the possibility was entertained by some women at the time. There was a realization that the hegemony of medical science arose from the suppression of the 'other' as a patient, madman, child, woman and animal, that the liberation of women from medicine could only be brought about by liberating these suppressed others. We shall now turn to the strategies theosophist feminism employed in formulating this awareness.

To understand occult feminism, one must remember three facts. First, there was a realization among theosophist feminists that while liberty for women at one level was a result of secularization and rationalization, this liberty had a price. Woman's participation in the eugenics and family planning movements had led to what may be called the semantic impoverishment of the feminine

[25] Patrick Geddes and Arthur Thomson, *Sex* (London: Williams and Norgate, 1914), pp. 233–4.

body, that is, the availability of signs, symptoms and symbols centring around the body diminished in the new social contract between the feminists and the medical establishment. The asexualism of the industrial life was already eroding the essentially feminine and, by 1917, there were already anxious reports about the decline of breast-feeding among working women.[26]

Second, the occult feminists realized the importance of treating the patient as a woman of knowledge. They realized that the mechanomorphic body of vivisectionist medicine, the elitism of eugenics, and IQ psychology gave little scope for the free play of the patient's knowledge or self-expression, and also, that the oppositions between nature and culture, woman and man, and the domestic and the professional had to be redrawn, and to do so they had to reshuffle the relationships between man, nature and God. Occult provided the space for both sets of activities. Occult pluralized the materialist concept of the body by multiplying the number of bodies. The sheer availability of other bodies—the causal body, the astral body, the etheric body—created multiple realities and spaces within which new possibilities could be worked out. The reductionism of the materialist body was no longer able to account for the emergence of forms of consciousness and psychic powers that the presence of the astral and etheric body provided for.

Helena Blavatsky remarked that it never occurred to the physician that it was in the physiology of the mind—in the relationship of the conscious self and the body—more than in the material body that the causes of many maladies were to be found. It was in that relationship that the secret of healing was to be sought rather than in the molecular structure on which generations of doctors had toiled with little success.[27]

Third, with the multiplication of bodies and forms of consciousness, the innumerable nervous disorders associated with women were re-read. Hysteria, spirit communication, telepathy, clairvoyance became spaces for a new freedom. They became spaces where the rules and regimentation of the official medical

---

[26] G. Srinivasmurthi, *The Slaughter of The Innocents* (Madras: 1917).

[27] Helena P. Blavatsky, *Collected Writings* (1879–80) (Illinois: Theosophical Publishing House, 1966), *3*, p. 189.

body were irrelevant. Simultaneously, an attempt was made to remove the various nervous disorders associated with woman from the domain of pathology to the domains of the normal and the supra-normal. Charles Leadbeater cites one of the earlier instances, that of Anton Mesmer. He says:

> [T]hroughout his early experiments, he [Mesmer] was under the impression that magnetic sensitiveness was always a symptom of ill health; and it seems to have been a great surprise to him when he found that one of his patients retained her power after recovery. Further investigation led him to understand that it was not a question of health but a psychic faculty; and he conjectured correctly enough, that all in reality have the power to a greater or lesser degree; but in some it is only able to come to the surface when ordinary physical faculties are weakened by sickness.[28]

Partly as a result of such formulations, there was a virtual epidemic of occult and spiritualist happenings, in which women were the primary medium of occultism and spiritualism. There was literally a celebration of telepathy, spirit healing, reincarnation and clairvoyance. It was one of the few surrealistic periods in the annals of medical science.

The period also emphasized the importance of language and communication in the doctor–patient relationship. As Blavatsky remarked, not all prophecies and communications 'could be reduced to the same level with the hallucinations of the ventroloquist Mlle Amonda, whose delusions were due to vapours caused by the hysterical swelling of the large intestine'.[29] The statement of mediums, the language of hallucinations became important. Though Blavatsky did add in a wry aside that

> the great majority of spiritual communications are calculated to disgust investigators of even moderate intelligence. Even when genuine, they are trivial, commonplace and vulgar. During the past twenty years we have received messages purporting to come from Shakespeare, Byron, Franklin, Napoleon, Josephine and even Voltaire. The general impression made upon us was that the

---

[28] Charles Leadbeater, 'The Rationale of Mesmerism', *The Theosophist*, October 1904, *2*, pp. 29–40; see p. 30.

[29] Helena P. Blavatsky, 'Three Months in the Blue Mountains near Madras', *The Theosophist*, June 1910, *31*, pp. 113–20; see p. 119.

> French conqueror and his consort had forgotten to spell words correctly; Shakespeare and Byron have become inebriates and that Voltaire has become an imbecile.[30]

Yet occult medicine was a genuine effort to restore the importance of speech in the doctor–patient relationship. In attempting this, it did add a truly semiotic dimension to modern medicine. It went beyond the reductionism of cause and effect, stimulus and response, to the world of signs, symptoms and symbols.

In such an exercise, the patient and the world of the patient became central. As important was the reconceptualization of the mother–child bond and the way it linked the doctor–patient relationship. The diagram below gives an idea of the alternative visions of childhood so central to the theosophical exercise and the concept of medicine which went with it.

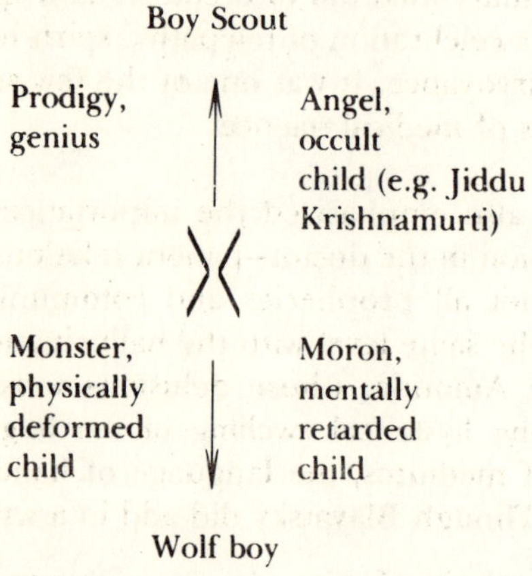

The concept of the patient in such a framework gave free play to a number of woman's basic selves—the pregnant woman, the patient, the mother seeking to understand childhood outside the narrow world of eugenics and modern medicine. The framework raised questions like: What is a foetus? What makes some foetuses become 'monstrous' and others angelic? How does one

[30] Helena P. Blavatsky, *Isis Unveiled* (1877), (Los Angeles: The Theosophy Company, 1968).

cope with or explain prodigies and morons? Does the foetus have rights?

The emphasis in these questions shifts from the demands of the scientific–medical world to the systems of meaning that women find relevant as women, mothers, patients and as parts of the folk imagination. The questions cut across nature and culture, and across the boundaries between the human, sub-human and animal. It is ethnoscience at its most autonomous, formed not by rejecting medical science but incorporating some aspects of it into a more meaningful bricoleurian world.

The problem of the monster—the entire teratology of deformed babies, those born with little tails, excess hair, withered feet, strange birthmarks, and other stigmata—was something that had always boggled the folk imagination. Theosophy, when it concerned itself with the problem, found evolutionist teratology neither sufficient nor convincing, for it left no place for reincarnation which was so important to the folk imagination. For the theosophists, too, only the cycles of birth and rebirth endowed biology with any sense of natural justice.

The re-emergence of the monster was accompanied by the resurgence of stories about the wolf boy, about children who had lived so close to animals that culture seemed minimal in them. The wild boy of Aveyron was part of both the folk and the scientific world. Attempts to treat him by doctors like Jean Itard were later to inspire Maria Montessori, well-known educationist and the first Italian woman to receive a medical degree.[31] While working at a psychiatric clinic in Rome, she frequently visited the city's asylums where she found idiot children grouped indiscriminately with the insane. The early work on the wolf boy had convinced her 'that mental deficiency presented chiefly a pedagogical rather than medical problem'.[32]

If Montessori's first radical step was to demedicalize the problem, her second move, as many theosophists observed, was to alter the interventionist frame of mind. For Montessori, education was not what we do for the child, but largely something we refrain from doing, so as not to interfere with its

---

[31] Harlan Lane, *The Wild Boy of Aveyron* (London: Paladin, Granada, 1979).
[32] Ibid., p. 280.

growth.[33] The child to Montessori was a little messiah.[34] Finally, according to her, account had to be taken not only of the child's physical but also its psychic life—which for the theosophists included the spiritual life. Partly as a result, for Montessori, every parent, especially the mother, became a true scientist caring for the child. This spiritual humility, too, was radically different from the interventionist eugenics of the time.

The radical imagination of Montessori-as-a-doctor captured the spirit of the theosophists with remarkable sensitivity. There was no distancing of the professional from the nonprofessional here, for every woman could locate a Montessori within herself. Montessori's science was a science of demedicalization and deregimentation. It was not a medicine that preached the surveillance of the body in a barrack-like school. It did not pathologize the child in order to objectify him and thus legitimate further intervention. And though there was innocence here and though the retreat of power was temporary—for her teachings were soon incorporated in courses of home science and scientific social work—for a while she represented the ideal medical scientist working as a participant observer.

The feminist–theosophist imagination also counterpoised the wolf boy against the boy scout. If the former represented nature which had to be recovered for culture, the other represented culture reaching back to nature. However, theosophists had little sympathy for Baden-Powell's concept of scouting which was steeped in social Darwinism and coloured by imperialism.[35] Scouting was a form of social hygiene established to counter the threat of English national decadence and lack of enthusiasm for the empire. Baden-Powell was against free-feeding, old age pensions, and strike pay, 'for they did not make for the hardening of the nation'.[36]

What theosophy sought to do was to recover the other part of Baden-Powell and integrate it in an alternative frame—the

[33] C. Jinarajadasa, *The New Humanity of Intuition* (Adyar, Madras: Theosophical Publishing House, 1938), p. 129.

[34] Ibid., p. 134.

[35] John Springhall, *Youth, Empire and Society* (London: Croom Helm, 1977), p. 57.

[36] Ibid.

ecological consciousness, the romantic woodcraft naturalism of Ernest Thomson Seton, who had inspired the sections on woodcraft in Baden-Powell's book. A central feature of Besant's dissident idea of the boy scout, embodied in the Hindustan Boy Scout movement, was that the boy scout was kind to animals. The child thus became part of the anti-vivisectionism so crucial to the theosophist critiques of medicine as well as part of the movements for the rights of animals and women in the West. There was frequent debate on the intelligence of animals (such as reports on horses that could count), in theosophist journals. Scouting lore, too, was full of anthropomorphic anecdotes. As Gerald Carson remarked, 'the zoologists may shudder but the anthropomorphic anecdote has made more friends for the animal kingdom than they have'.[37]

One last observation. As we have already said, there was an air of surrealistic biology about the theosophical framework. The theosophists produced a picture of a circus rather than that of a museum. The museum as a representative of modern science classifies defeated systems and alien bodies into the rigidity of a linear, evolutionary framework. The circus domesticates such alien bodies but allows for free-wheeling imagination. The surrealistic bricoleur of bodies in theosophy challenged the conventional ideas of the normal and pathological. It was reminiscent of the role of the carnival in medieval times. To mix metaphors, Blavatsky and other feminists were like intellectual Barnums who had turned the world of medical knowledge into a circus juxtaposing folk jugglers and psychologists, Paracelsus and Darwin, the magician and the scientist, so that formal medical science lost its priority. To condemn this as quackery, fraud or pseudo-science is to miss the point. It is like saying Salvador Dali could not see straight. Theosophist attacks were like sociological stances, tactics against the hegemony of a domineering medical science. The strategy was simple: pluralize the number of bodies and modern medicine would find it difficult to regiment them. And this strategy had to involve India; for the theosophists discovered their circus in India.

---

[37] Gerald Carson, *Men, Beasts and Gods* (New York: Charles Scribner, 1972), p. 121.

India, according to them, showed all the signs of being the site for an alternative medical imagination.

But the Swadeshi movement in India was already finding scientific medicine seductive. Lala Har Dayal had already said, 'a little science confers more happiness on mankind than all the piety of the middle ages'.[38] He noted that while Pasteur and Koch were not saintly ascetics, they were still greater benefactors of humanity than all the nurses of the religious organizations. For Har Dayal, modern science would be the Vedas of the resurgent India, and the scientist the model for the *ṛṣi*-hood of the future. 'Do not... follow the old footsteps of the rishis. Benares and Puri have had their day. What is there in Benares but... fat bulls and fat priests. What is there in Puri but cholera...?'[39] The theosophists, on the other hand, were afraid that Indian nationalism in its quest for liberation might internalize the violence of a desacralized western science. In fact, in the specifics of its critique of the Swadeshi movement, theosophy became a critique of the Swadeshi internalization of vivisectionist medical science.

Vivisection has been defined as the justified infliction of pain on animals in the pursuit of science. As a scientific ritual it includes starving, baking, crushing, beating with mallets, fracturing bones, varnishing with pitch, subjecting to varying atmospheric pressures or to none, blowing up the body by forcible inflation, poisoning, amputating, burning and irradiating. The anti-vivisection movement in the early part of this century attempted to show how modern science legitimized the violation of the integrity of the other when that other could be defined as animal or, for that matter, as criminal, black, monster, poor or colonial subject.

This attack on vivisection has to be understood in terms of the career of public health in India. The introduction of vivisection in India involved what a gathering of Jains once called the rise of Haffkinism and Pasteurism in India. We borrow an example from Helen Bourchier's classic paper read at the 1909 Anti-

---

[38] Har Dayal, 'The Health of the Nation', *Modern Review*, July 1912, *12*, pp. 43–9; quote on p. 48.

[39] Ibid., p. 49.

Vivisection and Animal Protection Congress.[40] Bourchier contrasts the Hippocratic view of medicine as an ethical art and the modern laboratory view of medicine. She shows the contrast by examining two differing empirical approaches to plague—the first evident in the case of the plague in Egypt in the late nineteenth century and the second in the Great Plague of Bombay, which began in 1896 and lasted twelve years.

When plague struck Egypt, Sir John Rogers, who was then Director General of the Sanitary Department, immediately instituted a series of measures. Persons found infected were isolated and those who came into contact with the patients were quarantined, fed and compensated for the loss of their time. These measures were supplemented by others, such as the lime-washing of infected houses and the disposal of garbage away from the city precincts. As a result, the epidemic subsided within six months, the eventual death toll being a mere 45. Today, the Egyptian case is hardly remembered in the annals of science while the Bombay plague is cited as an example of the success of medical science.[41]

Bourchier shows that when the epidemic was raging in India and millions were dying, a group of doctors brought to Haffkine's notice the importance of introducing sanitary measures similar to the ones employed in Egypt. But Haffkine represented what they called 'the laboratory point of view'; he had come 'to test on man the remarkable results which he had obtained on animals in the laboratory with the cholera bacillus'.[42] He rejected their suggestions and ensured that no sanitary measures were undertaken while his vaccine was being tried out. He had his own ideas about experimental and control groups and about how far people in a colony could be used as guinea pigs for the sake of the progress of science. It is indicative of the culture of modern medicine that not only has the modern medical profession half forgotten the Egyptian plague, it has deified Haffkine as a great healer and benefactor of the non-

---

[40] Helen Bourchier, 'The Use to which Men and Animals Alike are Put to by Men of Science', in Lind-Af-Hageby (ed.), *The Animal's Cause* (London: Animal Defence and Anti-Vivisection Society, 1907), pp. 75–98.

[41] Ibid., pp. 84–5.

[42] Ibid., pp. 85, 78.

western world. Theosophist editorials warned that the vivisectionist rituals of the laboratory state would soon envelop a whole series of 'others'. They referred to the proposed measure to legalize the vivisection of criminals sentenced to capital punishment in Ohio in North America. They warned that the logic of vivisectional science was such that the

> capitally sentenced criminals would be utterly insufficient to meet the demand for living human subjects and accordingly paupers, lunatics, hospital patients would have to be utilized. In a short time, no poor and friendless person would be safe and at length all classes would find themselves exposed to this danger.[43]

Already hospitals had become so blatant that opportunities for vivisection were widely advertised in medical directories. Lind-Af-Hageby cites the example of the Charing Cross Hospital at London which claimed in an advertisement in 1907:

> From the extensive outpatient department, the most instructive cases were drafted into the wards for the benefit of the pupils and the outpatient practice as well as the special departments for female disorders; children's diseases, eye diseases and skin diseases are similarly admitted, affording valuable opportunity for surgical practice.[44]

St Bartholomew's Hospital recommended itself in the following words: 'Hospital contains 670 beds, in addition to 70 beds for convalescent patients at Swanley, in Kent, there is therefore an abundance of clinical material.[45]

The theosophist campaign against vivisection thus became a virtual charter of civil rights for the victims of medical violence, a violence which was now increasingly backed by the state. The theosophists insisted that the violence of modern medicine was not merely directed against distant or pathological others; it was also the banal violence of everyday science. Thus, Annie Besant warned Swadeshi pedagogues against unnecessary dissections in science classrooms. Referring to schools in Europe she said,

---

[43] 'Cuttings and Comments', *The Theosophist*, March 1903, *24*, p. 382.

[44] Lind-Af-Hageby, 'Vivisection and Medical Students: The Growing Distrust of Hospitals and Their Remedy', in Hageby, *The Animal's Cause*, pp. 88–97; see p. 95.

[45] Ibid., p. 95.

> they repeat experiments of advanced scientific men in order to watch with their own eyes the results which they read in their text books. This is not done for the gaining of new knowledge, but is merely idle repetition of fact well established. For instance, a dog will be taken and laid upon the dissecting table, then the nerves will be exposed along the neck and under the skin of the legs, and while strapped in this condition, a sudden injury may be caused by the application of a red-hot iron, to a particular part of the brain and the dog will bark and the professor will brutally say to the public, 'See how we make the dog bark by stimulating this position of the brain.'[46]

Besant warned against such early brutalization in schools, and other theosophists argued that the entry of such a science into society could be dangerous. It was in this context that they opposed the inauguration of the Pasteur Institute in India.[47]

The advocates of vivisection, on the other hand, first propagated the fear of a disease, rabies in the case of the Pasteur Institute, and then offered science as a solution. Of this a theosophist said,

> westerners are awfully afraid of hydrophobia. It means death to them. Pasteur's Institute is supposed to be the only saviour and those that cannot bear the expense of going to it, must succumb to it sooner or later.[48]

'Yet in Indian villages', the essay pointed out, 'there are always pariah dogs which bite villagers. They can never hope to get to Kasauli and are cured and live.' The theosophists emphasized the importance of vegetable therapeutics, of herbs from other systems, of alternative systems of medicine in general, particularly in the context of resisting vivisection. For instance, they pointed out that the usual prescription for rabies was the juice of the *ummetha* plant mixed with jaggery.[49] They seemed to feel the need to create life-giving myths or, if that was not possible, to

---

[46] Annie Besant, *Against Vivisection* (Benares: Theosophical Publishing House, 1896), p. 7.

[47] 'Cuttings and Comments', *The Theosophist*, June 1903, *24*, pp. 565–8.

[48] K. Perraju, 'Extraordinary Virtues of Indian Plants', *The Theosophist*, October 1902, *24*, pp. 23–7; see p. 23.

[49] Ibid., p. 23.

give to the dominant medical system what, loosely following Arne Naess, we can call 'postulates of impotency'.[50]

The ideas of homeopathy were often used by the theosophists as examples. Samuel Hahnemann and his collaborators had experimented on themselves with about 97 drugs. The results had been 'astonishing'. The symptoms of the drugs had produced faithful 'pictures' of everyday illnesses. Hahnemann's 'provers', in expressing their abnormality, had used the exact phrases encountered in interviews with patients. Hahnemann had also found that nine-tenths of the symptoms produced were subjective, that is, they required human speech to articulate them. These he had classified, a classification which has survived in homeopathy till today. All this would have been impossible had he employed animals.[51]

There is one other reason why the theosophists might have found homeopathy attractive. We have already noted that one criticism of modern medicine is that it sees the patient not as a person but as a table of symptoms. Homeopathy shares this critical view and, to counter what may be called the impersonalization of sickness, advocates the individualization—and re-personalization—of the patient's symptoms. For the homeopath, every case is unique. The disease for which different patients may be consulting him may be the same, but the treatment should be different in each case. The physician has to consider the mental, emotional and physical pathology of each individual and the unique way in which the individual reacts to his illness. The clinical interview, therefore, becomes crucial for the homeopath's work.

Let us now turn to another major, if indirect, theme in the theosophical critiques of modern medicine. To articulate the theme we have first to recognize that the history of power has become in many ways the history of the body as well as a historical catalogue of the various forms of body technique and discipline devised to control the body in laboratories, barracks,

---

[50] Arne Naess, *Pluralist and Possibilist Aspect of the Scientific Enterprise* (London: Allen and Unwin, 1972).

[51] E. Petrie Hoyle, *Homeopathy and Vivisection* (London: Animal Defence and Antivivisection Society, n.d.).

hospitals and schools. To the theosophists, as to other dissenters of their times, medicine was becoming a legitimizing principle of the state. It allowed the state to inspect, survey and classify people in terms of medical categories—as insane, criminal or sick.[52] Sometimes the state even used these categories to exterminate or liquidate entire communities and races. The grand traditions of political theory have ignored this 'mundane' politics of everyday life. The abstract celebrations of market, state and sovereignty have time and again suppressed the awareness that medicine is politics, that it has provided the dominant metaphors of control and collectivization. Alfred Wallace once remarked that only two certificates were required from a registered doctor to send a feminist to an insane asylum.

This compact between western medicine and the nation-state worried dissenters of the era. They realized that if health was power and the state a form of hygiene, the civil society must contain alternative notions of health, pathology and cure. The availability of such alternative imaginations was fundamental to contain, ecologically, the hegemony of the medical state. In the next section we shall return to this issue.

At a less ambitious level, there were the works of Wallace, a British advocate of the Swadeshi movement, and Geddes. Wallace exerted a great influence on the theosophists in India. To him the very success of science-as-a-mode-of-being was a sign of concern, for science could be coercive in its cognitive style and difficult to domesticate once you granted its concept of method. The heretical impulse behind nineteenth-century mesmerism and homeopathy was, to Wallace, an ethico-scientific imperative, which some scientists must follow to prevent the dominant system of science from becoming hegemonic. Wallace's book *The Wonderful Century*, a history of nineteenth-century science, has an intriguing second half.[53] There he develops, after outlining the triumphs of western science, the ideas which were regarded as heretical by the scientifically minded—psychic research, phrenology, critiques of vaccination. (The heretical impulse also found expression in the theosophical movement's paradigmatic

[52] Michel Foucault, *Power/Knowledge* (London: The Harvester Press, 1980).
[53] Alfred Wallace, *The Wonderful Century* (1898) (London: George Allen and Unwin Limited, 1908).

scientist, Jagadis Chandra Bose. Bose introduced into modern plant physiology totally disjunctive ideas of life and matter which unfortunately were to get domesticated and absorbed eventually in the dominant structure of science.[54])

The effort of Geddes was more collective. A maverick biologist, Geddes believed that the hegemony of a mechanistic science had coloured major areas of western thought—the physical sciences, economics, pedagogy, health and even the Haussmanic city with its celebration of linear planning and mechanical grids of roads, cutting across vital communities merely because they were poor or disease-prone. Geddes saw in his neo-vitalist biology the possibilities of a dialogue the West had suppressed, both within itself and in other traditions. It was in this context that he felt that India should be the site for a post-Germanic university.[55]

For Geddes, no university system was complete without its dissenting academics. The career of the university as an organism often reflected a violent dialogue with competing notions of knowledge and pedagogy resident in its environment. Its very success lay in its ability to provide a working synthesis. For instance, the medieval university itself arose out of an attempt to reconcile the doctrines of the Christian church with the rediscovery of Aristotle. Similarly, he argued, the ideal culture of medicine should have physicians of many faiths, comparing not only their drugs but also their doctrines.

India, Geddes felt, could start such an exercise, which would, he hoped, lead to the revival of a rural view of science. He claimed that the economics of the leaf colony and the economics of metals were coming into conflict and that the first would once again have a larger significance, as it had in the rural world of old. He hoped that young doctors from Edinburgh, London and Paris would go to study Indian diseases and interpret India's diverse cultural contexts to throw new light on European bacteriology, as Calmette had brought back to the Pasteur Institute at Lille, to its brewers and bakers, a new yeast from old

---

[54] Ashis Nandy, *Alternative Sciences: Creativity and Authenticity in Two Indian Scientists*, second edition (New Delhi: Oxford University Press, 1995), part 1.

[55] P. Geddes, *On Universities in Europe and India, Five Letters to an Indian Friend* (Madras: National Press, 1904).

China, thus taking an industrial and a chemical step in one.[56] In pursuit of such an idea of the university Geddes wanted Vishwabharati at Shantiniketan to embody both a scientific and aesthetic encounter with the West, but the concept lost out in Tagore's final blueprint for the university. Swadeshi nationalists, on their part, defeated Geddes' hopes of designing the new university at Benares.

The other strategy to work out new relationships among various medical systems was a political one. In England, in the 1920s during the debate over the registration of medical practitioners, Lind-Af-Hageby convened a conference on medical liberty and declared the right to medical freedom to be a civil right. It included the right to choose one's treatment, the right to do without a doctor, the right to resist the fashions of orthodox and unorthodox medicines.[57] In fact she forwarded a scheme for a parliamentary party on medical freedom with some of the following objectives.[58]

1. To resist legislation by which the right of the individual to reject orthodox treatment could be abrogated and by which the prevalent theories of allopathic medicine would be identified with the state.

2. To spread knowledge of the various schools of nonconformist medicine and to demand for them the same liberty and independence as has been obtained by non-conformists in religion.

3. To work for the extended recognition of unregistered medical practitioners and thereby giving facilities for the demand for systems of healing which were those in advance of the accepted modern school of medicine.

4. To safeguard the public against fraud by encouraging the various societies and bodies concerned with unorthodox practice to qualify and register their own practitioners and to promote an act of Parliament by which such qualified practitioners will be able to exercise their powers of healing without being molested and subject to criminal charges.

---

[56] Ibid., p. 1.

[57] Lind-Af-Hageby *et al.*, *Progress and Freedom in Medicine* (London: Animal Defence and Antivivisection Society, 1934), p. 2.

[58] Ibid., p. 7.

Hageby felt that given the power of the state, these rights had to be built into the social contract between the citizen and the state.

When the same question of registration and recognition of medical systems was debated in India, the emphasis was not only on contract but on the idea of the medical system as a commons. The practitioners of traditional medicine argued that it was a system of cure suited to the environment and lifestyle of the community both in terms of economics and culture. They presented these arguments in a series of reports, the most famous of which was the report of the Madras Committee under the chairmanship of Mohammed Usman (1923). What was revealing about these reports was the nature of the questions asked and the answers offered. The response of the traditional practitioners was similar to that of craftsmen facing the political hegemony of the factory. It was not that the modern factory was more efficient; efficiency after all can be judged by a myriad yardsticks. But the modern factory facilitated greater control over and surveillance of workers.

The basic question the traditionalists had to confront was whether traditional systems of medicine were scientific. The practitioners realized that what was being challenged was not the efficacy of the system but an alternative civilizational style.

> When we speak of our medical science they ask us with great wonder if there is indeed such a thing. Instead of posing such a question, if we first agree that there is such a thing as a Hindu people and they also like others have a religion, a language and a science and a great ancient civilization.[59]

The traditional doctors tried to show that their medicines were suited to the genius of the Indian people. They argued for instance that the ayurvedic system was particularly suited to the poor, that the food they prescribed was as cheap as their medicines. They did not require 'ice, icebags, thermometers, or even pearl barley, malted milk, essence of chicken, but could manage with herbs available right in their back-yards'.[60] Only

---

[59] See 'Responses of Indigenous Medical Practitioners to the Madras Enquiry Sixty Years Ago', *PPST Bulletin*, June 1984, *4*, pp. 64–95; see p. 92.

[60] Ibid., pp. 71, 74. For an elegant parallel description of the same tragic process from the point of view of the Unani system, see Sardar, 'Medicine and Metaphysics'; also Madras Group, 'What is the Role of Indigenous Medical Sciences'?

gradually did the traditional doctors realize that the efforts were futile, for what was being built was an industrial grid.

The report of the Industrial Commission had appeared in 1918 and although it had been shelved by the colonial government, it provided the rudiments of the classificatory grid that was to underwrite modern society in India. Dissent and difference would have a different value in such a system.

Central to the emerging discourse on development, represented by the report of the Industrial Commission, was the following classification. In it industry, science (medicine) and the nation-state were to be parallel rubrics:

Modern industry	Western medicine	Nation-state
Intermediate or medium-scale industry	Traditional medicine	Major religious or ethnic grouping
Cottage industry, Craft	Folk medicine	'Little culture'

Under each of these rubrics, the first category encompasses all those below it. It is primary, allegedly more stable and efficient, more bureaucratizable; it is literally paradigmatic in the sense Thomas Kuhn defines the term. The lower forms represent not the 'other' as a possibility, but defeated, 'unscientific' structures, to be absorbed, assimilated or marginalized. Thus ethnicities and local cultures were to be homogenized through the school, marginalized in the reservation, or museumized if disappearing. The logic of the intermediate or craft traditions could survive in the short run but would eventually yield, the argument went, to the all-absorbing power of the multinational industrial empires. It was not that modern medicine was not sensitive to folk or traditional forms of medicine but it did not see them as parties to a dialogue or as an 'other' to be preserved; it saw them as a bag from which products had to be taken out.

III *Gandhi as a Medical Scientist*

Two issues remained to be discussed: the possibility of every one becoming a doctor and the survival of a society without western medical doctors. Both were forcefully articulated in Mohandas Karamchand Gandhi's *Hind Swaraj*.[61]

Gandhi's contribution to the debates on science and technology is usually described as a strange, anti-industrialist amalgam of an oriental Ned Lud and Ruskin. But the *gestalt* is radically different if one looks at Gandhi through his own eyes. Gandhi thought of himself as a scientist and regarded others as such. His autobiography, *My Experiments with Truth*, was literally what it claimed to be, the life and experiences of a scientist.[62] Viewed thus, his *Hind Swaraj* becomes a fascinating science policy document of the post-Swadeshi era, trying to resolve many of the problems that nagged the debate on science and technology. We shall briefly focus on the two texts to examine the alternative view of medical science they project.

Hind Swaraj has all the immediacy of a contemporary statement on science policy. Like all science policy statements, it presumes a relationship between truth and power. However, it grounds that relationship not in a political economy but in an ecological politics organized around a set of ethico-religious principles. Overtly, *Hind Swaraj* includes only a brief, trenchant critique of modern doctors, to parallel its critique of modern lawyers. Implicitly, it takes on the principle of the professionalization of modern scientific disciplines and the fact–value dichotomy which prompts modern society to locate the ethical controls on science outside scientific knowledge.[63] In this respect, the aphoristic essay resembles a Euclidean list of axioms. It holds that:

1. All critiques of technology must be ecological (*oikos*, house). (For Gandhi, ecology, like charity, began at home. The household and neighbourhood were the prime units of concern.)

---

[61] M.K. Gandhi, *Hind Swaraj*, in *Collected Works of Mahatma Gandhi* (Delhi: Publications Division, Government of India, 1963), *4*, pp. 81–208.

[62] M.K. Gandhi, *The Story of My Experiments with Truth* (Ahmedabad: Navjivan, 1927).

[63] Cf. Sunil Sahasrabudhe, 'Hind Swaraj and the Science Question', in Nageshwar Prasad (ed.), *Hind Swaraj: A Fresh Look* (New Delhi: Gandhi Peace Foundation, 1985), pp. 99–105.

2. All notions of ecology are eventually ethical.
3. All ethics are eventually religious.
4. All religions are civilizational and, therefore, a critique of science and technology has to be a civilizational critique, encompassing the ideas of polity, economy and consciousness. (For Gandhi, however, civilizations could be both baselines for and subjects of social criticism.)

The Gandhian concept of modernity encompassed more than the fact of British colonial rule; modernity was the principle of modern western civilization. The British were the vehicles of oppression, carriers of a disease called modernity, and just as captive to its technological power. Thus, the Swadeshi analysis was inadequate for him because it failed to unravel and cope with the logic of modernity.

Underlying the argument of *Hind Swaraj* is the metaphor of the body, relating the human body to the body politic. Bodily scale defines not only the nature of activity, but prescribes its limits. Modern mechanistic civilization is a disease because it violates the integrity of the body. The real tool, argues Gandhi, should be a natural extension of the body, not disjunctive with it. From these simple premises he outlines a critique of modernity, arguing that like colonialism, it is a self-inflicted disease, reflecting the dissipation of both the colonizer and the colonized. He illustrates it through his criticism of the railways in India. The simple fact of two styles of locomotion, on foot and by train, becomes a parable of modernity:

> God set a limit to man's locomotive ambition in the construction of his body. I am so constructed that I can only serve my immediate neighbourhood, but in my conceit I pretend to have discovered that I must with my body serve every individual in the universe. In thus attempting the impossible, man comes into contact with different natures, different religions and is utterly confounded. According to this reasoning, . . . railways are a dangerous institution. Owing to them man has gone further away from his maker.[64]

The railways disrupted the Indian body politic, which Gandhi saw as a huge body digesting and assimilating different cultural

[64] Ibid., p. 28.

elements. He then showed how the two technologies, reflected in pilgrimage on foot and by rail, represented memory and erasure respectively. The pilgrim's progress was an act of faith. The arduous act of pilgrimage to different corners of India gave the pilgrim a sense of both neighbourhood and nationhood, helping him to internalize both similarities and differences. The mechanical negotiation or 'ingestion' of territory through rail travel erased the sanctity of places and turned them into physical spaces. For Gandhi, the modern machine set off a decline into the pathology called history, which was a movement away from nature. A return to nature presupposed a spiralling back to body time and body scale, to bodily discipline. According to him, Indian civilization reflected the social construction of such spirals of conduct.

Gandhi also argued that the modern machine was an expression of unbridled appetite. Modern civilization was hedonistic, gauging progress in terms of calories and comforts and, thus, was necessarily hostile to the Indian concept of good conduct. He wrote:

> Our ancestors saw happiness as largely a mental condition. It is not that we did not know how to invent machinery but our forefathers knew that if we set our hearts after such things, we would become slaves and lose our moral fibre. They, therefore, after due deliberation decided we should only do what we could with our hands and feet. Real happiness consisted of the proper use of hands and feet.[65]

In a fundamental sense, Gandhi, J. C. Bose (1858–1937) and P. C. Ray (1861–1944) were the critical scientists of the Swadeshi and post-Swadeshi era. For each, the encounter with the colonial West became a crisis of identity. Each had to construct a social self in which modern science and technology were crucial targets of love and/or hate. Very self-consciously, each contributed to the social development of the scientist's role in India: Ray as the ascetic savant-entrepreneur, Bose as the scientist who used native ideas of vitalism to confound scientific classifications of life and non-life, and Gandhi as one defining the role of the dissenting scientist in modern India and reaffirming the scienti-

---

[65] Ibid., p. 37.

fic role of the humble craftsman embedded in the folk traditions. However, Gandhi managed to do something more. He challenged the deeper axioms of science—the dualism of knowledge and power, religion and science, and the laity and the expert.

As part of this challenge, Gandhi chose a medical science which was everyday in its immediacy, dietetics and hygiene. There was a certain playfulness about this, a 'cognitive indifference' to the products of modern science, as philosopher Ramchandra Gandhi puts it. Science, like western manners and dress, became something to be tried on, modified, or discarded. After all, borrowed etiquettes ultimately have to yield to the demands of hygiene and self-image. At another plane, the project was more serious and holistic. Dietetics, sexuality, technology, for him all were exercises in the pursuit of truth. The autobiography became an account of a continuing experiment, with the body as the test-tube; the discipline of the body served as a model for the civics of the body politic. For he was concerned about how to embed science in everyday life and yet save everydayness from becoming banal, non-critical and coercive.

The answer Gandhi tried to give, according to his account of his formative years, involved a split-level encounter with the West. At one level, he was the young man from the colonies playing the anglicized dandy, with gold watch chain, Gladstone collar and gloves, taking violin lessons, and speech lessons from Bell's *The Standard Elocutionist*. At another, he was a staunch vegetarian whose vegetarianism stemmed originally only from a promise made to his mother but was slowly becoming a philosophy. One of his friends, trying to dissuade him from it, suggested that he read Bentham on utility. Instead he picked up at a restaurant Henry Salt's *A Plea for Vegetarianism*, which he read and re-read.[66]

Vegetarianism in Gandhi's youth was not always a fad; it was a site for the location of alternative worldviews. It introduced him to the other West of occult philosophy, theosophy, various versions of socialism, and anti-vivisectionism; to Blavatsky, Anne

[66] Henry Salt, *A Plea for Vegetarianism and Other Essays* (Manchester: The Vegetarian Society, 1886).

Kingsford's critique of diet and to Louis Kuhne's naturopathy.[67] They combined with John Ruskin and Leo Tolstoy to provide not only an alternative view of the West but also to help him anchor his own identity in traditions. Vegetarianism linked a traditional religious view of health to an alternative western philosophy of medicine. The writings of the vegetarians, the theosophists, Ruskin and Tolstoy had in common not only a hostility to mechanistic–vivisectional science but contained also the concept of the patient as his own doctor. Instead of experimenting on others, one experimented on oneself. Above all, as Salt put it, it was in the science of diet and hygiene that the opposition betwen western science and religion was resolved, creating the possibility of a moral science. Salt's work convinced Gandhi that food reform could lead to social reform. Indeed, vegetarianism not only equipped the Mahatma with particular kinds of political–ideological skills, as a number of his biographers note, it enabled him to work out the outlines of a critique of modern medicine.

The critique was underpinned by a philosophical sensitivity to three political–ethical issues. First, Gandhi's vegetarianism sought to recover the body for the individual as part of a search for individual autonomy, in turn representing a community-based search for the autonomy of small human aggregates—the notorious Gandhian village republics. For this the vegetarian had to practise poverty, chastity and other forms of discipline, to accept the ethical and cognitive responsibility for his body and, thereby, reject medical processing by the state and by state-licensed medical practitioners.

Second, Gandhi identified in the body politic the pathological expression of three forms of violence—racism, prostitution and vivisection. These were not arbitrarily lumped together. Each form reflected a particular violation of the body and all three were epitomized in the parasitism of the city. The city was the home of censuses, epidemics and medical science. His experiences in South Africa had led him to connect racism, urbanity and medicine. Both in Natal and the Transvaal, the presence of Indians in towns was objected to on sanitary and medical

[67] Anne Kingsford, *The Perfect Way in Diet* (London: Kegan Paul, Trench, Trubner, 1889); and Louis Kuhne, *The New Science of Healing* (Leipzig: Author, 1892).

grounds, and the doctors had helped drive Indians out of towns into 'locations'. In response to this ultimate form of medical surveillance and to confront the triad of violence in a mechanical city, Gandhi encoded within his idea of a non-industrial way of life, along with vegetarianism and anti-vivisectionism, traditional agriculture, and the use of *khādī* and the *charkhā*. For him they signposted the road to the recovery of the body.

Finally, Gandhi's thought incorporated the idea of iatrogeny but went beyond it. *Hind Swaraj* not merely located the science of medicine in the colonial structure—'to study European medicine is to deepen our slavery', it says—the tract held the patient responsible for the persistence of the iatrogenic regime. Modern doctors helped perpetuate the urban–industrial civilization by disconnecting overconsumption from its bodily consequences. As a result, they both destroyed the 'natural' resistance to an expropriatory system, and actually aided the patient to lose control over himself. From such a viewpoint, the immorality of modern hospitals was axiomatic and recovery of the body from the medical expert by the laity became both a moral statement and an affirmation of political–moral autonomy.

This was a more radical set of proposals than theosophy offered. Theosophy rejected birth-control and vaccination intuitively because they militated against its vision of childhood. Gandhi rejected citizenship of a polis where to be was to be inoculated. The clash between Gandhi and Besant is often interpreted as the struggle between Home Rule and Swaraj. Actually it was also a clash between the occult body and the mystic body. Gandhi's radicalism lay in offering a more playful, though less Borgesian, critique of science. In it not only does every man become a scientist and every village a science academy, but there is a demand for a cognitive resistance to the gross appetite of modern science.

Few accepted his offer. The satyagrahi remained a political resister, too sedate to accept this invitation to an alternative vision of science.

IV *A Traditional Critique*

The theosophists, despite being fascinated by the mysterious East, were primarily carriers of the underground traditions of western science. Their critique of modern science had to be sometimes a play on the absurd, given the near-total dominance of the target of their criticism. Gandhi's critique, on the other hand, was a more down-to-earth attempt to represent both the dissenting traditions of the West and the surviving traditions of medicine in his own society. Because he linked his theory of the body to the theory of politics on the one hand, and the politics of culture on the other, his resistance to medicalization was necessarily part of a larger theory of resistance.

A third possible baseline of criticism still remains to be marked out. We have not asked till now which way a critique of western medicine would go if the point of view is that of a traditional Indian medical system, unaffected by critical western thought?

We shall try to answer this question by briefly describing what in many ways was a brilliant critical response to western medicine, given in the post-Swadeshi era by G. Srinivasmurthi on behalf of Ayurveda. A remarkably versatile man, Srinivasmurthi was an outstanding Sanskrit scholar and man of letters who had translated the *Merchant of Venice* into Telugu. Though he described himself as a 'humble votary' of western medicine, he was a trained modern doctor, fashionable enough to become personal physician to John Barrymore, the actor. But while he respected western science, Srinivasmurthi was not awed by it. In fact, he was prescient enough about modern science to remark in 1923, 'fortunately for the world, western scientists have not been able to release this [atomic] energy'.[68] He had the bilingual's confidence that a dialogue between different medical systems was possible. His minute on indigenous systems was part of the Usman Committee Report but can be read independently as an argument for a more plural encounter among medical systems.

Srinivasmurthi realized that the official history of western science acted as a filter, preventing the possibility of such an encounter. For the official history saw the authorities derived

[68] G. Srinivasmurthi, 'Secretary's Minute', *Report of the Committee of Indigenous Systems of Medicine* (Madras: Government Printing Press, 1923), p. 20.

from the scriptures and science as antithetical. Such a history could not be sympathetic to a medicine which cited the authority of the scriptures as one of the guides to right knowledge. Western science, he realized, would read such an appeal to authority as a 'petrified dogma', which denied the freedom of individual action so essential to their pursuit of science.

The idea of scriptural authority in indigenous knowledge, however, was radically different from that in the West, Srinivasmurthi argued. Scriptural authority in India did not have 'the sterilising touch... that sought to burn away the tender seed of science which Galileo planted at the risk of his life'. The minute says,

> no one who has not entered into the very soul of Hindu thought can appreciate what scriptural authority means to the Hindu and how two persons paying the profoundest possible veneration to the same scriptural texts can yet interpret them in ways as diverse as the poles; a classic example that occurs to my mind is how all schools of Vedanta–from uncompromising duality (Dvaita) to absolute non-duality (Advaita)—purport to be based on the same scriptural text.[69]

The minute observes that no orthodox pandit would admit that the Vedas were in error, but one pandit could claim that his commentary was more in conformity with the truth of the texts than that of others. 'In other words, differences of views were expressed through commentaries on texts rather than by altering the texts themselves.'[70] This absence of dogma, and this playful invitation to a festival of interpretations, allows for as many commentaries and editions of the scientific method as of a religious text.

Srinivasmurthi notes that there are historical precedents for similar exercises in the West. He quotes William Osler's observation:

> The quarrels of doctors made a pretty picture in the history of medicine. Each generation seems to have had its own... the Arabians and the Galenists, the Brunonians and the Broussonians, the Homeopaths and the regulars have in different centuries rent the robe of Aesculapius.[71]

---

[69] Ibid., p. 11.

[70] Ibid.

[71] Ibid., p. 8.

Such differences, Srinivasmurthi feels, could lead to 'not unhealthy disputations'. And he invites one to a dialogue of medical systems similar to a dialogue of religions. The dialogue would not be a search for uniformity through a search for similarities. Nor would there be an attempt to mechanically translate terms such as *vāyu, pitta, kapha* into wind, bile and phlegm, thus reducing Ayurveda to the old abandoned humoral theory of the Greek physicians.[72] Rather it would be an attempt to grapple with systems and systemic differences, without strapping indigenous systems to the procustean bed of western medicine. It would not even be a search for equality between the intellectual systems of the colonizer and the colonized but a fraternal disputation on differences.

The minute stresses the differences in the construction of the two systems, allopathy and Ayurveda, and specifically mentions the mix of science, philosophy and religion in the native system. It points out that in Madhavacārya's *Sarva Darśana Sangraha*, which is a discussion of roughly sixteen religio-philosophical faiths of India, each discussion constitutes a chapter. One finds here, along with discussions of Buddhism, Jainism and Advaitism, a full chapter on *raseśvara darśanam* or chemistry.[73]

To the western mind such an arrangement of chapters would mean a confusion of the categories of science, philosophy and religion. A Hindu perceives it differently.

> The one supreme object of life is to attain the state of self realization or *Mukti*.... Now the study of Chemistry helps me to achieve this object by intelligently using mercury and other chemicals in the healthy regulation of my physical and other bodies; here we see at once how the philosophy ... of chemistry is indissolubly associated with the science of chemistry and with certain ethical and physical practices broadly included under the name of 'Religion'—the religion if you please of Chemistry. As in chemistry so it is in Mathematics, Grammar, Exegetics, Ayurveda, or any other branch of study....[74]

We should mention here the recommendation of the Usman Committee that support to native systems of medicine should

---

[72] Ibid., p. 16.
[73] Ibid., p. 13.
[74] Ibid.

not be left only to the state but also be the responsibility of temples. The report recommended that some of the great south Indian temples take on the task of encouraging Ayurvedic and Siddha systems. This attempt to move beyond the secular idiom of the modern public realm reminds one of A. L. Basham's observation on the relationship between the Ayurvedic and Unani systems:

> The practitioners of the two systems seem to have collaborated, because each had much to learn from the other and whatever the ulama and the brahmans might say, we have no record of animosity between Hindu and Muslim in the field of medicine.[75]

It is in this spirit that Srinivasmurthi ventures a critique of western medicine from an Ayurvedic vantage ground. An elaborate exercise, it centres on three related sets of ideas: (1) the opposition between external and internal conceptions of disease; (2) the relationship between the disease and the patient; and (3) the relationship between clinical and laboratory conceptions of disease.

Sociologically, one of the major oppositions between Ayurveda and allopathy has centred on the germ theory of disease. While modern western theory has generally looked at disease in terms of the diverse objective agents that invade the body, Ayurveda has looked at disease in terms of internal processes, triggered by external factors. Srinivasmurthi notes that while Ayurveda recognizes the role of micro-organisms, it does not grant them the centrality they possess in allopathy.

> They [the Ayurvedis] merely looked upon the germ as one among the many causative factors capable of producing disease, if the soil or field (*Kṣetra*) was suitable for the growth of the germ seed. It is when the bodily constitution was undermined by the non-observance of the laws of health such as *Ṛtucaryā* (hygienic rules for various seasons of the year), *Dinacaryā* (hygienic rules for daily conduct), *Brahmacarya* (hygienic rules for celibacy or regulated social life) and so on, that the *Kṣetra* becomes suitable for the growth of germ seeds, which were powerless to do mischief in the case of people who lead pure and healthy lives. . . .[76]

---

[75] A. L. Basham, 'The Practice of Medicine in Ancient and Medieval India', in Charles Leslie (ed.), *Asian Medical Systems* (Berkeley: University of California, 1976), pp. 18–44; see p. 40.

[76] Srinivasmurthi, 'Secretary's Minute', p. 42.

Srinivasmurthi goes on to ask:

> Can the germ enthusiast say definitely that the cholera vibrio or the tubercule bacillus is *everything* in the causation of cholera or tuberculosis? ... Certain germs may be living for years in our intestines on terms of neutrality or even of harmonious helpfulness; but the moment something untoward happens to the intestines, they may at once grow unfriendly and declare war. Now all these years the so-called exciting cause was there but powerless to excite ... why should we not call the injury to the intestines the exciting cause and the bacterium the predisposing cause. They are apparently like seed and soil.... It seems the *tridośa* theory looks at the question from the standpoint of the soil, while the germ theory looks at it from the standpoint of the seed.
>
> 'Keep out the seed—away with all germs and you are safe'—that is the slogan of the germ enthusiast. 'It seems impracticable to keep out germ seeds which are ubiquitous. Therefore keep the soil in such a condition that no seed can grow, even if it gets there.' So urges the Ayurvedist.[77]

The question, Srinivasmurthi points out, is whether one should regard bacteria as the result or the cause. He asks as an example whether the term influenza denotes merely a group of clinical signs and symptoms or whether it signifies that influenza is caused by a specific germ. The answer, he believes, is unclear and unsatisfactory, and leaves one wondering why the germ theory has become such a fetish.

Ayurveda's 'agricultural view' becomes relevant in this context. Srinivasmurthi notes that western medicine has been prone to classify bacteria by their morphological characteristics, ignoring the wisdom of agriculturists who insist that what the bacteria do is more important than what they are. For example, an attack of Shiga dysentery or cholera will be mild or severe depending upon the intestinal content. If amino-acids are present in abundance, Srinivasmurthi points out, toxic amines will be produced, and the attack will be severe. If the diet has left little protein residue in the intestines, the bacteria will produce little toxic amines, and the attack will be mild.[78]

Srinivasmurthi goes on to say that even western medical

---

[77] Ibid., p. 13.

[78] Ibid., p. 46.

theory has been moving away from the germ theory and assuming a more Ayurvedic position of attending to the soil, keeping it so that germ seeds cannot thrive on it. Even the informed layman, according to him, had realized that the active campaign to abolish bacteria is futile. He quotes a comment in *The Times* of London: 'The control of human resistance offers a brighter future than the direct attempts to eliminate disease.'[79]

Apart from the possibility of a dialogue on the conceptual difference between external and internal concepts of diseases lies the scope for a dialogue on styles of diagnosis. Srinivasmurthi cites Yamini Bhusan Roy to make the point that 'western doctors do not possess the key to the proper diagnosis of the patient though they were correct in their diagnosis of the disease'.[80] Allopathy pays little attention to the *prakṛti*, the inherited constitution and idiosyncracies of the patient. The system has no place for ideas of *jāti* (race), *kula* (tribe), *deśa* (place), *kāla* (time), *vayas* (age) or the *pratyagātma niyata* of body temperament (individual peculiarities).

On the basis of Gananath Sen's observations, Srinivasmurthi discusses the possible consequences of such a bias:

> While western medicine cannot help us to tell beforehand which of our patients is likely to suffer from quinine idiosyncracy, and which not, we are able, if we know how to diagnose our patient (especially his *prakṛti*), according to Ayurvedic methods, to avoid making any mistakes about quinine administration... Western medicine has at present no means of recognising the patient's *prakṛti*.... It has to act more or less blindly, and learn from the bitter experiences of its patients.[81]

The stress on disease by itself rather than on disease-and-patient is identified as a by-product of the shift from the clinical to the laboratory view in western medicine.

> The laboratory worker obtains his results by a delicate mechanical contrivance, but the physician has to train his senses to recognize these different sensations. As a consequence of his inability to acquire this knowledge, he ignores information which it reveals particularly about the early signs of disease.[82]

---

[79] Ibid., p. 44.
[80] Ibid., p. 59.
[81] Ibid., p. 60.
[82] Ibid., p. 54.

Prognosis, according to the Ayurvedis, has been given inadequate significance in allopathy, even though much information exists about the stages of a disease. To the Ayurvedi, it seems strange that the importance of interrogation, the elaborate liturgy of procedures by which the doctor interrogates the patient, is disregarded in allopathy.

The laboratory view of treatment is found objectionable not merely morally, as an instance of objectification, but cognitively:

> ... experiments on healthy animals may easily lead us astray; and it is fallacious to judge the effect of a drug on a human being by the effect it produces on an animal; ... it is also fallacious to judge the effect of a drug on a diseased human being by the effect it produces on a *healthy* animal; ... then again there is the clinical fact that two persons may not react to the same drug in the same way in two different conditions of ill health; in a very real sense, then, every dose of a drug that we administer to a patient is a new experiment.[83]

Srinivasmurthi therefore wonders, given the discoveries of the botanist J. C. Bose, if one may some day obtain from experiments on plants the sort of help presently derived from experiments on animals.[84]

Srinivasmurthi makes one final point about the cognitive capacities of the two systems of medicine. The Ayurvedic classification of diseases and treatments seems elaborate enough to provide 'readymade niches' for other forms of treatment such as allopathy, homeopathy, osteopathy, Kuhne cure, vaccine therapy, psychotherapy, etc. This has saved it from the two perils of western medicine, namely, faddism and hyper-specialization. In Ayurveda (as in Hindu thought), there is no need to set up a closed or overdefined sect and proclaim it as owning a universal panacea. On the other hand,

> With our western brethren the case seems to be quite different. There, we have an ever-increasing number of medical sects, each with a special nostrum or formula wherewith to cure or charm away all the ills that flesh is heir to. Each may undoubtedly have a limited field of usefulness and applicability, but the danger lies in the attempt to transform it into a universal panacea.... One

[83] Ibid., p. 69.

[84] Ibid.

would cure all ills by osteopathy, another by chromopathy, yet another by homeopathy, a fourth by allopathy, others by electricity baths, food reform, vaccine therapy, charms, incantations, miracle workings, magnetic healing, faith cures, denial of diseases, affirmation of health, and so on, till one fails to see the forests from the trees.[85]

Then Srinivasmurthi quotes Bernard Shaw on western medicine:

> Now Heartbreak House was a hypochondriacal house, always running after cures. It was superstitious, and addicted to table rapping, clairvoyances, materialization, seances, palmistry, crystal gazing and the like to such an extent that it may be doubted whether ever before in the history of the world did soothsayers, astrologers, and unregistered therapeutic specialists of all sorts flourish as they did during this half of the century.... The registered doctors and surgeons were hard put to compete with the unregistered. They were not clever enough to appeal to the imagination and sociability of the heartbreakers by the acts of the actor, the orator, the poet, the winning conversationalist. They had to fall back on the terror of infection and death. They prescribed inoculations and operation. Whatever part of the human being could be cut out without necessarily killing him they cut out and he often died (unnecessarily of course) in consequence. From such trifles as uvulas and tonsils, they went on to ovaries and appendices until, at last, no one's inside was safe....[86]

V *Knowledge, Consciousness and Dissent*

We have here told the same story twice, once in our own language and then, in a more long-winded and colourful way, with reference to three strands of consciousness which emerged during the first three decades of this century in India. The second retelling of the story has some specific implications. Through it, we have described three modes of dissent from modern medical philosophy in this part of the world. Each of these modes is simultaneously an attempt to understand modern medicine and to cope with the typical clinical, social and

---

[85] Ibid., p. 62.

[86] Ibid., p. 63.

philosophical problems this mode of healing introduces into the world of applied knowledge.

These constructions of modern medicine in non-modern terms are, therefore, three forms of meaning-seeking when confronting a politically powerful knowledge system which shows immediate practical results in some areas but is intellectually, socially, and morally disorienting. From the irrationality-as-defiance of some of the theosophists to the culture-as-resistance of Gandhi to the indigenous-as-the-theory-of-the-exogenous of Srinivasmurthi, each construction revalues the past in the light of the present, to keep possibilities open for the future. Each construction also in turn produces its own set of problems which is no less formidable than that produced by modern medicine. It is however an indicator of the power of the empiricism of life, as opposed to the empiricism of the academe, that the three responses together almost fully anticipate our summary description of the contemporary critiques of modern medicine in the first part of the essay. Admittedly, this anticipation is only sometimes self-conscious; admittedly, it often uses specific formulations which verge on the absurd; admittedly too, the anticipation is mostly the product of a self-exploration which sometimes tells us more about the attempts to restore self-esteem in the Indian middle classes than about the inner logic of modern medicine. Yet the fact remains that in some mutually potentiating way, the critiques converge because, even though they diagnose the illness of modern medicine differently, the clinical acumen which informs them helps the critiques to identify the broad contours of the problem similarly.

Beyond this convergence lies a paradox. Six decades ago, modern medicine was already triumphant in the West. But it was yet to become hegemonic on the South Asian medical scene. What is easy to identify today, when the crisis of modern medicine has 'matured', was then the concern mainly of cranks and visionaries. And the two categories, as we well know from the growing literature on the nature of human creativity, are rarely if ever exclusive categories. We have shown that, to judge by the responses to modern medicine, 'demented' and otherworldly 'sages' diagnosed the crisis of modern medicine with greater clinical and philosophical perspicacity than did specialists and 'normal' scientists. Perhaps it is in the nature of a 'successful' modern knowledge system to push to the periphery all criticisms of the system and to ensure that they survive only in the form of artistic or fantastic imagination.

That these criticisms can sometimes return as the unconscious of the modern world is part of the same story. The story has to be retold only to reaffirm that even criticism with limited access to empirical data, even criticism couched in the language of anti-empiricism, can, when backed by an ethical vision, show greater empirical sensitivity than criticisms wedded to empiricism but unwilling to confront the problems of suffering without reifying them.

An Intelligent Critic's Guide to Indian Cinema

I *The Cultural Matrix of the Popular Film*

One of the most remarkable changes taking place in India is the expansion of urban, middle-class culture and the pace-setting role it has begun to play in the public realm. The changes are not so marked in terms of aggregate data—for instance, the proportion of Indians living in cities has increased by only about 5 per cent in the last fifty years—and the data give no clue to the way urban middle-class culture has begun to dominate the culture of politics today. Such domination would have been unthinkable only two decades ago. For the first time ever, India now has a popular culture which includes not only folk forms such as *jātrā, kathā* and *Rāmalīlā* but also a whole range of products with a number of common characteristics which include television serials, commercial Hindi films, cricket (particularly one-day cricket), ghazals and urban gurus.

The urban middle classes in India, thanks to the size of the country, have for a long time been large in absolute terms, even though small as a proportion of the Indian population. If urban India, which is roughly one-fourth of India, declares independence, rural India would still remain the world's second largest country but urban India would be, by itself, the world's fifth largest country. This urban India would also have enormous economic muscle and a huge pool of professional skills. It might go down one or two notches as an industrial power, thanks to Indian development policies which locate many industrial units away from cities, but it would still have the world's third largest scientific manpower, and be the world's third largest democracy as well as the world's largest producer of films. It would also have traditions. It would include the world's oldest city and represent the unbroken continuity of a civic tradition some four thousand years old, and it would house much of India's artistic treasures, from the Elephanta caves to the Taj Mahal. Urban India would also continue to provide a critical mass sustaining a level of intellectual activity and creative initiative difficult or impossible to achieve in smaller Third World societies.

It is the sheer size and political presence of urban India that has allowed the Indian middle classes to give the country, during the last 150 years, rather more than what other Third World societies have been given by their westernized bourgeoisie. The middle classes in India have often successfully processed, that is, creatively endogenized or ritually neutralized on behalf of the society, disturbing inputs from the modern West and simultaneously helped update or renew the society's traditions. In other words, these classes have often provided the baseline for a critique of modernity as well as of tradition. The great thinkers and social reformers of nineteenth- and twentieth-century India all operated from within the perimeters of urban middle-class India, even when they themselves were *haut bourgeois* like Rabindranath Tagore, even when they attacked middle-class culture the way Bankimchandra Chattopadhyay and Gandhi did, and even when they, like Bhimrao Ambedkar, came from the lowest stratum of the society.

That is why Tagore understood and respected Gandhi's enterprise despite his fundamental disagreement with it. They shared an idiom and a culture, within which most creative Indians, be they from the world of art cinema (from Satyajit Ray and Ritwik Ghatak to Mrinal Sen and Adoor Gopalakrishnan), contemporary art (Amrita Sher-Gil to Jamini Roy to M. F. Hussain) or literature (from Saratchandra Chattopadhyay and Premchand to U. R. Ananthamurthy and Sunil Gangopadhyay), operate today. All these figures can be seen as mediating between the classical and the non-classical or folk, and between West and East.

Concurrently, there has grown a parallel style of low-brow mediation between the same sets of variables–classical and non-classical, and East and West—from the middle of the nineteenth century. It, too, has had substantial popular support in India's urban centres. However, given the nature and reach of the creativity the Indian middle classes have shown for about a century, given the power and energy of living classicism and the living traditions of folk culture, that low-brow middle-class culture has not played, until very recently, a pace-setting role in Indian society. It has shaped public consciousness, but done so outside the normal angle of public vision and beyond public earshot. The quasi-yellow press of urban Bengal, thriving since the last decades of the nineteenth century and popularly known as *bat-talā*, and the flourishing calendar art of many parts of India, expressing in a new 'vulgate' the emerging concepts of the sacred and the secular, illustrate the point I am making, namely, that low-brow mediation has acted as a cultural 'underground' rather than as a legitimate form of popular culture.[1]

That underground has come above ground; it is now threatening to corner the high culture of the middle classes. Popular astrology, popular psychology, popular constructions of international cricket, and fast food, do not represent so much the vulgarization of astronomy, psychology, Victorian cricket and colonial cuisine, or the semi-modern incarnations of their folk counterparts in *jyotiṣ*, village wisdom, rural games and the *dhābā*. They are actually extensions of the *bat-talā*, calendar art, and the uniformed waiter in the cheap back-street restaurant who has simultaneously fascinated and intimidated the first-generation immigrant to the city since the last century.

The reasons for this new self-assertion of the low-brow are well known; only one need be mentioned here. The accelerating process of social change in India has uprooted increasing numbers of people from their folk traditions. The psychological needs of these newly uprooted are not those of the more settled middle-class culture of what used to be called, under the colonial dispensation, the presidency towns. For various reasons, the culture of the presidency town middle classes was more open to the Sanskritic traditions of the upper castes and to western upper-class classicism (which was often taken in colonial India to be the popular culture of Britain). At the same time, despite the

[1] See, for example, Sumanta Banerjee, *The Parlour and the Streets: Elite and Popular Culture in Nineteenth Century Calcutta* (Calcutta: Seagull, 1989).

lip service paid by middle-class intellectuals to the beauties of the people's culture, middle-class culture was noticeably less than hospitable to the folk traditions of both East and West.

This middle-class partiality towards the classical made its culture less able to meet the psychological needs of the newly uprooted in the second phase of modernization of independent India. The poor man's melting pot called modern India needed a more self-confident and abrasive culture which could be analogous to the mass culture of the West. (In parts of India and in some sectors of life, the problem was apparently resolved by the accidental emergence of a middle-brow medium of self-expression to serve as a new urban folk expression and a popular form of classicism. Many non-Bengalis, disturbed by the devotion to Tagore's songs shown by discriminating music lovers in West Bengal and Bangladesh, are unwilling to recognize that Tagore's music serves as a new form of popular culture for the Bengalis. So, along with commercial popular film songs, a space in the popular culture of that part of the world has been reserved for Rabindrasangit, mediating between the classical and the folk, East and West and, in this case, between music and poetry.)[2]

Though the emerging mass culture has taken to their logical conclusion some elements of what used to be popular middle-class culture, there are noticeable differences between the two. These differences are reflected in the line drawn by many viewers between the 'innocence' of Bombay Talkies, New Theatres and Prabhat Studios, on the one hand, and the hard-eyed commercialism of the Manmohan Desais and Ramesh Sippys, on the other; between Ravi Verma and calendar art, Rabindrasangit and film music, and so on. Some of these differences are as follows:

First, the new mass culture is low culture in two important senses: it includes more low-brow elements from the dominant, 'universal' mass culture of the West and it tends to reject elements from the western high culture, once so prominent in Indian middle-class culture. The new culture has conspicuously

[2] That there was space for such in the realm of the arts was intuitively sensed by a section of the left movement. Some in the movement, such as composer Salil Chowdhury, occasionally made highly creative use of this awareness in the early years of Independence. Analogous examples from the world of dance would be the efforts of Uday Shankar and, later, Sachin Shankar.

shed the comical, bowdlerized versions of western classicism which could be found in, say, Indian commercial theatre's and commercial cinema's 'remakes' of Shakespeare, or in Bankimchandra Chattopadhyay's more serious use of Walter Scott's work as a model for his historical novels. The new mass culture similarly underplays the classical elements of Indian culture without rejecting them fully. This attenuated presence of the classic is accompanied by an indirect but clear dependence on the epic or *purānic* worldview.

Second, there is a sliding scale of audience participation: folk culture encourages bilateral and multilateral modes of communication: never is the folk artist a purely professional entertainer and the audience a passive receiver of messages. In a Rāmalīlā, the viewer participates through his knowledge and experience of the genre, through his familiarity with the story, and through the scope which the genre gives to a person or community to be both audience and performer simultaneously. For a traditional viewer of a Rāmalîlā, the story as performed by the actors reveals something new not because the story is not known or because its unravelling keeps the viewer glued to his seat, but because something new is heard or seen every moment of the performance. It is a mode of renewal and, simultaneously, rediscovery, for each performance absorbs something new from life and reconstructs itself as a new commentary on life.

The popular culture of the urban middle classes inherited something of this tradition. It too had about it an apparent predictability or repeatability; it, too, spoke the language of continuity. Most commercial films still express something of this popular culture, even though they are increasingly influenced by the principles of mass culture.

In urban mass culture, on the other hand, communication is mostly one-way. 'Creativity' is seen as a packageable characteristic of the individual; it is the productivity of the writer, the director or the performing artist. Creativity is not seen to emerge from the interaction between the producer and consumer of art. The writer, the artist and the producer–director are seen to hold the story-line in their hands; the viewer views the unfolding. In the folk tradition, the artist, if he regards himself at all as a distinct individuated entity, sees himself as a vehicle of larger social forces. In popular culture, the creative artist still has this option though otherwise he is already a clearly identifiable individual producer. In mass culture, the artist uses his art as a vehicle for individual self-expression and tries to homogenize the audience into a passive source of applause and patronage. (This is one area where the principles of mass and modern élite cultures overlap; both emphasize the individuality of the artist. However, mass culture must try in addition to make the individual's peaks of creativity fully accessible to the consumer; it cannot demand from its audience prior exposure, or a trained or cultivated response.)

Third, popular middle-class culture, playing its mediatory role between the classical and the folk, the modern and the traditional, has usually been fragmented. It varies from region to region; that of Tamilnadu, Maharashtra and Bengal each bears the stamp of its own local culture and memories of its own unique past. For instance, Bengal's encounter with the West, its exposure to the Brahminism of the Gangetic plain, and even the ethnic and class composition of Bengali society have all been distinctive, and left their mark on Bengali popular culture. (Witness, for instance, the stylistic differences between Bengali and Marathi commercial cinema that developed as early as in the 1930s.)

Such distinctions are less conspicuous in the emerging mass culture, which is pan-Indian and, as I have already said, bears the strong impress of the 'universal' mass culture of the modern West. The major modes of self-expression in the modern world such as commercial movies, one-day cricket, and fast-food chains try to locate themselves on that universal grid. They may have distinct styles or schools which may self-consciously use regional or ethnic differences but such schools are perfectly commensurable, as far as mutual understanding and participation on the common grid goes.

Fourth, mass culture is relatively uncritical of the ruling political culture and political stereotypes; indeed it is partly shaped by them. In the popular middle-class culture, dissent tends to take a predictable form imposed by conventional concepts of sanity, normality and maturity. In mass culture, dissent is even more constrained by these concepts, for they operate in the form of a set of easy, neatly organized categories. To be successful, both dissent and dissenter must be advertised, packaged and sold like any other consumable.

Some of the common features of and differences between art films, middle-brow cinema (which for a while was called, quite appropriately, middle cinema) and commercial films in India are now perhaps clearer. All three depend on the middle classes for legitimacy and critical acclaim. Even those producers and performers who stridently proclaim the supremacy of popular taste, or denounce the élitism of the art-film critics, are on the defensive when there is sharp criticism of their wares in the media. Indeed, the way the producers of each of these kinds of movies try to win friends and influence middle-class opinion give the lie to their declared dependence on only the opinions of the 'common Indian'. The common Indian is rarely influenced by what Kumar Shahani says of Manmohan Desai. But Desai *was* distressed when Shahani took him on while Shahani in turn resents that his films do not get the patronage or support of those for whom his radical heart bleeds, whereas Desai mobilizes such support with casual ease.

Nevertheless, there are clear differences in the cultural thrusts of the three; to gauge the appeal or lack of appeal of any of these forms, one must first identify the thrusts.

First, the commercial film tends to reflect and be protective towards the implicit cultural values of the society. If it criticizes traditions, the criticism tends to be indirect, latent or unintended. If for instance there is criticism of untouchability, it is grounded on the traditional concept of a humane society; if there is criticism of religious violence, the criticism invokes not so much the secular values of a modern polity as the perennial values of the religions involved.

Of course, this emphasis on cultural self-expression or cultural self-defence is also simultaneously a defiance and unwitting criticism of middle-class values. The commercial cinema in India does tend to reaffirm the values that are being increasingly marginalized in public life by the language of the modernizing middle classes, values such as community ties, consensual non-contractual human relations, primacy of maternity over conjugality, priority of the mythic over the historical. But even such indirect criticism of middle-class values is cast not in the language of social criticism but in that of playful, melodramatic, spectacles.

In art films and middle cinema, on the other hand, the

emphasis on the expressive function of art or the reaffirmation of cultural values tends to be muted. High-brow films usually provide sharp criticisms and deep analyses of the social pathologies associated with tradition, which contrasts markedly with their shallow or superficial criticisms of the violence and exploitation associated with modern institutions. The high cinema in India has never been particularly sensitive to the growing threats to lifestyles, life-support systems and non-modern cognitive orders, or for that matter to the values of those in the 'survival sector' of the society—a sector not primarily concerned with the goal of a good life (as it is defined by modern India), but with mere survival and the protection of whatever little the survivor has by way of access to the global commons, traditional technologies, knowledge of health care, and community self-sufficiency outside the monetized sector of the economy. The feelings, attitudes and values associated with the survival sector are the ones that the commercial cinema consciously or unconsciously exploits but in the process also unwittingly supports, even if only partially and even while mouthing the slogans of the dominant culture of politics. Commercial cinema romanticizes and, given half a chance, vulgarizes the problems of the survival sector, but it never rejects as childish or primitive the categories or worldviews of those trying to survive the processes of victimization let loose by modern institutions. The makers of commercial cinema cannot indulge in the luxury of such rejection, given the kind of audience they seek. (This tacit refusal to reject cultural values and embrace modernity uncritically also partially explains the enormous popularity of the Indian commercial cinema in parts of the erstwhile Soviet Block which had rich native traditions of art cinema patronized by the state.)

Second, the middle cinema is—some may say was—the true heir to pre-Independence popular cinema and its occasional, mostly unsuccessful attempts to be arty (by which I simply mean the scattered attempts by some movie-makers to turn cinema into a new artistic medium of cultural and personal self-expression in India). P. C. Barua, V. Shantaram, Debaki Bose, and Bimal Roy did not make art films, nor did they lay down the basis for future directors of art films. (Satyajit Ray has often claimed that he learnt little from these makers of what were popularly seen as clean, socially relevant, technically competent films; he had virtually to create his own medium and style.) Though the middle cinema is often viewed as a compromise between art and commercial cinema, it could be more appropriately seen as a further development of the style that once catered to the middle-class culture of the 1930s and 1940s. The middle cinema has in fact a tradition to build upon, the tradition of the 'good popular cinema' of yesteryears.

Indeed, the middle cinema can claim to originate from an even wider cultural current—the current represented by a galaxy of well-crafted, less-than-great creative products, from the work of Ravi Verma to Premchand, Girish Chandra Ghose to Prithviraj Kapoor, from Marathi stage music to K. L. Saigal. Viewed thus, the middle cinema caters to that part of the middle-class consciousness which has during the last century and a half played a creative role in Indian society by sustaining a dialogue at the popular plane, however imperfect, between the traditional and the modern, the East and the West, the classical and the folk.

What we call popular cinema today is certainly popular but its links are now weakening with the pre-war popular cinema and the middle-class experiences that sustained that cinema. Popular cinema now (for the sake of clarity I shall stick to the term commercial cinema) has more links with the growing mass culture in India. However, though these links are getting stronger every day, they do not monopolize commercial cinema; nor are they likely to do so in the near future. Certain basic character types, stock situations, subplots survive. So do distinctive ways of telling a story, the styles of acting, and the set-piece interactions of stereotypes. Above all survives a structure of myths that has proved remarkably resilient to all demands for change.

Third, commercial cinema has to take an instrumental view of cultural traditions and worldviews and present them theatrically and spectacularly. To do so, it has to *generalize* the specific problems of its different audiences and then *exteriorize* the psychological components of these problems. To this extent such cinema is anti-psychological: it presents psychological conflicts as if they were conflicts among social types or products of a unique conjunction of external events.[3]

---

[3] Ashis Nandy, 'The Popular Hindi Film: Ideology and First Principles', *India International Centre Quarterly*, 1981, *9*, pp. 89–96; and *The Tao of Cricket: On Games of Destiny and the Destiny of Games* (New Delhi, Viking and Penguin, 1989), Ch. 1.

Thus, for instance, the grandiloquent stylization of the Muslim aristocratic traditions of north India, Goan Christian simplicity and love of a good life, Rajput valour, Bengali romanticism; they are all essential to the basic style of the commercial cinema. Thus also the dependence on stereotypical 'external' events or situations to sustain its story-line. Together they allow commercial cinema to 'spectacularize' and de-psychologize everything it touches–violence, dance, music, death, dress and love–and subject every sentiment and value to the judgment of the market.[4]

I sometimes suspect that this double-edged 'sensitivity' to culture is one of the few valid grounds for a social criticism of popular movies, not the violence and sex they depict nor what urbane critics say about their irrationality, crudity and use of stereotypes. In fact, the lack of realism and the dream-like quality—the 'cultural dream work', one may call it—is deployed to deal with the concerns of low-brow viewers, concerns which most art films and middle cinema do not touch upon. The basic principles of commercial cinema derive from the needs of Indians caught in the hinges of social change who are trying to understand their predicament in terms of cultural categories known to them. The strength of the commercial cinema lies in its ability to tap the fears, anxieties and felt pressures towards deculturation and even depersonalization that plague a growing number of Indians who do not find the normative framework of the established urban middle-class culture adequate for their needs and yet have been pushed to adopt it in everyday life.

There can, of course, be political and aesthetic criticism of films catering to the mass culture. But it is possible that public lamentation about the alleged aesthetic and moral failure of the commercial film only reinforces its appeal for its audience which is unconcerned about the aesthetic and the ethics, the absurdity and 'immorality', because it has the secret code by which to decipher the film's latent social message in the context of its life-world. It is actually willing to read such lamentations as final and satisfactory proof of the commercial film's defiance of culturally alien aspects of middle-class morality.

---

[4] On commercial film as a spectacle in Roland Barth's sense of the term, see Nandy, 'The Popular Hindi Film'.

Fourth, there are differences in the way art films and commercial films, so to speak, see themselves and see each other. The main difference is that for the art film there is a clear artistic break between it and commercial films; for the commercial film there is only a commercial break. The partisans of art films see themselves as champions of a proper medium of individual and cultural self-expression; to them, commercial films are technically competent, high-paying financial ventures with no artistic legitimacy or social relevance. When the votaries of art cinema grant social relevance to the commercial film, they do so in negative terms, seeing the commercial cinema only as an index of social pathology.

To the partisans of commercial films, on the other hand, art films constitute an artistic continuum with the commercial cinema. They hold that the art-film maker is usually careless about the producer's money and can therefore afford to indulge in useless, baroque detailing as a private ego trip at public expense. The applause the art-film maker receives is primarily the work of pedantic film critics pretending to be entertained when they are actually bored to tears. Such art films are distinguished mainly by their cultivated inability to gauge public sentiment and their ability to fail at the box office.[5]

The two kinds of film-makers also regard censorship differently. Commercial film-makers dislike censorship for the same reasons that businessmen hate social controls on business. They are out to sell their wares to the public and they feel that censorship, reflecting middle-class prudery, interferes with entrepreneurial freedom. Like other sections of the corporate

---

[5] The situation is actually more complicated. Like Hindu nationalists who constantly speak of themselves as representatives of Hindu sentiments but have never managed to get more than one-fifth of the Hindu vote, commercial film-makers are no great prognosticators of the public taste. As already mentioned, according to informal trade estimates, in India 80 per cent of all commercial films fail at the box office; another 15 per cent barely recover their costs. Less than 5 per cent are hits. Obviously, there is no one-to-one relationship between popular taste and commercial cinema. To get an idea of what popular taste may be reading into commercial cinema, see Nandy, 'The Popular Hindi Film'.

There is also the fact that many famous and commercially thriving film producers have, at some stage of life, approached distinguished directors of art cinema, such as Satyajit Ray and Mrinal Sen, to make films for them.

world, they are convinced that what is good for the commercial film is also good for India. However, there is in them a deeper acceptance of censorship, as is evident from their frequent attempts to justify their films by pointing out how standard family values and politically correct public norms are upheld in them and by their spirited denial that their films include pornographic elements and anti-woman attitudes or that they promote consumerism and violent vigilantism. Commercial film-makers never argue openly for greater freedom to express eroticism or realistic violence or political dissent. They only argue that they are even more conventional in these respects than many others (such as the makers of low-brow Hollywood films that get past the Indian censors).

Art-film makers, in closer touch with the *haute bourgeoisie*, take a different line. They feel that their work need not be censored, for all art films by definition have mature and responsible viewpoints, unlike the commercial films which are (by definition again) infantile, irresponsible and deserving of censorship. True, art-film makers would like the censorship not to be too prudish or anti-political. But, on the whole, they consider the makers and consumers of commercial films to be eminently educable in matters of public morality and they believe censorship to be an instrument of discipline and socialization. The partisans of art cinema do not deny that the appeal of the commercial cinema lies precisely in its 'immaturity' and 'childishness'; they merely deny that immaturity can be defiance and regression rebellion, for they equate the child with the primitive waiting to be civilized and educated. The champions of the art film cannot afford to keep a space in the public realm for the undersocialized self of the viewer that registers, however imperfectly or crudely, the political presence of Indians at the margins of modern India.

I shall now restate some of these propositions about the Indian cinema using three examples. I shall try to give an idea of how the different genres of film handle—if they do—the social problems they pose. In these examples, each kind of film is seen as the confluence of the four strands of consciousness mentioned above: the traditional classical, the traditional folk, middle-class popular culture and emerging mass culture. However, the presence and salience of each strand is seen to vary with the genre, according to the principles enumerated above. (The influence of western high culture and western mass culture on each genre, though important, has not been considered any further here.)

In the first example I explore an aspect of the political psychology of *Shatranj ke Khilari*, the most explicit political–historical film made by Satyajit Ray.[6] I try to show the shortcomings of historical judgment itself and suggest that, to the extent the modern concept of political history pervades Ray's majestic creative vision, the vision is philosophically and psychologically limited. At the same time, some kinds of political and ethical sensitivities enter his work defying his self-consciously historical, rational self.

My second example is a film version of the Mahabharata, *Kalyug*, made by a respected film-maker, Shyam Benegal.[7] I describe the treatment of the character of Karṇa in the film in the context of the ambivalent fascination the Indian middle classes have had with the character during the last hundred years or so. There can be endless debate about whether Benegal represents art films or middle cinema, but there is likely to be full agreement that *Kalyug* is proper middle cinema. I use *Kalyug* to illustrate the continuities between the middle cinema and the popular middle-class culture, and to demonstrate how, like art cinema, middle cinema, too, bypasses certain issues central to Indians experiencing major cultural changes.

The third example has to do with one of the most frequently used devices in commercial cinema, the double. Here, for reasons which will become obvious, I shift the emphasis partly from the individual film to a major theme and to the stereotypical mode of handling the theme. The aim is to show the social concerns the commercial film unwittingly articulates and the methods it unwittingly employs for this purpose.

I must warn my readers that none of the three examples is a

---

[6] Satyajit Ray, *Shatranj ke Khilari* (Calcutta: D. K. Films Enterprise, 1977); producer, Suresh Jindal; script, Satyajit Ray, based on a short story by Premchand.

[7] Shyam Benegal, *Kalyug* (Bombay: Film-Valas, 1981); producer, Shashi Kapoor; script, Girish Karnad and Shyam Benegal.

pure or ideal type. I do not believe that an artist can ever be unconcerned with the preferences of his or her audience or with his or her relationship with the political and social élites. (The Ravi Shankars, M. F. Hussains and Yamini Krishnamurthys are frequently no less eager to establish an equation with the political authorities and with their audiences than the Raj Kapoors and Amitabh Bachchans. Both kinds of artist have paying patrons in mind and both are aware of the charms of political conformity.) I also believe that even the crassest commercial movie-maker secretly nurtures the self-image of a flawed artist. I have read interviews with highly respected directors of art cinema, virtually pleading for the forced feeding of their beloved Indian masses with their radical ware; I have read interviews with the crudest of commercial film-makers lamenting that they are not recognized as creative artists but damned as hard-boiled businessmen. The illustrations I shall use in the next section, therefore, show three modes of social awareness; they do not represent three mutually exclusive categories of films.

Two other caveats. It may be thought that I have been overly respectful towards the commercial film. This is not accidental; this is basically an introduction to the social meaning of mainstream cinema, and its political and moral appeal. Second, I have not taken into account the popular regional cinema. Despite the inroads made by a pan-Indian mass culture, the regional popular cinema occasionally retains strong links with local cultures and local concerns. To this extent this analysis remains a partial one. The more so because the following analysis has obvious political overtones and the links between politics and cinema in places like Tamilnadu and Andhra Pradesh are distinctive.

II *Beyond Oriental Despotism: Politics and Femininity in Satyajit Ray*

Like most great Indian myth-makers of the last two hundred years, Ray is at his most creative when dealing with problems of women and femininity. There can be no better way of acknowledging his 'presence' in the contemporary Indian consciousness than by recognizing the social criticisms his construction of womanhood offers. I shall try to give some flavour of this presence by partly re-reviewing a film of his which is apparently concerned with only men and with a 'manly' pursuit, politics. This film, *Shatranj ke Khilari* (*Chess Players*), is based on a famous short story by Munshi Premchand and is Ray's only full-length Hindi film, directed at what may be called a pan-Indian audience. That it failed to reach its intended audience is of course well known. We do not know how far the failure was due to the film itself and how far to the structure of the Indian film industry, but that is not a specially relevant question in this context. For my concern in this re-review is to show that there is not only a politics of statecraft but also a politics of culture, and that all great artists have to deal with the second kind of politics, even when overtly refusing to challenge its basic axioms.

Second, I hope to show that both as a pioneer of the Indian art cinema and as a self-conscious representative of the nineteenth-century 'renaissance' of Indian culture, Ray cannot but venture a criticism of both the West and the East; and that his criticism of the East cannot but bear the imprint of values popularized by the modern West. I also hope to show that the film's attempt to give expression to Indian cultural values and to the struggle for cultural survival is incidental to Ray's artistic purpose. This is because Ray's critique of the modern West is internal to modernity and does not use Indian traditions, which in *Shatranj* happens to be the culture of the victims, as the baseline for the film's implicit theory of oppression.

My point of departure is a controversy that was reported some years ago in the pages of a popular weekly, in which Ray and the film critic Rajbans Khanna debated a central character in *Shatranj*, Nawab Wajid Ali Shah.[8] As is well known, Wajid ruled over Awadh till his kingdom was annexed by the British in 1856. To the utter contempt of most contemporary British historians and Indian nationalists, he gave up Awadh without firing a shot. In his critique of Ray's film, Khanna tries to be more fair than Ray

---

[8] Rajbans Khanna, 'Ray's Wajid Ali Shah', *The Illustrated Weekly of India*, 22 October 1978, pp. 49–53; Satyajit Ray, 'My Wajid Ali is not "Effete and Effeminate"', ibid., 31 December 1978, pp. 49–53.

to the defeated Nawab. Khanna argues that Wajid was not an effeminate feeble ruler, devoid of political acumen and military sense, that Ray had depicted Wajid as such following biased British historians and their Indian factotums, ignoring the views of more reliable chroniclers. Ray, always pugnacious when faced with hostile criticism, replied that his political history was sounder than Khanna's; that his Wajid was a more complex figure than Khanna made out and was, in essence, truer to historical fact, as a personification of the feudal decadence and timidity that helped establish the British empire in India.

Actually, despite Ray's defensiveness, the 'truth' of *Shatranj* is not dependent on the 'historical truth' of the personality of Wajid. Khanna partly misses the point of a story built around two apolitical aristocrats who are members of the political élite of Awadh. Being compulsive chess-players, they spend their time placidly playing chess while the forcible annexation of Awadh to the British empire takes place. The movie shows how the players make a mess of their lives because of their addiction to the game; how they, after being momentarily disturbed by the more serious political chess going on in their society, prepare to go back to their private game. It seems to be Ray's argument—and also Premchand's—that the easy carelessness of the two protagonists, both about their own lives and about public life in general, reflects their and their kind's distorted sense of reality and their unconcern with the fate of their people.

The 'real' personality of King Wajid—primarily a poet, musician, bibliophil, dancer and lover—is incidental to such a story. He forms part of the feudal backdrop against which the game called British colonialism in India was played, which in turn is the backdrop against which the private game of the two aristocrats has been portrayed. In any case, for his purposes Ray has every right to defy history and depict Wajid as a feudal prototype, a king who fails to perform his kingly functions, who is first an aesthete and only then a ruler. And that is how Ray as a creative artist and as a historically self-aware commentator on colonial India consciously depicts his Wajid. At this plane, Ray's commitment to the value of masculine kingliness is no less than Khanna's. He merely differs from his critic in his estimate of Wajid's conformity to these values.

However, the film-maker Ray is more sensitive than the

political historian Ray and the psychological and political issues which he raises in his movie are deeper than the historical issues he debates with Khanna. Statecraft, measured by masculinity and skill in realpolitik, and the politics of cultural clash, within persons and outside, are the two intersecting themes that give *Shatranj* its touch of poetry as well as critical content. General James Outram, British Resident at the Court of Awadh and the man who negotiates the surrender of Wajid, is certainly, as depicted by Ray, more cognizant of these themes than Ray himself. Ridden with moral doubts, Ray's Outram knows that the British are flouting their treaty with the Nawab and trying to oust him from the throne of Awadh. Outram makes peace with his conscience by reminding himself that Wajid dances with dancing girls, writes poetry and sings. What could be more unkingly, decadent and—this remains half-articulated—unmanly. At one place in the movie, Outram upbraids his English ADC for being infected with the dangerous virus of the oriental concepts of rulership and with sympathy for a king popular with his subjects for his artistic creativity and scholarship, a king willing to forego martial hypermasculinity to actualize his authentic, more androgynous self. But at the same time, Outram senses the faultlines in his own monolithic concept of politics; he suspects that somehow the king, despite losing his kingdom, has articulated a deeper and more healthy concept of governance.

The dénouement comes when James Outram faces Wajid Ali Shah for the final negotiations; in effect, to deliver the ultimatum to surrender. Wajid, determined to avoid bloodshed, takes off his crown and offers it to a highly embarrassed Outram. Outwardly, modern statecraft wins but, against the historical judgment of Satyajit Ray, the traditional vision of the public realm reaffirms its moral stature. And that through the primary agent of modern statecraft, Outram himself.

It is possible to argue that, unknown to Ray, *Shatranj* is an essay on the clash of two perspectives on womanhood, power and culture. These perspectives arise not from two irreconcilable sets of cultural categories represented by the East and the West; they provide an element of contradiction within each of the two confronting cultures too. Wajid borrows from the indigenous concept of self-realization which equates saintliness with the ability to transcend the barrier of gender. But he also deviates from the dominant concept of kingship in Indian Islam as well as in the Hindu tradition of Kṣatriyahood. Most of his courtiers and many of the ordinary citizens of Awadh know this, and Wajid occasionally appears to be a lonely man fighting a lonely battle with less than complete sanction for his lifestyle in his society. However, even if only partial, the sanction is there. In his culture, he could create a legitimate space for himself in the public realm.

In Outram's world, too, the legitimacy of hypermasculinity and pure politics is not complete. As his ADC's ambivalence shows, in the jungle of colonial politics persists a vague British disapproval of overt aggression, an almost pathetic attempt to justify the intervention in Awadh in terms of the rules of fair play, a hesitant cognitive respect for the creative androgyny of Wajid, and an uncomfortable ambivalence towards softness, femininity and poetry. In spite of the needs of colonialism, the demands of a civilizational mission and masculine Christianity, there remains in the English characters of the movie a certain self-doubt, an awareness of elements of their culture that have become recessive but are not entirely dead. Even Outram, that redoubtable hero of British colonialism, is not free of this doubt. There is an unspoken dialogue between him and Wajid which transcends the barriers of culture.

This dialogue reveals the common predicament of the principal antagonists. Both Wajid and Outram are torn men. Apparently, Wajid has full confidence in his own way of life and kingly identity. 'Can your Queen write poetry like me', he asks a perplexed Outram, 'and do people sing her lyrics the way they sing mine?' But he also nurtures the feeling that he has failed as a man, that perhaps his is not the correct model of kingship. There is a long monologue in the movie where the king accuses his court of political and administrative failure. The criteria by which he judges his officers are no different from the criteria by which he himself is judged by Outram and Ray.

At this plane, *Shatranj* holds Wajid responsible for not living up to his own declared values of masculine statecraft. In fact it underscores these values by connecting the Wajid who admonishes his court to the colonial–bureaucratic self of Outram through a speech by the Queen Mother of Awadh to Outram, in which she invokes the principles of fair play and statesmanship.

For Ray, there *is* a domain of discourse in which Indian passivity and cowardice meet their match in British power politics and perfidy, and the Queen Mother's vision of politics marks out that domain. He therefore tries, through the uncharacteristic use of Wajid's and his mother's long speeches, to make peace with his overt values and to deny the alternative political statement that his creative self makes throughout his movie. For if there are two Outrams here, there are two Satyajit Rays, too.[9]

Himself a self-conscious product of the dialogue between East and West absentmindedly brought about by colonialism, Ray depicts Outram's ethical discomfort as if it mainly involved modern concepts of justice and treaty obligations. Yet he hints at Outram's fear that not merely his ADC but he himself might become 'soft' towards the king's androgynous political style. If Wajid is guilty of trying to transcend the 'rightful' divisions between male and female, work and leisure, pleasure and responsibility, the soft and the hard, the political and non-political, Outram is no less guilty of wavering in allegiance to the dominant motif of his culture and the ideology of colonialism. His moral discomfort is even more patent, given the minimal sanction he gets from his own immediate environment, the British-Indian colonial culture, to defy the historical and cultural role imposed on him.

The world's largest empire ever, the empire on which the sun obligingly never set, was a costly affair. To the natives of course, but also to the insecure rulers fearful of losing face and caught in an unending, self-defeating search for power, prestige, success and potency. The 'victory' in Awadh, as retold by Ray, reveals the predicament of a colonial agent caught between manliness and compassion, hardness and empathy, and pure politics and justice. It predicts the crisis of a dominant society with a false sense of destiny, trying to disown aspects of its authenticity for the sake of values that a part of it has set up as primary.

How does this crisis tie up with the long-term concerns of Indian civilization and with the sensitivities of the creative Indian?

---

[9] See 'Satyajit Ray's Secret Guide to Exquisite Murders' below.

To answer this question one must first separate the problem of woman from that of femininity. The two problems are interrelated but they are not the same. The former is concerned with social stratification; the latter with hierarchy of qualities. The former may be even more important than the latter but cannot by itself alter the ideological power and legitimizing capacity of the latter. Even in this century, some men have subverted the ideology of masculinity more successfully than many women have, and some women in turn have been very imperfect carriers of the feminine qualities. Attacking specific problems of women while ignoring the hierarchy of qualities only allows the ideology of masculinity to find new and perhaps more effective expression in other spheres of life.[10]

Sensitive internal critics of Indian society during the last two centuries have recognized this, directly or indirectly. They have not merely fought for the cause of women, they have resisted the worldview that overvalues masculinity as a set of qualities and devalues femininity as low status, non-classical and impure. These critics have recognized that India's long colonial history endorsed the masculine principle in Indian culture as the only authentic form of Indianness, and that the theory of the martial and nonmartial races was an unavoidable part of this endorsement.

Contemporary Indian attitudes to woman and womanhood, when they are less than creative, are often the obverse of the colonial theory of statecraft: that is, they accept the hierarchy of gender qualities and either try to make 'men out of Indians' or to equal the West—or, as sometimes happens, Muslims—in masculinity. That is why between Vivekananda's theory of masculine Hinduism and Kipling's theory of the martial races there is such a beautiful fit. It is this fit which has induced some of the great social reformers and thinkers of India—Gandhi is the obvious example—to emphasize the feminine at the expense of the masculine and to move out of the dominant

---

[10] For a more detailed treatment of this theme, see Ashis Nandy, 'Women versus Womanliness: An Essay in Cultural and Political Psychology', *At the Edge of Psychology; Essays in Politics and Culture* (New Delhi: Oxford University Press, 1980), pp. 32–46.

culture of politics, even at the risk of sounding mystical or romantic.

Satyajit Ray, when he is fully in control of himself, fails to take a stand on the two strands of consciousness or to establish a dialogue between the two in *Shatranj*. However, his less tamed artistic self, as I have tried to show, did not falter in its social sensitivity. It remained, against his rational self, true to the socially and intellectually more creative elements in the culture of Indian politics.

Yet this reading of *Shatranj* is only a second-order one; it is the product of a self-conscious interpretation and, in a manner of speaking, refracted through the prism of Ray's less conscious, creative self. For, everything said, the dice is loaded against this reading by the director of the film himself. I shall return later to a parallel process in the commercial cinema, in which the Indian culture is not refracted but caricatured, and yet the crisis of the culture is captured directly, even if gaudily. If there was a commercial version of *Shatranj*, all the problems Ray poses in terms of the inner contradictions of the characters would have become external conflicts, and the hero would have been shown coping with these externalities spectacularly and crudely. But perhaps the hero would have expressed more directly the theory of life which Ray articulates indirectly and in spite of himself. In the absence of a clear-cut comparable commercial version, I can only try to capture some flavour of the theory through the third example below.

III *Shyam Benegal and the Case of the Missing Kṛṣṇa*

On 22 May 1899, in his forty-second year, Jagadis Chandra Bose, one of the founding fathers of modern science in India, wrote a long letter to his friend and contemporary Rabindranath Tagore, already recognized as one of the custodians of Indian self-consciousness. The letter carried a request to the poet to write on Karṇa, the tragic, internally torn, king of Bengal in the epic Mahabharata.

Karṇa, Bose wrote, was a grossly misunderstood character.

Even though he fought for the ungodly Kauravas, Karṇa did not deserve to be in the pantheon of anti-heroes of the Indian epics. For Karṇa had defied fate and his manifest identity as the son of a humble charioteer. Bose argued that through *puruṣakāra* and *pauruṣa*—that is, through self-creation, personal achievements and masculine courage—Karṇa transcended his caste and family origins, defied his ordained fate, and actualized his true status in life and in death. He proved to the world that he was a son of Surya, the mighty sun god, even though born of an earthly mother, Kuntī, who had abandoned him at birth.

Kuntī was of course also the mother of the five Pāndavas, one of whom was Arjuna, Karṇa's arch-enemy and arch-rival, sired by another powerful god, Indra. But unlike Karṇa, Arjuna was not rejected by his mother at birth or reared by humble foster parents. He was brought up as a much-admired young prince. The story of Karṇa's life, the way it gradually got entangled with Arjuna's through a series of 'fated' events, the way Karṇa was set up to lose, can justifiably be read as a replay of the cosmic rivalry between the god of light, Sūrya, and the god of thunder, Indra. That rivalry reached its dénouement in the climactic battle of Kurukṣetra. In the eighteen-day battle Karṇa fought valiantly but was killed treacherously towards the end by Arjuna, egged on by Lord Kṛṣṇa. Arjuna did not know that Karṇa was his brother; Karṇa knew and that held him back. Kṛṣṇa, Arjuna's charioteer at Kurukṣetra, knew too, but would not tell Arjuna lest the latter flinched from his duty to fight the ungodly Kauravas.

Karṇa would not have been killed but for his generosity. He was invincible in battle because of a magical cuirass given to him at birth by his divine father. He had magnanimously given away the cuirass to Indra who, in the guise of a Brahmin, had begged for it some years before the battle of Kurukṣetra. Also, during the battle, Karṇa's sacred javelin (which could be used only once) had to be spent to save the Kauravas in a difficult situation. Even so Karṇa might not have been defeated, but for the fact that Arjuna flouted the canons of Kṣatriya warfare by attacking Karṇa while he was dragging his chariot out of the mire it was stuck in.

Tagore agreed to retell this story of Karṇa in response to Bose's request and did so in his own way—by writing an elegant, brief verse-play, *'Karṇa-Kuntī-Sambād'*.[11] In it, the poet chose to describe the tragedy of Karṇa through an episode in Karṇa's life—his moving encounter with his mother just before the final battle, when she visits him to persuade him to change sides and fight with his brothers. It is then that Karṇa hears for the first time the story of his birth and also learns that the battle is fated to go against the Kauravas. Though he refuses to change sides—'Do not tell me to leave the side which is going to be defeated', he says—he promises not to kill any of the Pāṇḍavas except Arjuna. He also reaffirms his humble 'origins', his self-made self or acquired identity, and his duty and loyalty to his friends in the Kaurava camp.

I have used this episode involving Bose, Tagore and Karṇa elsewhere in a biographical essay on Bose, to show the way the character of Karṇa might have summed up the middle-class Indian need, at that point of time, to legitimize some of the psychological traits associated with modernity.[12] These traits had already entered the culture as necessary evils but had not become an acceptable part of the Indian self-definition. Simultaneously, the life of Karṇa invoked the imagery of a magnificent origin shrouded by a modest social status unjustly imposed by fate—imagery that had a special appeal for the parity-seeking élites of colonized India. I want to recapitulate that argument in a different way here.

For both Bose and Tagore in *'Karṇa-Kuntī-Sambād'*, Karṇa is the hero of the Mahabharata. This was the first time that such a claim had ever been made; Indian epics do not really have heroes in the Greek sense. However, if one looks at the Mahabharata from the western point of view, there are three characters that can be considered candidates for the status of the hero: Arjuna, Kṛṣṇa and Yudhisṭhira. While Arjuna probably comes closest to the conventional western idea of the hero, Kṛṣṇa, combining manifest divinity with occasional forays into realpolitik, had previously inspired creative minds like Bankimchandra Chattopadhyay who had seen in the figure of Kṛṣṇa a

[11] Rabindranath Tagore, *'Karna-Kunti Sambād'*, in *Rabindraracanābalī* (Calcutta: West Bengal Government, 1962), 5, pp. 578–82.

[12] Ashis Nandy, *Alternative Sciences: Creativity and Authenticity in Two Indian Scientists*, second ed. (New Delhi: Oxford University Press, 1995), Part 2.

possible model for a reinterpreted, semiticized Hindu godhead, capable of legitimizing modern statecraft and positivist science.[13] But with the deep inroads modernity had made into Indian social life, one needed a corresponding figure from among the lesser mortals. A new god by himself was not enough.

Probably that was why Bose, himself struggling to create a cultural space for modern science in India, stumbled on Karṇa as a possible mythic paradigm for the modern Indian. Perhaps that was also why Tagore who was trying to build an Upaniṣadic basis for a new universalism in India, quickly accepted the scientist's suggestion. It is an indicator of the way the process of modernization has gone in India that, during the last hundred years, a large number of creative minds have followed their lead, often without knowing that they were doing so. Two well-known recent examples are the Marathi novel *Mṛtyuṇjaya* by Shivaji Sawant and the Bengali verse-play *Prathama Pārtha* by Buddhadev Bose.[14] They have Karṇa as hero and both interpret Karṇa on Tagore's lines. Two even more recent efforts are Ramesh Menon's *The Hunt for K* and an unpublished play by Kiran Nagarkar.[15]

It is in this context that one must view Shyam Benegal's film *Kalyug*, a modern Mahabharata scripted by Girish Karnad and Benegal himself which, predictably, retells the story from the point of view of Karṇa. It is the latest in a series of attempts by Indian middle-class culture to reinterpret the core epics of an epic civilization to make them compatible with the psychological needs of the middle classes and update the traditional mythic consciousness of the society for that purpose. (The only reinterpretive effort of our times that seeks to retain Karṇa as one of the ungodly characters of the Mahabharata is by a sociologist. In a well-known essay, Irawati Karve makes a valiant attempt but

---

[13] Bankimchandra Chattopadhyay, '*Kṛṣṇacaritra*' (1886), *Racanābalī* (Calcutta: Sahitya Samsad, 1958), 2, pp. 407–583.

[14] Shivaji Sawant, *Mṛutyuṇjaya* (Pune: Continental Prakashan, 1967); Buddhadev Bose, *Anāmi Angana o Prathama Pārtha: Duti Kāvya Nātya* (Calcutta: Ananda Publishers, 1970), pp. 73–156.

[15] Ramesh Menon, *The Hunt for K* (New Delhi: Ravi Dayal, 1992); Kiran Nagarkar, 'Bedtime Story'.

fails to rediscover Karṇa as a proper villain.[16] This despite the serious scholarship she brings to bear upon the subject. The issue after all is not one of scholarship but of sensitivity to cultural conflicts.)

In *Kalyug* the hero Karan Singh is, as his name suggests, the contemporary Karṇa. Appropriately enough, he is an uprooted north Indian Hindu situated in India's commercial capital, Bombay, and a business executive. Like Karṇa, he gets caught in a fratricidal business war between two industrial houses—owned by two branches of the same family—because he works for one of them. Like Karṇa, he comes to know that he is the illegitimate brother of the side he is fighting against. Karan Singh is ultimately murdered the way the original Karṇa was, while attending to the wheel of his car.

There are, however, significant differences between *Kalyug* and the original Mahabharata. First of all, as film critic Anil Dharker pointed out in an early review, in Benegal's Mahabharata there is no Kṛṣṇa to guide the forces of good against those of evil. True to its title, the modern Mahabharata is not located in the *dvāpara yuga*, when, according to the scriptures, piety and truth were still important factors in social relationships, despite the decline in righteousness from the earlier *satya* and *tretā yugas*. The modern Mahabharata is located in the *kali yuga*, the final *yuga* of the four-*yuga* cycle, characterized by moral decline and decadence. (Unknown to the makers of the movie, one sociologist has read the *purāṇic* texts on *kali yuga* as the simultaneous description of a traditional Indian dystopia and as an anticipatory description of Weberian modernity.)[17]

A particularly lonely search for a personal moral framework and the absence of any theory of transcendence are, therefore,

---

[16] Irawati Karve, 'Karṇa', *Yugānta: The End of an Epoch* (Pune: Deshmukh Prakashan, 1969), pp. 167–88. Now, of course, another popular version of the Mahabharata is available in the form of a TV serial in which the 'standard' image of Karṇa has been retained.

[17] Krishna Prakash Gupta, 'Social Science and Modern Consciousness: The Exhaustion of a Vision', paper presented at the seminar on 'Towards a Critique of Modernity', New Delhi, 9–10 November 1978; and 'The Kaliyug Syndrome or the Ascent of Istrogenic Systems of Healing Modernity', paper presented at the seminar on 'Asian Peace Research in the Global Context', Yokohama, 1–5 December 1980.

the distinguishing features of Benegal's movie. A clear set of norms, divinity of the kind that guides action in morally ambiguous situations, and simple piety are clearly in short supply in *Kalyug*. Their place has been taken by morally and culturally empty suppliers of instant piety and piety-as-a-consumable. Even the unknown sire of Karan Singh and his brothers turns out to be, not a mighty god, but a decrepit, small-time guru, seemingly motivated by common lust and greed. He is of the kind which usually hangs around the urban rich, cut off from their traditional moorings and eager to buy a manageable frame of piety vaguely compatible with modern living and business norms.

Second, as in the original Mahabharata, there is a mixture of good and evil in all the characters of *Kalyug* but the subtle moral dividing line between the two sides in the original has been erased. In Vyasa's Mahabharata the evil in the Pāṇdavas is part of a larger framework of good, while the good in the Kauravas is part of a larger framework of evil. That the choice is a choice between two frames, rather than between absolute concepts of good and evil is made clear by Kṛṣṇa and his practical ethics.

Between them, Karnad and Benegal ensure that the spectator of *Kalyug* is left ethically uninvolved with either side because, according to the makers of the film, there is very little to choose between the two. The design of *Kalyug* is such that the spectator is encouraged to judge the opponents in battle impartially and negatively, and to work with an ethical framework outside the life-world of the characters. If one can conceive at all of an invisible Kṛṣṇa providing an ethical frame, he is located partly in the spectator, partly in the writer and director. In a desacralized world, in a *yuga* in which righteousness is scarce and transcendence scarcer, the charisma of Kṛṣṇa has been distributed more 'democratically'.

Third, the grandeur and power of womanhood that is projected in the Sanskrit epic is conspicuously missing in *Kalyug*. There is no celebration of femininity or of feminine power and magicality in the film. Kuntī in her new incarnation is still a strong woman and fragments—only fragments—of the original Draupadī are also visible in the wives of the modern Pāṇdavas. But the strength of the women in *Kalyug* is of a different order from that of the Mahabharata women who constitute the active principle of the epic in conformity with the traditional mythopoetic links between activism, power and womanhood.

I must hasten to say that this is not because the film is slanted against women; Benegal has shown in his other works that he can portray women and their problems sensitively and with creative acuity. It is because the makers of *Kalyug* cannot but be aware that realism in an urban–industrial setting demands the repudiation of the traditional idea of continuity between femininity in everyday life and the power and majesty of the feminine principle in the cosmos. The locus of activism and power in *Kalyug* has to be in its male characters and partly in the modern Kuntī, the most traditional of the women depicted in the film. The latter, one suspects, is a compromise with the most endurable archetype of popular movies, the Indian mother.

Once you understand these changes, you know how this new interpretation of the Mahabharata locates itself in middle-class culture. You also know why the film failed to appeal to a sizeable section of Indians when it was released, despite being the Mahabharata and being an elegantly made film. I do not want to enter into a debate on the artistic quality of the film, for even its critics would admit that *Kalyug*, by most canons of aesthetics, is superior to the usual pot-boiler that borrows themes from the Mahabharata (the legendary don of popular cinema in India, Manmohan Desai, has said that his success was partly due to his ability to lift themes from the Mahabharata). Yet neither its Mahabharata connection nor its quality saved *Kalyug* at the box office; they only allowed Desai his famous wisecrack, '*Kalyug* is a very interesting movie; I would like to see it again. This time with subtitles'.

I propose that the values and concerns of *Kalyug* provide a clue to its greater acceptance by critics than by the common run of movie-goers. First of all, the absence of piety brings into the film a hard materialism which, while trying to be a materialist-critique-of-materialism, is unable to provide an adequate critique of modernity for those viewers who live with modernity but not in it. For the latter, only that critique of materialism is acceptable which includes, in however muted a form, a theory of anti-materialism if not of transcendence. The critique offered in the film, on the other hand, seems quite adequate to fully modern Indians, including most film critics. It is faulted not on the grounds that it lacks a touch of the transcendent view of life but because of the ideological line of the film-maker.

Second, values which cannot be defended or protected 'realistically' are not defended at all in *Kalyug*, whereas most Indian movie-goers prefer even an unrealistic defence of the right values to a realistic refusal to take notice of them. For instance, bypassing the theme of womanhood-as-the-active-principle-of-the-cosmos may go well with the emerging Indian mass culture (in which the main debate now is on how women will 'equal' men within the modern sector). It may even be justifiable artistically, given that the modern business culture in India, which *Kalyug* depicts, is mostly an all-male affair. But for those seeking a restatement or reaffirmation of the androgynous at the mythic plane, those for whom realism or the aesthetics of 'proper' social criticism are not the only concerns, there is little to a Mahabharata which fails to link up normatively with traditions and only gives right answers to the wrong questions, for fear it might give wrong answers to the right questions.

Similarly with traits like the achievement drive, the primacy given to professional obligations and peer-group relations over family obligations, and the defiance of fate in Karṇa. For the modern Indian, these traits are ends in themselves. To the non-modern or semi-modern Indian, they are instruments. When they can be hitched to the right ends—as must have seemed possible to Bose and Tagore at the turn of the century in that particular phase of Indian nationalism—they become acceptable. When seen as self-justifying, the traits associated with *puruṣakāra* or self-creation are likely to arouse ambivalence, anxiety and even moral repulsion.

Thus, whatever 'moral guidance' *Kalyug* offers—I am aware that contemporary art criticism rejects the idea of such guidance—is not sufficiently relevant to the needs of viewers newly uprooted from their traditional ways of life or living with fears of such uprooting. Such viewers do not want good to win always, but they do demand that the moral questions be correctly posed every time.

We shall come back to this issue by a different route in the following section.

IV *The Double in Commercial Films*

The idea of the double has fascinated the human mind since ancient times. Stories about twins or unrelated strangers who look identical are perennial favourites. In the West such doubles occur mostly in comedies—the best known perhaps being Shakespeare's play *The Comedy of Errors*—but they are also found in adventure stories or romances, such as Alexander Dumas's *The Man in the Iron Mask* and the English novel, *The Prisoner of Zenda*, that has been filmed several times.

Though Sigmund Freud had already grappled with the subject of doubles, perhaps the first systematic psychological study of the literary double was Otto Rank's *The Double: A Psychoanalytic Study*, published in 1914.[18] Rank and his admirers like Ralph Tymms built on Freud's theory that the adult capacity for self-criticism, combined with heightened narcissism, accounts for doubling;[19] the double depicts the relationship of self to self. And neurotic narcissism, so elegantly depicted by Oscar Wilde in *The Picture of Dorian Gray*, is their main diagnostic and nosological category.

Later, Rank's thesis underwent some elaboration. In his *Beyond Psychology* he argued that the double could also symbolize the author's search for an immortal self and become a rational portrayal of an irrational drive for self-perpetuation.[20] However, his main argument remained unchanged: in an 'over-rationalized civilization' the double integrates in fantasy two parts of the self which cannot be otherwise integrated.[21]

The commercial Indian film—I refer primarily to the commercial Hindi film—provides a perfect validation of Rank's theory and he would have been delighted to make its acquain-

[18] Sigmund Freud, 'The Uncanny', *Collected Works* (London: Hogarth, 1924), *4*, pp. 368–407; Otto Rank, *The Double: A Psychoanalytic Study*, tr. and ed. H. Tucker, Jr. (Chapel Hill, N.C.: University of North Carolina Press, 1971).

[19] Ralph Tymms, *Doubles in Literary Psychology* (Cambridge: Cambridge University Press, 1949).

[20] Otto Rank, *Beyond Psychology* (New York: Dover, 1941).

[21] Later scholars have tried to update some of the insights. See, e.g., Doris L. Eder, 'The Idea of the Double', *The Psychoanalytic Review*, 1978, *65*, pp. 579–613.

tance. For a major clue to the role popular films play in contemporary Indian consciousness lies in the integrative role the double has in relation to self-concepts fragmented by uprooting and deculturation. I shall give only three examples of this role, even though such integration goes on at several levels and in many sectors. My examples involve the contradictions between two images of womanhood which Indian culture has mostly found difficult to reconcile (instance of an inner conflict within tradition itself); contradictions between the old and the new or—as has often turned out in contemporary India—between eastern and western (including conflicts between native and exogenous definitions of Indianness); and contradictions between two essentially identical selves differently favoured by 'fate' or destiny (a conflict between the traditional explanation of a person's lifecycle and new challenges to it).

The first theme, probably the most persistent of the three, expresses itself not only through the device of actual doubles but also in instances of quasi- or crypto-doubling (two close sisters instead of twins; two childhood friends who might substitute for each other in odd situations, including situations involving the opposite sex; mother and daughter, split-image of each other, played by the same actress). The theme uses the divided image of woman in the Indian mythic consciousness on which new categories and new splits have been superimposed by social changes. The Indic civilization, particularly the Indian epic culture, has always worked with a fractured concept of femininity. The woman is seen at one plane as a nurtural, devoted, maternal presence; at another, as an unreliable, seductive, primal being who tends to act out her passions, particularly her destructive impulses.[22] These two aspects of womanhood, one good and one evil, are used as explanatory devices in crucial sectors of life; in birth, productivity and fecundity; in conformity, dissent and deviance; in messianic or millennial movements; in transcendence and immortality; and in illness and death.

---

[22] For instance, G. Morris Carstairs, *The Twice Born: Study of a Community of High-Caste Hindus* (Bombay: Allied, 1958); Philip Spratt, *Hindu Culture and Personality* (Bombay: Manaktalas, 1966); and the more nuanced, Sudhir Kakar, *The Inner World: A Psychoanalytic Study of Childhood and Society in India* (New Delhi: Oxford University Press, 1978).

The Indian commercial film further dramatizes the split with the help of new stereotypes, simultaneously giving meaning to these stereotypes in terms of old polarities. This is done in various ways: by having two sisters who look alike but are totally different in character, or by having two look-alike women whose character differences pose a problem of choice for the hero. He oscillates between the openly seductive, aggressive schemer who at the beginning seems to win every battle and the coy, delicate, subtly seductive, discreetly manipulative, motherly girl who by her style finally wins the war. The defeat of the former at the end of the story is, one suspects, the 'cathartic' defeat within the viewer of the surging feelings triggered by the fantasy of a treacherous, fearsome, unreliable femininity and a reaffirmation of the other, more nurtural and protective symbol of motherliness and, by extension, of the benevolent feminine principle in the cosmos.

The second example, of the conflict between old and new, is often superimposed on that between the fearsome and the benevolent, the good and the bad. The aggressive, openly alluring woman is also often a modern, western-educated, slickly dressed, professional woman and the shy, nurtural, submissive one is frequently an old-fashioned, semi-literate village woman with a heart of gold. The depiction of intra-cultural tension becomes here the story of an intergenerational or intercultural conflict.

Frequently, these conflicts are resolved by reconciling two persons who are stereotypical representations of two confronting cultures. Thus two look-alike boys, one laughably traditional and the other aggressively westernized, are revealed in the last reel to be twins separated at birth by some natural calamity or by the unrivalled villainy of some one-dimensional crook. That they belong to the same genetic stock and in the critical climatic moment come to each other's help—say in facing a common enemy or a common disaster—makes the point that both have a core of goodness derived from their common origin and that there is a certain continuity between the old and the new. Neither is the old entirely retrogressive or comical, nor is the new totally immoral.

The double here dramatizes the discontinuities introduced into Indian society by new social and political forces and simultaneously neutralizes them 'ritually', in terms of available cultural categories. So the ultra-modern, arrogant, super-competent, western-educated professional has ultimately to turn to his twin—a rustic, good-hearted, spirited but nevertheless oppressed boy from the backwaters of village India—to defeat the hard-hearted smuggler or black-marketeer who in turn is a negative model of modernity and negative mix of the East and the West. The script may even strengthen the argument by having the westernized brother ultimately marry the more traditional girl in the film and having the traditional brother marry the westernized girl who in the earlier reels had despised everything non-modern.

The third theme establishes the continuity between king and commoner, the good and the bad, the lucky and the unlucky. This is done by showing through the double that it is fate that determines who is king and who is commoner, who is ethical and who is not, who is the privileged and who the underdog, who is modern, and who is not.

Take for instance a minor variation on the example of twins separated at birth, one becoming, say, a surgeon trained in the West, the other a harassed farm-hand in a remote village. One can view the example differently and raise a somewhat different set of questions. Why does one brother remain faithful to traditions and suffer poverty and indignity, while the other becomes a highly competent, prosperous crook or hard-boiled professional? Is this an elaborate, indirect depiction of the nature-versus-nurture controversy, where ultimately blood speaks despite the vicissitudes of nurture? Or is it a plea for acceptance of the principle of nurture in a culture theoretically committed—as anthropologist Nirmal Kumar Bose and historian D. D. Kosambi believed—to biogenetic determinism?[23]

I hazard the guess that the double in the Indian pop movie restates a new folk version of Advaita that proposes that the most concrete, conspicuous, existential expression of *māyā* or unreality is fate, and only a reasonably serene acceptance of the language of fate can help one to cope with the vagaries of nature as well as nurture. This is not a restatement of the cliché of Hindu fatalism; the 'serene' acceptance of fate may include major interventions, as it almost invariably does in the popular movies with their persistent commitment to an inverted form of

---

[23] See, for instance, Nirmal Kumar Bose, *Culture and Society in India* (Bombay: Asia, 1967).

realism. But the interventions must be legitimized and cast in the language of fate, the way all acceptance of transience in the culture must be framed in the language of continuity.

Splits in personality take place not merely in fantasy, as in film or literary doubles, but also in reality, as in schizophrenia. The self of a schizoid, R. D. Laing in a philosophical aside once affirmed, is an attempt to achieve 'secondary security from the primary dangers facing him in his ontological insecurity'. Schizophrenia is only a 'special strategy' that a sensitive person invents in order to cope with an unliveably inconsistent situation in a totally insensitive world.

Perhaps what is true of persons is also true of cultures. Certainly the double in popular Indian films does seem to externalize an inner struggle to cope with two disjunctive parts of the Indian's cultural self. Facing serious encroachments from the modern world, Indian culture is complex enough to be 'burdened' with elements within it that are receptive to these encroachments. The West today is only partly an external category; it is also an inner vector of the Indian self, an acceptable and legitimate aspect of Indianness activized by the society's long exposure to occidental despotism. Traditionally, the society handled such exposure by fitting the intruding cultural strains within its age-old scheme of things. But now that the West has found more powerful allies within Indian culture, now that it has altered the priorities of the culture by entering the interstices of at least the middle-class Indian mind, the conflict between East and West has become a matter of inner contradiction. No longer is the West a sub-theory of life by which powerful foreigners and a handful of Indians live; the West is a way of life throbbing around one and challenging the basic assumptions of one's life. It is everywhere—in one's workplace, school and family. It has become a prototypical instance of a double-bind.

To reuse the examples already given, not only has the Indian's concept of fate been increasingly challenged, the challenge has been mounted in terms of the traditional themes of *puruṣakāra* (self-creation through self-reliance and effort) and *pauruṣa* (courage). Not only have the new, the modern and the exogenous quickened the existing tensions between the two images of woman that the Indian carries within him; the new, the modern and the exogenous have themselves acquired meaning in terms of the old dichotomy. Thus, the various conflicts the double represents are interrelated and cumulative.

In such a situation, there can be no escape. Not only because the unacceptable aspects of the self are overwhelming, but also because they are supported by forces outside one's control. However crude, melodramatic and maudlin the use of the double in popular Indian cinema may seem, psychologically it helps exteriorize inner tensions (through the mix of the projections and the concretizations that go into such doubling) to help maintain the integrity of one's self-system. This is the final reason for the surfeit of doubles in commercial movies. They give clarity, mythical though that clarity may seem to many, to the inner confusion and disintegration produced by inescapable outer predicaments.

I cannot after all resist the temptation of illustrating some of the points by marshalling examples from a film that seems to provide a counterpoint to Ray's *Shatranj* and Benegal's *Kaliyug*.

The film, *Kishen Kanhayia*, is certainly not unique; it can be easily substituted by other films.[24] It is also an eminently forgettable production. However, it does represent a mix of popular and mass cultures that has become an identifier of many a recent movie. It is through that mix that the film copes with the problems of old and new, tradition and modernity, East and West, the mythic and historical. It does so in a fashion that neatly documents some of the points already made.

Kishen Kanhaiya involves a double in the classical mode of the Hindi commercial cinema, in that all the standard ingredients of a film involving doubles is present in it. However, unlike some commercial films of recent years, the film falls squarely within the genre of popular cinema; it has comparatively few elements of mass culture.

True to its name, the film is about two aspects of *purāṇic* Kṛṣṇa, represented by a pair of twins, Kishen and Kanhaiya. The story is about—what else?—twins separated at birth by fate aided by the enthusiastic help of two unscrupulous but later contrite servants. They are a childless couple who steal one of the twins and and bring him up as their son. The twins are the only children of an extremely rich business tycoon, inexplicably

[24] Rakesh Roshan, *Kishen Kanhaiya* (Bombay: Film Kraft, 1990), written by Anil Kapoor and Mohan Kaul.

staying in the popular cinema's idea of a typical Indian village called Rampur.[25] Their mother has died in childbirth, and the father remarries so as to have a mother for his only son (he does not know that he has another son who has been stolen). Soon enough he discovers that his remarriage has been a mistake; he finds the newly wed bride already pregnant. Remonstrating with her on that score, he falls from a stairway and is paralysed. He can now see and hear everything but cannot speak or intervene. His palatial house and factory are taken over by his wife and her brother who not only ill-treat him and his son, but also his employees.

The two brothers are thus brought up differently and have different personalities. They are also brought up in two different worlds, but they share a common moral frame. They also have a paranormal attachment to each other, without knowing that the other exists. When one is beaten up, the other feels the pain; when one is unhappy, the other suffers too. 'Blood calls', as Kanhaiya's contrite foster-father diagnoses when revealing to Kanhaiya the secret of his birth. However, blood calls Kanhaiya more frequently than it does Kishen.

The girlfriends of the two brothers underscore their different personalities. Despite his inherited wealth, Kishen is in every way a village boy and has a village girl as his lover. Appropriately enough, she is a milkmaid called Radha. Kanhaiya who is a city slicker has an attractive girlfriend called Anju, as urbane and sleek as he is. Like him, she is mad about popular films and looks upon Kanhaiya primarily as the incarnation of a romantic film hero. (This is a deviation from the norm; typically, the village girl falls for the smart brother, the city girl for the rustic charm of the villager. However, the story tries to establish Anju's Indianness through her love for Indian films; it is contrasted with the love for English films that Kishen's stepmother's villainous son displays.)

From childhood onwards Kishen has been made to suffer by his oppressive maternal uncle, stepmother and her son and has been constantly subjected to physical abuse. As a result, he is

[25] The script writers have hit upon an appropriate name. Rampur is the commonest name for an Indian village; according to the Census, there are hundreds of Rampurs in India.

passive, fearful, tongue-tied and shows signs of masochism. All he can usually do is suffer in silence or beg for mercy. His rustic girlfriend tries to protect him from his vicious step-uncle in her own innocent way, without conspicuous success. The stepmother and her brother are after the wealth Kishen would inherit at the age of twenty-five.

Through a series of accidents and without at first knowing their true relationship, Kanhaiya gets involved in his brother's life and has to substitute for Kishen. Though Kanhaiya too has an androgynous touch in his looks, he is steel within. And the evil uncle, stepmother and her son suddenly find themselves confronting an altogether different adversary in the form of Kanhaiya. The villains have to keep Kishen alive till he is twenty-five; then they will force him to sign away his property to them. Kanhaiya takes advantage of that and their limitless greed to divide the three criminals—and, later, when that does not work and they turn nasty—to bring the sadistic triad literally to their knees. The two brothers with Kanhaiya in the lead defeat the hoodlums the villains have hired in a gory encounter that ends, as if to compensate for the earlier violence, almost comically. In the last scene, when the ungodly are unceremoniously thrown into a marsh, not only is their humiliation complete, they also look ludicrous.

It is obvious that, like many such films, this one also invokes a *purāṇic* theme. As its name indicates, the film is about Kṛṣṇa, split into two selves. Kishen is the Kṛṣṇa of the Bhāgavata Purāṇa—non-martial, playful, erotic (the eroticism is underlined with the help of an actress known for her sex appeal playing the role of Kṛṣṇa's consort, Radha). As the alert reader must have suspected, the problem of Kishen, too, is a variation on the main theme of the Bhāgavata. The evil maternal uncle is obviously King Kamsa, Kṛṣṇa's maternal uncle as well as antagonist. Kishen's only means of self-expression is his flute which, like Kṛṣṇa, he plays beautifully. (As it happens, Kishen also represents an entire generation of pre-war heroes of Indian films and literature. His androgynous touch is a link with times past. Indian viewers can probably see in him a reflection of the composite picture of the hero projected by the likes of Saratchandra Chattopadhyay in literature and played by Dilip Kumar, Raj Kapoor and Guru Dutt in the days when popular cinema was less massified.)

Kanhaiya is the Mahabharatic Kṛṣṇa. He is Kṛṣṇa the king and the warrior, willing to take up arms to protect the good and destroy the evil. Despite the less-than-virile looks of the actor playing him, this Kṛṣṇa is tough, masculine and aware of this-wordly realpolitik. For this Kṛṣṇa there may not be a prototype in literature but his personality is summed up in some of the biggest box-office hits of the 1970s and 1980s, most of them starring Amitabh Bachchan. (To this extent *Kishen Kanhaiya* marks out a cultural space for the Bachchan films in a way that they themselves perhaps cannot.) The Mahabharata Kṛṣṇa comes to the rescue of the Kṛṣṇa of Bhāgavata, presumably because in our evil times, *kali yuga*, the innocence and naïveté of the latter are inappropriate and ineffective.

Kishen Kanhaiya establishes its distinctiveness from Ray's *Shatranj* and Benegal's *Kalyug* not so much by dealing in a radically different way with the problem of evil in our times, but by responding to the crisis of Indian culture more directly on behalf of the 'massified' and uprooted sections of Indian society. One instance is the way the film recapitulates the hundred-year-old debate in modern India on the character and contemporaneity of Kṛṣṇa. Since the beginning of the nineteenth century, a number of attempts have been made by westernized Indians to supplant the Kṛṣṇa of the Bhāgavata by the Kṛṣṇa of the Mahabharata. While the likes of Rammohun Ray rejected Kṛṣṇa altogether as a model of divinity because of the 'immorality' of the Bhāgavata Purāṇa as early as the 1820s, others like Bankimchandra Chattopadhyay rejected the Kṛṣṇa of the Bhāgavata as an interpolation into the Hindu pantheon, an embarrassment caused by the decline of Hinduism in medieval times; they sought to grant divinity solely to the Mahabharata Kṛṣṇa and to revalue the Gita as a *śruti* or canonical text. Both Rammohun and Bankimchandra sensed that the Mahabharata Kṛṣṇa had become much more acceptable than the Bhāgavata Kṛṣṇa to the westernized middle classes as it was closer to the semitic concept of divinity.[26] In *Kishen Kanhaiya* popular consciousness comes as close to self-awareness as possible to register that effort and herald its triumph. As a song in the film puts it, in an unintended *double entendre*:

---

[26] See Ashis Nandy, *The Intimate Enemy: Loss and Recovery of Self Under Colonialism* (New Delhi: Oxford University Press, 1983), especially pp. 22–6.

> Kanhaiya has come in western dress...
> to make the new world dance to new tunes.

Yet, and this is perhaps a clue to the power and pull of commercial cinema, the victory of the Mahabharata Kṛṣṇa over that of the Bhāgavata one is not allowed to be complete in *Kishen Kanhaiya*. Even though the former is the obvious victor in the mortal combat between good and evil in the film, at the end of it, when the two brothers rediscover each other and return to their ineffective father, an attempt is made to restore even the Bhāgavata Kṛṣṇa to his appropriate, deserved place. (Though by the time that happens, the space previously occupied by him has shrunk and the idyllic sylvan world of Vṛndāvan contaminated by contemporary evil, and Kanhaiya has been established as a more comprehensive character than Kishen who is shown to be more one-dimensional.[27]) There are however hints throughout the narrative that each Kṛṣṇa constitutes a secret self of the other, that even the Kṛṣṇa of the Mahabharata and Gita is not complete or fully legitimate without the Kṛṣṇa of the Bhāgavata.

This thematic structure is obviously not a part of the film-makers' self-conscious project. It is a projection elicited by the bonding of the undersocialized selves of its makers and viewers—the dream work of a medium that brings to the child 'the vistas of a desirable adulthood tantalizingly close' and helps the adult 'to keep the road to childhood open'.[28] The bonding is harder to achieve in art cinema which, being a more serious effort, has to be more self-conscious, unilinear and personalized. Its makers simply cannot submit happily to the vagaries of public sentiment and become their projection.

V *Cultural Space and Aesthetic Choice*

The cases used here indicate some of the reasons why art films

---

[27] Not only is Kanhaiya's telepathic bond with Kishen stronger than Kishen's with him, Kanhaiya can act the role of Kishen, whereas Kishen can only be himself.

[28] Sudhir Kakar, *Intimate Relations: Exploring Indian Sexuality* (New Delhi: Viking, 1989), p. 26.

cannot and, perhaps, should not hegemonize the entire cultural space available to the Indian cinema, why there is a felt need for at least a vague tripartite division of spoils among the high, middle and low-brow cinema.

While none of the examples fully represents a genre, they do all represent the kind of political–psychological problems each genre has to grapple with. Thus, Ray's *Shatranj*, however impressive artistically, has to invoke the idea of oriental despotism to allow its creator to blind himself to the subtler cultural onslaught of western colonialism unleashed on Indian society. The film is, in the final analysis, the product of a cultural stream which has consistently legitimized the model of domination used by India's urban, westernized, middle-class élites. This model emphasizes the political naïveté of India's non-modern citizens and demands a special place in the state apparatus for those who understand modern statecraft and can initiate the rest of the gullible society into the intricacies of national security and the beauty of hard-eyed, secular politics. Not that Ray's social criticism is insensitive to colonialism, but it simply cannot take into account the full contours of occidental despotism—and the imperialism of categories—that forces its victims to accept the colonizers' concept of statecraft and its gendered underpinnings.

In other words, while *Shatranj* includes a component of cultural criticism, the criticism is slanted against the worldview of the victims. The criticism of the political culture of the modern West which exists in the film is only covert, and has to be teased out through an interpretive exercise that pierces through the director's conscious self. One is forced to recognize that Ray and the stream of Indian nationalism he represents tend to hold western imperialism and Indian culture equally guilty for the colonization of India. For the criteria of political judgment employed in *Shatranj* are those of the victors.

Benegal's cultural criticism too is not fully sensitive to the changing politics of modernization in India. Like Ray, Benegal too seems only partly aware of the major cultural concerns of India's non-modern and semi-modern peripheries. His Karṇa captures and yet does not capture the anguish of the Indian, surviving by living according to the principles of what, to him, is an illegitimate way of life. His Karṇa does not even define the possible terms of any protest, for he does not re-examine the values he has lived by, even though, unlike the Mahabharata Karṇa, he lives in a corporate world that swears by individual achievement, denial of ascriptive status and self-creation. Thus, Benegal's Mahabharata—though it comes close to one particular version of the middle-class reading of the Mahabharata and thus is truly contemporary—locates itself too deeply within that version to negotiate the full range of debate between East and West, and past and present for Indians at the margins of modern India.

Ray's Wajid and Benegal's Karan Singh are tragic figures with only partial clues to the changing world around them. The popular cinema's village boy, searching for and ultimately rescuing his long-lost brother cannibalized by the urban–industrial world, shows more self-confidence in tackling modernity. Even though his self-confidence makes him somewhat ludicrous, the rustic hero has at least an alternative understanding of his modern brother. It is the modern brother who does not understand and truly value his twin. In fact, the popular cinema not only recognizes the siblings' equal worth; but by occasionally making the city-bred, sleek brother eat dust and humbly survive with the help of his rustic twin, the popular cinema seems to offer a critique of modernity from the point of view of 'eternal India'. This critique almost always verges on coarseness, but by unwittingly locating its normative fulcrum in a threatened tradition trying to self-express, it becomes a crucial part of the life of the culturally threatened Indian.

One might add in conclusion that as long as modernity was only a marginal strain within Indian society, art cinema and middle cinema could justify their ideological line of an overall critique of traditions and a partial critique of modernity. Now that modernity has become the dominant principle in Indian public life, when much of the oppression and violence in society is inflicted in the name of categories such as development, science, progress, and national security, there has grown a tacit demand for a different kind of political attitude towards cultural traditions. However much we may bemoan the entry of mass culture through the commercial cinema, the fact remains that it is commercial cinema which, if only by default, has been more responsive to such demands and more protective towards non-modern categories.

Both art cinema and the middle cinema, on the other hand, avoid facing this changed politics of culture and the newer concerns and anxieties of society. As a result, such cinema is often constrained to survive in India on institutional patronage and subsidy, depending on the Indian state to underwrite its social status and lamenting at every opportunity the aesthetic immaturity, political crudity and non-critical consciousness of Indian cinema-goers. This dependence on the political establishment for survival and significance can only increase over time unless the makers of art films and middle cinema fundamentally re-examine the politics of a culture of which they have become willy-nilly a part.

Satyajit Ray's Secret Guide to Exquisite Murders: Creativity, Social Criticism, and the Partitioning of the Self

Many years ago, in the 1940s and 1950s in Calcutta, I read some of the science fiction of H. G. Wells (1866–1946). I had then just crossed the boundaries of childhood. On reading Wells, I remember being especially impressed by *The Time Machine* (1895), *The Island of Dr Moreau* (1896), *The Invisible Man* (1897), and *The War of the Worlds* (1898). The last two novels I read in Bengali, my English being still somewhat uncertain.

While all four novels intrigued me, two did something more; they jolted me out of conventionality. They made me aware that everyone in the world did not look at science the way my school teachers and parents did, or said they did. The criticism of science in *The Invisible Man* and *The Island of Dr Moreau* was so direct and impassioned that it could not be ignored even by a teenager being constantly exposed to the then-new slogans about scientific rationality, being vended systematically by India's brand-new, youthful prime minister.

It was therefore a surprise when, more than a decade later, I began to read Wells on history and society. For I discovered that there was not a whiff of the criticism of modern science that I had confronted in my teens in his novels; there were criticisms only of the social relations of modern science. When Wells wrote on the political sociology of science self-consciously, as for instance in his *Outline of History* (1920), he was prim, predictable, and just like some of my teachers and relatives. This was disappointing at the time but also consoling in strange ways, for his criticisms of science *had* shaken me.

Everyone tries to forget one's childhood heroes. Mine were going out of fashion right before my eyes during my adolescence. Wells, like George Bernard Shaw (1856–1950), Bertrand Russell (1872–1970) and Aldous Huxley (1894–1963), was yielding place to the new heroes of the times. Before long, I was keeping the company of others. I had nearly forgotten the two Wells until, many years later, I discovered that one of the other heroes of my teens, Arthur Conan Doyle (1859–1930), was a practising spiritualist and theosophist. Here was a major writer of crime fiction—whose hero Sherlock Holmes had done so much to sell the ideas of induction, empiricism, and value-neutral, dispassionate, rational knowledge to us in our teens—and he turned out to be, in his other incarnation, a direct negation of all the right values.[1]

I was to remember both Wells and Conan Doyle yet again when, two decades later, I read some of Salman Rushdie's non-fiction soon after reading his *Midnight's Children* and *Shame*.[2] When I read *Midnight's Children*, I had not even heard of Rushdie. Parts of the novel, therefore, came to me as a revelation. Few had written about the Indian middle-class consciousness of our times with such sensitivity. The middle classes Saratchandra Chattopadhyay (1878–1938) wrote about with such deep understanding were no longer there, and few had sensed the new pot-pourri of multicultural life of the middle-class Indian of the 1960s and 1970s. Before Rushdie, even fewer had tried to capture the interplay among the popular, the folk, and the nascent pan-Indian mass culture in urban India, creating new contradictions and absurdities for millions. Only a handful of writers have matched the insight with which Rushdie speaks in *Midnight's Children* of elements of the new popular culture in urban India, such as Bombay films and professional wrestling bouts, entering the interstices of the middle-class worldview. Rushdie's novel recognizes the inner dynamics of India's upper-middle-brow metropolitanism better than almost anyone else's—the fragments of self derived from the parochial,

[1] For a discussion of this issue, see Ashis Nandy, *The Tao of Cricket: On Games of Destiny and the Destiny of Games* (New Delhi: Viking and Penguin, 1989), Ch. 1.

[2] Salman Rushdie, *Midnight's Children* (London: Pan, 1982); and *Shame* (Calcutta: Rupa, 1982).

the local and the cosmopolitan; the peculiar, shallow mix of East and West which defines many western-educated Indians; a cauldron of emotions bubbling with the profound, the comic, and the trivial in a startling amalgamation.

Rushdie's formal social and political comments are a direct negation of these sensitivities. They have all the 'right' values in a predictable social-democratic format, but, on the whole, what he has to say in his non-fiction is cliché-ridden and pathetically dependent on categories derived from the popular Anglo-Saxon philosophy of the inter-war years. Rushdie's social and political comments could well be what Jawaharlal Nehru might have said about the public realm today if he were recalled in a séance by an enterprising medium. And when Rushdie writes on public issues in non-fictional form, he seems even to lack Nehru's grandfatherly charm. He speaks in a tone that may be very comforting to the ageing Left, but that is not even good radical chic, being at least thirty years out of date.[3]

Nothing reveals the insensitivity of the self-declared political sociologist Rushdie, compared to the novelist Rushdie, better than his article on Mohandas Karamchand Gandhi (1869–1948), written soon after Richard Attenborough's block-buster *Gandhi* was released and had captured the imagination of film-goers, if not of film critics.[4] Rushdie's essay is ostensibly on the film, but it also tells a lot about his understanding of the subject of the film. Rushdie's Gandhi is a slippery partisan of things medieval—a shrewd, if not slimy politician who could be forgotten but for his tremendous capacity to mobilize public

---

[3] Though Rushdie is Bombay-born, in his adult life he may have been in closer touch with Pakistan. And his social and political naïveté may have something to do with the Pakistani connection; I have noticed this touching, unqualified Nehruism in many Pakistani intellectuals. I suspect that certain social and cultural processes were short-circuited in Pakistan by the country's obtuse military rulers and what was a natural and necessary phase in Indian politics has become an unfulfilled dream in Pakistan. Perhaps Pakistanis need Nehru more today than Indians do. I say this not in empathy with the unthinking though understandable anti-Nehru posturing of many Indian intellectuals, but in the belief that Nehru's humane, 'progressivist' concept of the public realm once had an important role to play in Indian politics but has been, alas, badly mauled by time and almost entirely co-opted by India's ruling élite.

[4] Salman Rushdie, 'Gandhi: How and Why the British are Continuing to Distort our History', *The Telegraph*, 5 June 1983.

sentiments for irrational, primordial causes. Implicitly, it is a Gandhi who was responsible for the partition of India on religious grounds, a better-edited version of that spokesman for Muslim atavism, Mohammad Ali Jinnah (1876–1948). Rushdie's Gandhi is not even the ultimate social base of the bicultural, alienated Nehru but the political equal of the future prime minister of India, debating crucial issues with the young, modernist social reformer and hero of India's middle classes.

Not being a Gandhian, Rushdie's criticism of Gandhi did not disturb me. What did disturb me was my discovery of Rushdie as the last serious disciple of the late Professor Harold Lasky and Rajani Palme Dutt, and the shocked recognition that this lost child of the 1930s was behind the creation of *Midnight's Children*. Later, it was to help me understand better the reaction of the Islamic world to his *Satanic Verses*, but the discovery, when I first made it, was somewhat disheartening.

After reading Rushdie, I was back to the curious case of H. G. Wells and the vague awareness it had spawned in me years ago—about the ability of the highly creative to partition their selves, disconcertingly but effectively. Effectively, because by now I had begun to suspect that this partitioning was something Wells and Rushdie had to do to protect their creative insights—their painfully dredged-out less accessible self—from being destroyed by their 'normal', 'sane', rational self. It was as if they sensed that their conventionalities would overwhelm their deeper but vulnerable insights into the changing nature of the human predicament, unless they took care to defend that conventionality morally in another sphere of life, a sphere in which 'pure cognition' and 'rationality' dominated.

Perhaps psychoanalysis tells only part of the story. The conditions under which human passions get less contaminated by interests than do human cognition have remained an understudied aspect of personality theory. As a result, the pathologies of irrationality today are more vividly recognized than the pathologies of rationality and intellect. Perhaps the trend began not with Sigmund Freud but with the crystallization of the culture of Galilean Europe—with Francis Bacon (1561–1626) himself. After all, over the last three hundred years, only a few thinkers such as William Blake, John Ruskin, Joseph Conrad, Hannah Arendt, and Herbert Marcuse in the western world have paid some attention to the pathology of rationality, though it has continued to be a major concern of many non-western thinkers, Gandhi being the most conspicuous recent example. The great minds of Europe after the Enlightenment—from Giovanni Vico to Karl Marx to Sigmund Freud—have all been more keen to unravel the pathologies of human irrationality.

Both Wells and Rushdie, professed champions of western modernity and the Enlightenment, demonstrate in their own ways the perils of this intellectual imbalance. To make my point in a more roundabout way (after all, that is what scholarship is all about) I shall now discuss the same process in more detail in the case of a highly creative, contemporary Indian film-maker, Satyajit Ray.

II

Satyajit Ray was born into a well-known family of littérateurs and social reformers in 1921. It was originally a Kayastha family that had probably come from Bihar to settle at Nadia in western Bengal in medieval times. Since the sixteenth century, the Rays also had an East Bengali connection through their estates in Mymensingh, now in Bangladesh. They had acquired the surname Ray (originally Rai, a Mughal title) when an ancestor held office under the Mughals. Previously, they had been known as Deos and then Debs. Unlike the majority of Bengali Kayasthas who are Śāktos, the Rays were Vaiṣṇavas.[5]

By the time Satyajit was born, the Rays were already an important presence in Calcutta's social and intellectual life. Satyajit's grandfather, Upendrakishore Raychowdhury (1863–1915), had renounced orthodox Hinduism and embraced Brahmoism early in his life, as an act of social defiance and a statement of commitment to social reform. He had joined the Sadharan Brahmo Samaj, the most radical of the Brahmo sects, and married into a well-known family of Brahmo social refor-

---

[5] On the psychological correlates of Śākto and Vaiṣnava cults, see a brief discussion in Nandy, *Alternative Sciences: Creativity and Authenticity in Two Indian Scientists*, 2nd edition (New Delhi: Oxford University Press, 1995), part 2.

mers. Upendrakishore's father-in-law, Dwarkanath Ganguli, was one of the founders of Sadharan Brahmo Samaj, and Dwarkanath's wife and Upendrakishore's stepmother-in-law, Kadambini Ganguli, was the first woman graduate in the British empire, South Asia's first modern woman doctor and a delegate to the fifth session of the Indian National Congress. Despite these connections, however, Upendrakishore managed, in life as well as in death, to avoid being typed as an abrasive activist. He was primarily known as a famous writer of children's literature, a printer and publisher.

Upendrakishore's eldest son and Satyajit's father, Sukumar Ray (1887–1923), has been described by many as India's greatest writer of children's stories and verses in modern times. He began to publish from the age of nine, specializing in writing nonsense verse. Apart from Gijubhai of Gujarat, one cannot think of another major Indian writer during the past hundred years whose fame depended so entirely on writing for children. Sukumar was also a talented printing technologist, illustrator, actor, and the editor of Bengal's finest children's magazine *Sandeś*, which had been founded by Upendrakishore.[6]

There were other eminent persons in the family, too. Sukumar's cousin, Leela Majumdar, was a gifted humorist and writer of children's fiction; so was Sukhalata Rao, Sukumar's elder sister. Upendrakishore's brother Sharadaranjan pioneered the game of cricket in eastern India; another brother, Kuladaranjan, was a recognized artist. Kuladaranjan and his younger brother Pramadaranjan translated into Bengali popular English science fiction and crime thrillers for children.

On the whole, the family had a special relationship with children's literature, art, and theatre—having written and published for children for so long, it turned that specialization into a family tradition. Each member of the family had to support the weight of the tradition and, simultaneously, affirm his or her own distinctive style of creativity. This balance was in turn influenced by the ideological tilt of the family; by the time Satyajit was born, the family culture had become, through the Brahmo connection with late Victorian culture, aggressively

[6] The most elegant and charming invocation of Sukumar Ray as a person is in Leela Majumdar, *Sukumar Ray* (Calcutta: Mitra o Ghose, 1969).

rationalist, anti-hedonistic, and, despite their nationalism, Anglophile. The Rays were proud of their British connection, of the fact that many of them were trained in England, and that they played the civilizing role demanded of them by the modern institutions introduced by the Raj into the country.[7]

The problem of harmonizing these diverse strains was, however, complicated for young Satyajit by Sukumar's tragic death at the age of 36, when his only child was less than two years old. Sukumar died of *kālājvar*, literally black fever. At that time it was a fatal disease that, like tuberculosis in Victorian England, had acquired a special meaning for some sections of Bengalis. *Kālājvar* carried the contradictory associations of pastoral life and the new threats to it, the growing chasm between city and village, the lurking fear of the abandoned countryside, taken over by the darker forces of nature and thus no longer hospitable or nurtural, as well as associations of fatalism, melancholia, and self-destruction. When offset against Sukumar's robust humour and zest for life, the disease must have had a strange, ominous, tragic significance. Its impact was certainly magnified by the family's awareness that Sukumar's impending death would also mean the end of the family's publishing business and lead to their financial decline. They were not wrong; the business folded up soon after Sukumar died, and the family's fortunes fell sharply.

A joint family protects its children from the full impact of such bereavement. In Satyajit's case, for instance, there were his uncles and cousins to cushion the loss of his father.[8] It is likely that for Satyajit his father survived in his memory mainly as a mythic, larger-than-life figure, serving both as a prototype of charismatic but distant male authority, and as a figure that was vaguely vulnerable and fragile. The theme of a childlike gifted adult in whom loneliness masquerading as search for privacy

[7] The ideological bias was reflected in Ray's youthful indifference to and perhaps contempt for Indian cinema, music and painting. Till his college days his tastes were completely western. His sojourn at Shantiniketan, where he went on his mother's insistence, reluctantly leaving his beloved Calcutta, changed his attitude radically. Partha Basu, *'Garpār theke Shantiniketan'*, *Anandalok*, 9 May 1992, pp. 16–21; esp. p. 21.

[8] Ibid., p. 17.

combined with obsessive preoccupation with creative work would later on be an important one for his son both in his life and his work.[9]

Satyajit naturally grew up close to his young widowed mother, an impressive, firm, self-disciplined woman and a good singer. Suprava constituted not only his first and immediate model of care and adulthood but also of power and resilient authority. Indeed, one critic has hinted that she was for her only son also an authoritative symbol of purity and expiation through widowhood that was to recur in his work in two different guises—as a nurtural mother who invests in her son her all (as in *Aparajito*) and as a seductive, eroticized presence, fighting against and finally yielding to the demands of her 'lost' conjugal self (as in *Aranyer Din Ratri*).[10]

In addition, Suprava might have become an immediate, 'real' authority for her young son and even have been for him a sturdier, more tenacious, nuanced, and acceptable target of ambivalence. He may have been spared the sharper edges of Oedipal tussles in a crypto-Victorian family in the tropics, not the problems of authority common in a culture with a marked substratum of matriarchy. Many years afterwards, he remarked:

> In my movies I have brought in a certain detachment in the women. I like to think of women as lonely, unattached and self-absorbed. I can understand the power and the beauty of women easily. I think women have more power of mind.[11]

But that power of mind was not isolated from feelings:

> Many among the women around us keep us alive emotionally.... The qualities in women that I admire most are intelligence, grace and sophistication. Much of the beauty of women is captured in their patience and tolerance.... In some areas, men are much

[9] Aparna Sen, '*Purono Ālāp*', *Sananda*, 15 May 1992, 6(21), pp. 63–7; esp. pp. 63–4.

[10] Ranjan Bandopadhyay, *Viṣaya Satyajit* (Calcutta: Navana, 1988), p. 39. Bandopadhyay reads the second image differently. He sees in it Ray's inability to discover in his widowed characters the stern, sanitized standards set by his own mother. Satyajit Ray, *Aparajito* (Calcutta: Epic Films, 1956), story: Bibhutibhushan Bandopadhyay; and *Aranyer Din Rātri* (Calcutta: Nepal and Ashim Datta, 1970), story: Sunil Gangopadhyay.

[11] Ibid., p. 32.

more fragile than women. In those areas only women can protect men.[12]

In sum, one guesses that the family culture and mythologies underpinning it were to shape Satyajit's life and work through four dominant themes. First, the Ray family encompassed and summarized within itself the cataclysmic changes that had taken place in the social world of the Bengalis over the previous 150 years. Marie Seton and Chidananda Dasgupta have summarized these changes and shown how the Rays represented as well as responded to the changes and turned them into distinctive strains—and sources of creativity—within the family.[13] Indeed, the very fact that the family had arrived at a large frame of reference, within which could be located these representations and responses, brought the family traditions close to being a worldview that could not be easily defied but within which there was some scope for dissent.

Second, since the end of the nineteenth-century the family had consistently been in the forefront of social change in Bengal and faced the consequences of it. The emphasis on humour and children's literature, and the self-confident style most of them cultivated, often obscured the fact that they were part of a small minority and perhaps even felt isolated and beleaguered. When Seton speaks of the combination of 'sensitivity' and 'imperviousness' in Satyajit the film-maker, one is tempted to relate it to the experience of the Rays over the previous hundred years, to the peculiar mix of respect, love, social distance, and defiance with which the family had learned to live.[14]

Also, it was a dissenting family, and in that dissent the ideology of modernity had played a major part. The ideology justified their nonconformism and gave meaning to their 'odd', occasionally 'eccentric', experimental careers. The Rays had reason to be grateful for the process of westernization in Indian society

---

[12] Ranjan Bandopadhyay, *'Satyajiter Chabir Nārīrā'*, *Anandalok*, 9 May 1992, pp. 92–5; see pp. 93, 95.

[13] Marie Seton, *Portrait of a Director: Satyajit Ray* (London: Dennis Dobson, 1971), Chs. 2–3; Chidananda Dasgupta, *The Cinema of Satyajit Ray* (New Delhi: Vikas, 1980), pp. 1–14.

[14] Seton, *Satyajit Ray*, p. 64.

and to post-Renaissance Europe for the distinctive style of creativity they evolved.

Third, their Brahmo faith—a quasi-puritanic protest against the hedonism of the babus of greater Calcutta, in turn triggered by the disorienting and violent entry of the colonial political economy into eastern India—gave a sharp edge to moral issues, especially those that involved sexual norms and the channelling of violence in society. In a culture that was traditionally not greatly inhibited in the matter of heterosexual relationships, this quasi-puritanic strain was, paradoxically, not an indicator of conformity but of dissent.

As part of this attempt to reinstate a moral universe, emphasis on the public role of women and on the problems of women was something more than a matter of ideology for the Rays; the emphasis represented an unselfconscious, probably latent, attempt to rediscover one's relationship with a culture that included an identifiable substratum of matriarchy and with a society that, in facing the alienation and anomie produced by the colonial intrusion, had begun to wreak vengeance on women, seeing in them symbols of continuity with a capricious maternal principle in the cosmos that had begun to falter and sometimes failed altogether.[15]

Finally, as a result of this configuration of cultural and psychological strains, there persisted in the Rays an inner tension between unfettered imagination and disciplined rationality, perhaps even a tendency to live at two planes, which they could not fully reconcile. The imaginativeness was primarily reserved for what they wrote, drew, and fantasized for children; the rationality for organized intervention in society and for defining their social responsibility in an adult world in which children, too, were part of one's trust.

III

> Because you believe in the indivisibility of life, you seem to me to be the most Indian of all film directors.[16]

---

[15] For an analysis of this process, see Ashis Nandy, 'Sati: A Nineteenth Century Tale of Women, Violence and Protest', in *At the Edge of Psychology: Essays in Politics and Culture* (New Delhi: Oxford University Press, 1980), pp. 1–31.

[16] Ranjan Bandopadhyay, open letter to Satyajit Ray, quoted in Bandopadhyay, *Viṣaya Satyajit*, p. 10.

Against these details of Ray's background and early life, I shall now attempt a capsuled reading of his creativity and the 'controlled split' and divisibility of self the creativity presupposes, hoping that my reading will also have something to say about the relationship between popular culture and high or classical culture in South Asia.

Satyajit Ray lived simultaneously in the East and the West and operated at two levels. As a film-maker, which is what Ray at his best was, he was a classicist; his style was classical, even though heavily influenced by post-World War II neo-realism. In the context of the Apu trilogy, Dasgupta defines this classicism as follows:

> The depth of feeling which Ray creates...., all his fragile and ineffable evocations of beauty and mortality, are contained firmly within the story framework and expressed with the utmost economy....
>
> Ray's own stories are even more tightly constructed, to the point of being over-structured.[17]

As a person, however, Ray lived in the pre-war, bicultural world of Rabindranath Tagore that had a touch of Edwardian England. 'Ray's classicism like so much else in his outlook is derived from Tagore', for 'it was in Tagore that the restless reformism of the "Bengal Renaissance", of the East and West, had found its equilibrium'.[18] The ideological basis of that equilibrium was, to a significant extent, constituted by the values of the Enlightenment—scientific rationality, uncritical acceptance of the theory of progress, and secularism being the most conspicuous among them—and aspects of Indian high culture. Among the latter were certain readings of Vedānta and the Upaniṣads, once aggressively pushed by the Brahmo Samaj in Bengal and the Prarthana Samaj in west India. These readings were monistic—many would say monotheistic—and puritanic in scope and rationalist in orientation. To this mix of West and East, some of the nineteenth-century social reformers of India, including Ray's Brahmo forebears, gave respectability.

The 'Tagorean synthesis', as Dasgupta names it, had, however, its own strengths and weaknesses: 'At its best,... it resulted

---

[17] Dasgupta, *The Cinema*, pp. 65–6.

[18] Ibid., p. 68.

in the emergence of noble images of character; at its worst, it was hypocritical, a little puritan, a little afraid of Freud. It was never suited to the depiction of life in the raw.'[19]

The passions that drove the Bengali social reformers of the last century have long since subsided, but they do survive as an intellectual and cultural underside of modern consciousness in Bengal. Understandably, in this world, neither the mass culture of the post-World War II West nor Indian folk or popular culture has any say. An exception is made for some elements of Bengali non-classical culture, but that is probably an accidental by-product of personal socialization in most instances.

As part of the same cultural–psychological baggage, Ray was not satisfied with being a mere film director. He saw himself as a Renaissance man in the tradition of the great Calcuttans of the last century, and his movies are witness to this self-definition. Like Charles Chaplin and Orson Welles he was more than a director. He usually wrote the scripts and the music for his films, and, reportedly, at least one cameraman, Subrata Mitra, left his unit on the grounds that Ray only technically hired cameramen for his films, for he was primarily his own cameraman. Ray also wrote the stories for a number of his films.

Apart from the cinema, Ray had a number of other interests—he was a famous art designer and editor of a highly respected children's magazine. He was best known, however, as a writer of immensely successful crime thrillers and science fiction. He did try to maintain a distinction between the two genres but frequently did not succeed. Much of his science fiction, too, revolves around crime, and violence remains the central concern of both genres. During the last two decades of his life, Ray published nearly thirty books of popular fiction, two of which he also turned into successful films.[20]

Though his popular fiction was apparently meant for children, Bengalis of all ages adored Ray's thrillers and science fiction and eagerly waited for the next adventures of the young private detective Pradosh C. Mitter alias Feluda—the anglicization of

[19] Ibid., p. 69.

[20] Ray's popular fiction also includes some brilliant stories that cannot be classified as science fiction or tales of detection. I have not taken them into account in this essay except tangentially.

the surname is Ray's—and Professor Trilokeśvar Śanku—some of whose western friends affectionately call him Shanks—a researcher-inventor who looks like Professor Calculus of the Tin Tin series and lives alone in a small town near Calcutta, while keeping in touch with the best scientific minds in the world.

For those acquainted with late nineteenth-century thrillers and science fiction, Feluda is the more predictable of the two characters. He is a young professional detective who works in tandem with his teenage cousin, Tapeś. Tapeś, unlike Dr Watson in the Sherlock Holmes stories, is bright and observant; nonetheless, he acts as a foil to Felu because of his Watson-like inability to fathom the master's analyses and game plans. His pet name, 'Topse', reminds the Bengali reader of *topse* fish, known for its perplexed and blank look. There is a third person in the team, the famous thriller-writer Lalmohan Ganguli, better known by his pen name Jatayu, who provides comic relief of the Dr Watson variety. However, it is not Jatayu but young Topse who narrates the Feluda stories, often making snide comments on Jatayu's style of narration in his highly popular crime thrillers. The events usually take place within India, though one story has been set in Kathmandu and another in England.

Professor Śanku's diary—recovered by chance from a crater left by the eccentric professor when he took off in a home-made space rocket—is the basis for the Śanku stories. Śanku is a peculiar familiar-but-strange surname. It is usually a shortened form of Śankara in Bengal but unknown as a surname. The name gives Ray's hero a region- and caste-less identity, somewhat in the manner of the conventional hero of popular Bombay commercial films, who is rarely given a surname. The diary was written in a magic notebook that was fireproof, elastic and chameleon-like in its ability to change colour. Each Śanku story is a long extract from the diary.

Prima facie Śanku is a more original character than Felu, for he resurrects a romantic model of the creative scientist who has nothing to do with the practising research scientists of today. He is a lonely researcher who works in a laboratory in his own home in Giridi, a small insignificant town on the Bengal–Bihar border that has for decades served as a summer resort for Bengali babus. His loneliness is mitigated by his cat, Newton, his very human robot with a very Bengali name, Vidhuśekhar, and his devoted servant Prahlād, who is courageous but foolish, given to the kind of 'simple faith' which prompts him to read the Ramayana while travelling on a space rocket. Śanku is a physicist, but he conveys the impression of being a gifted amateur in a number of other sciences also. His discoveries and inventions span a wide range of disciplines—from archaeology to chemistry, from weapons research to biology, and from computer science to botany. He even builds an interplanetary rocket in his backyard and discovers a drug, miracurall, which miraculously cures all illnesses except the common cold (though in one story it cures colds too). As one would expect, Śanku loves to work alone.[21] However, his work and inventions bring him in touch with a wide variety of people from all over the world. So, unlike Feluda's adventures, Śanku's take place in different continents.

For the psychologically minded reader, both genres deal with all-male worlds, though the 'homoerotic' impulses in them are differently patterned. In the crime stories, by making the elderly novelist a comic figure and the assistant a cousin, Ray leaves little scope for explicitly sexual spoofs of the kind that have dogged the Sherlock Holmes stories in recent decades. In his science fiction, the homoeroticism has been given a Hegelian master–slave dimension. It is playfully done but there is in it just the hint of sado-masochistic content which is, in turn, legitimized by a conventional theory of progress and Baconian scientific rationality. Thus, in the stories there are instances of Śanku harassing Prahlād by means of some newly invented drug or contraption, not in spite but in fun. We shall come back to this.

The Bengali middle classes may respect the film-maker Satyajit Ray but they love the popular-fiction writer Ray. The writer Ray reminds them of his father, Bengal's most loved humorist and writer of nonsense verse, and his grandfather, Bengal's most popular writer of fairy tales in this century.

In response to the respect and the love, Ray partitioned his self into two neat compartments. Into one he fitted his 'classical' ventures—the feature films he had made over a period of three

[21] These personal details of Śanku are scattered in a number of stories, most prominently in Satyajit Ray, '*Byomyātrir Diary*', *Professor Śanku* (Calcutta: n. d.), pp. 9–38.

decades. Into the other he fitted his popular, low-brow ventures—his thrillers and tales of mystery, adventure, and violence.

The first category has a number of identifiable features. The most prominent of them is the centrality given to women and his use of women as windows to some of the core social problems of his society and his times. This place given to women's issues is not unique to Ray. From Rammohun Roy (1772–1833), who made the cause of women central to his platform of social reform in the first decades of the nineteenth century to Gandhi, who saw the role of women as vital to his movement for winning political freedom for India and for expanding the sector of freedom for all humanity, nearly all great thinkers and social reformers in India have viewed womanhood as the arena where the moral consciousness of the Indic civilization has to be recontextualized in response to the new social forces emerging on the Indian scene.[22]

This is equally true of the creative writers who have influenced Bengali social life. From Bankimchandra Chattopadhyay (1838–1894) to Rabindranath Tagore and Saratchandra Chattopadhyay (1876–1938) the great Bengali writers have been consistently concerned with the problems of women and used them to mirror the crises of Indian society. (I deliberately avoid using here the examples of women reformers and writers, lest their attempts to make the problems of women central to the society look interest-based and sectoral.)

In Ray's case, however, both these strands of awareness have been further underscored by the experiences of his family. No wonder he saw himself as heir to the nineteenth-century Bengali 'Renaissance' and, though some scholars now find the term inadequate and misleading in the context of Bengal, the term and its progressivist implications did not lose their shine for Ray. For he lived intellectually and morally in the pre-war world of Tagore.[23] To Ray, the continuity between the problems of women and the crisis of the Indian society seemed obvious and

---

[22] This issue is discussed in some detail in 'Woman Versus Womanliness: An Essay in Cultural and Political Psychology', in Nandy, *At the Edge of Psychology*, pp. 32–46.

[23] Even Ray's favourite actor, Soumitra Chatterji, who often played the hero in his films, looks remarkably like the young Tagore (Dasgupta, *The Cinema*, p. 71).

inevitable. And women constitute a formidable maternal as well as conjugal presence in his important films. Even in those where there are few women characters—for instance, *Parash Pathar, Jalsaghar* and *Goopi Gyne Bagha Byne*—the issues of gender and potency enter the scene indirectly and constitute a salient theme.[24]

In Ray's world femininity is not merely an important principle, it is given added power by telescoping into all situations of conjugality a clear touch of maternity. Here Ray is in the company of the great myth-makers of late nineteenth- and early twentieth-century Bengal, and also perhaps of the great Indian myth-makers of all time.

The second major feature of Ray's movies is exclusion of the sentimental and dramatic. Ray loved to tell a story in his films; he does not provide a political or philosophical text. He considered movies that do away with a proper story-line self-indulgent. On the other hand, he would take great care not to overload his films with events, to have too dense a plot, or to assume too partisan a tone. One critic repeatedly speaks of Ray's *parimiti-bodh*, sense of restraint, and considers this restraint part of Ray's personality.[25] Another has gone so far as to say:

> Ray is not naturally drawn towards contradictions in mental make-up.... The grace in Ray's films often comes from the way he approaches confrontations, averts actions, decisions, events. Where he tries to be direct, the result is often ineffective or jarring.[26]

Even *Charulata* and *Ghare Baire*, movies that stick closely to the novels on which they are based, de-dramatize their originals to some extent.[27]

The fear of being melodramatic or maudlin that dogs many

[24] Satyajit Ray, *Parash Pathar* (Calcutta: L. B. Films International, 1957), story: Parasuram; *Jalsaghar* (Calcutta: Satyajit Ray Productions, 1958), story: Tara-shankar Bandopadhyay; and *Goopi Gyne Bagha Byne* (Calcutta: Purnima Pictures, 1969), story: Upendrakishore Raychaudhuri.

[25] Bandopadhyay, *Viṣaya Satyajit*, p. 13.

[26] Dasgupta, *The Cinema*, pp. 70, 80–1.

[27] Satyajit Ray, *Charulata* (Calcutta: R.D. Bansal, 1964), story: Rabindranath Tagore; and *Ghare Baire* (Calcutta: NFDC, 1984), story: Rabindranath Tagore.

contemporary creative writers in Bengal is partly a reaction to the somewhat maudlin world of Saratchandra Chattopadhyay, who dominated Indian middle-class consciousness in the inter-war years. Ray is no Ernest Hemingway or Bertolt Brecht (two random examples of western authors who made tough-minded detachment their hallmark), but even when he deals with a subject as cataclysmic as the Bengal famine of the early 1940s, he makes a special effort not to be emotionally too involved with his subject. As a result, when *Ashani Sanket* was released, some of his critics accused him of producing a pretty picture postcard on a subject as grim as famine.[28] They interpreted his somewhat detached gaze as an indicator of inadequate social commitment.

Partly, however, this *parimitibodh* and 'distance' come from the fact that Ray usually avoided dealing with subjects with which he was directly acquainted.[29] By underplaying the stress and anomie of urban India, by concentrating on rural India about which he knew little, Ray had paradoxically acquired a comprehensive, dispassionate view of the gamut of macroscopic changes to which his family had been an important witness. He saw it whole, Dasgupta says, because he saw it from a distance.[30] There were obvious deep, unresolved passions behind his restraint; however, the demands made on him for direct, impassioned social commitment only cramped his style. He was never able to match the creativity of his first decade as a director, when his cinematic voice was soft and his commitments understated.

Third, despite his emphasis on femininity, Ray's films are characterized by a low-key, almost hesitant, treatment of sex. As a recent assessment puts it:

> In nearly every film where a frank treatment might have been appropriate, a natural barrier to intimacy has existed. In *The Goddess* it was Doyamoyee's reluctance, in *Charulata* Amal's, in *Kapurush* Amitava's, in *Days and Nights in the Forest* Sanjoy's (although intercourse between Hari and the tribal girl is suggested), in *The Chess Players* Mirza's, and in *Pikoo* the mother's (though semi-nakedness is shown because the film was being made for French television).[31]

---

[28] Satyajit Ray, *Ashani Sanket* (Calcutta: Sarbani Bhattacharya, 1973), story: Bibhutibhushan Bandopadhyay.

[29] Bandopadhyay, *Viṣaya Satyajit*, p. 19.

[30] Dasgupta, *The Cinema*, pp. 43–4.

[31] Andrew Robinson, 'Ray's View of the World', *The Telegraph*, 3 December 1989, pp. 6–9.

This avoidance of sexuality is matched by an avoidance of overt conflict.

> In *Charulata*, intensity of love is expressed without the lovers even holding hands; there is a rather impulsive, rather brotherly, embrace, but it contributes only a minor note in the tension created between the two. The fascinating scene of the memory game in *Aranyer Din Ratri*, together with the walks, the interplay and repetition of themes, creates a musical statement in which the seduction scenes are only the fortissimos, not raucous even in violence.[32]

Dasgupta recognizes in the context of *Apur Sansar* that Ray's ambition, given his anti-hedonistic Brahmo heritage, is nothing less than to redress the overemphasis on conjugality at the expense of maternity and to re-emphasize love in its all-embracing sense:

> Apu and Aparna's love for each other is only another aspect of Sarvajaya's love for her children or theirs for their aunt or father—a comprehensive all-pervasive, non-sexual love which has seldom been celebrated in the cinema with such purity.[33]

The first time Ray showed a couple kissing in his films was in *Ghare Baire*, made in the mid-1980s; even when he made an avowedly adventure film such as *Abhijan*, he took care to avoid showing extreme violence.[34] Many have attributed this restraint to his Brahmo puritanic upbringing; others have seen in it a compromise with conventionality and an inability to 'let go'. Ray himself is clear on the subject:

> People do not seem to bother about what you say as long as you say it in a sufficiently oblique and unconventional manner—and the normal-looking film is at a discount.... I don't imply that all the new European film makers are without talent, but I do seriously doubt if they could continue to make a living without the very liberal exploitation of sex that their code seems to permit.[35]

Certainly in Ray's world sex enters stealthily and fearfully,

---

[32] Dasgupta, *The Cinema*, p. 81.

[33] Ibid., p. 22. Satyajit Ray, *Apur Sansar* (Calcutta: Satyajit Ray Productions, 1959), story: Bibhutibhushan Bandopadhyay.

[34] Satyajit Ray, *Abhijan* (Calcutta: Abhijatrik, 1962), story: Tarashankar Bandopadhyay.

[35] Satyajit Ray, quoted in Dasgupta, *The Cinema*, p. 67.

whether he is dealing with conjugality directly or with eroticized maternity (as in *Charulata*). Similarly with violence. It enters Ray's world as something that is sinister by virtue of what it implies or what it can be, rather than by what it is. Often the violence is not physical but involves injuries to a person's or a group's dignity, self-definition, or way of life. For instance, *Abhijan*, *Pratidwandi* and *Seemabaddha*, particularly the first two, offer ample scope for disturbing, if not spectacular, violence.[36] The temptation is consciously avoided. Even in the two movies Ray has made out of his own crime thrillers, overt violence is minimal.

To begin with, this restraint may have been Ray's attempt to mark off his work from the Indian and western commercial films and create a specific audience for his kind of cinema. He pioneered art films in India; he did not have a ready audience at least for his early works. Later, such restraint became part of his style.

Some of these features extend into Ray's fiction. But there are important distinctions in the way they appear in their low- or middle-brow incarnations, primarily designed to amuse children.

First, Ray's popular fiction is set in a nearly all-male world. If Ray's cinema tends to shrink from the details of man–woman relations,[37] the tendency is even more apparent in his fiction. Women enter this world rarely and as subordinate presences, much as they do in classical Victorian thrillers, in Arthur Conan Doyle's and G. K. Chesterton's works. The deeper relationships, whether of love or hate, are invariably between men. Not only is the device of pairing the sleuth with a somewhat obtuse imperfect man of science imported from Victorian England for the Feluda stories, even Ray's science fiction introduces a similar

---

[36] Satyajit Ray, *Pratidwandi* (Calcutta: Nepal and Ashim Datta, 1970), story: Sunil Gangopadhyay; and *Seemabaddha* (Calcutta: Bharat Samsher Rana, 1971), story: Sunil Gangopadhyay.

[37] Bandopadhyay, *Viṣaya Satyajit*, p. 25. It seems that Ray once confided to writer Sunil Gangopadhyay that he was not comfortable creating women characters. Gangopadhyay thinks that that might be the reason why Ray liked to write for children and not for adults. Memorial meeting on Satyajit Ray, organized by the Sahitya Akademi at the India International Centre, New Delhi, 15 May 1992.

doubling: Professor Śanku has an innocent, loyal servant on whom he tries out his ideas. Occasionally, Śanku goes farther than Holmes; the scientist literally tests some of his new inventions on his servant Prahlād. To make this inoffensive, there are the 'mitigating' aspects of the relationship—Śanku's paternal concern for the welfare and 'upliftment' of Prahlād, Prahlād's poor intelligence and 'distorted' awareness of the world (which places him in an intermediate category between his master, representing scientific rationality and professional expertise, and the 'things' his master has mastered), and the load of the inferior culture Prahlād carries by virtue of being embedded in the local and parochial. Together they ensure that his subjecthood is complete and Ray has no self-doubt about it.

Second, Ray's popular fiction places much emphasis on scientific rationality which is identified entirely with Baconian inductionism and empiricism. The stories usually posit a clear-cut division between the cognitive on the one hand, and the affective and normative on the other, and here again Ray's direct inspiration is the Victorian crime thriller. The underlying assumption in both cases is that objective reality lies hidden behind manifest reality, and the detective, using superior techniques and unencumbered scientific rationality—that is, by disjuncting cognition from affect—tears the mask off false innocence. The detective, thus, not merely reveals the objective reality underneath, but ensures that authentic, informed innocence reasserts itself socially. As I have discussed the psychological profile of such thrillers in more detail elsewhere, I shall leave this issue at that.[38]

Third, Ray's detective stories and science fiction are two forms of adventure story. But his idea of adventure has a geographical content. Many of his stories assume that while crime is universal both in theory and practice, science is universal more in theory than in practice. The criminals in Ray's stories of detection are home brewed; in his science fiction, they are usually whites with German names or what the South Africans once used to identify as honorary whites.[39]

---

[38] Nandy, *The Tao of Cricket*, Ch. 1.

[39] Of the twenty-one villains in the Śanku stories, only two are Indian. Most of the villains are immoral scientists misusing their scientific talent. See the excellent 'guide' to these stories in Anish Deb, 'Professor Śanku', *Anandamela*, Satyajit Ray Special No., 13 May 1992, pp. 15–31.

The reasoning seems to be as follows. To do 'great science', as the moderns define it, one has constantly to rub shoulders with western scientists, for creative science is primarily a western pursuit. Naturally, Śanku's status in the world of science can only be established through his jet-setting participation in the 'global' community of first-class scientists, a community that is predominantly white. Śanku's Indianisms, his home in a small town (not too far from a metropolis, though), his family traditions (his father was a well-known Ayurvedi and great-grandfather a *sannyāsī* who renounced the world at the tender age of sixteen), his and his occasional *khādī*-clad associate Nakurbabu's openness to things such as telepathy and clairvoyance, and the contradiction between his self-image as a pure scientist and his actual life lived out as a brilliant practising technologist and inventor—they are all hitched to this global hierarchy of scientists. If, however, the hierarchy is accepted, its obverse, too, has to be stipulated: the great scientific frauds and the great scientist-psychopaths, like the great creative scientists and the great scientist-savants, must also come mainly from the West.

Fourth, many elements of the commercial Bengali and Hindi movie, the exclusion of which negatively define Ray's concept of good cinema, are introduced in his popular fiction. Not only do magical elements return in the guise of superscience to play an important part in his science fiction, so does the element of predictability in his crime stories. One knows for instance that Śanku as well as Felu will negotiate all crises in style and emerge intact. It is the content of the style—the events through which the style unfolds–that are less than predictable for readers. And to ensure this unpredictability, there is an emphasis on dramatic events—and an avoidance of details—that would be unthinkable to the film-maker Ray. In this respect, the popular writings of Ray fit in with the dominant frame of popular cinema in India.[40] Within that frame, the search of both the popular film-maker and the viewer is not for the entirely unpredictable, the original

[40] Ray himself has contrasted the enormous 'respect given to detail' in traditional Indian art with the 'poverty of detail' in Indian cinema. According to him, all great artists except the abstract ones are set apart by their emphasis on detail. Satyajt Ray, '*Detail Samparke Du'cār Kathā*', *Viṣaya Calaccitra* (Calcutta: Ananda Publishers, 1976), pp. 26–9.

or the unique, but for a new configuration of the familiar, updated in terms of contemporary experience and therefore found novel.[41]

In this configuration, there is hardly any semblance of the patient, leisurely—some would say laboured—development of character and setting one finds in Ray's serious movies. As in popular Bombay films, the narratives in Ray's popular fiction are built almost wholly around a structure of fast-moving events. The characters are revealed, to the extent they are, through the drama of the events.

Fifth, one suspects that Ray's identification with his scientist-hero and detective-hero is at least partly powered by his self-image as a Renaissance man, straddling the disjunctive cultures of the humanities and science to defy the likes of C. P. Snow. The identification is located in a self-definition on which three generations of Rays and modern Bengalis have worked diligently for nearly a century. It also seems to be powered at the personality level by a certain insecure narcissism of a once highly protected child who has been the carrier of his mother's hopes, ambitions, and feelings of insecurity, and who has internalized the image of a male authority that is overwhelming as well as vulnerable.

The result is again an uneven distribution of certain qualities between Ray's films and his popular fiction. There are in his films reflections of what appear to be conspicuous forms of anxiety-binding strategies—enormously detailed technical work and workmanship and a search for complete dominance or control over the entire technical process of film-making. In popular fiction, however, his commitment to the worldview of science is romanticized. Specially in his science fiction, the events on which he builds his stories often reveal an openness to experiences (such as paranormality and extra-sensory perceptions of various kinds) that might be taboo to the other Ray. Ideologically, he may be more closed in his popular works, methodologically he is much less encumbered. Even a casual reader quickly finds out that Ray is not a perfectionist in his popular writings: he is less careful about his workmanship and his imagination is less controlled.

---

[41] See 'An Intelligent Critic's Guide to Indian Cinema', above.

Finally, there is a distinctive quality of violence in Ray's popular works. It is immediate, concrete, and personalized. It is often physical, though carefully sanitized. This difference can be traced to the different ways Ray treats evil in the two genres. In his films, the source of evil is usually diffused and not easily identifiable (a feature Ray fails to maintain in his lesser films) and the carriers of evil do not stray beyond the reach of humanity and morality. They are driven by uncontrollable forces and motivations. As in many traditional Indian epics, Ray gives his audience a choice between reading his 'villains' as villains and reading them as twisted figures bent by life.

The focus and concreteness of evil in Ray's lesser work come from characters which are guided—as in the works of Conan Doyle and other Victorian writers of crime thrillers—by a scientific rationality that is untouched by any insight into social ethics. The villains are only villains; they are openly guided by amoral passions and self-serving greed backed by a value-neutral science. The clash is usually between two kinds of reason—the self-interest-backed psychopathic reason of the criminal and the socially acceptable moral reasoning of the sleuth. (Actually, the criminal expertise of the sleuth is also amoral; only the sleuth as a person is governed by conventional social morality.)

All three features make Ray the producer of popular fiction complementary to Ray the film-maker. And in this respect, he is not unique. All the persons we have mentioned in this essay show similar relationships between their partitioned selves. Thus, the Wells of science fiction is not conceivable without the Wells of *The Outline of History* (which is, of course, a history of western civilization, even though it is written in the innocent belief that it is a global history which does full justice to the non-western world). The Conan Doyle of the Sherlock Holmes stories neatly complements Conan Doyle the theosophist; and the Rushdie of *Midnight's Children* is possible only because there is the other Rushdie, the brain-child of the easy theories of progress of the 1930s.

Is this complementarity a matter of *ex post facto* search for order, the artificial imposition of a deterministic theory of aesthetics on these authors? Possibly not. Psychologically, the Ray of the Apu trilogy, *Devi* (1960) and *Ghare Baire* seems to have been made possible by Ray the tame, uncritical believer in the emancipatory and educative role of Enlightenment values. In this respect, the complementary is not merely aesthetic; it is personological. By writing for children and by upholding the conventional Victorian norms as the embodiment of Enlightenment values—thus intervening in child-rearing and education to inculcate, institutionalize, and perpetuate these values—Ray does appear to make peace with his social conscience. He can then be more daringly 'free associative' and give controlled expression to his less socialized, less tamed, less 'educated', more intuitive self in his serious cinematic work. It is Ray's way of making peace with himself and using the integrative capacities at the disposal of his self.[42]

Such forms of partitioning, one suspects, come more easily to the South Asian, traditionally accustomed to live in many cultures and, in fact, in many worlds. This alternative is available, of course, to creative writers in the modern West but they have to search more self-consciously for internal consistency in their work. Perhaps that is why, in Wells' case, the more well-thought-out cognitive ventures are conventional and conformist, whereas in someone like Ray, the more serious and carefully thought-out ventures are more imaginative and less constrained by values derived from the dominant culture. Wells is more conventional in history, Ray in fiction, which, for him, is a 'freer' medium than cinema.

Note that Rushdie, too, driven by his internalization of the West, tries in his non-fiction to be allegiant to Enlightenment values, to win through such conformity the freedom to be more careless about these values in serious fiction. In the West, you can be playful only in fiction, not in science, not even in scientized social analysis. When Rushdie self-consciously tries his hand at serious social analysis through playful fiction, as in *Satanic Verses*, it ends in disaster.[43] He loses almost entirely the targets of his reform, who feel humiliated and provoked by his style of social analysis and intervention.[44]

---

[42] On ego strength being a crucial personality factor in the highly creative, see for instance, Frank Barron, 'The Psychology of Creativity', in *New Directions in Psychology II* (New York: Holt, Rinehart and Winston, 1965), pp. 1–134.

[43] Salman Rushdie, *Satanic Verses* (New York: Viking, 1988).

[44] See, for instance, an impressive analysis of the responses to *Satanic Verses* among the Muslims in B. C. Parekh, 'Between Holy Text and Moral Void', *New Statesman*, 24 March 1989, pp. 29–33.

One may also note that in Wells' serious novels, such as *Ann Veronica* and *Tono-Bungay*, the political and social ideology of the author intrudes to shape the narrative more perceptibly than it does in Ray's work. Wells is more influenced by his ideas of scientific history and rationality in serious literature; Ray, in popular fiction. It is a minor paradox that both emerge as better social analysts when they cease to be self-consciously social scientific and socially relevant.

Some of these comments apply to another tormented, internally split writer, Rudyard Kipling (1865–1936). He, too, came close to partitioning his self in his works in the manner we have described, but failed to contain his highly conventional, imperial values when writing even his more creative, intellectually daring novels. As Edmund Wilson points out, it is something of an anticlimax that in *Kim*, which comes close to being one of the great novels of our times and one of the most sensitive ever written about India—Bernard Cohn calls it the best fictional ethnography of India—the hero, after all his encounters with the mysteries of nature and human nature and after all his encounters with an alternative worldview and an alternative vision of human potentialities (represented in the novel by the kaleidoscope of India's cultural diversity and by the haunting figure of the Lama respectively), ultimately decides to become a servitor of the Raj.[45]

The two Satyajit Rays are not in watertight compartments. There is an occasional leak. He made charming films based on two of his own thrillers, and once wrote a script for a science fiction movie, *The Alien*, on which two Hollywood block-blusters, *ET* and *Close Encounters of the Third Kind* were reportedly based.[46] Likewise, some of the early Professor Śanku stories, such

[45] Edmund Wilson, 'The Kipling that Nobody Read', in Andrew Rutherford (ed.), *Kipling's Mind and Art* (Stanford: Stanford University Press, 1964), pp. 17–69.

[46] Amrit Rai, 'Satyajit Ray: A Rare Creative Genius', paper presented at the memorial meeting on Satyajit Ray, 15 May 1992, mimeo. Rai's unwitting source was writer Arthur C. Clarke who wanted Ray to sue the producers of the two Hollywood films.

The main attraction of Ray's script for Hollywood film-makers might have

as the charmingly Gothic '*Professor Śanku o Robu*', do have a latent critique of science built into them.[47] However, here I am not talking of such self-conscious bridges but of the subtler communication and 'division of labour' between the two selves. Thus, what we have identified as an understatement of violence in Ray's cinema often becomes a form of sanitized violence in his popular fiction. Professor Śanku's discovery, the anihilin gun, is as its name indicates a weapon that not only kills instantly but does so cleanly, smokelessly, and soundlessly. It vaporizes its target, leaving no messy blood-drenched body or injured victim to be taken care of.

However, the seepage is usually in the other direction. The identification with the ordinary person confronting life incompetently but nobly—as in *Aparajito, Apur Sansar, Mahanagar, Abhijan* or even *Parash Pathar*—does enter the world of the other Ray.[48] It even acquires a touch of romantic grandeur in a story such as '*Bankubābur Bandhu*', cast in the mould of science fiction, about a harassed schoolteacher who is the constant butt of the crude humour of a village landlord and his cronies. The teacher acquires a new sense of dignity and self-confidence when he accidentally encounters and befriends extraterrestrial beings in the village woods. Technology here puts one in touch with things larger than oneself and with an awareness that positivist knowledge knows nothing about.[49]

---

been its positive attitude to the unknown, the strange, and the other-worldly. For Hollywood, the alien has traditionally been an evil and hostile presence, a source of fear. For it, the prototypical science fiction movie is *The War of the Worlds*. For Ray, the strange is a self-enriching and self-expanding experience.

This belief colours not merely Ray's science fiction but his fantasy life in general. His last film, *Agnantuk* (Calcutta: NFDC, 1991, story: Satyajit Ray) can be read as a moving effort by its maker to reaffirm this faith. In it, Ray defies the conventions of his own thought and his self-definition as a chosen carrier of the European Enlightenment in India even more dramatically than he usually does in his more ambitious movies. The defiance comes through a painful process of self-transcendence and self-negation; he has to set up a formidable anti-self in the form of a truant anthropologist who rejects all progressivist definitions of civilization and gracefully lives out his faith.

[47] Satyajit Ray, '*Professor Śanku o Robu*', in *Professor Śankur Kāndakārkhānā* (Calcutta: Ananda Publishers, 1970), pp. 1–18.

[48] Satyajit Ray, *Mahanagar* (Calcutta: R.D. Bansal, 1963), story: Narendranath Mira.

[49] Satyajit Ray, '*Bankubābur Bandhu*', *Ek Dozen Gappa* (Calcutta: Ananda Publishers, 1970), pp. 17–28. For a fascinating discussion of the theme of lower-

Notwithstanding such leaks or exchanges, there are reasonably clear principles by which the selves are separated. We have already hinted at the presence of three of the principles. First, the second self is primarily a pedagogic self. (Though the public stereotype about the selves is exactly the reverse—the film-maker Ray is seen as being serious, the popular writer Ray as fun.) It may be true that 'in Ray's stories there is no crude attempt to provide a moral',[50] but the Brahmo concept of what is good for children informs much of Ray's crime thrillers and science fiction indirectly. Ray's aunt, Sukhalata Rao, another gifted writer of children's literature, once started a brief controversy in Bengal by arguing that ghost stories should not be written, for they were bad for the character—read moral development—of children.[51] Others may not have taken Sukhalata's advice seriously but her nephew has, for though Ray *has* written ghost stories and often brilliantly, his popular fiction always has a series of unstated morals and is guided by an implicit concept of 'healthy pastime' or 'healthy fun', parallels to which can only be found in some writings on cricket produced in Victorian England and in Lord Baden-Powell's concept of the boy scout movement.

Second, the second Ray is distinguished by a 'masculine' concern—the term is not entirely appropriate—with the world of machines, power, intrusive or invasive curiosity, competition for priorities and dominance, combined with an often astonishing insensitivity to nature, including human nature. As if Ray's concern in his popular fiction was nothing more than telling a story in which his hero would solve a proper criminal puzzle. All subtleties of characterization are seen as diverting from a good, strong narrative line. The androgynous sensitivities of Ray, so evident in cinema, seem to give way to a romanticized, two-dimensional, materialistic, phallocentric world where puzzle-solving and a certain toughness predominate. I use the word 'romanticized' advisedly, for the element of romance does not

middle-class, humble persons living a life of imagination or in touch with things larger than themselves, see Sen, '*Puroṇo Ālāp*', pp. 63–4.

[50] Bandopadhyay, *Viṣaya Satyajit*, p. 52.

[51] Buddhadev Bose, '*Bhuter Bhaya*' (1932), *Racanāsamgraha* (Calcutta: Granthalay, 1982), *5*, pp. 466–72.

run counter to the materialism and the tough, positivist view of the world. Rather, Ray works with a romantic vision of materialism and positivism with which many non-western ideologues of scientific rationality feel comfortable and which was first popularized in India in the nineteenth century by the babus of Calcutta. There is a perfect and innocent continuity between Father Eugène Lafont's physics classes at St Xavier's College and Mahendralal Sarkar's science movement in *fin-de-siècle* Calcutta, and the dreary enthusiasm for modern science shown by many like Ray in post-Independence India, blissfully unaware of the altered social relations of science in the country.

Third, readers may have noticed that, in the partitioning of the self, the values and concepts associated with the European Enlightenment have a special role to play. Among these values are scientific rationality; the idea of dispassionate, impersonal, falsifiable knowledge, obtainable through a scientific method strictly defined by positivist criteria; the idea of expertise, represented by the experimental scientist and the private detective-as-a-professional-criminologist; and a wholly instrumental concept of knowledge that allows one to see true knowledge as value-neutral, usable either for good or for evil. Ray's crime thrillers and science fiction pay homage to these values.

Ray's message in cinema is profoundly different. We have already described it. It is that message which makes his films, to borrow an expression from Ronald Laing, an experience of experience.

IV

A creative person can be at times a sounder critic of himself than his critics are. There are at least three stories by Ray, all formally classifiable as science fiction, that try to capture the tragedy of the creative person in a conformist society. In all three, but particularly in '*Āryaśekharer Janma o Mṛtyu*', Ray depicts how the creative are forced to opt for survival at the cost of creativity because, in the environment in which they live, the extra-normal is no different from the abnormal and both are repressed by the society to protect and restore the domain of normality.[52] All

[52] Bandopadhyay, *Viṣaya Satyajit*, pp. 53–4; Satyajit Ray, '*Āryaśekharer Janma o Mṛtyu*', *Tin Rakam* (Calcutta: Kathamala, n.d.), pp. 9–24. See also '*Professor Śanku o Khokā*', *Professor Śanku* (Calcutta: Newscript, 1987), pp. 169–90.

three stories carry the latent message that creativity is often destroyed because the creative fail or refuse to internalize the social need to repress the strange and the mysterious in them. For instance, in '*Āryaśekharer Janma o Mṛtyu*', the saddest and most direct of the three, the hero, a child prodigy in mathematics, first loses his gifts and then dies because he is uncompromising in his scientific curiosity and recklessly confronts his staid, unimaginative father with his socially daring 'scientific theory'. When dying, in pain and perhaps with an awareness of the futility of it all, it is only his mother that he remembers.

That is about all I can say. We have no direct clue as to whether Ray saw himself as a survivor who had made realistic compromises, or as an uncompromising rebel who nurtured a latent fear of being destroyed by his surroundings, or, more likely, as one who had in him elements of both. Ray's stories, usually pitched in a low key, do not seem to address themselves to other questions that dog the steps of psychologists researching creativity: Which way do the ego defences of a creative person operate? In what kind of work can the creative 'let go'? Where does he or she tighten the reins of imagination?

No clear answers to these questions emerge from Ray's life story either. The only additional comment I can make on the subject sounds, therefore, so naïvely Freudian and speculative to my own ears that I shall have to ask the reader to take it as entirely tentative.

Creativity—to the extent that it involves the interplay of the conscious and unconscious, the regressive and the ego-integrative, the rational and nonrational or irrational—must at some point encounter the creative person's own moral self. Behind this clinical platitude lies the fact that over the last three hundred years the structure of morality in the dominant culture of the world has gradually come to include a number of Baconian values: a specific form of rationality, a specific concept of knowledge, and a specific set of methods to live by that rationality and to generate that knowledge. In the dominant global culture today, these, too, are part of our socialized—one may say, oversocialized–self and an aspect of the demands of the modern superego. Whoever does not know that while all selves are equal, some selves are more equal than others.

As a consequence, it appears that creativity has begun to

demand from the creative person both defiance of conventional morality and also some conspicuous conformity to an aspect of morality which is not overtly conventional. To meet this demand, the creative person sometimes creates a kind of shadow self which is perfectly compatible with dominant social ideals and one's oversocialized self, but wears successfully the garb of unconventionality. This shadow self allows freer play to one's undersocialized self, having greater access to the primitive, the non-rational and the intuitive.

The partitioning of the self we have seen in Ray and others is, it seems to me, part of this larger dynamic. It allows greater play to the internalized aspects of social processes which would otherwise have been irreconcilable. Some manage to do this partitioning painlessly, others painfully; some do it with self-conscious finesse, others clumsily and unselfconsciously. But in each case, they pose a challenge to the students of creativity to crack the code of this shadowy self and decipher the writer's language of communication with the other self as a crucial component of the creative process.

This issue of communication often becomes part of a larger politics of cultures, too. The reader may have noticed that, in the case of Wells and Rushdie, their imaginal products are less encumbered by the authors' prim theories of life; with Ray, it is the lighter works that are more encumbered. Is this accidental? What about the fact that in all three cases, time and the changing concepts of social knowledge have shown that their concepts of reliable, valid, scientific social knowledge were less reliable and valid than they might have thought? Does not the very fact that these two questions can be asked today have something to tell us about the changing landscape of the intellectual world?

I shall leave the reader with these questions, in the belief that all questions cannot—and should not—be answered by those who raise them.

Index